YOUNG GRAPHIC DESIGNERS AMERICAS

daab

INTRODUCTION

North and south – despite the many socio-cultural and economic differences, there seems to be a unifying thread that crosses boundaries. Not just drinking from the same sources of influence in music, fine art, street art, and cinema, but ironically, thanks to the dreaded concept of globalization, one could argue that there is also a visual alliance through pop culture, whether the reference is mainstream or niche. All brought directly to your doorstep, whether you live in the heights of the Andes or reside in the heart of Minnesota, by the weird, wonderful, and sometimes very frightening world-wide web. There is evidently a widespread awareness of how to accomplish things, thanks to the availability of information, which wasn't quite so accessible during the humble beginnings in this line of work. Secondly, there is a steady rumor that design invokes not just an understanding of problem-solving, but also notions of gusto, of expressing ideas and beliefs, and of articulating original thought. Of being more eclectic. It seems designers are reluctant to let the medium control their design, or at least to impose limits on them. It makes sense that they look to what is outside their traditional design field. Many people originally got involved with design because they recognized that their interests were very diverse, spanning over various fields, and were not necessarily coherent in one traditional career. This approach of course directly conflicts with professional criteria, which encourage specializing in one professional path and developing a reputation in ones own particular field. However, students in design schools nowadays are strongly drawn to this multi-disciplinary approach. Other designers embark on parallel activities where they can use their acquired skills and designer flair simply as a result of the difficult graphic-design market, and the need to earn a living through other pursuits. Lastly, there is an increased concern about the designer's role as far as transmitting an ethical and responsible message. The last few years have been a time of political and environmental upheaval, and there is a clear voice emanating from designers, both in the north and south, whose view of the world is filled with feelings of doubt and nonconformity, yet importantly also altruism and optimism. However, as ever, looking and enjoying is more important than any explanation – Follow your eyes.

Norden und Süden. Über die soziokulturellen und wirtschaftlichen Unterschiede hinaus scheint es einen grenzüberschreitenden, vereinenden Gedankengang zu geben. Es sind vergleichbare Einflüsse in der Musik, der etablierten Kunst, der Straßenkunst und im Kino zu beobachten; auch die Globalisierung führt zu einer Verbindung der unterschiedlichen Bereiche durch die Popkultur – im Mainstream wie auch in schwerer durchschaubaren Strömungen. Und all das wird bis an die Türschwelle geliefert, ob man sich nun in den Anden oder im Herzen von Minnesota befindet, und zwar durch das eigenartige, wundervolle und manchmal beängstigende World Wide Web. Es verschafft uns umfassende, allgemein verfügbare Informationen, die in den bescheidenen Anfängen der Kreation von Design nicht so leicht zu beschaffen waren. Wir sind uns aber auch alle über die Informationsflut und ihre Vor- und Nachteile bewusst. Außerdem weiß man, dass man als Designer nicht nur Probleme lösen muss, sondern auch über Geschmack verfügen und Ideen ausdrücken können sollte, und zwar auf originelle Weise. Man muss vielseitiger sein als früher. Es scheint auch, dass Designer nur zögernd zulassen, dass ihre Kreationen durch das jeweilige Medium beeinflusst werden, und sie versuchen zu verhindern, dass es ihnen Grenzen auflegt. Diese Herangehensweise führt zu einem Konflikt mit den beruflichen Anforderungen, die eher eine Spezialisierung im eigenen Fachgebiet erfordern. Designstudenten fühlen sich durch eine multidisziplinäre Herangehensweise stark angezogen, und es ist auch durchaus sinnvoll, sich auf Methoden zu konzentrieren, die über traditionelles Design hinausgehen. Manche Designer setzen aufgrund des schwierigen Marktes auf parallel verlaufende Betätigungen, die es ihnen erlauben, ihre Kenntnisse und ihr Fingerspitzengefühl anzuwenden, um ihren Lebensunterhalt zu verdienen. Schließlich ist auch ein verstärktes Interesse an der Rolle des Designers als dem Übermittler einer ethischen und verantwortlichen Botschaft zu erkennen. Die letzten Jahre waren eine Zeit des politischen und umweltpolitischen Umbruchs, und man kann ganz klar die Stimme von Designern aus dem Norden wie aus dem Süden vernehmen, deren Weltsicht voller Zweifel und Nonkonformismus ist, aber auch voller Altruismus und Optimismus. Doch Schauen und Genießen ist viel wichtiger als jegliche Erklärung. Lassen Sie sich von Ihren Augen führen.

BIG SHOT MAGAZINE
DJ MUSIC
ART / CULTURE
GEAR

Norte y Sur. Rebasando múltiples diferencias socioculturales y económicas, hay un hilo conductor que cruza fronteras. No sólo por beber de las mismas fuentes musicales, de bellas artes, arte urbano y cine, sino por la tan temida globalización, podría decirse que existe un vínculo visual entre la cultura popular, sea de carácter convencional o absolutamente subversivo, que llega a cualquier rincón del mundo a través de la extraña, fascinante y a veces inquietante Internet. A la conciencia de lo que puede lograrse gracias a la disponibilidad de la información, inexistente en los orígenes de esta profesión, así como de los efectos de su sobrecarga –tanto positivos como negativos–, se suma un rumor incesante que insiste en que el diseño comprende no sólo la solución de problemas, sino también las nociones de «gusto», la expresión de ideas y creencias y la articulación de un pensamiento original. En que es más ecléctico. Los diseñadores parecen mostrarse reticentes a que el medio controle su labor o, al menos, a que les imponga límites, una actitud que entra en conflicto directo con el criterio profesional, que anima a especializarse y a forjarse una reputación en un ámbito específico. Los alumnos de las escuelas de diseño de hoy se sienten fuertemente atraídos hacia un enfoque multidisciplinario. Resulta de lo más natural que sus ojos se fijen en aquello que se encuentra fuera del ámbito tradicional del diseño si tenemos en cuenta cómo llegan a él: con intereses muy diversos, que abarcan varios campos, y no necesariamente afines. Otros diseñadores se embarcan en actividades paralelas en las que aplicar sus habilidades adquiridas y su talento sencillamente como consecuencia del complejo mercado del diseño gráfico y la necesidad de ganarse la vida. Por último, existe una mayor preocupación acerca del papel que desempeña el diseñador en cuanto a la transmisión de un mensaje ético y responsable. Estos últimos años han sido tiempos de desasosiego político y medioambiental, y una voz clara emana de diseñadores del Norte y del Sur, con una visión del mundo llena de dudas e inconformismo, pero también de altruismo y optimismo. Pero mirar y disfrutar vale más que cualquier explicación: déjate guiar por los ojos.

Du Nord au Sud– et en dépit de nombreuses différences socioculturelles et économiques, un fil d'Ariane semble traverser les frontières. Puiser aux mêmes sources d'influences, à savoir, musique, beaux-arts, street art et cinéma, n'en est pas la cause unique. En effet, l'ironie veut que, grâce à ce concept de globalisation tant redouté, nous puissions prétendre à l'existence d'une alliance visuelle via la culture pop- que ce soit un courant majeur ou une niche. Car, grâce au web, étrange, merveilleux et parfois effrayant, vous trouvez tout sur le pas de la porte, du sommet des Andes au cœur du Minnesota. De toute évidence, une conscience générale sur la manière d'accomplir les choses est née de l'accès à l'information, plus facile aujourd'hui qu'à la naissance de cette ligne artistique. Qui plus est, selon la rumeur, le design n'invoquerait pas uniquement l'appréhension d'un problème à résoudre, mais aussi des notions de goût, d'expression d'idées et d'articulation de pensées originales. L'art d'être plus éclectique. Les designers semblent réticents à laisser les moyens techniques contrôler leur design, ou du moins, à ne pas leur imposer de limites. Et on comprend qu'ils tournent leurs regards hors du design traditionnel, quand on sait pourquoi les gens se sont impliqués, à l'origine, dans ce domaine : parce qu'ils ont reconnu la grande diversité de leurs intérêts, regroupant des domaines variés, sans nécessairement former un ensemble cohérent dans une carrière traditionnelle. Cette approche entre directement en conflit avec les critères professionnels, qui incitent à se spécialiser dans une direction professionnelle et à se faire un nom dans son propre domaine. Pourtant, de nos jours, les étudiants des écoles de design sont fortement attirés par cette approche pluridisciplinaire. Vu la situation difficile du marché du design graphique et la nécessité de gagner sa vie par le biais d'autres activités, certains designers s'engagent tout simplement dans des activités parallèles où ils peuvent utiliser leur talent et les compétences acquises dans le design. Enfin, on s'interroge de plus en plus sur le rôle du designer en tant que passeur d'un message éthique et responsable. Les dernières années ont connu une période de bouleversements politiques et écologiques. Du nord au sud, les designers font entendre une voix claire, forts d'une vision du monde remplie de sentiments de doute et de non-conformisme, mais aussi d'un altruisme et optimisme important. Ceci étant, regarder et apprécier valant mieux que toute explication, laissez votre regard flâner sur les pages suivantes.

BY:AMT
BADGE
HONOR OF
SM/LG
BY:AMT
www.byamt.com
info@byamt.com
BY:AMT
RING
5/6/7/8/9
10/11/12
BY:AMT
www.byamt.com
info@byamt.com
Styles:
Band/Diamond/
Pearl/Signet
BY:AMT
BLING
BRACELET
SM/LG
BY:AMT
www.byamt.com
info@byamt.com

Nord e Sud: messe da parte le differenze economiche e socio-culturali, sembra che vi sia un filo unificante che supera questa frontiera. Non solo perché ci si abbevera alle stesse fonti nel campo della musica, delle belle arti, dell'arte di strada e del cinema, ma anche perché, grazie al temuto vocabolo (globalizzazione) è lecito supporre che esista un'alleanza visuale trasversale nella cultura popolare, sia nelle sue correnti principali sia in quelle più sotterranee. E tutto ciò viene consegnato fresco a domicilio, sia per chi risiede sulle vette andine sia nel cuore del Minnesota, grazie al Web, quella rete mondiale così imprevedibile, meravigliosa e a volte sconcertante. Oggi è possibile conseguire risultati grazie a una disponibilità di informazioni che era impensabile negli umili esordi della Rete, e siamo tutti coscienti dell'iperinformazione, dei suoi pro e contro. Inoltre, si è radicata l'idea che il design non faccia appello solo alla risoluzione di problemi funzionali, ma anche alla nozione di gusto, all'espressione di idee e convincimenti nonché all'elaborazione di un pensiero originale. In definitiva, all'essere più eclettici. I designer sono riluttanti a permettere che lo strumento condizioni le loro creazioni o almeno cercano di limitarne l'influenza, e questo approccio è in controtendenza rispetto al mondo del lavoro, che incoraggia l'iperspecializzazione. Se si pensa a come un tempo ci si avvicinava al mondo del design, si comprende l'importanza dell'approccio multidisciplinare degli studenti di oggi. È significativo che i neofiti del design orientano il loro sguardo verso ciò che sta al di fuori dal tradizionale campo del disegno industriale, perché sono consapevoli della varietà dei loro interessi, che nel loro insieme non sono necessariamente coerenti con una carriera tradizionale. Alcuni intraprendono attività parallele nelle quali mettere in pratica le capacità di designer, dato che le difficoltà del settore rendono necessario guadagnarsi da vivere in altri campi. Infine, c'è una preoccupazione crescente riguardo al ruolo del designer in quanto divulgatore di un messaggio etico e responsabile. In questi anni di rivolgimenti politici e di sensibilizzazione per l'ambiente, i designer – del Nord e del Sud – hanno lanciato un chiaro messaggio nel quale la visione del mondo appare impregnata di incertezze e di anticonformismo, ma al contempo di ottimismo e altruismo. Ma saper guardare e apprezzare è più importante di qualunque spiegazione: lasciatevi guidare dal vostro sguardo.

ABCDEFGHI
JKLMNOPQR
STUVWXYZ

abcdefghijklmn
opqrstuvwxyz
1234567890

ACCENT CREATIVE | SAN DIEGO, CA, USA

Miguel Vega

Miguel Vega is an Argentinean creative director who is just as happy designing vector sets or crafting record packaging as he is working on live video art or his own electronic music. Accent.tv is his online creative portfolio, where he puts into practice his beliefs that a good idea and thorough research are always a project's starting point.

www.accent.tv

1 Promotional poster | Self-initiated, 2007
2 Packaging and identity | Brandon Zamudio, 2007
3 Promotional poster | Freewaves, 2007
4 Magazine spread | Sunshine Distribution, 2007
5 LP sleeve design | Brendan Collins, 2007
6 Promotional poster | Crosswired, 2007

2

PROPER CHILLAGE
SOUL PROVINCE
ADMIT ONE
PROPER CHILLAGE
SOUL PROVINCE
ADMIT ONE

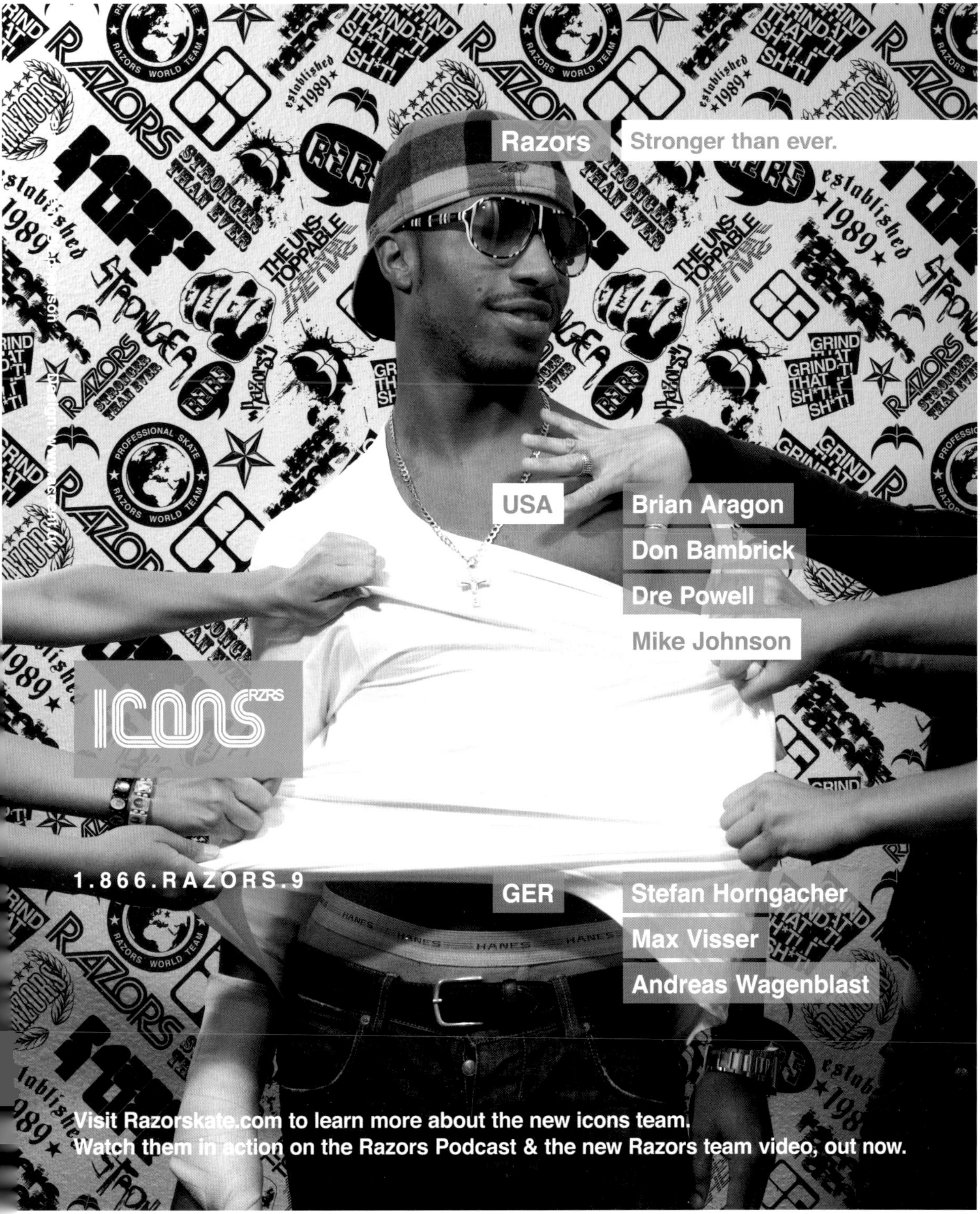
Razors
Stronger than ever.
USA
Brian Aragon
Don Bambrick
Dre Powell
Mike Johnson
ICONS RZRS
1.866.RAZORS.9
GER
Stefan Horngacher
Max Visser
Andreas Wagenblast
Visit Razorskate.com to learn more about the new icons team.
Watch them in action on the Razors Podcast & the new Razors team video, out now.

MATRIX &
FUTUREBOUND

5

Label:
Catalog#:
Format:
Country:
Released:
Genre:
Style:
Insert label name
insert catalog name
12"
UK
November 2006
Electronic
Drum n Bass
A: Universal Truth
AA: Skyscraper
VIPER
©2006 Matrix & Futurebound. All rights reserved. Unauthorized duplication is a violation of applicable laws

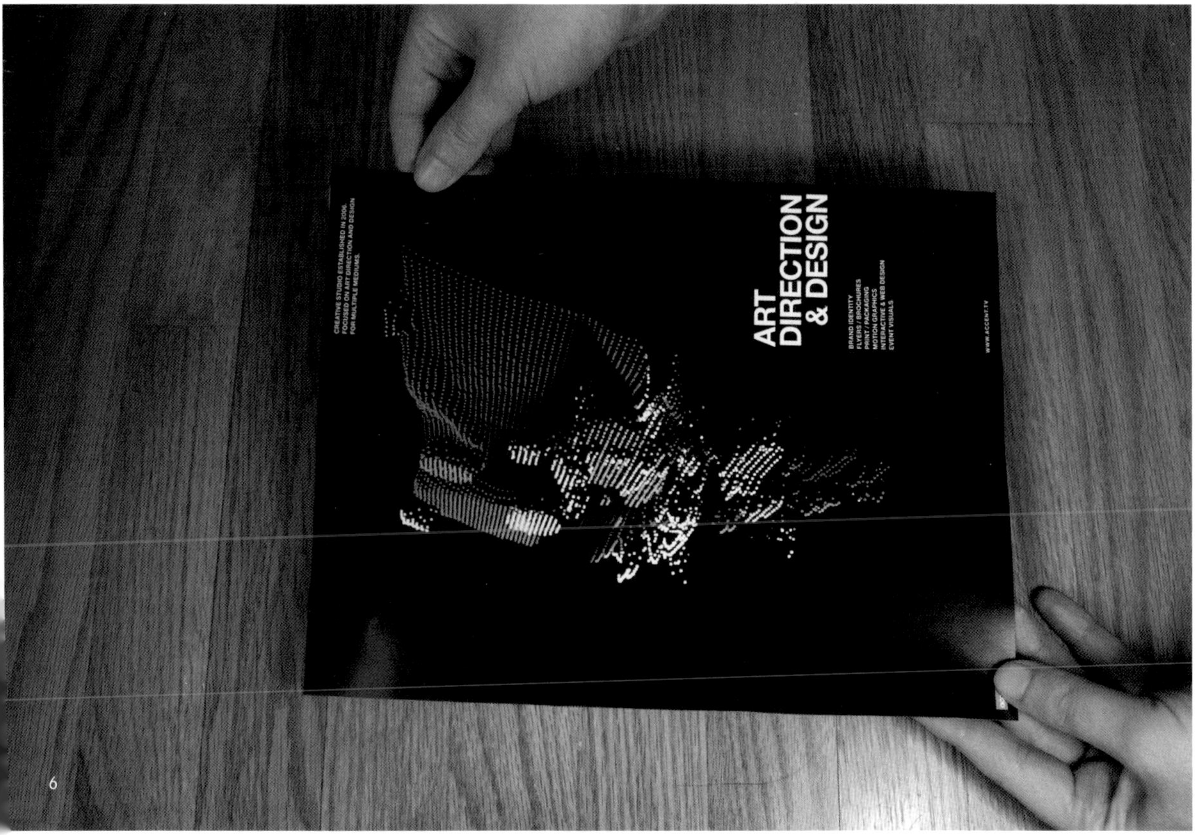
CREATIVE STUDIO ESTABLISHED IN 2006,
FOCUSED ON ART DIRECTION AND DESIGN
FOR MULTIPLE MEDIUMS.
ART
DIRECTION
& DESIGN
BRAND IDENTITY
FLYERS / BROCHURES
PRINT / PACKAGING
MOTION GRAPHICS
INTERACTIVE & WEB DESIGN
EVENT VISUALS
WWW.ACCENT.TV
6

ALEX LIN | NEW YORK, NY, USA

Alex Lin is a New York-based designer whose work is never short of exciting, whether his own freelance projects or in conjunction with Anisa Suthayalai as Default Office. Since previously working at 2x4, his work has been exhibited at the Cooper Hewitt Design Museum, and in 2006 he was a recipient of the Art Director's Club Young Guns 5 award.

www.alexlin.org, defaultwebsite.org

1 Flocked wallpaper | Illinois Institute of Technology, 2004
Designed at 2x4
2 Book design | Guggenheim Museum, 2004
Designed at 2x4, director Susan Sellers
3 Magazine special feature | Idea Magazine, 2005
Designed at 2x4, director Michael Rock
4 Promotional publication | Studio Museumin Harlem, 2005
Designed with Glen Cummings and Katie Andresen at 2x4
5 Artist monograph | Power Plant Art Gallery, 2005
Designed at 2x4, director Georgie Stout
6 Identity and promotional material | Citigroup Art Advisory Service, 2005
Designed at 2x4, director Michael Rock
7 Mural portrait | Illinois Institute of Technology, 2004
Designed at 2x4 with Karen Hsu, director Michael Rock

Walter De Maria
Cross, 1965–66

Aluminum
4 x 42 x 22 inches
(10.2 x 106.7 x 55.9 cm)

Solomon R. Guggenheim Museum,
New York
73.2033

Walter De Maria
Museum Piece, 1966

Aluminum
4 x 36 x 36 inches
(10.2 x 91.5 x 91.5 cm)

Solomon R. Guggenheim Museum,
New York
73.2034

2

It is an activity that he has done brilliantly well, and his work for Braun has haunted the imagination of Richard Hamilton and other artists. He made the perfect calculator, from which nothing more could be removed without compromising its performance. He did the same for Braun's stereo system, as well as for its television sets. And yet, at a deeper level, he failed. He made perfect, timeless objects beyond fashion and applied decoration, but entire categories of objects he devoted his life to have become redundant. Who needs a calculator the size of a book anymore, when the function can be performed by a cell phone? The LP record is no longer the primary means for disseminating music, and its player is now three generations of technology out of date. Rams's designs for Braun are revealed as an impossible, Canute-like campaign against change that, in retrospect, was a beautiful failure.

The term "Minimal" first began to be applied to architecture twenty years ago in connection with Pawson, who emerged as an architect at the beginning of the 1980s. In contrast to the architectural landscape of the time—dominated by a last decorative flourish of pastel postmodernism before it vanished into Disneyland resort hotels, the high-water mark of militant neoclassicism led by the Prince of Wales, and its counterpoint, the muscular high tech of the British school that could verge on fetishism—what was called "Minimalist architecture" seemed like something entirely different. Certainly, it was fresh, but it wasn't new, and it probably didn't have much to do with Minimalism in the sense that it was understood at the time. The term has perhaps served only to confuse the issue.

Pawson designed a first apartment for himself that owed a debt to the much admired Japanese designer Shiro Kuramata, in the form of a pink finish on the cornice—Pawson's only recorded use of applied color. The furniture he used showed his interest in AG Fronzoni from Milan. The interior caused something of a sensation in the overheated climate of 1984. It appeared to have nothing in it. Not just no furniture or pictures, but no shelves, no books, no door handles, no washing machine, no sofa, and no bed—just nothing. He went on to design a commercial art gallery on Cork Street that demonstrated his

pursuit of the art of almost nothing and that looked to be entirely unpublishable: in all the photographs, you find yourself looking at the art, focusing on a prancing Flanagan hare rather than on the architecture.

I wrote about this gallery, using the word "Minimalism" much too casually to describe it. Pawson was as close to the art camp as any architect, but his work could not really be equated with the art movement of the same name. Pawson was certainly fascinated by Donald Judd. And to this day, his office has a Dan Flavin fluorescent on the wall, leaking red light wantonly across the white plaster. His architecture, however, has a different sensibility. In his buildings, technique matters a great deal: the sensual properties of materials and the calculations of proportion matter even more. It is, in some ways, a highly traditional view of architecture. In the twentieth century, architectural minimalism is an idea that can be seen to link Loos—certainly a minimalist, both in his writings and, equally, in his sensuous but restrained use of rich materials—with Ludwig Wittgenstein, whose house designed for his sister in Vienna certainly fully lived up to Judd's idea about "proportion being reason made visible."[2] Minimalism is a concept that can provide insights into the work of Mies van der Rohe, with his infinite spaces, and also that of Kahn, with his sense of monumental enclosure. Kuramata's delicacy and directness with materials and Luis Barragán's manipulation of

2 *Donald Judd: Complete Writings, 1959–1975* (Halifax: Nova Scotia College of Art and Design Press; New York: New York University Press, 1975).

Above: Ludwig Mies van der Rohe
Farnsworth House, Plano, Illinois, 1946–51

Facing page: John Pawson, Pawson House, London, 1999

ærice Marden, March 1–April 27, 1975,
Solomon R. Guggenheim Museum,
New York, installation view

Robert Morris: *The Mind/Body Problem*,
February 3–April 17, 1994, Solomon R.
Guggenheim Museum, New York,
installation view

2

Dan Flavin
the nominal three (to William of Ockham),
1963

Fluorescent light fixtures with
daylight lamps
Edition 2/3
Height: 72 inches (183 cm); overall
dimensions variable

Solomon R. Guggenheim Museum,
New York, Panza Collection
91.3698

idea 3: Pin-Up
Show the changing studio wall as a site for work in progress.
ピンナップ
Theatre
Museum Moving Image
loving
working

3

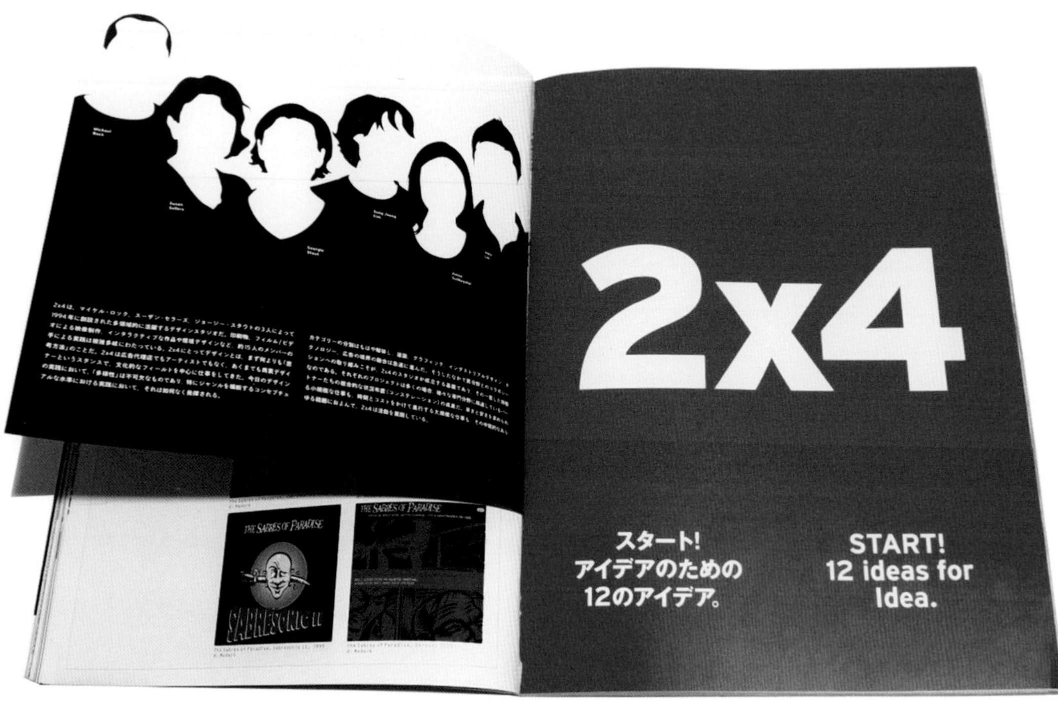
2x4
スタート!
アイデアのための
12のアイデア。
START!
12 ideas for
Idea.
THE SABRES OF PARADISE

3

4

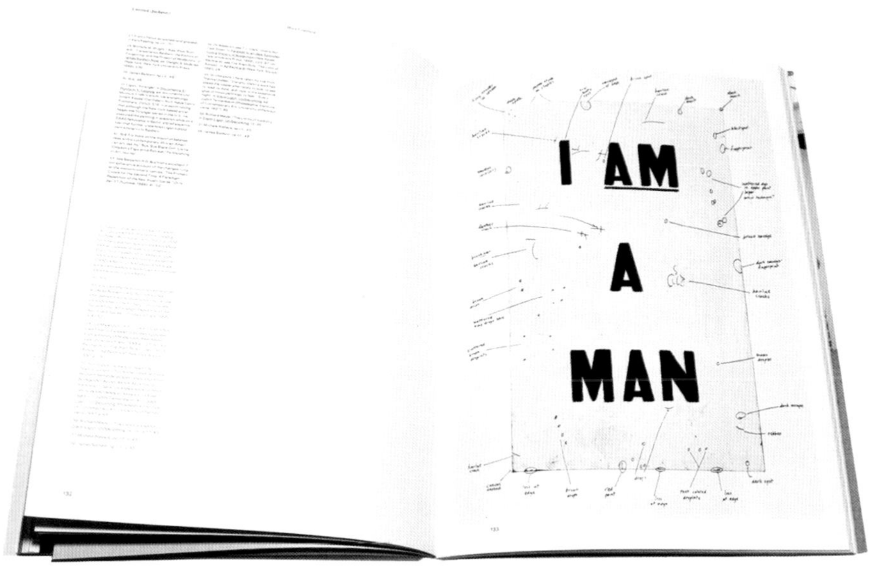

5

6

7

PORTUGAL. THE MAN
EURO TOUR
23.05.07 RÜSSELSHEIM RHEIN MAIN DAS RIND
25.05.07 HANNOVER CAFE GLOCKSEE
26.05.07 ROSTOCK MAUCLUB
28.05.07 SAARBRÜCKEN KLEINE GARAGE
29.05.07 DÜSSELDORF ZAKK
30.05.07 HAMBURG FÆT KNUST
03.06.07 HEIDELBERG KARLSTORBAHNHOF
04.06.07 STUTTGART SCHOCKEN
05.06.07 KONSTANZ KULTURLADEN
06.06.07 INNSBRUCK WEEKENDER
07.06.07 ZÜRICH HAFENKNEIPE
08.06.07 LUZERN KONZERTHAUS SCHÜÜR
09.06.07 OBERENTFELDEN BÖRÖM PÖMPÖM
TICKETS UNTER: WWW.KARTENHAUS.DE
DEFIANCE RECORDS
FUZE
laut.de
myspace.com a place for music.
target
VISIONS empfiehlt

AUSTIN SELLERS | PORTLAND, OR, USA

Originally from Indiana, Austin Sellers is a freelance graphic designer who settled in Portland, Oregon because of his love of all things mossy and fresh smelling. Though he cannot yet snowboard or surf, (sledding is a "yes") he specializes in print design, in particular the kind that is hand-made, and if possible the sort that is related to music.

www.austinmadethis.com

1 Promotional poster | Defiance Records, 2007
2 Promotional posters | Holocene, 2006, 2007
3 CD sleeve art | Blue Cranes, 2006
4 Promotional posters | Holocene, 2007, 2006

HOLOCENE PRESENTS
GIRL TALK
AUSTINMADETHIS
$8 ADV
AT BROWNPAPERTICKETS.COM + HOLOCENE.ORG
MACRO'S MANTICS
DJ BEYONDA (CD RELEASE)
DJ 1996 OLYMPICS
21+ 9PM
HOLOCENE
1001 SE MORRISON
WWW.HOLOCENE.ORG
FRI. NOV. 10TH

HOLOCENE PRESENTS
DAN DEACON
VIDEOHIPPOS
SHOW ME THE PINK
DJ BEYONDA
FRI JUNE 22ND 9PM 21+
$7
TICKETS AT JACKPOT RECS + BROWN PAPER TICKETS.COM
HOLOCENE
1001 SE MORRISON · WWW.HOLOCENE.ORG

BCM003
BLUE CRANES
LIFT MUSIC! FLOWN MUSIC!
1. RETURNING TO PORTLAND
(Reed Wallsmith)
(7:16)
2. ALUVIÓN/ SONG FOR AUDREY
(Reed Wallsmith)
(6:06)
3. POLARIS (7:19)
(Charley Westmoreland)
Black And Gold Music (BMI)
4. CRISTO DE PALACAGÜINA
(Carlos Mejia Godoy)
(SDRT)
(7:08)
5. COMING UP ROSES
(Elliott Smith)
Spent Bullets Music (BMI)
(4:09)
6. DEAR HOWARD
(Reed Wallsmith,
Lyrics: Nico Alvarado-Greenwood)
(8:01)
7. GREENWOOD
(Reed Wallsmith)
(4:45)
8. THIRTY OUGHT SIX CIRCUS
(Reed Wallsmith)
(7:39)
© 2007 Blue Cranes

BLUE CRANES
LIFT MUSIC!
FLOWN MUSIC!

3

BLUE
CRANES
LIFT
MUSIC!
FLOWN
MUSIC!

BLUE
CRANES
LIFT
MUSIC!
FLOWN
MUSIC!

HOLOCENE PRESENTS
White Magic
Plants
White Rainbow
WED
NOV.21
HOLOCENE
9PM
21+
$10
1001 SE MORRISON WWW.HOLOCENE.ORG
ADVANCE AT JACKPOT RECS, BROWNPAPERTICKETS.COM+HOLOCENE
AUSTINMADETHIS

HOLOCENE &
BLACKBIRD PRESENT
SAT. MAY 6
HOLOCENE
9PM 21+ $7
ADVANCE AT
JACKPOTS & BROWNPAPERTICKETS.COM
HOLOCENE.ORG BLACKBIRDPRESENTS.COM

BLACK MARMALADE | MILWAUKEE, WI, USA
DeChazier P. Stokes-Johnson

DeChazier Stokes-Johnson started actively working under the pseudonym Black Marmalade in 2005, as a way of exploring the ideas and design experiments that he was otherwise not able to execute in his 9 to 5 job. His involvement with the design world has led to themarmaspot.com, his site dedicated to interviews and commentary on creative culture.

www.black-marmalade.com

1 Promotional illustration | MKE, 2007
2 Stickers and CD | Dork Magazine, 2007
3 Illustration | Bon Iver, 2007
4 Graphics | Royal Magazine, 2007
5 Magazine cover and titles | Rockpile magazine, 2006-07
6 Promotional illustrations | Kareem Black and Black Marmalade, 2006
7 Poster | Obama Summer Benefit Party, 2007
8 Logos and type | Black Marmalade, Dert, Shift, Forty8One, Two Step, OIO, Nire, MammaJamma, Sweetface, 2005-07

dork
magazine
www.dorkmag.com

NO
MORE
FUSSING
-AND-
FIGHTING
www.dorkmag.com

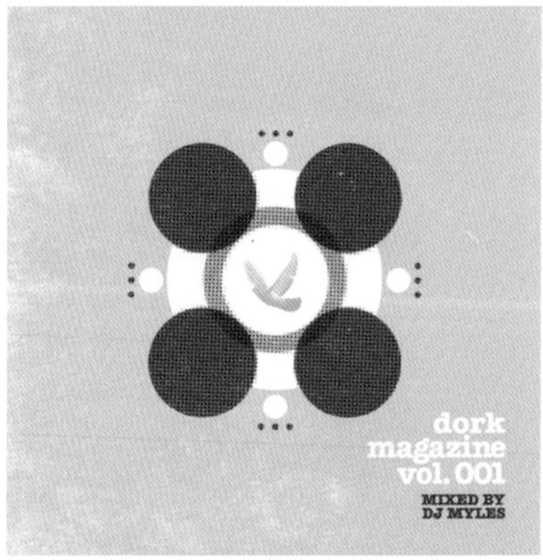
dork
magazine
vol. 001
MIXED BY
DJ MYLES

visit dorkmag.com
Liner Notes from DJ Myles:
On this mix I've put some new, some exclusive, and some old music. It is a celebration of everything soulful. This is all music that has excited and moved me. I hope you enjoy this mix as much as I've enjoyed making it.
Thanks to James and Taj at Dork Magazine, the love of my life Lindsey, Mom and Dad, Deirdre, Brad and Jen, Kit, Mike, Josh, Arty, Peter, Meg, Matzu, Nicolay, Ali Shaheed Muhammad, Uncle Mike, Rich Medina, Rob Swift, Akalepse, Waajeed, Ge-ology, J. Rawls, Alec @ APT, Justin @ Nublu, Ty and Kory, Jack and Blayke, and of course R.I.P. to the late great James Yancey.

bon iver

We print NEW YORK
Custom Publishing. Full Service Printing.
Promotions. Out of Home. Look Books

4

AND THAT'S JUST THE HALF -*of my*- WAR PATH

Rockpile

INDEPENDENT MUSIC AND CULTURE

121
May/Jun 2006

USA $4.50 Canada $5.50
www.Rockpile.net

COMM-
UNICATION
BREA-
KDOWN
Deconstructing Art, Business and Identity on the Road with Bloc Party

ISN'T
WICKED
TO CARE
Belle And Sebastian
Visit Palestine

Harmony
in my
Head
Catching Up
With the Futureheads

KAREEM BLACK + BLACK MARMALADE

OBAMA '08
SUMMER
BENEFIT
PARTY
SATURDAY
JUNE 9TH
10PM-4AM
THE ONE
& ONLY
RICH MEDINA
ON THE ONES & TWOS

BLACK-MARMALADE

BMAR

BLACK-MARMALADE

DERT WIND & FIRE

DERT THUMB NAILS

SHIFT

FORTY ONE

two step

NIRE

YAMMA YAMMA

Sweet face

Flopa
VIERNES 14 02 07
23:00HS
CENTRO CULTURAL
TORQUATO TASSO
Defensa 1575 - San Telmo

BRAVO | BUENOS AIRES, ARGENTINA
Juan Pablo Caballé, Rina Di Maggio, Marcos Girado

Bravo is a design and communication studio founded in Buenos Aires in 2006. Formed by a trio of designers each coming from different communication disciplines, Bravo boasts of a versatile style, specialized skills, and a creative process that takes experimentation as a starting point for developing fresh trends and ideas.

www.bravosite.tv

1 Promotional poster | Flopa, 2007
2 Promotional posters | Ian Cyborg, 2007
3 Promotional poster | Girazul, 2007
4 CD packaging | Flopa, 2007
5 Notepad and folder | MTV Latin America, 2006

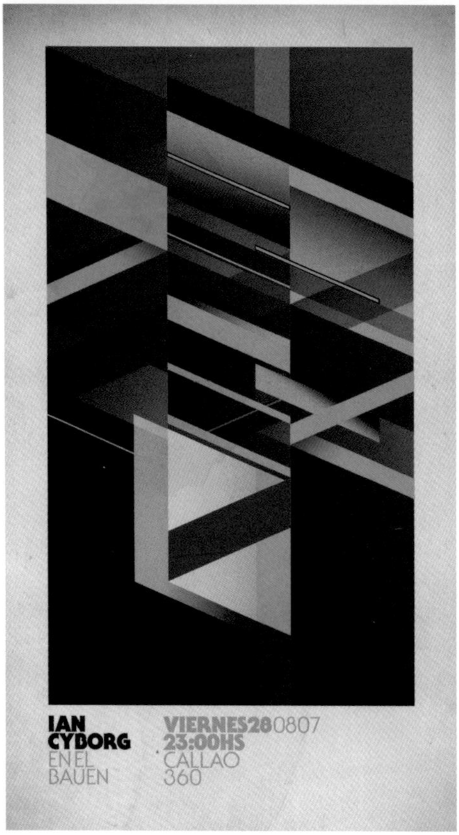
IAN
CYBORG
EN EL
BAUEN
VIERNES280807
23:00HS
CALLAO
360

iancyborg
17 DE NOVIEMBRE 22HS
BAHUEN — CALLAO 360

2

IAN
CYBORG
EN EL
BAUEN
VIERNES280807
23:00HS
CALLAO
360

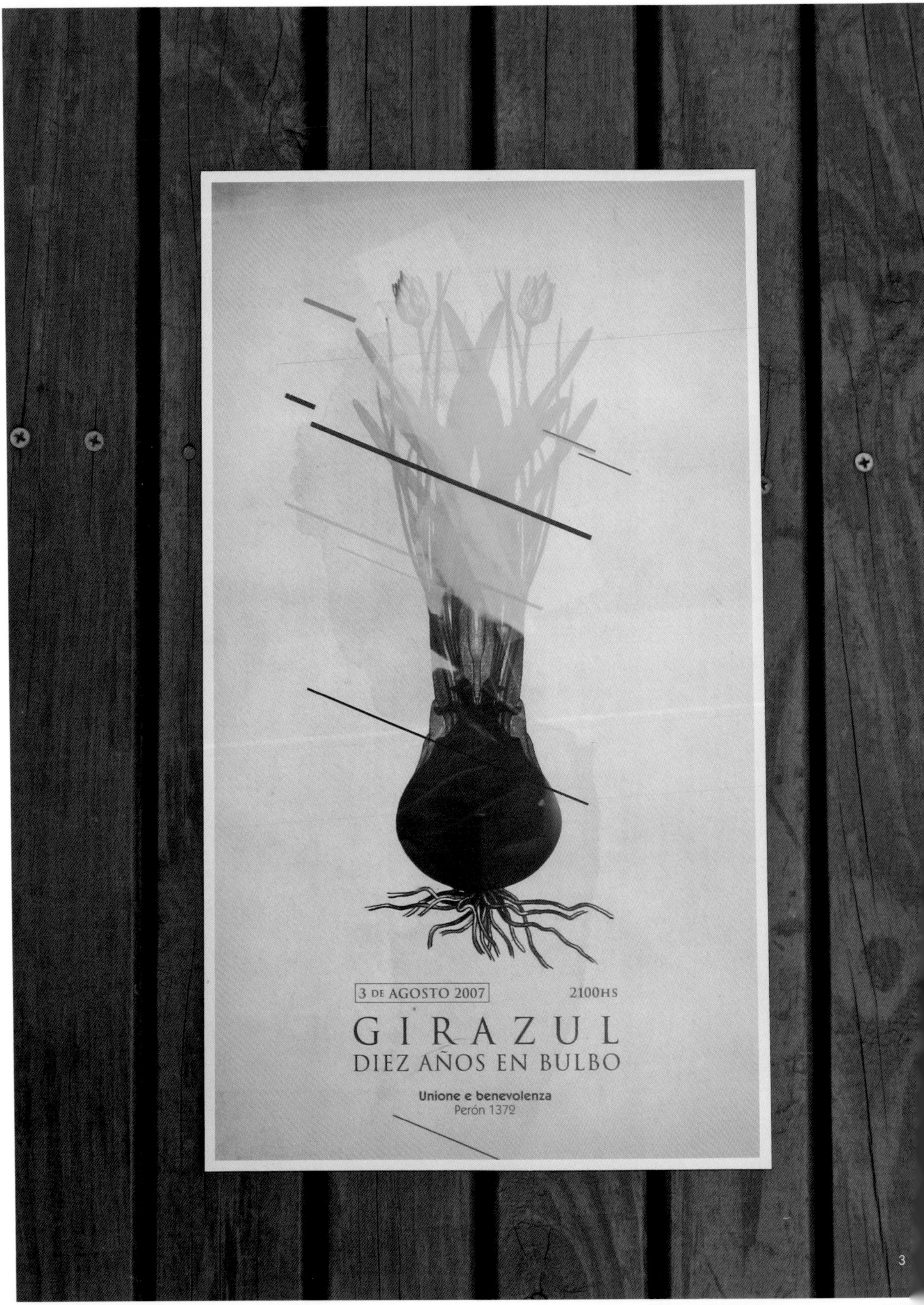
3 DE AGOSTO 2007
2100HS
GIRAZUL
DIEZ AÑOS EN BULBO
Unione e benevolenza
Perón 1372

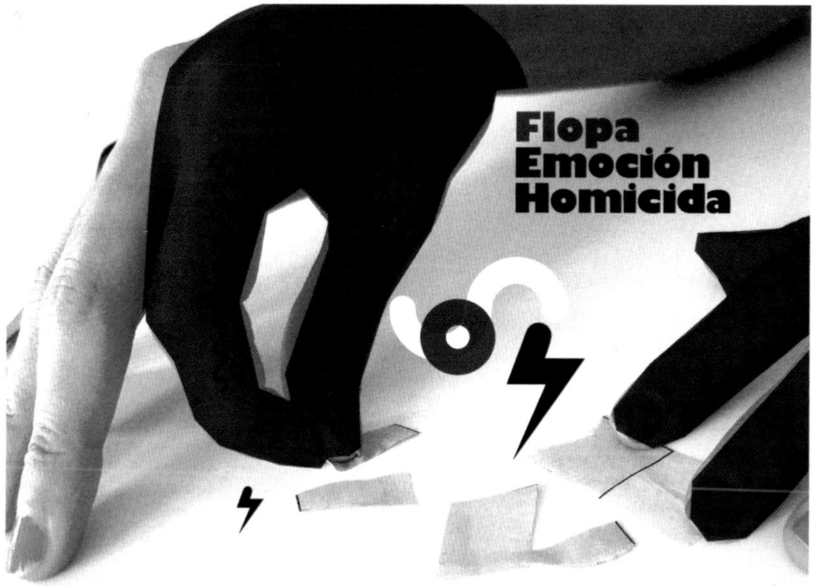

Flopa
Emoción
Homicida

MTVLA.COM

MTVLA.COM

5

MTV Networks Latin America
1111 Lincoln Road
Miami Beach, FL 33139
© MTV Networks Latin America. Todos los derechos reservados.

MUSIC TELEVISION®

5

CONHECIDA POR TODOS
Gillette
MARCAS REGISTRADAS
W 4
INDÚSTRIA BRASILEIRA
200
250

CUBICULO | RIO DE JANEIRO, BRAZIL

Fabio Arruda, Rodrigo Bleque

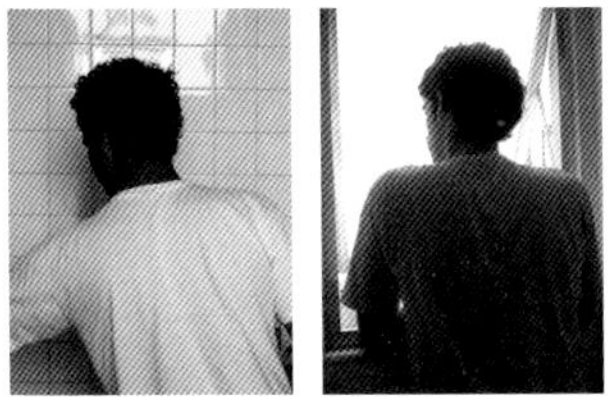

Fabio Arruda and Rodrigo Bleque share and develop their ideas at Cubiculo, a graphic design studio based in Rio de Janeiro. They have worked together since 2001 and most of their projects are related to cultural areas like exhibitions, music, fashion and theatre. They usually state unsatisfactory reasons to justify what they believe instinctively.

www.cubiculo.net

1 O Púcaro Búlgaro collage | Teatro Poeira, 2006
2 Catalogue for Fabulosas Desordens graffiti exhibition | Metropolis Produções, 2007
3 Flyers | MOO, 2006
4 Jean Nouvel book design | Centro de Arquitetura e Urbanismo, RJ, 2004
Art directors Fabio Arruda, Rodrigo Bleque and Marcos Leme
5 O Acidente theatre program | Signorini MKT, 2005
6 Layout and graphics | Jornal do Brasil, 2006

GRAFITE &
MAINSTREAM:
ALGUMAS APROXIMAÇÕES
GUY AMADO
A ponto de já existir a terminologia específica corporate grafite, empregada na América do Norte e na Europa para designar a produção de grafiteiros a serviço de grandes empresas.
2

CAIXA CULTURAL
apresenta
fabu
losa
expo/workshops/palestras
13 março → 29 abril
Caixa Cultural Rio de Janeiro

MOO
2 anos / edição especial

MOO—
28–10–2006

É indispensável a apresentação deste.
Convite válido para 1 pessoa
24FEV SEXTA 23H
AUDIO
Diogo Reis (moo)
Eduardo Christoph (moo)
Vince Watson (live-escócia)
Oblongui (brasília)
VIDEOS
Marcos Kotlhar
Eduardo Berliner
Cadu
LUZ
Tomás Ribas
Álvaro Ramos 414, Botafogo
mapa & infos: www.moo.com.br
classificação etária 18 anos
desenhado por cubiculo@2006

4

Situado em um ângulo do Quai Saint Bernard no término do Faubourg Saint Germain, o Instituto do Mundo Árabe efetua a transição delicada entre o tecido urbano parisiense tradicional e os edifícios precisos e modernos da faculdade de Jussieu. O edifício que segue a curva do cais e acomoda-se ao sul em direção à faculdade, de uma ampla esplanada, é fracionado de uma falha estreita orientada em direção ao jusante do rio Sena e mais precisamente à cabeceira da igreja Notre Dame.

Vitrine da cultura árabe, o IMA é um edifício ocidental no qual Nouvel associou alguns temas da arquitetura árabe tradicional. Abstração e geometria dos motivos repetidos, os jogos inteligentes de sombra e luz. A fachada Sul é constituida de um conjunto estrito de "diafragmas" com motivos de estrelas evocadores do "moucharabieh", a torre de livros e sua rampa em aspiral fazem alusão ao "ziggourat", a sala hipóstilo lembra lugares antigos, crípticos e sagrados. Por fim e sobretudo, o edifício inteiro constitui um filtro sutil da luz que transforma-se ao longo do dia e exibe um permanente jogo movimentado de reflexos e refrações entre painéis de vidro e de metal.

Louise Cardoso
Marcelo Escorel

5

Estava procurando um texto visceral que me desafiasse, que me revirasse as entranhas,
Cibele Forjaz e eu estávamos querendo trabalhar juntas, depois do nosso encontro no
Bonde Chamado Desejo, que eu ajudei na compra dos direitos autorais. Eu queria fazer um trabalho
que tivesse identidade, onde texto, direção, ator, cenário, luz, figurino, adereços, produção, viessem
da mesma fonte, e caminhassem pra mesma direção, juntos, interligados.
Marcelo Escorel me apresentou O Acidente, fizemos uma leitura pra Cibele e fomos arrebatados
universo do Bosco Brasil! O texto nos encantou e surpreendeu, os personagens nos apaixonou
trouxe a equipe da Cibele de São Paulo, misturei com a minha aqui do Rio, tudo
Fernanda Signorini, e o apoio do meu parceiro e sócio,

A CULTURA NU PODER

B
Jornal do Brasil
Domingo
24 de setembro de 2006
cadernob@jb.com.br

a cultura no poder e o poder nu.

Jornal do Brasil
Domingo
24 de setembro de 2006
cadernob@jb.com.br
B

Outro Brasil. Não precisa ser o paraíso terrenal das cartas de Rui Pereira, em 1560, a seus irmãos de fé portugueses. Mas não precisava ser tão difícil. Está bem, não é só o Brasil, é o mundo que está um inferno. Então, outro mundo. Em que, no juízo final, um italiano não precisasse xingar a mãe e a parentela toda de um francês e o francês não reagisse com uma cabeçada. Bom, é mais do que outro mundo, é caso de outro homem. Aí vai ser mais difícil, não dá para resolver numa edição de domingo. Mas um outro Brasil vale a pena ao menos tentar.

Na nossa tribo, estamos sempre falando que a cultura pode salvar (o Brasil, o mundo, o homem). Que tribo é essa? Bastava dizer, a tribo deste caderno b, um marco na cultura brasileira. Mas prefiro ser mais modesto, ou mais pessoal, ou mais romântico, ou mais nacional (para não ficar na carioca geração Paissandu). Assim: na Praça do Ferreira, mais perto do equador, nos anos 60, essa tribo era chamada de os culturais. Eram os que chegavam à praça depois dos halterofilistas e antes dos radialistas, dos jogadores de carteado e dos putanheiros, os últimos, que só chegavam quando acabava a noitada na zona, isso quando não dormiam por lá mesmo. Os culturais saíam da sessão das dez do cinema São Luiz para salvar o mundo a partir dos bancos da praça. Os primeiros que se mandavam, cansados desse papo furado, eram os halterofilistas. Tinham de acordar cedo para tomar sua dose diária de Charles Atlas, o açaí daquela época. Logo eles que podiam ser nossa tropa de choque. Ficava o pessoal do carteado, bocejando, e os putanheiros, em geral bêbados. Não tinha muita graça, pois só os culturais acreditavam que a cultura podia salvar o mundo.

Não deu naquela época, vamos tentar agora. Sei que vão me dizer, você entendeu mal, a gente disse a cultura pode salvar, não os culturais. O que eles fazem, não eles propriamente. Não venha querer salvar o mundo com o colaboracionista do Céline e o fascista do Pound. Vamos falar da Viagem ao fim da noite, dos Cantos, não desses cavalos (do candomblé).

Ora, eu respondo, um livro não pode presidir uma reunião ministerial, que, aliás, não pode ter só quadros, filmes, discos ao redor daquela mesa grande. Tem que ter gente para todas essas ações monumentais (como vender empresas públicas) que empurram um país pra frente (ih!) e, espera-se, trazem prosperidade e felicidade para sua gente. Os livros, os quadros, os filmes, os espetáculos de teatro, as músicas podem salvar, desde que uns pobres mortais cuidem da cozinha. Então, por que não os que pintam, escrevem, tocam, compõem, interpretam?

Trata-se, pois, de um Brasil imaginário, com a cultura e os culturais no poder. Mas não a Ilha Brazil, essa ilha fantástica ao sul da Irlanda, que só uns poucos escolhidos podem ver. Muito embora Brazil com Z lembre Glauber Rocha, extraordinário candidato a presidente se fosse vivo. Estou falando deste Brasil velho de guerra, talvez mais impossível do que aquela ilha, inexistente apesar de existente (como diria Campos de Carvalho), ou existente apesar de inexistente (como diria Drummond).

Então é isso aí, imaginar os poetas no poder.

E um outro Brasil, fértil, feminino, menstruando. Onde, sobretudo, o poder ficasse nu, com o corpo e a alma expostos à luz do dia e à luz elétrica, sem segredos, sem cinismo, sem hipocrisia. O poder nu, escancarado, a arte e a cultura inventando uma nova política. Quem sabe a impossível síntese do poder e da anarquia, a suprema utopia, tudo saudavelmente de pernas pro ar, como um filme da Atlântida, com Oscarito e Grande Otelo. Um país genial, como um filme do Glauber Rocha, um livro do Rosa ou do Callado, uma música do Pixinguinha, um poema do Bandeira, uma peça do Nelson Rodrigues, um quadro do Portinari.

Na hora de devolver o Brasil outra vez aos políticos, o poeta do poder podia simplesmente escrever como o prefeito de Palmeira dos Índios, Graciliano Ramos, em seu relatório ao governador das Alagoas: não sei se a administração do município, digo, do país, foi boa ou ruim; talvez pudesse ser pior.

Como diz o primeiro-ministro Oscar Niemeyer, "a gente tem é que sonhar, senão as coisas não acontecem".

Vamos nessa?

Aderbal Freire-Filho

Com esta edição o JB inaugura o **Projeto B Intervenção,** em que personalidades do meio cultural e artístico criarão edições especiais do Caderno B. O diretor e autor de teatro Aderbal Freire-Filho é nosso primeiro convidado.

Rela
Exte
Relações Exteriores
Hilde
... e a alta-sociedade das letras.
prf. B.Strb~

Uma página de inteira responsabilidade do búlgaro Prf. B. Strb~, interessado em não estar só em sua observação do Brasil.

Mesmo quando Stefan Zweig, Lévy-Strauss e outros mais votados saem para tomar um cafezinho (ou se suicidam), as repúblicas culturais muitas vezes se manifestam sobre o Brasil. Contra e à favor.

Michel Houllebecq é o maior escritor europeu de hoje, dizia Fernando Arrabal comendo bolinho de bacalhau no Rio Scenarium. O trecho é de seu romance Partículas elementares (Editora Sulina, 1999). A personagem Sophie diz a Bruno "adora as danças brasileiras". Pra quê?

Só para tranquilizar o Ministério das Relações Exteriores do governo Nu, é bom lembrar que o livro de Houllebecq é de 1998, ano, portanto, do auge da corrupção, da violência e da miséria.

Rubén Darío, o extraordinário poeta nicaragüense que deu régua e compasso ao idioma modernista espanhol, passou pelo Rio em 1906 e saudou em seus versos os novos tempos

Daniel Samper Pisano, romancista e cronista colombiano. O romance "Impávido coloso", com esse título, só podia se passar mesmo no Brasil e nos pávidos anos de ditadura. Os personagens fictícios do romance encontram-se com um personagem verdadeiro, D. Helder Câmara, o telefone toca, D. Helder atende e depois diz aos visitantes que foi o de sempre, outra ameaça de bomba

Miguel Torga, o escritor português de quem Jorge Amado dizia que "faleceu sem ter recebido o Prêmio Nobel, injustiça sem tamanho", viveu alguns anos de sua adolescência na fazenda de um tio no interior de Minas. Em "A criação do mundo" define o Brasil

prf. B.Strb~

Eduardo Portella

Arnaldo Niskier

Sábato Magaldi

Nélida Piñon

Cícero Sandroni

Marcos Vilaça

Celso Lafer

Padre Ávila

Murilo Mello Filho

Ana Maria Machado

Tarcísio Padilha

Antonio Secchin

José Mindlin

Evaristo de Moraes Filho

Ivan Junqueira

Afonso Arinos de Mello Franco

Moacyr Scliar

6

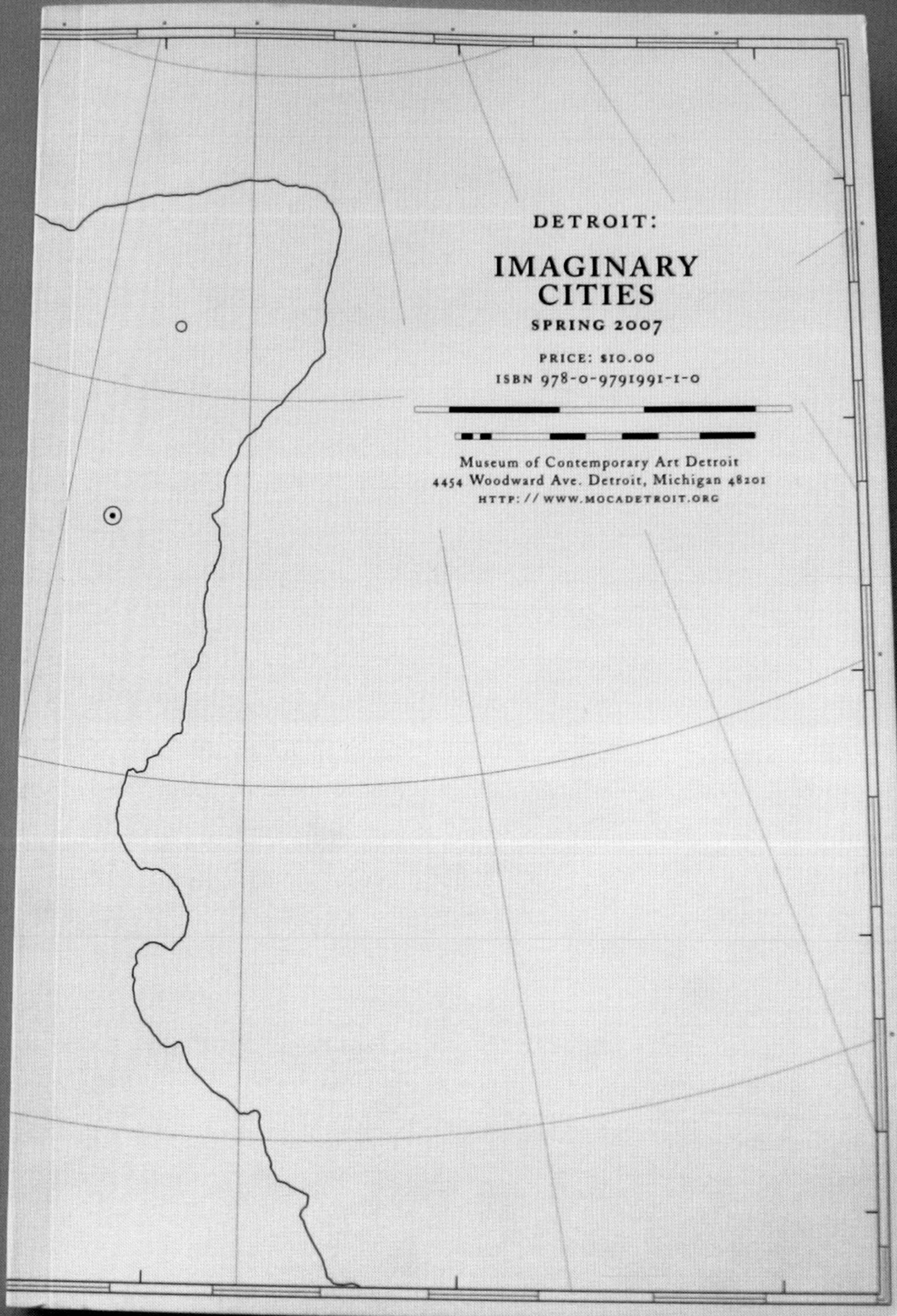
DETROIT:
IMAGINARY CITIES
SPRING 2007
PRICE: $10.00
ISBN 978-0-9791991-1-0
Museum of Contemporary Art Detroit
4454 Woodward Ave. Detroit, Michigan 48201
HTTP: // WWW.MOCADETROIT.ORG

1

DANIELLE AUBERT | DETROIT, MI, USA

Danielle Aubert has practiced graphic design in New York and Moscow, and is now based in Detroit, where she works regularly as a graphic designer for the Museum of Contemporary Art. Her book, 16 Months Worth of Drawings in Microsoft Excel, was published by Various Projects in 2006. She currently teaches at the College for Creative Studies.

www.danielleaubert.com

1 Journal | Museum of Contemporary Art Detroit, 2007
In collaboration with Nina Bianchi
2 Book | Self-initiated, published by Various Projects, 2006
3 Exhibition catalogue | Museum of Contemporary Art Detroit, 2007

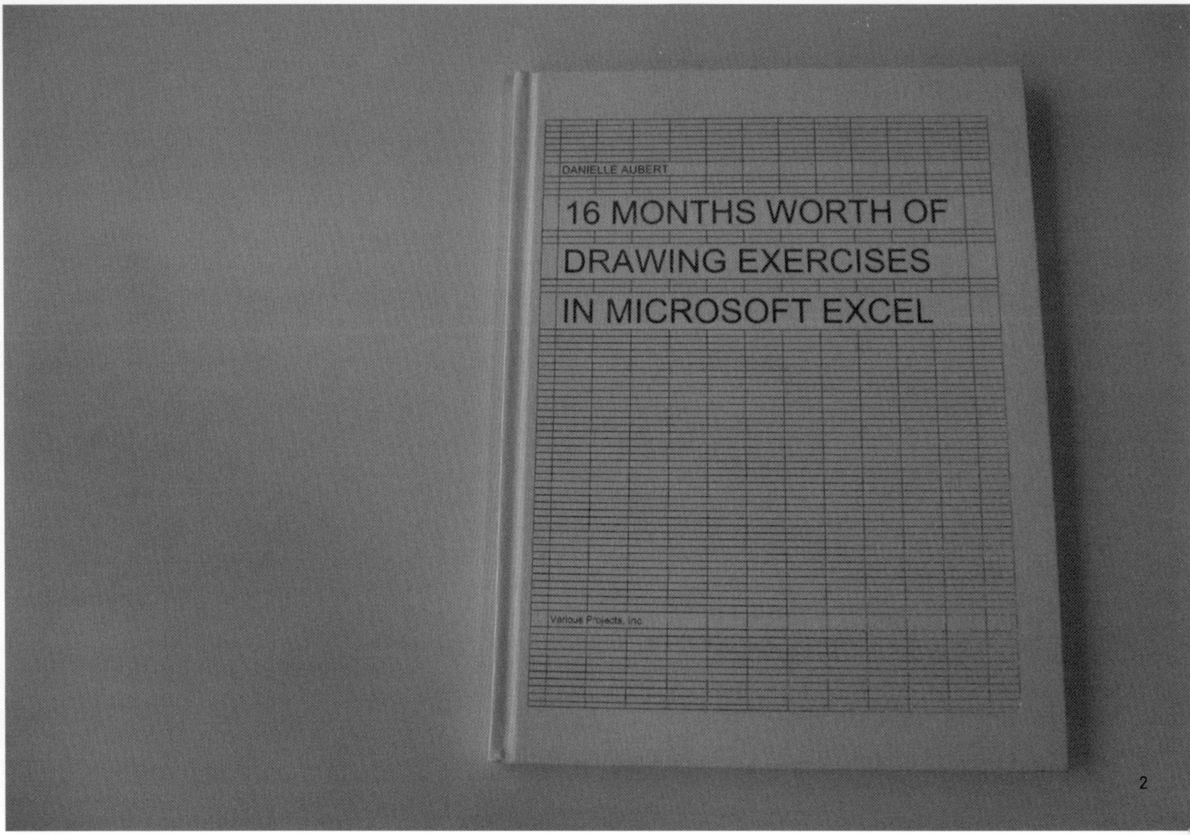
DANIELLE AUBERT
16 MONTHS WORTH OF
DRAWING EXERCISES
IN MICROSOFT EXCEL
Various Projects, Inc.

2

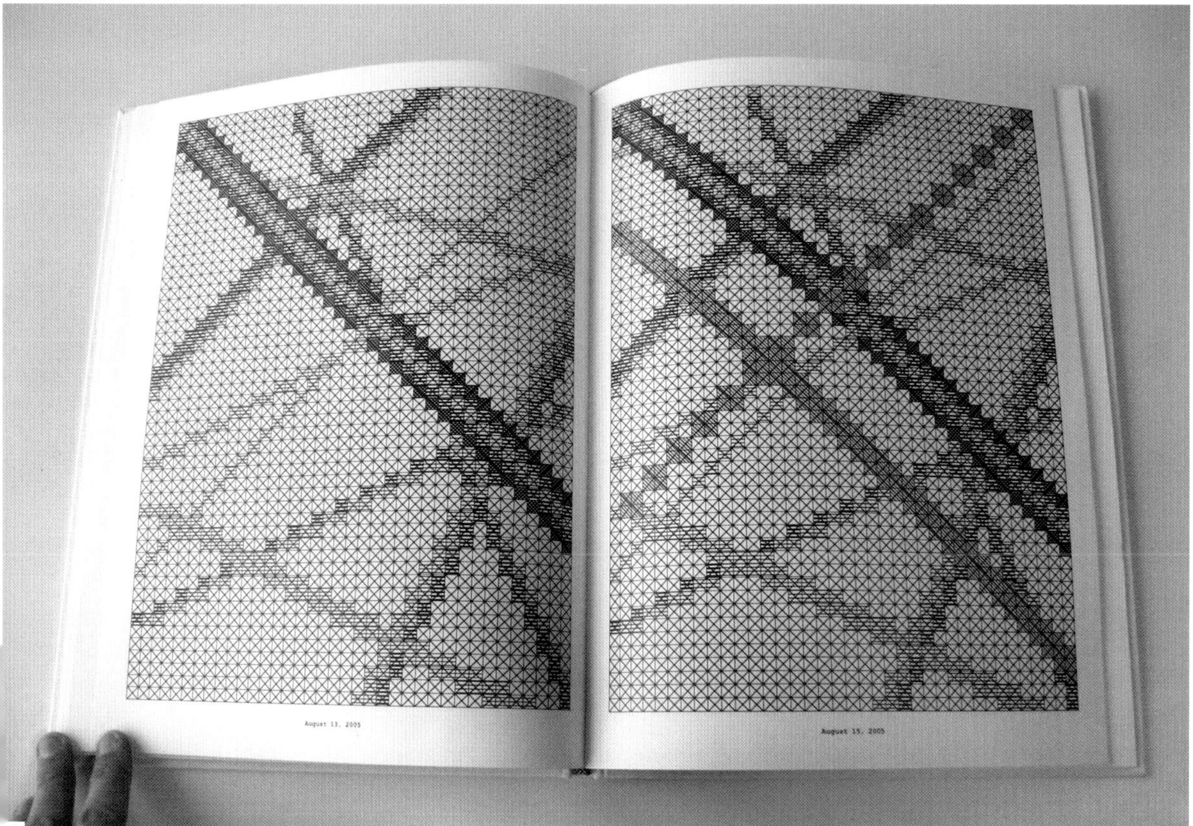

2

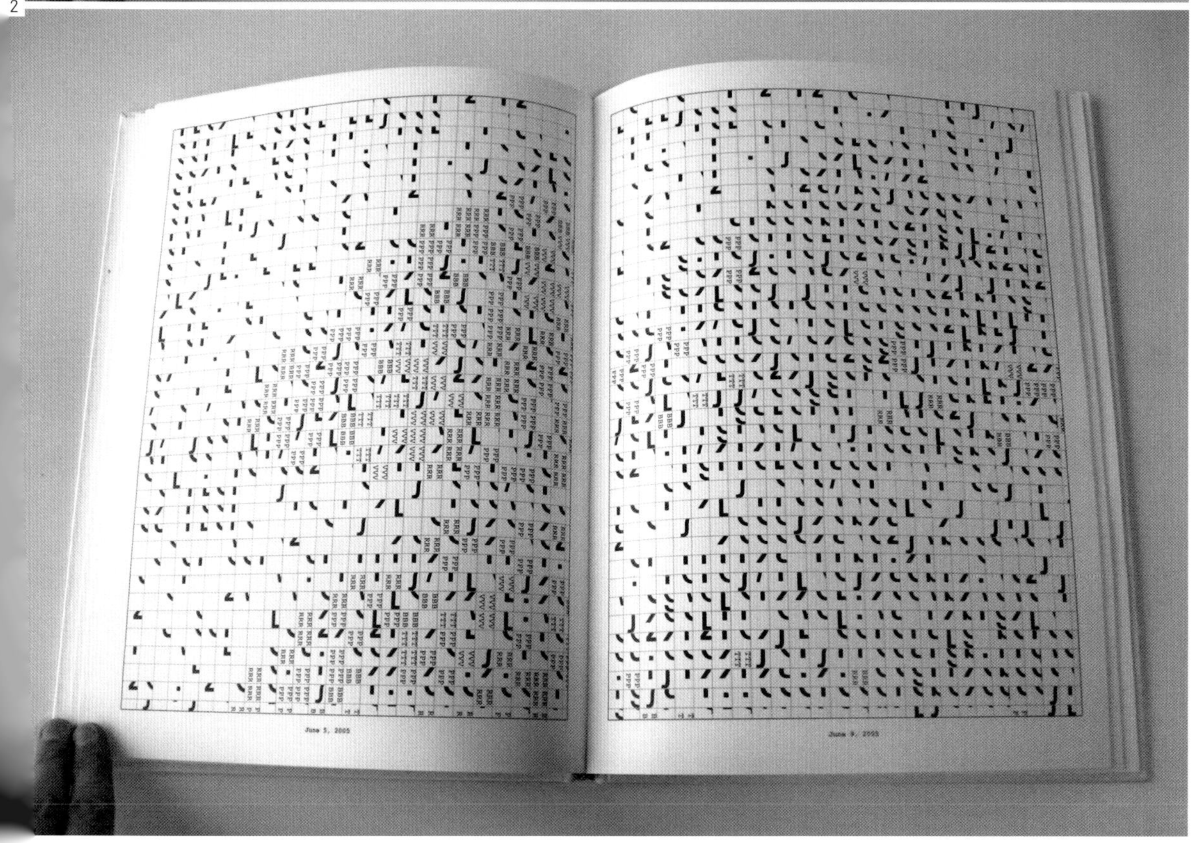

MEDITATIONS IN AN EMERGENCY
Mark BRADFORD, Christopher FACHINI, Barry MCGEE,
Roxy PAINE, Paul PFEIFFER, Jonathan PYLYPCHUK,
TABAIMO, Kara WALKER, Nari WARD
curator
Klaus KERTESS
MO
CAD
Museum of Contemporary Art Detroit

pages 54 - 57.
Paul PFEIFFER
Live from Neverland, 2006
Still images courtesy The Project Gallery
- 54 -
- 55 -

3

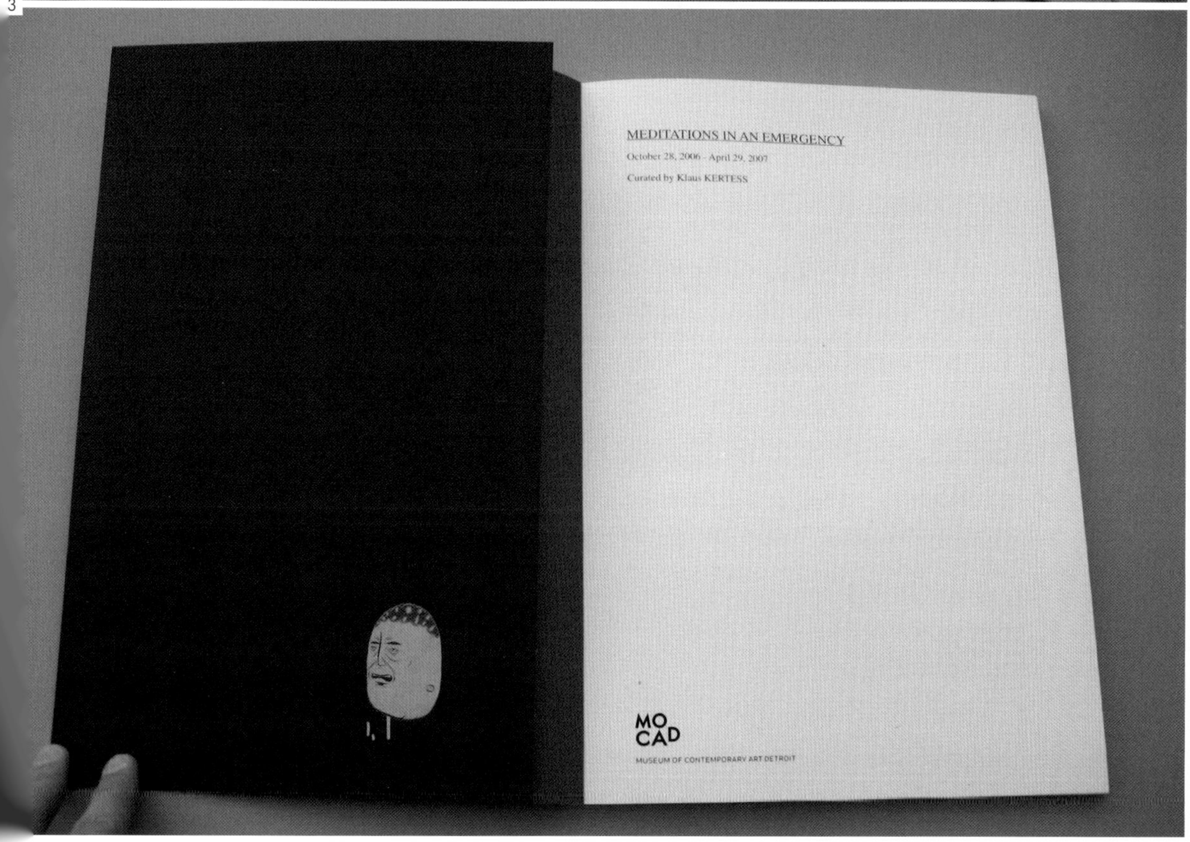
MEDITATIONS IN AN EMERGENCY
October 28, 2006 - April 29, 2007
Curated by Klaus KERTESS
MO
CAD
MUSEUM OF CONTEMPORARY ART DETROIT

DiOS
TE
SAL
MaRÍA

DELRANCHO | SANTIAGO DE CHILE, CHILE
Ricardo Villavicencio

Delrancho is the creative outlet of Ricardo Villavicencio. Born in Santiago de Chile, Ricardo started his professional career as art director for the multinational advertising agency network, Lowe, later leaving the advertising world to dedicate himself to art direction and freelancing for the Brand New School studio in New York.

www.delrancho.org

1 Promotional poster | Design Politics, 2006
2 Promotional poster | Cinesur, 2007
3 Graphics | El Cielo ayb, MTV2, 2006
4 Promotional poster | G2 Grey, 2005
5 Illustration | Plan C, 2007
6 Promotional poster | Bar Central, 2007
7 Promotional poster | Leche2, 2007

AMPARO NOGUERA | PAULINA GARCÍA | DANIEL MUÑOZ | TAMARA ACOSTA | ALFREDO CASTRO | LUIS GNECCO | LUZ VALDIVIESO | ALVARO ESPINOZA
FRANCISCA EYZAGUIRRE | LUIS BRAVO | DANIELA LLHORENTE | ANDRÉS EYZAGUIRRE | CLAUDIO ARREDONDO | CLAUDIO VALENZUELA
CASA DE REMOLIENDA
LA PUTA Y SANTA VERDAD
UNA PELICULA
DE JOAQUÍN EYZAGUIRRE

2

head
bangers
ball
New
24 A.M. THURSDAYS
MTV2

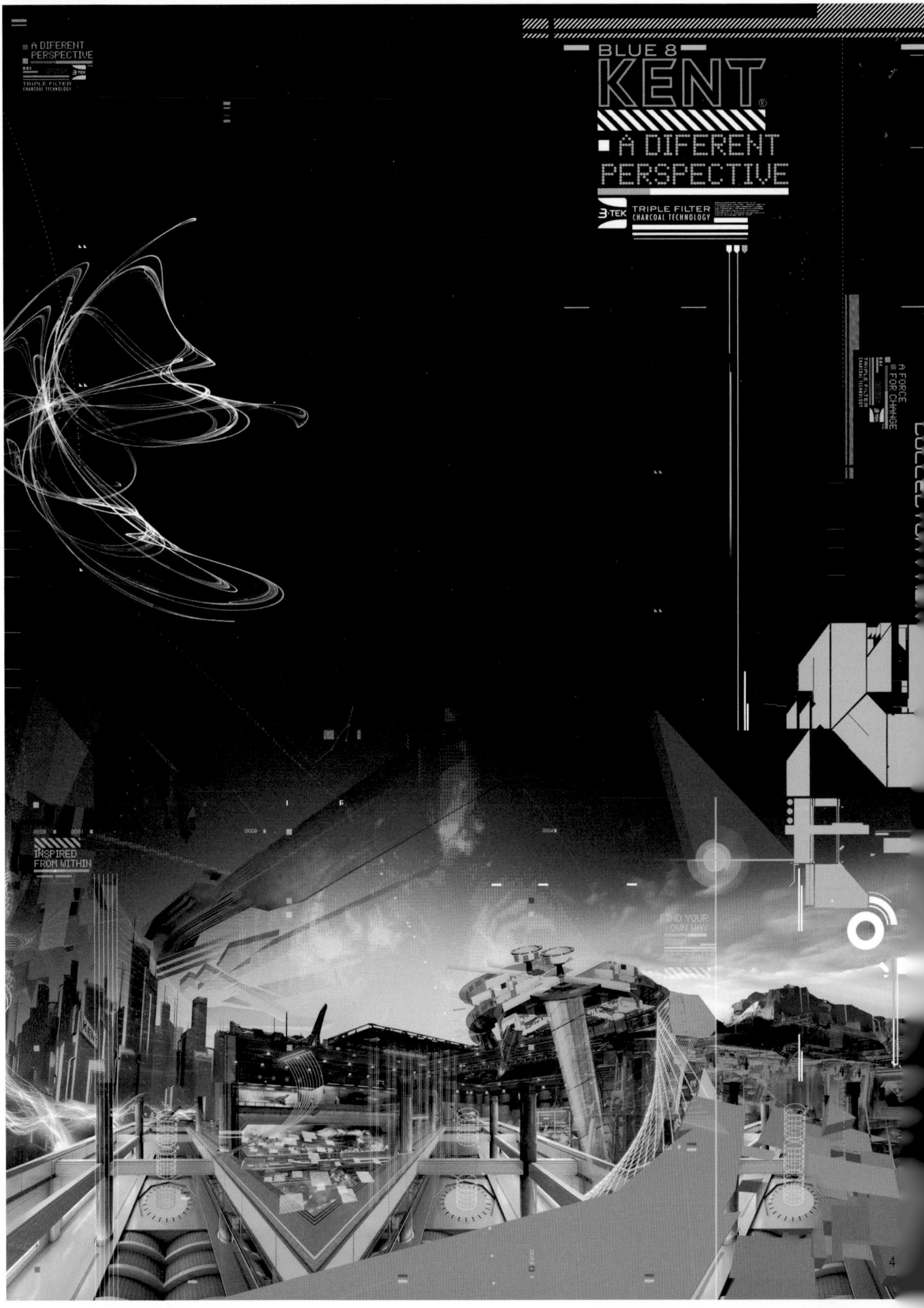
A DIFERENT PERSPECTIVE
TRIPLE FILTER CHARCOAL TECHNOLOGY
BLUE 8
KENT®
A DIFERENT PERSPECTIVE
3·TEK TRIPLE FILTER CHARCOAL TECHNOLOGY
A FORCE FOR CHANGE
TRIPLE FILTER CHARCOAL TECHNOLOGY
INSPIRED FROM WITHIN
FIND YOUR OWN WAY

R

7

COME OUT
AND PLAY
AIGA DC DESIGN FOR THE FUN OF IT LEVEL 8
THE GALLERIA AT LAFAYETTE CENTRE
1155 21ST STREET, NW, WDC 20036
MAY 22, 2001
6:30-9:30 PM
AIGA

DESIGN ARMY | WASHINGTON DC, USA
Jake Lefebure, Pum M. Lefebure

Founded in Washington DC by creative partners Jake and Pum M. Lefebure, Design Army is a studio that prides itself on being smart, strategic and selective. Only taking projects that are both challenging and rewarding, and keeping clients to a minimum ensures that their diverse client base has their full attention and the highest standard of work.

www.designarmy.com

1 Invitation | American Institute of Graphic Arts, D.C. Chapter, 2001
2 Book | Black Book, 2007
3 Invitation | Mohawk Paper, 2003
4 Mail campaign and brochure | Relish, 2005-06
5 Visual identity | Golden Triangle Business Improvement District, 2007
6 Promotional posters | Signature Theatre, 2006-07
7 Trivia game | Chronicle Books, 2007
Illustrations by Alex Fine
8 Promotional items | Self-initiated, 2005-06
9 Promotional kit | Cade Martin, 2006
10 Press kit and book | Signature Theatre, 2007
11 Poster | American Institute of Graphic Arts, D.C. Chapter, 2006

Now that the hard work is done
it's time to show off the goods.

THE BLACK BOOK

AR100

There's almost always room for improvement.

PERFECT 10

PRINTING

Alexandria Real Estate Equities, Inc. **2006**

Anderson Energy Ltd. **2006**

Distress Centres of Toronto **2006**

The George Gund Foundation **2005**

Golden Gate National Parks Conservancy **2006**

Intercontinental Exchange Inc. **2006**

The Royal Opera House **2005–06**

SAQ **2006**

Texas A&M Foundation **2006**

Visiting Nurse Service of New York **2005**

A designer's best friend

PERFECT 10

PHOTO GRAPHY

Anderson Energy Ltd. **2006**

Children's Home & Aid **2005**

Distress Centres of Toronto **2006**

Ford Foundation **2005**

The George Gund Foundation **2005**

Golden Gate National Parks Conservancy **2006**

IBM **2006**

Novartis **2006**

The Progressive Corporation **2006**

Stategic Hotels & Resorts Inc. **2006**

Perfection takes revision.

THE MOHAWK SHOW3
THE ROAD to HIGHER DESIGN
THE MOHAWK SHOW3
DC A DESIGN COMPANY
USE LESS
FIXIT
CHIP FARKUS
markspellman
DOGGY DO's
FULL MOON STUDIO

3

71
ODEUR 71
COMME des GARCONS

SOUNDS IN THE SQUARE
FARRAGUT SQUARE PARK
VISIT WWW.GTBID.COM FOR DETAILS

SOUNDS IN THE SQUARE
FARRAGUT SQUARE PARK
VISIT WWW.GTBID.COM FOR DETAILS

5

NEST
signature

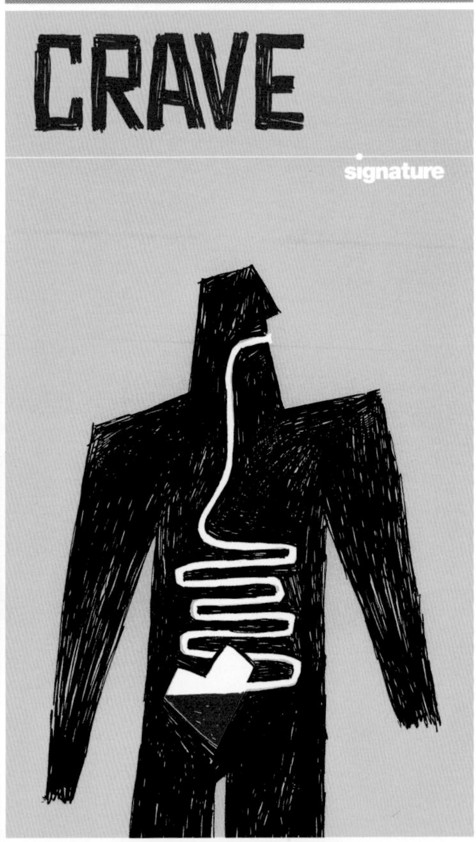
CRAVE
signature

6

1
GEORGE WALKER BUSH
BORN 7/6/46
Born again: 1985
NICKNAME Dubya, Shrub, 43, The Misleader
POSITION 43rd president of the United States of America
MISUNDERESTIMATION RATING ★★★★★

2
RICHARD BRUCE CHENEY
HATCHED 1/30/41
NICKNAME The Puppet Master
POSITION 46th vice president of the United States of America
SHOTGUN ACCURACY RATING ★★

3
CONDOLEEZZA RICE
BORN 11/14/54
NICKNAME Guru
POSITION Secretary of state
LOYALTY TO BUSH RATING ★★★★★

4
ANTONIN GREGORY SCALIA
BORN 3/11/36
NICKNAME Nino
POSITION Associate justice of the Supreme Court; nominated by President Reagan
ELECTORAL HANKY PANKING RATING ★★★★

5
WILLIAM JAMES O'REILLY, JR.
aka Bill O'Reilly
BORN 9/10/49
NICKNAME The Big O (Bestowed by George W. Bush), Falafel
POSITION Host of *The O'Reilly Factor* since 1996, best-selling author, including *The O'Reilly Factor for Kids.*
FAIR AND BALANCED RATING -★

6
JACK ABRAMOFF
BORN 2/28/58
NICKNAME Casino Jack
POSITION Federal inmate No. 27593-112. Currently serving five years and ten months for fraud, public corruption, and tax evasion; formerly a right-wing megalobbyist.
ABUSE OF POWER RATING ★★★★

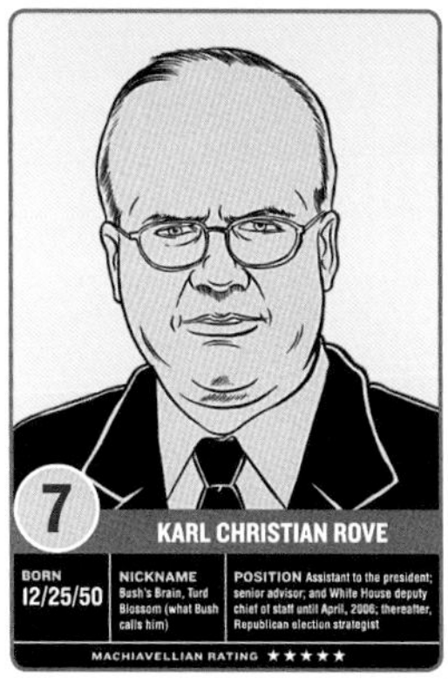
7
KARL CHRISTIAN ROVE
BORN 12/25/50
NICKNAME Bush's Brain, Turd Blossom (what Bush calls him)
POSITION Assistant to the president; senior advisor; and White House deputy chief of staff until April, 2006; thereafter, Republican election strategist
MACHIAVELLIAN RATING ★★★★★

8
RICHARD JOHN SANTORUM
"Rick"
BORN 5/10/58
NICKNAME Rooster (thanks to unruly hair in high school)
POSITION Former senator from Pittsburgh, Pennsylvania; forced into early retirement by voters, November 2006
LIKELINESS TO COME OUT OF CLOSET ★

9
RUSH HUDSON LIMBAUGH III
BORN 1/12/51
NICKNAME Rusty Sharpe, Jeff Christie (both fake radio names he has used)
POSITION Host of *The Rush Limbaugh Show*, the No. 1 nationally syndicated radio talk show in the United States
HYPOCRISY RATING ★★★

10
ARNOLD ALOIS SCHWARZENEGGER
BORN 7/30/47
NICKNAME The Austrian Oak, The Governator, Conan the Republican, Herr Gröpenführe
POSITION 38th governor of California
TIME-TRAVELING CYBORG RATING ★★★

11
ANN HART COULTER
BORN 12/8/61
or 12/8/63, if you believe Ann.
NICKNAME Coultergeist
POSITION Author; syndicated columnist; talking head for Fox Network; pundit
ACIDITY RATING ★★★★

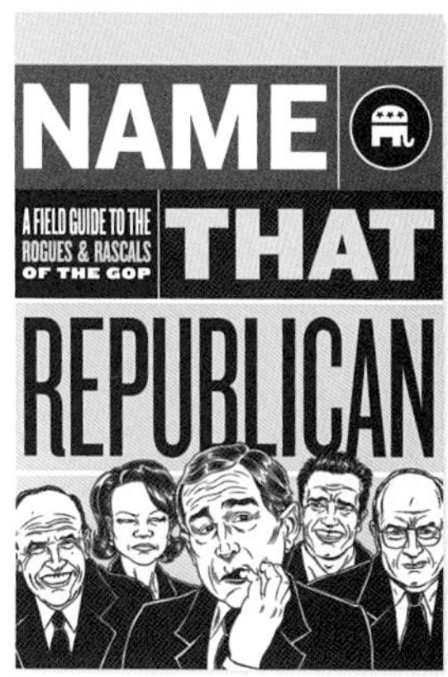
NAME
A FIELD GUIDE TO THE ROGUES & RASCALS OF THE GOP
THAT
REPUBLICAN

EMERGENCY
EVENT PREPAREDNESS CARD KIT

EVERYDAY
IS A HOLID★Y
HUGGING DAY
TWIN DAY
SEP05
S M T W T F S
01 02 03
04 05 06 07 08 09 10
11 12 13 14 15 16 17
18 19 ★ 21 22 23 24
25 26 27 28 29 30
designarmy.com

9

signature

THEATER WITH 50.
HONORED
299
SEAT MAX THEATRE
LOTS OF FREE PARKING
15
BETTER
16M
99
SEAT ARK THEATRE
2 GREEN ROOMS
STREET-ACCESSIBLE BOX OFFICE
COMPLIMENTARY
COAT CHECK
REHEARSAL ROOMS
signature
A Story in 3 Acts

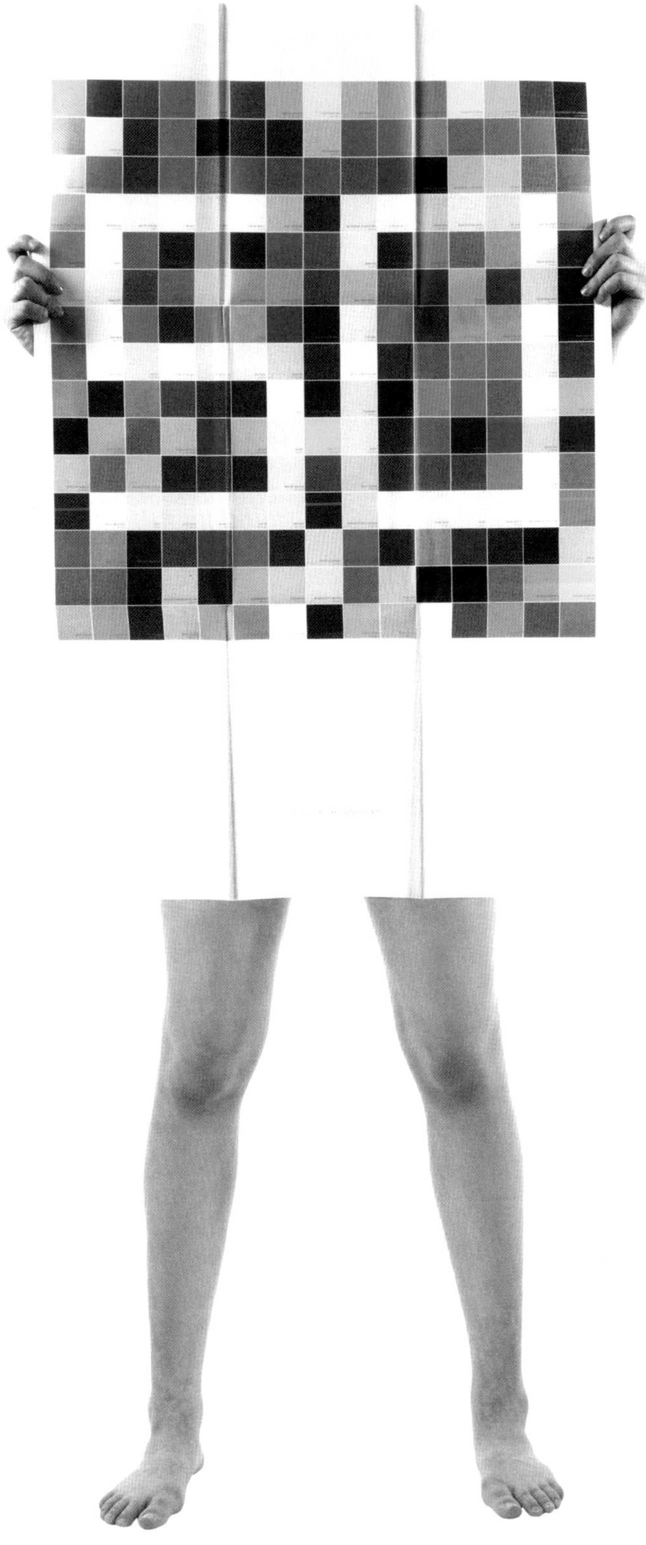

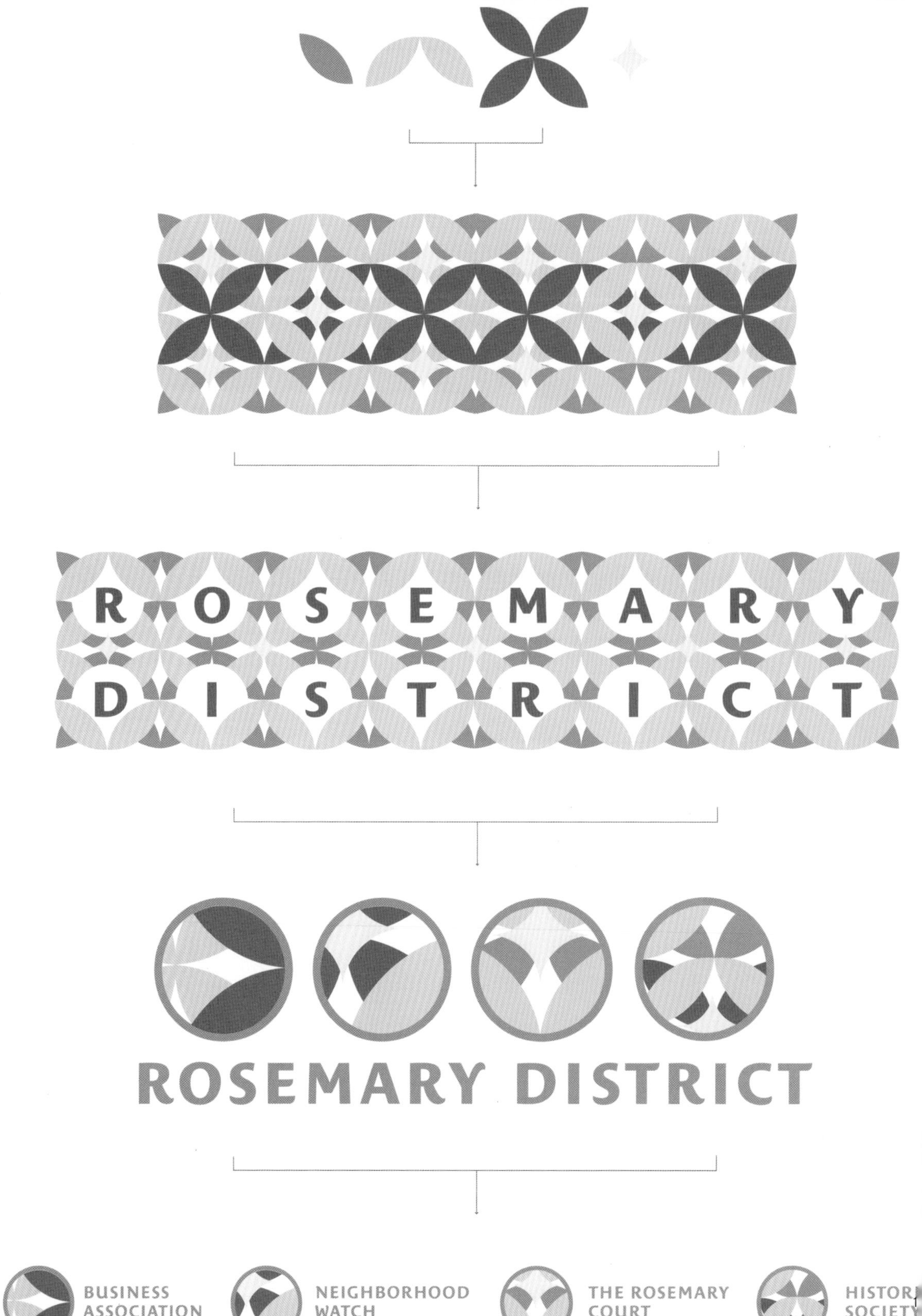

R O S E M A R Y
D I S T R I C T
ROSEMARY DISTRICT
BUSINESS ASSOCIATION
NEIGHBORHOOD WATCH
THE ROSEMARY COURT
HISTOR
SOCIET

ELSA CHAVES | NEW YORK, NY, USA

Elsa Chaves spent her childhood between her native Colombia and Florida, where she attended Ringling School of Art and Design. The fun factor is very important in her work – she aims to create engaging pieces that people can interact and play with. When not enjoying design, Elsa can often be found biking or finding new places to eat tacos.

www.hielsa.com

1 Logo system, postcards and newsletter | Student project, 2006
2 Packaging | Student project, 2006
3 Poster | Student project, 2006
4 Holiday card | Student project, 2006
5 Cross Stitch font | Self-initiated, 2007
6 Brochure | Student project, 2006
7 Packaging and flash cards | Student project, 2006

1

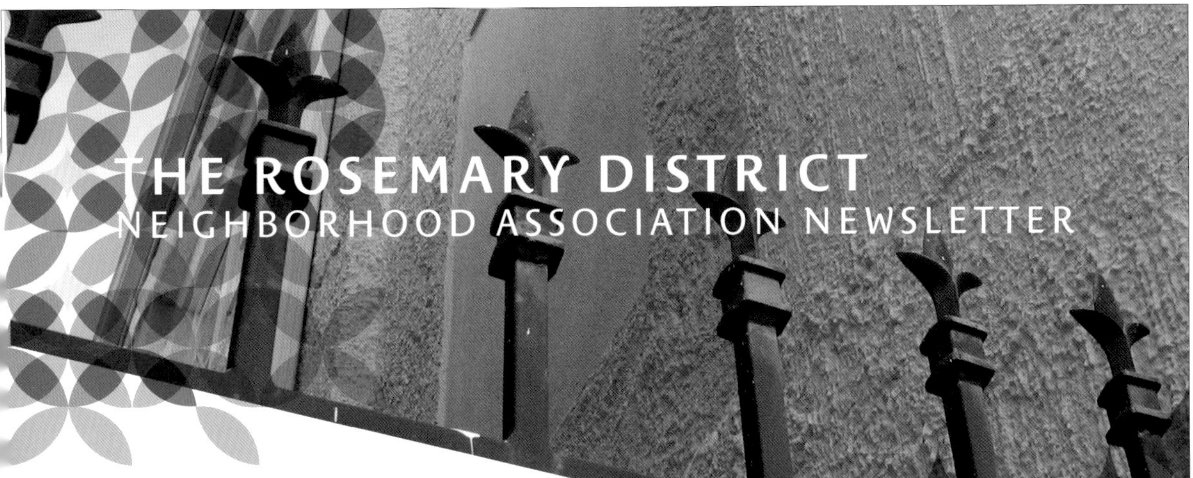

THE ROSEMARY DISTRICT
NEIGHBORHOOD ASSOCIATION NEWSLETTER

ROSEMARY DISTRICT REINVENTED INTO VIBRANT AREA

Business owners in the historical Rosemary District don't try to hide their excitement when they talk about the renaissance sweeping a neighborhood with a troubled past.

Hip. Energetic. Full of life. There's always something happening in Rosemary, its business tenants say. New Yorkers say it reminds them of SoHo. San Franciscans think it resembles Soma, the area south of Market Street.

A mixture of renovated buildings, new construction, retail, restaurants and services make up the business component of what was once an overlooked and segregated black neighborhood called Overtown.

White Sarasotans buried their dead in the Rosemary Cemetery, the city's first, beginning in the early 1900s. Col E. Morrill named the cemetery in 1906. The word symbolizes healing, safety and remembrance and in due course became the name for the entire district.

Overtown and Rosemary District now are recognized by th National Register of Historic Places as Sarasota's first documented black community.

In the past 18 months, about 18 new businesses have moved to the area bordered by U.S. 41, Fruitville Road, Orange Avenue and 10th Street. Today Rosemary is home to about 30 businesses, each eclectic and unusual.

The Rosemary District will host "Rosemary Rising," an evening street festival, on Friday, Dec. 9 from 5 to 9 p.m. Artists, musicians and performers will be featured with free bus tours of historical Overtown starting at the intersection of Seventh Street and Central Avenue. The Rosemary District is bordered by U.S. Highway 41, Fruitville Road, Orange Avenue and 10th Street. For more information, call 952-5280.

VOLUME 3, ISSUE 1 JANUARY 2006

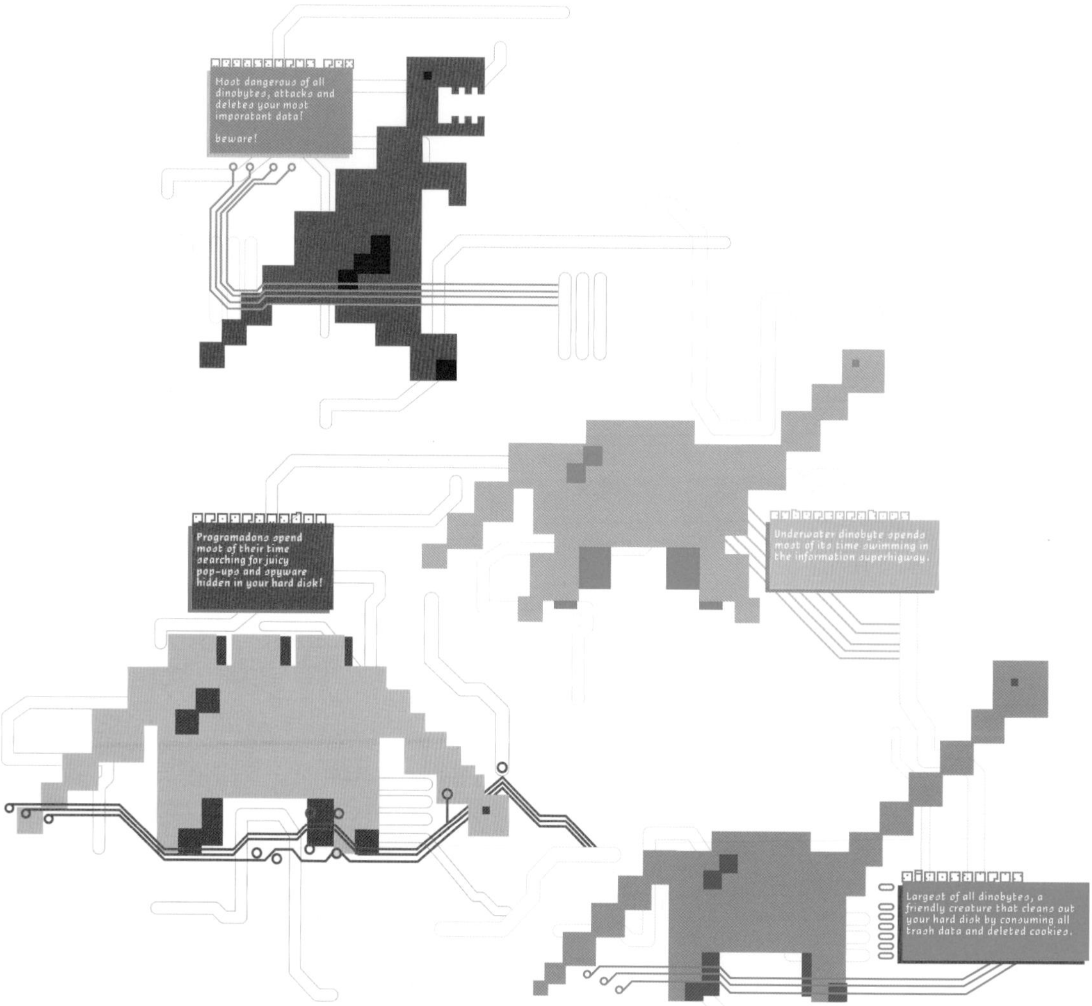
Most dangerous of all dinobytes, attacks and deletes your most imporatant data!
beware!
cyberceratops
Underwater dinobyte spends most of its time swimming in the information superhigway.
programadon
Programadons spend most of their time searching for juicy pop-ups and spyware hidden in your hard disk!
gigosaurus
Largest of all dinobytes, a friendly creature that cleans out your hard disk by consuming all trash data and deleted cookies.

Underwater dinobyte spends most of its time swimming in the information super-highway.

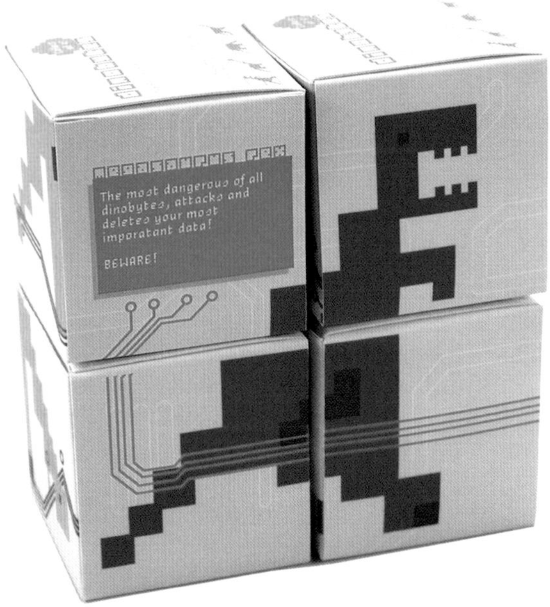
The most dangerous of all dinobytes, attacks and deletes your most imporatant data!
BEWARE!

REGROWTH

HURRICANE KATRINA | 08 · 25 · 2005

CROSS
STITCH
ABCDEFG ABCDEFG
HIJKLMN HIJKLMN
OPQRSTU OPQRSTU
VWXYZ VWXYZ

5

RINGLING SCHOOL OF ART AND DESIGN

6

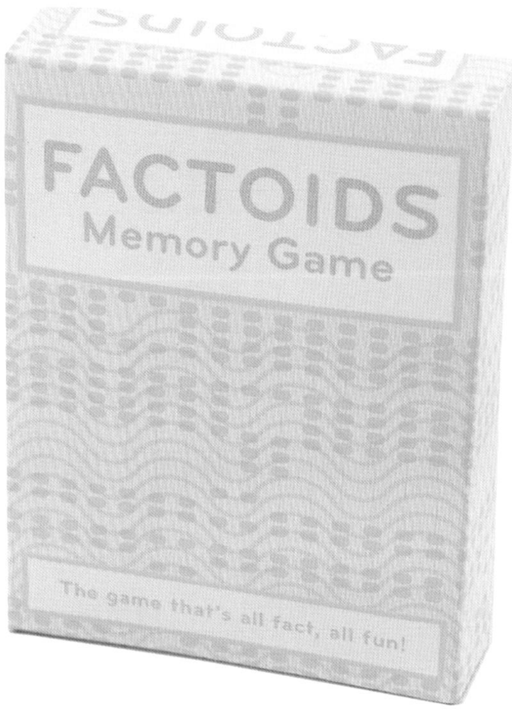
FACTOIDS
Memory Game
The game that's all fact, all fun!

7

PANDAS ARE REALLY GOOD AT MATH.

THE MAYANS DEVELOPED THE FIRST WORKING ESCALATOR.

MICE BORN IN TRIPLETS ARE ALWAYS BLIND.

DINOSAUR URINE GLOWS IN THE DARK.

THE PUPIL OF AN OCTOPUS' EYE IS RECTANGULAR.

HUGO
below
the
belt

FAKE I.D. | LOS ANGELES, CA, USA
Yván Martínez, Joshua Trees

Yván Martínez and Joshua Trees met while studying New Genres at the San Francisco Institute and teamed up to work towards an open practice of visual art and design. They believe that borderless experimentation produces the most relevant results, regardless of how it is categorized. Correspondingly, their work is nothing short of interesting.

www.wefakeid.com

1 In-store installation | Nike, 2003
2 Media kit | GLBT Historical Society, 2002
3 V magazine | Art Center College of Design, 2002-2007
4 Design and edition | Emigre magazine, 2002
5 Fake Forest eco-friendly stationery | Self-initiated, 2003-2007
6 In-store installation | Nike, 2003

Fake Forest
フェークフォレスト

GLBTHS
GAY LESBIAN BISEXUAL TRANSGENDER HISTORICAL SOCIETY OF NORTHERN CALIFORNIA

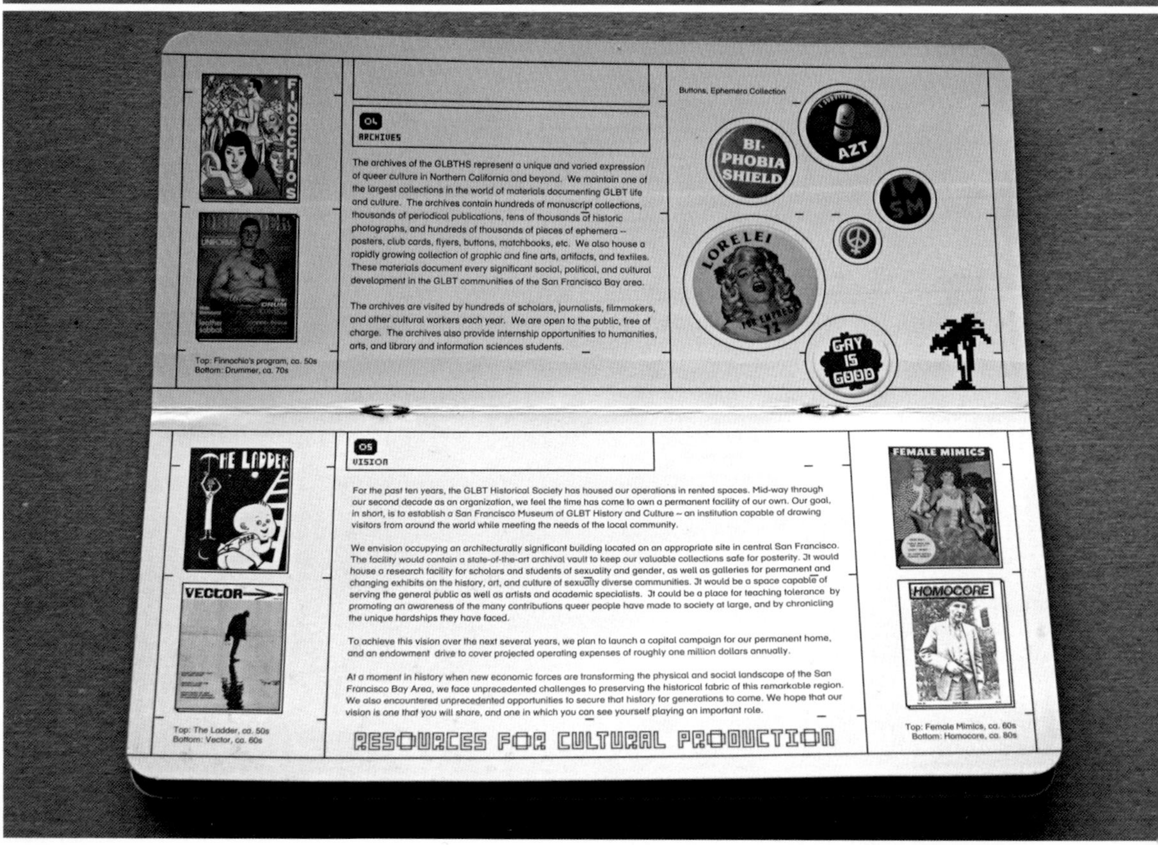
04
ARCHIVES
The archives of the GLBTHS represent a unique and varied expression of queer culture in Northern California and beyond. We maintain one of the largest collections in the world of materials documenting GLBT life and culture. The archives contain hundreds of manuscript collections, thousands of periodical publications, tens of thousands of historic photographs, and hundreds of thousands of pieces of ephemera -- posters, club cards, flyers, buttons, matchbooks, etc. We also house a rapidly growing collection of graphic and fine arts, artifacts, and textiles. These materials document every significant social, political, and cultural development in the GLBT communities of the San Francisco Bay area.
The archives are visited by hundreds of scholars, journalists, filmmakers, and other cultural workers each year. We are open to the public, free of charge. The archives also provide internship opportunities to humanities, arts, and library and information sciences students.
Top: Finnochio's program, ca. 50s
Bottom: Drummer, ca. 70s
Buttons, Ephemera Collection
BI-PHOBIA SHIELD
AZT
SM
LORELEI
GAY IS GOOD
05
VISION
For the past ten years, the GLBT Historical Society has housed our operations in rented spaces. Mid-way through our second decade as an organization, we feel the time has come to own a permanent facility of our own. Our goal, in short, is to establish a San Francisco Museum of GLBT History and Culture -- an institution capable of drawing visitors from around the world while meeting the needs of the local community.
We envision occupying an architecturally significant building located on an appropriate site in central San Francisco. The facility would contain a state-of-the-art archival vault to keep our valuable collections safe for posterity. It would house a research facility for scholars and students of sexuality and gender, as well as galleries for permanent and changing exhibits on the history, art, and culture of sexually diverse communities. It would be a space capable of serving the general public as well as artists and academic specialists. It could be a place for teaching tolerance by promoting an awareness of the many contributions queer people have made to society at large, and by chronicling the unique hardships they have faced.
To achieve this vision over the next several years, we plan to launch a capital campaign for our permanent home, and an endowment drive to cover projected operating expenses of roughly one million dollars annually.
At a moment in history when new economic forces are transforming the physical and social landscape of the San Francisco Bay Area, we face unprecedented challenges to preserving the historical fabric of this remarkable region. We also encountered unprecedented opportunities to secure that history for generations to come. We hope that our vision is one that you will share, and one in which you can see yourself playing an important role.
RESOURCES FOR CULTURAL PRODUCTION
THE LADDER
VECTOR
Top: The Ladder, ca. 50s
Bottom: Vector, ca. 60s
FEMALE MIMICS
HOMOCORE
Top: Female Mimics, ca. 60s
Bottom: Homocore, ca. 80s

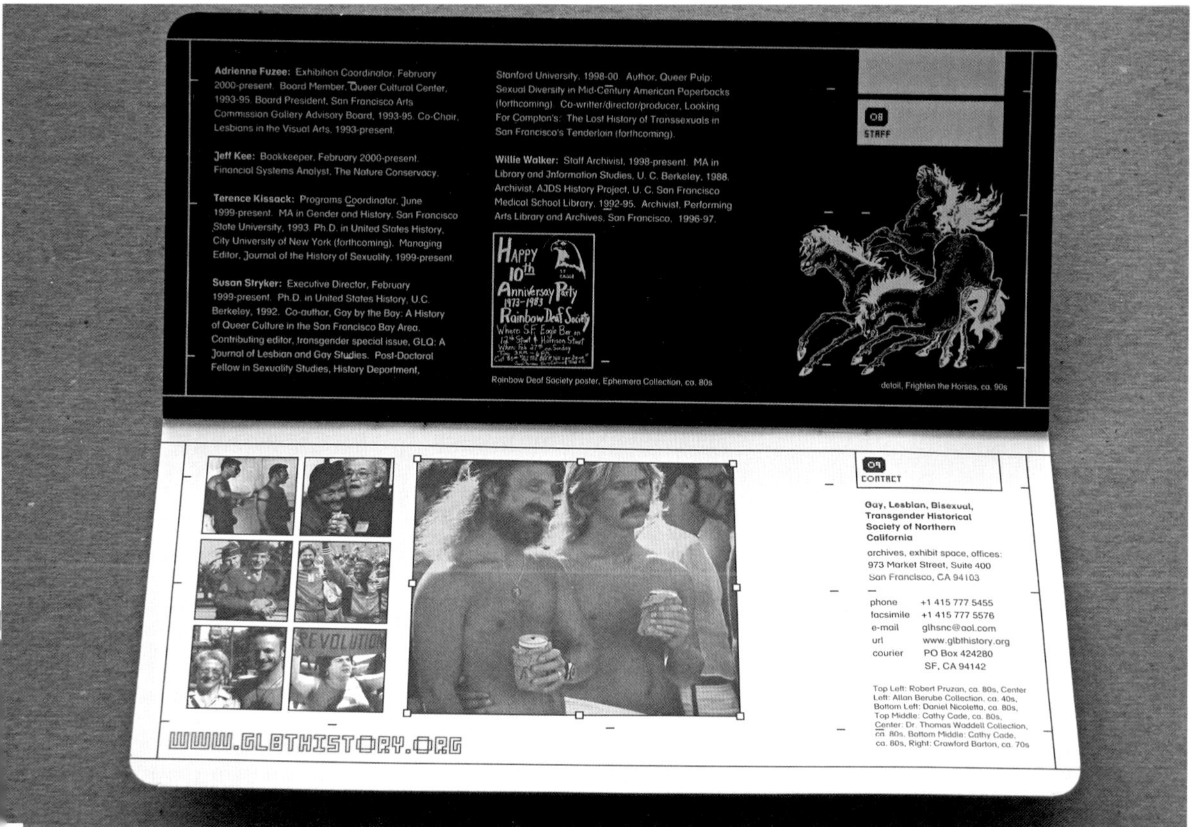
Adrienne Fuzee: Exhibition Coordinator, February 2000-present. Board Member, Queer Cultural Center, 1993-95. Board President, San Francisco Arts Commission Gallery Advisory Board, 1993-95. Co-Chair, Lesbians in the Visual Arts, 1993-present.
Jeff Kee: Bookkeeper, February 2000-present. Financial Systems Analyst, The Nature Conservacy.
Terence Kissack: Programs Coordinator, June 1999-present. MA in Gender and History, San Francisco State University, 1993. Ph.D. in United States History, City University of New York (forthcoming). Managing Editor, Journal of the History of Sexuality, 1999-present.
Susan Stryker: Executive Director, February 1999-present. Ph.D. in United States History, U.C. Berkeley, 1992. Co-author, Gay by the Bay: A History of Queer Culture in the San Francisco Bay Area. Contributing editor, transgender special issue, GLQ: A Journal of Lesbian and Gay Studies. Post-Doctoral Fellow in Sexuality Studies, History Department, Stanford University, 1998-00. Author, Queer Pulp: Sexual Diversity in Mid-Century American Paperbacks (forthcoming). Co-writer/director/producer, Looking For Compton's: The Lost History of Transsexuals in San Francisco's Tenderloin (forthcoming).
Willie Walker: Staff Archivist, 1998-present. MA in Library and Information Studies, U. C. Berkeley, 1988. Archivist, AIDS History Project, U. C. San Francisco Medical School Library, 1992-95. Archivist, Performing Arts Library and Archives, San Francisco, 1996-97.
Happy 10th Anniversay Party 1973-1983 Rainbow Deaf Society
Where: S.F. Eagle Bar on 12th Street & Harrison Street
Rainbow Deaf Society poster, Ephemera Collection, ca. 80s
08
STAFF
detail, Frighten the Horses, ca. 90s
WWW.GLBTHISTORY.ORG
09
CONTACT
Gay, Lesbian, Bisexual, Transgender Historical Society of Northern California
archives, exhibit space, offices:
973 Market Street, Suite 400
San Francisco, CA 94103
phone +1 415 777 5455
facsimile +1 415 777 5576
e-mail glhsnc@aol.com
url www.glbthistory.org
courier PO Box 424280 SF, CA 94142
Top Left: Robert Pruzan, ca. 80s, Center Left: Allan Berube Collection, ca. 40s, Bottom Left: Daniel Nicoletta, ca. 80s, Top Middle: Cathy Cade, ca. 80s, Center: Dr. Thomas Waddell Collection, ca. 80s, Bottom Middle: Cathy Cade, ca. 80s, Right: Crawford Barton, ca. 70s

2

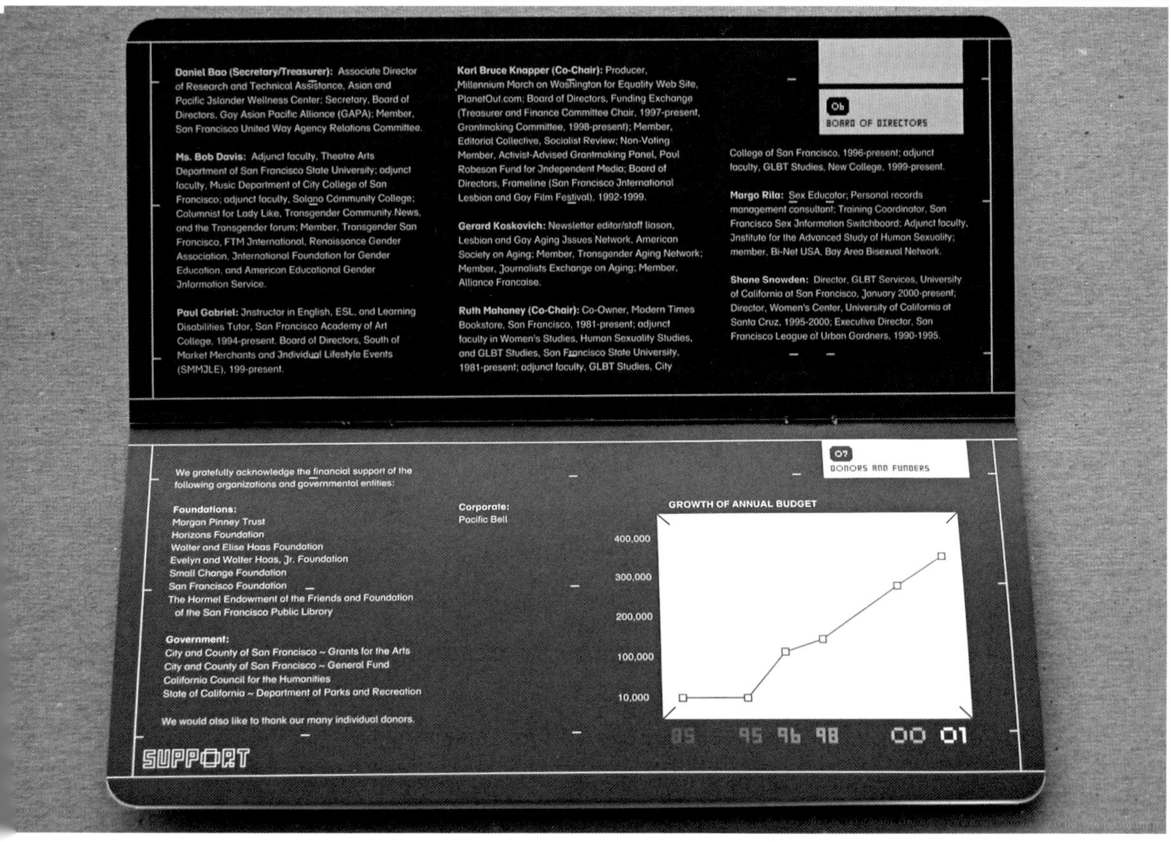
Daniel Bao (Secretary/Treasurer): Associate Director of Research and Technical Assistance, Asian and Pacific Islander Wellness Center; Secretary, Board of Directors, Gay Asian Pacific Alliance (GAPA); Member, San Francisco United Way Agency Relations Committee.
Ms. Bob Davis: Adjunct faculty, Theatre Arts Department of San Francisco State University; adjunct faculty, Music Department of City College of San Francisco; adjunct faculty, Solano Community College; Columnist for Lady Like, Transgender Community News, and the Transgender forum; Member, Transgender San Francisco, FTM International, Renaissance Gender Association, International Foundation for Gender Education, and American Educational Gender Information Service.
Paul Gabriel: Instructor in English, ESL, and Learning Disabilities Tutor, San Francisco Academy of Art College, 1994-present. Board of Directors, South of Market Merchants and Individual Lifestyle Events (SMMILE), 199-present.
Karl Bruce Knapper (Co-Chair): Producer, Millennium March on Washington for Equality Web Site, PlanetOut.com; Board of Directors, Funding Exchange (Treasurer and Finance Committee Chair, 1997-present, Grantmaking Committee, 1998-present); Member, Editorial Collective, Socialist Review; Non-Voting Member, Activist-Advised Grantmaking Panel, Paul Robeson Fund for Independent Media; Board of Directors, Frameline (San Francisco International Lesbian and Gay Film Festival), 1992-1999.
Gerard Koskovich: Newsletter editor/staff liason, Lesbian and Gay Aging Issues Network, American Society on Aging; Member, Transgender Aging Network; Member, Journalists Exchange on Aging; Member, Alliance Francaise.
Ruth Mahaney (Co-Chair): Co-Owner, Modern Times Bookstore, San Francisco, 1981-present; adjunct faculty in Women's Studies, Human Sexuality Studies, and GLBT Studies, San Francisco State University, 1981-present; adjunct faculty, GLBT Studies, City College of San Francisco, 1996-present; adjunct faculty, GLBT Studies, New College, 1999-present.
Margo Rila: Sex Educator; Personal records management consultant; Training Coordinator, San Francisco Sex Information Switchboard; Adjunct faculty, Institute for the Advanced Study of Human Sexuality; member, Bi-Net USA, Bay Area Bisexual Network.
Shane Snowden: Director, GLBT Services, University of California at San Francisco, January 2000-present; Director, Women's Center, University of California at Santa Cruz, 1995-2000; Executive Director, San Francisco League of Urban Gardners, 1990-1995.
06
BOARD OF DIRECTORS
We gratefully acknowledge the financial support of the following organizations and governmental entities:
Foundations:
Morgan Pinney Trust
Horizons Foundation
Walter and Elise Haas Foundation
Evelyn and Walter Haas, Jr. Foundation
Small Change Foundation
San Francisco Foundation
The Hormel Endowment of the Friends and Foundation of the San Francisco Public Library
Government:
City and County of San Francisco ~ Grants for the Arts
City and County of San Francisco ~ General Fund
California Council for the Humanities
State of California ~ Department of Parks and Recreation
We would also like to thank our many individual donors.
Corporate:
Pacific Bell
07
DONORS AND FUNDERS
GROWTH OF ANNUAL BUDGET
400,000
300,000
200,000
100,000
10,000
85
95
96
98
00
01
SUPPORT

CHRISTIAN ROCHA
3

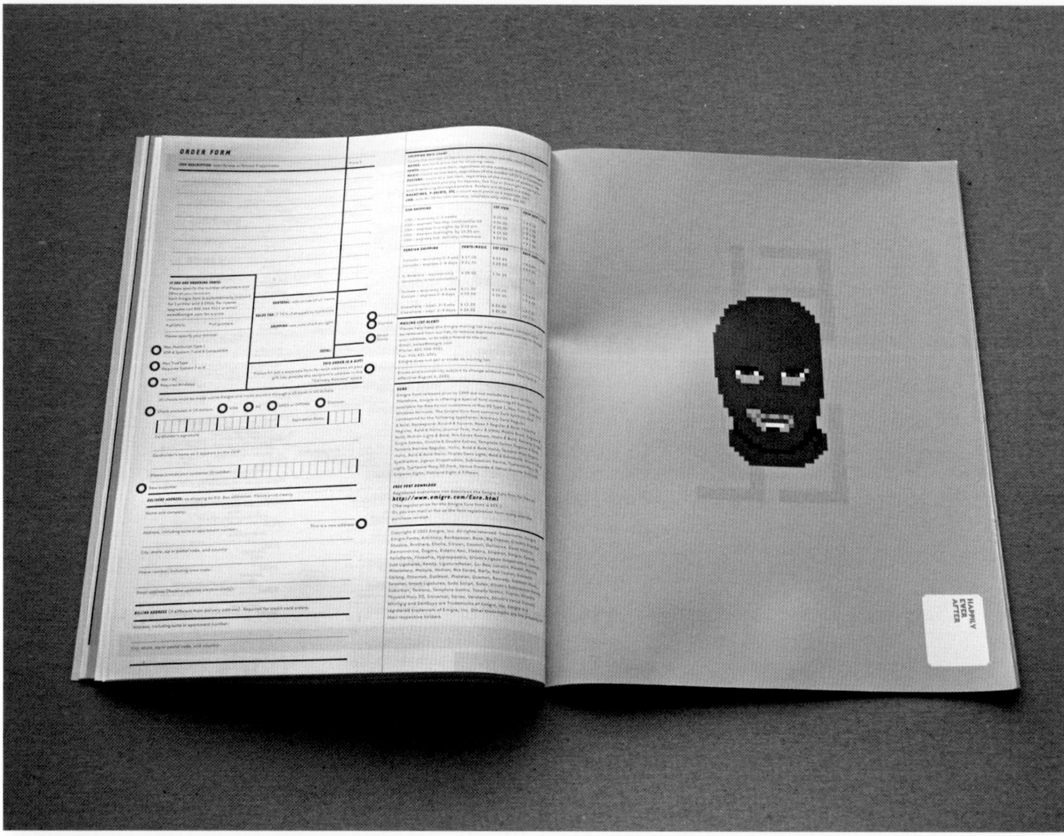

4

yes, we're
to post-consumer satisfaction!
EMIGRE
emigre.com

4

ERROR:
UNDEFINED
69

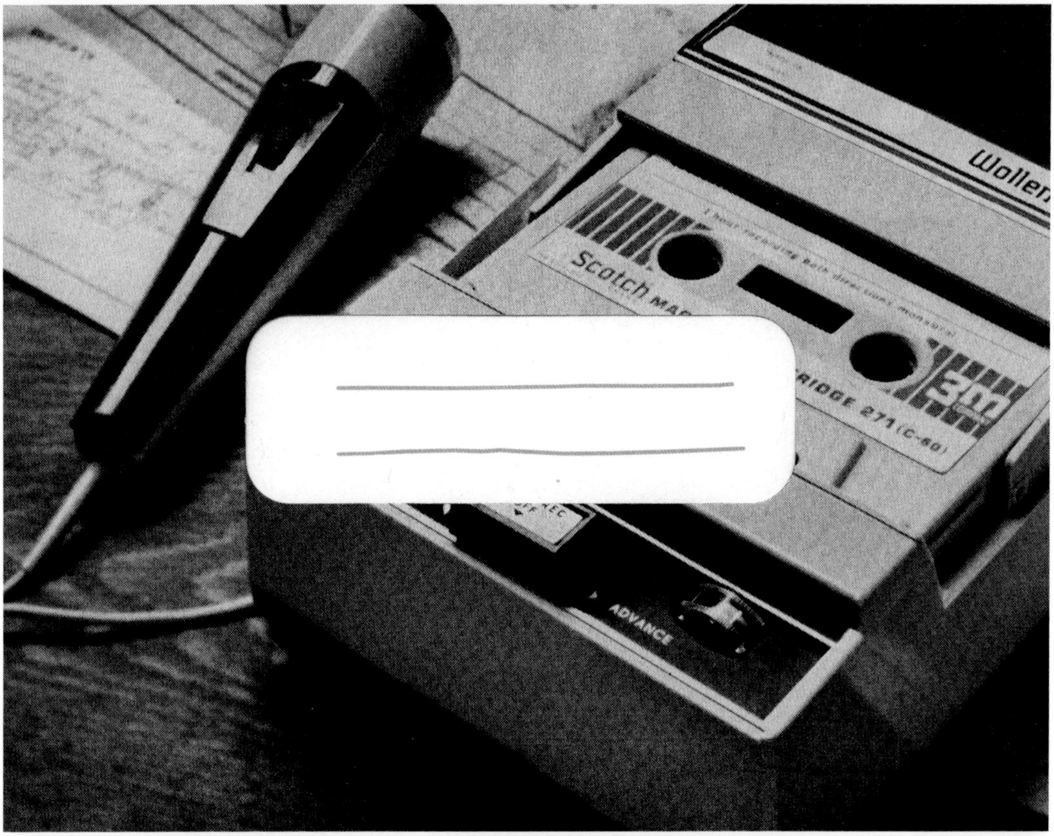
Scotch
ADVANCE

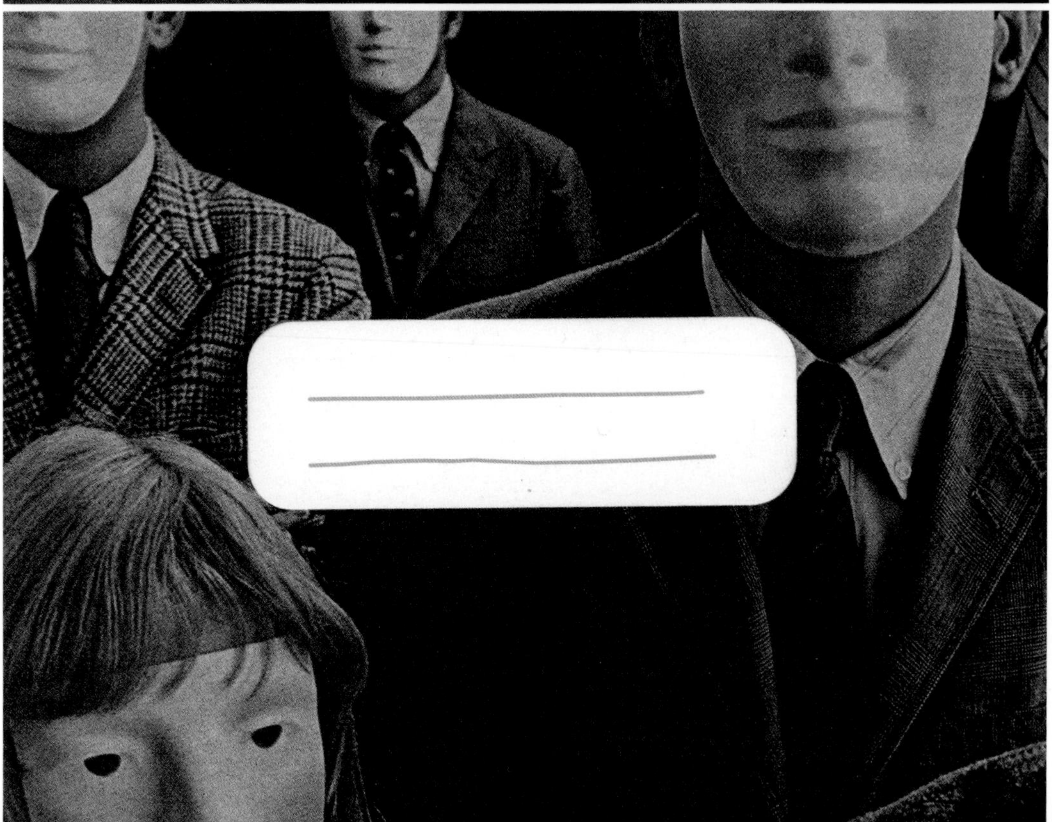

10

HOY
NO
TAXI
SEGURO
SITIO
TAXI
SIN
LIBRE
ALTO
SIGA
SUBALE
LO QUE
MARQUE EL
TAXIMETRO
MEXICO
100%
RULETERO
DF

HULA+HULA | MEXICO CITY, MEXICO

Cha!, Aldo Lugo, Quique Ollervides

Hula+Hula is the brainchild of Quique Ollervides and Cha!, a design studio that deals out corporate identity, editorial design. It directs art projects and has a special fondness for typefaces and CD sleeve design. Hula+Hula also runs Kong, the first Mexican shop and gallery to specialize in graphic design, illustration and urban art.

www.hulahula.com.mx

1 Illustration | Design Mexico magazine, 2007
2 Poster | Hematoma, 2006
3 Illustration | Absolut Vodka and Teran, 2007
4 CD sleeve design | Fobia and Sony BMG, 2005
Photography by Miguel Calderón
5 Mono font | Self-initiated, 2006
6 Illustration | Cartoon Network Latin America, 2007
7 Silk-screen | Self-initiated, 2006
8 Various logos | Cocinas Lejanas, Fobia, Kabah, Chinelo, Hula+Hula, 2006-07

2

ABSOLUT
LADY PURE
ABSOLUT CITRON
JARABE NATURAL
JUGO DE LIMÓN
JUGO DE PIÑA
JUGO DE MANGO
LICUAR CON HIELO & SERVIR
ABSOLUT
Country of Sweden
CITRON
Absolut Citron is made from
750 ML
YEAH
ABSOLUT
Citron

fobia

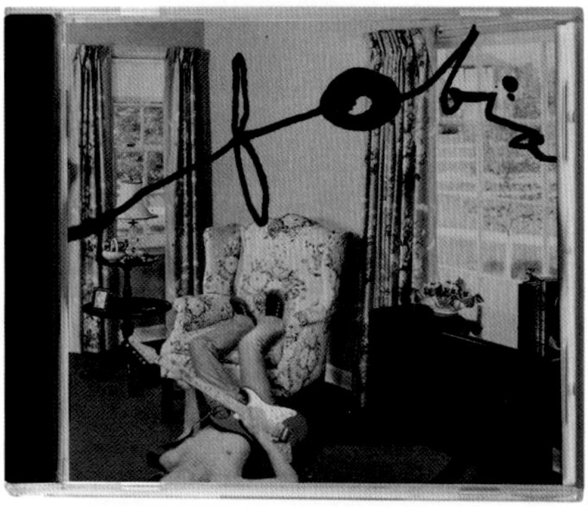
fobia

fobia

fobia
ROSA VENU

1 Rosa venus
2 No eres yo
3 200 sábados
4 No soy un buen perdedor
5 12 pasos
6 1 camino y un camión
7 2 corazones
8 Todas las estrellas
9 Una vida sencilla
10 Muy maniaco de mi parte
11 Sembrando estrellas
Bonus track:
12 Hoy tengo miedo
Una producción SONY BMG Music Entertainment (México), S.A. de C.V.
dirigida y realizada por Gordon Raphael & Paco Huidobro.
Co-director y co-realizador: Jay de la Cueva.

5

LOS AMIGOS INVISIBES
NORTEC
COLLECTIVE
PANTEON
MO
NO
ZOE
AUSTIN
BOOK
OF LOVE
LOS DE
ABAJO
seattle
washington
RO
CK
YEAH
YEAH
BASS&TREBLE

6

WE DO
WHAT
WE WANT

HULA HULA

Cocinas Lejanas

pic nic

Kabah

HULA HULA DIEZ AÑOS

HULA HULA DIEZ AÑOS

chinelo ENTERTAINMENT

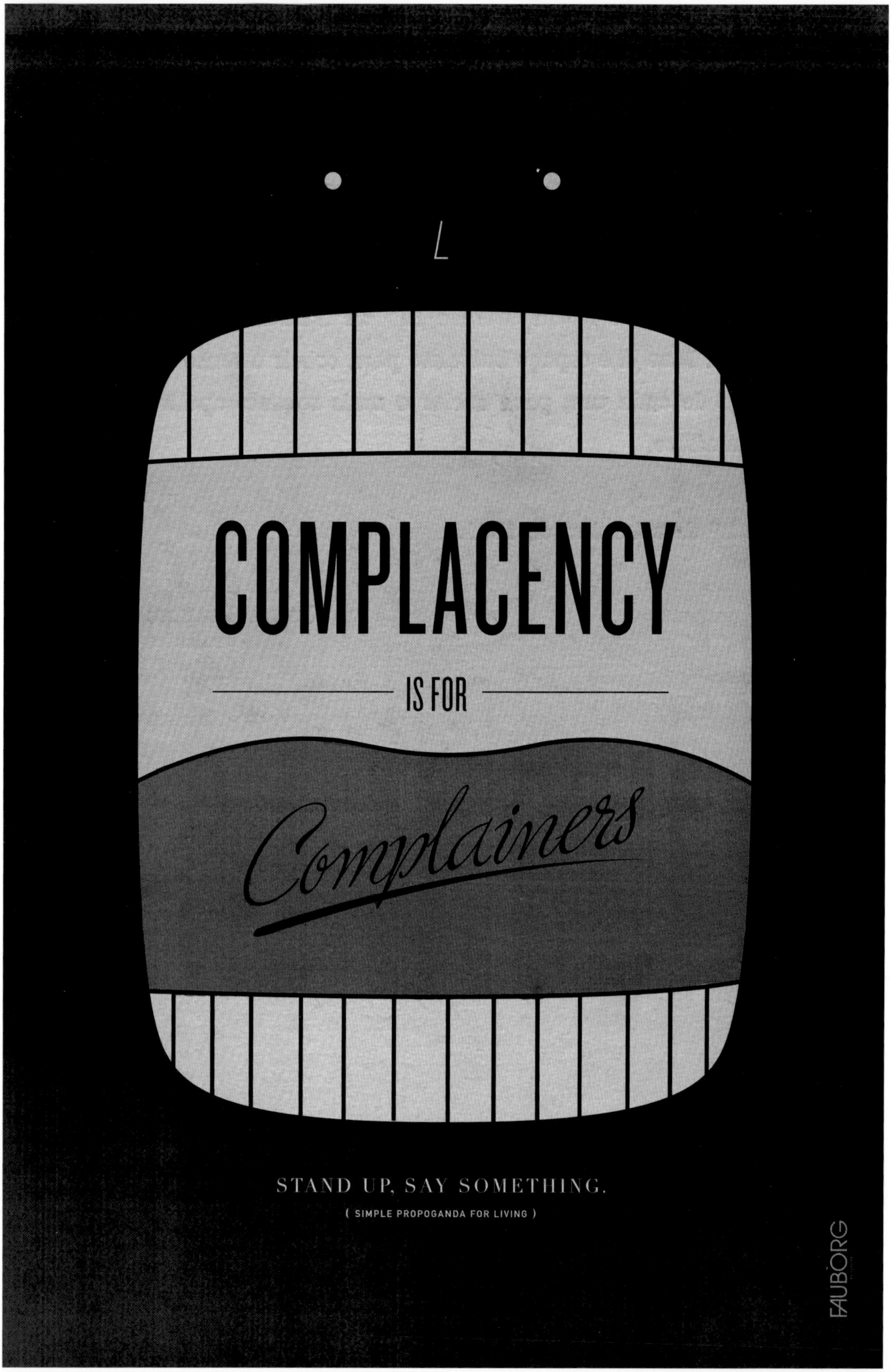
COMPLACENCY
IS FOR
Complainers
STAND UP, SAY SOMETHING.
(SIMPLE PROPOGANDA FOR LIVING)
FAUBORG

IAMALWAYSHUNGRY | NEW ORLEANS, LA, USA
Nessim Higson

Iamalwayshungry is the studio of Nessim Higson. Besides being a firm believer that design has the responsibility to not only contribute to the economic market, but to the social fabric of society as well, Nessim is a detester of the word mundane, a sucker for French films, and an advocate for the convergence of mediums.

www.iamalwayshungry.com

1 Poster | Faub.org, 2007
2 Promotional poster | Republic, 2007
3 Graphics | The One Show, 2007
In collaboration with John Finnell
4 Posters | Kellerhouse Studio, 2007
5 CD sleeve | Patternbased, 2007
6 Tshirt graphics | I-Manifest, 2007
7 Promotional publication | Personal project with Lee Crum, 2007
8 Graphics | Mike Ski, 2007

2

fig. 6A
fig. 2A
fig. 1A
fig. 5A

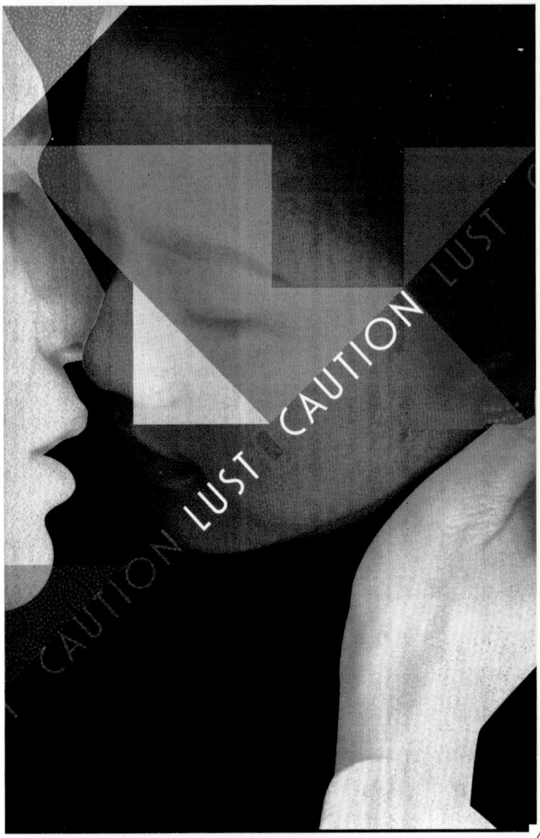
LUST CAUTION

LUST CAUTION

LUST CAUTION
LUST CAUTION

LUST CAUTION

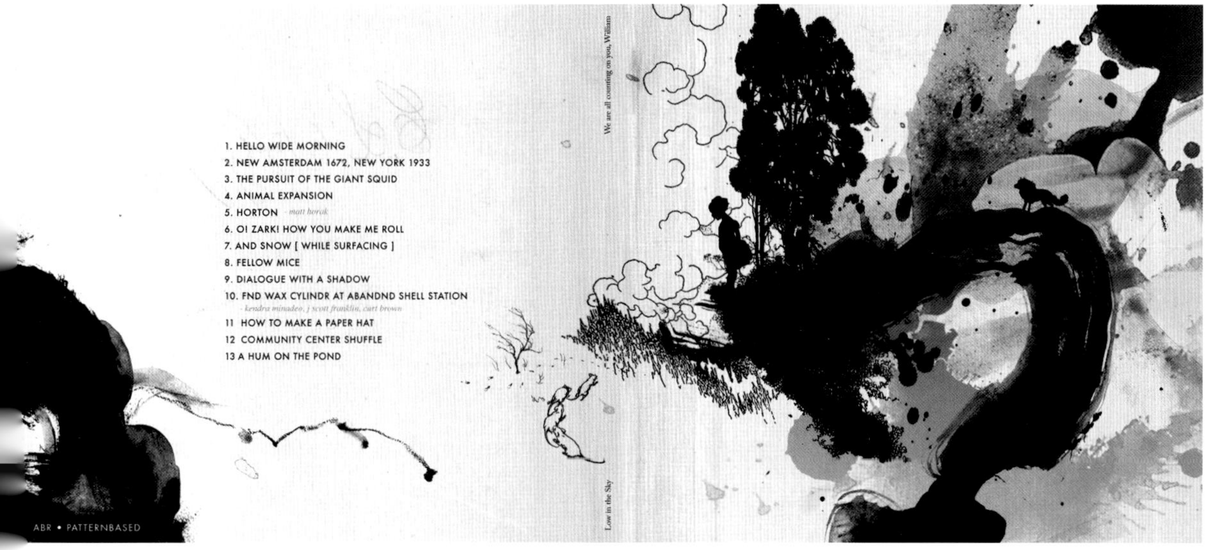
We are all counting on you, William
1. HELLO WIDE MORNING
2. NEW AMSTERDAM 1672, NEW YORK 1933
3. THE PURSUIT OF THE GIANT SQUID
4. ANIMAL EXPANSION
5. HORTON - matt horak
6. OI ZARK! HOW YOU MAKE ME ROLL
7. AND SNOW [WHILE SURFACING]
8. FELLOW MICE
9. DIALOGUE WITH A SHADOW
10. FND WAX CYLINDR AT ABANDND SHELL STATION
- kendra minadeo, j scott franklin, curt brown
11 HOW TO MAKE A PAPER HAT
12 COMMUNITY CENTER SHUFFLE
13 A HUM ON THE POND
ABR • PATTERNBASED
Low in the Sky

ANd
Curt Brown / Jim Franklin / Matt Horak

MOTHER
MOTHER
There's too many of you crying.

BROTHER
Bro
ther
brother

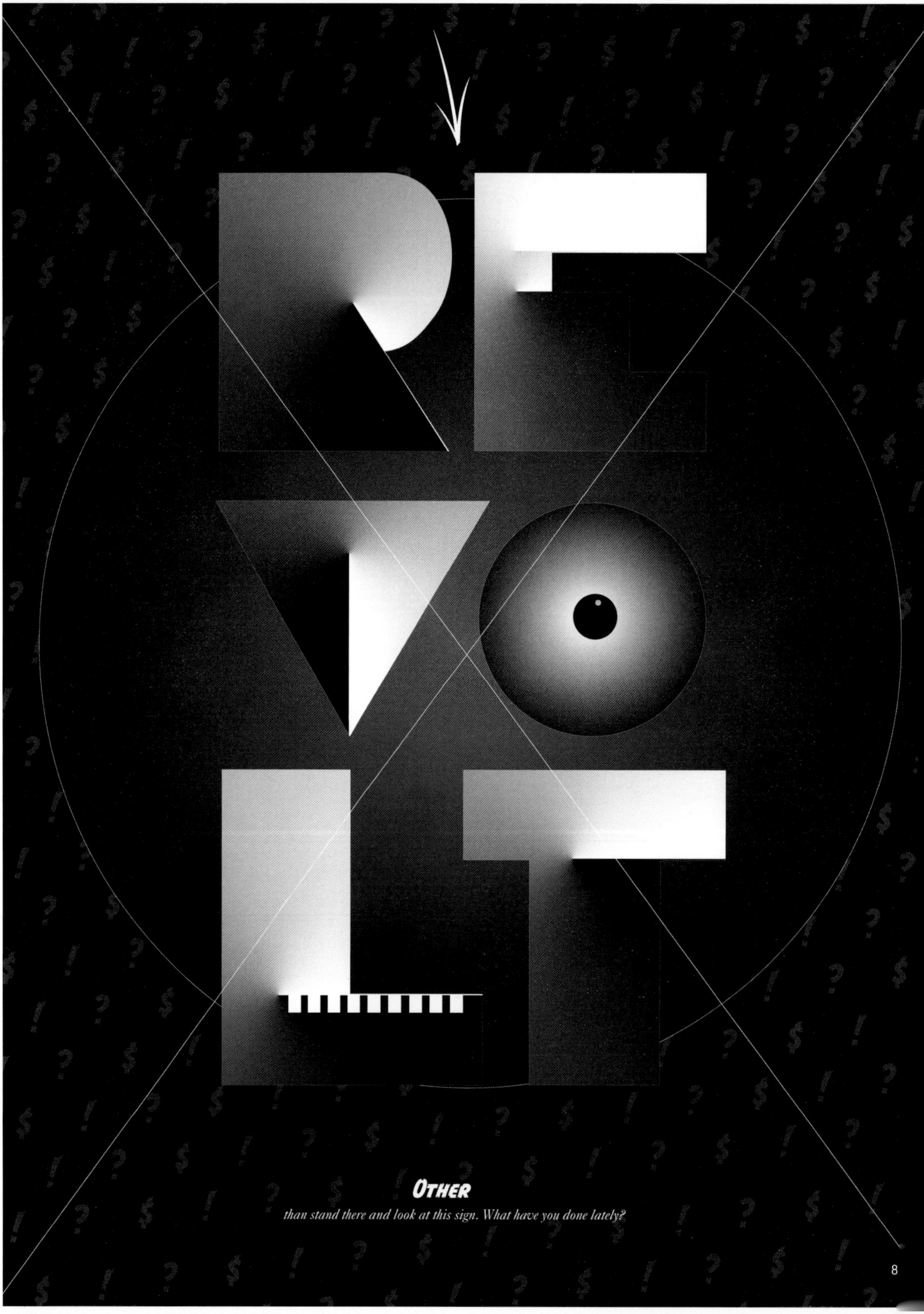
REVOLT
Other
than stand there and look at this sign. What have you done lately?
8

REVOLT
REVOLUTION
is not a monster.

BY:AMT
BADGE
HONOR OF
SH/LG
BY:AMT
www.byamt.com
info@byamt.com
BY:AMT
RING
5/6/7/8/9
10/11/12
BY:AMT
www.byamt.com
info@byamt.com
Styles:
Band/Diamond/
Pearl/Signet
BY:AMT
BLING
BRACELET
SH/LG
BY:AMT
www.byamt.com
info@byamt.com

JOSHUA DISTLER | NEW YORK, NY, USA

Born in New York City and raised in Southern Vermont, Joshua Distler is a designer, programmer and entrepreneur who strives to balance pure concept and functional execution in his work. He is praised by the likes of Communication Arts and the Type Directors Club. When not designing, he likes to pursue his study of sushi and fine curries.

www.joshuadistler.com

1 Packaging and font | BY:AMT, 2007
In collaboration with Mike Abbink
2 Book design | Tony Labat and New Langton Arts, 2005
In collaboration with Mike Abbink
3 CD packaging concept | Self-initiated, 2001
4 Sample cover designs | Shift, 2006

1

BY:AMT
BADGE OF
HONOR
SM/LG
BY:AMT
www.byamt.com
info@byamt.com
BY:AMT
RING
5/6/7/8/9
10/11/12
BY:AMT
www.byamt.com
info@byamt.com
Styles:
Band/Diamond/
Pearl/Signet
BY:AMT
BLING
BRACELET
SM/LG
BY:AMT
www.byamt.com
info@byamt.com

1

Trust Me. Tony Labat
New Langton Arts
Susan Miller
ISBN 0-9627010-4-1

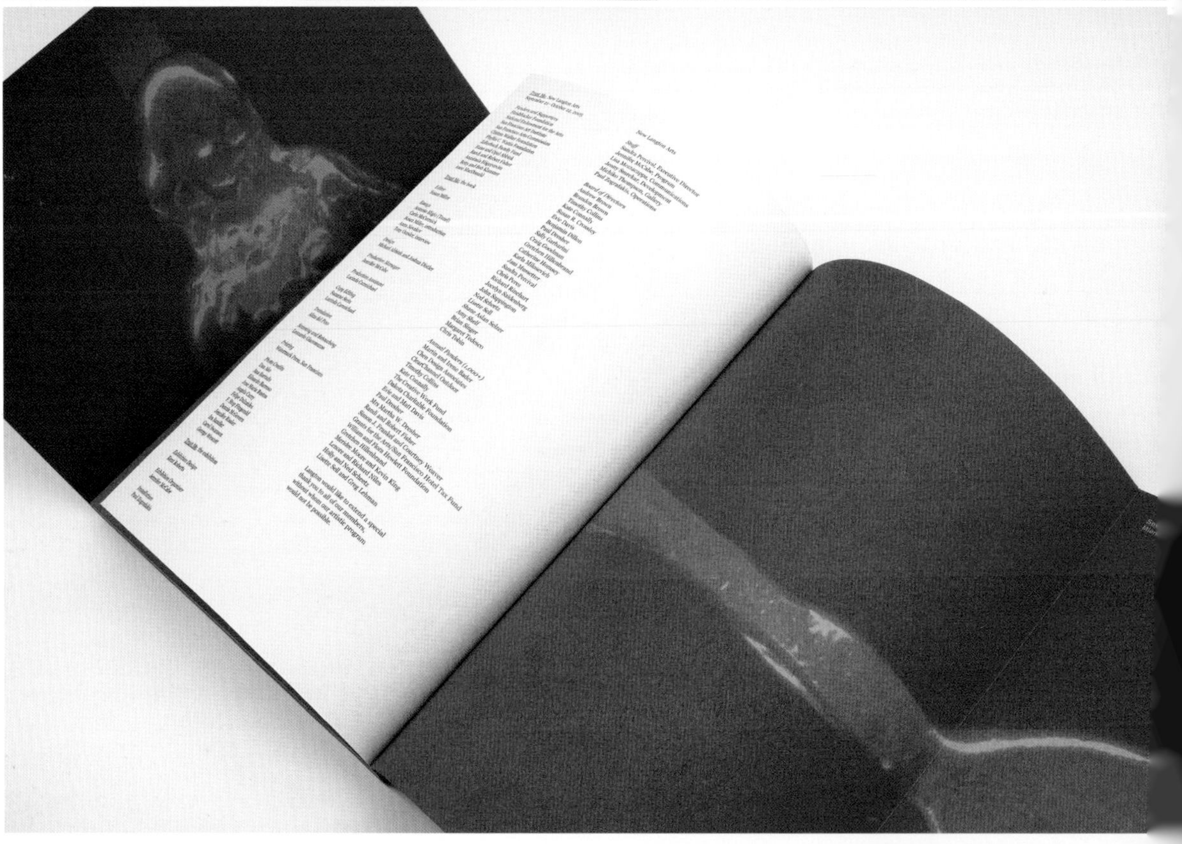

Contents
Hooters Project
shooting script, 1997
<31
Some of the national media coverage of Peace Sign proposal for Golden Gate Park, 1997
25
33
HOOTERS
PARKING LOT
ENTRANCE
By Dan Levy
Chronicle Staff Writer
The San Francisco Art Commission yesterday rejected a proposal to erect a giant peace sign at the entrance to Golden Gate Park, apparently killing an issue that started as a whimsical debate on public art but intensified into a fi
Peace Sculpture Plan
San Francisco
Art: Process
Well As Product
Some prefer to
forget the S
of Love.

Contents
11
Trust Me: Lessons in Good Salesmanship
Susan Miller
12
14
15
16
18
21
Phantom Dioramas
22
23
24
25
26
Against Expectations
Carlo McCormick
27
28
29
30
31
32
38
39
43
46
48
50
51
54
PROFESSIONAL BOXI
KEZAR PAVILIO
MAY
7

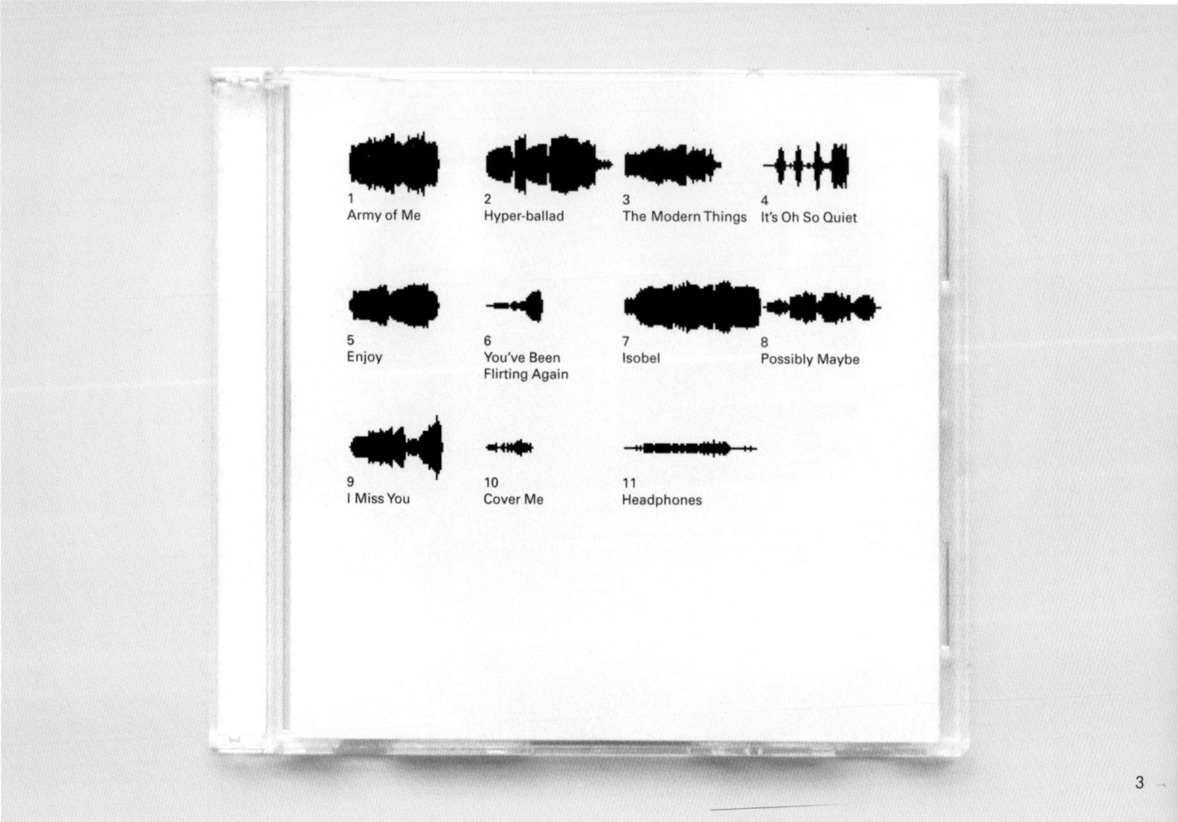
1
Army of Me
2
Hyper-ballad
3
The Modern Things
4
It's Oh So Quiet
5
Enjoy
6
You've Been
Flirting Again
7
Isobel
8
Possibly Maybe
9
I Miss You
10
Cover Me
11
Headphones

3

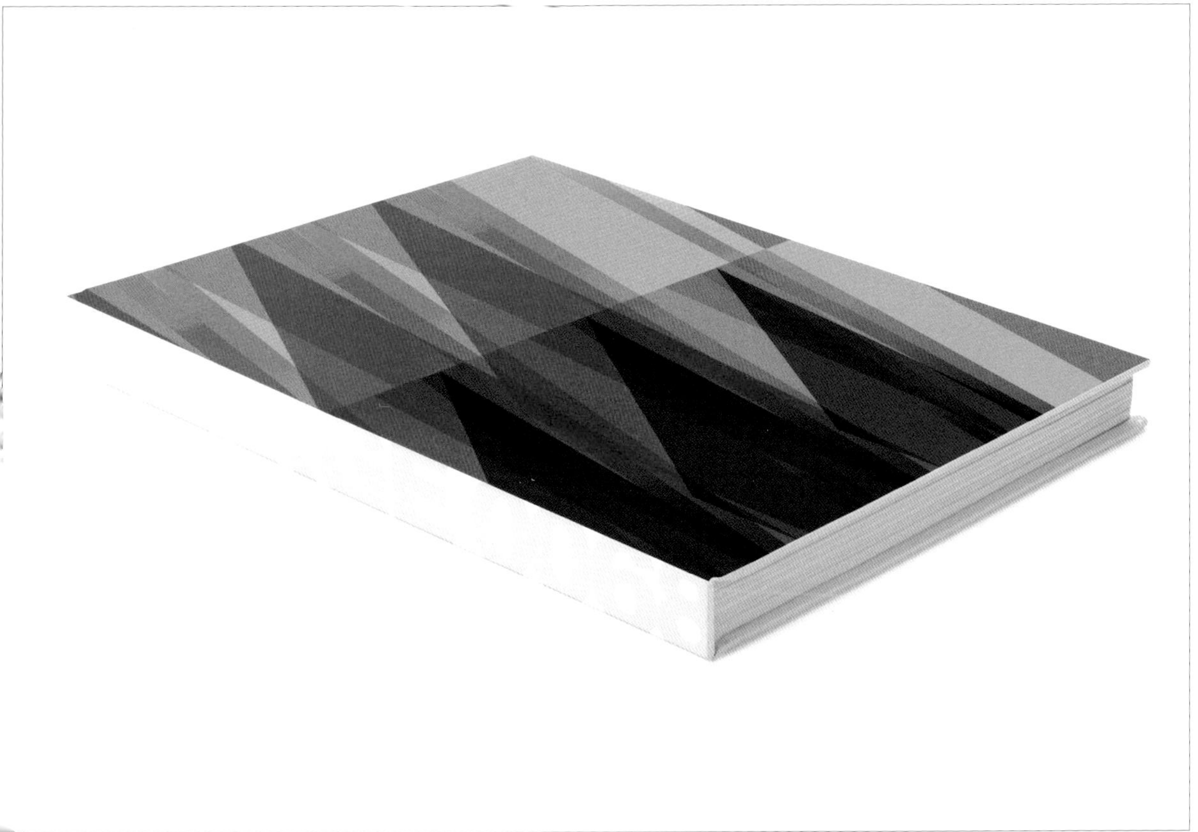

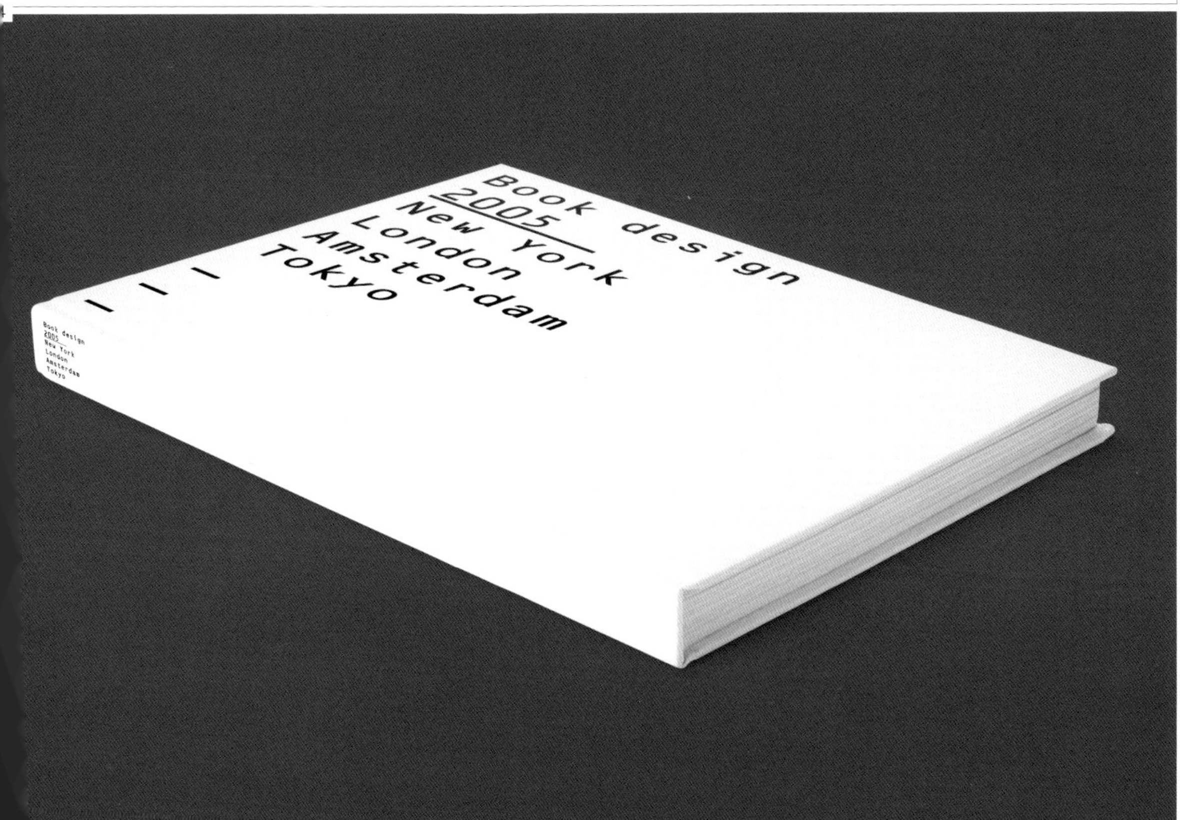
Book design
2005
New York
London
Amsterdam
Tokyo

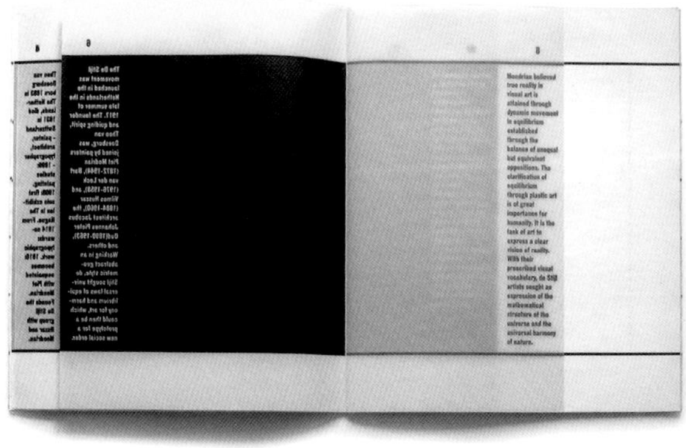

THEO VAN DOESBURG: THE INSTALLATION

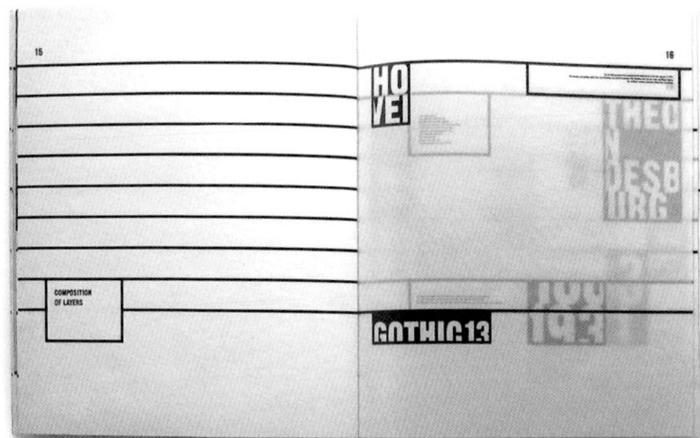
15
16
COMPOSITION OF LAYERS
GOTHIC13

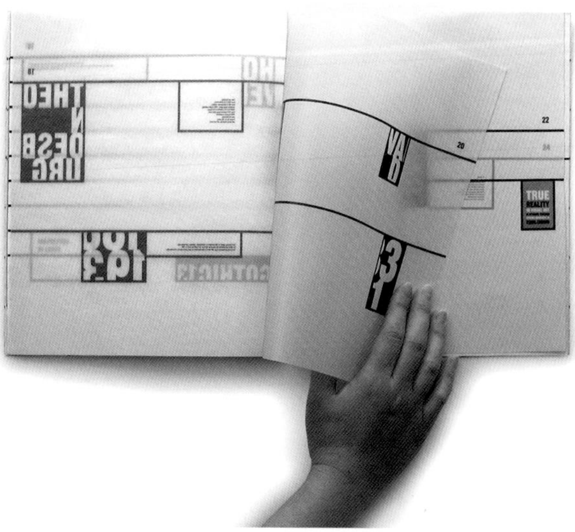
22
20
TRUE REALITY

3
THEO
VAN
DOESBURG
&
DE
STYJL

1

JUNE KIM | FORT LEE, NJ, USA

June Kim was born in Seoul, South Korea, and moved to New York in 1998, where he started to work at The New York Times designing special sections for the newspaper. Currently he works as a Senior Designer at the Iridium Group in New York City, with clients that include American Red Cross and the United Nations Federal Credit Union.

www.junekim.com

1 Theo van Doesburg guidebook and installation | Experimental work, 2002
2 Logo and Stationery | Sportology, 2003
3 Logos | June Kim, C&S Orthodontics Clinic, Monumonu Shanghai, 2002, 2005
4 Invitation | Saet Hwang, 2004
5 Diary and Stationery | Pansydaisy, 2004

THEO
WORKING
IN AN ABSTRACT
GEOMETRIC
STYLE
FOR ART
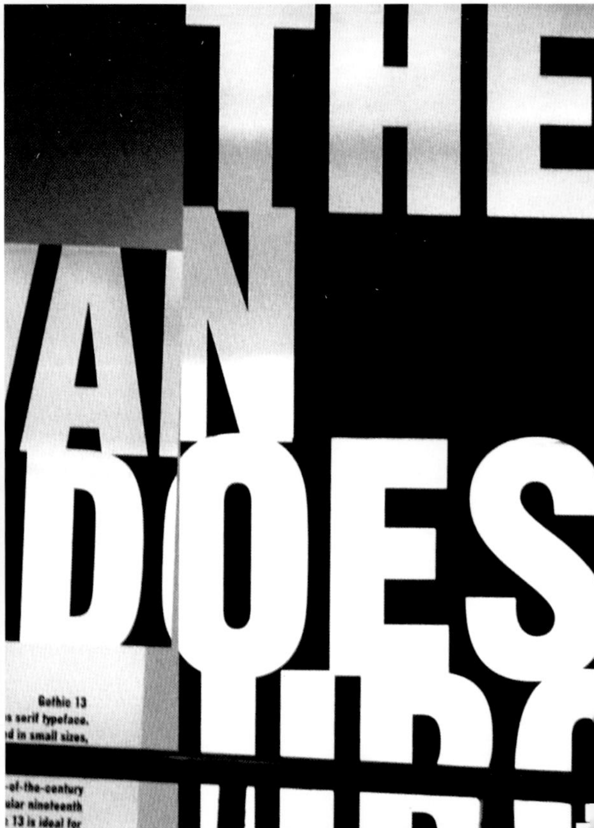
THE
AN
DOES
Gothic 13

THEO
OESB
URG
METRIC
STYLE
R ART

sportology
sportology
sportology
Taekwoong Chung, Principal Partner
Nasan Suite Building 2F, 1330-16 Seochodong, Seochogu, Seoul Korea 137-070
Office +82.2.3474.3303 | Mobile +82.16.9222.3003 | Fax +82.2.6249.1188
Nasan Suite Building 2F, 1330-16 Seochodong, Seochogu, Seoul Korea 137-070
Office +82.2.3474.3303 | Mobile +82.16.9222.3003 | Fax +82.2.6249.1188

C&S ORTHODONTICS

monumonu

4

5

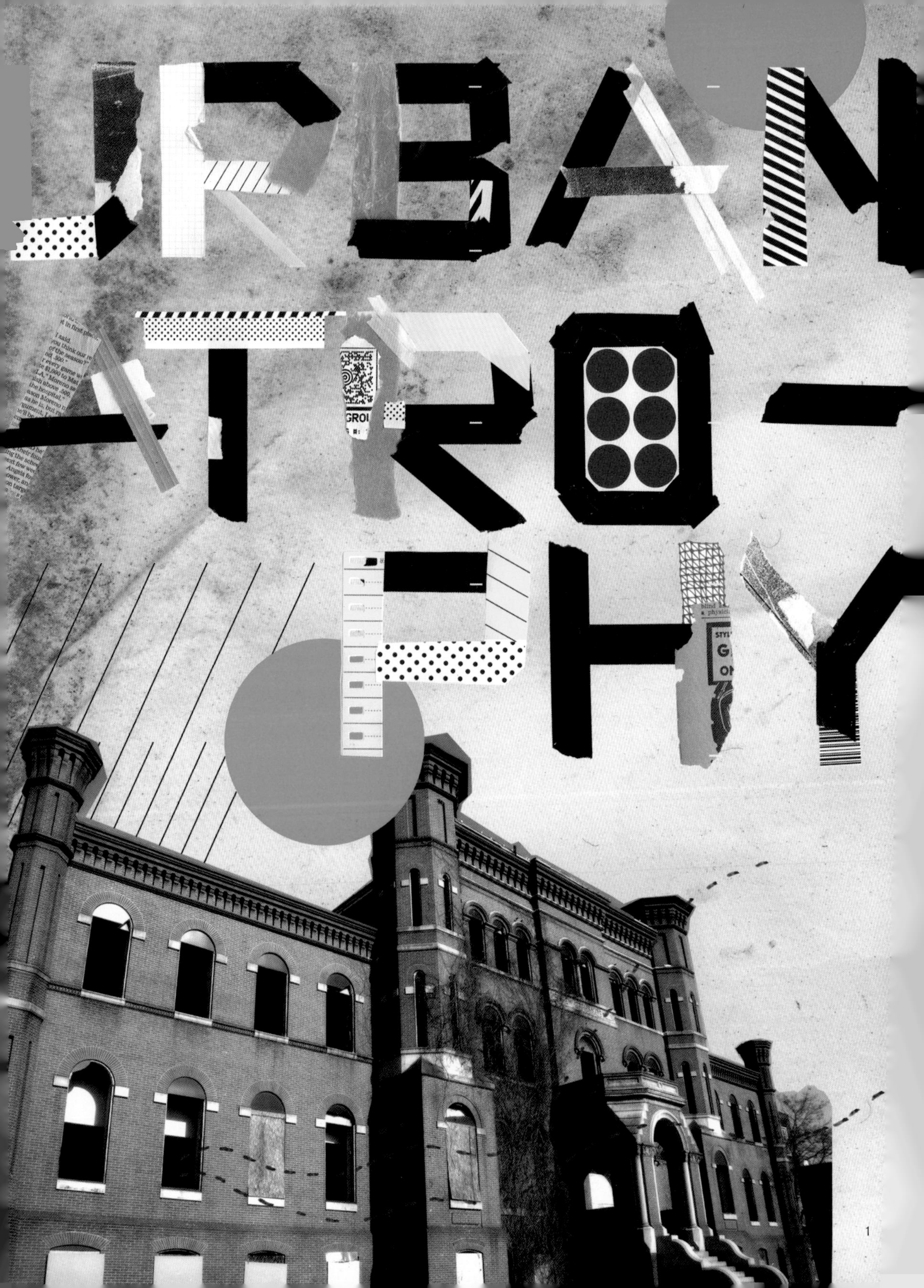
URBAN
ATRO–
PHY

KRISTIAN HENSON | LOS ANGELES, CA, USA

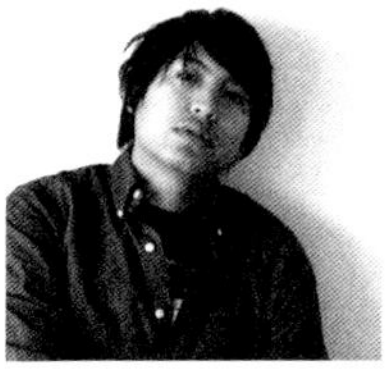

Kristian Henson was born and raised in Los Angeles. He graduated from the Art Center College of Design and was swiftly picked up by Studio Number One, the graphic design agency run by Shepard Fairey. Between working there full-time and frequent freelance projects, Kristian is about to launch his pet magazine project, Of Letters & Science.

www.tstfy.com

1 Magazine spread | Swindle magazine, 2007
Created at Studio Number One
2 Graphics | Motorola, 2006
Created at Studio Number One
3 Magazine concept | Self-initiated, 2006-07
4 CD and LP packaging | Stones Throw Records, 2007
In collaboration with Stephen Serrato

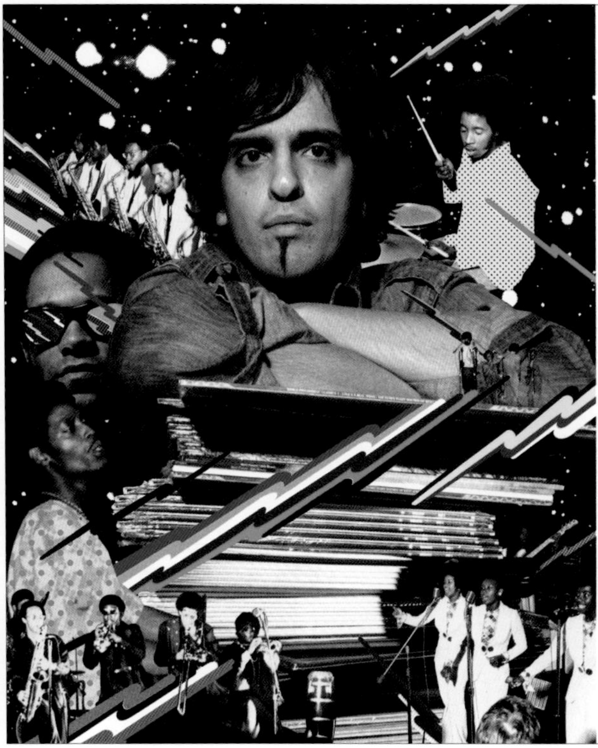

FROM THE DEEP END OF FUNK

By Caleb Neelon
Illustrated by Kristian Henson

EGON the manager and resident archivist of Stones Throw Records and its Now-Again imprint, is a reformed record collector. As he tells it, record collecting is hard to kick. Once an obsessive completist, beholden for years to the fraternal order of neurotic record dudes, he describes his period of collection addiction with fervor appropriate to a 12-step meeting: "I've fought the battle. I've lost friends over records."

These were the dark times. Times, he recalls, "when I removed myself from what I loved so much about James Brown and the feeling I got when I wanted to share it."

And although he discloses, "It still freaks me out sometimes," things have changed. He says, "I've been able to step back and say, 'What's the most important thing to me about this?' Well, I want to share the music, to share what I felt when I first heard James Brown." He leans forward and his voice drops: "I don't care if I have the record now. If I can find a friend that I can convince to give me a file of the record to master from, to release, that's more important to me."

Egon's redirected passion has yielded some of the most rare and coveted soul, jazz and funk reissues in recent memory. Below, this record collector turned Johnny Appleseed of rare music introduces three of the most interesting and important albums in his list of releases.

THE SOUTH DALLAS POP FESTIVAL 1970
Various Artists
CD/LP
Label: Now-Again
Re-release date: 2003

On a rainy summer night in 1970, Roger Boykin, local DJ and owner of storied Texas label Soultex, finally saw the result of his most recent effort: the First (and only) Annual South Dallas Pop Festival went off without a hitch. The event was called "pop," but as Egon says, "No question, it was a funk festival." Held at the musty Central Forest Club, a converted theater outside of downtown Dallas, the festival featured the cream of the local funk scene. In this, the evening wasn't much different from thousands of jubilant nights enjoyed and forgotten across the county. Roger explains, "There were funk fans, jazz fans, businessmen and women, hustlers, players, ladies of the evening, entertainers and ordinary people." However, unlike the vast majority of these fleeting parties, this one was recorded. Long after the motley crowd departed, the reels of two-track quarter-inch tape documenting these performances remained, guarded, but unissued, waiting like a time capsule in Roger's care.

Enter Egon. Like an archeologist rescuing a rare fossil from a sinking ship, Egon chose this long unrecognized gem as Now-Again's inaugural release: "It was just natural to start with something that I thought was really important, but was also a little bit, you know, off the beaten path," he says. Off the beaten path, maybe, but a worthwhile detour for anyone who'd enjoy a sweaty, gritty, funk party—a party from the days when "funk" was a term banned in polite company.

TEXAS THUNDER SOUL 1968-1974
KASHMERE STAGE BAND
CD/LP
Label: Now-Again
Re-release date: 2006

Imagine The JBs, James Brown's inimitable backing band during the first half of the '70s. Hold that thought. Picture a hip group of afro'd, platform shoe-wearing high school students from the same era. Now, conflate these images. Good. Through this exercise you've envisioned, roughly, the Kashmere Stage band (KSB), a rotating group of students from Houston, Texas' Kashmere High School who managed, over nearly a decade, to produce some of the most driving, heartfelt funk of its time. The Auntie Mame behind this joyful musical outpouring was bandleader Conrad Johnson, a slight, disarming man with roots in the early days of jazz. When he took charge of Kashmere High's stage band, in 1969, they were doing what was expected of a high school band: performing just listenable versions of Swing's tepid classics. Clearly, a situation guaranteed to inspire no one. Noting this, Conrad sought ways to make the stage band both compelling and challenging for his students. He lighted on the idea for changing KSB's musical direction, appropriately enough, when he went to an Otis Redding concert. As Conrad explained to NPR reporter David Brown, "[Redding] was kicking...and I went back and [asked my band], 'If I were to get you to do a show while you're playing and teach it to you, do you think you could do it?' My band said, 'If you believe we can do it, we can do it.'"

He believed. They did it. Not only did they do it, they excelled. Barrie Lee Hall Jr. is the conductor for the Duke Ellington Orchestra. He knew Johnson since he was a child, and played professionally with him in 1986, at the age of 11. Hall Jr. says, "It's a feat of magic, what [Johnson] could get out of the kids." Johnson picked up students who didn't have a ride to practice and created practice regimens for students who needed extra help. He dedicated himself to

1

1

OMAYRA AMAYA: MODERN GYPSY

by Shawna Kenney
Photos by Adam Amengual
Illustration by Kristian Henson

Clap your hands 12 times fast. Now do it again, clapping loudly on just the bolded beats: 1 2 3 4 5 6 7 8 9 10 11 12. Or, try it this way, clapping hard only on the "ones": 1 2 1 2 1 2 3 1 2 3 1 2. Do it over and over and you're clapping a Seguiriya, the most basic of Flamenco forms. Easy, right?

Flamenco is not just a form of dance. It is complex rhythms. It is intricate guitar. It is songs of passion and mourning accompanying dresses swishing, fringe flying, skirts twisting, chunky heels stomping, elegant arms and hands fluttering. And while its multiethnic ancestry is still being studied, most agree that it is a folk art born in 18th-century Andalusia, the autonomous community that makes up southern Spain.

Flamenco's cultural stew is made up of many groups--Gypsies, Jews, Moors, Muslims, and Latins--all of whom once lived in southern Spain, blending together in the lower levels of society until many were expelled during the Spanish Inquisition. While the word "flamenco" actually means "Flemish" in Spanish, etymologist Blas Infante claims the word "flamenco" is derived from the Hispano-Arabic word fellahmengu, meaning "expelled peasant." Others disagree. But despite its nebulous history, Flamenco as a form lives on in modern society, where it is still practiced, taught, debated, and celebrated in nearly every country.

Carmen Amaya, a legendary Barcelona-born dancer and subject of the book and documentary Queen of the Gypsies, wowed the world with Flamenco throughout the 1940s and '50s. She moved to America in 1936, acting in several box-office-breaking films and even performing for Presidents Roosevelt and Truman. She died in 1963 at the age of 50, but her legacy lives on through her grandniece, 34-year-old Omayra Amaya.

MOTO
space

MOTO
RAZR

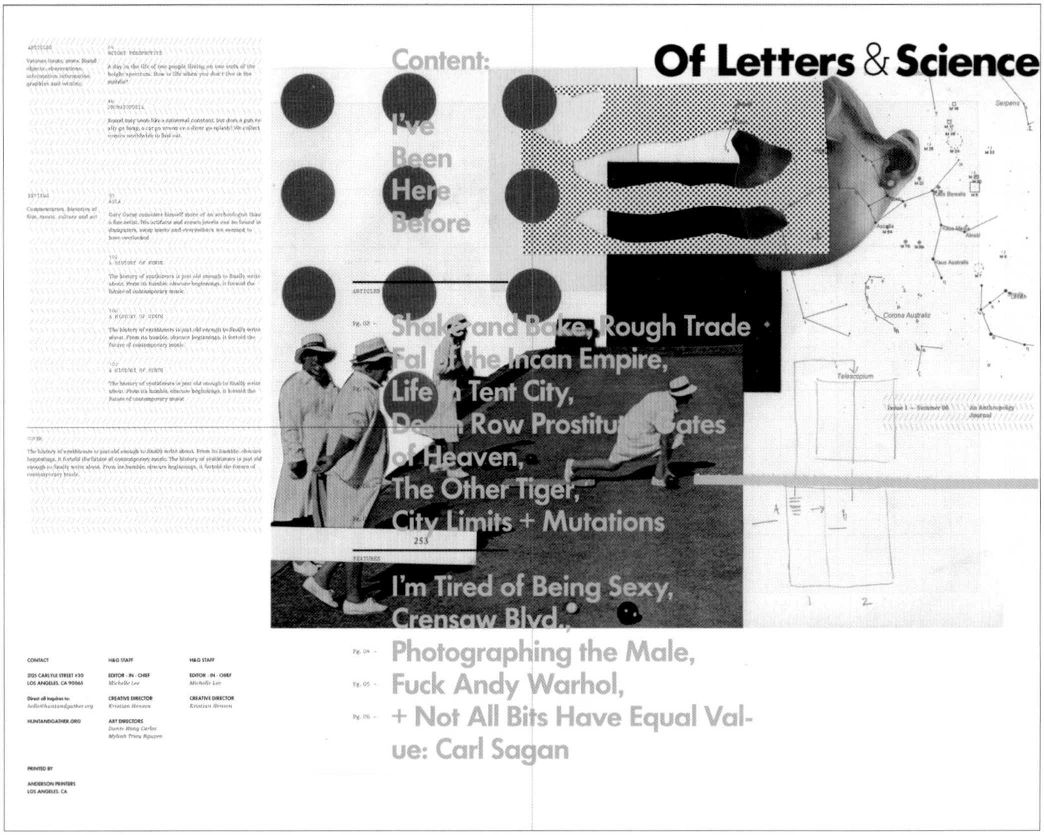
Of Letters & Science
Content:
I've Been Here Before
Shake and Bake, Rough Trade
Fal of the Incan Empire,
Life in Tent City,
Row Prostitu ates
of Heaven,
The Other Tiger,
City Limits + Mutations
253
I'm Tired of Being Sexy,
Crensaw Blvd.,
Photographing the Male,
Fuck Andy Warhol,
+ Not All Bits Have Equal Val-
ue: Carl Sagan

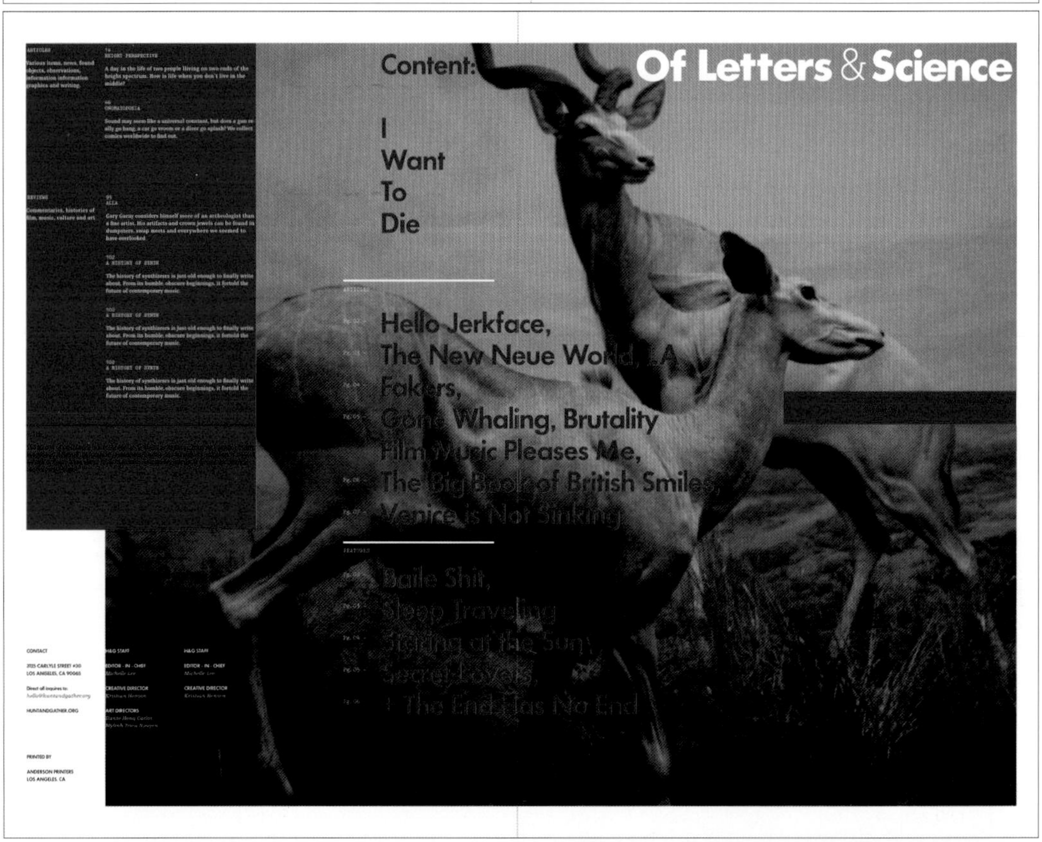
Of Letters & Science
Content:
I Want To Die
Hello Jerkface,
The New Neue World, LA
Fakers,
Gone Whaling, Brutality
Film Music Pleases Me,
The Big Book of British Smiles,
Venice is Not Sinking

4

la tortilleria
Atelier Visuel & Couleur Gestionnaires
CORREGIDORA 410 SUR
SAN PEDRO CENTRO
66230 GG NL MÉXICO
T. 52 (81) 8192 0448 & 49
LA TORTILLERIA
LATORTILLERIA.COM
SONIA SALDAÑA
CORREGIDORA 410 SUR
SAN PEDRO CENTRO
66230 GG NL MÉXICO
T. 52 (81) 8192 0448 & 49
LATORTILLERIA.COM

LA TORTILLERÍA | SAN PEDRO GARZA GARCÍA, MEXICO

Zita Arcq, Carolina Díaz, Sonia Saldaña

Originally based out of a former tortilla factory, La Tortillería was born when Zita and Sonia joined forces to turn the space that they shared as an art studio into the headquarters for their freelance design projects. Later joined by Carolina, the studio grew to specialize in sophisticated editorial design and exquisite brand identities.

www.latortilleria.com.mx

1 Visual identity | Self-initiated, 2007
2 Invitation | Ortiz & Arcq, 2006
3 Brochure | Grupo Constructor Armadillo, Plate, 2007
4 Art direction and design | Porcelana magazine, 2004-05
5 Identity | Cráftika, 2005
6 Identity | Lemon Chic, 2005
7 Brochure | Chino Moro, 2007
8 Brochure | Trendsétera, 2007
9 Magazine spread | File magazine, 2005
10 Identity | Teddy & Co, 2007

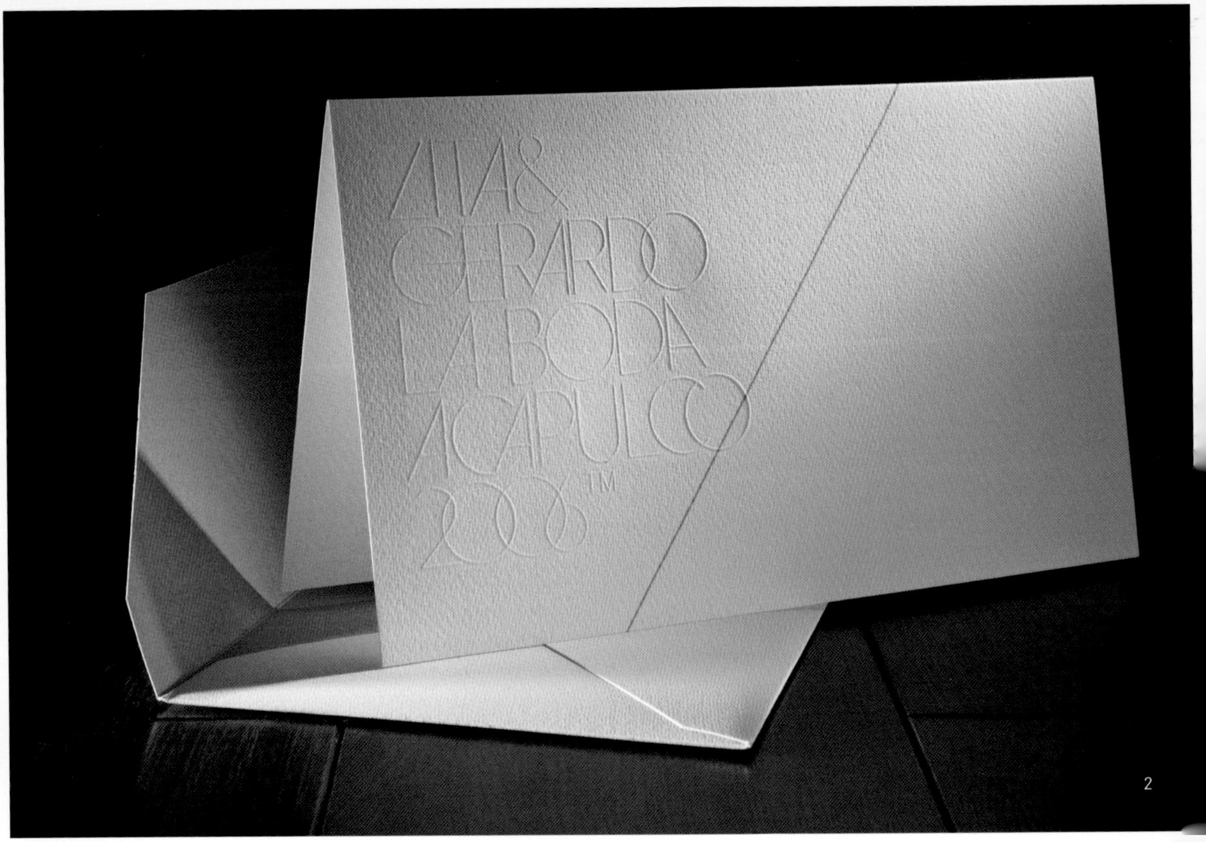

2

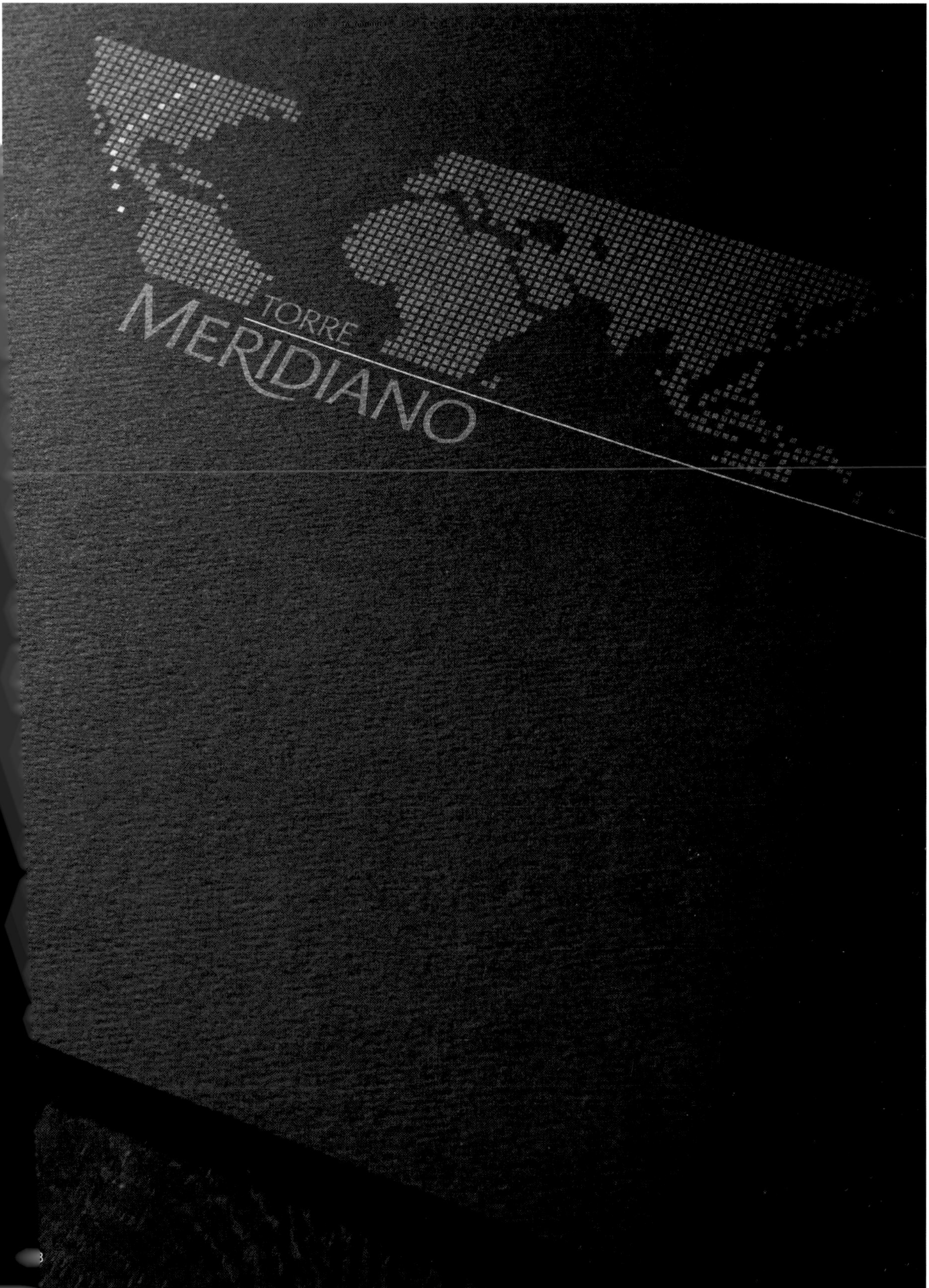
TORRE
MERIDIANO

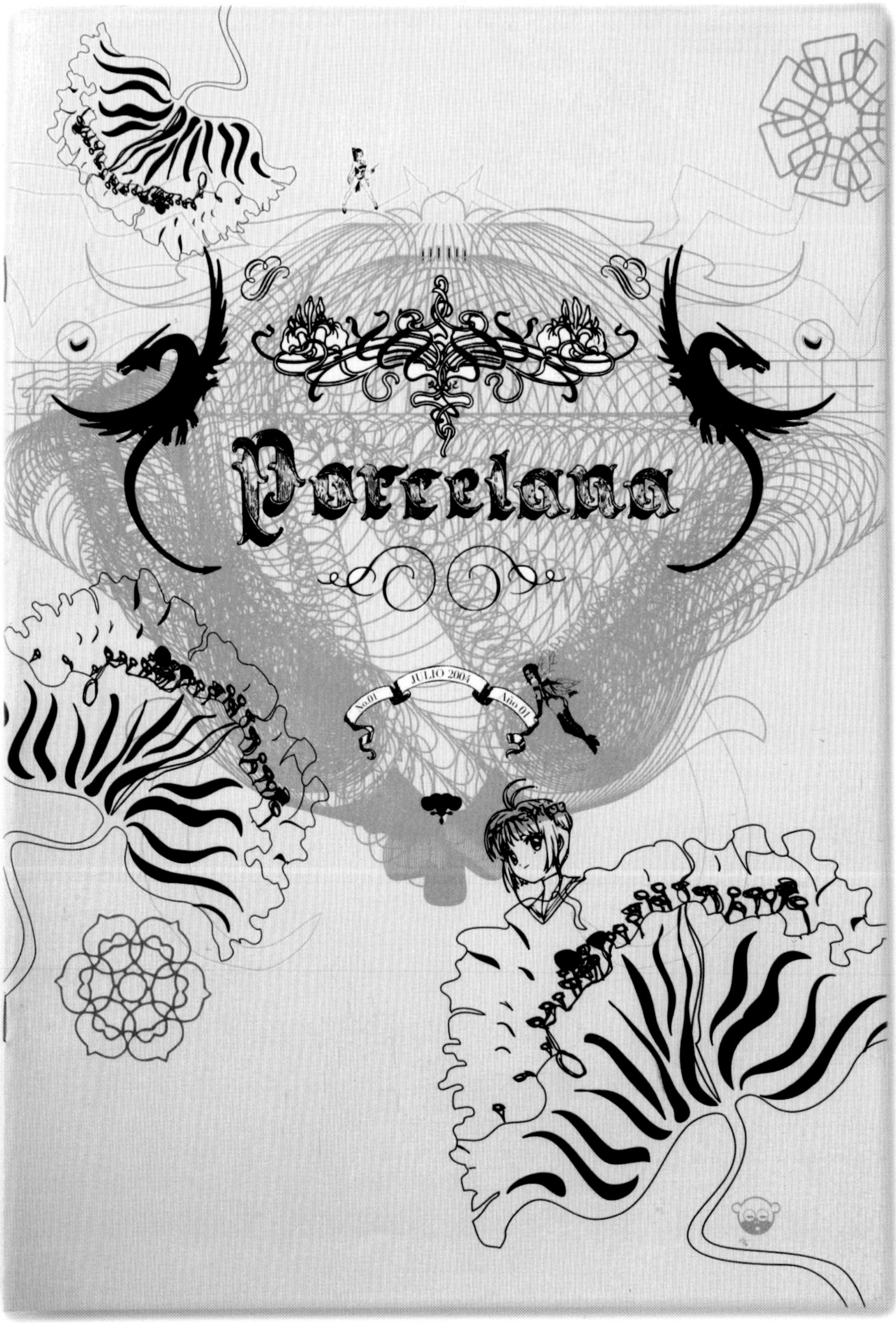
Porcelana
No.01
JULIO 2004
Año 01

PORCELANA
No. 02 / SEPTIEMBRE 2004 / Año 01

CRAFTiKA

CRAFTiKA™
CRAFTiKA
CRAFTiKA
CRAFTiKA

LEMON CHIC
SWEET AND SOUR GLAM
REBECCA TAYLOR · CATHERINE MALANDRINO · CHLOÉ · BARTAK
TRACEY REESE · MIGUELINA · YANUK · BALENCIAGA · FRANKIE
ADRIANO GOLDSCHMIED · EARNST SEWN · JOYSTICK · BLUE CU
JOE´S · ROCK AND REPUBLIC · GERARD YOSCA · NANETTE LEP

LEMON CHIC
SWEET AND SOUR GLAM

Musa

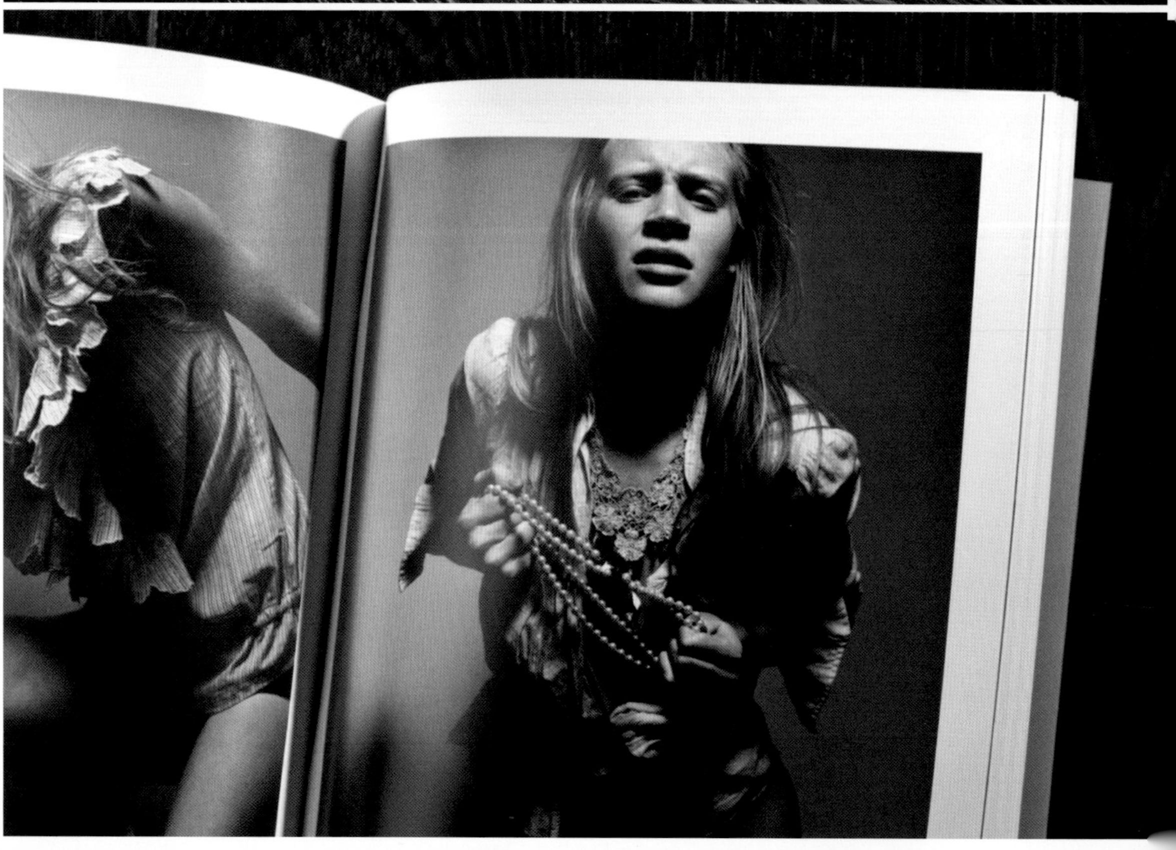

SAVOIR
FAIRE

THE PLACE
TO EAT
NO INHIBITIONS

Magicuento
Flora Martínez, Manolo Cardona y Unax Ugalde protagonizan la producción México-Colombia Rosario Tijeras, que se estrenará próximamente.
Fotografía: Oleg Kovtun
Coordinación de moda: Annie Lask
Maquillaje y pelo: Vinicio Conti para Twiggy Fashion Team
Gráfica: La Tortillería
Louis Vuitton
197

Flora: Blusa Adolfo Domínguez, falda Louis Vuitton. Unax: Camisa Libertine, sombrero nacho fila
203

Teddy&Co.

10

HORRIBLE
AWFUL
FEO
PUAJ
YOU ARE
HORRIBBLE

LAURA VARSKY | BUENOS AIRES, ARGENTINA

Laura Varsky is a designer and illustrator from Buenos Aires. Her first forays into the design world came through her involvement with the local independent rock scene. She gradually asserted herself as a designer specializing in the design of books and record sleeves. In 2006 she received a Grammy Latino for best record packaging.

www.lauravarsky.com.ar

1 Illustration | Die Gestalten Verlag, 2004
2 Book design | Retina, 2006
3 Book design | Ediciones del Eclipse, 2007
Illustrations by Christian Montenegro
4 Illustration | Monoblock, 2007
5 CD packaging | Árbol and PopArt Discos, 2007
6 CD packaging | Cuentos Borgeanos and EMI, 2007
Illustrations by Christian Montenegro
7 Business cards | Self-initiated, 2006
8 Illustration | Personal work, 2007
9 Illustration | Peri, 2006

VIRGINIA LUQUE

En el camarín de Virginia Luque en *El Viejo Almacén* hay una mezcla de tocador y altar en el que la foto de su madre, la gallega doña María, está entronizada junto al espejo, entre un Señor de los Milagros y un Jesucristo que debe conocer la noche mejor que el príncipe de las tinieblas: lleva años recorriendo tanguerías con su devota propietaria. "Roberto Goyeneche me decía: '¡Ay, hermana, qué lindo es! ¿Me dejás darle un beso al barbudo?'". Cantante, actriz y última diva porteña, la Luque filmó decenas de películas y tuvo tanto éxito en Japón como en Centroamérica. Pero dice pertenecer a una época en la que, a despecho de cualquier otra conquista, "si uno no se asomaba al escenario de esta catedral del tango, no existía", y que, por lo tanto, está aquí para cumplir un deseo: "El de ser. Soy, existo: estoy en *El Viejo Almacén*".

En los años 60, su misteriosa vida sentimental y sus disputados pases televisivos obsesionaban a la revista *Radiolandia*. Era la época en la que deslumbraba con un guardarropas de más de doscientos diseños de su modisto exclusivo, Luis Bocú, y declaraba: "¡Quieren endilgarme idilios y amoríos que no están ni en mi imaginación! ¡A veces, utilizando el nombre de algún compañero de trabajo o el de algún caballero que tiene la osadía de hacerme llegar el testimonio de su admiración!". Hoy confiesa los gustos sencillos y las rutinas domésticas de una señora reposada: "Soy muy casera. Vuelvo casi a la una de la mañana, tomo algo caliente, me relajo. A veces hago *zapping*, me encuentro con una película mía y me engancho. Me hace feliz ver las películas, aunque el cine no era lo que más quería: yo amo el teatro. En cine empezás por la escena final, al día siguiente filmás una escena anterior y es muy difícil entrar en materia, a veces, salvo cuando el director es uno de aquellos grandes. Lucas Demare fue extraordinario. Con él hice *Sangre y acero*, filmamos en un pueblo ferroviario. Yo hacía dos personajes, madre e hija, y había que marcar bien la diferencia entre el personaje lleno de luz de la hija y el personaje un poco sufrido de la madre. No era sólo cuestión de vestimenta y maquillaje: había que componerlo. Lucas era tremendo, no sabe lo que me hizo llorar hasta lograr lo que me pedía".

Peleonas, Mentirosas y Haraganas
con texto de
Didi Grau,
ilustraciones de
Christian Montenegro
y diseño de
Laura Varsky
Peleonas, Mentirosas y Haraganas
Didi Grau, Christian Montenegro y Laura Varsky

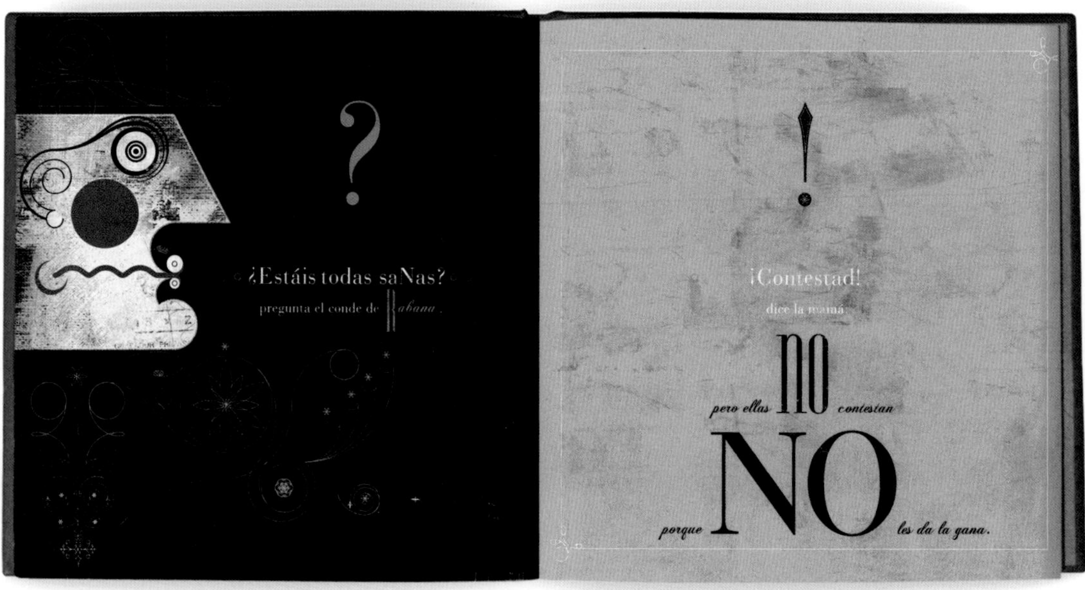
?
¿Estáis todas saNas?
pregunta el conde de Habana.
!
¡Contestad!
dice la mamá
pero ellas no contestan
porque NO les da la gana.

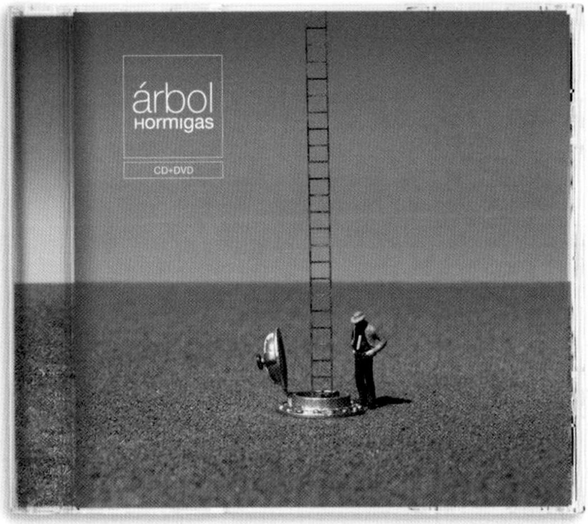
árbol
Hormigas
CD+DVD

árbol
Hormigas

www.arbol.com.ar

felicidades
cuentos
borgeanos

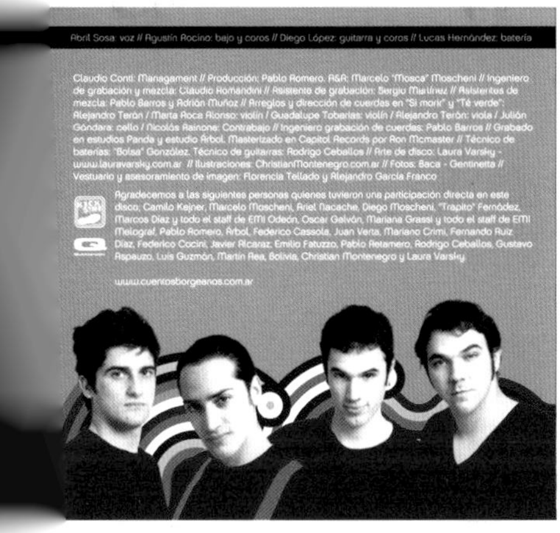

Abril Sosa: voz // Agustín Rocino: bajo y coros // Diego López: guitarra y coros // Lucas Hernández: batería
Claudio Conti: Managament // Producción: Pablo Romero. A&R: Marcelo "Mosca" Moscheni // Ingeniero de grabación y mezcla: Claudio Romandini // Asistente de grabación: Sergio Martínez // Asistentes de mezcla: Pablo Barros y Adrián Muñoz // Arreglos y dirección de cuerdas en "Si morir" y "Té verde": Alejandro Terán / Marta Roca Alonso: violín / Guadalupe Tobarias: violín / Alejandro Terán: viola / Julián Góndara: cello / Nicolás Rainone: Contrabajo // Ingeniero grabación de cuerdas: Pablo Barros // Grabado en estudios Panda y estudio Árbol. Masterizado en Capitol Records por Ron Mcmaster // Técnico de baterías: "Bolsa" González. Técnico de guitarras: Rodrigo Ceballos // Arte de disco: Laura Varsky - www.lauravarsky.com.ar // Ilustraciones: ChristianMontenegro.com.ar // Fotos: Baca - Gentinetta // Vestuario y asesoramiento de imagen: Florencia Tellado y Alejandro García Franco
Agradecemos a las siguientes personas quienes tuvieron una participación directa en este disco: Camilo Kejner, Marcelo Moscheni, Ariel Nacache, Diego Moscheni, "Trapito" Fernádez, Marcos Díaz y todo el staff de EMI Odeón, Oscar Galvón, Mariana Grassi y todo el staff de EMI Melograf, Pablo Romero, Árbol, Federico Cassola, Juan Verta, Mariano Crimi, Fernando Ruiz Díaz, Federico Cocini, Javier Alcaraz, Emilio Fatuzzo, Pablo Retamero, Rodrigo Ceballos, Gustavo Aspauzo, Luis Guzmán, Martín Rea, Bolivia, Christian Montenegro y Laura Varsky
www.cuentosborgeanos.com.ar

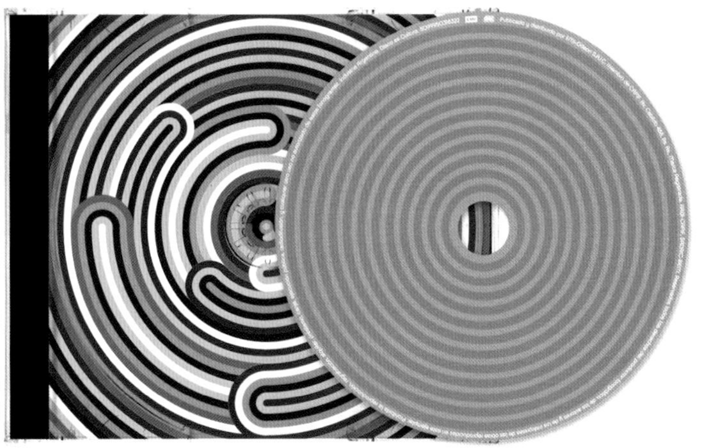

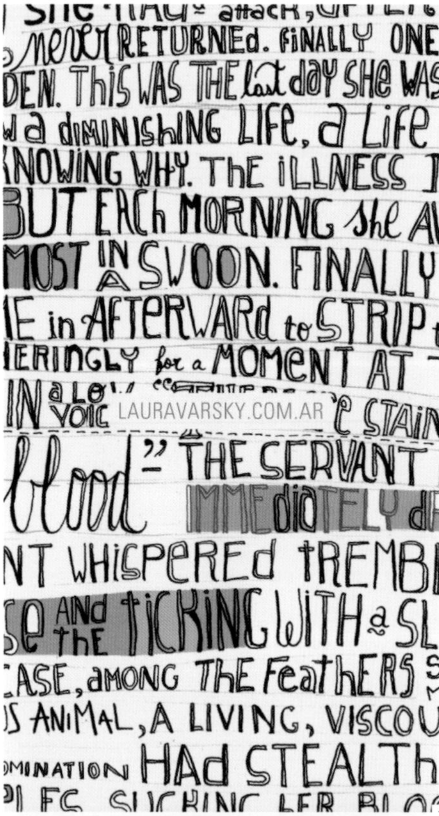
never RETURNED. FINALLY ONE
DEN. THIS WAS THE last day SHE WAS
a diminishing LIFE, a Life
KNOWING WHY. THE ILLNESS
BUT EACH MORNING she A
MOST IN A SWOON. FINALLY
E in AFTERWARD to STRIP
HERINGLY for a MOMENT AT
IN a LOW VOICE
E STAIN
blood" THE SERVANT
IMMEDIATELY
NT WHISPERED TREMBL
se AND the TICKING WITH a SL
CASE, AMONG THE FEATHERS
S ANIMAL, A LIVING, VISCOU
OMINATION HAD STEALTH
LAURAVARSKY.COM.AR

LAURAVARSKY.COM.AR

7

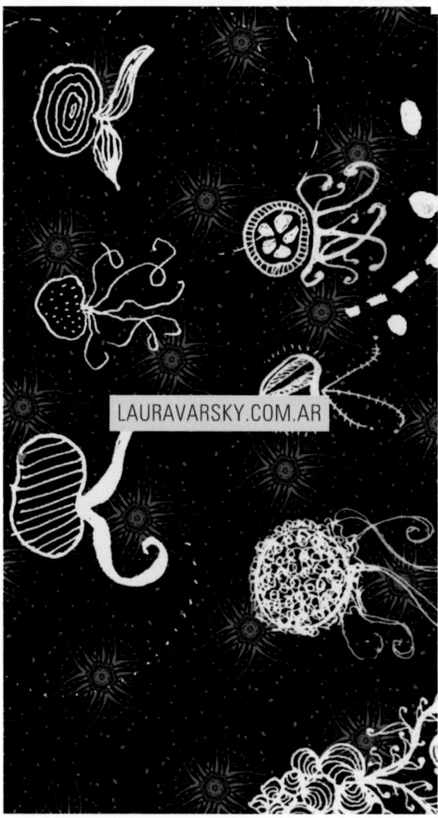
LAURAVARSKY.COM.AR

LAURAVARSKY.COM.AR

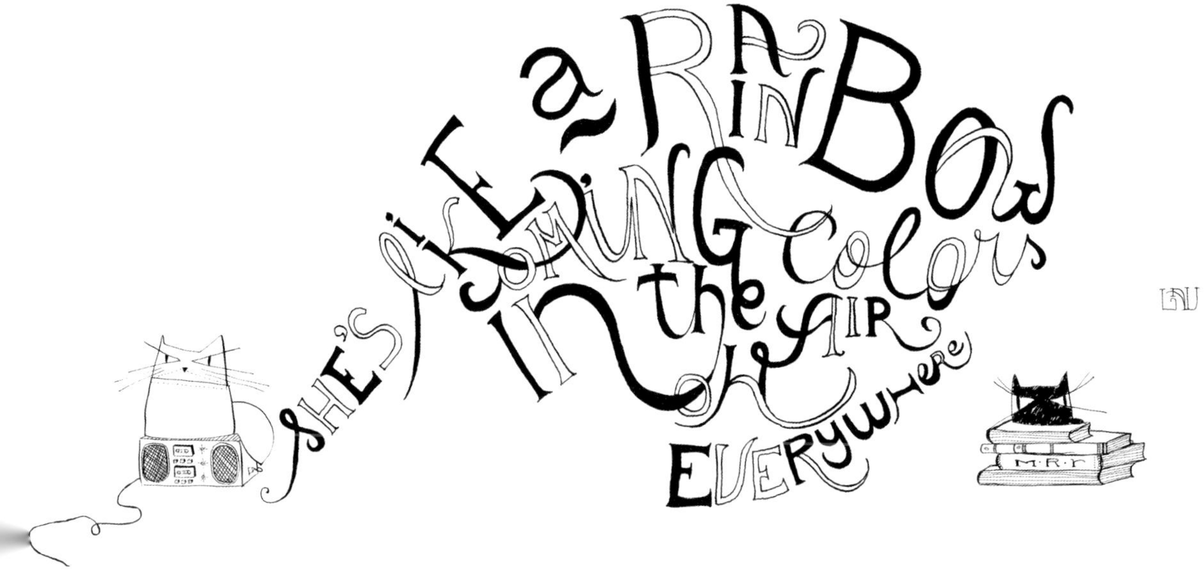
SHE'S LIKE a RAINBOW
COMING COLORS
IN the AIR
OH
EVERYWHERE
M·R·T

QUERO·VOCÊ·MEU·BEM
FIM·DA·LINHA
DÓ·ME·MIM
DEIXA·DE·DRAMA
FARINHA
PRA·TE·VER
DEDO·DE·DEUS
ladainha
DIGA·QUE·ME·AMA
FALAR DE DENTRO
NÃO·TER
DEPRESSA
NEM·TENTE
JUREMA
Barcelona
A·CAMA·E·A·TV
Falar DE Dentro
CAMOMILA
O INDIVISÍVEL
FINA TARDE
REDEMOINHO
UM·ALGUEM

1

LETTER BY CIRCLE | SAN FRANCISCO, CA, USA

Dante Carlos

Letter by Circle is Dante Carlos's personal portfolio, showcasing projects that aim to be relevant, beneficial and informed. Interests include culture, music, documentary, film, performance, science, technology, the environment, philosophy, and education. Dante is a graduate of the Art Center College of Design, and now lives in San Francisco.

www.letterbycircle.info

1 Supply publication | Self-initiated, 2005
2 Large-format posters | Self-initiated, 2006
3 Sagan typeface | Self-initiated, 2005
4 Visual identity posters | Self-initiated, 2005
5 Pilot plan book | Self-initiated, 2005

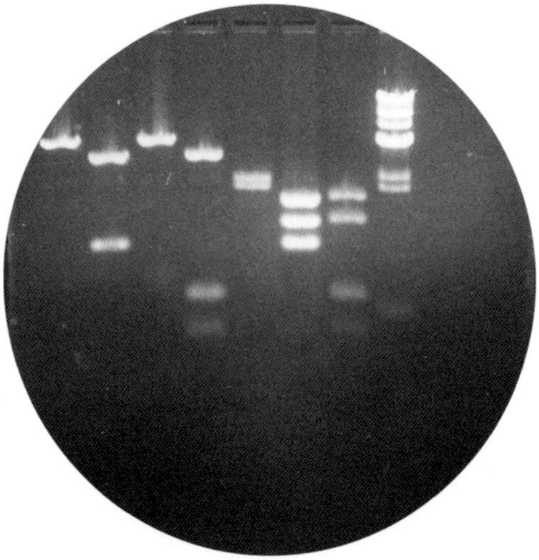

Chromosomes and their role | **DNA Transcription** | **DNA Translation**

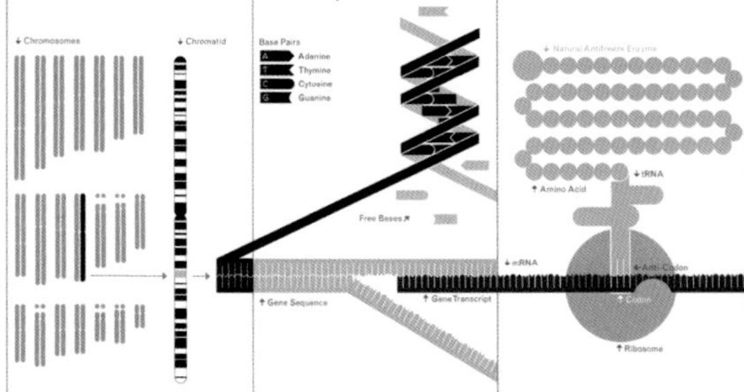

Every organism has genetic material in all of their cells. This material is responsible for the expression of all characteristics passed down from generations before. These characteristics, or genes, determine a whole host of functions, such as pigmentation, metabolism and susceptibility to certain diseases.

Within a gene, the sequence of nucleotides along a DNA strand defines a protein, which an organism is liable to manufacture or "express" at one or several points in its life using the information of the sequence.

The relationship between the nucleotide sequence and the amino-acid sequence of the protein is determined by simple cellular rules of translation, known collectively as the genetic code. The genetic code is made up of three-letter 'words' (termed a codon) formed from a sequence of three nucleotides (e.g. ACT, CAG, TTT). These codons can then be translated with messenger RNA and then transfer RNA, with a codon corresponding to a particular amino acid.

Since there are 64 possible codons, most amino acids have more than one possible codon. There are also three 'stop' or 'nonsense' codons signifying the end of the coding region, namely the UAA, UGA and UAG codons.

In many species of organism, only a small fraction of the total sequence of the genome appears to encode protein. The function of the rest is a matter of speculation. It is known that certain nucleotide sequences specify affinity for DNA binding proteins, which play a wide variety of vital roles, in particular through control of replication and transcription.

During translation, a small ribosomal subunit attaches to a mRNA molecule. At the same time, an initiator tRNA molecule recognizes and binds to a specific codon sequence on the same mRNA molecule. tRNAs carry specific amino acids that correspond with codons within the nucleotide sequence. A large ribosomal subunit then joins the newly formed complex. When a specific tRNA recognizes the codon sequence, it will attach itself to it. As the ribosome moves down the sequence, another tRNA molecule with another amino acid that corresponds with the next immediate sequence will attach. Both amino acids join, and the spent tRNA detaches itself from the mRNA. This process continues until the desired protein is created.

2

2
7
1
0
4
6
0
5
0
9

SPACE

ABCDEFG

HIJKLMNOPQRS

TUVWXYZ

1234567890

Æ CH TH HT

FF CT AT CK FL

ET EH SS FK HE FJ

EC ER Œ ER FO

EF FE FB FH

Washington Mutual

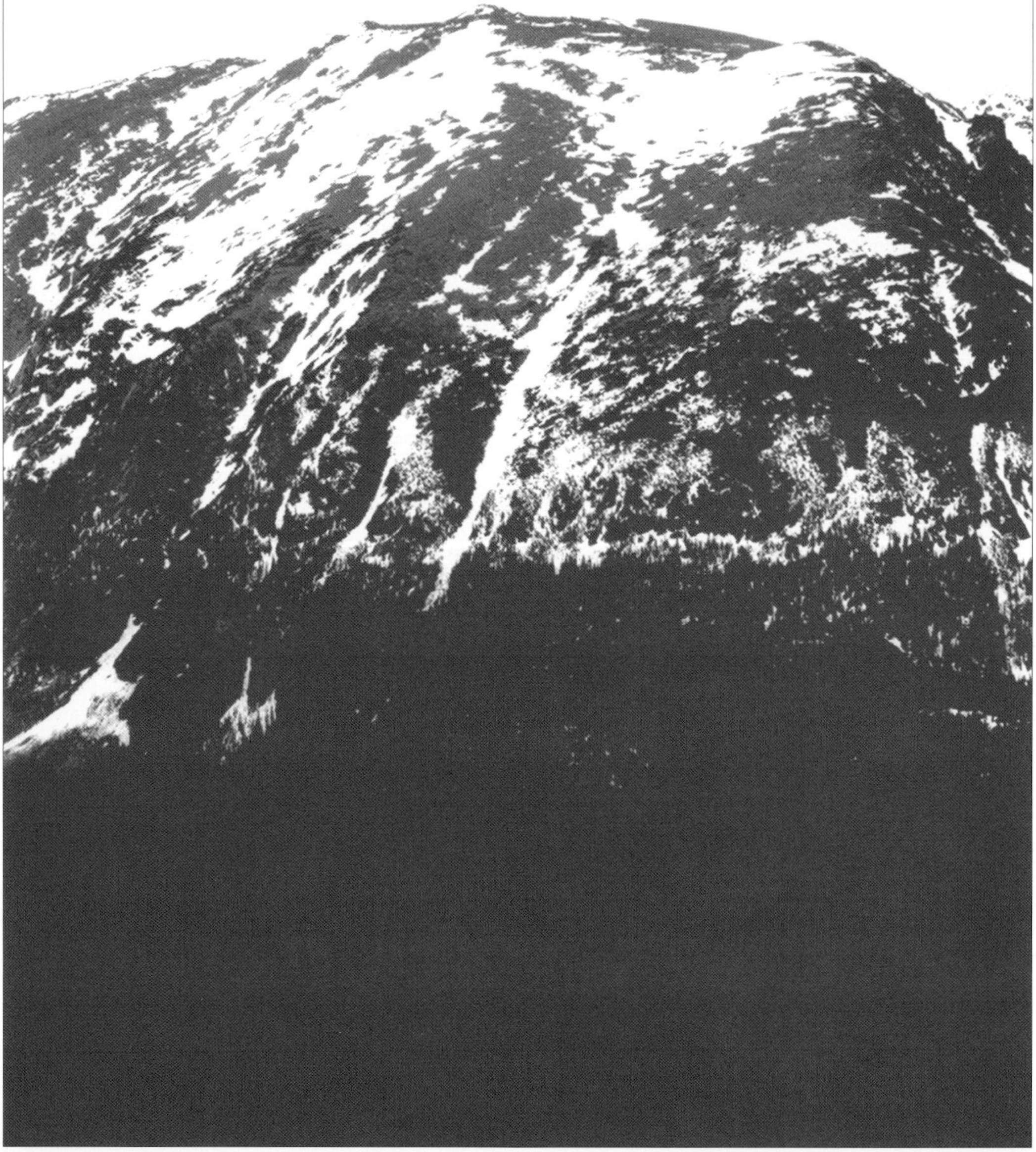

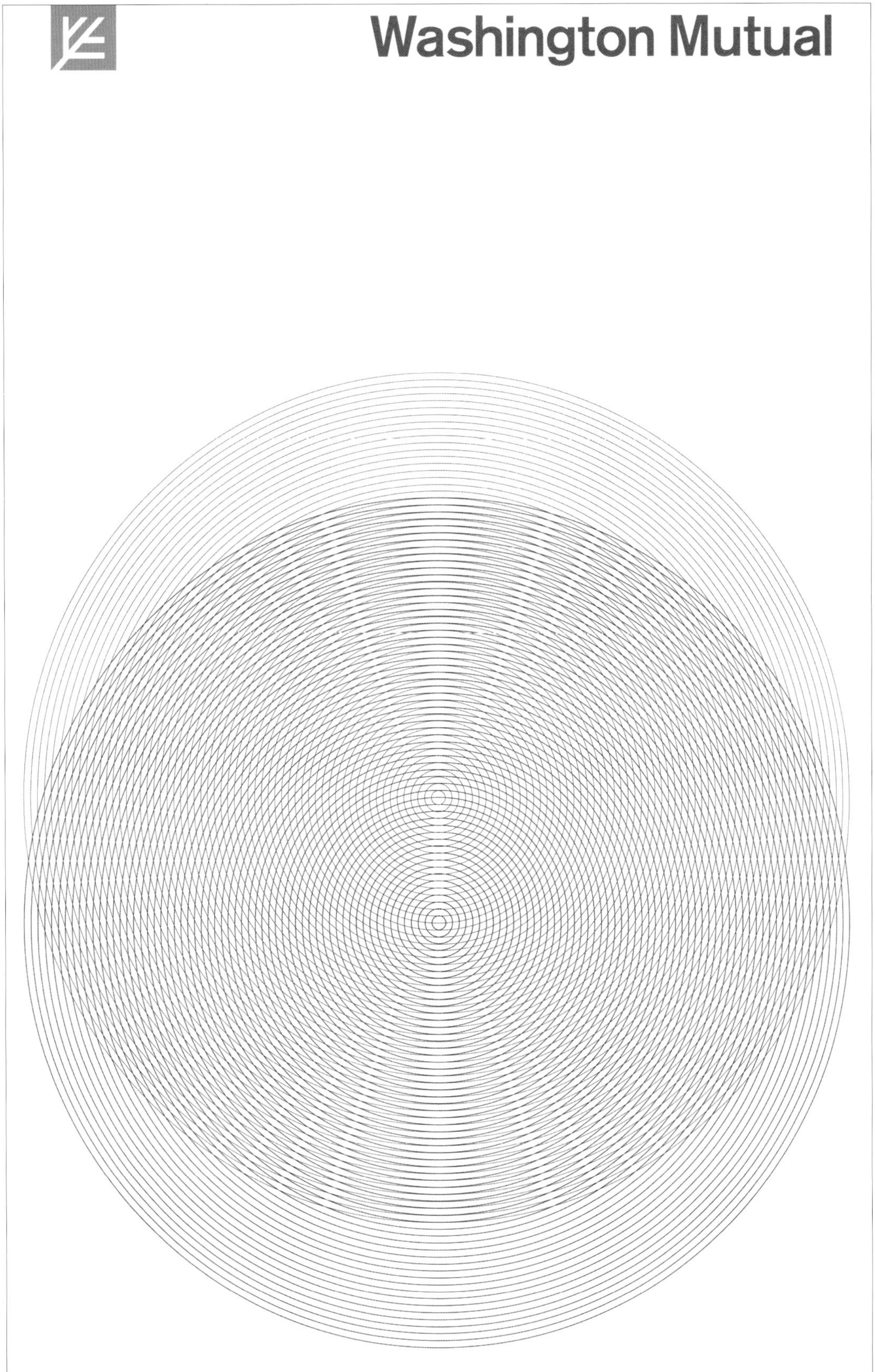
Washington Mutual

AOS TRABALHADORES
DE BRASILÍA, QUE
CONSTRUÍRAM A NOVA
CAPITAL;
AOS TRABALHADORES
DE BRAZIL, QUE
PAGARAM.
PILOT PLAN
AN EXAMINATION ON THE CITY OF BRASILIA

the world, and the interpretations and social processes they engage. This study requires that we differentiate between the various components of the planned city: between the architects' intentions for social change, embodied in its design, and the government's intentions to build and occupy it. In evaluating the former, I present Brasilia as an exemplar of the tenets of modernist architecture and city planning. Proposed by avant-garde groups in Western Europe and the Soviet Union and adopted in Brazil, these tenets constitute a radical re-conceptualization of city life. Brasilia is probably their most complete realization. Nevertheless, what is found as a totality in Brasilia is found as fragments large and small in cities throughout the world because in this century of phenomenal urban growth architectural theory, debate, education, and practice have been set in modernist terms. It is therefore not too great a generalization to say that the modernist vision of a new way of life has fundamentally altered the urban environment in which nearly half the world's people live. Postmodern critics tell us today that this modernism is now finished/ its creativity exhausted. Yet I would suggest another aspect of the problem: if modernism is dying it nevertheless remains dominant, at the very least in the third world. A study of Brasilia therefore offers an opportunity to evaluate its dominant assumptions in a context in which they are expressed with particular clarity. In analyzing the second set of intentions—the government's plan to build Brasilia—I suggest a number of different but related points about development. On the one hand, I analyze the role of modernist architecture and city planning in development projects which require massive state intervention and centralized coordination. This issue is especially important in third-world countries/ where the modernist aesthetic appeals to governments across the political spectrum. To explain this unusual appeal, I suggest a number of affinities between modernism as an aesthetic of erasure and reinscription and modernization as an ideology of development in which governments, regardless of persuasion, seek to rewrite national histories.

On the other hand, I examine Brasilia as an example of a common type of development project founded on a paradox. In portraying an imagined and desired future Brasilia represented a negation of existing conditions in Brazil. This Utopian difference between the two is precisely the project's premise. Yet, at the same time, the government intended it as a means to achieve this future—as an instrument of change which would of necessity, have to use the existing conditions it denied. My point in analyzing this apparent paradox is not to dispute the need for Utopia in imagining a better world. Indeed, in the course of the book I shall oppose the postmodern abandonment of alternative futures. My aim is rather to determine the ways in which, in the construction of the city and the making of its society the paradoxes of Utopia subverted its initial premises. On this subversion—on the way in which the people of Brasilia engaged these premises at their points of contradiction to reassert the social processes and cultural values Utopia intended to deny—I focus my ethnographic account.

5

MANSI SHAH | VALENCIA, CA, USA

Mansi Shah, born in India and raised in Southern California, is interested in all things sublime and beautiful. Her Indian background brings a love for vibrant color and mysticism to her work, while calm Californian attitudes leave her mind to dream and wander. Present goals include pursuing a career in textiles and illustration as well as design.

www.mansishah.com

1 Silk-screened poster | California Institute of the Arts, 2007
In collaboration with Silas Munro
2 Illustrations | California Institute of the Arts, 2007
3 Illustration | Faesthetic Magazine, 2006
4 Poster | Elisa Maria Lopez, 2006
In collaboration with Beau Johnson
5 Illustration | Shadrach Lindo, 2007
6 Posters | Cat Lamb, 2005, 2004
7 Hand-drawn typography | Self-initiated, 2007
8 Silk-screened poster | California Institute of the Arts, 2006

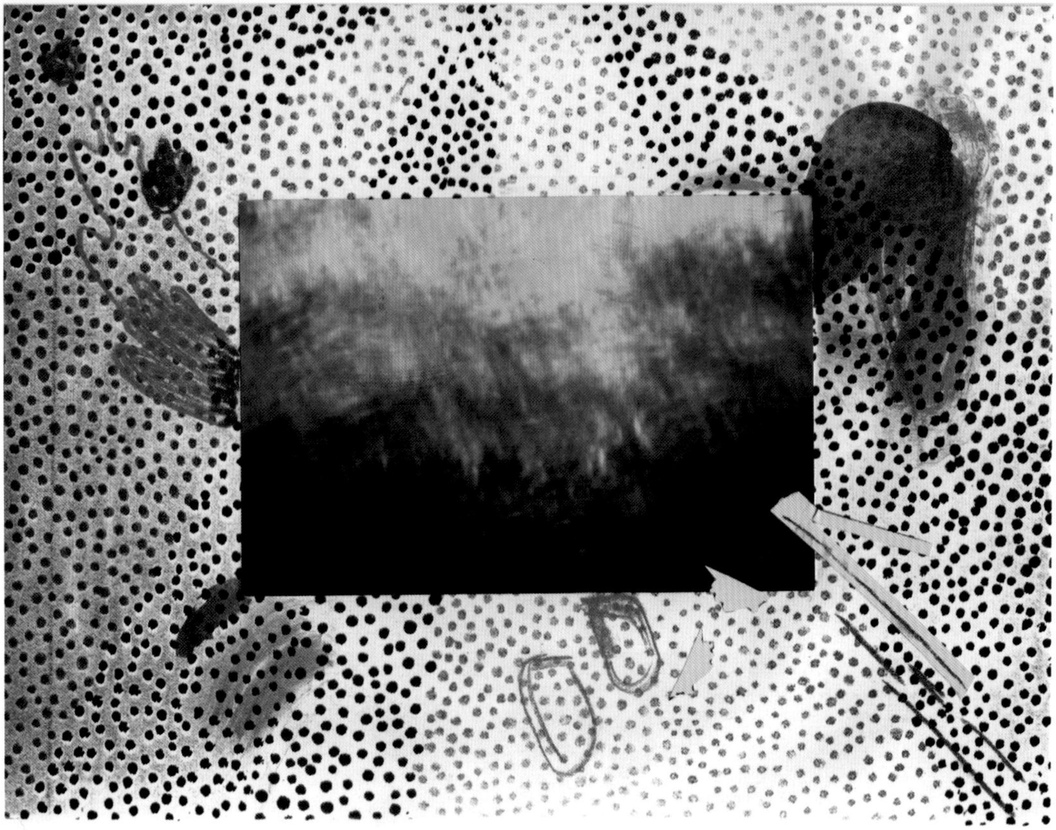

2

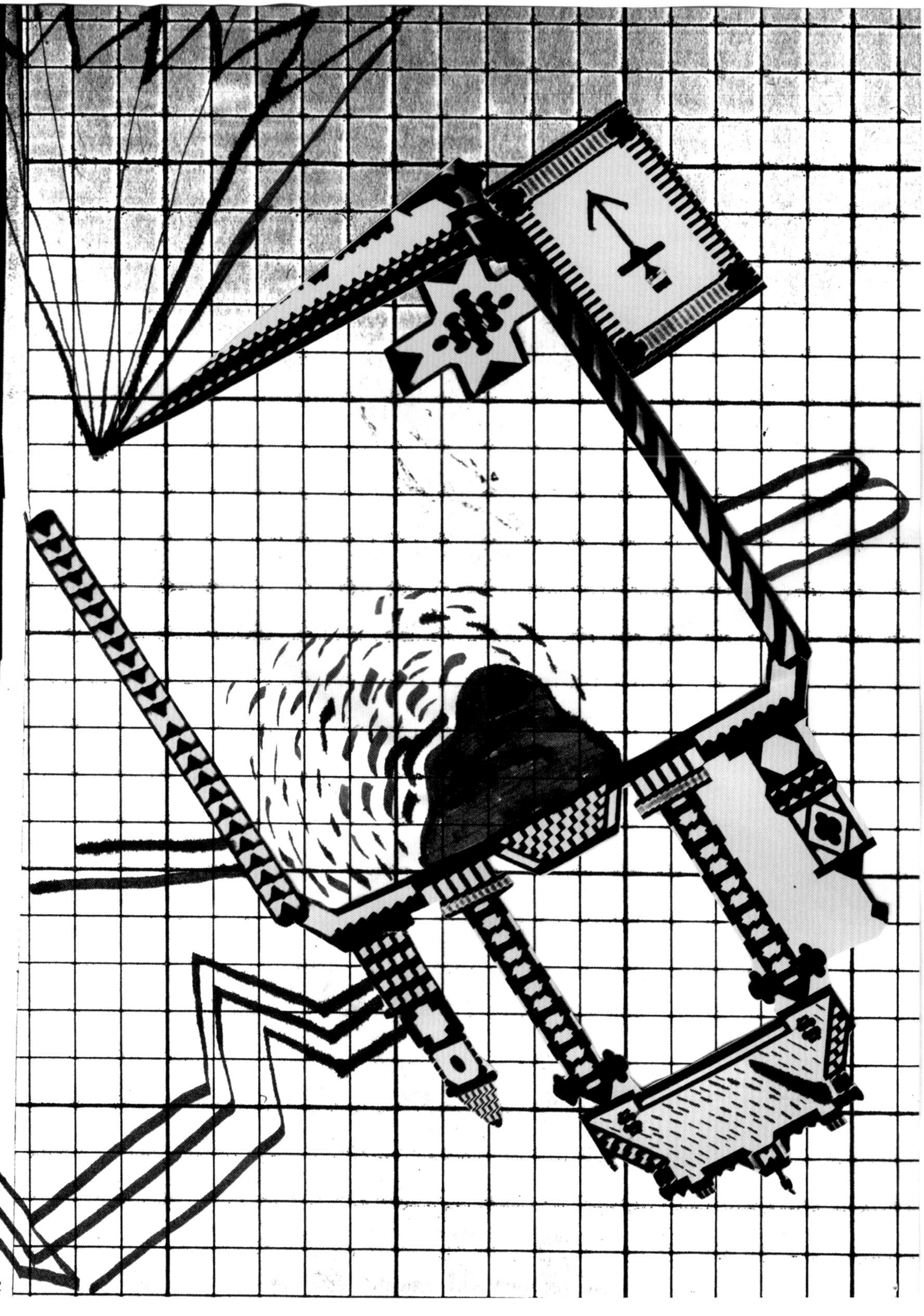

THE THEORY IS RELIGION
THE PRACTICE IS MAGIC
ELISA MARIA LOPEZ
Thesis Exhibition March 5-11, 2006
Pinatas to be opened Thursday, March 9
at 12 pm, 6:30 pm, 10 pm
Reception March 9, 10 pm Lime Gallery, Cal Arts
Performances by Fireworks and Vitamin Wig C

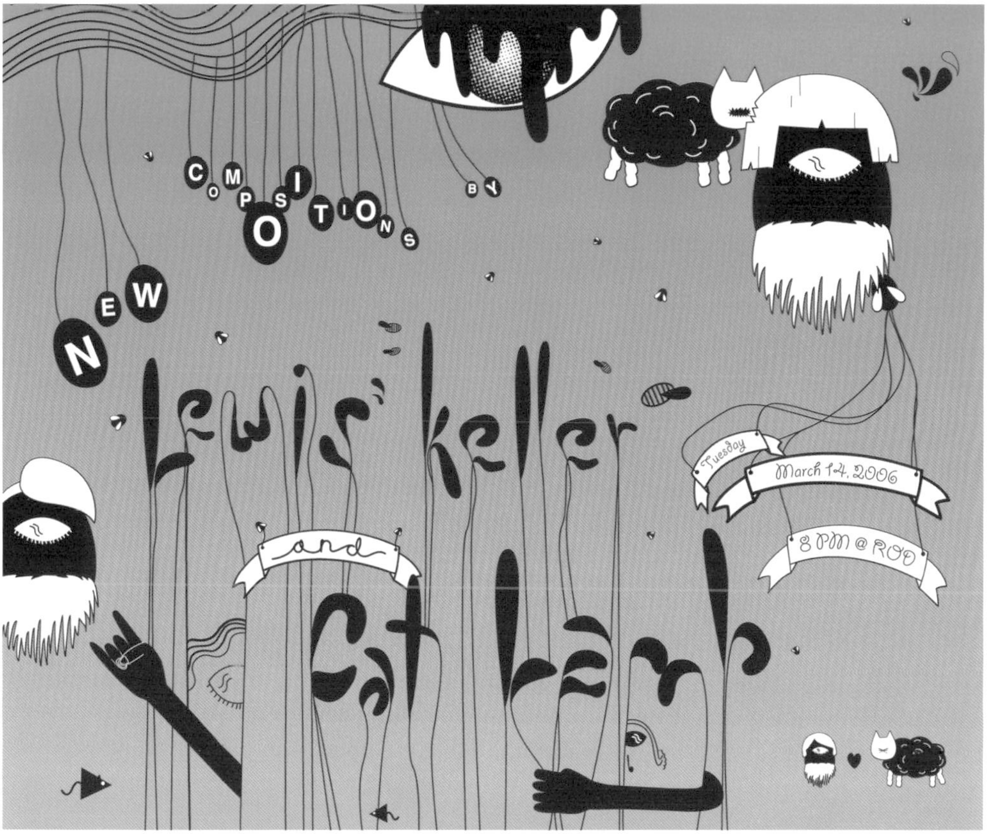
NEW COMPOSITIONS BY
Lewis Keller
and
Cat Lamb
Tuesday
March 14, 2006
8 PM @ ROD

Come hear a poem
A Viola Poem?
An afternoon performance by
Cat Lamb
Performers
Composers
Saturday
December 3rd, 2005
2PM @ R.O.D

JOSHUA

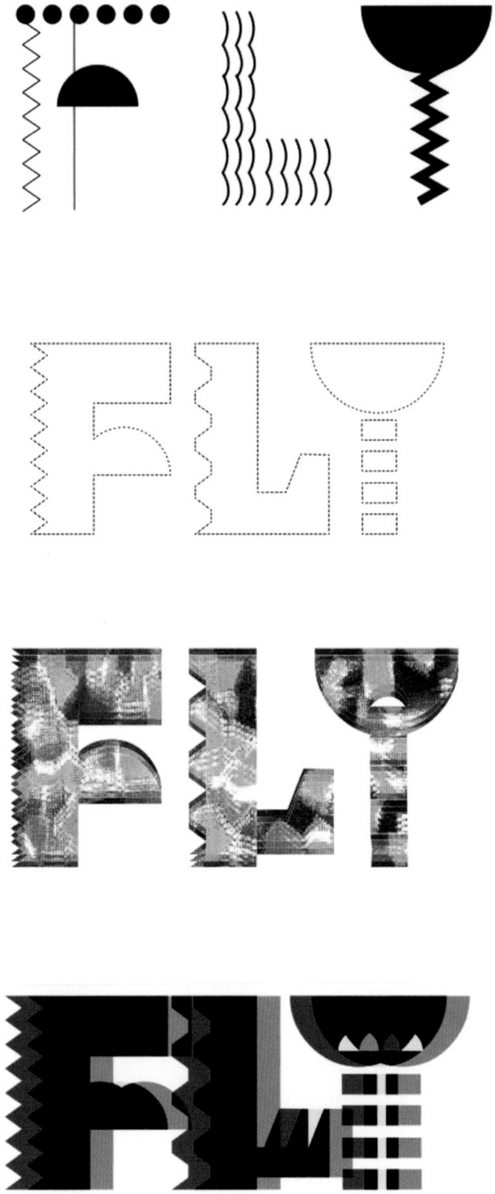
FLY
FLY
FLY
FLY

LISTEN
Saturday May 13, 2006, 4 PM
Roy O. Disney Music Hall
California Institute of the Arts
LIVE PERFORMANCE
SOUND INSTALLATION
AND WRITINGS

"IF YOU GO INTO ANY OFFICE BUILDING, WHO IS THE COOLEST PERSON? THE JANITOR."

Mike D of Beastie Boys, premiere issue

"Anyone who wants to know about Brooklyn history, they can't go on without knowing Lil' Kim."

Lil' Kim, June/July 2003

"I REMEMBER WHAT IT WAS LIKE TO BE FUCKING NOBODY, AND NOBODY WANTED TO FUCK ME."

Iggy Pop, Aug 2001

"I'm not politically aimed to be anti-anything."

Kaws, Feb 2001

"I never knew I wanted to be a film director. Now, looking back on it, it seems obvious. All the things I've been doing these past ten years have been teaching me things in order to direct a film."

"I've never worn this much pink in my life—and I love it!"

"I GOT SPANKED FOR THE TOOTHBRUSH INCIDENT."

Nylon Magazine
7th Anniversary
1999—2006

"In my position, it's my job to be emotional. Doctors cure diseases and shoemakers make shoes. It's my job to go through emotions and describe them to other people."

"I don't go looking for publicity, it comes looking for me."

"I'D LIKE TO BE MORE APPROACHABLE —NOT LESS WEIRD"

Chloë Sevigny, Nov 2003

"You've gotta think fast."

Steven Sprouse, Feb 2001.

"I wish I could put all the player-haters on one planet. So they could just go hate on each other by themselves."

Missy Elliott, Sept/Oct 1999

[redacted] "I don't remember a single show we've ever played."

Paul Banks of Interpol, Sept 2002

"WHY CAN'T WE GET A GIG ON DAWSON'S CREEK?"

Casey Spooner, June/July 2001

"People often tell me that they think I am an old soul. I really don't know what that means."

"I am not here to dress women to go shopping in Monoprix. Sorry. Get into the spirit of haute couture, girls."

John Galliano, Mar 2002

"You're thinking all the time that there must be like six other bands doing what we're doing and then you realize that no one else is doing anything even close."

Alex Turner of Arctic Monkeys, Feb 2006

"Popular culture is a contradiction in terms: if it's popular it's not culture."

Nylon Magazine
7th Anniversary
1999—2006

"I was in love with Mao, because I am more on the left side, you know, and I am a rebel, so I identified with him."

"I INJECT ANGER INTO EVERYTHING I CREATE."

MICHAEL PERRY | NEW YORK, NY, USA

Michael Perry runs a small design studio in Brooklyn where he doodles away night and day. He creates new typefaces and sundry graphics that inevitably evolve into new work. He firmly believes generating piles of stuff is the sincerest form of the creative process. Notorious clients include MTV, Brooklyn Industries and the *New York Times*.

www.midwestisbest.com

1 Book | Princeton Architectural Press, 2007
2 EP packaging | Hail Social, 2006
3 Invitation | The School at Columbia University, 2007
4 Illustrations for Arkitip | Self-initiated, 2006
5 Promotional poster | Thinktopia, 2007
Curators Pernille Albrectsen and Jacob Fabricious
6 Untitled Magazine | Self-initiated, 2007
7 Anniversary poster | Nylon magazine, 2006
8 Illustration | Modest Mouse, 2007
9 Logo | Urban Outfitters, 2006

ALL HAIL TO MY HANDS
- SPARKY HARDISTY
One.
FLOR DE MICHO
SIEMPRE LO NATURAL
ES MEJOR
Puerto Escondido, Mexico 2005
PAGE 12 | HAND JOB | ALL HAIL TO MY HANDS | SPARKY HARDISTY

SOME THINGS ARE BEST LEFT UNSAID.
THE KIDS WILL HAVE THEIR SAY
LOUSY LIVIN
Photo by: Anna Wolf
Michael Perry spends his days and nights in Brooklyn, New York, usually staring at his computer or sheets of paper. He does hand type whenever possible, probably more than he should. But it is hard to not want to do it. It is just so damn fun. He has done hand type for such clients as Urban Outfitters, American Eagle Outfitters, MTV, Rome SDS, Polyvinyl Records, Amelia's Magazine, and so on. Michael looks forward to a long life of making letters.
WWW.MIDWESTISBEST.COM
MAKE ME MONSTER
DUB CARTEL SOUND SYSTEM
LIKE OH MY GOD
CONSUME.
I WILL ONLY COMPLICATE THINGS FURTHER
Honey Bun
A WISE BRAND IS AN EVIL BRAND
a Different Kind of HIT On.
ONE-MAN SUPERGROUP
FRIENDS FOREVER

PUBLISHED BY
PRINCETON ARCHITECTURAL PRESS
FOR A FREE CATALOG OF BOOKS, CALL 1 800 722 6657
©2007 PRINCETON ARCHITECTURAL PRESS
ALL RIGHTS RESERVED
PRINTED AND BOUND IN CHINA
EDITING: JENNIFER N. THOMPSON
HAND JOB
DEDICATED TO MY FATHER AND GRANDMOTHER!
SPECIAL THANKS TO MOM, JIM GENTRY, GRANDPA, ANNA WOLF, DAN KEENAN, DAMIEN CORRELL, JIM DATZ, AND EVERYONE ELSE WHO HELPED THIS BECOME REAL ♡

B 45RPM
HAIL SOCIAL

HAIL SOCIAL
WARNING SIGN
45 RPM

Please join us for a

Commencement Celebration

in honor of

The School at Columbia University's

Graduating Class of 2007

6:30 PM, Wednesday, June 13

Low Memorial Library Rotunda

Columbia University Campus

We are delighted to have Alan Brinkley, Provost and the Allan Nevins Professor of History at Columbia University, joining the celebration as The School's first commencement speaker.

RSVP

Jessica Jimenez
jjimenez@theschool.columbia.edu
or 212 851-4284

4

Success is for the people at the precipice. The entrepreneurs, innovators, risk takers, and dreamers. We remind you to never stop thinking. Proactively seek out fresh answers. Find partners. Remember that you are only as smart as the people you surround yourself with. Seek out people who are smarter than yourself. Nurture them. Reward them. Because they are the future. Become cosmonauts of change. Move forward. Find your buzz. Remember that life is a continual uncovering. Most of all, discover the things that thrill you and do them. In the end, they are the only reason to get up in the morning. Thinktopia® is an idea engineering company dedicated to building communities around brands. We work in a variety of media, from designing brand futures to media development. Better thoughts through thinking. www.thinktopia.com

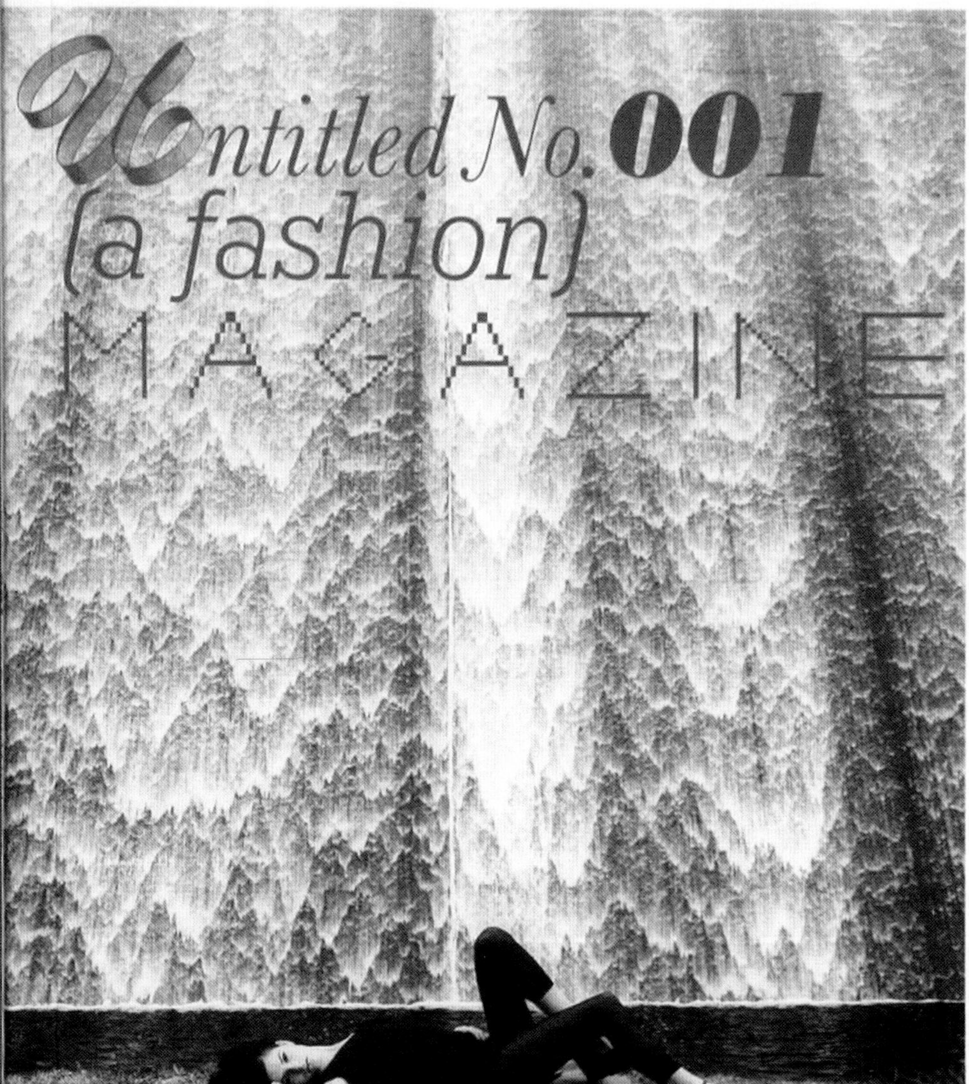

untitled No. **001** *— Featuring: Alessandra Petlin, Lane Coder, Brigitte Sire, Eric Ray Davidson, and More…*

Page 48

BY
MYSELF

A CATALOG OF TYPE
HAND JOB
By Michael Perry
BACKYARD BOUNCE
Everything
Chillin

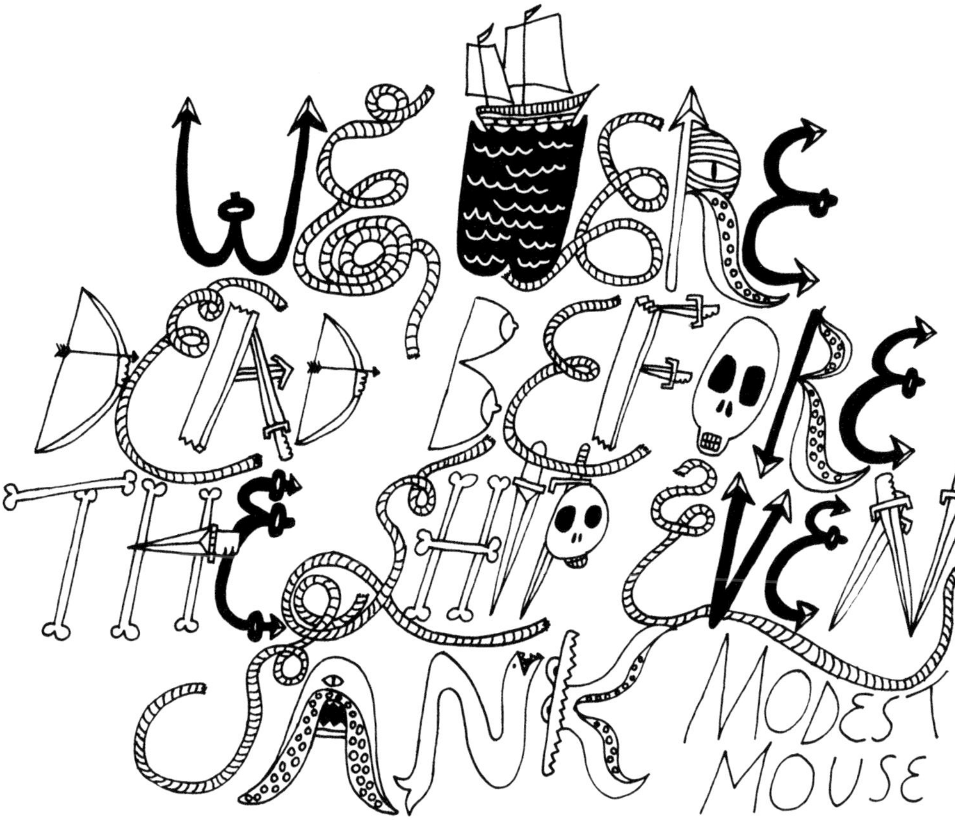
WE WERE DEAD BEFORE THE SHIP EVEN SANK
MODEST MOUSE

8

URBAN OUTFITTERS

9

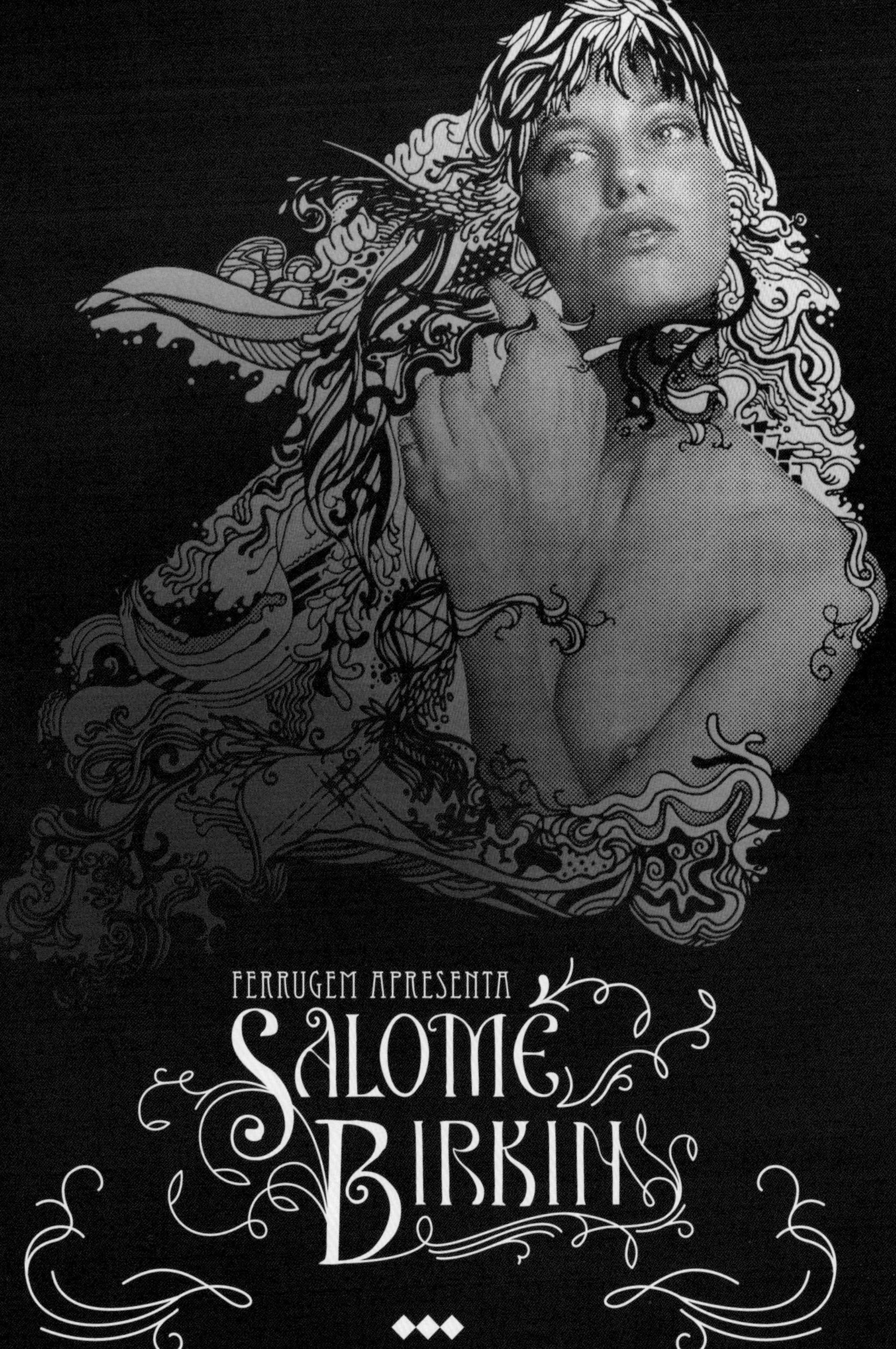
FERRUGEM APRESENTA
SALOMÉ BIRKIN

MOPA | BRASÍLIA, BRAZIL

Daniel Gizo, Felipe Medeiros, Felipe Mello, Rogério Lionzo, Alline Luz

Mopa is an illustration and graphic design studio, which was founded in 2006 in Brasília. The artists place great value on the social aspect of their work; personal growth and developing projects in a more humanized way, resulting in varied styles and visual resources that perfectly suit each individual project. They love you. Please love them back!

www.estudiomopa.com

1 Promotional image | Fernanda Ferrugem, 2007
2 Index illustration | Bizz magazine, 2007
3 Illustration | Self-initiated, 2007
4 Illustration | Sopro design, 2007
5 Lameira typeface | Self-initiated, 2007
6 Amanda typeface | Self-initiated, 2006
7 Goteira typeface | Self-initiated, 2007
8 Tshirt graphics | Owl Movement, 2007
9 Pattern | Self-initiated, 2007

2

o Amor
é

NAS CURVAS DE SEU CORPO, CAPOTEI MEU CORAÇÃO

NA VIDA TUDO É PASSAGEIRO, MENOS O MOTORISTA E O COBRADOR

CAMINHÃO

SEIS PNEUS CHEIOS E UM CORAÇÃO VAZIO

A BELEZA É PROFUNDA, A FEIURA SE VÊ LOGO

PRÁ QUEM SABE LER, UM PINGO É LETRA.

NÃO TENHO TUDO QUE AMO, MAS AMO TUDO QUE TENHO!

PASSARINHO NÃO COME PEDRA PORQUE SABE O BICO QUE TEM

NAVIO IMITA TUBARÃO
AVIÃO IMITA GAVIÃO
SÓ MEU CAMINHÃO
NÃO TEM IMITAÇÃO

NO BARALHO DA VIDA ENCONTREI APENAS UMA DAMA

LAMEIRAS

AMANDA

ABCDEFGHIJKLMNOPQRSTUVWXYZ
abcdefghijklmnopqrstuvwxyz
0123456789 - + = { } . , : ; ? ¿ | " ! @ # $ % & * ( )

Amanda likes ICE CREAM

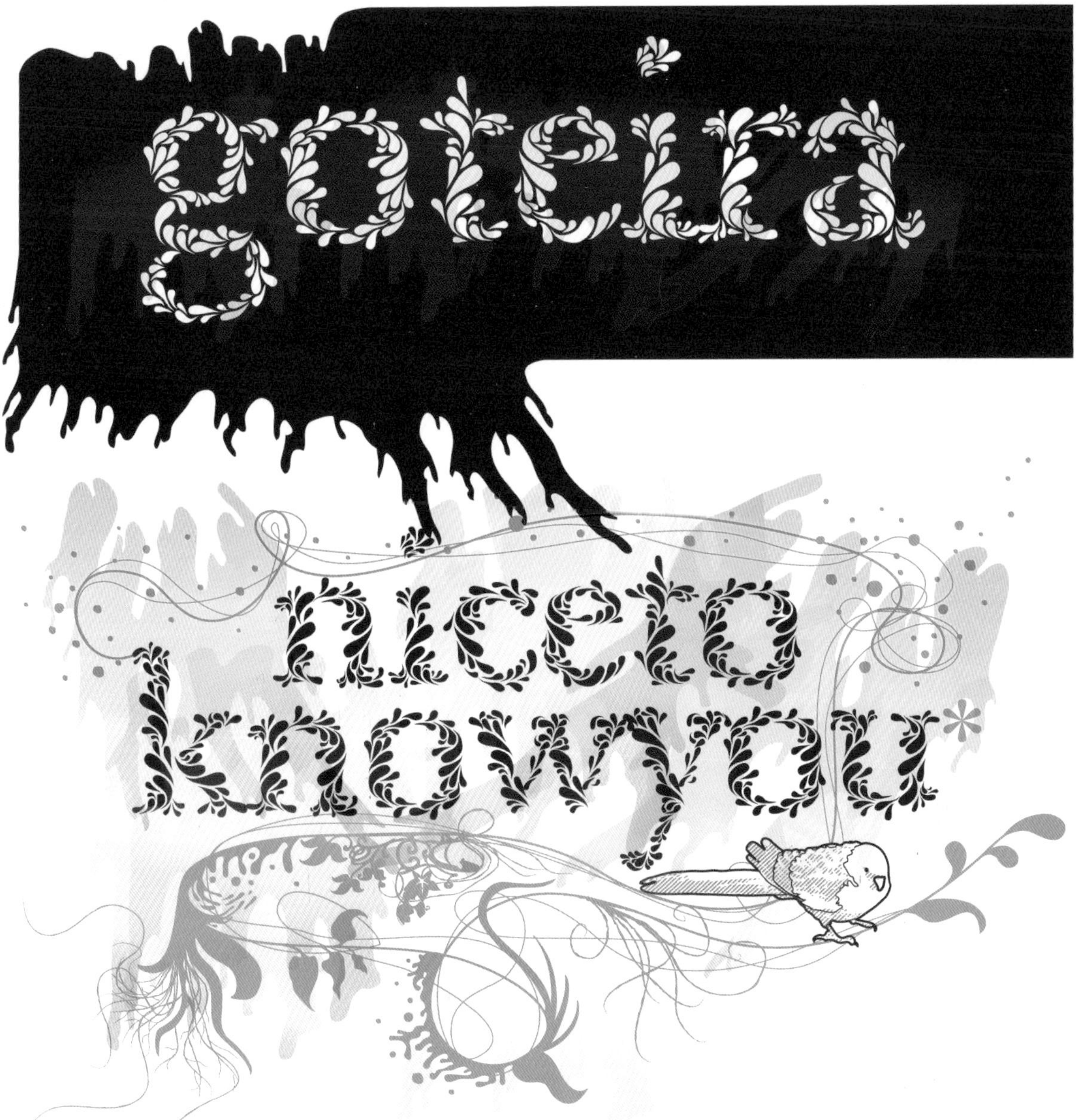

ABCDEFGHI abcdefghijklmn
JKLMNOPQR opqrstuvwxyz
STUVWXYZ 1234567890

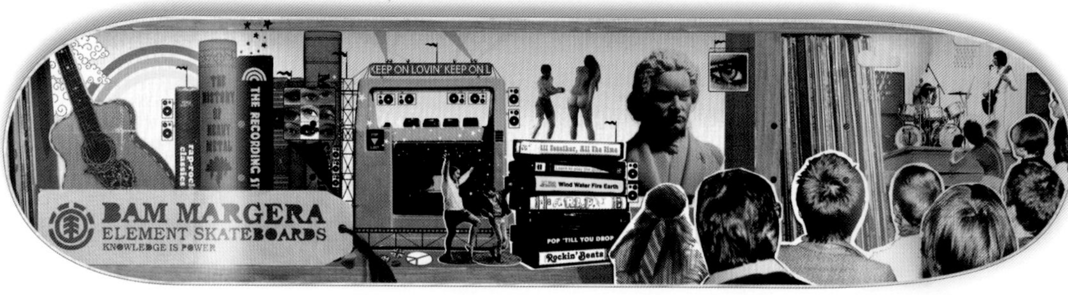
BAM MARGERA
ELEMENT SKATEBOARDS
KNOWLEDGE IS POWER
KEEP ON LOVIN' KEEP ON L
THE RECORDING ST
POP 'TILL YOU DROP
Rockin' Beats
Wind Water Fire Earth
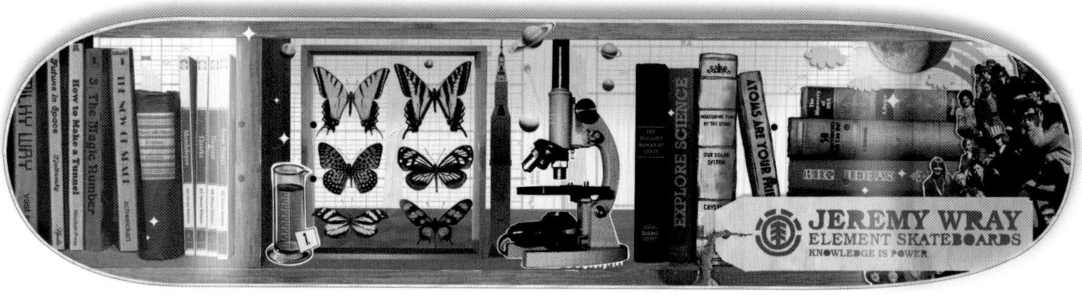
JEREMY WRAY
ELEMENT SKATEBOARDS
KNOWLEDGE IS POWER
EXPLORE SCIENCE
ATOMS ARE YOUR FRI
BIG IDEAS
How to Make a Tunnel
3 The Magic Number
Future in Space

JAKE RUPP
ELEMENT SKATEBOARDS
KNOWLEDGE IS POWER
WHAT IS ART?
Anatomy for the Artist
Be Creative
Tales of the Avant-Garde
Constructional
THE PIRATE IN AR
Just A Smidgen Of...
History of a typeface

TOSH TOWNEND
ELEMENT SKATEBOARDS
KNOWLEDGE IS POWER
Capturing the Seas
Onward Ho!
Wanderlust
Along The Equator
History of the Hot Air Balloon
Cultures of the World
Traveler

COLT CANNON
ELEMENT SKATEBOARDS
KNOWLEDGE IS POWER
Marco Polo
For All Mankind
THE CAMEL & THE CANO
The GAME of LIFE
THE TREASURES OF HORYU-JI
GENGHIS KHAN
It Began In Afric
The French Revolution

NATIONAL FOREST DESIGN | LOS ANGELES, CA, USA

Henry Dieu, Steven Harrington, Justin Krietemeyer,
Mylinh Trieu

National Forest Design is a full-service creative think-tank with expertise in project completion. Members apply their respective artistic backgrounds, love of culture and a collaborative approach to all tasks. From traditional print campaigns and advertising, to product, web and interior design, the goal is to keep their work in the vanguard graphically.

www.nationalforest.com

1 Skateboard graphics | Element Skateboards, 2007
2 Visual identity | Starr Restaurant Organization, 2007
3 Promotional posters | Be The Riottt, 2006
4 Logos | Element Skateboards, Stones Throw Records, 2007
5 Catalog design | Urban Outfitters, 2007
6 Demolition Derby visual identity | Self-initiated, 2006

2

the Continental
Lunch Menu
the Continental
Dessert Menu

The Continental
Lunch : Menu

Steven Harrington

Steven Harrington

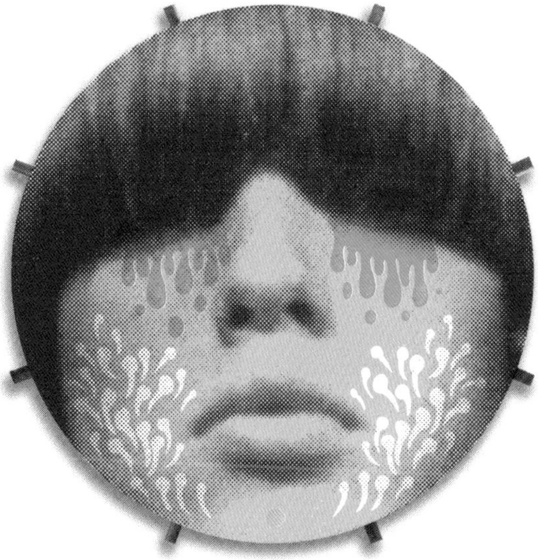

Steven Harrington

3

Steven Harrington

Steven Harrington

Element

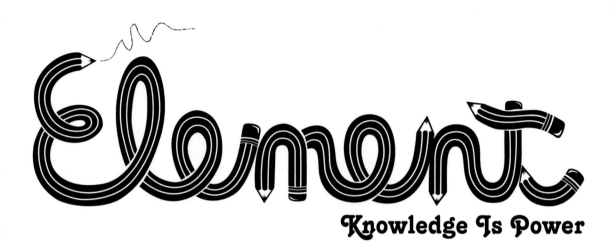

Knowledge Is Power

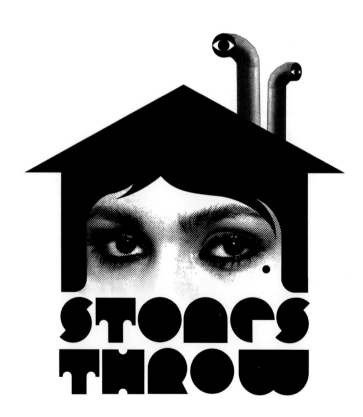

Stones Throw

Future Is Nature

ONE LOVE
element skateboards

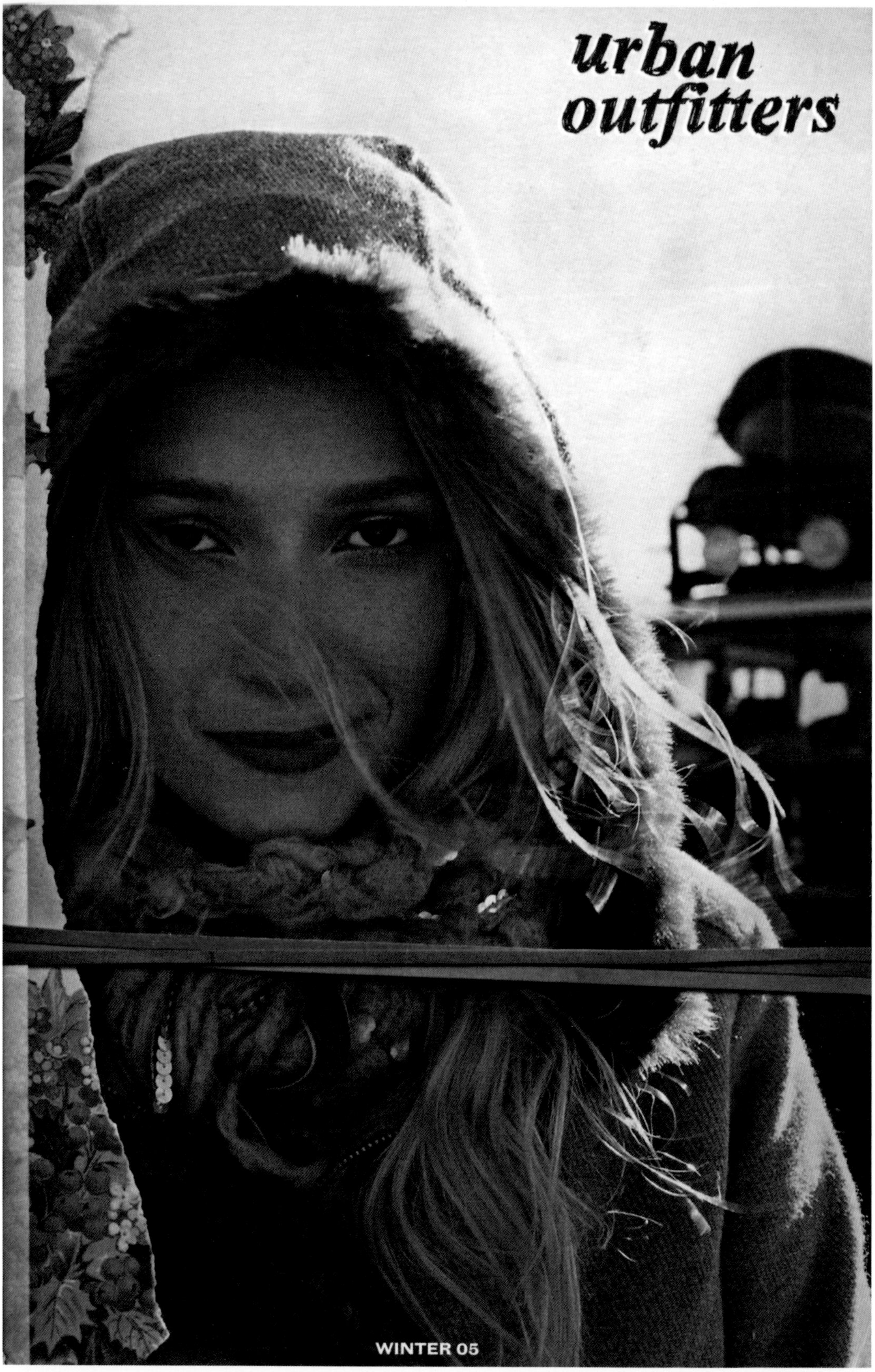
urban
outfitters
WINTER 05

PIT PASS
WEST COAST
RIPPERS
V.I.P.
WEST COA
RIPPERS
WEST COAST
RIPPERS
W.C.R.
7th CHAPTER
WEST COAST
RIPPERS

6

lumina mi camino.
Guíame hasta el fin de mis días.
Light my night.
With respect!
Trash Sudamerica

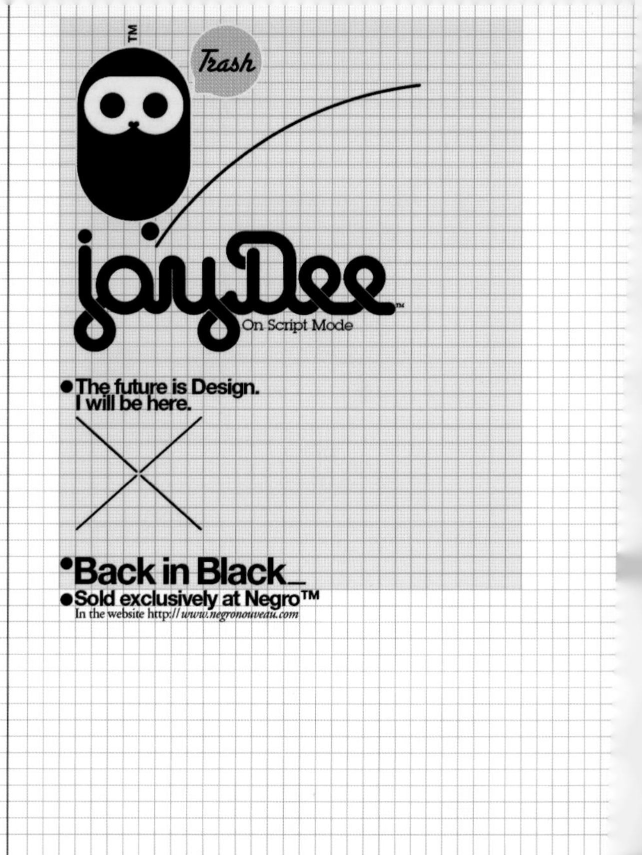
TM
Trash
jayDee
TM
On Script Mode
The future is Design.
I will be here.
Back in Black_
Sold exclusively at Negro™
In the website http:// www.negronouveau.com

By Negro
OOD
BYE
AS LAS FOTOS DE TRASH™ FUERON TOMADAS
LEICA D-LUX 3
E IN JAPAN
Page30
JD has been many things: singer, songwriter,
velist, ladies'man, artist, buddhist monk & poet.
e one time ladies' man is a poet, a prophet, and snappy dresser.
This is the end.
See you soon.
be here when you want.
Arg.
Last Page
Trash Sudamerica
acias por haber estado acá.
hank you for your visit

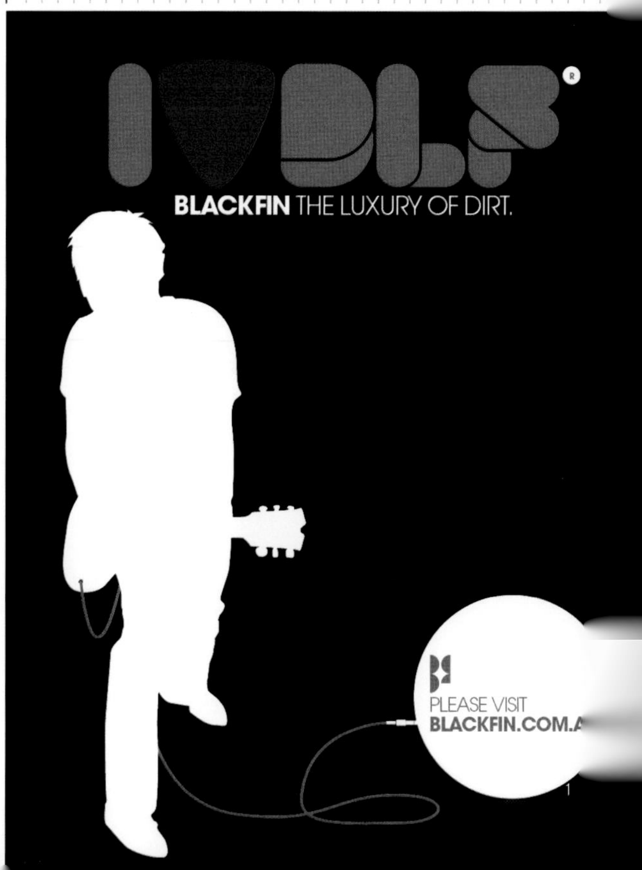
BLACKFIN THE LUXURY OF DIRT.
PLEASE VISIT
BLACKFIN.COM.A

NEGRO™ | BUENOS AIRES, ARGENTINA
Ariel Di Lisio

Negro™ is Buenos Aires based designer Ariel Di Lisio's personal portfolio. It ranges from classic print and editorial design to graphical experimentation and creating fonts. Recent his hotly acclaimed projects include LOVE magazine, an interesting mix of images of beautiful naked ladies and cutting-edge typography.

www.negronouveau.com

1 Trash Sudamerica magazine | Self-initiated, 2007
2 Invitation | Ernesto Catena Fotografía Contemporánea, 2007
3 Invitation | Love magazine, 2007
4 Promotional image | Self-initiated, 2007
5 Miscellaneous logos | Self-initiated, 2007

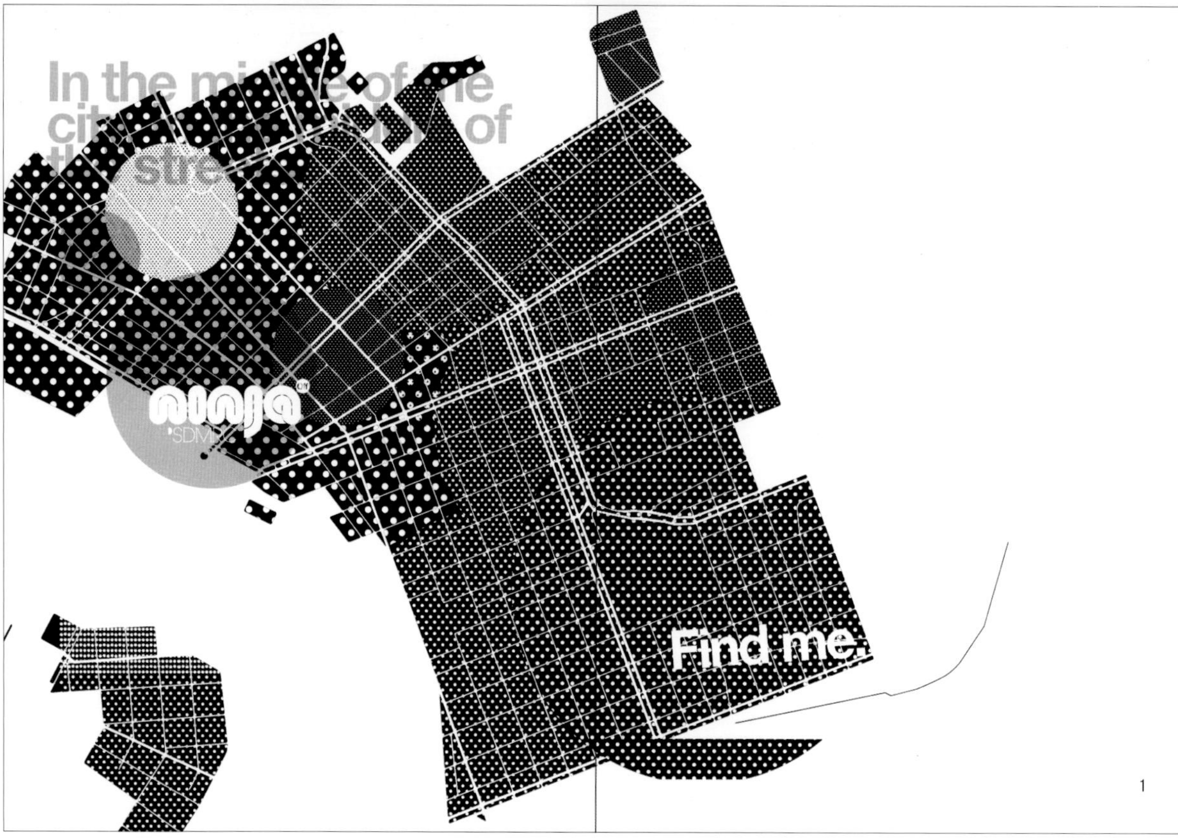

1

Trash Sudamerica™ es una publicación de Negro™ / Idea y diseño Ariel Di lisio / Textos Agustín Riso Bancalari / Fotografías Alejandro Billiris / Ilustraciones Santino Di lisio /

info@negronouveau.com
http://www.negronouveau.com

When something comes from your heart...without [illegible] that's the best, most concise criteria of what makes something good.

Gracias a todos los que colaboraron de una u otra forma [illegible]
A mi familia, Pity y mi amor del alma Santino. A [illegible]
Agustín, Eleo, todos en Negro. A mis amigos. A Dios.

Impreso en DeFerrari durante el mes de Octubre de 2007.
Printed in Argentina.2007

Cuatro franjas de color en el cielo se podían vislumbrar antaño. Pero en épocas tecnológicas como la de este relato sólo hay contaminación en el aire y desde hacía años que en la ciudad sólo se veían horizontes oscuros. Pero ese día no.

Entre el humo y las nubes, se pudo ver desde diversas ubicaciones geográficas, una extraña claridad. Por la mañana se manifestó como un débil resplandor, al mediodía cobró intensidad, y por la tarde traspasó diferentes zonas de esas negras formaciones allá arriba, afirmando su presencia.

El segundo día la luz se intensificó. Temprano salieron todos de sus casas para admirar el fenómeno, algunos llevaban consigo un simple pedazo de vidrio cortado y oscurecido por alguna llama, mientras que otros observaron el milagro con complicados cristales ahumados elaborados durante la noche. Los ojos de los habitantes, acostumbrados a las penumbras, se habían convertido con el tiempo en débiles receptores, y el brillo detrás del telón fácilmente hubiese quemado las retinas de quien apreciara sin adecuada protección aquel evento, considerado por muchos el acontecimiento de la década.

Así, día a día, todos pudieron ver esa inusual luz abriéndose paso por entre las nubes. Al principio, diferentes astrónomos y científicos se preocuparon por establecer antes que sus colegas, diversas teorías de lo que estaba ocurriendo, sin saber precisamente, o mejor dicho, sin tener la más mínima idea de lo que estaba sucediendo en realidad. Conforme avanzaban los días el brillo se intensificaba más y más, pero nadie podía explicar razonablemente los motivos de tal incandecencia.

Los dirigentes preocupados reunieron en las salas de debate y estudio a los más destacados profesores y sabios que había. Durante semanas estuvieron discutiendo distintas posibilidades y haciendo complicados esquemas en función de las más descabelladas teorías.
Todos los cálculos y fórmulas utilizados fueron probando, con gran consternación al gobierno, su infructuosidad.

Los días, cada vez más enceguecedores, y las noches cada vez más claras, tuvieron un efecto noscivo en los relojes corporales de las personas. Pronto comenzaron a circular distintas enfermedades de la piel, y se hicieron frecuentes los defectos de pigmentación epidérmica en los recién nacidos, denominados por los historiadores como el Estigma del Brillo.

Asimismo el sentido de la vista, genéticamente preparado para otro entorno, mutó, haciéndose cada vez más resistente y generando un extraño y rojo iris. Cabellos blancos y calvicies coronaron las cabezas de los ciudadanos.

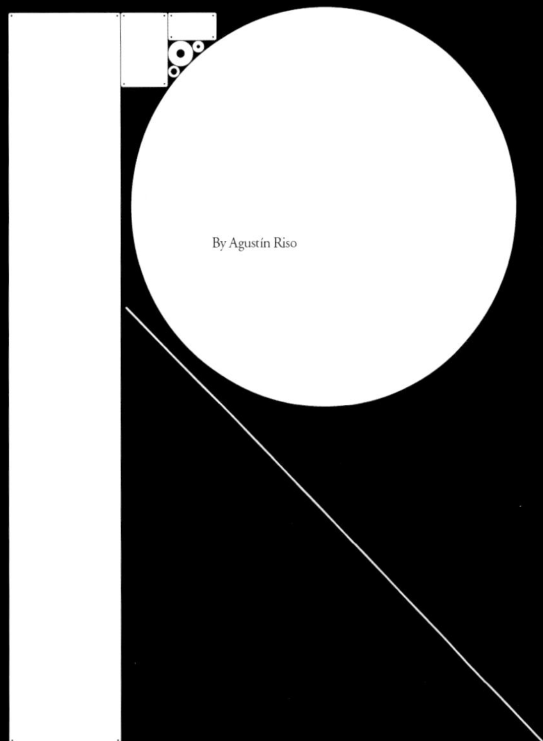

E.CATENAPARTY
En el marco de ArteBA'07
By
Ernesto Catena
Fotografía Contemporánea
Design by Negro™
http://www.negronouveau.com

Honduras 4882, 1er Piso, Capital, Arg.
Tel 48339499 /9399 Fax 48346800
info@ecfotografiacontemporanea.com
www.ecfotografiacontemporanea.com
EC
ErnestoCatena
Fotografía
Contemporánea

•2007
Catena Party
Jueves/
17/05/2007
23:00hs.
Locate: http://www.
ecfotografiacontemporanea.com
Honduras 4882, 1er Piso. Capital, Arg.
Tel 48339499/9399 Fax 48346800
info@ecfotografiacontemporanea.com
Ernesto Catena Créateur du vins
Director: Hernán Zavaleta

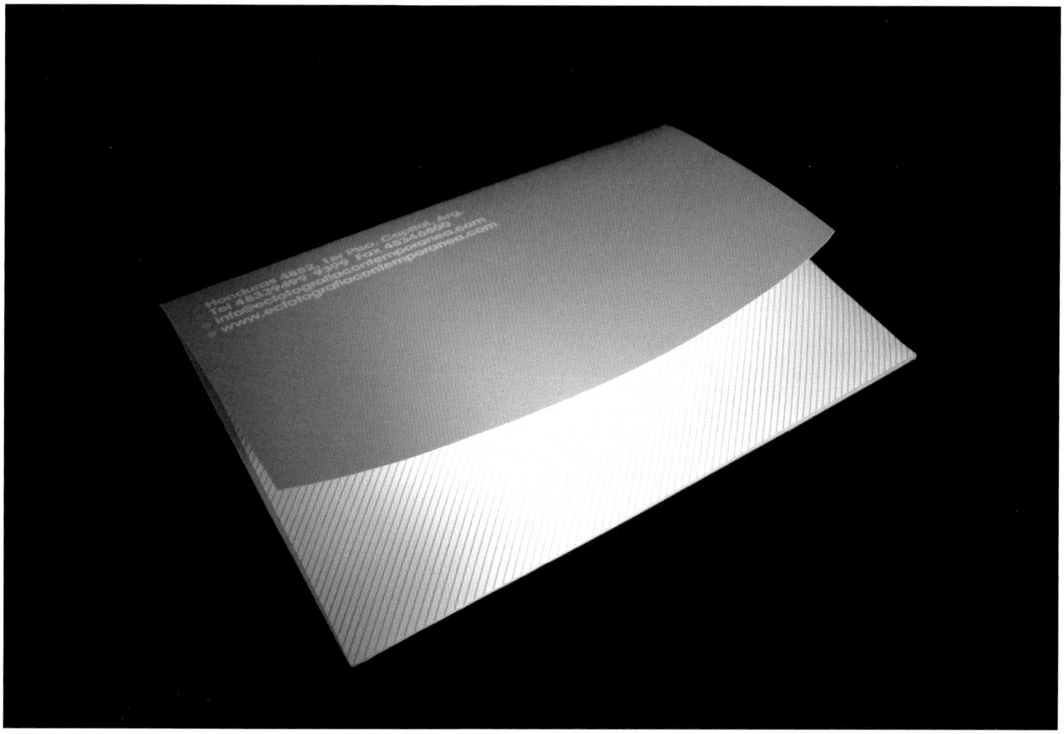

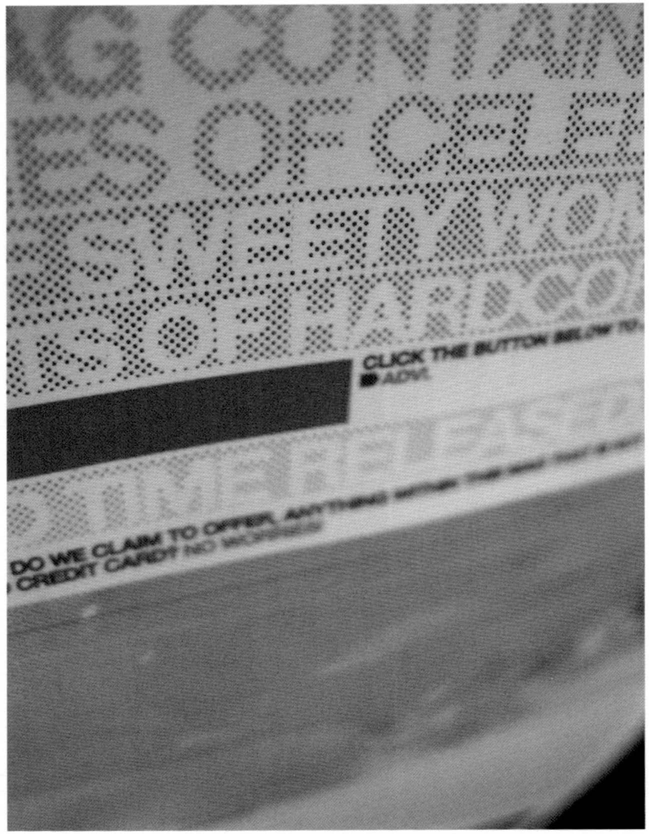
CLICK THE BUTTON BELOW TO
DO WE CLAIM TO OFFER,
CREDIT CARD?

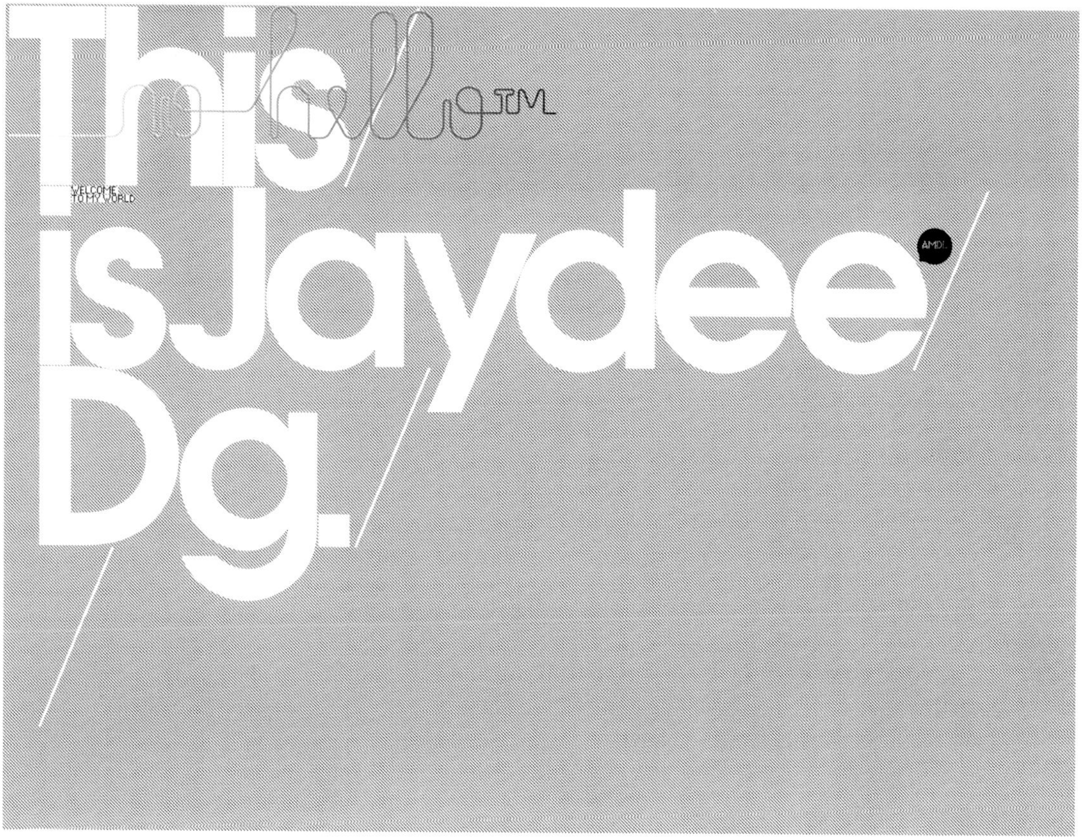
This is Jaydee Dg.
WELCOME TO MY WORLD
AMDL

3

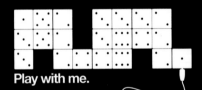

Miscelaneas Varias / 2007

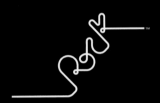

AND NOW
WE ARE AS ONE/.
MADE IN ♥
BA.

THE ART DIRECTORS CLUB 106 West 29th Street, New York, NY 10001
THE ADC SPRING PAPER EXPO 2005
NEW LEAVES. PAPER PROMOTIONS AND SAMPLES. REFRESHMENTS. FRIENDS.
/
THE ADC SPRING PAPER EXPO 2005
/
THURSDAY, APRIL 28, 2005, 5:30PM–8:00 PM
106 W. 29TH ST, NEW YORK
/
ADC MEMBERS FREE. APC, SPD, TDC MEMBERS $5
ALL OTHERS $10
/
RSVP 212-643-1440, OR RES@ADCGLOBAL.ORG
/
PROFESSIONALS ONLY. STUDENTS ARE INVITED TO PICK UP SAMPLES ON FRIDAY, APRIL 29TH, 11AM–2PM.
/
PARTICIPATING COMPANIES:
APPLETON COATED
CRANE
FOX RIVER
GMUND
MEADWESTVACO
MOHAWK
MONADNOCK
NEENAH
TRU-TECH
WAUSAU
/
AND:
ALDINE
L.P. THEBAULT
LITHO-ART INC
/
POSTER DESIGN: NATASHA JEN, NJENWORKS
PAPER: MOHAWK SUPERFINE SOFTWHITE SMOOTH
PRINTING: LITHO-ART INC.

NJENWORKS | NEW YORK, NY, USA
Natasha Jen

After leaving her native Taiwan, Natasha Jen relocated to New York where she honed her graphic design skills, soon collecting numerous awards and merits thanks to her distinctive and elegant designs. Clients include Puma, Le Book and Flaunt Magazine. As a diversion, Natasha also likes to create series of conceptual and poetic objects.

www.njenworks.com

1 Paper Expo Poster | Art Directors Club, New York, 2005
2 Packaging and identity | Kiki de Montparnasse, 2006 Work for Base NYC
3 Proposed catalogue | Ahmet Kaleli, 2005
4 Holiday wrapping paper | American Institute of Graphic Arts, New York Chapter, 2007

KIKI DE MONTPARNASSE

MASSAGE OIL
DRY BODY OIL
WATER
personal lubricant
SILICONE
personal lubricant
BODY CRÈME
BODY CRÈME
KIKI DE MONTPARNASSE
SILICONE
personal lubricant
KIKI DE MONTPARNASSE
MASSAGE OIL
KIKI DE MONTPARNASSE
WATER
personal lubricant
KIKI DE MONTPARNASSE
DRY BODY OIL
KIKI DE MONTPARNASSE

SEAMED THIGH HIGH
4
KIKI DE MONTPARNASSE

SAUCE L'AMOUR
dark chocolate
KIKI
DE
MONTPARNASSE
SAUCE L'AMOUR
milk chocolate
KIKI
DE
MONTPARNASSE

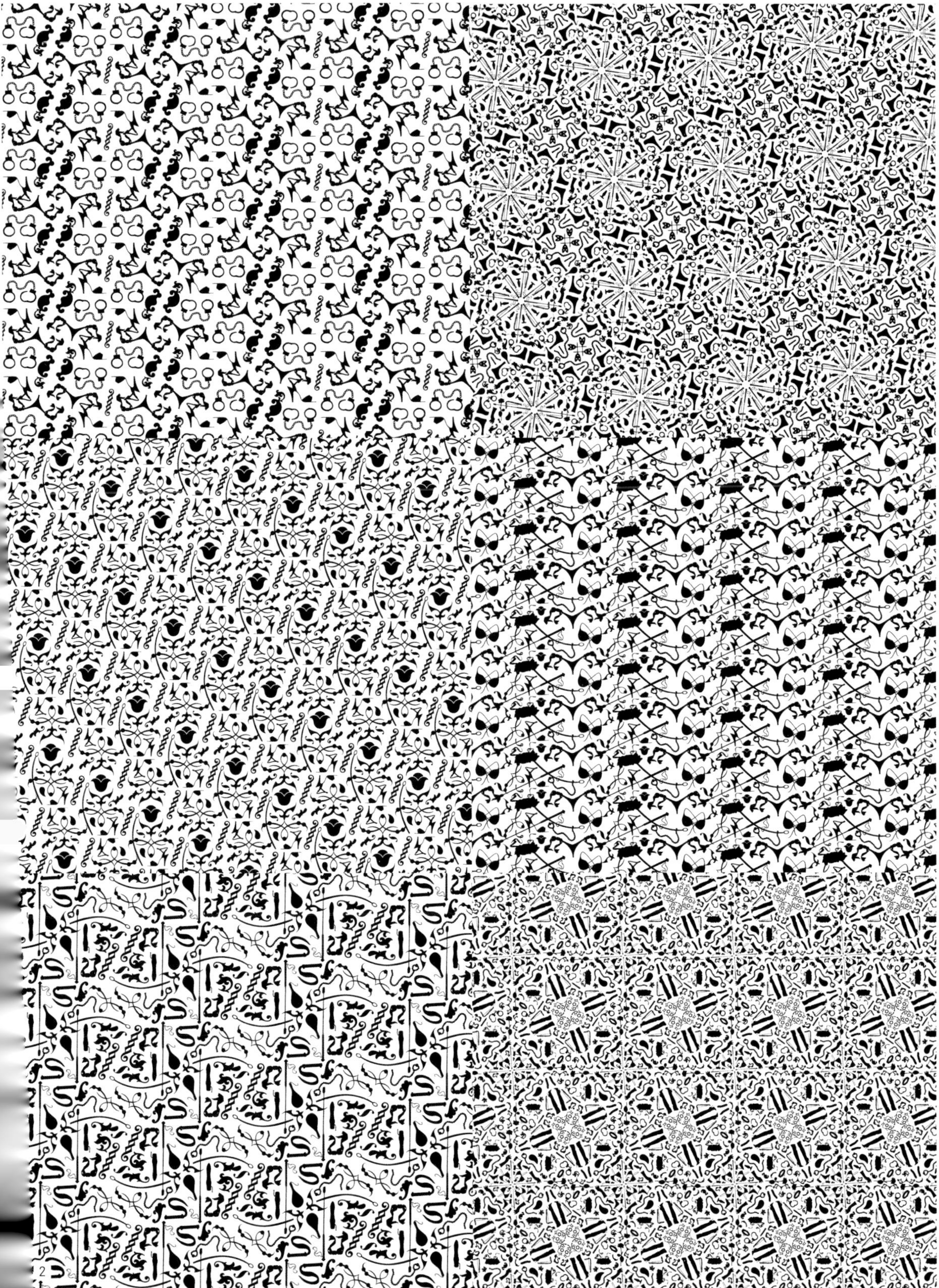

2005–2006:
Bug/ClP/Giraff
Vagon/Manta
Forma/Memo
Puf/Kılıf/Sedir
Butler/
Kanepe/Zulu

AHMET
KALELİ

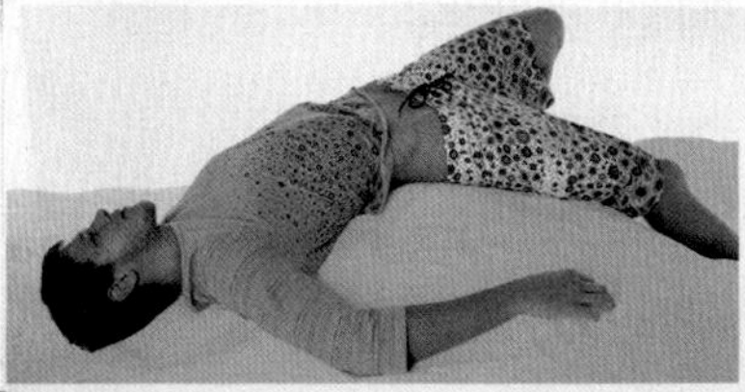

QUINTA-FEIRA | RIO DE JANEIRO, BRAZIL
Tonho

Far from the clichés of Samba, football and Carnival, Quinta feira, based in the hills of Rio de Janeiro, is the product of improvisation, an open mind, and no preconceptions. Quinta-feira's varied range of work has graced the pages of international heavyweights Die Gestalten Verlag, Creative Review and The New York Times.

www.quinta-feira.org

1 Catalogue | Cavalera, 2006
  Photography by Murillo Meirelles
2 Visual identity | Tarantula, 2007
3 Poster | Casa do Vaticano, Burti, 2003
4 Poster | V-ROM, 2005
5 Illustrations | Die Gestalten Verlag, 2003
6 Poster | Agnès B. Gallery, 2007
7 Poster | SESC, RJ, 2004
8 Illustration | The New York Times, 2007

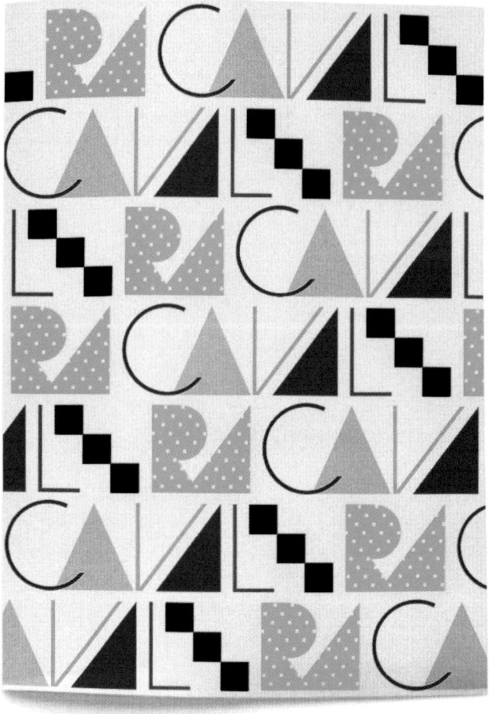

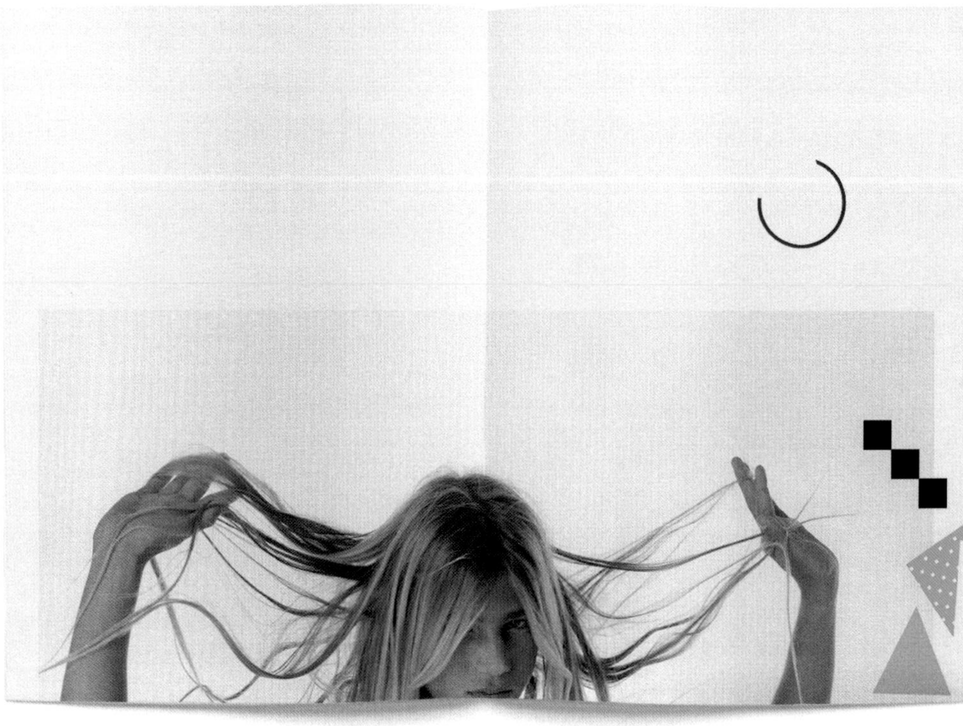

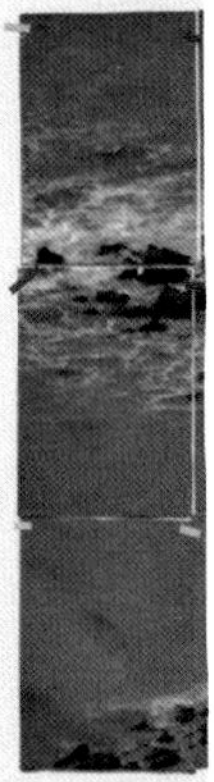

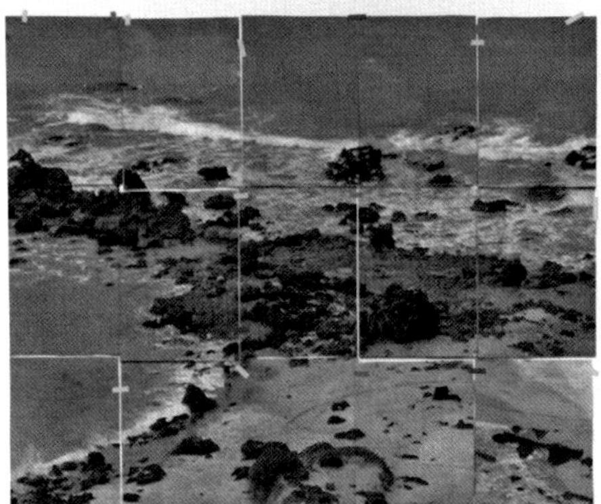

Nesta coleção, a Cavalera homenageou o litoral brasileiro.
E foi na Paraíba que escolhemos a nossa praia: Tambaba.
Com paisagens belíssimas e ainda selvagens, é uma das poucas onde pratica-se o naturismo no país.

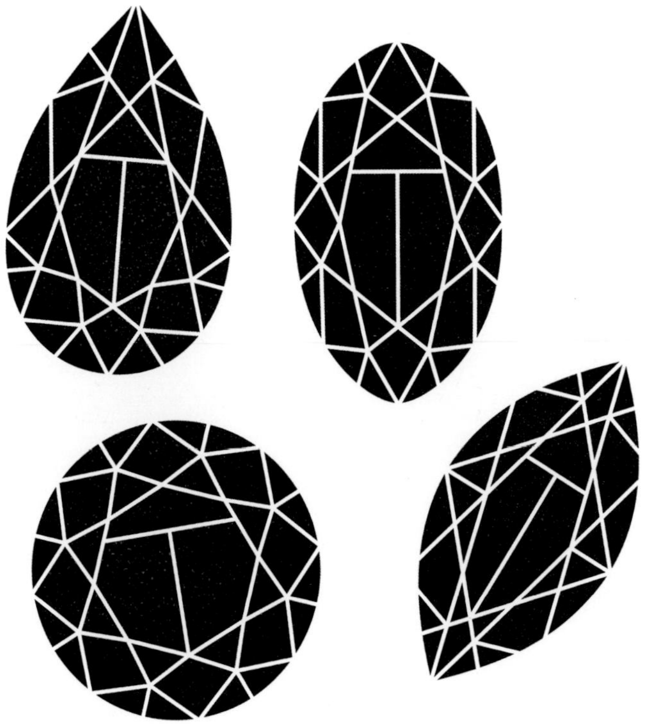

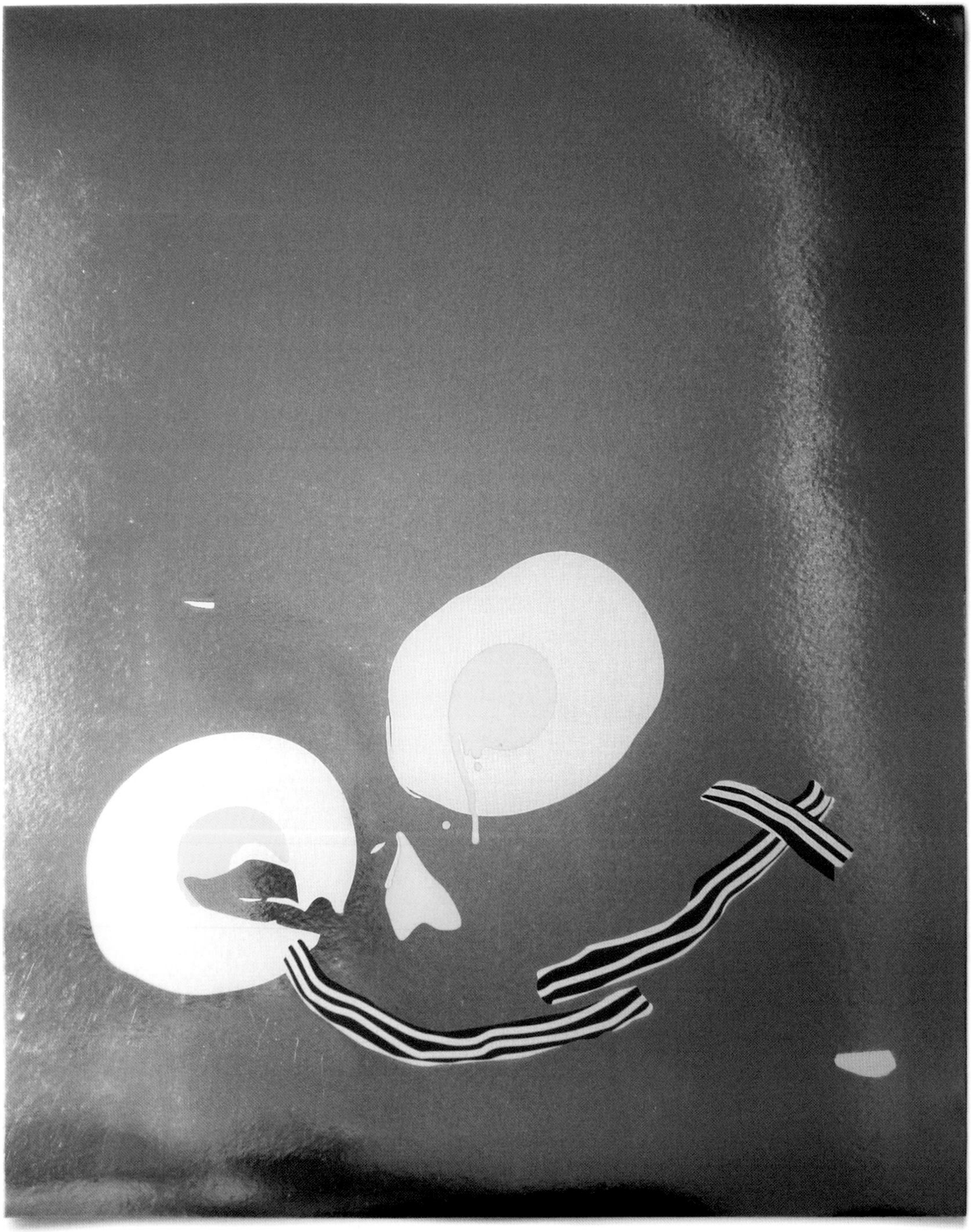

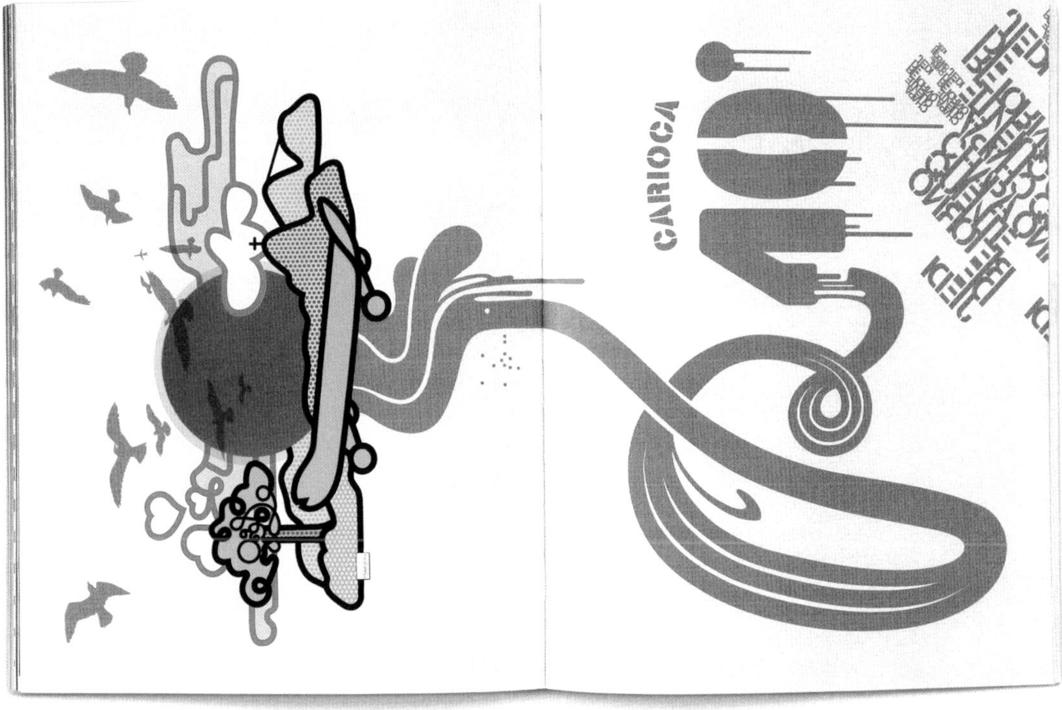

5

6

RIO PREFEITURA CULTURAS

e

SESC RIO DE JANEIRO

apresentam:

— Queridinha,

Conto de Tchekhov

Direção de Gilberto Gawronski
Com Ricardo Blat e Regina Gutman
Tradução de Boris Schnaiderman

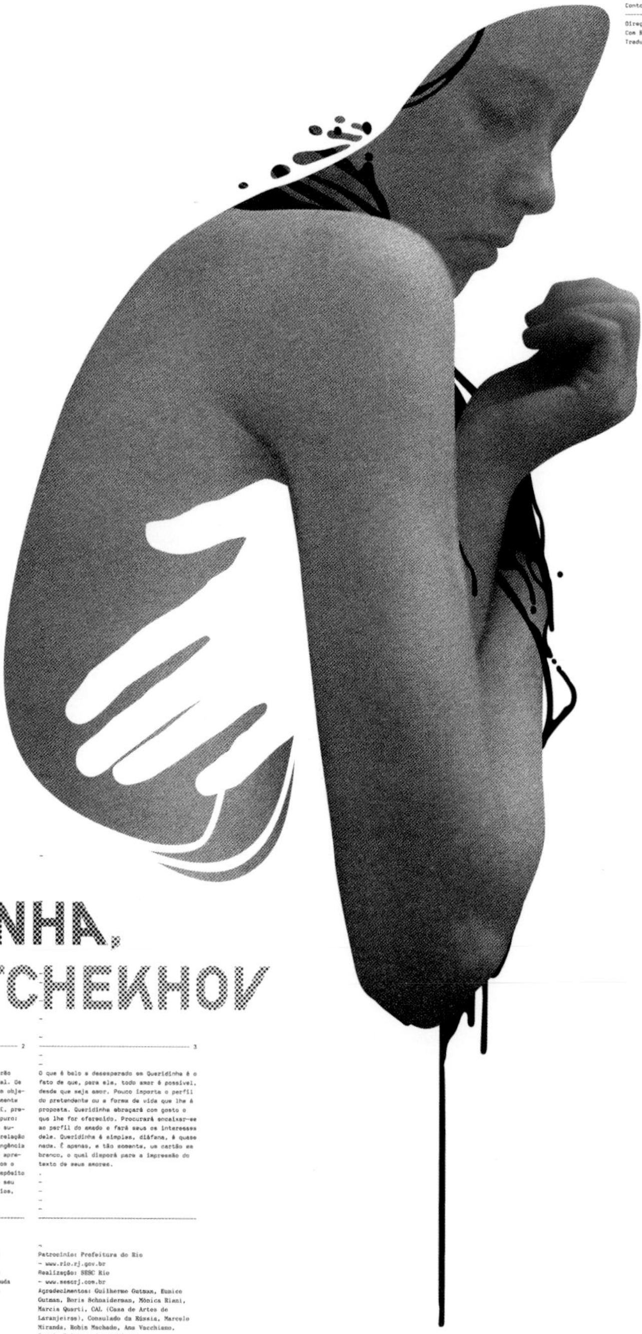

Estréia sexta-feira, dia 5 de março
Sala Multiuso – Espaço SESC

Rua Domingos Ferreira, 160 – Copacabana
tel. 2547-0156

Curtíssima temporada: 5 a 14 de março

Sexta a domingo às 20h

Reestréia sexta-feira, dia 2 de abril
Espaço Cultural Sérgio Porto

Rua Humaitá, 163 – Humaitá
tel: 2266-0896

Curta temporada: 2 a 18 de abril

Sextas e sábados às 21h
Domingos às 20h

— QUERIDINHA, CONTO DE TCHEKHOV

Queridinha — 1
por Guilherme Gutman, psicanalista

Há em "Queridinha" uma frase pungente, espécie de síntese deste conto de Tchekhov: "Ólenka estava sempre amando alguém e não podia viver sem isso". Há, ainda, outra frase que funciona como complemento da primeira: "Precisava de um amor que tomasse conta de todo o seu ser, alma e entendimento, que lhe infundisse idéias, desse um sentido à sua vida, aquecesse o seu sangue, que envelhecia".

— 2

Ao longo da vida de Ólenka, se sucederão personagens que amará com entrega total. De tal forma e a tal ponto que, sem algum objeto de amor, ficará à deriva: completamente só, sem opiniões, vazia e apavorada. E, precisamente aí, revela-se algo de mais puro: os homens de sua vida são apenas como suportes de algo mais fundamental: sua relação direta com o amor. Ela aceita a contingência dos encontros amorosos que a vida lhe apresentou, mas a sua relação não é nem com o dono do circo, nem com o gerente do depósito de madeiras, nem com o veterinário ou seu filho; seu diálogo é, sem intermediários, com Eros.

— 3

O que é belo e desesperado em Queridinha é o fato de que, para ela, todo amor é possível, desde que seja amor. Pouco importa o perfil do pretendente ou a forma de vida que lhe é proposta. Queridinha abraçará com gosto o que lhe for oferecido. Procurará encaixar-se ao perfil do amado e fará seus os interesses dele. Queridinha é simples, diáfana, é quase nada. É apenas, e tão somente, um cartão em branco, o qual disporá para a impressão do texto de seus amores.

Ficha Técnica

Direção: Gilberto Gawronski
Elenco: Ricardo Blat e Regina Gutman
Tradução de Boris Schnaiderman
–in A Dama do Cachorrinho – Editora 34
Direção de Produção: André Schmidt
Produção Executiva: Angela Pecego
Iluminação: Paulo César Medeiros
Cenografia: Cláudia Moraes
Desenho de Figurino: Marcella Virzi
Execução de Figurino: Ticiana Passos

Supervisão de Movimento: Cláudia Mele
Visagismo: Hélio Dias
Assistente de Direção: Fábio Cordeiro
Assistente de Produção: Francisco Arruda
Assessoria de Imprensa: Angela Pecego e Ana Wambier
Fotos de Divulgação: Deborah Engel
Design Gráfico: tonho/Quinta-feira

Patrocínio: Prefeitura do Rio
– www.rio.rj.gov.br
Realização: SESC Rio
– www.sescrj.com.br
Agradecimentos: Guilherme Gutman, Eunice Gutman, Boris Schnaiderman, Mônica Riani, Marcia Quarti, CAL (Casa de Artes de Laranjeiras), Consulado da Rússia, Marcelo Miranda, Robin Machado, Ana Vecchiano, Sergio Britto e Angel Vianna.

Apoio:

editora 34 — HARMONIA & SAÚDE — CACO — zen — TON SOR — espaço

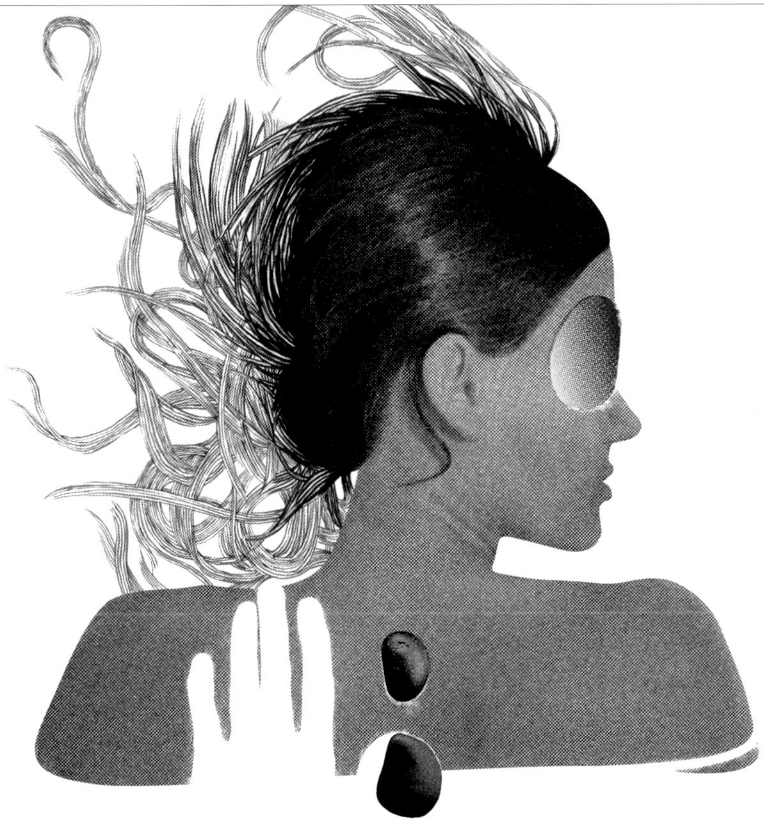

8

work
CHOPP

RENAN MOLIN | CURITIBA, BRAZIL

Renan Molin started his graphic design career working for a number of design studios like Doma Design, Garn, and the celebrated Estudio Crop, of which he is now a full-time member. His free time is spent on graphic experiments and his plans to start up a band and eventually become its singer. If you'd like to say hello, you're more than welcome.

www.dmolin.com

1 Illustration | Clube de Criação do Paraná, 2007
2 Illustrations | MTV Magazine, 2007
3 Illustrations | Capricho Magazine, 2007
4 CD sleeve art | Roof magazine, 2007
5 Business card | Self-initiated, 2007
6 Brochure | Camerata de Curitiba, 2007
7 Illustration | Self-initiated, 2007

SONORO

FiRE

DMOLIN.COM •
DESIGNER •
RENAN MOLIN
41 9604 5185 •
RENAN@DMOLIN.COM •

Tempo e Som
Fundação
CULTURAL
DE CURITIBA

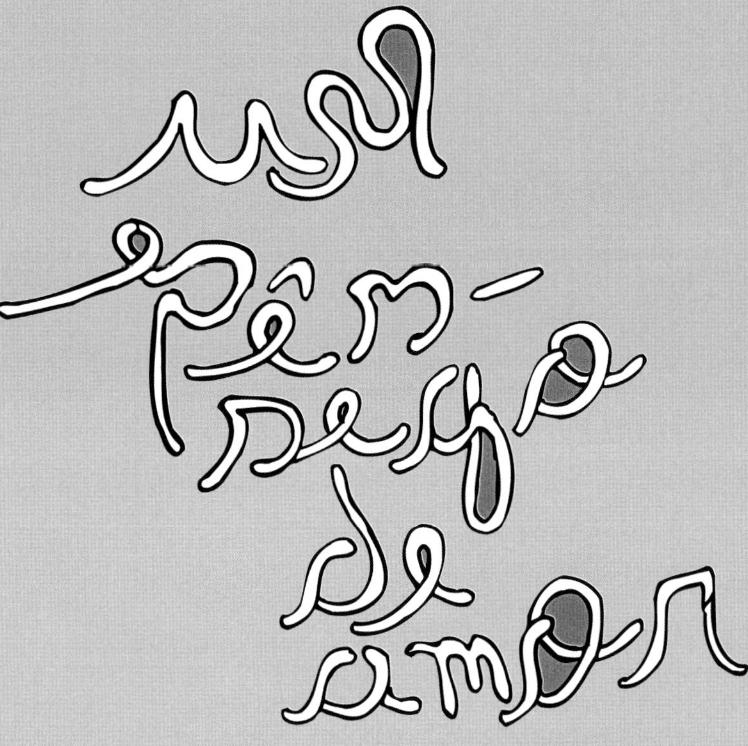

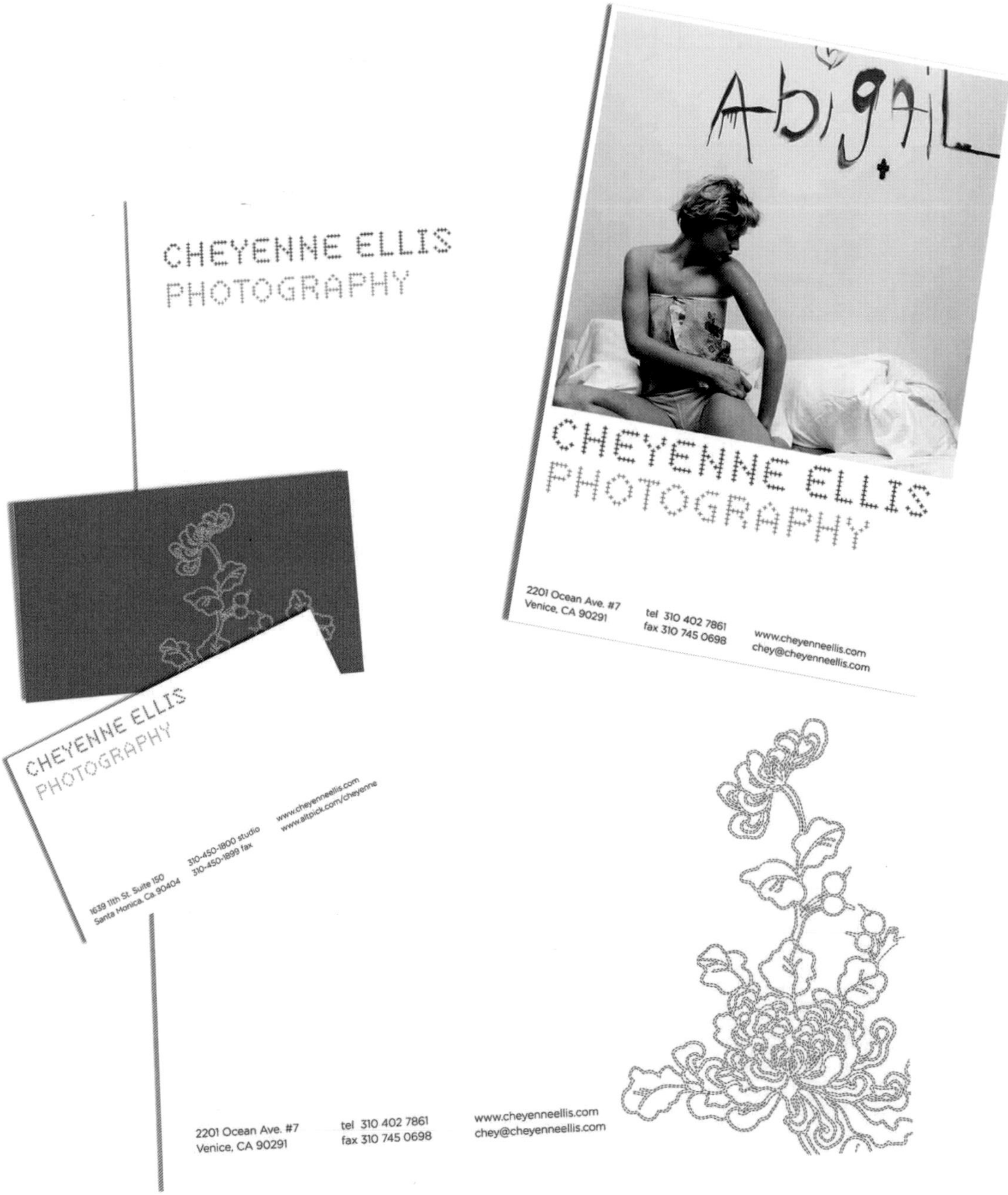

CHEYENNE ELLIS
PHOTOGRAPHY
Abigail
CHEYENNE ELLIS
PHOTOGRAPHY
2201 Ocean Ave. #7
Venice, CA 90291
tel 310 402 7861
fax 310 745 0698
www.cheyenneellis.com
chey@cheyenneellis.com
CHEYENNE ELLIS
PHOTOGRAPHY
1639 11th St. Suite 150
Santa Monica, Ca 90404
310-450-1800 studio
310-450-1899 fax
www.cheyenneellis.com
www.altpick.com/cheyenne
2201 Ocean Ave. #7
Venice, CA 90291
tel 310 402 7861
fax 310 745 0698
www.cheyenneellis.com
chey@cheyenneellis.com

1

ROANNE ADAMS DESIGN | NEW YORK, NY, USA

Roanne Adams is a designer and art director working in New York, and runs a multi-disciplinary design studio in TriBeCa. Project types include brand identity, managing creative magazines, book design, web design, managing art projects, and any other creative consultation needed, always executed with ingenious freshness and visual consistency.

www.roanneadams.com

1 Stationery | Cheyenne Ellis, 2005
2 Invitation | Honolulu Academy of the Arts, 2007
Illustration by April Lee
3 Identity and stationery | Sebastian + Barquet, 2006
4 Objective magazine design and art direction | Self-initiated, 2003
Photos by Cheyenne Ellis and Blossom Berkofsky
5 Poster | One Globe One Flag poster exhibition, 2007
In collaboration with Eric Wrenn
6 Logo design | Lwala charity, 2007

2

The Director and Trustees of the Honolulu Academy of Arts cordially
invite you to attend the members' opening-night preview reception for
ARTISTS
OF HAWAII
2007
Exhibition Juror
Russell Ferguson
Chair, Department of Art
University of California, Los Angeles
Wednesday, June 6, 2007
6:30–9:30 p.m.
Please present this invitation to attend the reception
Entertainment by DJ Mark Chittom
Refreshments in Luce Pavilion
The Academy Shop will be open until 9:30 p.m.

SEBASTIAN + BARQUET
SEBASTIAN + BARQUET
SEBASTIAN + BARQUET
SEBASTIAN + BARQUET

SEBASTIAN + BARQUET

SEBASTIAN + BARQUET

Design Miami/ Booth N4
Gallery 212.644.0535 544 W. 24th St. NYC 10011
Showroom 212.488.2245 601 W. 26th St. NYC 10001
SEBASTIAN + BARQUET
www.sebastianbarquet.com
info@sebastianbarquet.com

objective
Rachel Comey
Mira Schor
Emily Woods
Kathleen Hanna
No.1

Rachel Comey
When someone asks you what you do for a living, how do you respond?
Usually I tell the truth. Im a clothing designer.
What brought you into the fashion world?
I was making costumes and sets for various bands (such as Phish and more recently GoGol Bordello) and small theater groups when the musicians and actors began wearing the costumes in their daily lives, I started getting phone calls from other people and stylists asking about the items.
Do you prefer designing for men or women?
They present different challenges for me. I think about what I am attracted to in men, like what what makes them sexy or interesting, and I design for them based off of those characteristics. With women, I think about how I would like to be perceived. So, I don't really prefer one to the other.
How would you describe the style of your designs?
Timely. Detailed. Funny.
What is the best piece of advice you could give to an aspiring fashion designer?
learn your craft and technique.
How do you define femininity versus masculinity?
like a key and a keyhole.
What would you say is feminine about yourself?
I tend to nurture relationships with the people around me and the people I work with (my assistants, patternmakers, vendors, and ups man).
What about you is masculine?
I'm daring, resiliant, and strong.
What was the last inspiring thing you saw on television?
I can't think of anything on television, but I am in love with the recent movie, "Lilya 4 ever".
What music do you listen to while you work?
All kinds. itunes.
Where have you lived?
Clove Hill, Main St., North Union St., Peru St., Monroe St., Ridge St., East 4th St., Elizabeth St.
7

DEANNE CHEUK
What about you is masculine?
I like to be the boss.

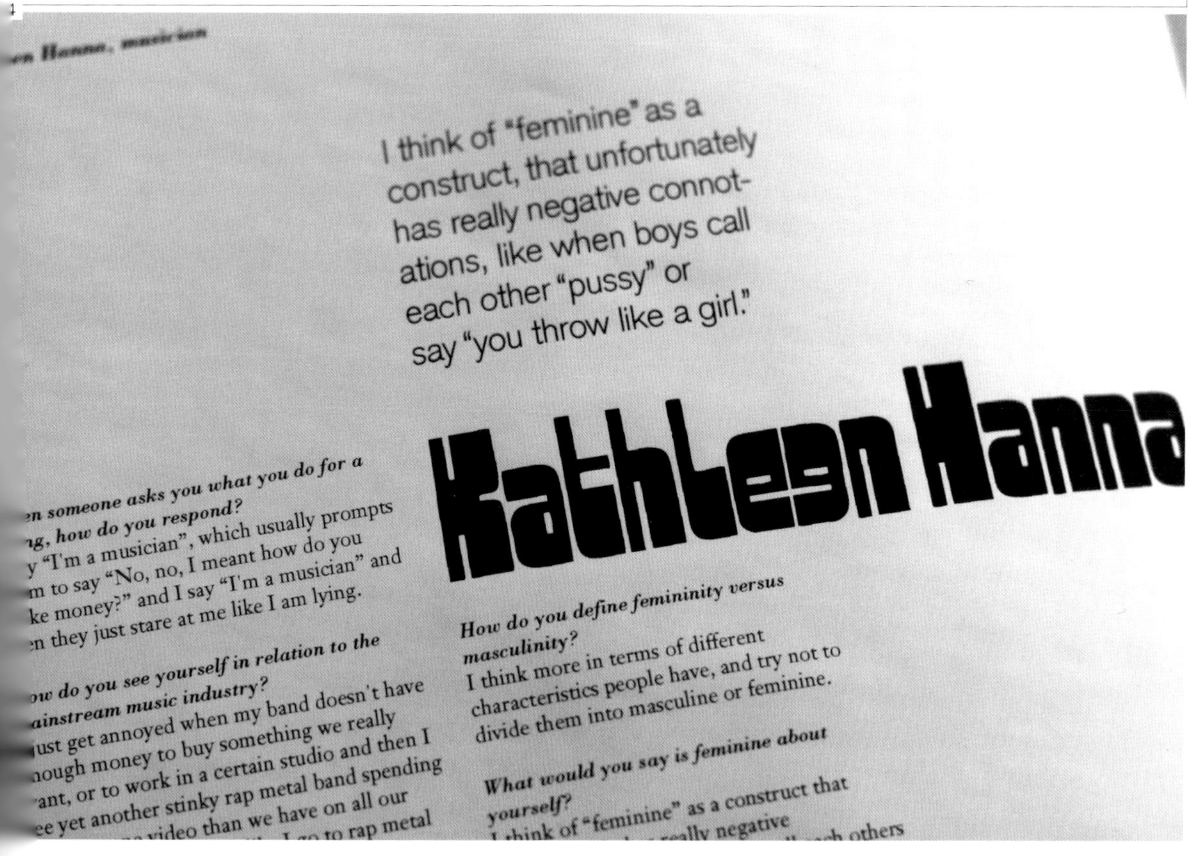
I think of "feminine" as a
construct, that unfortunately
has really negative connotations, like when boys call
each other "pussy" or
say "you throw like a girl."
Kathleen Hanna
en someone asks you what you do for a
ng, how do you respond?
y "I'm a musician", which usually prompts
m to say "No, no, I meant how do you
ke money?" and I say "I'm a musician" and
en they just stare at me like I am lying.
ow do you see yourself in relation to the
ainstream music industry?
ust get annoyed when my band doesn't have
nough money to buy something we really
ant, or to work in a certain studio and then I
ee yet another stinky rap metal band spending
How do you define femininity versus
masculinity?
I think more in terms of different
characteristics people have, and try not to
divide them into masculine or feminine.
What would you say is feminine about
yourself?
I think of "feminine" as a construct that

LOVE
SEES
NO
COLOR

6

01 – Protect forests
02 – Protect endangered species
03 – Protect marine life
04 – Grow more wind power
05 – Embrace solar power
06 – Be aware of global warming
07 – Embrace energy efficient appliances
08 – Prevent forest fires
09 – Carpool
10 – Embrace public transport
08 – Promote use of biofuels
12 – Walk instead of driving close distances

SAVIO ALPHONSO | SANTA ANA, CA, USA

Savio Alphonso was taught how to draw by his commercial artist father at an early age. A graphic design Master's Program at California State University Fullerton saw his skills to communicate strong meanings and ideas flourish, and he has since received several accolades from the likes of AIGA and the International Design Awards.

www.savioalphonso.com

1 Pictograms | MFA thesis at California State University, 2007
2 Concept labels | Concept project, 2007
3 Postcard | Downtown Santa Ana Business Council, 2007
4 Posters | California State University, 2004
5 Magazine concept | Concept project, 2005
6 Exhibition catalogue | Jesse Benson, Grand Central Press, 2006
7 Solo show catalogue | Laurie Hassold, Grand Central Press, 2006
8 Identity | @Space Contemporary Art Gallery, 2007

2

{H}
{H}
{H}
PRIVATE RESERVE
2004
IVES
NOIR
{ HYBRID CELLARS }
CHAMBOURCIN
{ HYBRID CELLARS }
PRIVATE RESERVE
2003
AURORE
PRIVATE RESERVE
{ HYBRID CELLARS }
2004

ORANGE COUNTY ARTS GRANT
FOR DRAWING, PAINTING & PRINTMAKING
DOWN TOWN
SANTA ANA BUSINESS COUNCIL

ORANGE COUNTY ARTS GRANT
A GRANT FOR DRAWING, PAINTING & PRINTMAKING
Send Info. To:
DSABC – Art Grant
125 N Broadway
Santa Ana CA 92701
DOWN TOWN
SANTA ANA BUSINESS COUNCIL
3 CATEGORIES:
Working Artist: $1000 Grant
Graduate Student: 3 $500 Grants
Undergraduate Student: 5 $100 Grants
SUBMIT:
High resolution digital images ready for print (jpg, tiff, psd)
Current resume & contact info.
Include SASE, if you want your disk back
DEADLINE:
October 5, 2007
AWARDS:
December 1, 2007
Plant featured: Common Money plant

BLAME! BLAME!
MUSLIM OR HINDU ?

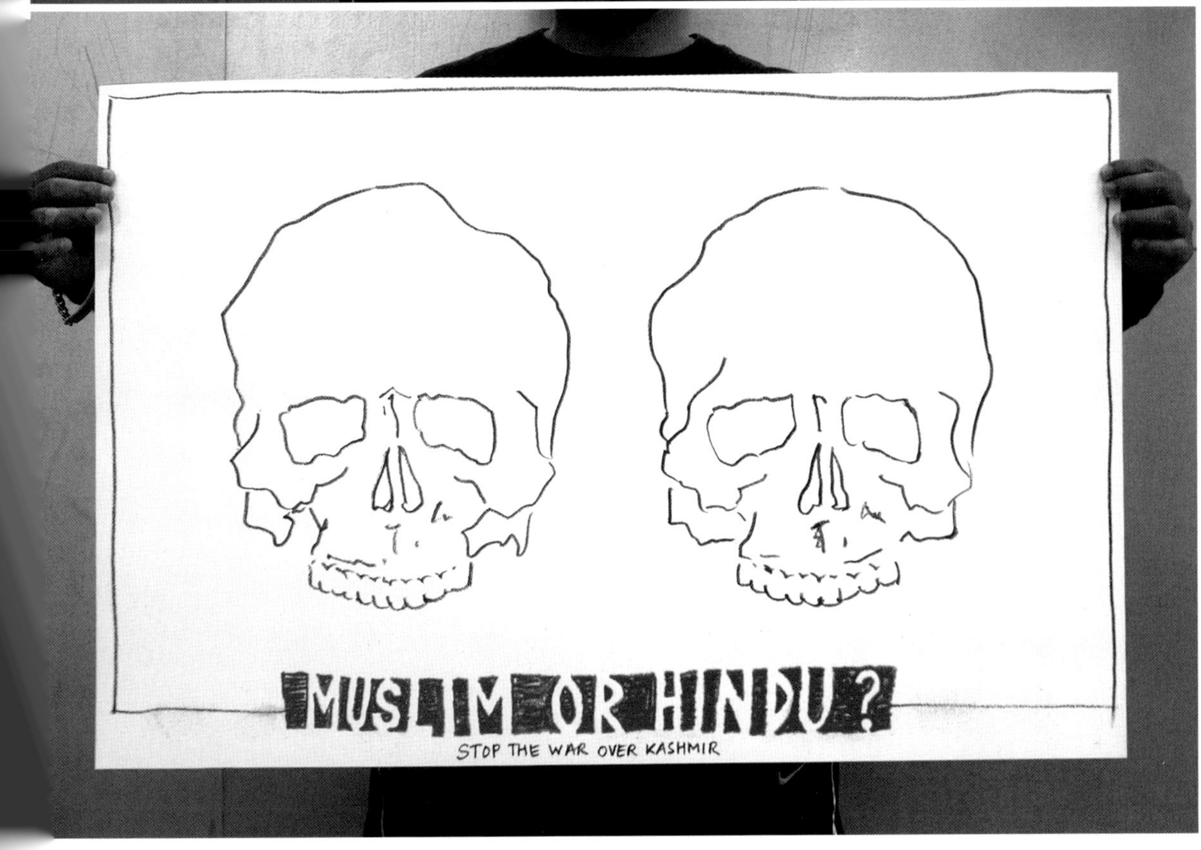
MUSLIM OR HINDU ?
STOP THE WAR OVER KASHMIR

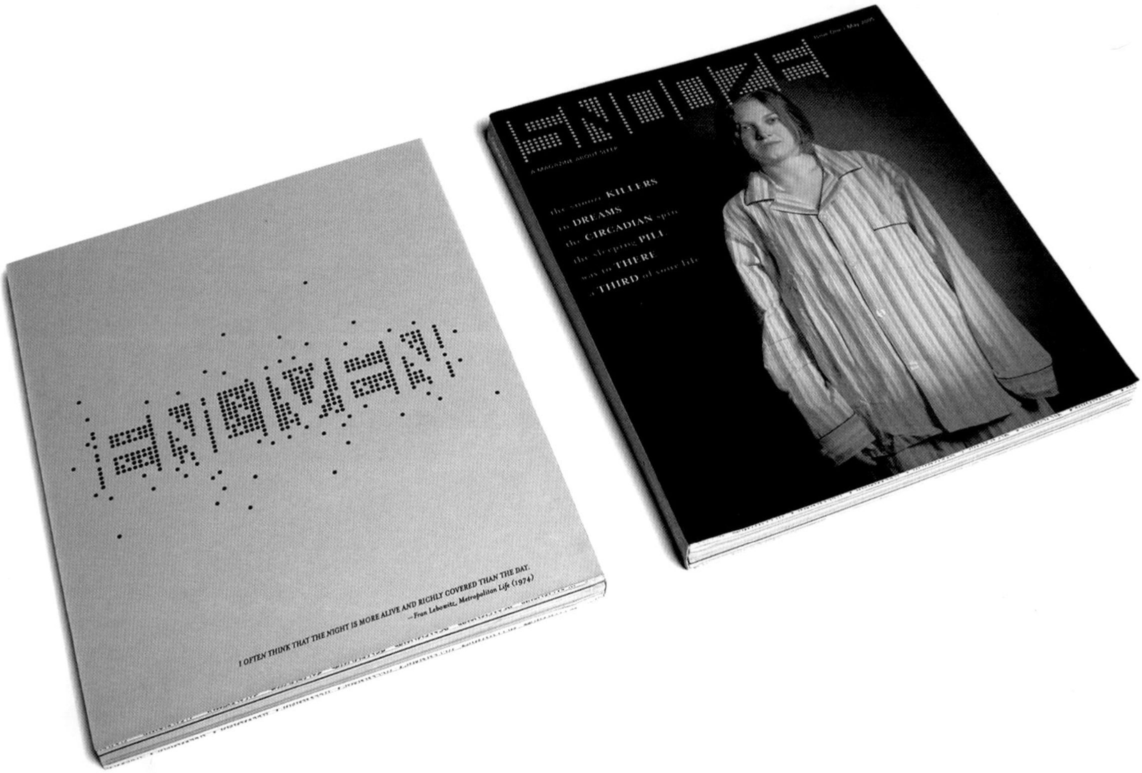
I OFTEN THINK THAT THE NIGHT IS MORE ALIVE AND RICHLY COVERED THAN THE DAY.
—Fran Lebowitz, Metropolitan Life (1974)

44

THE SNOOZE KILLERS
SIX INSOMNIACS FROM ST. JOSEPH'S MEDICAL HOSPITAL GIVE THEIR VIEWS ON WHAT IT FEELS LIKE BEING THE ONLY SOULS AWAKE THROUGH THE DARK HOURS OF THE NIGHT.

Dreams set the stage for your actions the following day, priming you to either rise and shine and conquer the world, or crawl back under the soft covers of your bed and duck all the challenges that lie ahead.
dreams and color

DELU
SIO
NARI
UM

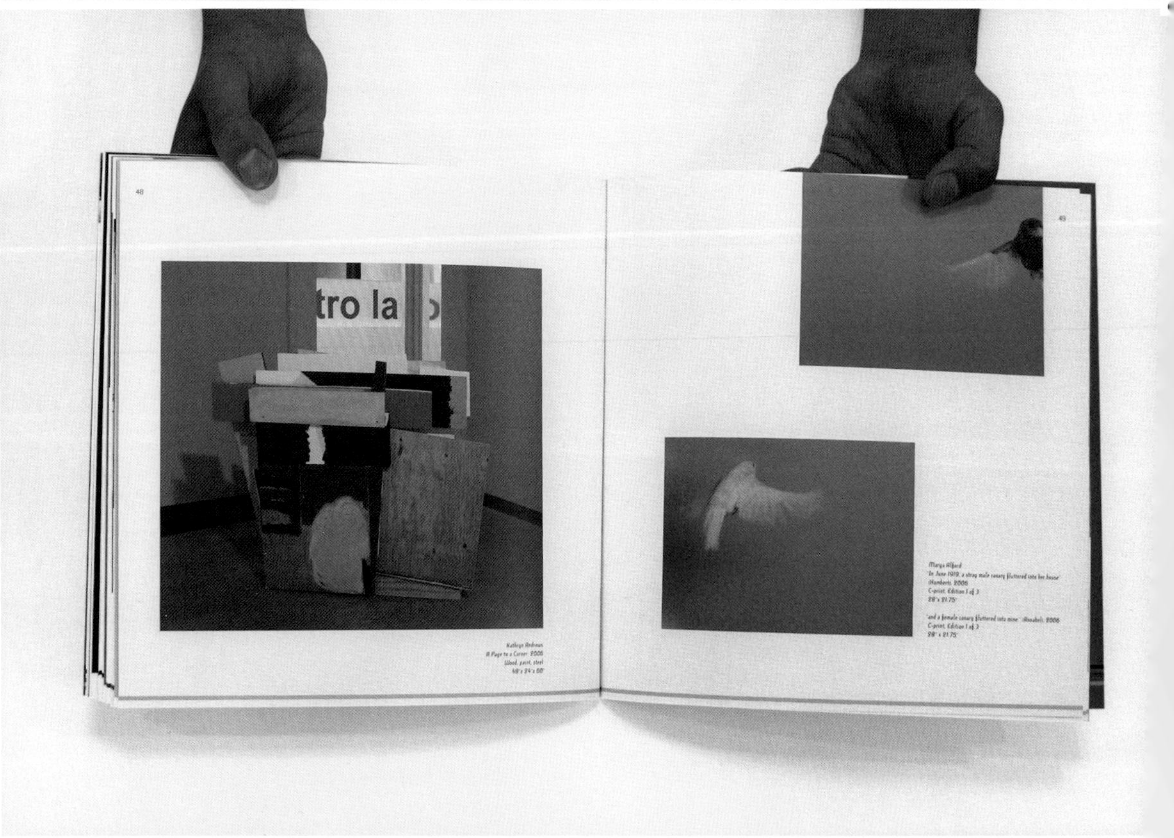
48
49
tro la
Wood, paint, steel
"In June 1919, a stray male canary fluttered into her house"
C-print, Edition 1 of 3
"and a female canary fluttered into mine"
C-print, Edition 1 of 3

ORB
AND ONE DAY WE DIDN'T NEED TO BREATHE

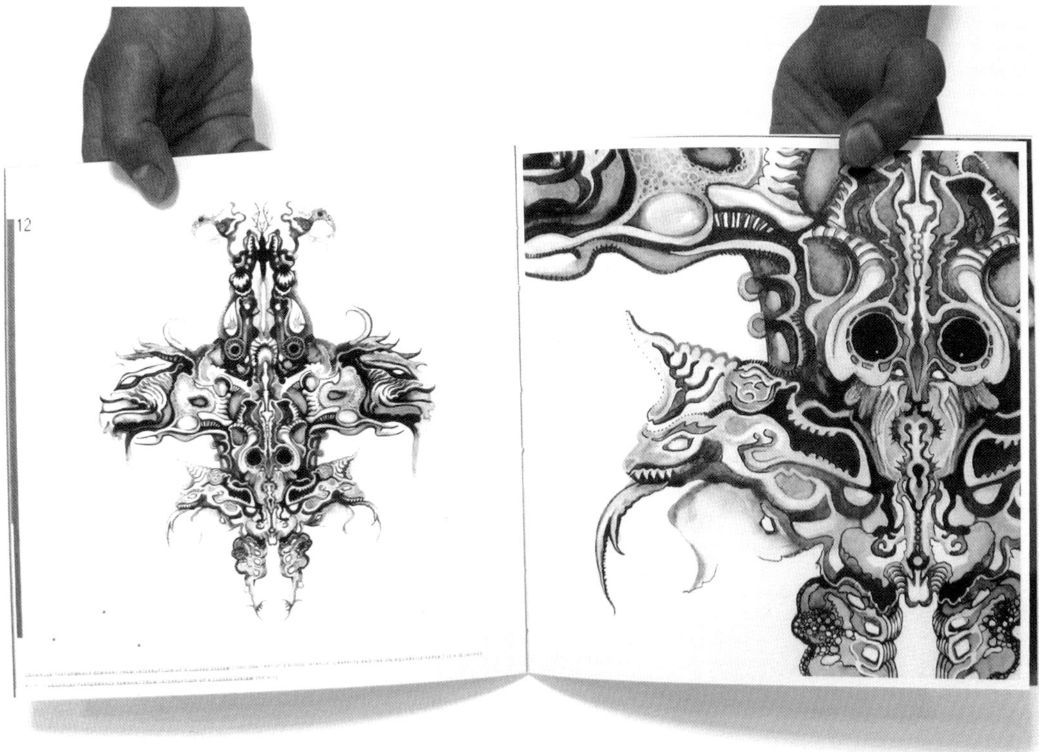
12

JACK HAMILTON
ATSPACEGALLERY.COM
JULIE PERLIN LEE
GALLERY
DIRECTOR
2202 N MAIN ST.
SANTA ANA, CA 92706
714 835 3730
JPERLIN@ATSPACEGALLERY.COM
ATSPACEGALLERY.COM

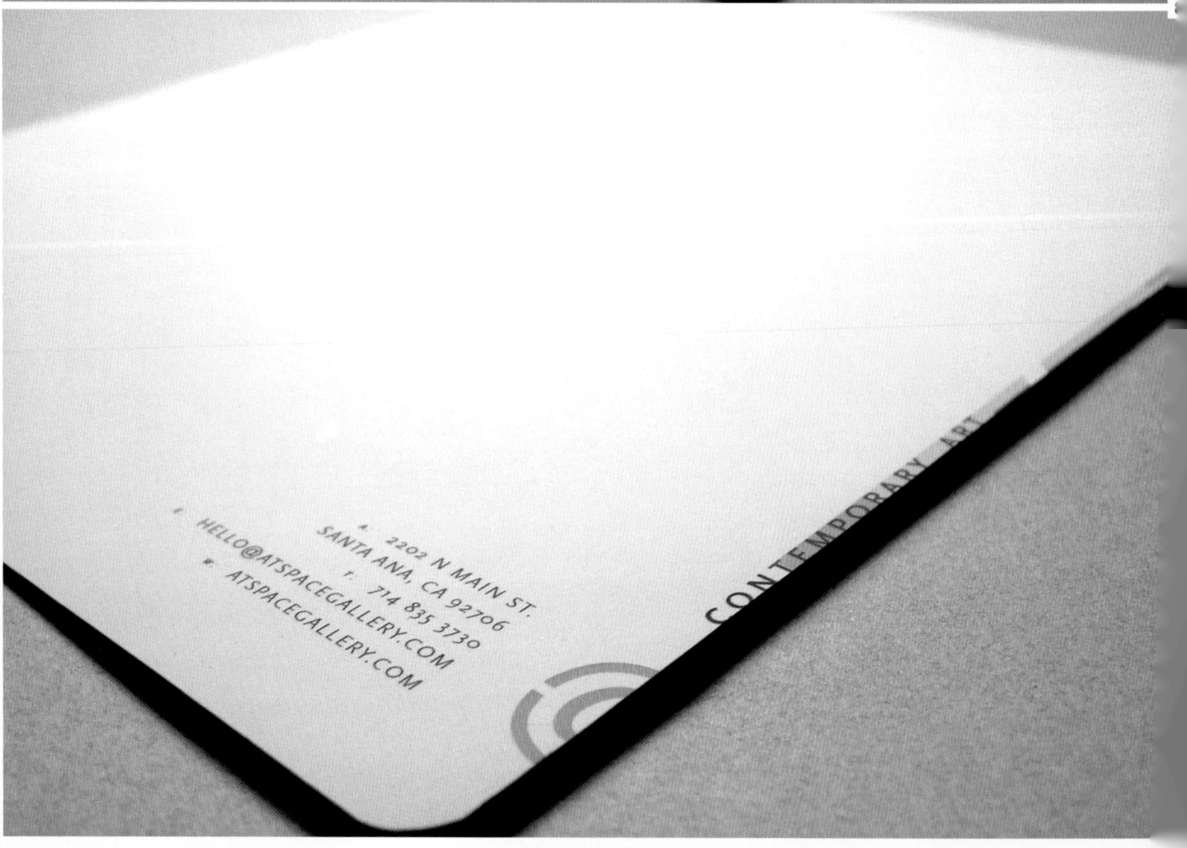
A. 2202 N MAIN ST.
SANTA ANA, CA 92706
T. 714 835 3730
E. HELLO@ATSPACEGALLERY.COM
W. ATSPACEGALLERY.COM
CONTEMPORARY ART

8

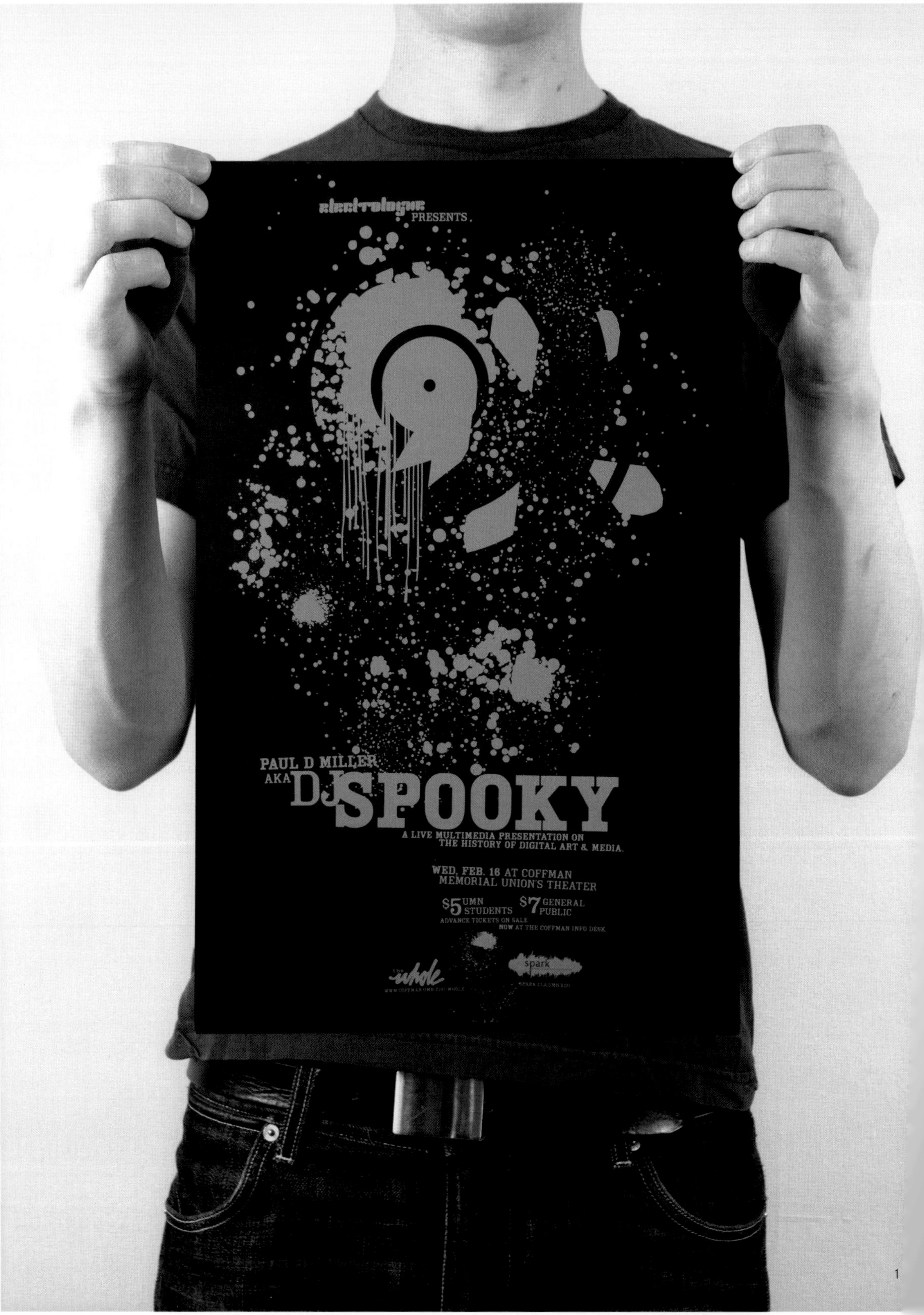
PRESENTS
PAUL D MILLER
AKA DJ SPOOKY
A LIVE MULTIMEDIA PRESENTATION ON
THE HISTORY OF DIGITAL ART & MEDIA.
WED, FEB. 16 AT COFFMAN
MEMORIAL UNION'S THEATER
$5 UMN STUDENTS
$7 GENERAL PUBLIC
ADVANCE TICKETS ON SALE
NOW AT THE COFFMAN INFO DESK
spark

SKWIOT-SMITH | SAINT PAUL, MN, USA
Peter Skwiot Smith

After six months in Amsterdam at the Gerrit Rietveld Academie of Art & Design, Peter Skwiot Smith returned stateside to settle in Saint Paul, Minnesota. The many projects at hand include running a design boutique and Five to Nine pdf magazine, creating minimal beautiful freelance work, looking after his cats, cooking and drinking beer.

www.skwiotsmith.com

1 Promotional poster | Electrologue, 2005
2 Wedding invitation | Michael & Meredith Gordon, 2005
3 Magazine design | Self-published, 2007
4 Album artwork | Minutes to Midnight, 2005
5 Promotional DVD and buttons | Worrell, 2007
6 Tshirt graphics | Self-initiated, 2007

2

hope
michael + meredith

IN
TRO
DUC
TION

KA
RL
WH
O?
ARCHIVED PHOTOS (19.10.03)
BY PETER SKWIOT SMITH

MINUTES TO MIDNIGHT
I WISH YOU WELL
ALL SONGS BY MINUTES TO MIDNIGHT.
© 2005 MINUTES TO MIDNIGHT.
ALL RIGHTS RESERVED.
WWW.MINUTESTOMIDNIGHT.COM
1. STORY OF MY LIFE
2. SHOULDER THE BURDEN
3. FAR AWAY
4. ADORE
5. DECOMPOSE

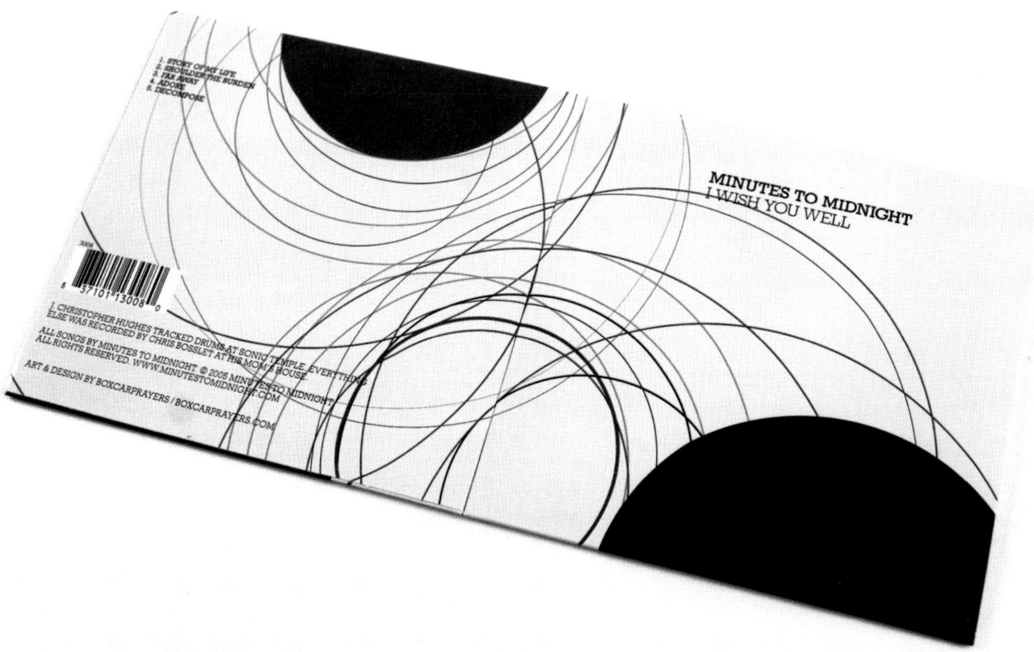
1. STORY OF MY LIFE
2. SHOULDER THE BURDEN
3. FAR AWAY
4. ADORE
5. DECOMPOSE
MINUTES TO MIDNIGHT
I WISH YOU WELL
J. CHRISTOPHER HUGHES TRACKED DRUMS AT SONIC TEMPLE. EVERYTHING
ELSE WAS RECORDED BY CHRIS BOSSLET AT HIS MOM'S HOUSE.
ALL SONGS BY MINUTES TO MIDNIGHT. © 2005 MINUTES TO MIDNIGHT.
ALL RIGHTS RESERVED. WWW.MINUTESTOMIDNIGHT.COM
ART & DESIGN BY BOXCARPRAYERS / BOXCARPRAYERS.COM

WORRELL
STORIES

5

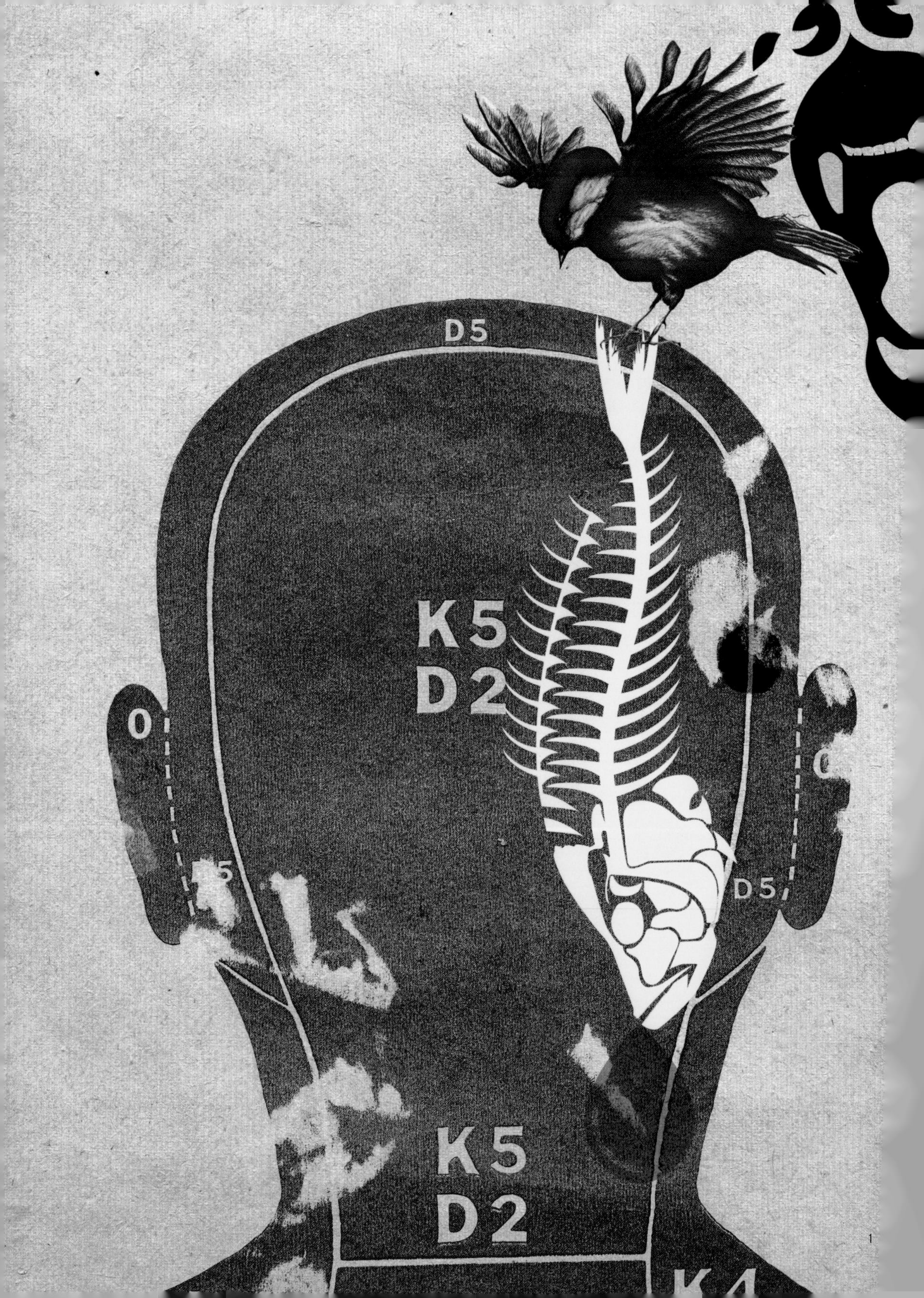
D5
K5
D2
O
D5
K5
D2

SOCITY | NEW YORK, NY, USA
Jesse Raker

Jesse Raker operates his one-man graphic design practice, SoCity, from his sunny 12th floor studio/home in the East Village. Drawing inspiration from urban decay and thrift finds as much as he does from street art and photography, the streets of New York provide an endless source of the stimulating ideas, which are expressed in his work.

www.socity.com

1 Illustration | Semi-permanent, 2006
2 Illustration | Self-initiated, 2006
3 Magazine spreads | Cooleh Magazine, 2005-06
4 Graphics | Start Mobile, 2005
5 Tshirt graphic | Brooklyn Industries, 2007
6 Graphics | Brooklyn Industries, 2006
7 Branding | 3rd Ward, 2006
8 Tshirt graphics | Brooklyn Industries, 2006-07

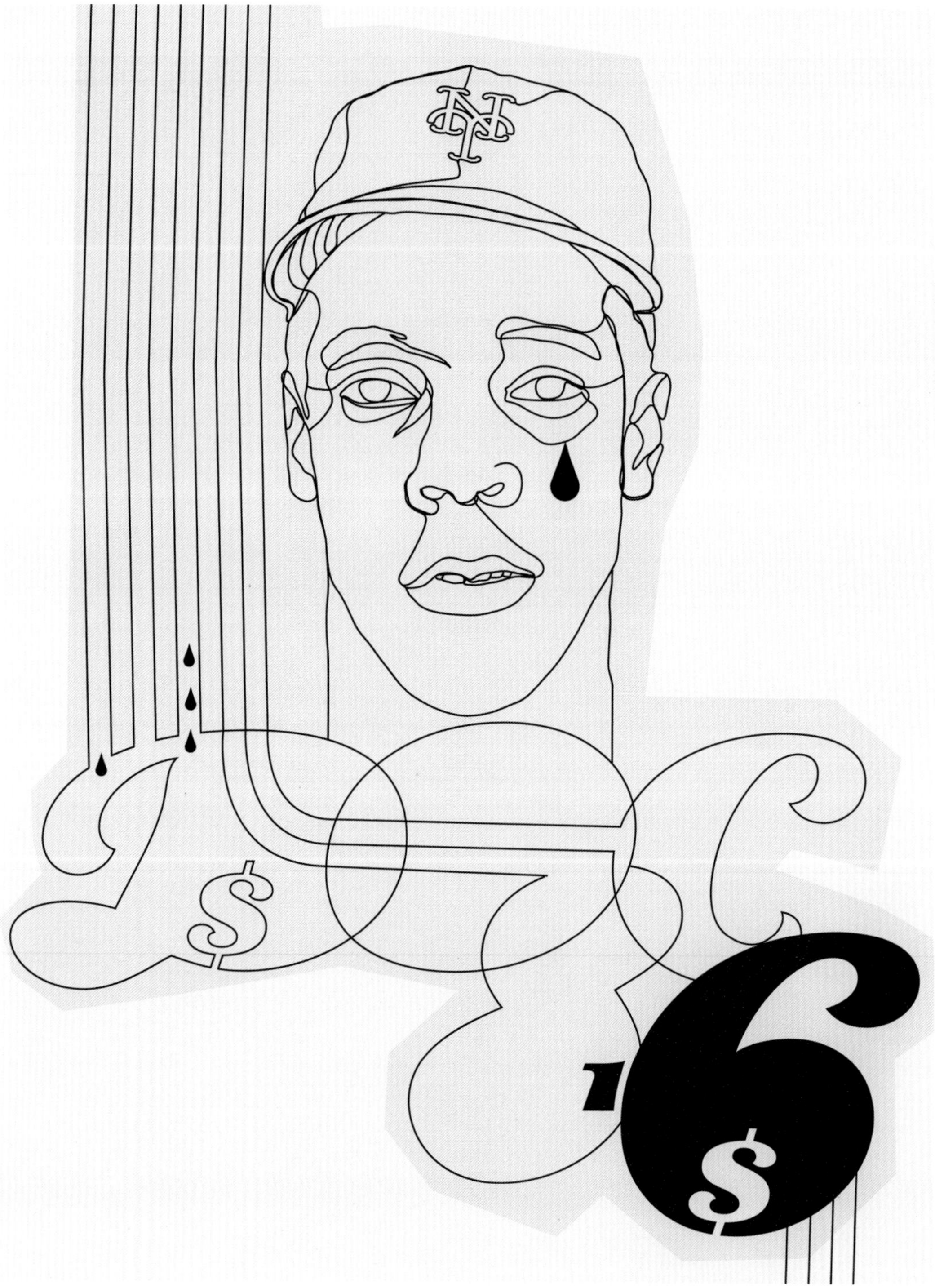

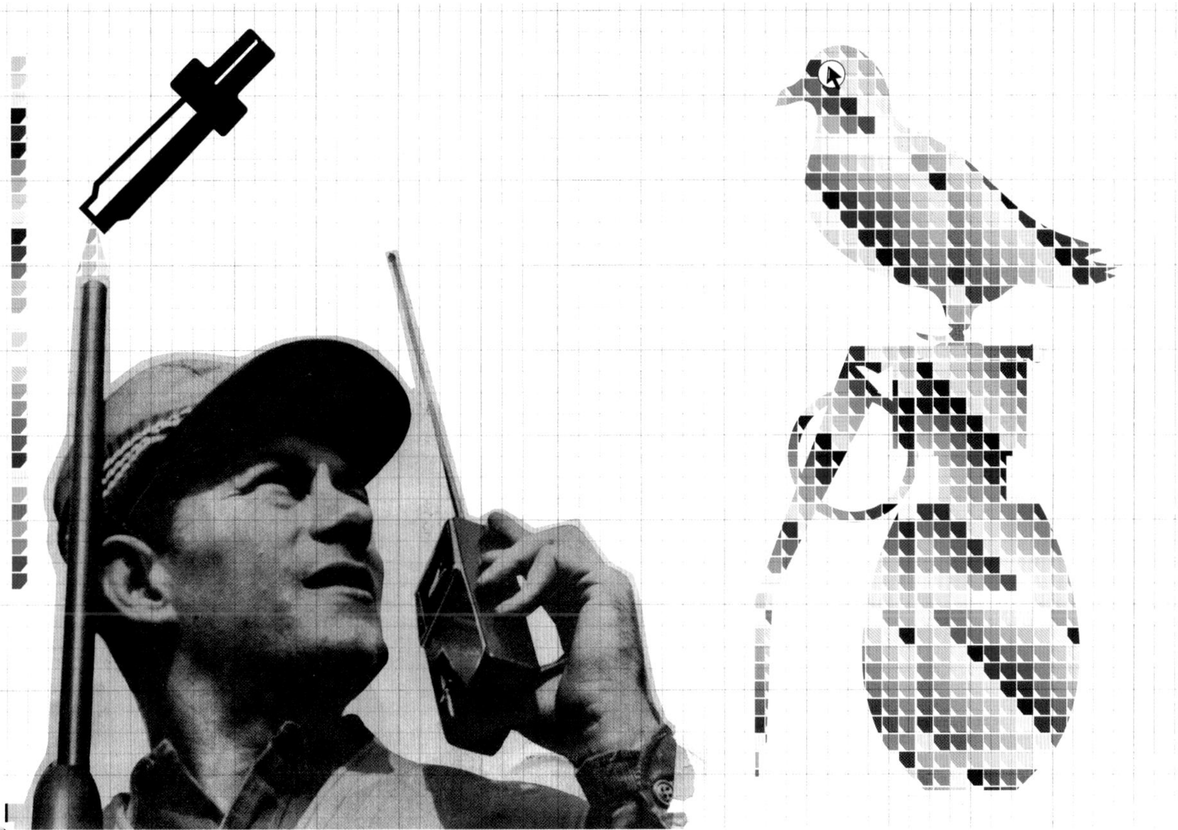

NEW YORK
DAILY NEWS
DOIN IT
AFTER DARK
DOIN IT
IN
THE PARK

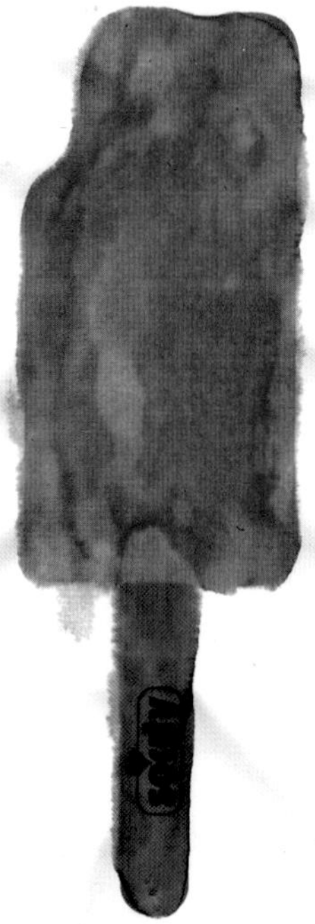

MiAMQR

7

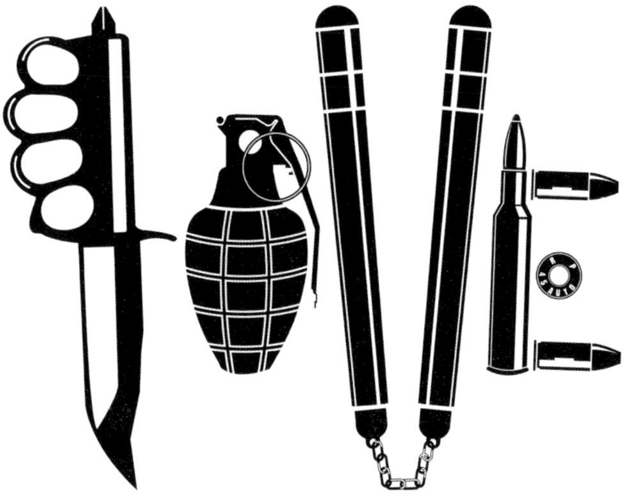

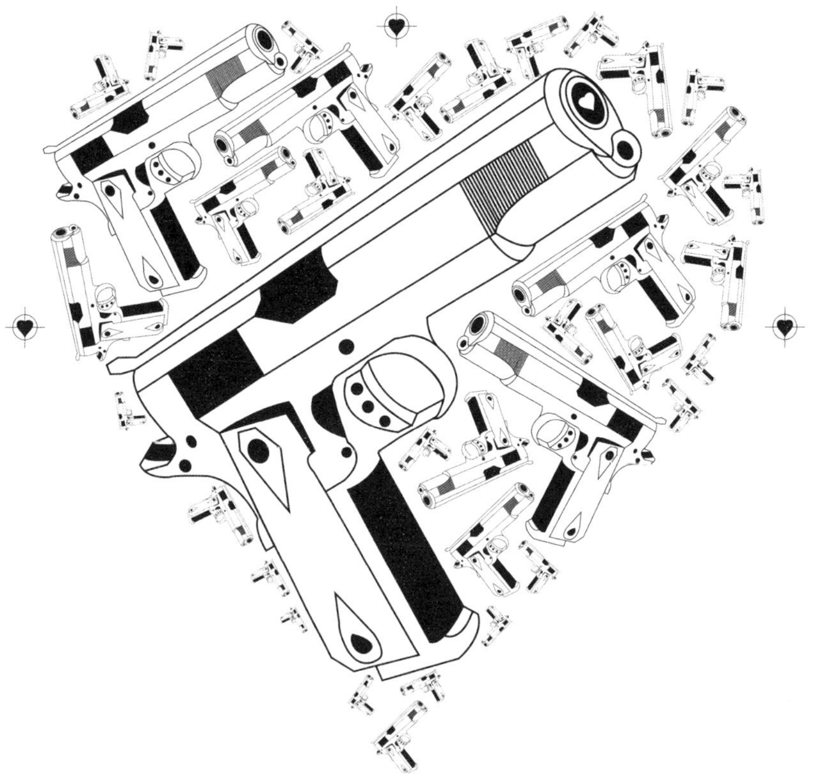

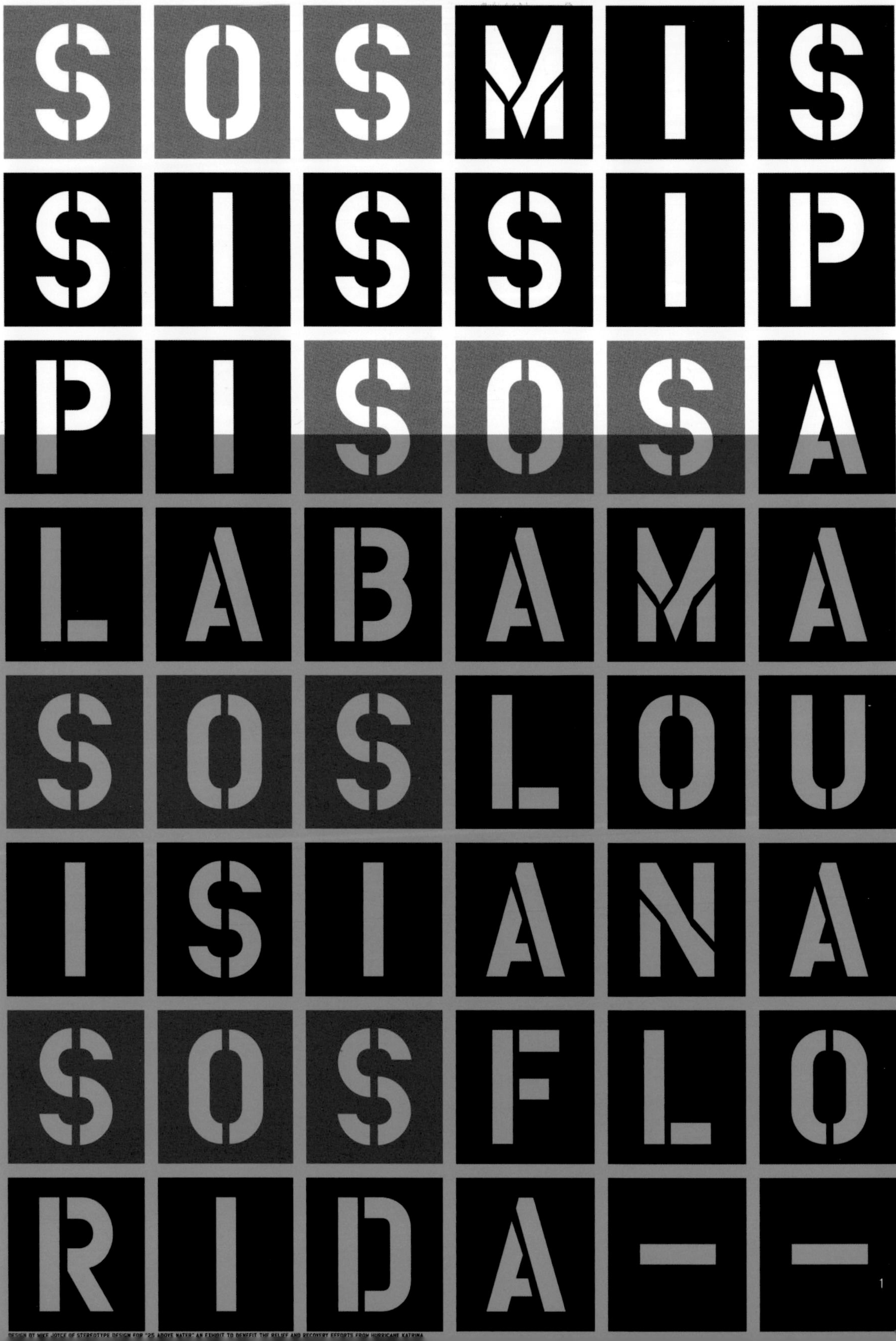
SOSMIS
SISSIP
PISOSA
LABAMA
SOSLOU
ISIANA
SOSFLO
RIDA——
DESIGN BY MIKE JOYCE OF STEREOTYPE DESIGN FOR "25 ABOVE WATER" AN EXHIBIT TO BENEFIT THE RELIEF AND RECOVERY EFFORTS FROM HURRICANE KATRINA

STEREOTYPE DESIGN | NEW YORK, NY, USA
Mike Joyce

Mike Joyce founded Stereotype Design in 2002, a graphic design studio developing projects for commercial, cultural and corporate clients. Mike also teaches typography and design to 3rd and 4th year students at the School of Visual Arts in New York, and may be the only graphic designer with absolutely no interest in collecting sneakers.

www.stereotype-design.com

1 Poster | 25 Above Water, 2007
2 Box set packaging | Hachette Audio, 2006
3 Promotional brochure | Matthew Salacuse Photography, 2005
4 Promotional posters | Fueled By Ramen, 2005-06
5 Promotional poster | Agent Orange, 2004
6 Promotional poster | Virgin Records, 2005
7 Box set packaging | 2005
8 Invitation | MTV Networks International, 2003
9 Tshirt design | 2K By Gingham, 2007

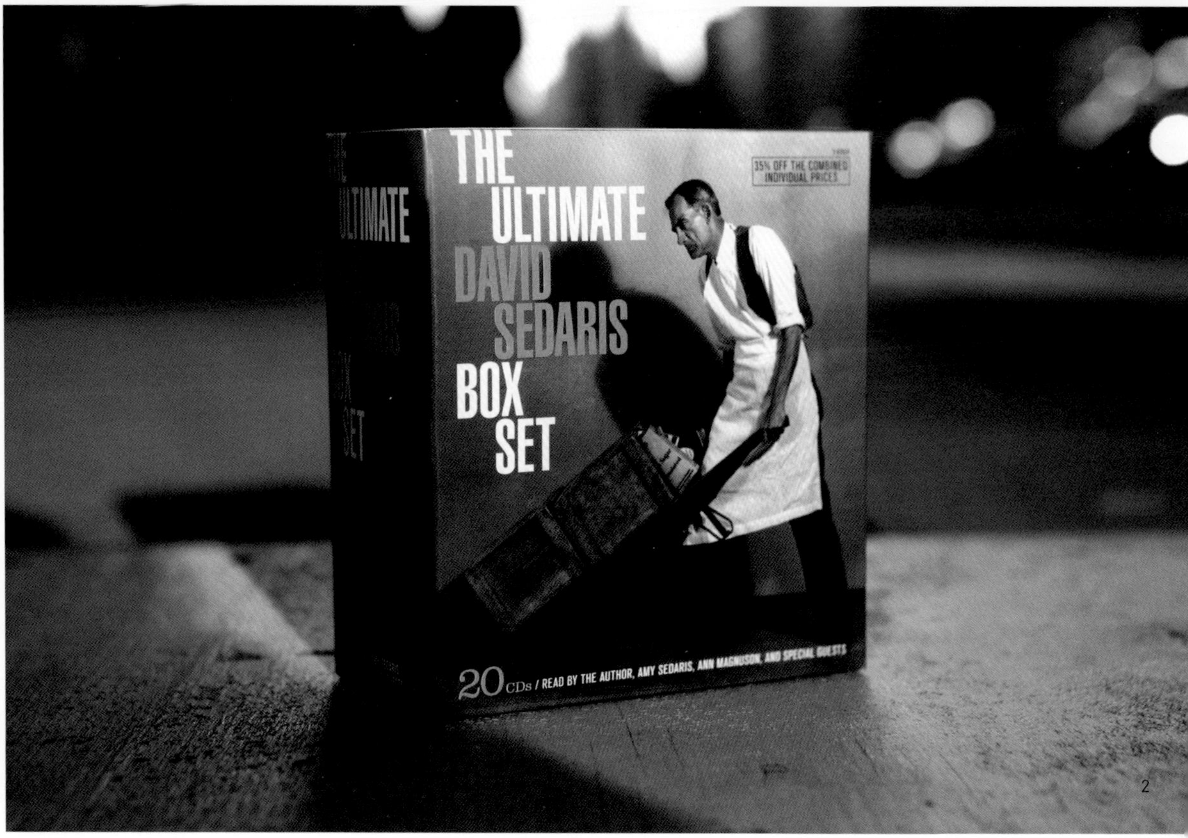
THE
ULTIMATE
DAVID
SEDARIS
BOX
SET
35% OFF THE COMBINED INDIVIDUAL PRICES
20 CDs / READ BY THE AUTHOR, AMY SEDARIS, ANN MAGNUSON, AND SPECIAL GUESTS

2

ROCK
MATTHEW SALACUSE
PHOTOGRAPHY
WWW.SALACUSE.COM
646.418.1084

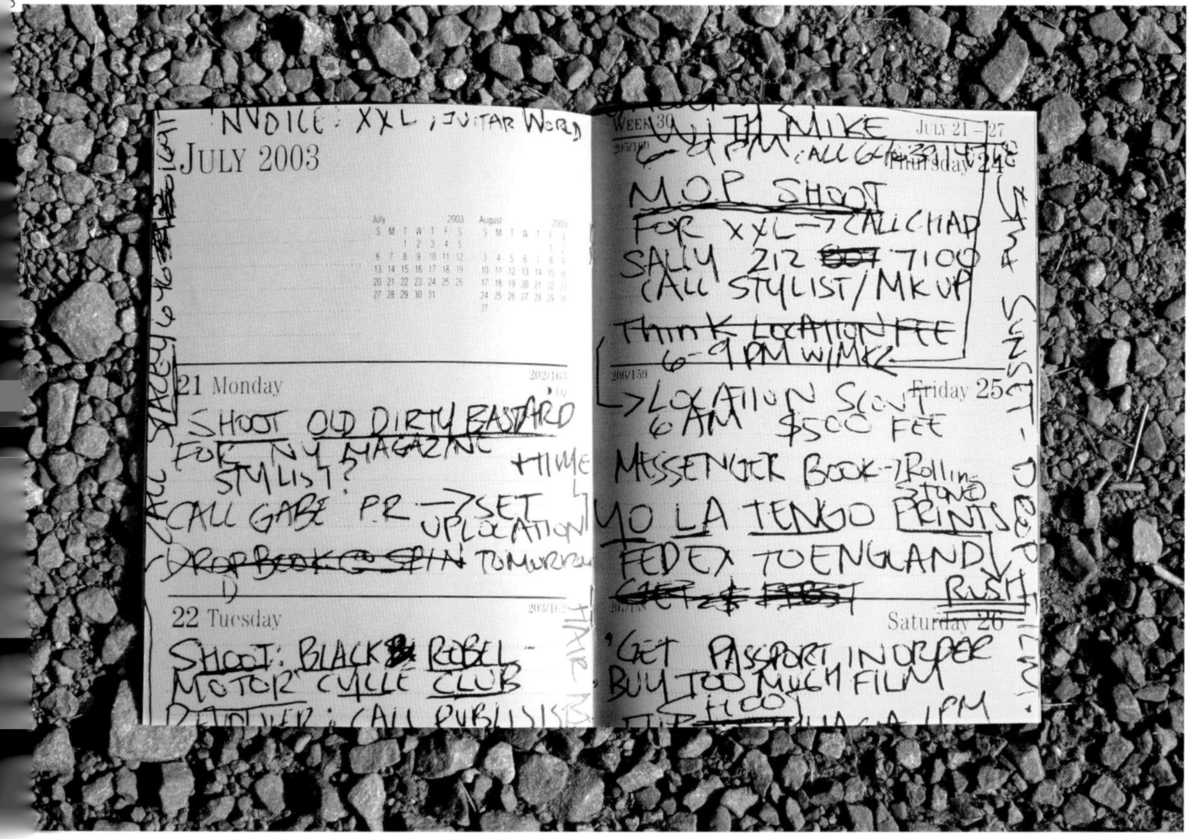
JULY 2003
21 Monday
SHOOT OLD DIRTY BASTARD
FOR NY MAGAZINE
STYLIST?
22 Tuesday
SHOOT: BLACK REBEL
MOTOR CYCLE CLUB
WEEK 30
JULY 21 – 27
Thursday 24
M.O.P. SHOOT
FOR XXL
CALL STYLIST/MK UP
Friday 25
6 AM $500 FEE
YO LA TENGO PRINTS
FEDEX TO ENGLAND
RUSH
Saturday 26
GET PASSPORT IN ORDER
BUY TOO MUCH FILM

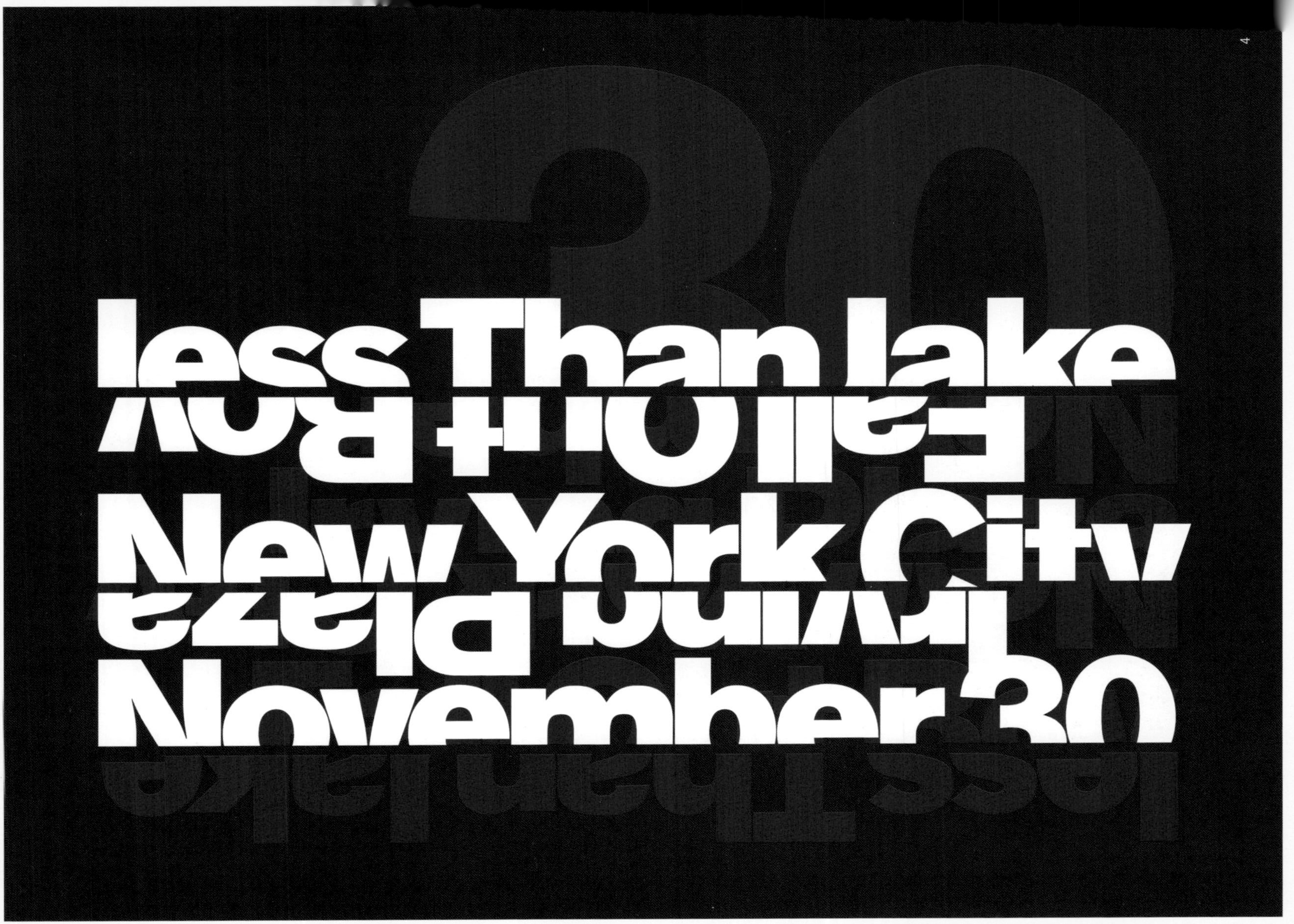
Less Than Jake
Fall Out Boy
New York City
Irving Plaza
November 30
30

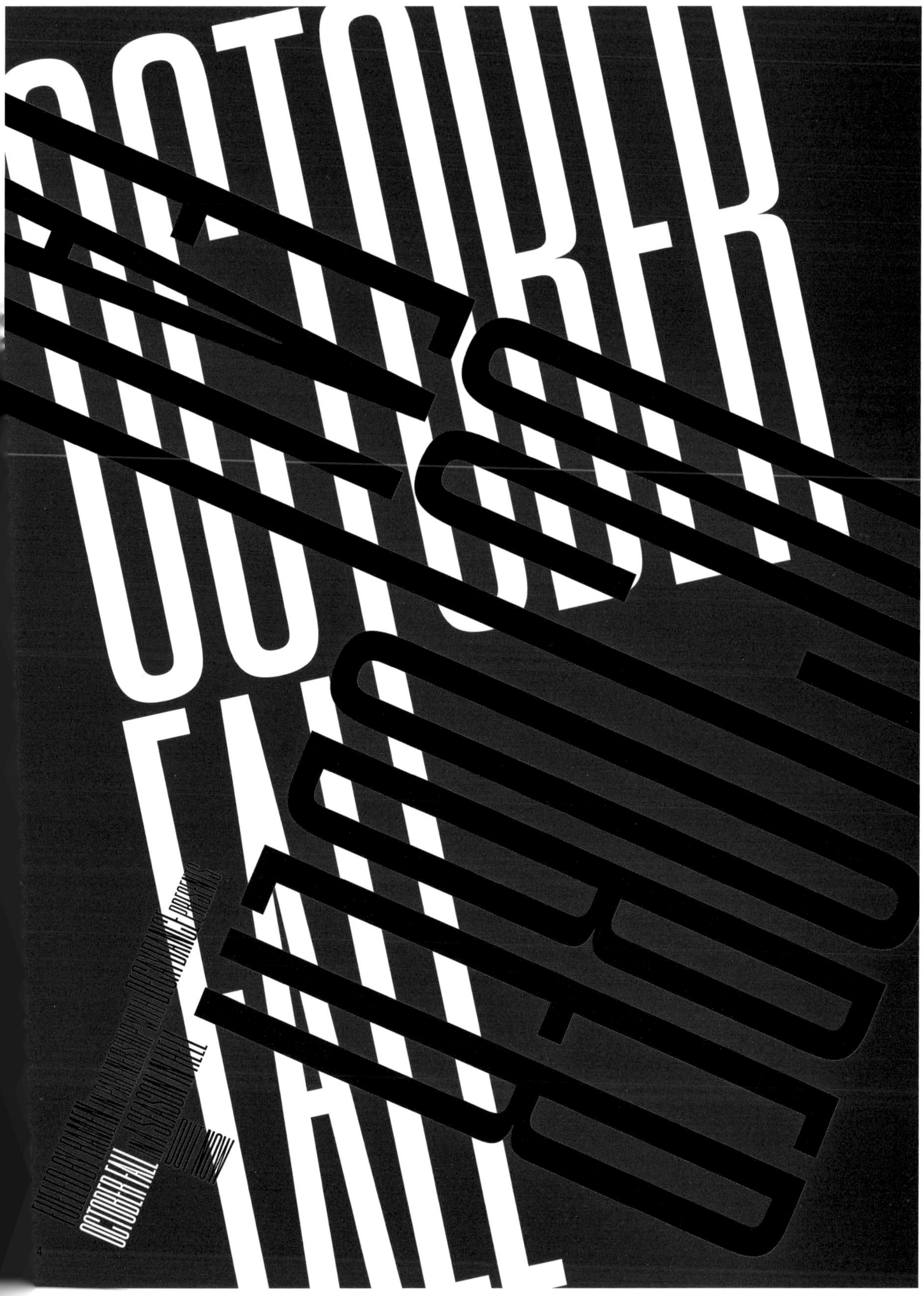
OCTOBER FALL
OUT NOW

AGENT ORANGE
LIVE AT THE AUTRY MUSEUM
OF WESTERN HERITAGE
LOS ANGELES CALIFORNIA
JUNE 22

GORILLAZ
SEATTLE, WA : SAN JOSE, CA : PORTLAND, OR : MONTEREY, CA : RIVERSIDE, CA : SAN FRANCISCO, CA : SAN DIEGO, CA
SANTA BARBARA, CA : PHOENIX, AZ : RENO, NV : TULSA, OK : TAMPA, FL : ORLANDO, FL : WEST PALM BEACH, FL
ATLANTA, GA : CHARLOTTE, NC : RICHMOND, VA : NORFOLK, VA : WASHINGTON DC : PHILADELPHIA, PA : MONMOUTH, NJ
NEW YORK, NY : PROVIDENCE, RI : BOSTON, MA : PORTLAND, MN : BURLINGTON, VT : ALBANY, NY : ROCHESTER, NY
PITTSBURGH, PA : DETROIT, MI : GRAND RAPIDS, MI : COLUMBUS, OH : NASHVILLE, TN : ST. LOUIS, MO : KANSAS CITY, MO
MILWAUKEE, WI : CHICAGO, IL : MADISON, WI
INVASION TOUR SUMMER 2005
VIRGINRECORDS.COM
Virgin RECORDS
Music from EMI
Parlophone
GORILLAZ

Virgin RECORDS
Music from EMI
* TURN-TABLE FOR SALE *
EXCELLENT CONDITION WITH CORDS AND POWER SUPPLY
* CLASSIC CAR IN PERFECT CONDITION *
equipped with power steering, brakes, windows and locks
FOR SALE
Brand new Virgins!
FOR RENT
Vintage Virgins!
*** VIRGIN RECORDS ***
GET IN BED WITH US!
GET IN BED WITH US.
Hot 20-year old VIRGIN
seeks perfect partners to make
beautiful music together.

7

OCT1103
YOU'RE INVITED TO THE MTV NETWORKS INTERNATIONAL COCKTAIL PARTY AT MIPCOM
LE BÂOLI RESTAURANT, PORT PIERRE CANTO
BD DE LA CROISETTE 06400 CANNES
SATURDAY, OCTOBER 11, 2003
6:30PM - 9:30PM
TO RSVP:
TEL / 212.846.2519 FAX / 212.258.7938
E-MAIL / MTVNINT@MTVN.COM
XXXXL®
100% MTV NETWORKS INTERNATIONAL
BIGGER, BETTER
AND BURSTING WITH
PROGRAMMING.
SEE REVERSE SIDE FOR MIPCOM PARTY INSTRUCTIONS.
MTV NETWORKS
INTERNATIONAL

8

9

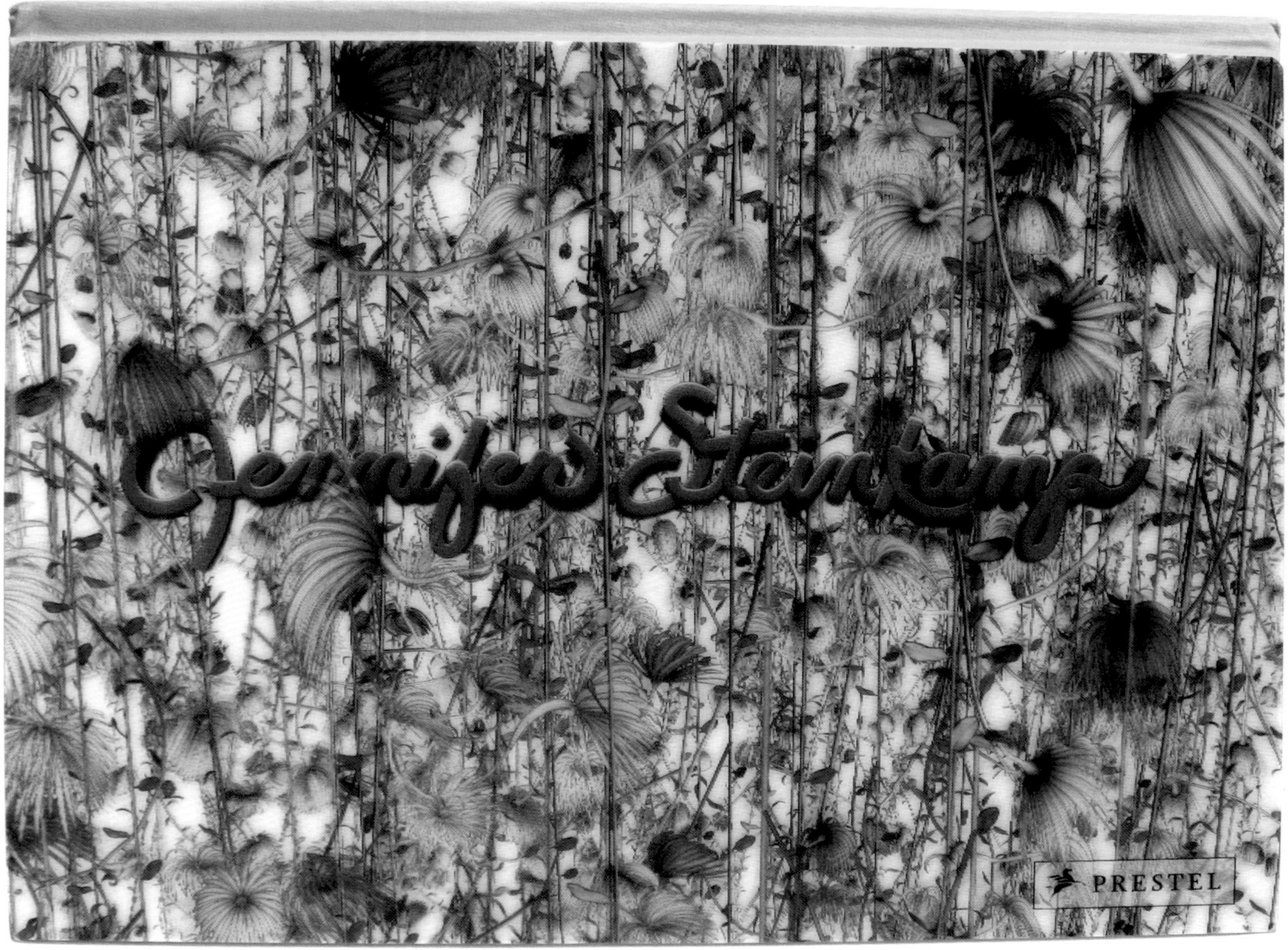
Jennifer Steinkamp
PRESTEL

STRIPE | LOS ANGELES, CA, USA
Jon Sueda, Gail Swanlund

A native of Hawaii, Jon Sueda has practiced design everywhere from Honolulu to the Netherlands. Gail Swanlund cut her teeth writing for the experimental and influential typography journal Emigre. They founded Stripe, a full-service design studio with a taste for the offbeat or strange, a lot of curiosity, and remarkable collaborators.

www.stripela.com

1 Jennifer Steinkamp exhibition catalogue | San Jose Museum of Art, 2006
Designed by Gail Swanlund, Geoff Kaplan (General Working Group) and Jennifer Steinkamp
2 Laura Owens exhibition catalogue | Laura Owens, 2002
Designed by Gail Swanlund and Laura Owens
3 USC promotional posters | USC Roski School of Fine Arts, 2007, 2006
4 CalArts Tshirt exhibition poster and catalogue | CalArts, 2005
5 CalArts Admissions Bulletin | CalArts, 2004
Designed by Gail Swanlund and Scott Taylor
6 Rebellion Acceptance Overdrive: CalArts Type Design 1988-2001 exhibition catalogue | CalArts, 2003
7 Margaret Kilgallen exhibition catalogue | REDCAT Gallery, 2005
Designed by Jon Sueda and Michael Worthington (Counterspace)
8 Andrea Bowers exhibition catalogue | REDCAT Gallery, 2006
9 Black Clock literary journal | CalArts, 2006
Designed by Gail Swanlund
10 UCLA promotional poster | UCLA, 2002
Designed by Gail Swanlund and Geoff Kaplan (General Working Group)

2

LAURA
OWENS

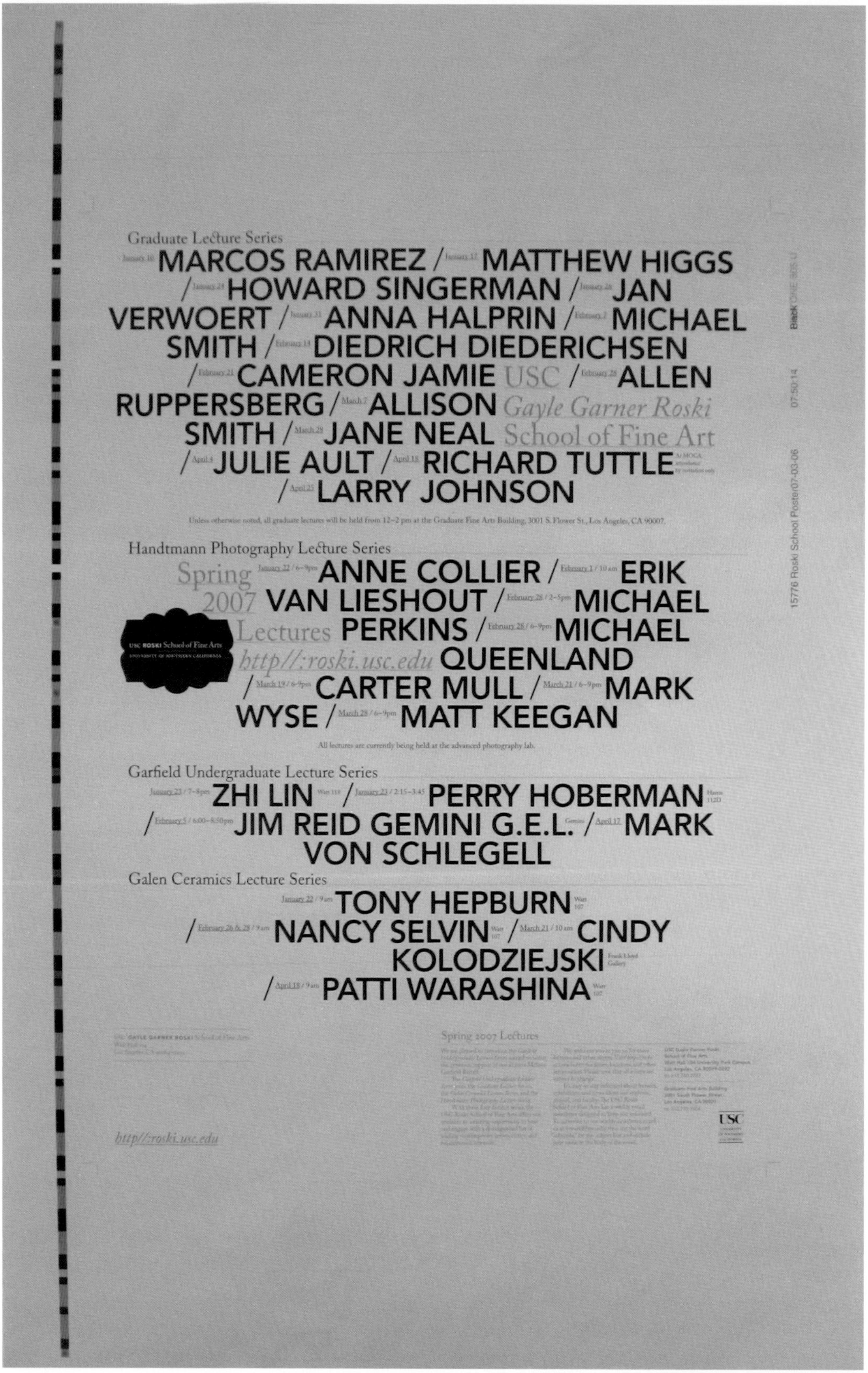

Graduate Lecture Series
MARCOS RAMIREZ / MATTHEW HIGGS
/ HOWARD SINGERMAN / JAN
VERWOERT / ANNA HALPRIN / MICHAEL
SMITH / DIEDRICH DIEDERICHSEN
/ CAMERON JAMIE USC / ALLEN
RUPPERSBERG / ALLISON Gayle Garner Roski
SMITH / JANE NEAL School of Fine Art
/ JULIE AULT / April 18 RICHARD TUTTLE
/ April 25 LARRY JOHNSON
Unless otherwise noted, all graduate lectures will be held from 12–2 pm at the Graduate Fine Arts Building, 3001 S. Flower St., Los Angeles, CA 90007.
Handtmann Photography Lecture Series
Spring January 22 / 6–9pm ANNE COLLIER / February 1 / 10 am ERIK
2007 VAN LIESHOUT / February 28 / 2–5pm MICHAEL
Lectures PERKINS / February 28 / 6–9pm MICHAEL
http//:roski.usc.edu QUEENLAND
/ March 19 / 6–9pm CARTER MULL / March 21 / 6–9pm MARK
WYSE / March 28 / 6–9pm MATT KEEGAN
USC ROSKI School of Fine Arts
All lectures are currently being held at the advanced photography lab.
Garfield Undergraduate Lecture Series
January 23 / 7–8pm ZHI LIN / January 23 / 2:15–3:45 PERRY HOBERMAN
/ February 5 / 6:00–8:50pm JIM REID GEMINI G.E.L. Gemini / April 17 MARK
VON SCHLEGELL
Galen Ceramics Lecture Series
January 22 / 9am TONY HEPBURN
/ February 26 & 28 / 9am NANCY SELVIN / March 21 / 10 am CINDY
KOLODZIEJSKI
/ April 18 / 9am PATTI WARASHINA
Spring 2007 Lectures
http//:roski.usc.edu
USC
15776 Roski School Poster/07-03-06

USC
Roski
School of Fine Arts
Bachelor of Fine Arts | Bachelor of Arts 2005–06
USC Roski School of Fine Arts
Bachelor of Fine Arts | Bachelor of Arts 2005–06

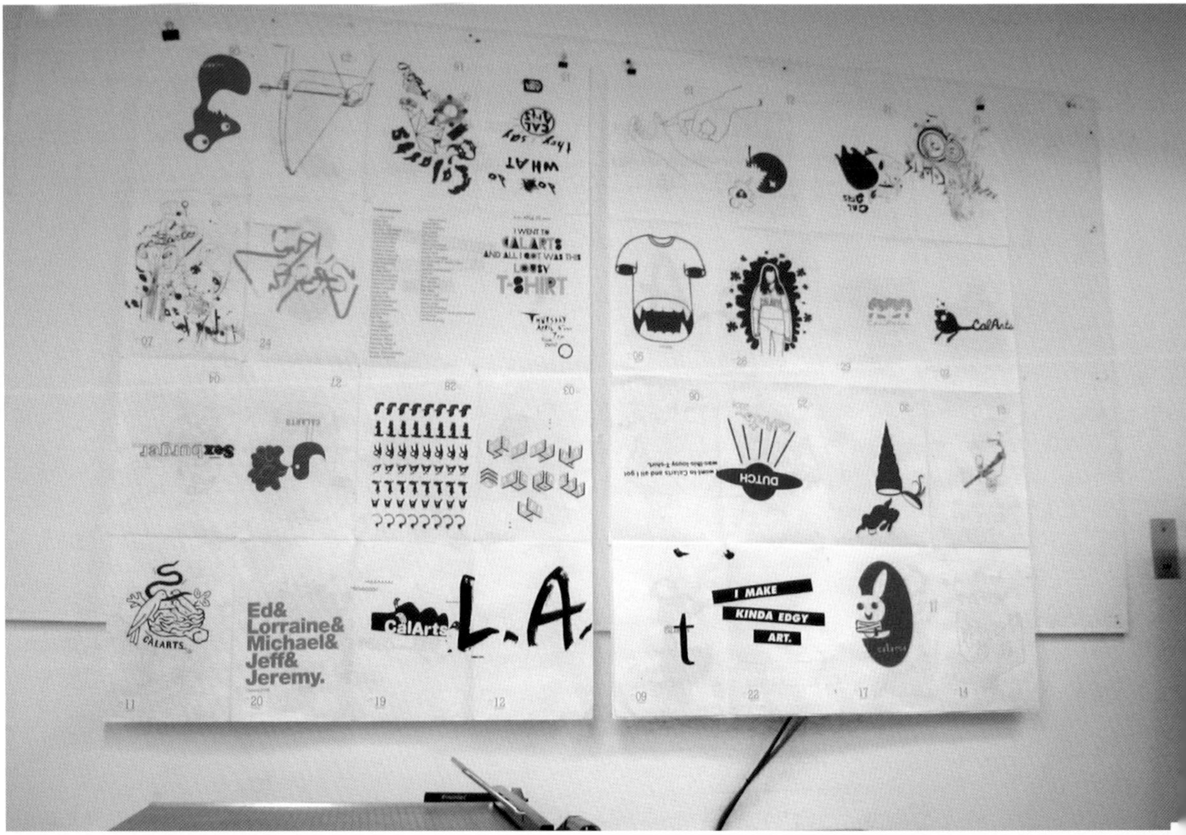
I WENT TO
CALARTS
AND ALL I GOT WAS THIS
LOUSY
T-SHIRT
CalArts
Ed&
Lorraine&
Michael&
Jeff&
Jeremy.
CalArts
L.A.
DUTCH
I MAKE
KINDA EDGY
ART.

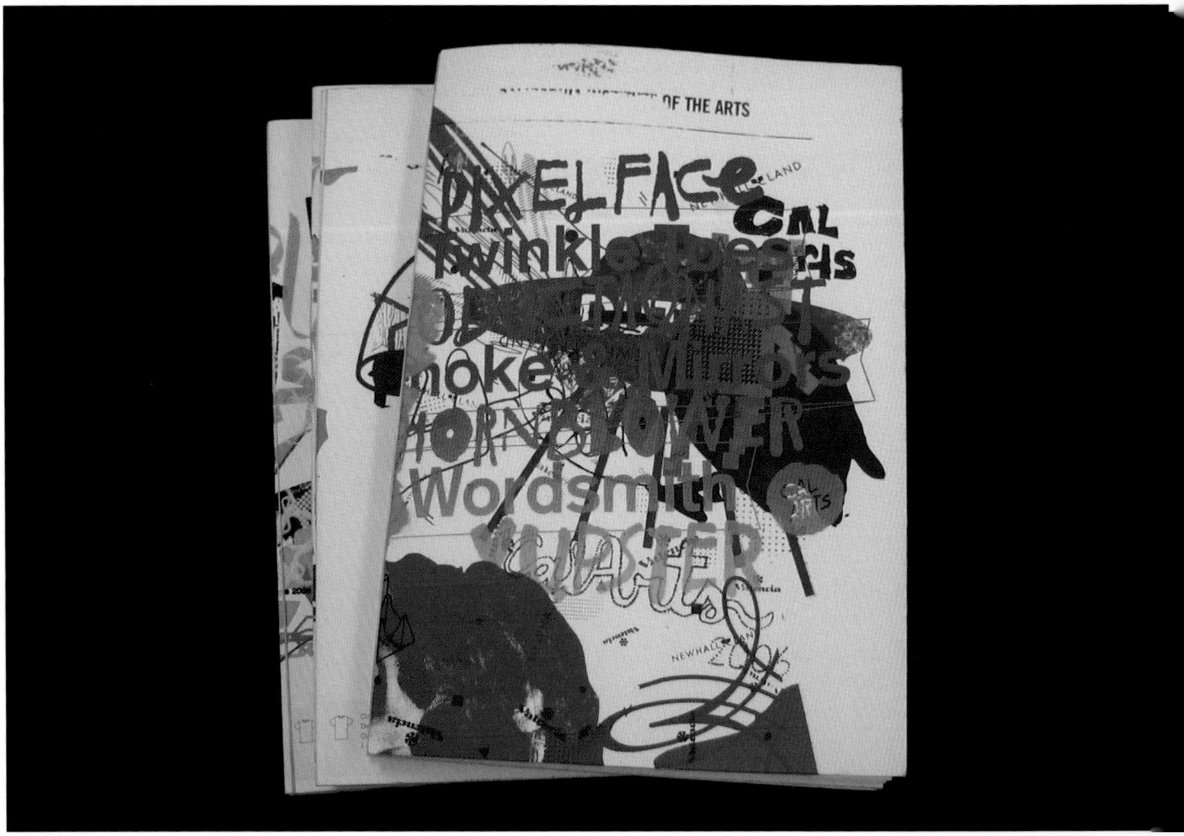
OF THE ARTS
PIXELFACE
CAL
Wordsmith
NEWHALL

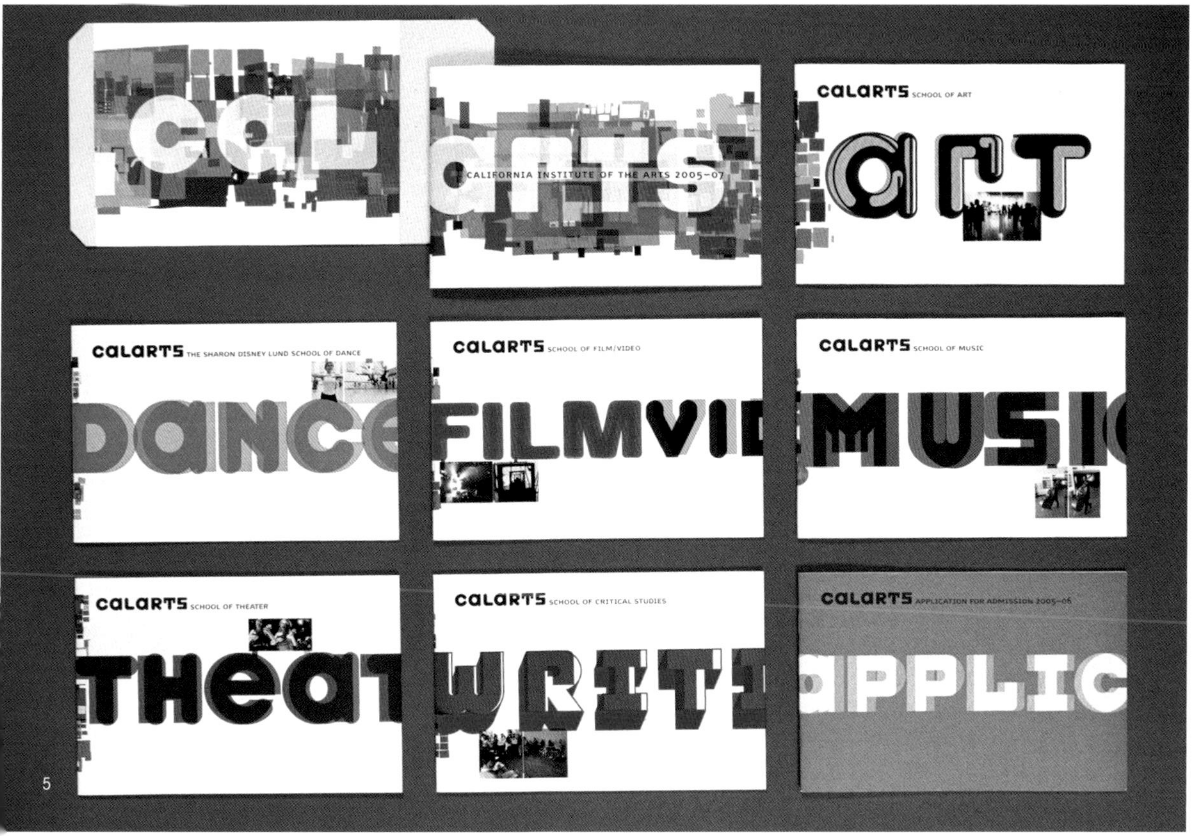
calarts
CALIFORNIA INSTITUTE OF THE ARTS 2005–07
calarts SCHOOL OF ART
art
calarts THE SHARON DISNEY LUND SCHOOL OF DANCE
DANCE
calarts SCHOOL OF FILM/VIDEO
FILMVID
calarts SCHOOL OF MUSIC
MUSIC
calarts SCHOOL OF THEATER
THEAT
calarts SCHOOL OF CRITICAL STUDIES
WRITI
calarts APPLICATION FOR ADMISSION 2005–06
APPLIC

5

REBELLION ACCEPTANCE OVERDRIVE:
CalArts Type Design 1988-2001
2nd Edition Catalog
Rebellion Acceptance Overdrive (exhibition poster)

6

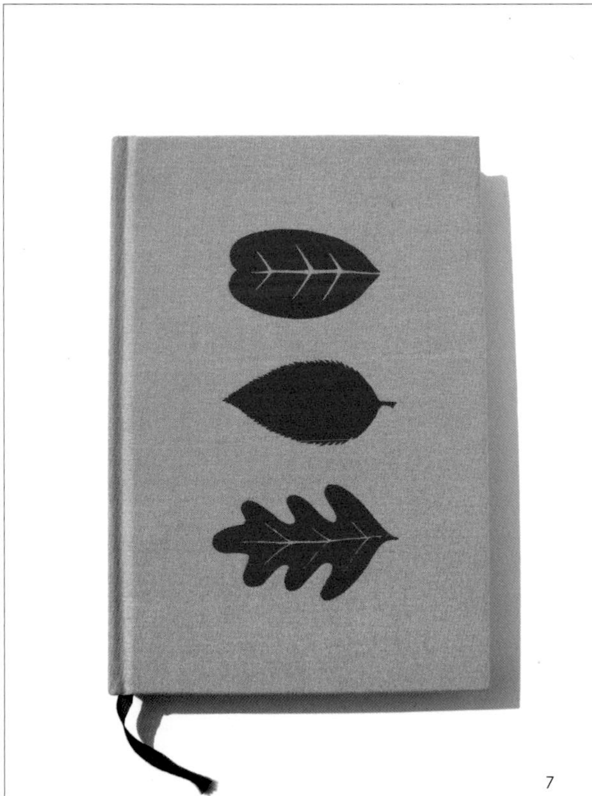

7

7

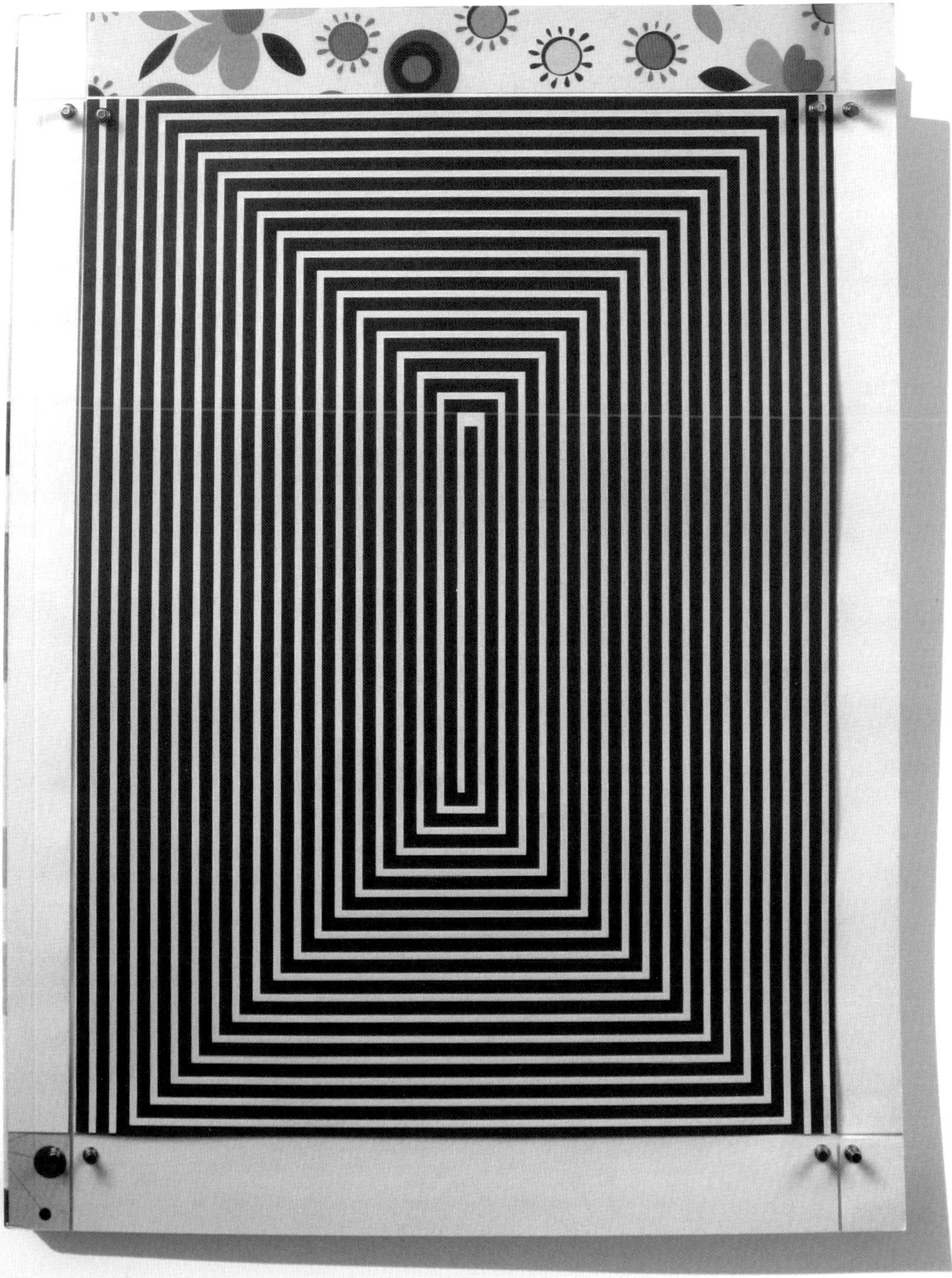

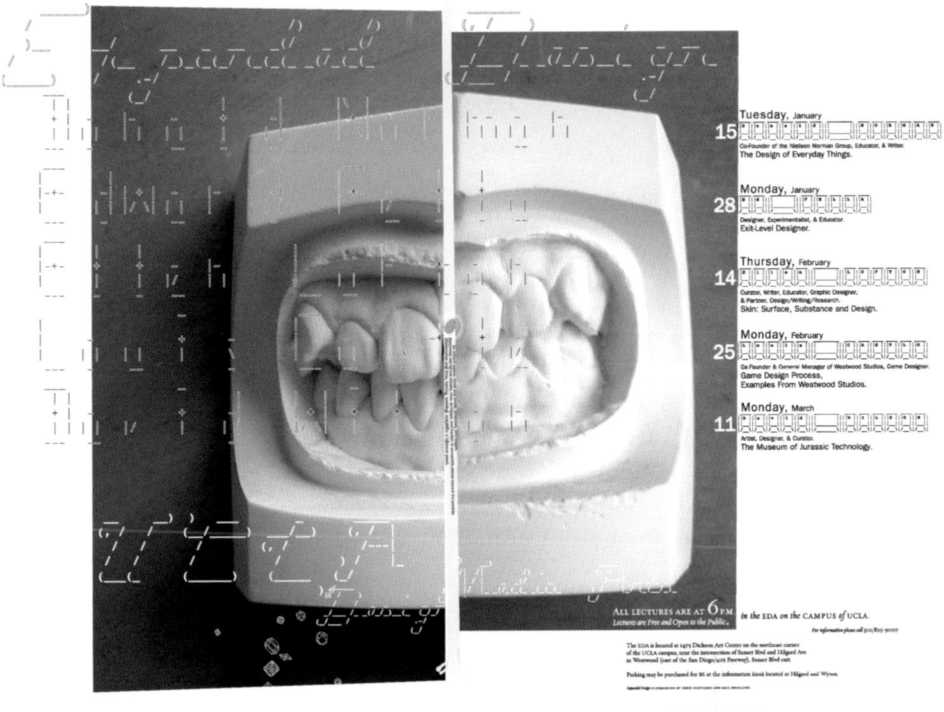
Tuesday, January
15
Co-Founder of the Nielsen Norman Group, Educator, & Writer.
The Design of Everyday Things.
Monday, January
28
Designer, Experimentalist, & Educator.
Exit-Level Designer.
Thursday, February
14
Curator, Writer, Educator, Graphic Designer,
& Partner, Design/Writing/Research.
Skin: Surface, Substance and Design.
Monday, February
25
Co-Founder & General Manager of Westwood Studios, Game Designer.
Game Design Process,
Examples From Westwood Studios.
Monday, March
11
Artist, Designer, & Curator.
The Museum of Jurassic Technology.
All lectures are at 6 P.M.
Lectures are Free and Open to the Public.
in the EDA on the CAMPUS of UCLA.
For information please call 310/825-9007
The EDA is located at 1473 Dickson Art Center on the northeast corner
of the UCLA campus, near the intersection of Sunset Blvd and Hilgard Ave
in Westwood (east of the San Diego/405 Freeway), Sunset Blvd exit.
Parking may be purchased for $6 at the information kiosk located at Hilgard and Wyton.

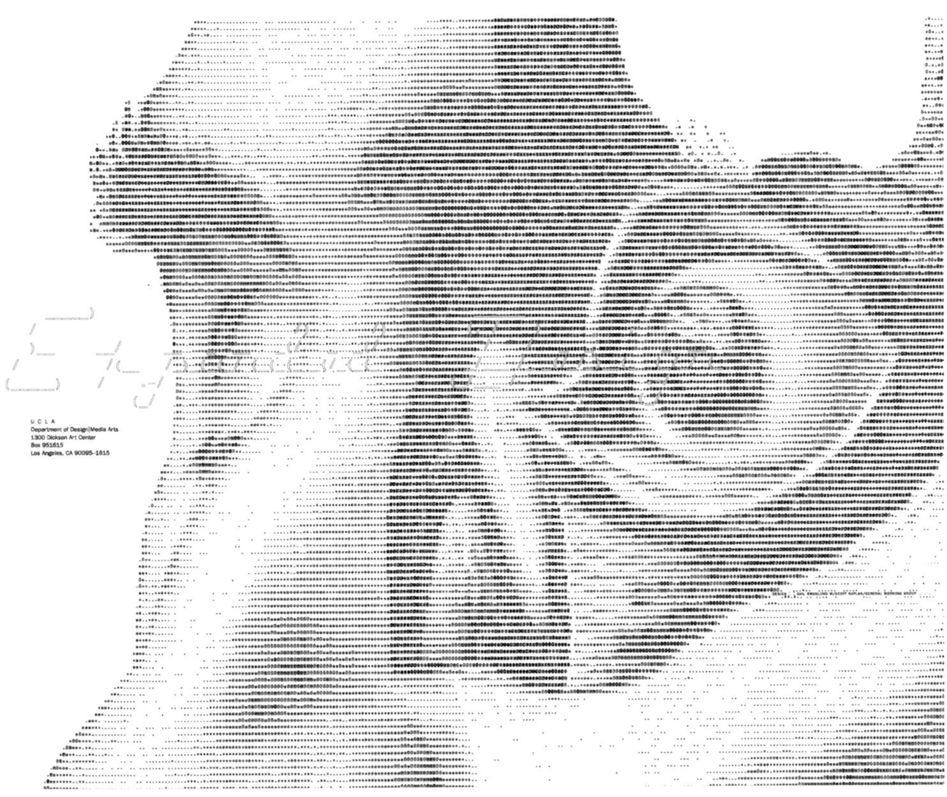
U C L A
Department of Design|Media Arts
1300 Dickson Art Center
Box 951615
Los Angeles, CA 90095-1615

DJ MUSIC
ART/CULTURE
GEAR

TRIBORO | NEW YORK, NY, USA
David Heasty, Stefanie Weigler

Originally from Dallas, David fled to New York and worked at Design Machine. Originally from Dusseldorf, Stephanie traveled to New York and settled at Design Machine also. Today the pair are, respectively, founder and art director of Triboro, their own much acclaimed design firm started in 2003 and based in the heart of Brooklyn.

www.heasty.com

1 Poster | Bigshot magazine, 2005
2 Magazine layouts | Bigshot magazine, 2004-05
Photos by Bert Spangemacher, Michael Sugrue and Kareem Black
3 Logo and spreads | Artworld Digest, 2007
Seed logo photo by Rachel Sussman
4 Logos | Alfred A. Knopf, 2007
5 Bussines Card | Self-initiated, 2007
6 Magazine spread | Vertical Inc. Publishing, 2007
7 Verrazano typeface | Bigshot Magazine, 2004

Contents / Issue 6

Cover photo and this page by Bert Spangemacher

Rebirth of Cool

Matthew Dear grooms techno's next micro-wave. Words Justin Paul photography Michael Sugrue

Who would've thought that a frat party would be responsible for discovering one of the country's best underground labels on the map? It's true. That's where Ghostly International's Sam Valenti IV, then a first-week freshman sampling University of Michigan's Welcome Week, walked in on Matthew Dear rockin' an empty basement with an old synthesizer, a sequencer and a sampler.

"I wanted to show a different aspect of what minimal techno can do."

"That was the only one of those parties Sam went to," Dear recalls while en route from his Detroit apartment to his Tuesday night residence at Ann Arbor's Goodnight Gracie. "Nobody was into it. Sam was one of 10 people that stopped down there that night." Impressed, Valenti introduced himself and recommended the two meet for lunch. A few months later, Valenti's GI label and Dear turned heads at the DEMF with their disco-house flavor debut, "Hands Up for Detroit."

Dear, 24, has come a long way in the past five years. Working under the False alias on Richie Hawtin's Plus 8 label and the Jabberjaw moniker for German tastemakers Perlon, his two click-heavy EPs (*EP1* and *EP2*) released in early 2003 on Ghostly, continue to haunt the inner canals of minimal techno and micro-house heads. "I'm an idol of German minimal music," says Dear. "Right now, I think a lot of the [American] guys are taking it to a different area. There's a kind of little rebirth going on."

Leave Luck to Heaven, the first full-length under Dear's own name, takes his style one step further. Dripping with an understated glide and shuffling rhythms that chew deeper into you than a pitbull on an ankle, the album pockets 4/4 thumps inside lush melodies, keyboards and vocal edits that often share more with pop emotion than machinated visions. "I wanted to show a different aspect of what minimal techno can do," he explains of the album's aim for "songs you can listen to at home or in the car or on the dancefloor."

Thus, "Reason and Responsibility" stakes its hushed addiction on a bassline pacing the cusp of invisibility, while laptop slips, time-stretched murmurs and a shimmering synth run interference upfront. Elsewhere, Dear edges away from stack tracks and toward song structure. "*When will you come clean/with all the lies you're telling me*," begin the lyrics of "Just Us Now" as layers of warm chord rushes and pops draw that eyelid-drooping surrender typically reserved for soft-dry hoodies at dawn.

In stark contrast to his recent album, Dear's next project is bangin', "post nuclear-war techno" where he introduces his latest code-name: Audion. "It's real rugged and jagged—dirty drums and early programming," he says. A polar opposite to *LLTH*, the alias illustrates his take on the genre. Quirky, microtic, heavy or hard, Dear hears a vastness of sound waiting exploration.

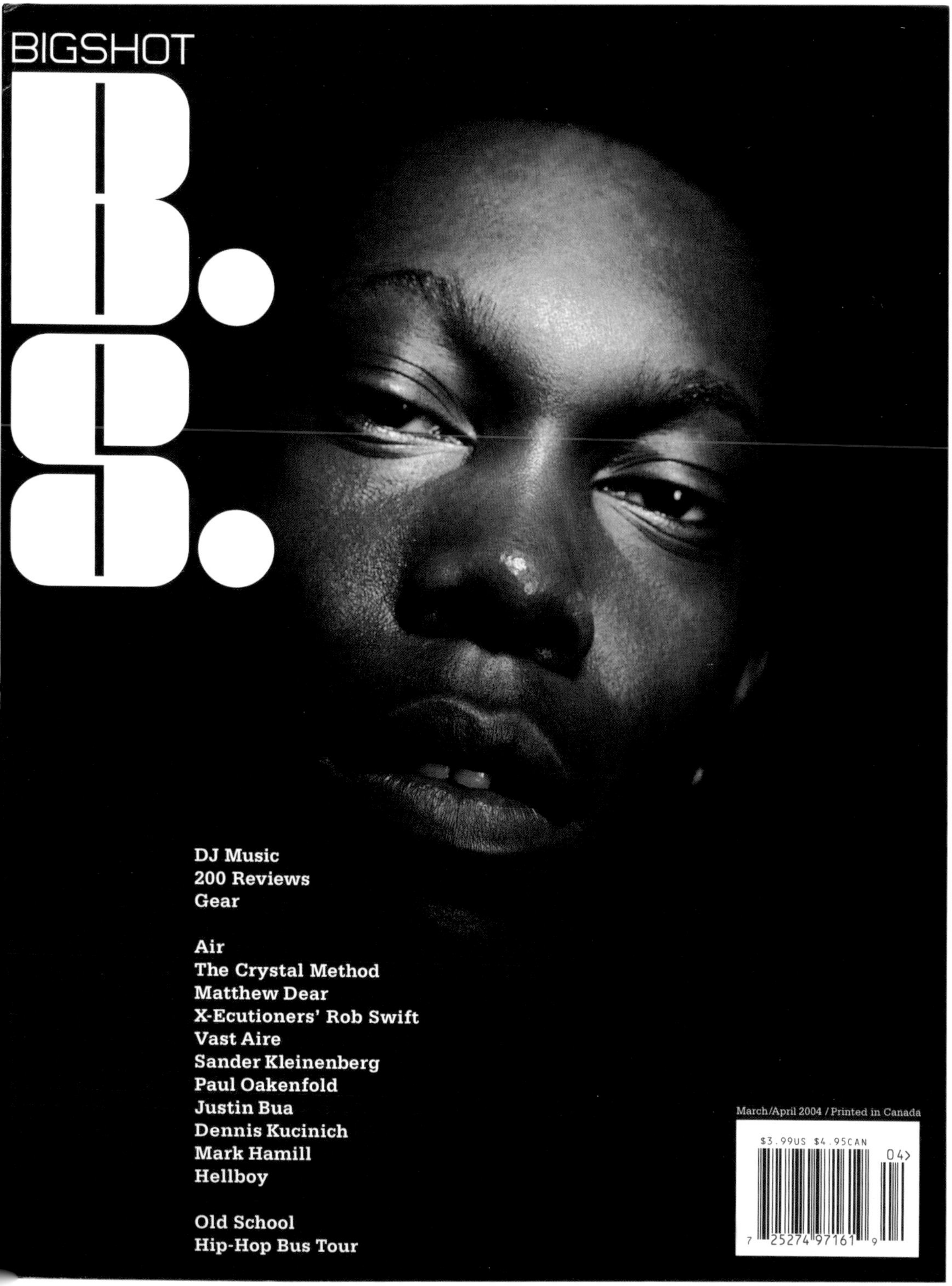
BIGSHOT
B.S.
DJ Music
200 Reviews
Gear
Air
The Crystal Method
Matthew Dear
X-Ecutioners' Rob Swift
Vast Aire
Sander Kleinenberg
Paul Oakenfold
Justin Bua
Dennis Kucinich
Mark Hamill
Hellboy
Old School
Hip-Hop Bus Tour
March/April 2004 / Printed in Canada
$3.99US $4.95CAN
04>
7 25274 97161 9

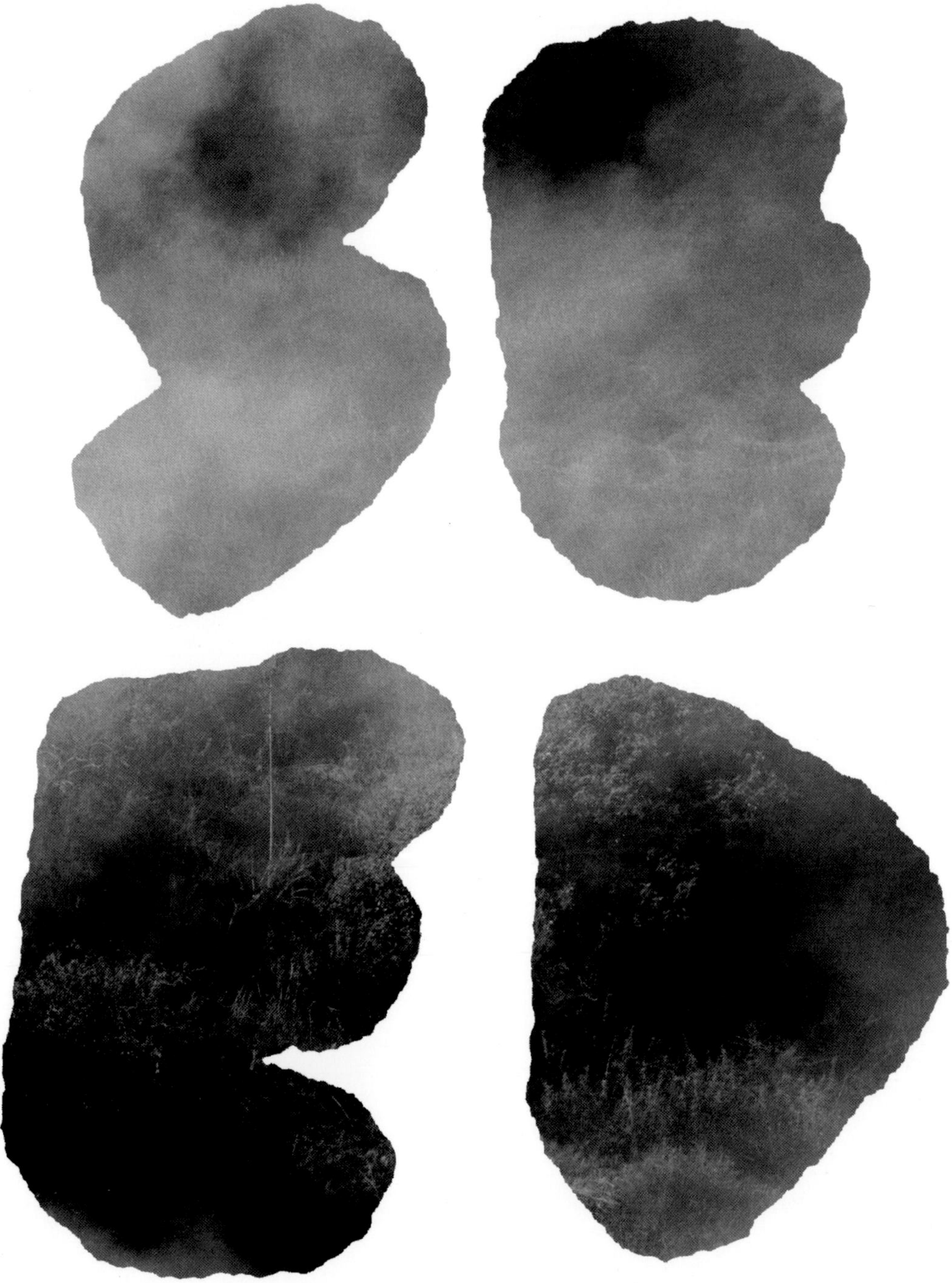

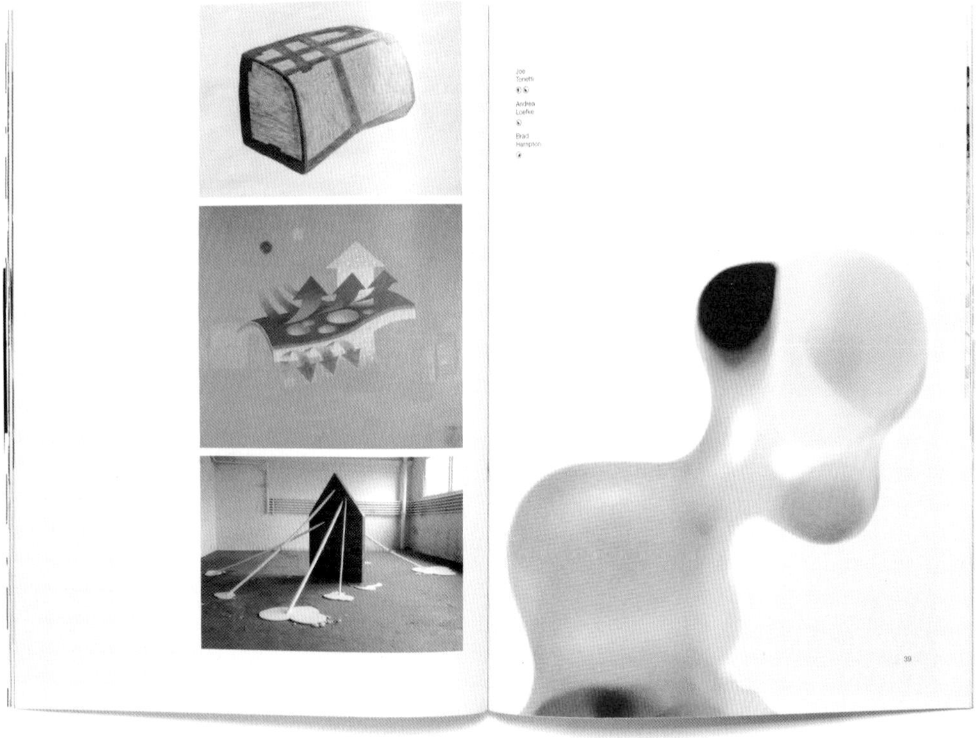

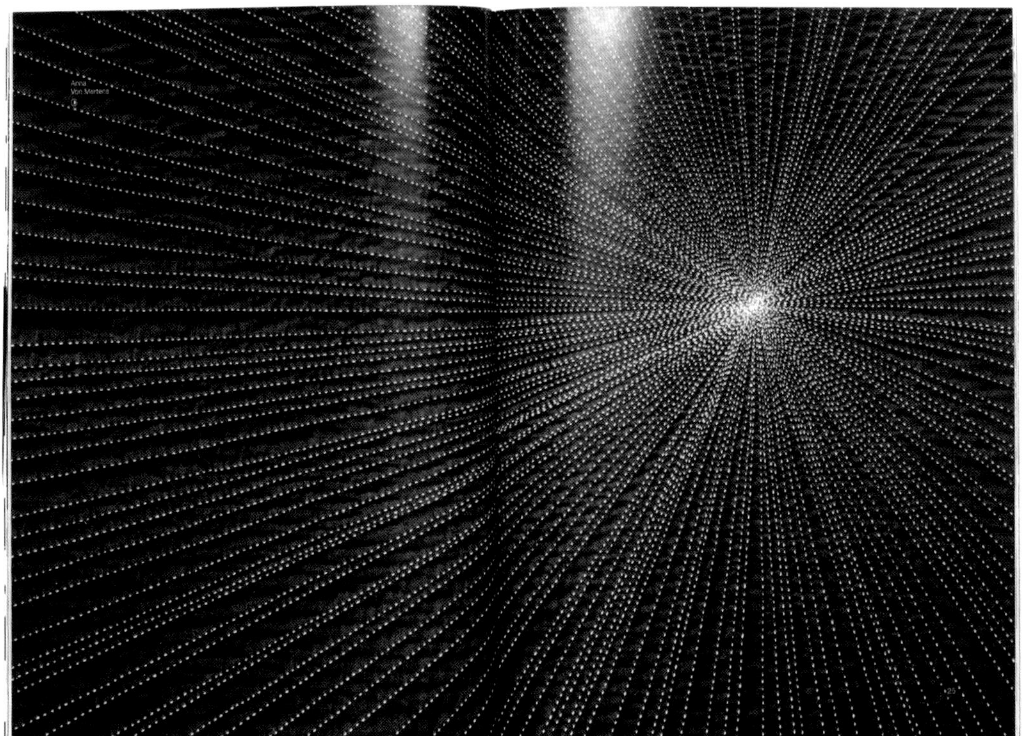

3

KNOPF

KNOPF

STEFANIE WEIGLER CO
119 NASSAU AVENUE 4
BROOKLYN, NY, 11222
PHONE: 646 248 1436
STEFANIEWEIGLER.COM

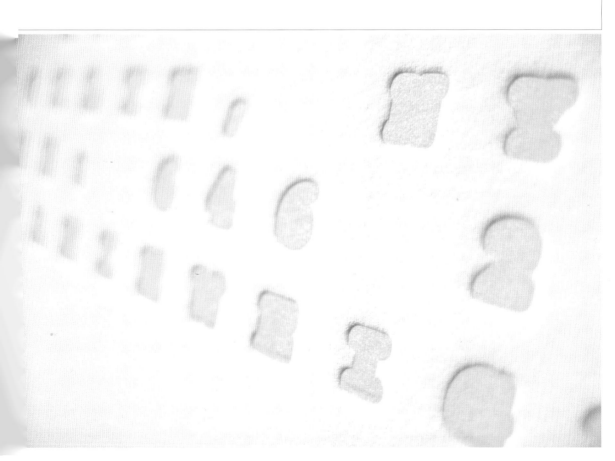

6

bigshot
compilations
albums
singles
gear
personals
7 charts

ELLIOTT
a
pril 30
7pm
CalArts Visiting Designer Lecture
F200
2007
EARLS

VICTOR HU | LOS ANGELES, CA, USA

Victor Hu was born in 1977 in Orange County, California, where he studied Graphic Design at the California Institute of the Arts. He currently resides in Los Angeles, where he works designing books, and generally enjoying computers, bicycles, and snorkeling. Other big favorites include the color blue and tuna sandwiches.

www.victorhu.com

1 Promotional poster | Elliot Earls, 2007
In collaboration with Kristen Coogan
2 Book | Fantality, 2006
3 Promotional poster | Miranda July and Phil Elverum, 2007
In collaboration with Florencio Zavala
4 Magazine | China Net Review, 2006
5 Flyer | Work Study, 2006
6 Promotional poster | Bartleby the Scrivener, 2006
7 Poster | All Around You..., 2006
8 Promotional poster | Mark Allen, 2006

Date Due
JUN 14 1972
JUL 15 1997
APR 23 2004
MAY 11 2006
1000
CALIFORNIA PLACE NAMES
Semiotics of
So-Cal

2

WEDNESDAY, APRIL 11TH 2007
Miranda July &
Phil Elverum
(Mt. Eerie, Microphones)
VISITING ARTIST MYSTERY ACTIVITY
IN THE SCHOOL CAFETERIA
Upcoming in
Thinking Small:
7:30pm-potluck
8ish-mystery activity
Thinking Small

3

Butterfly Lovers: Most Famous Lovers in All of China

ACT I — THE COURTSHIP

Chu Ying-tai (trans. Heroine Platform) was a very beautiful young lady who wanted to go to school and study like boys did. In ancient China, only boys were allowed to do certain things such as joining the Army or going to school. In order to do so, a girl had to disguise herself as a boy and hope that her identity was not revealed. So Chu Ying-tai dressed up herself as a boy and off she went to school in the next city.

On the way to the city, Ying-tai met a boy named Leung Shan-po (Mountain Uncle) who was also going to the same school. The two soon became good friends.

Three years had passed and Shan-po still did not know that his school friend was actually a girl who had a crush on him. One day, she received a letter from her father asking her to come home. Shan-po escorted her all the way, still not knowing that "he" was a girl even though she had given many hints that she had fallen in love madly with him. When they departed, Ying-tai told him that she had a younger sister and "he" would ask "his" family to arrange a marriage with Shan-po.

ACT II — FORCED MARRIAGE

As Ying-tai returned home to see her parents, she heard some shocking news: her parents had arranged to marry her to the next door neighbour, Mr. Mah Man-choi, the son of a very rich merchant. During feudal times in China, practically all marriages were arranged by the parents, and due to the prevailing Confuciun notion that children must obey their parents unconditionally, she had no choice but to accept the arrangement.

Shan-po arrived at the village and the two lovers met at a local Pagoda. Tragically however, their first date turned out to be their last. The two lovers had to be separated.

Shortly afterwards, Shan-po died of heartbreak and was buried next to the village.

ACT III — REBIRTH AS BUTTERFLIES

Ying-tai's wedding day was far from happy. As the bride and her procession passed by Shan-po's tomb, a roar came from Heaven. A thunderbolt had hit her lover's tomb and cracked it opened. Immediately, Ying-tai jumped into the tomb and killed herself. Then, Heaven roared again, striking the tomb with another thunderbolt. Miraculously, the tomb closed up again to return to its normal shape.

Just then, a pair of butterflies appeared flying among the flower beds—the two lovers had been reborn and would live happily together in their next life. After death, Buddhists typically wish to be reborn in the higher realms as humans or divas. But China's most famous lovers found happiness in being reborn as a pair of butterflies.

The Rice University Transnational China Project

The Transnational China Project seeks to expand the study of the influence of the transnational circulation of people, technologies, commodities, and ideas on contemporary culture in Chinese societies by sponsoring original commentary and analysis, developing curriculum materials, and fostering networks of scholars.

The mission of the Transnational China Project is to develop innovative approaches to the study of contemporary China through the use of advanced technologies and by means of new forms of both personal and inter-institutional collaboration. The central goal of this interdisciplinary effort is to identify, bring together, make accessible, and analyze the multiplicity of views emerging from the complex interplay between the forces of both global and local change. In so doing, this initiative seeks not only to clarify the issues involved in these debates but also to contribute to the debates themselves.

China Net Review
Spring 2007
1
Internet Culture

CalArts
Graphic Design
WORK
STUDY
Lots of fun!
3–5 hrs. / week working on the Graphic Design Program website!
Contact if interested, reliable and have web (HTML) experience!
Louise: lu@lsd-studio.net
Victor: vhu@alum.calarts.edu
GREAT JOB!

Pigeon Press is pleased to Announce:
In a Special new Printing,
Herman Melville's Shocking Tale of Existential Horror!
BARTLEBY
THE SCRIVENER
A STORY OF WALL STREET
Available at
Barnes & Noble

ALL AROUND YOU IS TIME... *and Space*
PSALMS 37:7 BE STILL BEFORE THE LORD AND WAIT PATIENTLY

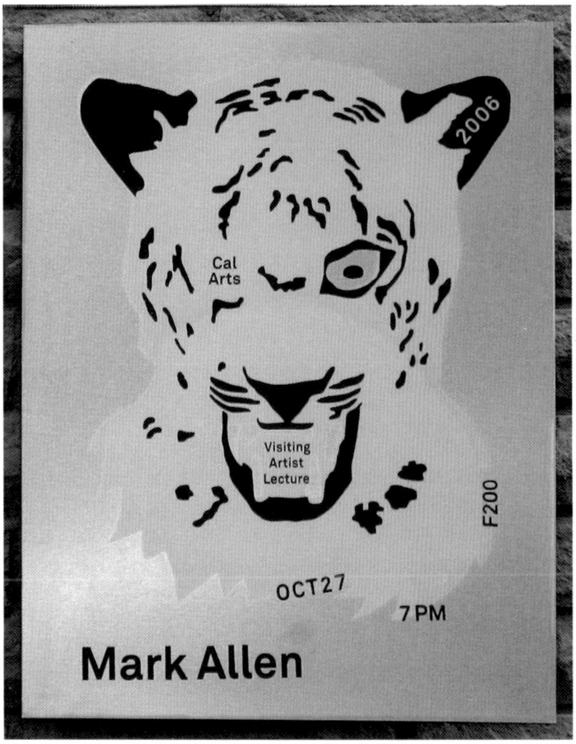
2006
Cal
Arts
Visiting
Artist
Lecture
F200
OCT27
7PM
Mark Allen

2006
Mark Allen
Cal
Arts
VISITING
ARTIST
LECTURE
OCT27
F200
7 PM
roooaarrrr

8

10th Anniversary
Los Angeles Times Festival of Books
UCLA Campus
April 29–30, 2006

1

WAY SHAPE FORM | SAN FRANCISCO, CA, USA
Matthew Boyd, River Jukes-Hudson

Way Shape Form was born when River Jukes-Hudson and Matthew Boyd met at the Art Center College of Design in Pasadena. Coming from California and Ontario respectively, the two share similar backgrounds. They both have artistic families and attended Montessori schools– enthusiastic influences on their free approach to design and creative expression.

www.wayshapeform.info

1 Campaign poster and booklet spreads | Self-initiated, 2005
2 Proof folders | Anderson Printing, 2006
3 Promotional poster | Daniel Rosenberg, 2006
4 Exhibition catalogue | Sonoma County Museum, 2005
5 Literary publication | Art Center College of Design, 2005

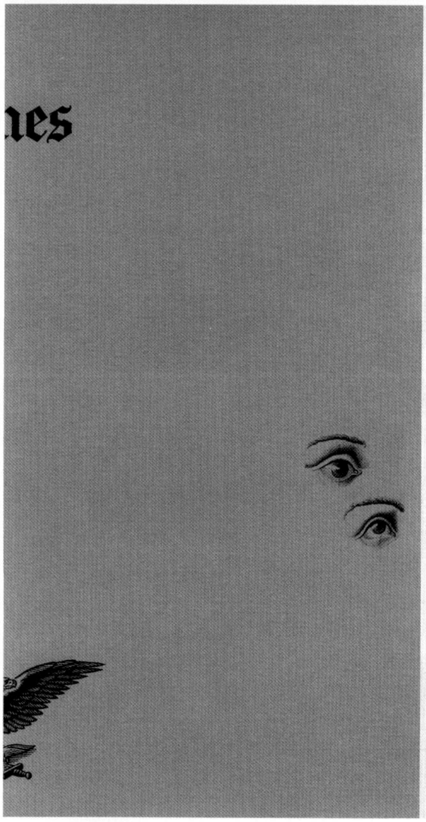

nes

10th Anniversary
Los Angeles Times Festival of Books
UCLA Campus
April 29–30, 2006

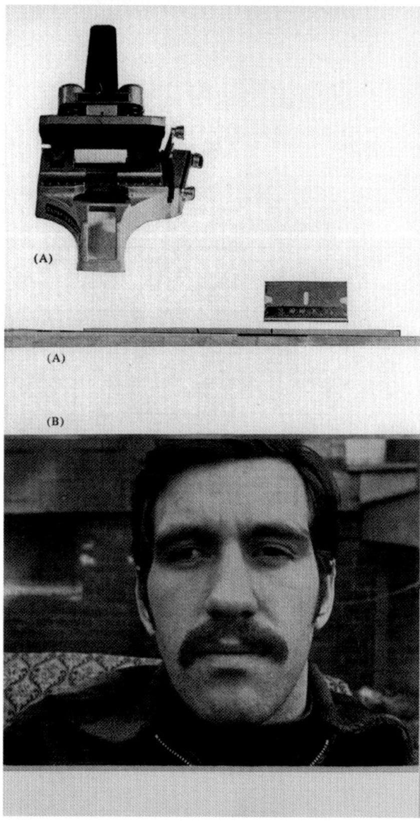

(A)
(A)
(B)

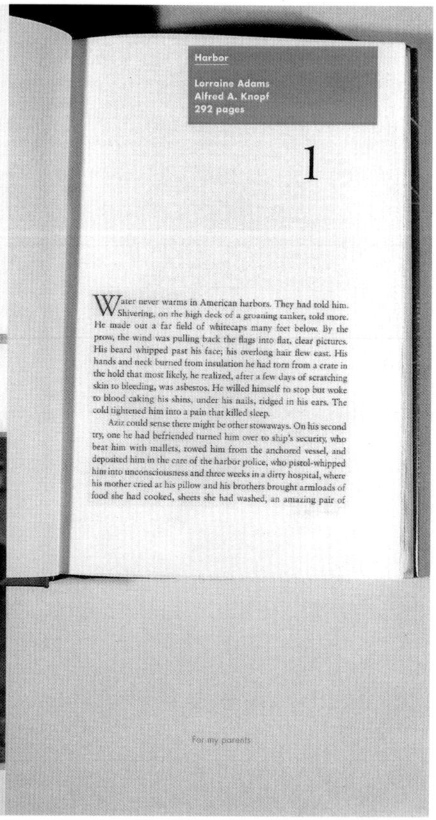

Harbor
Lorraine Adams
Alfred A. Knopf
292 pages
1
Water never warms in American harbors. They had told him. Shivering, on the high deck of a groaning tanker, told more. He made out a far field of whitecaps many feet below. By the prow, the wind was pulling back the flags into flat, clear pictures. His beard whipped past his face; his overlong hair flew east. His hands and neck burned from insulation he had torn from a crate in the hold that most likely, he realized, after a few days of scratching skin to bleeding, was asbestos. He willed himself to stop but woke to blood caking his shins, under his nails, ridged in his ears. The cold tightened him into a pain that killed sleep.
Aziz could sense there might be other stowaways. On his second try, one he had befriended turned him over to ship's security, who beat him with mallets, rowed him from the anchored vessel, and deposited him in the care of the harbor police, who pistol-whipped him into unconsciousness and three weeks in a dirty hospital, where his mother cried at his pillow and his brothers brought armloads of food she had cooked, sheets she had washed, an amazing pair of
For my parents

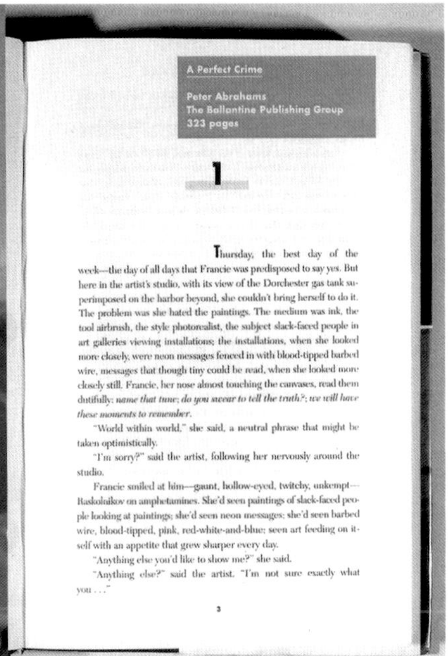

A Perfect Crime

Peter Abrahams
The Ballantine Publishing Group
323 pages

1

Thursday, the best day of the week—the day of all days that Francie was predisposed to say yes. But here in the artist's studio, with its view of the Dorchester gas tank superimposed on the harbor beyond, she couldn't bring herself to do it. The problem was she hated the paintings. The medium was ink, the tool airbrush, the style photorealist, the subject slack-faced people in art galleries viewing installations; the installations, when she looked more closely, were neon messages fenced in with blood-tipped barbed wire, messages that though tiny could be read, when she looked more closely still. Francie, her nose almost touching the canvases, read them dutifully: *name that tune; do you swear to tell the truth?; we will have these moments to remember.*

"World within world," she said, a neutral phrase that might be taken optimistically.

"I'm sorry?" said the artist, following her nervously around the studio.

Francie smiled at him—gaunt, hollow-eyed, twitchy, unkempt—Raskolnikov on amphetamines. She'd seen paintings of slack-faced people looking at paintings; she'd seen neon messages; she'd seen barbed wire, blood-tipped, pink, red-white-and-blue; seen art feeding on itself with an appetite that grew sharper every day.

"Anything else you'd like to show me?" she said.

"Anything else?" said the artist. "I'm not sure exactly what you . . ."

3

To Alan Cohen

2

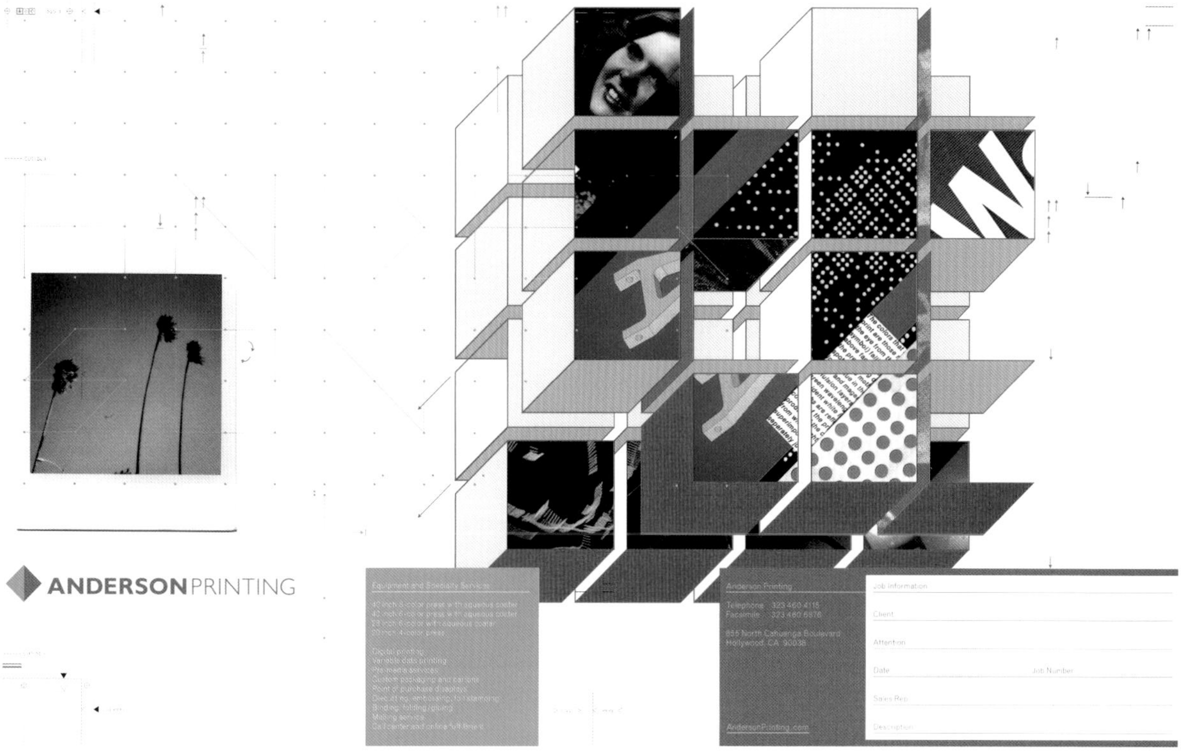

ANDERSONPRINTING
Equipment and Specialty Services
42 inch 8-color press with aqueous coater
40 inch 6-color press with aqueous coater
28 inch 6-color with aqueous coater
20 inch 4-color press
Digital printing
Variable data printing
Pre-media services
Custom packaging and cartons
Point of purchase displays
Diecutting, embossing, foil stamping
Binding, folding, gluing
Mailing service
Call center and online fulfillment
Anderson Printing
Telephone 323 460 4115
Facsimile 323 460 6876
855 North Cahuenga Boulevard
Hollywood, CA 90038
AndersonPrinting.com
Job Information
Client
Attention
Date
Job Number
Sales Rep
Description

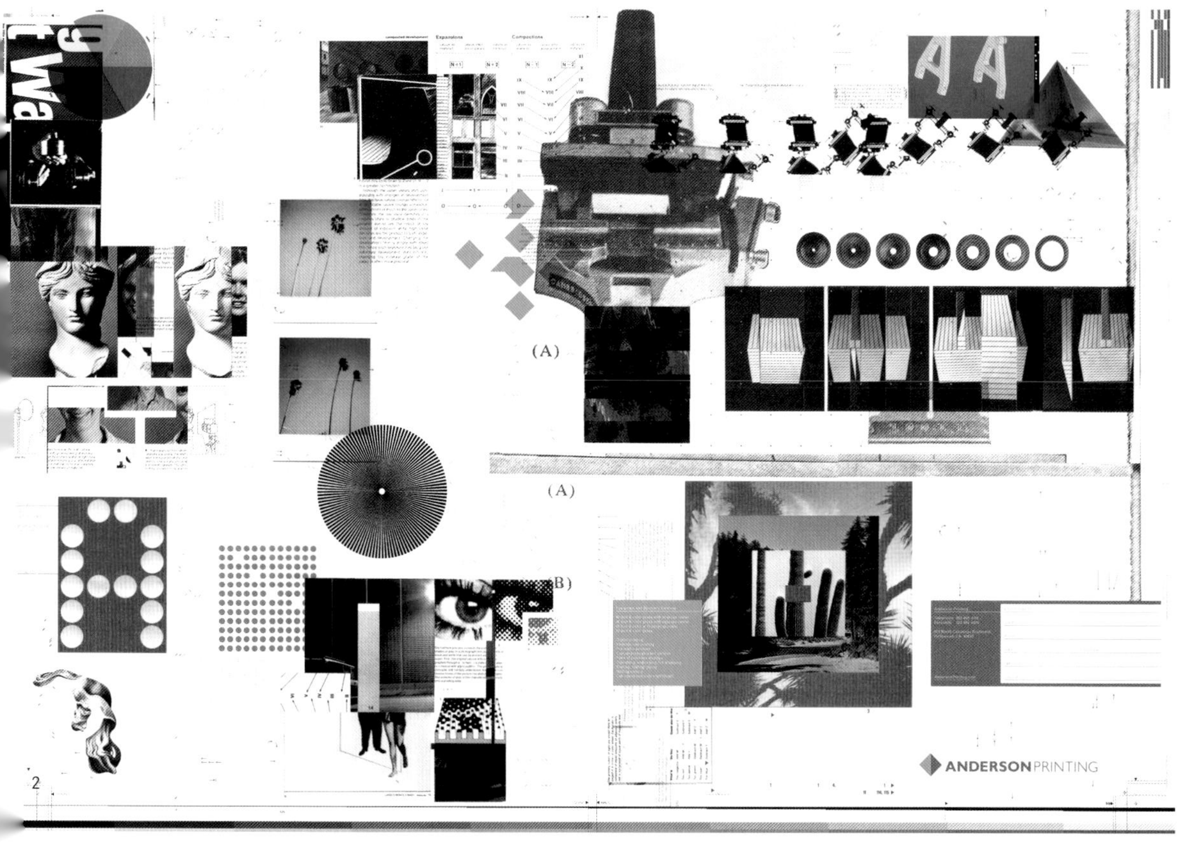

Expansions
Compactions
(A)
(A)
(B)
ANDERSONPRINTING

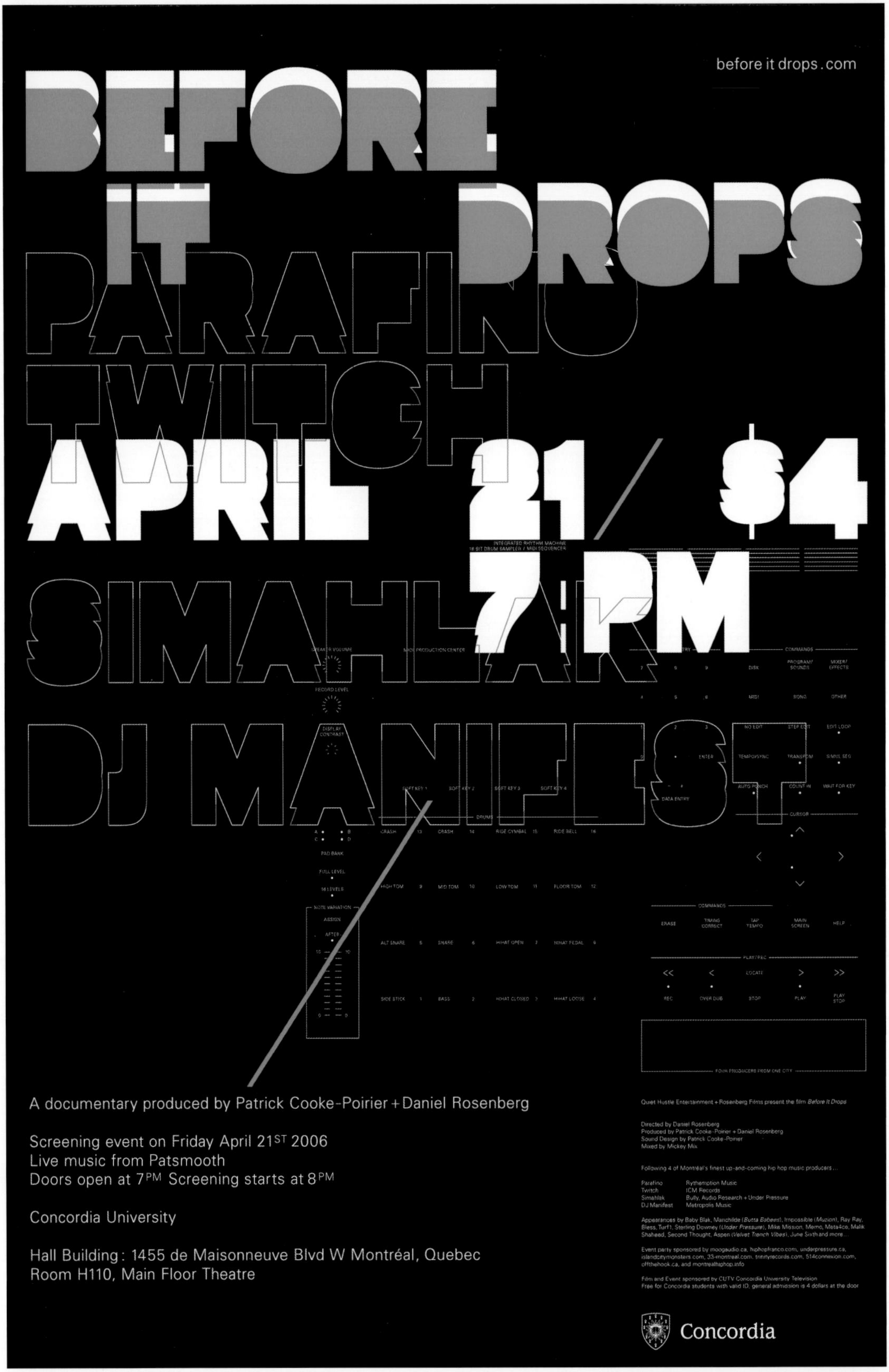
before it drops.com
BEFORE
IT
DROPS
PARAFINO
TWITCH
APRIL 21/ $4
7 PM
SIMAHLAK
DJ MANIFEST
FOUR PRODUCERS FROM ONE CITY
A documentary produced by Patrick Cooke-Poirier + Daniel Rosenberg
Screening event on Friday April 21ST 2006
Live music from Patsmooth
Doors open at 7PM Screening starts at 8PM
Concordia University
Hall Building: 1455 de Maisonneuve Blvd W Montréal, Quebec
Room H110, Main Floor Theatre
Quiet Hustle Entertainment + Rosenberg Films present the film Before It Drops
Directed by Daniel Rosenberg
Produced by Patrick Cooke-Poirier + Daniel Rosenberg
Sound Design by Patrick Cooke-Poirier
Mixed by Mickey Mix
Following 4 of Montréal's finest up-and-coming hip hop music producers…
Parafino Rythemption Music
Twitch ICM Records
Simahlak Bully, Audio Research + Under Pressure
DJ Manifest Metropolis Music
Appearances by Baby Blak, Manchilde (Butta Babees), Impossible (Muzion), Ray Ray, Bless, Turf1, Sterling Downey (Under Pressure), Mike Mission, Memo, Meta4ce, Malik Shaheed, Second Thought, Aspen (Velvet Trench Vibes), June Sixth and more…
Event party sponsored by moogaudio.ca, hiphopfranco.com, underpressure.ca, islandcitymonsters.com, 33-montreal.com, trinityrecords.com, 514connexion.com, offthehook.ca, and montrealhiphop.info
Film and Event sponsored by CUTV Concordia University Television
Free for Concordia students with valid ID, general admission is 4 dollars at the door
Concordia

Working the Wheel, 1993 (L)
48 × 4[illegible] in. [illegible] enamel, collage on paper
collaboration with William Allan and William T. Wiley

Outrigger, 1983–84 (R)
[illegible] in. enamel on steel, cast iron, antlers

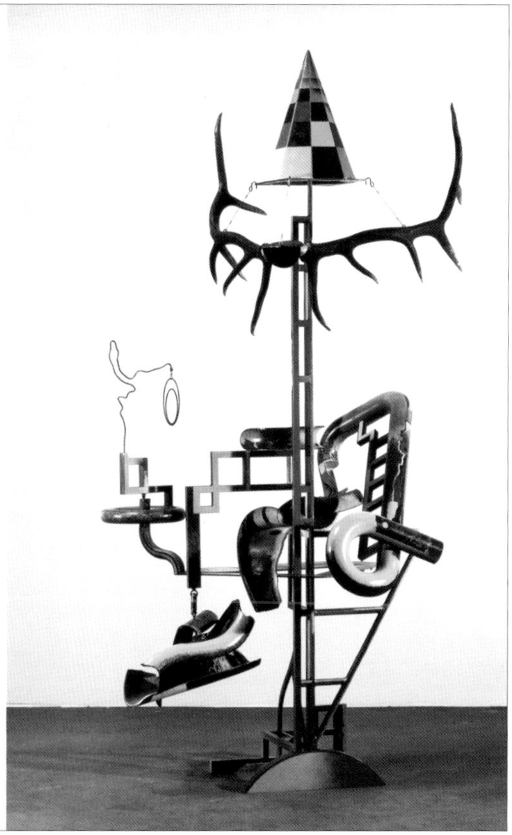

It is a sincere honor for the Sonoma County Museum to present a significant survey of the work of Robert Hudson. The opportunity is especially timely as the museum celebrates its 20th anniversary year, dedicated to connecting the region's rich history with contemporary artistic and cultural currents. *Robert Hudson: The Sonoma County Years, 1977–2005* showcases Hudson's vast oeuvre created in his Cotati studio over the past twenty-eight years.

Robert Hudson is indeed a national and international treasure of the art world, a celebrated artist whose work is collected by major museums and patrons. Has his prolific output been influenced by the landscape and culture of his adopted home of Sonoma County? While no obvious conclusion can be drawn from the work, we can indeed claim him as our own. We delight in Hudson's daft mastery of impossible materials, his use of intense color, his humor and irony, and his empathetic touch – all evident in this rich and fulfilling collection of work.

The Sonoma County Museum thanks Michael Schwager, guest curator, for his singular vision in conceiving this survey – and for his passion, depth, rigor and sensitivity in crafting it. His keen understanding of Hudson's work and life is evident in this catalog's essay. We thank River Jukes-Hudson and Matthew Boyd, exhibition and catalog designers, for their exquisite talent, forthcoming generosity and impeccable grace. We thank lenders to the exhibition and our patrons for their commitment, support and friendship, the Board of Trustees, members of the Sonoma County Museum, and our program staff: Patricia Watts, Eric Stanley, Maureen Cecil and intern, Debra Lehane. We thank Mavis Jukes and the Jukes-Hudson family for input and support. Most of all, we extend our deepest gratitude to Robert Hudson for sharing with us the joyous celebration that is his art.

Ariege Areguel, *Executive Director*

Robert Hudson: The Sonoma County Years, 1977–2005

FISHWRAP V | MMV–MMVI

all I can think about is tadpoles. I can't remember what it was my brother was so worried about and what it was that was inside that box he had delivered, which was indeed now missing; in fact, it is the only thing missing. This thought alone instantly pisses me off. Fuck, my brother sends me a package and it turns out to be the only thing worth hitting me in the head with a fucking baseball bat for. Damn, they didn't even take my Otis Redding collection.

I have my brother on the phone within five. He has me off the phone and a plane ticket in his hand within sixty. In three hundred and sixty I rip open a third packet of Alka Seltzer as I watch him pace back and forth with the cell phone jammed into his ear. He surfaces, grabs a Mickey's out of the fridge from the twelve pack he brought (he never likes my beer), pops it back and burps, "Am I ever fucked!"

He ignores my question, "What was in it?" for another sixty so it becomes an easy-ass eight hours before my brother ever gets around to telling me what it was that he had mailed to me. Yet, I still can't figure out its significance and why in the hell anyone would ever bother stealing it--much less, fuck them,--hit me in the side of the head with a baseball bat. I didn't even own a baseball bat, so that meant they had to premeditate that crap and bring one with them.

It was bonsai Linden tree sealed in a terrarium. A nest for a magic caterpillar that snores in its sleep.

I choke on a stench of sulfur as I light a match.

What?

It is a rare tree. Extinct, actually, except for two. One of which I possessed.

Until you mailed it to me. Why?

To keep it safe.

Of course.

He fails to get my humor. Tosses the Mickey's bottle in the sink. It shatters. He rips open another bottle and burps.

Got any Xanax?

SOMNAMBULISM
POSTURING
HOLLYWOOD RAZZLE-DAZZLE
the RHYTHYM METHOD
LOGICAL POSITIVISM
OBLIQUE STRATEGIES
PRODUCT
MAGICAL REALISM
COGNITIVE DISSONANCE
le NOUVEAU RICHE
PATHOS
VORTICISM
CYBERNETICS
CRITICAL METHOD
OPTICS
the JERSEY
LEISURE
the NOT

WYETH HANSEN | NEW YORK, NY, USA

Born in the suburbs of central California and raised on psychedelic poster art and early Talking Heads albums, Wyeth relocated to the East Coast to attend college and start work as a freelancer. You may also spot him art directing experimental documentaries for television, designing typefaces or developing Casual Aesthetics, his creative manifesto.

www.wyethhansen.com

1 Tshirt graphic | 2K By Gingham, 2004
2 Promotional poster and conference materials | MOVE Conference and American Institute of Graphic Arts, 2006
In collaboration with Ryan Dunn
3 Student yearbook | Rhode Island School of Design, 2003
In collaboration with Ryan Waller, Joe Marianek, Lily Williams and Adriana Deleo-Stubbe
4 Silkscreened graphics | Unbearable Brightness of Neon show at the Selective Hearing Gallery, 2004
5 Graphics | True Believers exhibition at the Riviera Gallery, 2007
6 Silkscreen poster and flash card set| Free Library exhibition, 2005
7 Magazine cover | Commissioned by Kimberly Lloyd for CMYK magazine festival, 2005

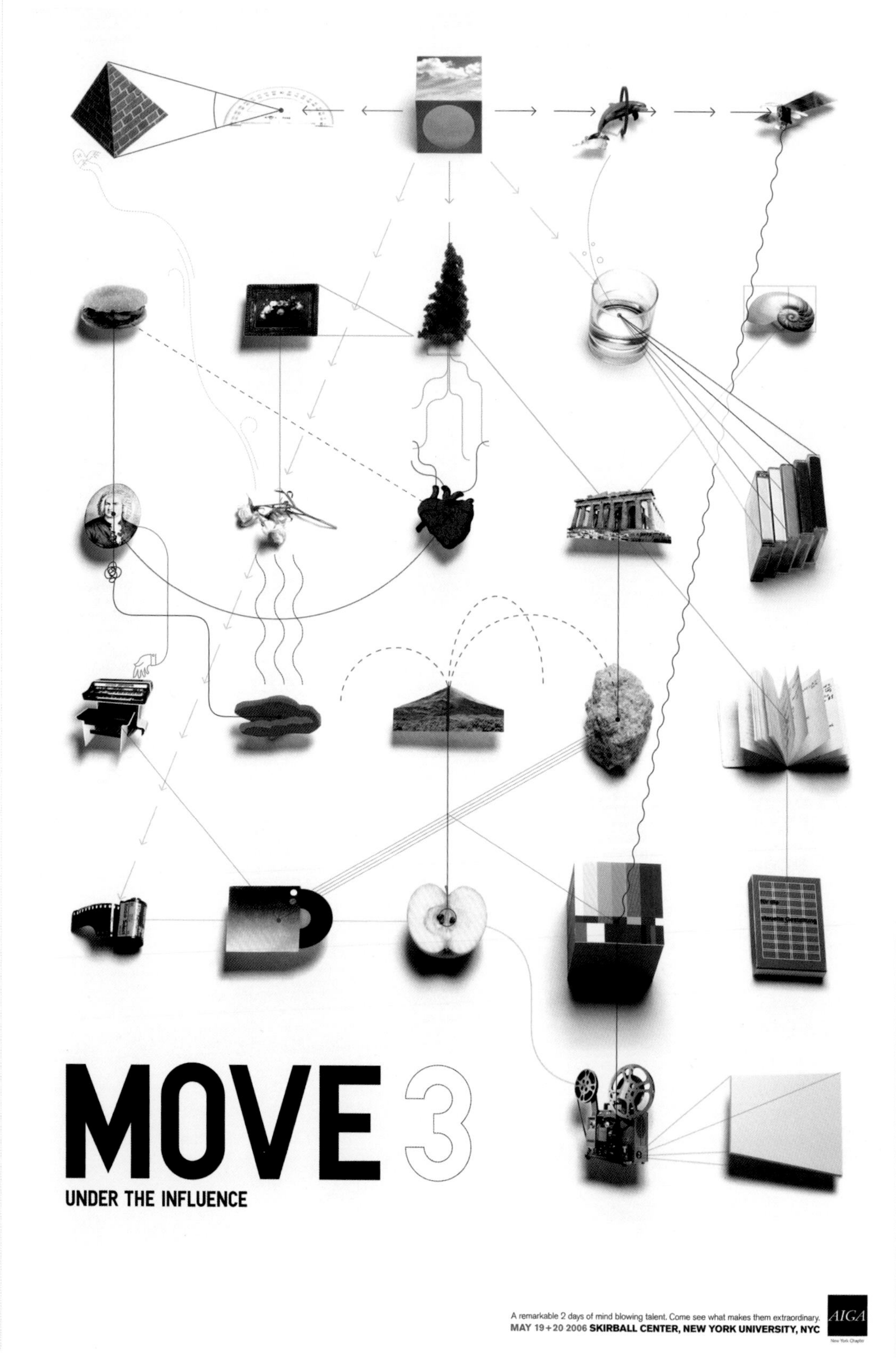
MOVE 3
UNDER THE INFLUENCE
A remarkable 2 days of mind blowing talent. Come see what makes them extraordinary.
MAY 19+20 2006 SKIRBALL CENTER, NEW YORK UNIVERSITY, NYC
AIGA
New York Chapter

2

AIGA

A conference that will explode the definition of motion graphics and the boundaries of storytelling.

APRIL 29 + 30 2005 SKIRBALL CENTER, NEW YORK UNIVERSITY, NYC

2003
PARADISE
YOU GOT IT!
UP HIGH!
kisses
CZECH
YOU'RE PRETTY WHEN I'M DRUNK

3

hot STUFF
NEVER AGAIN
BITCH
PICASSO IS MY FAVORITE
Champ
WHAT A DRAG
COOL
HOW HIGH
YOU GOT IT!
SINGING LESSONS
KATHERINE DIKA

5

Residence of the Soul

Primal Fears

The Humanzee

Phantom Limbs

Telepathy

Ether

Ancient Astronauts

Cone of Silence

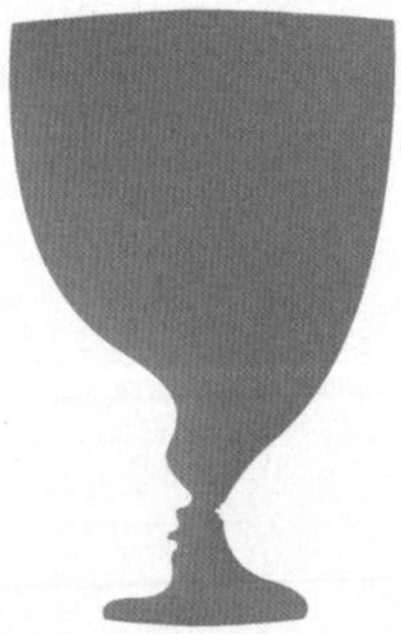
Divine Symmetry

Messages from Beyond

Unicorns of the Deep

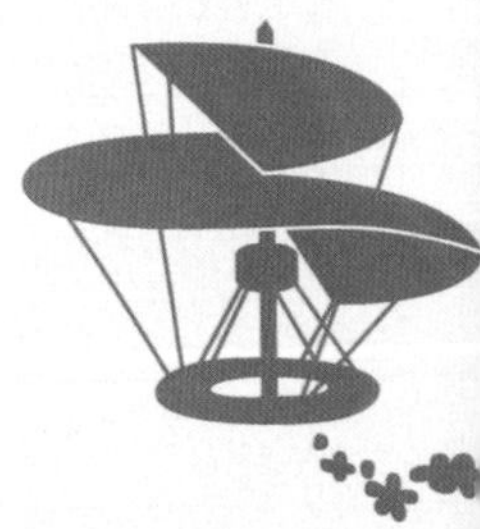
UFOs

Secrets

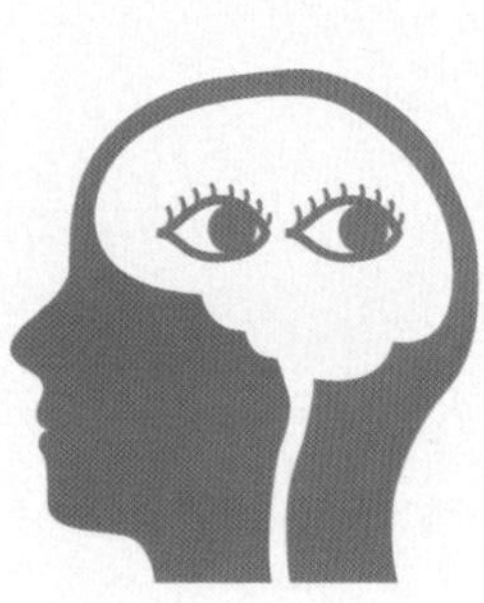
Extrasensory Perception

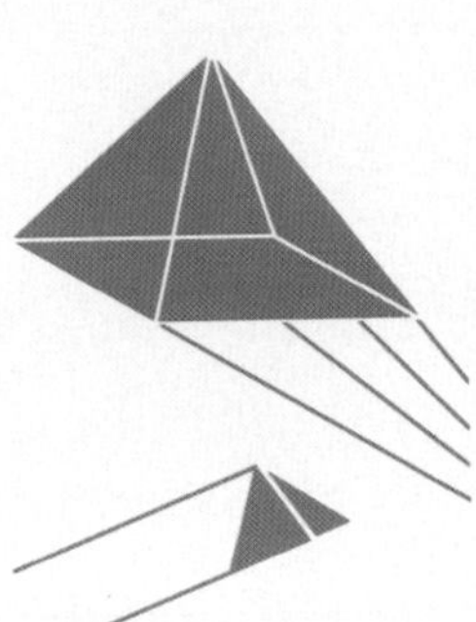
Flying Pyramids

Wormholes

PLOP

for finicky fellows

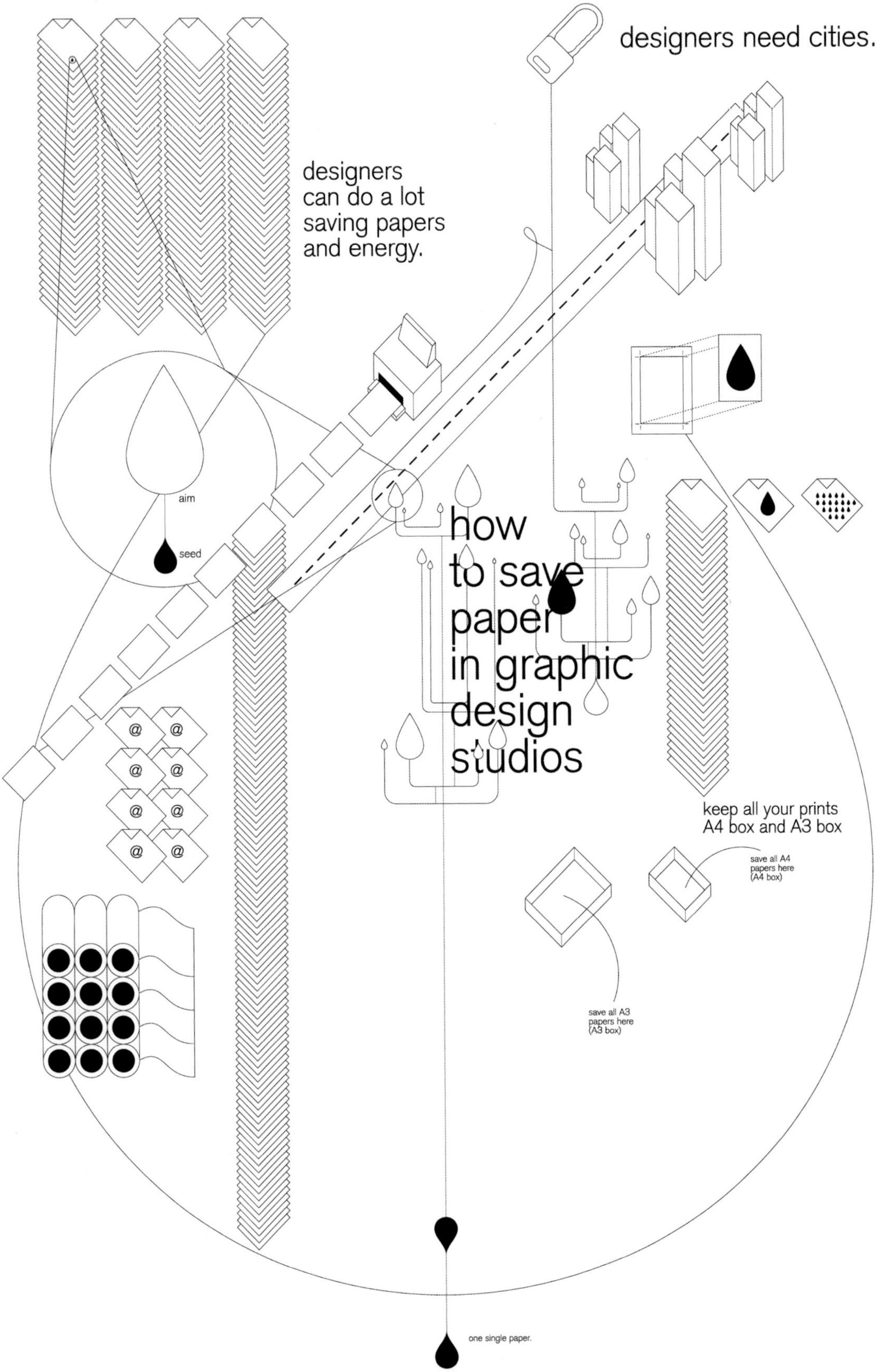
designers need cities.
designers can do a lot saving papers and energy.
aim
seed
how to save paper in graphic design studios
keep all your prints A4 box and A3 box
save all A4 papers here (A4 box)
save all A3 papers here (A3 box)
one single paper.

YOMAR AUGUSTO | RIO DE JANEIRO, BRAZIL

Hailing from Brazil, Yomar Augusto is as passionate about typographic exploration and calligraphy as he is about graphic design. The unusual and highly expressive ways in which he combines these elements have earned him international clients and artistic collaborations featuring calligraphy and painting at Nankuza Underground gallery in Tokyo.

www.yomaraugusto.com

1 Poster | Self-published, 2007
2 Illustrations | Redley, 2005
Art direction by Edu Campos
3 Spreads | Oi! magazine, 2005
4 Portfolio | Self-initiated, 2004
Bookbinding by Rosa Guimarães
5 Illustrations | Nike, 2005

2

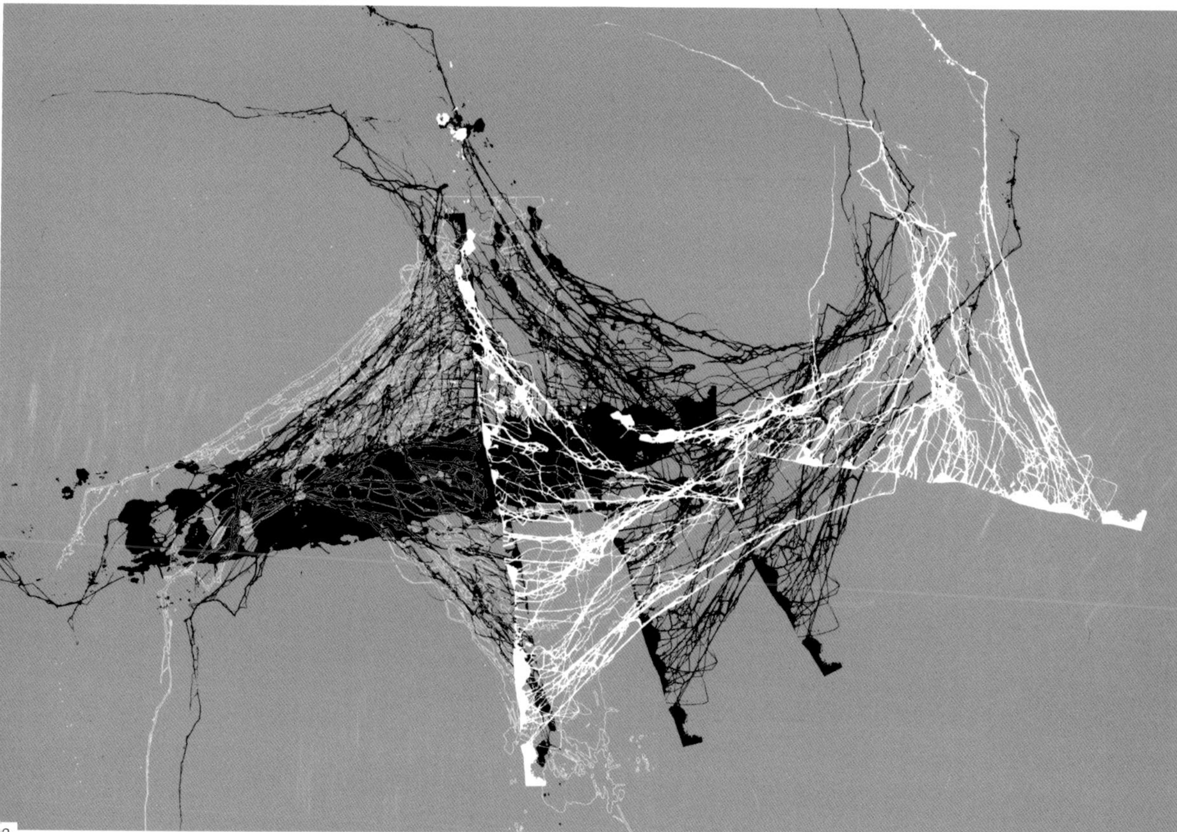

2

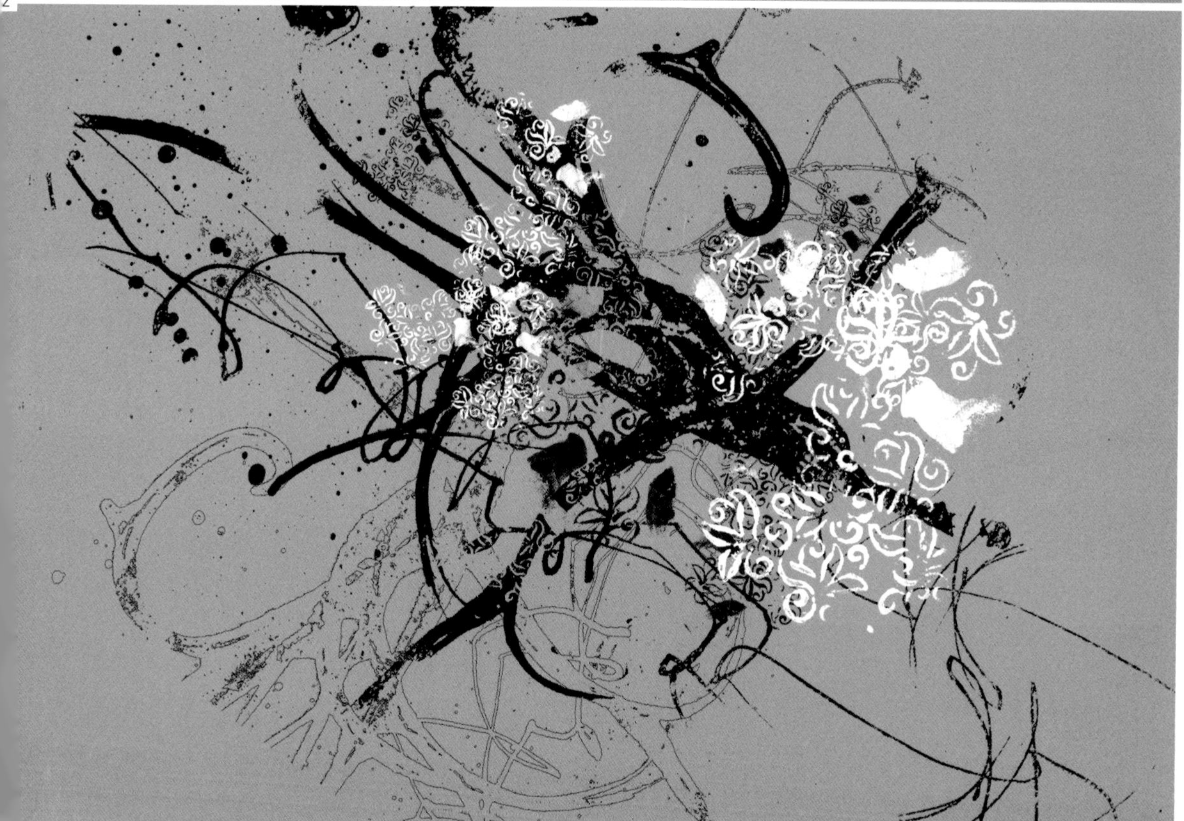

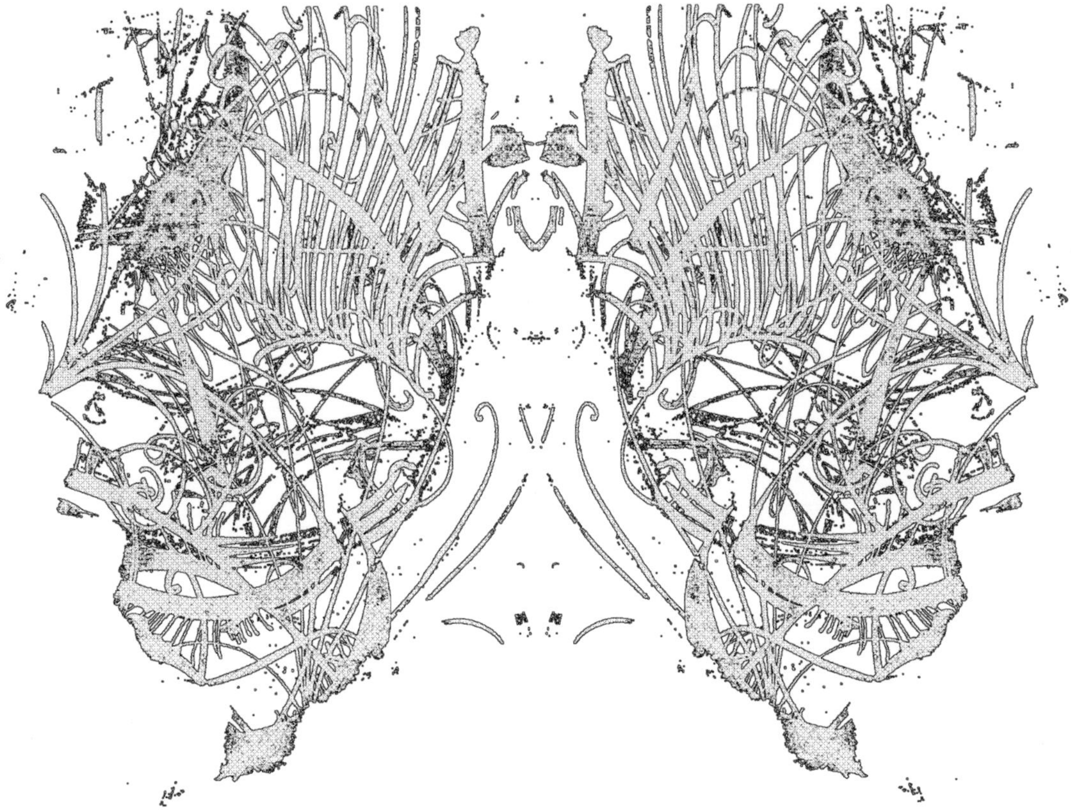

3

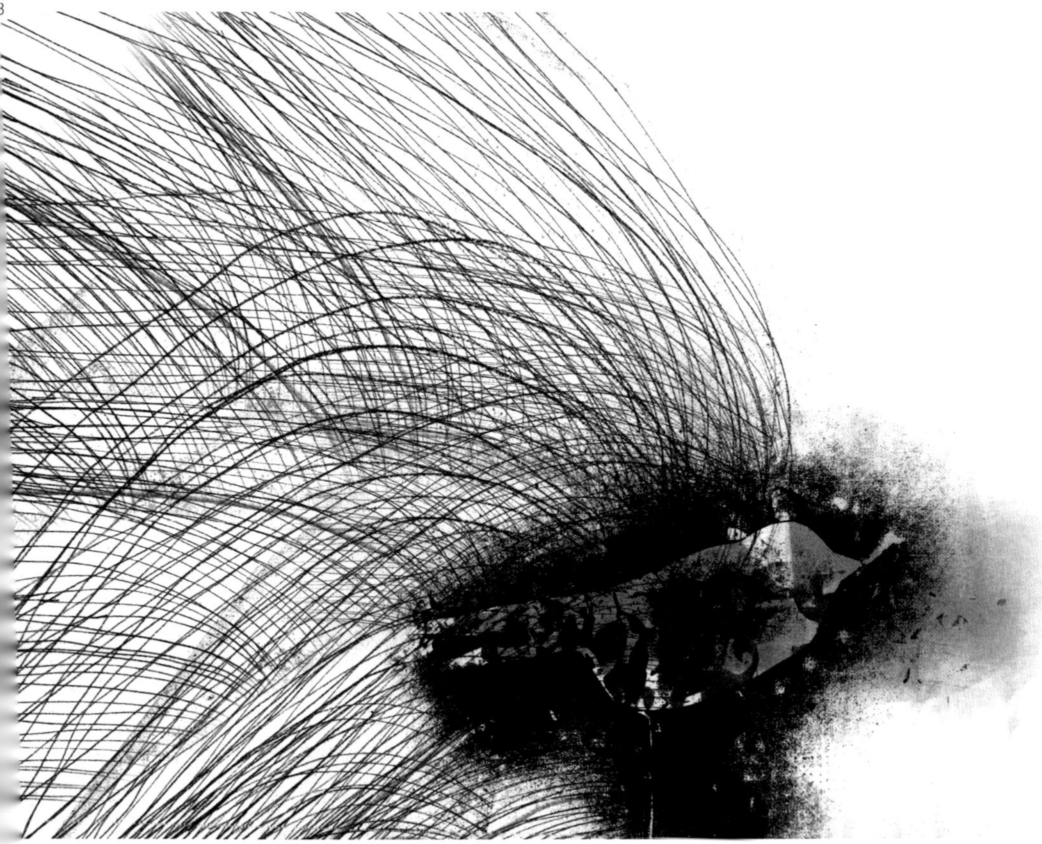

gentes

4

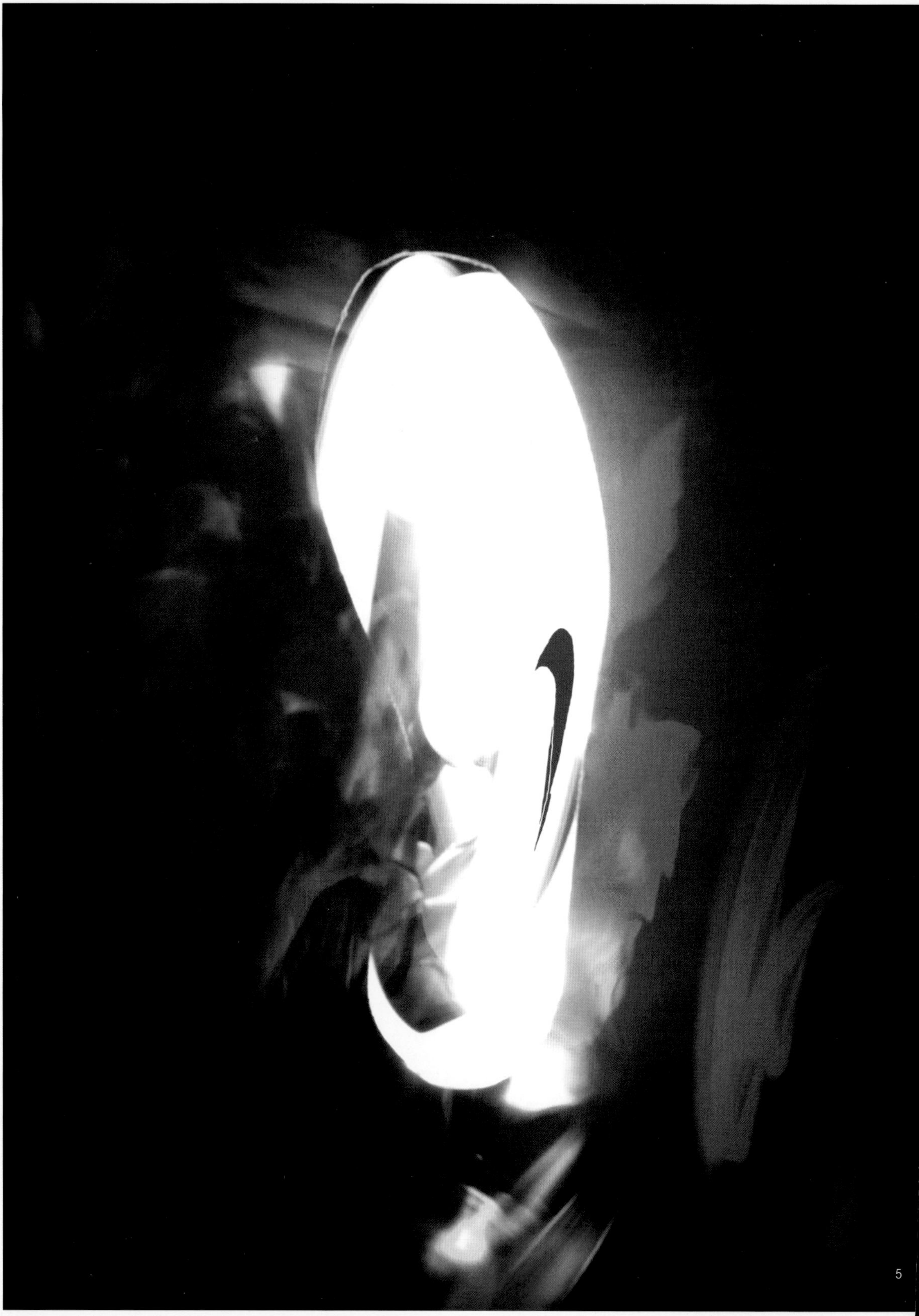

9.00 kr. pr zone
Gyldighed
1 zone
62743
1 zone
62742

INDEX

published and distributed worldwide by
daab gmbh
friesenstr. 50
d-50670 köln

p + 49-221-913 927 0
f + 49-221-913 927 20

mail@daab-online.com
www.daab-online.com

publisher ralf daab

creative director feyyaz

editorial project by maomao publications

editor and text claire dalquié

layout gemma gabarron vicente

credits
cover front mopa
cover back socity
introduction page 7 triboro, 9 joshua distler, 11 mopa
french translation marion westerhoff
italian translation marco zincone/buysschaert-malerba
german translation susanne engler
spanish translation cymbeline núñez

printed in italy
www.zanardi.it

isbn 978-3-86654-016-3

ASHGATE
RESEARCH
COMPANION

THE ASHGATE RESEARCH COMPANION TO MEDIA GEOGRAPHY

ASHGATE
RESEARCH
COMPANION

The *Ashgate Research Companions* are designed to offer scholars and graduate students a comprehensive and authoritative state-of-the-art review of current research in a particular area. The companions' editors bring together a team of respected and experienced experts to write chapters on the key issues in their speciality, providing a comprehensive reference to the field.

The Ashgate Research Companion to Media Geography

Edited by

PAUL C. ADAMS

University of Texas at Austin, USA

JIM CRAINE

California State University, Northridge, USA

JASON DITTMER

University College London, UK

ASHGATE

Published by
Ashgate Publishing Limited
Wey Court East
Union Road
Farnham
Surrey, GU9 7PT
England

Ashgate Publishing Company
110 Cherry Street
Suite 3-1
Burlington, VT 05401-3818
USA

www.ashgate.com

British Library Cataloguing in Publication Data
A catalogue record for this book is available from the British Library

The Library of Congress has cataloged the printed edition as follows:
Adams, Paul C.
The Ashgate research companion to media geography / edited by Paul C.Adams, Jim Craine and Jason Dittmer.
pages cm
Includes bibliographical references and index.
ISBN 978-1-4094-4401-5 (hardback: alk. paper) -- ISBN 978-1-4094-4402-2 (ebook) -- ISBN 978-1-4724-0608-8 (epub) 1. Communication and geography. I. Craine, Jim. II. Dittmer, Jason. III. Title. IV. Title: Research companion to media geography.

P96.G47A327 2014
302.2309--dc23

2014010314

ISBN 9781409444015 (hbk)
ISBN 9781409444022 (ebk – PDF)
ISBN 9781472406088 (ebk – ePUB)

MIX
Paper from responsible sources
FSC www.fsc.org FSC® C013985

Printed in the United Kingdom by Henry Ling Limited,
at the Dorset Press, Dorchester, DT1 1HD

ASHGATE **RESEARCH** COMPANION

Contents

List of Figures and Tables

Figures

Tables

Notes on Contributors

Paul C. Adams is Associate Professor of Geography at the University of Texas at Austin. His research addresses place images in the media, the historical geography of communication technologies, mediated experience and virtuality, and the incorporation of communication technologies into particular places. His previous books include *Geographies of Media and Communication* (2009), *Atlantic Reverberations* (2007), *The Boundless Self* (2005), and *Textures of Place* (with Steven Hoelscher and Karen E. Till, 2001). He is the founder of the Communication Geography Specialty Group of the Association of American Geographers.

Stuart C. Aitken is Professor of Geography at San Diego State University and the Director of the Center for Interdisciplinary Studies of Young People and Space (ISYS). He has also worked for the United Nations on issues of children's rights, migration, and dislocation. His research interests include film and media, critical social theory, qualitative methods, children, families, and communities. He has written five books including *The Awkward Spaces of Fathering* (2009) and *Geographies of Young People* (2001) and has collaborated on five others including *The Fight to Stay Put* (2013), *Young People, Border Spaces and Revolutionary Imaginations* (2011), *Qualitative Geography* (2010), *Global Childhoods* (2008), and *Place, Space, Situation and Spectacle: A Geography of Film* (1994). He has published more than 200 articles in academic journals.

James Ash is a lecturer in Media and Cultural Studies at Newcastle University. He received his PhD in Human Geography at the University of Bristol in 2009. His thesis investigated practices of videogame design and use. His current research is concerned with developing post-phenomenological accounts of body–technology relations. He has published work on videogames and technology in a variety of journals including *Transactions of the Institute of British Geographers, Theory Culture and Society, Body & Society, Environment and Planning D: Society and Space* and *Environment and Planning A*. More information about his research is available at his Web site: www.jamesash.co.uk/.

Michael Bull is Professor of Sound Studies at the University of Sussex. He has published widely in the field of Sound Studies. His books include *Sounding Out the City: Personal Stereos and the Management of Everyday Life* (2000) and *Sound Moves: iPod Culture and Urban Experience* (2007). He coedited *The Auditory Culture Reader* with Les Back (2003) and recently published a four-volume edited work on sound studies for Routledge (2013). He is a founding member of the European Sound Studies Association, a core member of the European Think Tank "Future Trends Forum," and the editor and cofounder of the Journal Senses and Society (Bloomsbury).

Brett Christophers is Associate Professor of Geography in the Institute for Housing and Urban Research at Uppsala University in Sweden. His research ranges broadly across economic and urban geography, with particular interests in the media and cultural industries, money and finance, and urban political economy. He is the author of three books: *Positioning the Missionary* (1998), *Envisioning Media Power* (2009), and *Banking Across Boundaries* (2013).

Jim Craine is Associate Professor of Geography at California State University, Northridge. He specializes in the geography of media and also works applying geovisualization theory to digital and analog cartography. He is a coeditor of *Aether: The Journal of Media Geography* (www.aetherjournal.org).

Julie Cupples lectures in Human Geography at the University of Edinburgh. Her work is positioned at the intersection of cultural geography, development studies, and media studies and has appeared in the *Annals of the Association of American Geographers, Transactions of the Institute of British Geographers, Antipode, Feminist Media Studies,* and *Television and New Media.* She is currently investigating the geographic dimensions of media convergence and the relationship between convergent media production and consumption and cultural citizenship through a focus on geopolitically inflected entertainment television and indigenous media.

Giorgio Hadi Curti is Adjunct Professor and Research Associate in the San Diego State University Department of Geography. Working at the intersections of society, culture, and media through post-structuralist sensibilities, he brings a spatialized and micropolitical perspective to discussions of urban transformation and change, the politics of place, and affect, emotion, and memory. His recent publications include an edited collection with Jim Craine and Stuart C. Aitken titled *The Fight to Stay Put: Social Lessons through Media Imaginings of Urban Transformation and Change* (2013). He currently holds the position of Ethnography Project Director and works as an ethnographer and cultural geography at HDR, Inc., where he is putting to practical use his research and interests in emotional and affectual geographies and memory, identity, and the politics of place.

Christina E. Dando is Associate Professor of Geography at the University of Nebraska Omaha. Her work explores the intersections of landscape, media, and gender and has appeared in *Acme: An International E-Journal for Critical Geographies, Aether: The Journal of Media Geography, Journal of Cultural Geography, and Cartographica, Gender, Place, and Culture.* Her current project examines Progressive Era women's use of geography, cartography, and media to improve their communities on local and national levels. She is an editorial board member for *Aether: The Journal of Media Geography.*

Ronald A. Davidson is Associate Professor of Geography at California State University, Northridge. His research focuses on humanistic geography, public space, and urban landscapes in the United States and Japan.

Jason Dittmer is Reader in Human Geography at University College London. His recent books include *Comic Book Geographies* (2014), *Captain America and the Nationalist Superhero: Metaphors, Narratives, and Geopolitics* (2013), and *Popular Culture, Geopolitics, and Identity* (2010). His current research considers the role of materiality and affect in geopolitical assemblages.

Deborah Dixon is Professor of Geography at the University of Glasgow. Her research addresses monstrous geographies, as manifest in feminist theory, art/science, critical geopolitics, topologies of touch, and the viralities of cinema. Her recent work has been published in *Science, Nature, Transactions of the Institute of British Geographers, Progress in Physical Geography, Dialogues in Human Geography, Geoforum, Cultural Geographies,* and so on. She is Editor of *Environment and Planning A.*

John C. Finn is a lecturer in Geography in the Department of Sociology, Social Work and Anthropology at Christopher Newport University. His research focuses on racialized urban landscapes, music, and space, and food and food culture in Cuba. He has conducted extensive fieldwork in Brazil and Cuba.

Colin Gardner is Professor of Critical Theory and Integrative Studies at the University of California, Santa Barbara, where he teaches in the departments of Art, Film and Media Studies, Comparative Literature, and the History of Art and Architecture. Working specifically on the intersection of art, film-philosophy, and Deleuze studies, his research focuses on issues of time, space, and memory. He is the author of *Joseph Losey* (2004), *Karel Reisz* (2006), and a new critical study of Samuel Beckett's film and television work entitled *Beckett, Deleuze and the Televisual Event: Peephole Art* (2012). He is currently on the editorial board of *Aether: The Journal of Media Geography*.

Steven Hoelscher is Professor of American Studies and Geography and is former Chair of the Department of American Studies at the University of Texas at Austin. He regularly teaches graduate seminars on the history and geography of photography at the Harry Ransom Center, where he is Academic Curator of Photography. His books include *Reading Magnum* (2013), *Picturing Indians* (2008), *Textures of Place* (with Paul Adams and Karen Till, 2001), and *Heritage on Stage* (1998), and he has published more than 50 book chapters and articles in such journals as *American Indian Culture and Research Journal, American Quarterly, Annals of the Association of American Geographers, Ecumene, Geographical Review, GeoJournal, History of Photography, Journal of Historical Geography, Public Historian,* and *Social and Cultural Geography*. In 2005, he received the President's Associates Teaching Excellence Award from the University of Texas.

Tamara M. Johnson is Research Associate for Academic Planning in the Office of Academic Affairs and an adjunct faculty member in the Department of Global, International and Area Studies at University of North Carolina (UNC) at Charlotte. She earned her doctorate in geography from the UNC Chapel Hill, completing a Fulbright-funded dissertation project that explored the emotional politics of marginalization, embodied memory, and inclusivity in Cape Town, South Africa. As an urban geographer, her research examines the ways in which continued conflicts and contestations over changes in the material, legislative, and symbolic infrastructure of the city play out in urban social spaces. Her pedagogical and policy research focuses on global service-learning, community engaged scholarship, and student success.

David Lulka is an independent researcher who has taught at several colleges in California. His research primarily focuses upon the ontological and ethical aspects of human relations with nonhuman animals. In addition to highlighting pervasive hierarchies among species, his work accentuates nonhuman agency so as to redefine the parameters for equitable relations in a posthuman world. His writings have been published in numerous books and geographic journals, including *Environment and Planning D: Society and Space, Transactions of the Institute of British Geographers, Urban Geography,* and *Geoforum*.

Derek P. McCormack teaches in the School of Geography and Environment at the University of Oxford, where he is an Associate Professor. He is the author of *Refrains for Moving Bodies: Experience and Experiment in Affective Spaces* (2013) and has written widely on nonrepresentational theory and spaces of affect. He is currently working on a book about atmospheric things.

Alasdair Pinkerton is a lecturer in the Department of Geography at Royal Holloway University of London. His research interests include geopolitics and political geography, with a particular interest in media and communications. His PhD and postdoctoral research have explored the political geographies of international radio broadcasting during and after the Cold War. More recently, his research has explored the both the geographies of rumor and social media technologies. Hi first book, *Radio*, will be published by Reaktion in 2014.

Ate Poorthuis is a PhD student in the Department of Geography at the University of Kentucky. His current research is looking at (im)possibilities of studying the everyday use of public spaces through "big data." His broader interests lie at the intersection of urban and Internet geographies with a predilection for a varied and eclectic use of both quantitative and qualitative methodologies. He is a member of the FloatingSheep research blog.

Darren Purcell is Associate Professor in the Department of Geography and Environmental Sustainability at the University of Oklahoma. His research interests are situated within the fields of political and communications geography, primarily focusing on how the state and other geopolitical actors use information technologies to achieve strategic goals such as articulating the nation, place promotion, branding, and governance. Other work has engaged the role of humor in popular geopolitics, social media and its use by nationalist groups, and film in popular geopolitics.

Pauliina Raento is Professor of Human Geography at the University of Helsinki and an associate editor of *Political Geography*. Her research interests include political and cultural geography, interdisciplinary leisure studies, and visual and field methodologies. Her work has appeared in, e.g. *Annals of Tourism Research, Geografiska Annaler Series B, Geopolitics, The Geographical Review, International Gambling Studies, National Identities, and Political Geography*. Among her recent books is *Gambling, Space, and Time* (coedited with David G. Schwartz).

Paul Simpson is a lecturer in Human Geography in the School of Geography, Earth and Environmental Sciences at Plymouth University. His research interests relate to the social and cultural geographies of everyday life and the use of urban public spaces. He is currently pursuing these interests through a collaborative L'Agence nationale de la recherche funded research project that considers the significance of ambiances and atmospheres to understandings of the experience of urban mobilities. He has published on these themes in *Area, Cultural Geographies, Environment and Planning A, Geoforum, Social and Cultural Geography*, and *Space and Culture*.

Katrinka Somdahl-Sands is Assistant Professor of Geography at Rowan University and Coordinator for the New Jersey Geographic Alliance. Her research interests focus on the spaces of political communication, mediated spaces of performance, and geographic education. Her recent teaching areas include World Regional Geography, Political Geography, and regional courses on Africa, the Middle East, and Europe. She has published articles in various journals including *Cultural Geographies, Journal of Geography, Space and Polity, Geography Compass, Acme,* and *Aether*.

Barney Warf is Professor of Geography at the University of Kansas. His research and teaching interests lie within the broad domain of human geography. Much of his research concerns economic geography, emphasizing producer services and telecommunications. His work straddles contemporary political economy and social theory on the one hand and traditional quantitative, empirical approaches on the other. He has studied a range of topics that fall under the umbrella of globalization, including New York as a global city, fiber optics, the satellite industry, offshore banking, international producer services, and the geographies of the Internet. He has also written on military spending, voting technologies, the US electoral college, and religious diversity.

Matthew Zook is Professor in the Department of Geography at the University of Kentucky and researches technological change and the associated spatial structures and practices of society and the economy. His recent work focuses on the geographical web (the geoweb) and the phenomenon of user-generated data (both volunteered and unknowingly contributed) and seeks to understand where, when, and by whom geo-coded content is being created. He is the cofounder of the New Mappings Collaboratory at the University of Kentucky as well as the FloatingSheep research blog.

ASHGATE
RESEARCH
COMPANION

Introduction: Geographies of Media

Paul C. Adams, Jim Craine and Jason Dittmer

Planning this project took a great leap of faith. After all, we were doing most of the work during the final year in the thirteenth *b'ak'tun* in the ancient Mayan calendar. By some accounts, the world would end on December 21, 2012 – long before we could finish our project. As early as 2006, hundreds of Web sites in dozens of languages had appeared in anticipation of the calendrical event as well as "compact discs of music, videos, on-line discussion groups, and even commemorative t-shirts" (Sitler 2006: 24, 27). Maya-millennialism also spawned close to 2,000 books and tens of millions of Web sites, as well as television programs on the Discovery Channel and History Channel, and films such as Mel Gibson's *Apocalypto* and Roland Emmerich's *2012* (Sitler 2012). Many if not most of these texts profited from the craze while conveying little understanding of the Mayan people, their culture, or even their sense of time. Serious scholars, including scientists at NASA, joined the debate to expose some of the delusions, deceptions, and misunderstandings (Stuart 2011; Hoopes 2011; Restall and Solari 2011), but at least some of their arguments may have been beside the point. The event meant what people in 2012 wanted it to mean, not what the ancient Mayans intended.

The date came and went with neither Armageddon nor a radical heightening of human consciousness, but it *was* an event. It typified what Daniel Boorstin long ago labeled a "pseudo-event" (1961) in that the hype around the event constituted the event itself. The event included a handful of people moving to the Yucatan Peninsula to be close to Ground Zero at the time of transition, people watching movies and television, people taking "spiritual tours" to learn about "crystal skulls, ancestral ties to Atlantis, and a bond with Pleiadians" (Sitler 2012: 68), and people hoping to experience an "exponential acceleration of the wave harmonic of history as it phases into a moment of unprecedented synchronization" (Argüelles 1987: 159). As a media event, its origins reach back to the carving of glyphs into stone some 2,000 years ago, long before anyone could have imagined that they would eventually drive a billion dollar media market.[1] The turn of the *b'ak'tun* thus became a social, cultural, and economic event through media – to be precise, through transhistorical, international networks of cross-cultural communications, involving countless interpretations and reinterpretations.

Media are deeply implicated in historical geographical processes, some of which reside primarily within these media and others of which have their origins outside of mediation. But even events of the latter sort, like the tsunamis that struck Indonesia in 2004 and Japan in 2011, become known to all but a handful of people through media. Regardless of their degree of materiality, and even when they abound in unmet expectations, misrepresentations, and misunderstandings, mediated events are very real. This is true of events mediated by print and broadcast media as well as computer-mediated events. Indeed, the process of technological convergence renders this distinction increasingly problematic.

1 Emmerich's film alone grossed over $769 million (IMDB).

Turning from the history of mediated experience to the much shorter history of media geography as a research focus, it is over a quarter of a century since the publication of *Geography, the Media and Popular Culture* (Burgess and Gold 1985) – a foundational text that appeared at a time when the Commodore 64 was the state of the art home computer and DVDs had not yet been invented. How can we thank Burgess and Gold for their prescience? No doubt by looking in more than a cursory fashion at exactly what was going on in that book. The predominant methodological inspirations came from British cultural studies, particularly questions about how thoroughly dominant ideologies are imposed by the media versus the degree to which audiences actively shape the meaning of media products – a debate largely articulated at that time in terms of "encoding" and "decoding." While catch phrases have shifted, certain fundamental assumptions of this early work remain, not least of which is that it is taken for granted that the meanings and social relevance of all sorts of things, and even what constitutes a "thing," are constructs embedded in mediated discourses.

The editors of *Geography, the Media and Popular Culture* noted a fundamental dichotomy between European and American research. In a somewhat stereotyped characterization, the American scholars adopted a model of communication based on transmissions between sender(s) and receiver(s), conceiving of both primarily as individuals and focusing on the fidelity of this transfer, as well as its effects on people's perceptions and actions. In contrast, the Europeans framed communications as a social force, adopting a contestational model of society in which scholarly writing must work to unsettle, expose, and critique the dominant ideologies and paradigms. Interestingly, a quarter century later, this divide has largely disappeared. The European contributors to this volume cite North American theorists such as Marshall McLuhan, Robert Putnam, Judith Butler, and Donna Haraway, while the American participants cite Michel Foucault, Gilles Deleuze, Walter Benjamin, and Julia Kristeva among others. There are now important figures in the subdiscipline – for example, Manuel Castells – who defy categorization as either American or European. (And one of this book's editors has forsaken the former colony for the heart of the former empire.)

A third feature of *Geography, the Media and Popular Culture* was its attention to power, whether in the form of the power to produce cheap television programming (Gould and Lyew-Ayee 1985), the power to define notions like risk and danger (Liverman and Sherman 1985; Burgess 1985), the power to articulate a particular structure of space and time (Brooker-Gross 1985), or more generally the power to propagate dominant ideologies. Power remains a central concern in media geography, and the contributors to this volume address the power relations of media production (Dixon), the power of geopolitical iconography (Pinkerton, Raento, and Dittmer), the power of visibility in defining race relations (Finn), and a range of other power relations. Media geography emphasizes that power relations are embedded in spaces and places through communications, no less than through physical means such as violence. Media geographers still contend that the physical acts imposing power – violence, intimidation, and embodied resistance – become socially meaningful through lead-up and follow-up acts of communication. At the same time, media geographers have become a bit more careful to avoid blanket critiques that overlook contingencies of the places and circumstances of communication.

Geography, the Media and Popular Culture is a peculiarity among the geographical works of the 1980s as most of the foundational works in media geography did not appear until somewhat later – works such as Barnes and Duncan's *Writing Worlds* (1992), Duncan and Ley's *Place/Culture/Representation* (1993), Aitken and Zonn's *Place, Power, Situation, and Spectacle* (1994), and Crang, Crang, and May's *Virtual Geographies* (1999). Yet all of these later works owe something to earlier explorations focused primarily on literature – works such as Douglas Pocock's *Humanistic Geography and Literature* (1981), Buttimer and Seamon's *The Human Experience of Space and Place* (1980), and various writings of Yi-Fu

Tuan (1974; 1977; 1978). Research motivations and sense of purpose changed radically between the 1970s and the 1990s, with a wholesale reorientation from interpretation and understanding toward critique and intervention. Today there is a partial return indicated by the ebbing of the quixotic sense that attacking dominant ideologies is our raison d' être, yet there is a lingering concern with power's operation through discourse.

The early corpus in media geography includes some, like James Duncan (1993), who entirely rejected literal meaning and the principle of mimesis, finding in representation *nothing but* ideological distortions and operations of authorial power. Other early contributors extolled the place perceptions and existential insights in what they saw as artful expressions of transpersonal aspects of experience, although if one reads closely they also recognized representations as constructs (Tuan 1978). We would venture to suggest that here again the dividing line between opposing poles has blurred with time, in large part because an interest in the body and embodiment has brought attention not only to biological differences (e.g. sex and age) but also to aspects of embodied sameness in the human encounter with the world (e.g., eating, moving, seeing, hearing, touching). This is in many ways a return to concerns that animated the works of humanist geographers, such as age (Rowles 1978), mobility (Tuan 1977; Seamon 1980), and the senses (Tuan 1974).

This phenomenon illustrates that as media geography has grown forwards it has also grown outwards, encompassing a widening range of issues, which in turn lead back to the root stock of geography, linking to other specialties in the discipline. This process now includes political geography, economic geography, and critical landscape studies. Specifically, these rerouted roots of media geography include insights about bordering as an ongoing process of social construction and attention to humor as a form of critical engagement with mainstream geopolitics (Paasi 1996; Dodds 1996; Purcell, Brown, and Gokmen 2010). Key texts now include landmarks of economic geography such as David Harvey's *The Condition of Postmodernity* (1990) and J.K. Gibson-Graham's *The End of Capitalism (As We Knew It)* (1996). We also look back to landscape studies by authors such as Don Meinig (1979), Denis Cosgrove (1984), J.B. Jackson (1970), Richard Schein (1997), and Ken Foote (2003). Thus, media geography as a specialty has become less specialized (though hopefully no less special) over its two-and-a-half-decade lifespan.

Despite this luxuriant growth forwards, outwards, and backwards, our specialty is still new and there remain many gaps. More work needs to be done on nonvisual media such as radio, telephone, and portable music technologies. There has been relatively little research on the geographies of media production compared to the numerous geographies of media images, representations, and discourses. We are still quite vague about the meanings, spatial practices, routines, and audiences of humble, everyday media like postage stamps and advertisements. It is in some of these areas in particular that we have tried to fill in a few of the gaps with this collection, as well as engaging with the cutting edges of epistemology and methodology. Finally, the personal interests of the three editors bring certain emphases to this collection: virtuality, visualization, geopolitical discourse, nonlinear narrative, embodiment, language, and performance. The time has come, then, to consider more closely the state of the art in media geography.

State of the Art

In their contribution to this volume, Curti and Johnson argue that "media geography and its syncretic encounters offer an emerging promise for those who do not fit so comfortably into the confines of the pre-scripted, the conventional, the acceptable, or the 'appropriate.'"

We agree wholeheartedly with this argument, although we do not necessarily share their dismissal of the rest of geographical research. The value of media geography resides to a major extent in its propensity to test the boundaries of conventional worldviews. We are happy to adopt a kaleidoscopic vision of the world by looking at the world through whatever lenses have been provided by culture, with both a small *c* and a large *C*. An unsettling and creative tendency emerges from the combination of media studies with geography, because of ontological cross-currents when we see the world as something we (humans) always know through mediation (by language and all the rest), even as we insist that media themselves are not placeless but have particular place-based implications, depending on where they are used and how they facilitate interactions through space and at a distance. Rather than attempting to justify the neglect of one of these viewpoints, we submit that they coexist in a productive tension.

Media in Spaces/Places

On the one hand, the question Where am I? points us toward an "I" situated in geographical space/place. What we mean by this is that *communications form a connective tissue through space and between places*. From this standpoint, communication is both a product and a producer of myriad differences between here and there, but it also permits interdependency and interaction between here and there. Research indicates the marked spatial variability of media access and the digital (and predigital) divides between the information haves and the have-nots. This perspective also leads to a focus on the centers and peripheries as world cities accumulate access and control over global information flows while much of the world is left with sparse access to information and little ability to shape these flows. On this account, asking Where am I? takes us to a position in urban, regional, national, and global spaces where differences instrumentally assert and contest manifest structures of power.

This perspective leads to multiple foci. For example, one may interrogate the impact of having the state act as a media producer versus private enterprise. Questions arise concerning power relations and organizational arrangements at the place of production – for example, between actors and the production management team. Geographies of media distribution can be examined, from retail outlets to the mail system, to electromagnetic waves, to the Internet, each with peculiar characteristics structuring the flow of communications through space and time. Speed, directionality, funding, scripting, and many other attributes of communication relate in important ways to the uneven geographical patterns of communication flow and infrastructure. These geographies are all about power in its various forms – for example, the global south has limited broadcasting access owing to topography, political oppression, and poverty. But when noting this we must avoid determinism: "limiting a group's access to media does not necessarily render it powerless" (see Raento this volume).

The media in spaces/places-approach locates media infrastructure in map space, but also locates communications devices in interior spaces and places. Whether we examine how a home is transformed by the introduction of a radio or television, how a billboard gazing down on a street transforms that street, or how an onboard DVD transforms the inside of a moving vehicle, we repeatedly encounter the power of media to transform the places in which they are used. This power is not a mere conceit of human audiences; animals and even plants respond to the presence of media in their environments (see Lulka, this volume). Media transform a place from within, whether the place in question is the nation-state, the neighborhood, or the home.

Spaces/Places in Media

Returning to the question Where am I?, we may alternatively point toward topological relationships embodied within a network of communication flows. This view encounters space and place as contents rather than the contexts of communication. On this account, *media actively constitute spaces and places through techniques of representation, expression, and performance.* Many if not most human actions and sensations take place in and through media and the meanings of any given experience are always already embedded in texts and discourses (Ricoeur 1984; 1985; 1988). People inhabit the assumptions of particular discourses since what is taken for granted or unsayable includes the vast majority of geographies – known and fantastic, actual and ideal, past, present, and future. Thus, Where am I? leads not to a physical place but to the intersection of various publics as they engage with various media and a dizzying array of texts (Warner 2002).

Drawing on Gilles Deleuze, Brian Massumi, and others, the observers of this new environment employ tactile terms such as "smooth," "striated," or "folded," to capture how the things we encounter are felt to be inside or outside. This challenging new vocabulary charts a shift from a focus on objects to a focus on processes, doings, and verbs. We are no longer comfortable enumerating the objects that comprise "the media" – the screens, cameras, producers, and audiences – but alternatively want to consider an event, an identity, a place of refuge, a conflict, or a form of intergroup contact. A medium is a network of particular dynamics constantly slipping through various hybrid configurations. A major shift in interest has carried media geography in this direction over the past five to 10 years. From an interest in auditory and haptic spaces to the idea of video games as social architecture, to the idea of interior as exterior and vice versa, to the notion of social space as folded or "scrumpled" – non-Euclidean geographies have proliferated like mutants in a nuclear holocaust.

The earlier understanding that communication consists of codes and languages remains viable, if rather submerged with the waning of interest in naturalistic, positivistic, semiotic, hermeneutic, and deconstructive methodologies. The notion of decoding still helps us to recognize that to read the televisual/cinematic language requires that one learn to make sense of certain conventions regarding the meanings of these perspectival movements such as jump cuts, panning, tilting, and tracking. It is still instructive to recall that there is nothing natural about the way a particular medium produces a sense of setting, or a particular spatiotemporal configuration; each medium carries with it certain ways of communicating that have specific histories. But rather than stop with identification of codes, we must press onwards to ask how it is that one language or code inf(l)ects another. Spillover – for example, from film to dance, or from billboard to graffiti, or vice versa – is not merely semiotic but also sociospatial.

After a several decade hiatus, Marshall McLuhan has once again reared his homely head. Communication geographers are noticing that "changing media form, in and of itself, can be informative" (see Lulka, this volume). Armed with this sensibility to meaning as excessive, spilling over each and every symbolic system, familiar academic tropes (for example, the critiques of romanticism and anthropomorphism) collapse under the weight of a general skepticism regarding dichotomous thinking. The medium is now, once again, seen to be the message (or rather one of many messages).

Synthesis

These two approaches, space/place in media and media in space/place, are explored by Adams (2009; 2011), who divides the ontologial terrain into four quadrants by associating research approaches with positions on two axes. While we find this approach helpful, we would note the risk in imposing dichotomies. Place versus space is often more of a polarity than a productive tension. The other dialectic, between media-as-content and media-as-context, is more subtle and therefore less likely to be used in reductionist fashion, but it may still be employed in a way that creates impasses in our understanding. As Adams suggests (2011), rather than adopting one of two poles, research can occupy the center of the field, working with both elements rather than picking sides.

There is much to be gained by looking simultaneously, for example, at "the media connection between places of interiority and worldwide forces" (Aitken, this volume) while questioning the dichotomy between the represented spaces and the spaces where representations are produced, which in the case of film-geography reduces to a rejection of the fossilized distinction between "the real" and "the reel." A nationalist superhero like Captain America can be seen as a representation of the nation through a kind of idealized embodiment, but at the same time, the superhero exceeds representation and transcends borders by inspiring the creation of competing visions of the nationalist superhero in foreign countries (Dittmer 2013: 185). We can think of communication as occurring in a possibility space between the poles of space and place, as well as between the poles: in-media and media-in (more on this possibility space in a moment). Manifestations of this impulse include a nonrepresentational style of inquiry as advocated by Nigel Thrift (2007) and the distributed, hybrid actors that Actor Network Theory urges us to recognize (Latour 2005). It may help to think in terms of assemblages and hybrids – for example, the screen-body that exists through the linked performances on both sides of the screen, a body that is at once technical and pleasurable.

This synthesis of dichotomies motivates a turn toward the body, because whereas earlier writings in geography dismissed mediated place on the basis of its supposed disembodiment, recent contributions to the geographic literature find the body to be situated simultaneously in mediated encounters *and* in material environments. On the one hand, bodies make up much of the content of media:

> *Bodies are ubiquitous in media. Slim and fit bodies, obese and carnivalesque bodies, young and old bodies, murdered and mutilated bodies, alien and machinic bodies appear constantly on our television and computer screens, producing diverse modes of entertainment, engagement and contestation. (Cupples, this volume)*

On the other hand, bodies are required in order to engage the media. Deborah Dixon points to an ontology of touch while Derek McCormack suggests we think of moving bodies as "prosthetic technologies for inhabiting affectively mediated worlds" (McCormack, this volume). If we acknowledge Pinkerton's suggestion that radio can play to the mind's eye, then the seemingly frivolous pun employed in "The medium is the massage" (McLuhan and Fiore 1967) articulated a prescient understanding of our deep interdigitation with media – that "we do not simply partake of a message, but rather … are worked over by it because we are in the midst of the medium itself" (Lulka, this volume). Digital media have made us (once again) sensitive to this interdigitation.

One of the kinds of synthesis involves the way a medium such as radio works to "produce, reinforce or, indeed, to unsettle and undermine different kinds of sociocultural and political formations and at a range of different scales" (Pinkerton, this volume).

Here we are dealing with the constitution of particular publics or imagined communities (Warner 2002; Anderson 1991). Communication binds the public or community not only by *reaching* people, and therefore connecting through physical and social space, but also by *portraying* "the people," and therefore staking out boundaries in physical and social space. These simultaneous operations are suggested by Curti and Johnson, in this volume: "Approaching the world in this way requires an accounting for both the coming-together – *the syncretic amalgamated* – and breaking-apart – *the emergent migrating* – of the very living processes continually (re)composing the zones of variable intensities and integrities that are place and places." Yet even in this synthesis the dichotomies indicated above remain, if only as complementary impulses. New technologies of "augmented reality" reveal these complementary impulses as human mobility comes to depend on the ubiquitous hereness of georeferenced information as it is accessed through handheld devices and we make sense of this information by mobilizing our understanding of the intangible environments of games and simulations so that "the interface logics of game environments bleed into extended spaces of the world through such devices" (Ash, this volume). In short, representations of place are rendered as overlays that one accesses by moving through space, thereby infusing the experience of material, tangible spaces and places with preinscribed and reinscribed meanings linked to an abstract, geometrical coordinate system. But augmented reality devices are not the only means of moving through "real" space with a mediated awareness. Simply by internalizing the narratives of National Geographic television specials and programs on the Discovery Channel, we explore what it would be like to inhabit space and place as an animal (Lulka, this volume), and this internalized awareness may in turn motivate animal rights activism, environmentalism, and other systematic alterations of action.

The Chapters

This volume is divided into three parts, each of which highlights a different dimension of media geography, drawing from Adams's typology (2011). In the first part of the book, the authors turn their attention to specific media, if not arguing for their absolute uniqueness at least considering them as distinct forms. Some of these media have been well covered in the geographic literature while others were selected because of their unique geographical properties. The authors in this section were asked to specifically highlight the geographical dimensions of the medium in question: What is unique to this medium with regard to space and place? How is the medium productive of particular places and spaces? This section starts with media that, while continuing into the present-day, were developed in the late nineteenth and early twentieth centuries: photography, film, radio, comic books, the postal system, and dance. It concludes with media of more recent provenance: video games and the Internet.

The second and third sections delve into the qualities of mediated places and spaces. In the second section, place is imagined as the momentary crystallization of various flows and discourses within a particular context and also as a context in its own right where various events take place. Authors in this section were asked to speak to two questions: How is place produced through or embedded in various media? What kinds of spatiality enable this mediated place to exist? The chapters chart a flow from nature, the mysterious world-out-there, inward to the body and mind – the mysterious world-in-here, with its intuitions, desires, and emotions. The discussion builds in several ways on the notion of interiority, unfolding place or even turning it inside out to suggest a synthesis of space and place, a context in which proximity does not necessarily imply legibility or familiarity. In the remaining two chapters of this section, we learn about inscribing oneself onto place through graffiti and about the ways in which products are inscribed onto places and subsequently onto the mind by advertising.

The third and final section of the book shifts attention to media spaces, which is to say the contexts in which people and things interact by way of communication. Spaces push our attention outwards from the subjective to the intersubjective as the particular structured flows of sensation, meaning, action, and value help to constitute the contexts in which things happen. The authors in this section respond to two questions: How do spaces of communication differ with regard to the sensory modalities of the communication? What spatial patterns and topologies are associated with particular kinds of communication? The individual chapters cover a range of communication spaces, from spaces of live performance to social networks, ensuring not only that expected topics are covered but that our expectations of what constitute "communication spaces" are challenged. This section concludes with a chapter addressing capital, which by reducing the flows to their economic basis provides an encompassing view.

The three parts to this volume are intentionally overlapping in some ways. There are, for instance, several chapters relating to the Internet in some way, and dance comes up more than once. However, our intention was to show the various distinct ways in which such topics can be considered, and how they might be laid alongside one another in productive ways. In this, we hope that you agree we have been successful.

Media in Place and Space

The first section of the book is organized so as to introduce media dynamics that have a relatively long history – somewhat more than a century – and then turn to newer technologies and dynamics. Steven Hoelscher opens the section with a discussion of photography, a medium that has provided a mediated sense of "thereness" since the mid-nineteenth century. Photography offers a historical perspective that helps lay a foundation for subsequent chapters. In keeping with this attention to time, Hoelscher's chapter reminds us of the paradoxical relationship between the photograph as a momentary vision and the photograph as an enduring object, a relationship that has recently changed owing to digital photography. Through a case study of Magnum Photos, his chapter reveals media as a means of propagating a progressive sense of place.

In another analysis of a visual medium, Deborah Dixon excavates the complex and multifaceted geography of cinema. She tracks geographies of film from the early proposal that a film can show students "the field," to studies of the spatial organization of the entertainment industry and its laborers, analyses of the political and economic settings in which film is produced, and analyses of place representations with their systematic distortions and manipulations. Most recently, there is a rejection of Cartesian space and the primacy of the visual that transcends the artificial dichotomy between the "reel" and the "real" and takes us away from images and sites toward topologies of multisensory engagement. The latter aspects of film are more than representational as affect circulates among partial objects – networks of technologies and organisms that only temporarily appear coherent.

Departing from visuality but deepening our understanding of the early twentieth-century media complex, Alasdair Pinkerton draws our attention to radio – a medium too often forgotten by scholars. His contribution shows radio as inherently spatial. Radio was the first of many media to make use of electromagnetic waves; it once startled with its ability to pass through walls and over great distances. Radio remains an important vehicle for the promotion of place identities, but simultaneously transcends place – for example, promoting national interests beyond the borders of the state. In addition, radio permits continuous communication during mobility, an ability that still renders it useful (in tandem with newer technologies) so that one's sense of being "here" remains stable even while traveling between here to there. Radio resonates with other media we find somehow more impressive, but perhaps its most intriguing aspect is its ambiguous relation to the entire sensorium, because as Pinkerton argues, the voice of the radio activates not only to the ear but also the mind's eye.

The mind's eye is trained in childhood, and as Jason Dittmer argues, superheroes in comics provide an embodied symbol of the nation, functioning as "rescaling icons." To fit them (and vicariously fit ourselves) into superhero adventures, we need to learn our way around in the Bergsonian space-time of animated narrative. To the spatialities of national embodiment and visual montage we can add the place-based geographical process by which readings of comics are performed. A final geography that is brought to bear in this constellation is the geographical arrangement of comic book production and distribution, which enables all of the other geographies. As Dittmer notes, we must consider all four of these geographies not as disconnected but as co-constituting each other.

Pauliina Raento takes us on an excursion into the surprisingly complex geography of one of the smallest and least obtrusive media. Much more complex than it seems, the postage stamp affords insight into a range of geographic processes including iconographic representations of place and material flows of meaning and information through space. Much of the potency of the postage stamp derives from its official character as a display of national iconography as well as an indication of the conveyance that is prepaid, both of which in tandem create opportunities for subversion. A stamp stuck on the wrong way can be a challenge to the state political authority embodied both in the stamp's imagery and in the institution of the postal system. This subversion demonstrates the close connection between communication content and communication networks.

Derek McCormack's chapter explores the relation between dance and media, searching for a way past the too-obvious dichotomy between the live dancing body and the disembodied media image. He urges us to think of dance as a technicity of relational movement. On this account, sensation is always prosthetic regardless of whether it is technologically mediated. Both media and bodies participate in dance as a distributed flow of dynamic materiality. A key to this shift in thinking are "media ecologies," a term he employs to suggest dynamic relations in which bodies respond to screened dances by dancing differently. We perceive these ecologies whether we think of dance-centric movies such as *Footloose*, video-arcade games like *Dance, Dance, Revolution*, or the countless remakes of dance videos such as PSY's Gangnam Style. While dance is the oldest medium in this section of the book, this chapter raises issues that connect strongly to the last two chapters in the section.

James Ash considers video games with a flexible perspective, arguing that space in video games can be conceptualized in three main ways: spaces that appear on the screen, spaces of the game-player's body, and spaces constituted by assemblages of body and screen. Spaces of the screen construct space visually, as they scroll in various ways allowing the player to move beyond the visible field of the screen in different ways, depending on the game. Some games appear to surround the game player in three dimensions while others are two-dimensional. Screen-spaces of these various sorts are supplemented by the various spaces of the body where the player is embodied and his or her senses literally come into play. Integrating these spaces begins to allow us to perceive the game as an assemblage; constructed geometries limit player action even as players "corporeally and skillfully respond to these limitations using their embodied knowledge and sensori-motor skill."

Darren Purcell rounds out the section with a discussion of the Internet. His chapter cites the boundary-crossing potential of the Internet with the implications of such fluidity, in regard to human mobility and the evolving notion of intellectual property. While computer networking provides the means of overcoming spatial boundaries, its appropriation always reflects the local conditions of "real people, embedded in real places." The big picture also continues to show unevenness in the concentration of Internet bandwidth, raising skepticism about whether boundary-crossing necessarily leads to the smoothing out of spatial lumpiness. Nonetheless, as Purcell mentions, there are some tantalizing examples of resistant politics benefiting from digital networks and flows.

Place in Media

The second section attacks the concept of place, working on it through a wide-ranging set of theoretical inspirations. David Lulka's chapter provides a point of departure by questioning how mediated encounters with nature distort the distance between humans and nonhumans. To shrink the earth by picturing it from space, to draw a fantasy vision of a future earth without humans, to analyze nature via science or romanticize it via fiction, thereby engaging it via anthropomorphism or mechanism, is in any case to work on the conceptual distance between the human and the nonhuman. Whether in the anthropomorphic characters of *Bambi* and *Finding Nemo*, or in the "ecoporn" of *Blue Planet*, we are confronted by (re) constructions of this distance. However, as Lulka reminds us, it is not enough simply to critique media constructions for being constructions, because our critique itself is historically and geographically contingent.

Julie Cupples explores what she calls the "body-media interface." These concerns are not wholly different from those of Lulka, because in many ways it is through our own bodies that we connect with nature, whether through the shared experience of consumption and reproduction, or through the panoply of the senses and desires that are bequeathed to us by our mammalian (and specifically simian) ancestry. This discussion addresses a powerful current of media-critique: the allegations that spending time with media degrades the body to a tuberous state while media images themselves push us to strive for impossibly slender and muscular physiques. The chapter leaves room for progressive potentials in mediated forms of embodiment, acknowledging but also questioning such critiques.

Stuart Aitken takes us on a dizzying trip that starts on terrain similar to the previous chapter – the mediated body – but works toward a more general notion of interiority. On this account, places of interiority include not just the innards of the body but also the mind, as revealed by psychology, psychotherapy, and post-structural critiques, and interiority itself, as considered by Gilles Deleuze, certain "new" feminists, and the philosopher Henri Bergson. The filmic language of David Cronenberg provides a case study in which the boundaries between the inside and the outside of the body, and ultimately the boundaries of the self, are dissolved in a monstrous way.

Giorgio Hadi Curti and Tamara M. Johnson offer a perspective that nicely complements Aitken's interpretation. Their discussion of syncretic geographies, tied closely to the notion of hybridity, brings together an unlikely pair of media: Japanese anime film and Salsa dance. The assumed difference between these media serves to recall ways in which other things assumed to be different are, to greater or lesser degrees, the same, and more generally the ways in which place itself depends on mixture, combination, and blending. Calling for a relational sensibility, the authors urge us to compose maps of the world that can be unfolded like intricate origami creations so as to better capture the syncretic stew of affect.

The art installations of Canadian artist Stan Douglas form the focus of the chapter by Colin Gardner. These installations are not only places in their own right, but are meant to evoke other places, and in doing so they simultaneously rupture an ordinary sense of time. They linger on a past in which things obviously could have worked out differently, and if they had, here would not be here and there would not be there. Thus ultimately they disrupt the traditional relationships between space, place, and time to offer an alternative reality that is both haunted and haunting.

The chapter by Jim Craine, Ron Davidson and Christina Dando explores yet another ordinary and mundane medium with hidden geographic import. Advertising is so familiar that it is usually treated as "beneath" geographic study. Yet advertisements not only use place representations to promote consumption, which alters places, they also shade into architecture and thereby become places. The orange roof of the Howard Johnson's, McDonald's golden arches, or the obese homunculus in front of a Big Boy restaurant, all serve as media built into place for the purpose of increasing consumption. The identical façades and décor exist in tension with ads playing on the concept of the uniqueness of place, a uniqueness one must colonize, either literally or at least with the touristic gaze.

John Finn rounds out this section with a consideration of graffiti as a way in which people are able to write meaning directly onto the landscape. As a tool for reclaiming some degree of power over the spaces that urbanites inhabit, graffiti quite often responds to the other messages deployed in the city – for example, billboard advertisements. In Finn's analysis this reinscription intervenes in representation of race in the city of Salvador, Brazil, and contests this city's racialized landscapes.

Space in Media

The third and final section reframes the geographical not as place but as space. Paul Adams invites us to think of words as creating particular verbal spaces: tree-spaces, container-spaces, layer-spaces, particle-spaces, and area-spaces. While these spaces may be encountered through metaphors, like the term *root* when applied to an ancestral word fragment, there is something here that is more than metaphorical. How we interpret words and organize words, on the one hand, and how we use words, on the other, are coordinated in complex ways that imply the existence of spaces that coordinate the interactions between people, words, and things. Our ability to act through words depends on the varied logics of these spaces. If spaces are understood as systems of opportunity and constraint, then we literally inhabit the spaces created by words.

Michael Bull shows how the movement of people through urban space is increasingly overlain with the experience of mediated sound. People move around in what amount to "privatized sonic bubbles" as they employ headphones or earbuds to replace the auditory aspects of the spaces they inhabit. Sonic environments therefore become oddly dislocated even as they are privatized and fused (differently for each person) into a single melody and rhythm, and space is no longer shared in the way it once was.

Barney Warf explores social networking, or to be more precise, telemediated interpersonal interactions. While noting the unevenness of the diffusion of all of the associated technologies, he also shows the revolutionary situation induced by even modest levels of access to new interpersonal networking media such as cell phones. To a degree this change involves hardware but it is no less dependent on software, as Twitter, Facebook, and other applications form "telemediated networks" separate from the cell phones and computers on which they are carried. These networks permit daily life to constitute strange geographies, including wormholes, tunnels, and "origami-like spatialities."

Ate Poorthuis and Matthew Zook explore the relatively new and increasing interactivity of computer-mediated communication, or what is increasingly called VGI (volunteered geographic information). Drawing on the metaphor of a flaky, many-layered French pastry called a mille-feuille, they consider the countless layers of mediated social interaction that now characterize daily life. Creating and updating online maps, posting updates to one's online profile, broadcasting invitations to events, and responding to crises and disasters, people are increasingly at home in multiple discrete but relatively ephemeral and crumbly layers of space.

Paul Simpson's chapter seeks to avoid equating media with texts and textuality by taking up nonrepresentational themes, particularly the concept of affect. He considers the countless encounters when bodies impinge on other bodies, when emotions cross the bounds of the self, when a certain intensity passes from here to there and we are caught up in communications of a nonrepresentational sort. He attends to communication as a form of change and transformation without recourse to conventional notions of cause and effect that objectify communications as things passing between objects. Instead, he considers cinema, video games, and sound in relation to their various atmospheres.

The chapter by Katrinka Somdahl-Sands and Paul Adams takes us into spaces and places of performance that are undergoing transformation in response to the diffusion of various media. Performance has proven fully capable of evolving alongside contemporary technological and social transformations. Viral videos, for example, are performances. As such, they rework the boundaries between public and private. What would otherwise have remained private, such as a child bursting into tears, can become public on a grand scale. What is new about this publicness is not merely the geographical scale or audience numbers, but the particular ways in which technology reworks the boundaries between presence and absence, self and other, now and then, here and there. This reworked performance space brings together activists, artists, and artist-activists whose projects constitute new types of publics.

Brett Christophers rounds out the section and the book by considering the geography of media-related capital. There is, on the one hand, a concentration of productive power in the hands of giant media conglomerates in a few major cities where the vast majority of media products are created, packaged, marketed, and licensed. At the same time, media investment and production have become increasingly mobile, transnational, and decentralized through a process of deterritorialization. This process of concentration and dispersion profoundly affects all of the media geographies addressed throughout this book.

References

Adams, P.C. 2009. *Geographies of Media and Communication: A Critical Introduction*. London: Wiley-Blackwell.

Adams, P.C. 2011. A taxonomy for communication geography. *Progress in Human Geography* 35 (1): 37–57.

Anderson, B. 1991. *Imagined Communities: Reflections on the Origin and Spread of Nationalism*. Rev. and extended ed., 2nd ed. London and New York: Verso.

Argüelles, J. 1987. *The Mayan Factor: Path beyond Technology*. Santa Fe, NM: Bear & Co.

Barnes, T. and J. Duncan. 1992. *Writing Worlds: Discourse, Text and Metaphor in the Representation of Landscape*. London and New York: Routledge.

Boorstin, D. 1961. *The Image: A Guide to Pseudo-Events in America*. New York: Atheneum.

Brooker-Gross, S.R. 1985. The changing concept of place in the news. In *Geography, the Media and Popular Culture*. Edited by J. Burgess and J.R. Gold. London: Croom Helm, 63–85.
Burgess, J. 1985. News from nowhere: The press, the riots and the myth of the inner city. In *Geography, the Media and Popular Culture*. Edited by J. Burgess and J.R. Gold. London: Croom Helm, 192–228.
Burgess, J. and J.R. Gold (eds). 1985. *Geography, the Media and Popular Culture*. London: Croom Helm.
Buttimer, A. and D. Seamon (eds). 1980. *The Human Experience of Space and Place*. London: Croom Helm.
Cosgrove, D. 1984. *Social Formation and Symbolic Landscape*. Madison: University of Wisconsin Press.
Dittmer, J. 2013. *Captain America and the Nationalist Superhero: Metaphors, Narratives, and Geopolitics*. Philadelphia: Temple University Press.
Dodds, K. 1996. The 1982 Falklands War and a critical geopolitical eye: Steve Bell and the If… cartoons. *Political Geography* 15(6): 571–92.
Duncan, J. 1993. Sites of representation: Place, time and the discourse of the Other. In Place/Culture/Representation. Edited by James Duncan and David Ley. London and New York: Routledge, 39–56.
Duncan, J.S. and D. Ley (eds). 1993. *Place/Culture/Representation*. London and New York: Routledge.
Foote, K. E. 2003. *Shadowed Ground: America's Landscapes of Violence and Tragedy*. Austin: University of Texas Press.
Gibson-Graham, J.K. 1996. *The End of Capitalism (As We Knew It): A Feminist Critique of Political Economy*. Cambridge, MA, and Oxford, UK: Blackwell Publishers.
Gould, P. and A. Lyew-Ayee. 1985. Television in the Third World: A high wind on Jamaica. In *Geography, the Media and Popular Culture*. Edited by J. Burgess and J.R. Gold. London: Croom Helm, 33–62.
Harvey, D. 1990. *The Condition of Postmodernity*. Oxford: Blackwell.
Hoopes, J.W. 2011. A critical history of 2012 mythology. *Proceedings of the International Astronomical Union* 7(S278): 240–48.
Jackson, J.B. 1970. *Landscapes: Selected Writings of JB Jackson*. Boston: University of Massachusetts Press.
Latour, B. 2005. *Reassembling the Social: An Introduction to Actor-Network-Theory*. Oxford, UK: Oxford University Press.
Liverman, D.M. and D.R. Sherman. 1985. Natural hazards in novels and films: implications for hazard perception and behaviour. In *Geography, the Media and Popular Culture*. Edited by J.Burgess and J.R. Gold. London: Croom Helm, 86–95.
McLuhan, M. and Q. Fiore. 1967. *The Medium Is the Massage: An Inventory of Effects*. London: Penguin.
Meinig, D.W. 1979. The beholding eye: Ten versions of the same scene. In *The Interpretation of Ordinary Landscapes: Geographical Essays*. Oxford, UK: Oxford University Press, 33–48.
Paasi, A. 1996. *Territories, Boundaries, and Consciousness: The Changing Geographies of the Finnish-Russian Boundary*. New York: J. Wiley & Sons.
Purcell, D., M. Brown, and M. Gokmen. 2010. Achmed the Dead Terrorist and humor in critical geopolitics. *GeoJournal* 75(4): 373–85.
Restall, M. and A. Solari. 2011. *2012 and the End of the World: The Western Roots of the Maya Apocalypse*. Lanham, MD: Rowman and Littlefield.
Ricoeur, P. 1984, 1985, 1988. *Time and Narrative* (Temps et Récit), 3 vols. Translated by Kathleen McLaughlin and David Pellauer. Chicago: University of Chicago Press.

Rowles, G.D. 1978. Prisoners *of Space? Exploring the Geographical Experience of Older People*. Boulder, CO: Westview Press.

Schein, R.H. 1997. The place of landscape: A conceptual framework for interpreting an American scene. *Annals of the Association of American Geographers* 87(4), 660–80.

Seamon, D. 1980. Body-subject, time-space routines and place-ballets. In *The Human Experience of Space and Place*. Edited by A. Buttimer and D. Seamon. London: Croom Helm, 148–65.

Sitler, R.K. 2006. The 2012 phenomenon: New Age appropriation of an ancient Mayan calendar. *Nova Religio: The Journal of Alternative and Emergent Religions* 9(3): 24–38.

Sitler, R.K. 2012. The 2012 phenomenon comes of age. *Nova Religio: The Journal of Alternative and Emergent Religions* 16(1): 61–87.

Stuart, D.S. 2011. *The Order of Days: The Maya World and the Truth about 2012*. New York: Harmony Books.

Thrift, N. 2007. *Non-Representational Theory: Space, Politics, Affect*. New York and London: Routledge.

Tuan, Y.-F. 1974. *Topophilia: A Study of Environmental Perception, Attitudes, and Values*. Englewood Cliffs, NJ: Prentice-Hall.

Tuan, Y.-F. 1977. *Space and Place: The Perspective of Experience*. Minneapolis: University of Minnesota Press.

Tuan, Y.-F. 1978. Literature and geography: Implications for geographical research. In *Humanistic Geography: Prospects and Problems*. Edited by D. Ley and M.S. Samuels. Chicago: Maaroufa Press, 194–206.

Warner, M. 2002. Publics and counterpublics. *Public Culture* 14(1), 49–90.

PART I
Media

Photography

Steven Hoelscher

Introduction: An Oakland Bus Stop

Photography, at its most powerful, is a geographic medium unparalleled in shaping perceptions of place (van Gelder and Westgeest 2011). Whether viewed on a computer screen, in a gallery, through the pages of a book, or at a classroom lecture, photographic images of locations, near and far, can seem real and unmediated. They can transport people across vast distances of time and space.

This was made clear to me in early August 2010 at a bus stop in Oakland, California. I had just finished the first of a two-day oral history interview with Richard Misrach for the Smithsonian's Archives of American Art (Misrach 2010a). As a way to help prepare for our discussion the following day, Misrach – an environmental photographer whose large-scale prints of bombing sites in the Nevada desert, petrochemical plants in Louisiana, and beaches in Hawaii have earned him international acclaim – lent me an advance copy of a forthcoming book. *Destroy This Memory* is large, measuring 15" x 11," with the horizontal spine across the top, and printed at the highest possible quality in full color (Figure 1.1). Reading the book is like holding a slice of a museum in your hands with the pictures seeming to leap out from the page.

But that's not putting it quite right. It's more like a window through which viewers jump into another place – in this instance, post-Katrina New Orleans during the immediate months after the 2005 hurricane. Waiting for the bus back to Berkeley, I leafed through the photo book, lingering over every page, as the embattled city came into clear focus. New Orleans, through Richard Misrach's lens, was unpeopled – not one person is seen in the 70 images – but the human impact on the devastated environment was immediate and loud. Seeing the landscape meant hearing it, too, as the words of local residents appeared at the center of each uncaptioned picture. Spray-painted messages in bright red, violet-blue, deep carrot orange, and ghost white gave voice to frantic pleas for help, stories of traumatic loss, and angry indictments. Although Misrach (2010b) let the words of residents speak for themselves with no interpretative text, he arranged the graffiti-laced photographs in a distinct narrative, beginning with despair ("help" and "fuck, fuck, fuck") moving on to defiance ("I have a gun" or "to SOB that looted me I will kill you") to gallows humor ("yard of the month" and "yep, Brownie, you did a heck of a job") to a concluding, existential note ("what now?" "broken dreams," "destroy this memory"). The effect on viewers is haunting.

And affective. Emotions of confusion, sympathy, frustration, and anger are ones that I heard expressed at the Oakland bus stop. Within minutes, more than a dozen fellow passengers, also waiting for the F bus, joined me in studying Misrach's photographs. Sitting next to me and looking over my shoulder, they took turns thumbing through the photo book as I held it, stopping at every page, reading aloud its provocative words, and seeing the

Figure 1.1 Cover to Richard Misrach's *Destroy This Memory*, 2010
Source: Richard Misrach

wounded landscapes on which they were written. My bus stop companions offered shrewd, at times conflicting interpretations of the photographs' meanings: some knew little about the hurricane and were astonished that such disaster could be wrought by natural forces, while others remembered it well and were chilled by what they saw to be indictments against governmental ineptitude. It was made clear to me that there was no single right way to read these visual images. But also clear is that, for everyone that afternoon at the small corner in Oakland, we were somehow having contact with a place and a time that affected us in profound and surprising ways. We were responding to the *thereness* of photography.

The Thereness of Photography

So was Roland Barthes, when he looked at a nineteenth-century photograph of the Alhambra in Granada, Spain. "This old photograph touches me," he wrote, "it is quite simply *there* that I should like to live." The experience that Barthes (1981: 38, 84) describes – the sense that he is looking directly at a slice of geographic reality, "an immediate presence to the world" – is foundational to the medium. And it's not just among astute semiologists like Barthes that photographs exert the power of place. The most democratic of the geographic media, photography speaks an accessible language that's both multivalent and open to anyone who pauses to look at what's there.

"Thereness is a sense of the subject's reality, a heightened sense of its physicality, etched sharply into the image," writes Gerry Badger (2010: 17). "It is a sense that we are looking at the world directly, without mediation." Badger is describing the often-noted aura of machine objectivity that hangs over photographs, despite the subjective nature of both taking a picture and manipulating its visual qualities. It's often easy to forget, when looking at photographs, that one is looking at a mediated reality instead of reality itself. Marita Sturken and Lisa Cartwright (2001: 17) call this the *myth of photograph truth* and note that "although we know that images can be ambiguous and are easily manipulated or altered ... much of the power of photography still lies in the shared belief that photographs are objective or truthful records."

This constant tension between photography and reality – a slippery relationship at once straightforward and enigmatic – can be found at the extreme ends of the photographic spectrum: from modest snapshots emerging from a Brownie camera or cell phone to the most serious "art" photographs. Walker Evans (1974: 95), himself a master of the art, recognized that even the most modest and banal postcards, produced as they often are "as a routine chore by heaven knows what anonymous photographer," can be a "well-nigh perfect record of place." Such photographs can simultaneously present evidence and evoke a magical quality that evades definition – resulting in a complex set of feelings and associations specifically because of the allegiance with thereness.

What's more, the thereness of photographs means that such visual images "don't only show us things, they *do* things. They engage us optically, neurologically, intellectually, viscerally, physically" (Heiferman 2012: 16). For my bus stop companions, photographs of Katrina-wracked New Orleans demanded our scrutiny and interpretation, as they promoted conversation, stimulated thought, and shaped at least one person's understanding of the unnatural metropolis. Conceiving photographs this way, on the one hand, helps move beyond an unproductive impasse within human geography, where "representation" is counterposed to something called "practice" or "performance." As an agent of change, feeling, and affect, photography's active role in the practices and performances of everyday life makes it an especially important geographic medium (Abel 2012).

On the other hand, recognizing the thereness of photography suggests something about geography. As Felix Driver (2003: 227) argues, the idea that geography is a particularly visual discipline has a long history and "isn't simply the product of heightened anxiety about the politics of vision in recent cultural theory. For centuries, indeed, practitioners of the art of geography have been engaged in developing languages and techniques to capture what the eye could or should see in a landscape." Photography emerged in the nineteenth century as an ideal instrument for geographic research and education, evolving from lantern slides and stereographic views to 35 mm slides and PowerPoint presentations (Figure 1.2). So successful has the camera been to visualize a slice of the world that, as Tuan (1979: 413) astutely observes, "in the classroom, a geography lecture without slides is as anomalous as an anatomy lecture without bones."

Sometimes, as Gillian Rose (2003: 216; cf. Driver 2003; Matless 2003; Ryan 2003) observes, the photograph shown as a lecture slide "becomes the real," the photographs "confirm the truth of our words." This is an important point, and one that must be emphasized. It also should be extended beyond the geography classroom and become an initial point of departure for all photographic/geographic studies – namely, the recognition of the dual existence of photographs as physical objects and compelling imagery. Before a photograph can function as a representation of any kind, it begins its life as a three-dimensional thing, which has "volume, opacity, tactility, and a physical presence in the world" (Batchen 1997: 2). One might push this general observation even further to assert that a photograph's material form (whether a gelatin silver print or the bytes of a digital file), no less than the image it bears, is fundamental to its function as an object that carries social and cultural meaning.

This essential observation is easy to overlook, especially when viewing photographs of visually arresting imagery. As Elizabeth Edwards and Janice Hart (2004: 2) argue, "the

Figure 1.2 ***Children in a Geography Class Viewing Stereoscopic Photographs*, 1908. Photographer unknown**
Source: Library of Congress Prints and Photographs Division, Underwood and Underwood Collection, LC-USZ62-90216

prevailing tendency is that photographs are apprehended in one visual act, absorbing image and object together, yet privileging the former." While image content – what is depicted in a photograph – remains the principle interest of most viewers, much is lost if we leave it at that. It's worth considering, for example, this 1938 image of an isolated farm in the Texas panhandle by the American photographer Dorothea Lange (Figure 1.3). At one level, it offers evidence of the sort of vernacular structures and agricultural patterns that have long fascinated cultural geographers. Pushing a bit further, a geographer might take notice of the abandonment of the dwelling and the particularly neat rows of contour-plowed land surrounding it. Such descriptions, as important as they are, neglect the fact that Lange's Texas photograph is a mediated representation that performs cultural work.

An approach to this photograph that is aware of its thereness begins with its status as a material object. It would, furthermore, acknowledge that Lange created this image with a specific agenda in mind, that it served her and other's interests in competing ways. Finally, it would recognize that, over the years, the material object has circulated widely as different viewerships have seen it in multiple contexts. As a key member of President Franklin Roosevelt's Farm Security Administration (FSA), Lange was commissioned to

Figure 1.3 **Dorothea Lange, *Tractored Out*. Power farming displaces tenants from the land in the western dry cotton area, Childress County, Texas Panhandle, 1938.**
Source: Library of Congress Prints and Photographs Division, US Farm Security Administration/Office of War Information, LC-USF34-T01-018281-C

photographically document the social and economic relationships of American agricultural labor during the Great Depression. She became a severe critic of that system, using her photographs to expose its structural inequalities. This becomes evident only when the photograph's full caption, as Lange intended it, is matched to the image itself: "Tractored Out: Power farming displaces tenants from the land in the western dry cotton area, Childress County, Texas Panhandle. June 1938." Far from a value-neutral picture of a Texas landscape, Lange's photograph simmers with indignation and moral conviction (Spirn 2009).

Image makers like Dorothea Lange seductively deployed the thereness of photography to stake her claims about the troubled and uneven nature of American capitalist development. Other photographers may also strive to present a visual argument, but, like Trevor Paglen, are simultaneously concerned with the slippery relationship between photography and what is depicted. Trained as a geographer and a photographer, Paglen recognizes a contemporary suspicion of representation – "the days of believing that there's something out there in the world that can be transparently represented by a photograph or image are over" – at least in the realm of critical theory and the art world (quoted in Stallabrass 2011: 8). But rather than either retreating to pure abstraction or eschewing the visual altogether, he embraces the performative act of photography. Indeed, for Paglen photography is all about exploring limits – limits of visibility, representation, knowledge, and democratic society.

Each photograph he takes can be regarded as a record of political performance as he insists on his right to bring his camera to public space and document what is otherwise invisible.

And it is the generally invisible – and purposefully so – that intrigues Paglen and compels him to document the hidden spaces of military power. He has taken thousands of photographs of the "black world" – the covert defense projects and infrastructure that has grown exponentially since the Bush administration's 2001 declared War on Terror. In some cases, he uses high-end optical lenses designed for astronomical photography to document secret military bases in the United States. In others, he makes use of data generated by amateur satellite watchers to track and photograph classified spacecraft in the earth's orbit. "Nine Reconnaissance Satellites over Sonora Pass" from 2008 (Figure 1.4) is an example of the latter series and presents viewers with an immediate and interesting contradiction. With its striking, multicolored symmetrical lines set against the deep black background, the photograph is a four-hour time-lapse exposure of the northern sky over the Sierra Nevada. It at once belongs to the art world,[1] but its full significance only becomes apparent when considering the social process that went into making it. For the artist, it is an exposé of the "legal 'nowhere' that nourishes the worst excesses of power" (Paglen 2010: 276).

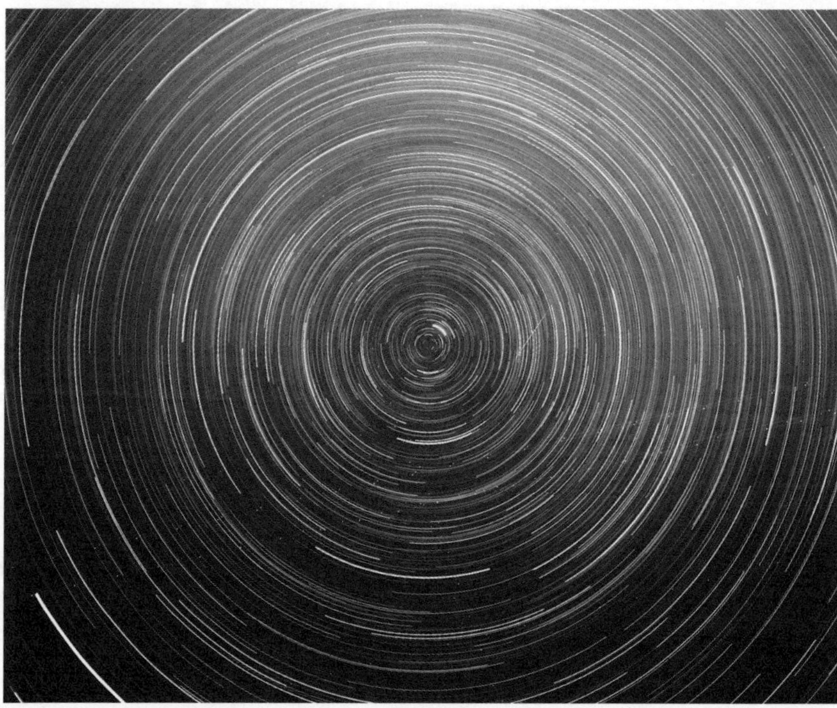

Figure 1.4 Trevor Paglen, *Nine Reconnaissance Satellites over Sonora Pass*, 2008
Source: Trevor Paglen; Altman Siegel, San Francisco; Metro Pictures, New York; Galerie Thomas Zander

1 Paglen is represented by the same Chelsea gallery, Metro Pictures, that represents superstar artists like Cindy Sherman, and his photographs have been exhibited at the world's most prestigious venues, including the Metropolitan Museum of Art, New York, and the Tate Modern, London.

Making the "nowhere" of covert operations into a somewhere through the troubled yet continued relevance of photography's thereness is what gives Paglen's work its geographic immediacy and political relevance.

The photographic work of Trevor Paglen, Dorothea Lange, and Richard Misrach point to something else – namely, that it behooves geographers to pay close attention to the work of photographers. This point is picked up by James R. Ryan (2003: 235), who notes that "geographers have tended to see the work of visual artists as merely illustrative of textual ideas or, at best, something to be deconstructed from a distance." Instead, he argues that there is much to be gained from a sustained dialogue between these two spheres. A sustained dialogue must, by definition, narrow the conversation to give it substance and depth, especially so with this ubiquitous, accessible medium. What makes photography – defined by its close, thorny connection with reality – ideal to enlist for politics and to illustrate things, also makes it elusive and easy to underestimate (Hoelscher 2012). A case-study perspective, one that engages critically with images and sociocultural context, would seem to offer the most direct route to photography's thereness.

In the following sections, I explore the possibilities of such a dialogue between geography and photography by closely examining the geographic lenses of one photo agency – Magnum Photos. Not only does Magnum – now in its seventh decade – offer a range of approaches and ways of handling the medium, it also has a distinctly geographic way of seeing and visually describing the world. Because photographs so seamlessly enter the relationship between observer and material reality, they have become "a functioning tool of the geographic imagination," write Schwartz and Ryan (2003: 3). The relationship becomes even more interesting when considering the work of photographers, like many associated with this particular photo agency, whose specific objective is to create visual records that actively shape perceptions of place. Exploring something of Magnum's geographical imagination sheds light on how geography and photography can be mutually entwined to the benefit of each.

The Geographical Imagination of a Photo Agency

In 1947, in the wake of the Second World War's unprecedented destruction, four of the most prominent photographers to cover that shattering event had a unique idea: to form a photographic cooperative that would allow for the creation and dissemination of visual images unencumbered by the constraints of for-profit photojournalism.[2] The experience of the war and its aftermath called into question the very foundation of Western civilization and its traditional means of conveying visual information. The resulting organization – Magnum Photos – has since become one of the modern world's most influential photographic communities, producing images of great diversity and distinction that have been viewed the world over.

It has been long understood that for Henri Cartier-Bresson, photography was a temporal matter. The decisive moment, he famously said, is the "simultaneous recognition, in a fraction of a second, of the significance of an event." But it was also, for this Magnum founder, a spatial concern: "the [re]discovery of the world around us" (Cartier-Bresson 1952: n.p.). Sometimes those worlds embody excruciating pain and at other times exuberant joy; they can exhibit breathtaking beauty or bleak unsightliness. Regardless of what they look

[2] This section is derived, with considerable modification, from Hoelscher (2013).

like, photographs of decisive places demonstrate the relationship between people and their environment as they shed light on other places without giving up their specificity – they create a distinct sense of that place.

"Place," no less than "story," is a central, organizing concept of the Magnum archive. As Chris Boot (2000: 4) has documented, "story" is "etched into the way Magnum has organized its work." Ever since the photo agency's beginning, "story" is a term used to "describe any body of work, whether an account of an historical event, or a set of entirely personal pictures," or a commercial, commissioned assignment. Thus, a "story" comprises photographs as diverse as Dennis Stock's pictures of James Dean walking through a rainy Times Square in 1955, Bruno Barbey's of the 1968 Paris street riots, or Susan Meiselas's mid-1970s series on American carnival strippers.

What each of these "stories" has in common is its geographic referent. As Matthew Murphy (2010), Magnum's current New York bureau archivist, explains, "the 'story' is a concept which defines a series of photographs, which have in common a place, anything from a kitchen to a continent." From a purely organizational perspective, it hardly matters if the resulting photograph ends up in a corporate annual report, a magazine cover, a textbook, or a gallery wall: in most cases, Magnum arranged its stories geographically, giving an otherwise potentially amorphous organizational system a common thread.

Significantly, that thread was there from the beginning. The 1947 certificate of incorporation for Magnum Photos, Inc., seeks as its mission: "to engage in a photographic, portrait, picture, and painting business; to make … representations of persons, places, landscapes, [and] scenes … and to carry on the business of photography in all its branches, in any part of the world" (quoted in Miller 1997: 52–53). A business model that defined Magnum's objectives in distinctly geographical terms is hardly surprising, given its early dependency on the picture magazines of the day. Moreover, it aligned the fledgling cooperative with the long history of photography itself. Photography, as one of the medium's earliest proponents declared in 1858, did something quite unique: through photographs, the world was "made familiar" and "brought in intense reality to our very hearths" (Price 1858: 1–2). This is to say that photographic images – from daguerreotypes in the nineteenth century to halftone reproductions in newspapers and magazines in the twentieth century to digital files on the Internet today – have played a major role in the making and dissemination of geographical knowledge (Schwartz and Ryan 2003). Magnum, with its ever-regenerating group of influential photographers, has been vital to that endeavor.

In order to achieve its goal of carrying the business to "any part of the world," each of the original photographers was assigned a world region: David "Chim" Seymour would cover Europe; Bill Vandivert had the United States; George Rodger was assigned the Middle East and Africa; Cartier-Bresson had Asia; while Robert Capa – the driving force behind Magnum's founding – was free to take on roaming assignments wherever stories might appear. As George Rodger put it, Magnum was formed, at least in part, to "make our own lives easier so that we could operate, each in his own field" – "field" meaning here both a particular photographic vision and geographic territory (Rodger quoted in Hill and Cooper 1979: 67).[3]

Magnum's geographic project emerged, according to Ernst Haas, at a "time when the world had to be rediscovered." Like his early Magnum colleagues, Haas simultaneously felt alienated from his home (he emigrated from postwar Vienna upon acceptance into Magnum and rarely returned) and also possessed by "a tremendous wanderlust." Emerging from the toxic cauldron of World War II, when place after place was "destroyed and separated,"

3 Because one of the charter members, Bill Vandivert, left Magnum one year after its founding, Robert Capa took over responsibilities for the US photographs.

Haas found that "suddenly there was peace and everybody ... wanted to know each other" (quoted in Sanghvi 1981: 16, 21). The idealistic internationalism at the heart of such sentiments was strongly influenced by larger political, ideological, and cultural imperatives to conceive a world beyond national boundaries and removed from a fascist ideology that emphasized racial and cultural "purity." The founders of Magnum, deeply influenced by the era's unrestrained atrocities, were substantial participants in an imperative that sought to create a world different from the one that led to two world wars.[4] Visually describing what that world might look like – embracing photography's thereness and making it the cooperative's aesthetic principle – became Magnum's immediate raison d'être.

Perhaps not surprisingly, the geographies that "had to be rediscovered" by Magnum photographers initially emphasized human experiences that transcended cultural and spatial differences. Earliest and most influential was an ambitious comparative photo-essay conceived by John G. Morris, recently hired as Editor at *Ladies' Home Journal* and soon to become the first and legendary Executive Editor of Magnum Photos. As Morris (1948: 43) put it, the photo-essay would "explain people to people in intimate, vivid terms, taking them not country by country, but trait by trait." More important than highlighting dissimilarity and conflict, the "series would show families in [12] countries every month, as they went about their quotidian business and engaged in the common preoccupations of humankind." The resulting 12-issue series – titled "People are People the World Over" and published between May 1948 and 1949 in both *Ladies Home Journal* and the German picture magazine *Heute* – proved to be a financial boon to the new photo agency (Figure 1.5). It also became a template for group projects to follow – and from which to depart.

With text by Morris and photos by Magnum members and three freelancers, the project adhered to a very strict script.[5] In addition to making a family portrait, Morris prescribed the following scenarios: farming, cooking, eating, washing, bathing, playing, studying, shopping, worshipping, relaxing at home, traveling, sleeping. The series was designed to satisfy *Journal* readers' curiosity about the geographies emerging from the embers of war ruin, and what they saw must have been comforting. Month after month, the visual evidence supplied by Capa et al. seemed to demonstrate that "people are pretty much people, no matter where you find them" (Morris 1948: 43).

By highlighting images of shared underlying values, "People Are People" was a direct contradiction of racist and fascist ideology. It also proved to be a great popular and commercial success. It inspired Robert Capa to launch an equally ambitious group project later that very year, called "Generation X," which sought to compare the postwar generation in 12 different countries. More noteworthy, "People Are People" was a major inspiration for Edward Steichen's seminal 1955 "The Family of Man" exhibition at the Museum of Modern Art. Arguably one of the most influential photography exhibits ever made, "The Family of Man" relied heavily on Magnum not only for its conception but also for many of its 500-some photographs (Sandeen 1995).[6]

---

[4] Much has been said about the impact the war had on the founders of Magnum: Seymour, whose Polish-Jewish family was murdered by the Nazi war machine; Cartier-Bresson, who spent three years as a POW and only escaped on his third try; Capa whose journey through the horrors of fascist-driven warfare famously began with the Spanish Civil War; and Rogers, whose war photographs ranged from the London Blitz of 1939 to the liberation of the Bergen-Belsen concentration camp.

[5] The sole, and notable exception, is Cartier-Bresson, whom Morris believed would not be able to "follow such a simplistic script" and was thus not included (Morris 1998: 116).

[6] Photographs from the following members or future members were included: Eve Arnold, Werner Bischof, Cornell Capa, Robert Capa, Henri Cartier-Bresson, Elliott Erwitt, Burt Glinn, Ernst Haas, George Rodger, Wayne Miller, David "Chim" Seymour, and W. Eugene Smith.

Japan: Familie Okamoto aus Oschika. Selbst ihre Kühe werden vom Staat, der insgesamt 12 Abgaben vorschreibt, gestaffelt besteuert.

Deutschland: Familie Stieglitz aus Wollau. Auf einem Dorftanz fanden sich Vater und Mutter Stieglitz vor mehr als 15 Jahren fürs Leben.

Tschechoslowakei: Familie Balogh aus Furolac. Hier in den Karpathen dauern die Hochzeitsfeierlichkeiten pausenlos 3 Tage und Nächte.

Vereinigte Staaten: Familie Pratt aus Glidden. Zuviel oder zuwenig Regen ist das Problem, das den Farmer in Iowa ständig beschäftigt.

Rund zwei Milliarden Menschen leben auf dieser Erde. Sie gehören verschiedenen Rassen und Völkern an, sie bekennen sich zu verschiedenen Religionen, sie sind durch politische Schranken getrennt. Als Menschen sind sie sich jedoch im Grunde genommen recht ähnlich. Die amerikanische Zeitschrift „Ladies Home Journal", deren Entgegenkommen HEUTE die Veröffentlichung dieser Bilder verdankt, illustriert diese Ähnlichkeit in einem großen Bildbericht: ihre Photographen haben das Leben von zwölf Familien in aller Welt festgehalten, die durch Erdteile und Grenzen, Hautfarbe und Glauben getrennt sind. Fern von jeder Politik entstand ein Bericht, der ohne Sensation einfach von den Menschen und ihrem Leben erzählt.

England: Familie Hiatt aus Hook Norton. Alle vier lesen am Abend für ihr Leben gern die neuesten Geschichten aus dem Wilden Westen.

Pakistan: Familie Mohammed Usman aus Patni. Sie kannten sich vor ihrer Heirat nicht — und sind jetzt schon 13 Jahre glücklich verheiratet.

JOHN GODFREY MORRIS

MENSCHEN WIE DU UND ICH

Die Familie ist der Grundstein der menschlichen Gesellschaftsordnung. Alle die Menschen, die auf den Bildern dieses Berichts gezeigt werden, leben auf dem Lande. Sie bestellen ihre Äcker und sind durch ihren arbeitsreichen Alltag so ausgefüllt, daß sie wenig Zeit haben, sich um die hohe Politik zu kümmern. Mit dem Alltagsleben dieser Familien werden sich die nächsten Folgen dieses Berichtes beschäftigen: mit dem Essen und dem Schlafen, mit dem Lernen und dem Einkaufen, dem Kirchgang und dem Waschtag. Und — auf den folgenden Seiten — mit dem häuslichen Herd.

China: Familie Ho Fu-Yuan aus Kia-Ting. Zuerst sollte die kleinste Tochter wegen der bösen Geister nicht mit auf das Bild kommen.

Ägypten: Familie El Gamel aus Manaye Schebein el Kanater. Ihre Lasttiere sind heute noch Esel, wie sie es schon in biblischen Zeiten waren.

Frankreich: Familie Redouin aus Fosses. Ihr größter Stolz ist ihre gute Stube, die aber nur benutzt wird, wenn einmal Besuch kommt.

Italien: Familie Guercini aus Greve. Sie haben ihr Haus gelb getüncht, weil alle Nachbarn ihre Bauernhöfe mit roter Farbe gestrichen haben.

Zentral-Afrika: Familie Zamba Aluma aus Lujulu. Für die Mädchen beginnt der Tag jedesmal mit dem Pflücken eines neuen Blätterrocks.

Mexiko: Familie Gonzalez aus Moravatio. Hier ist es noch Sitte, daß der Bräutigam die Braut ihren Eltern vor der Hochzeit entführen muß.

9 →

Figure 1.5 *"Menschen wie du und ich"* **[People Are People the World Over], a page from the July 1, 1948, edition of *Heute***

Source: Information Control Division, US Army

While the influence of "The Family of Man" remains strong (its catalog, after selling more than 4 million copies, is still in print), the ideological framework – what Michael Ignatieff (2003: 54) later called "liberal moral universalism" – has fared less well.[7] The liberalism of the postwar era was not to go unchallenged, even in its photographic expression. In 1957, Roland Barthes (1972: 100) disparaged the "sentimental humanism" of "The Family of Man" and questioned whether the broad generalizations about shared human experiences describe the world in its full geographical complexity. One can plausibly argue that "Family of Man" expressed the "core belief" of Magnum's founders; it is no coincidence that Steichen's assistant at MoMA, Wayne Miller, became a member of Magnum in 1958. Twenty years later, Susan Sontag (1977: 33) argued that "by purporting to show that individuals are born, work, laugh, and die everywhere in the same way, 'The Family of Man' denies the determining weight of history – of genuine and historically embedded differences, injustices, and conflicts."[8]

If this were all there was to Magnum's geographical project, the photo agency would surely not have survived, at least in its recognizable form. Although traces of a wish to find shared values across place remain, more recognizable is what Barthes also called a "progressive humanism." In contrast with sentimental humanism's search for a "rock solid of a universal human nature," a progressive inflection takes seriously the profound differences across the humanly constructed world. For Barthes (1972: 102), "progressive humanism" constantly "scours nature, its 'laws' and its 'limits' in order to discover History there, and at least to establish Nature as historical." Such an approach denies the supposition that people are basically the same under the veneer of culture, but also emphasizes the way that something – whether political-economic power or a shared historical experience – connects people from very different geographies. If sentimental humanism was premised on the belief in a common human nature beneath the incredible diversity of human beliefs, values, and geographies, then Barthes's progressive humanism finds this to be a myth.

In existence for more than 60 years, Magnum has successfully adapted progressive humanism as it has grown, diversified, and created ever-new conceptual frameworks for rediscovering the world. That is not to say that Magnum photographs have one "look" or point of view. With their broad conceptions of place – "anything from a kitchen to a continent" – Magnum photographers possess strikingly diverse geographical imaginations, which are recurrently reflected in their work. Some, like Bruce Gilden, frequently focus on the interplay of behavior and customs in urban spaces, while others, like Steve McCurry, emphasize regions where cultures and languages collide. Still other photographers, like Larry Towell, directly acknowledge their geographical imagination. Towell (2013) notes, "if there's one theme that connects all my work, I think it's that of landlessness; how land makes people into who they are and what happens to them when they lose it and thus lose their identities." Similarly, Jonas Bendiksen's continuing project of isolated communities and enclaves goes by the name "The Places We Live." While Gilles Peress is perhaps less explicit about how geographical imaginations play a role in his work, observers have noted how his projects ranging from Teheran and Belfast exhibit a distinct "politics of space" (Kozloff 1994: 170–77). Contemporary Magnum members, through a diverse set of geographical imaginations, share with their predecessors an enduring dedication to photographing "the world as it is."

By "geographical imagination," I simply mean a heightened sensitivity toward the importance of space, place, and environment in the making and meaning of social and cultural life on earth (Harvey 2005). Bringing that sensitivity to bear on their projects is

[7] Ignatieff astutely observes that Magnum's liberalism developed in conjunction with the United Declaration of Human Rights, drafted in the aftermath of World War II.

[8] A similar critique comes from Catherine A. Lutz and Jane L. Collins (1993: 277–78).

what enables many Magnum photographers to picture places as "decisive" and not as mere backdrops to important personalities or events. Cartier-Bresson, for one, was greatly influenced by the anarchist geographer, Élisée Reclus (1830–1905), and his belief that political emancipation and parity among global peoples and cultures goes hand in hand. Others, like Stuart Franklin, are geographers by training (he received BA and PhD degrees in geography from Oxford University). Yet, Magnum's photographers have been imbued more generally with a "habit of mind" that spirals well beyond the walls of the academy. They would seem to have taken in Reclus's central educational point that "It's outside of school that one learns the most, in the street, in the workshop, at the stalls of a fair, at the theatre, in railroad cars and on steamboats, in new landscapes and foreign cities" (quoted in Galassi 2010: 29).

Put differently, geographical imaginations are triggered by personal experience, but also by the visual and aural representations that we find in a variety of media, including photography. With both intellectual passion and modesty, Mikheal Subotzky (2013), one of Magnum's most recent nominees, describes his approach to photography's thereness: "For me, photography has become a way of attempting to make sense of the very strange world that I see around me. I don't ever expect to achieve that understanding, but the fact that I am trying comforts me."

Magnum's photographers seek to make sense of the world around them through a number of geographic lenses, two of which stand out: exploration/travel and insider/outsider visions. The progressive humanism at work in photographs of decisive places suggests a persisting attempt to *re*discover the world, to constantly question what is purported to be good, natural, and universal. Magnum's unique commitment to long-term, in-depth projects made such questioning possible and created photographs with evocative senses of place.

Decisive Places: Magnum's Geographic Lenses

Exploration/Travel

Photographers, whether on assignment for a magazine or working on personal projects, visually document the places they visit and the people who inhabit them. Beginning with George Rodger in Africa, Magnum's systematic geographic coverage of the world for the benefit of viewing audiences elsewhere make it part of a long-established tradition. To be sure, at the very core of the medium, photographic images provided the opportunity for vicarious visual exploration of distant places. Photography might be originally rooted in the development of pictorial illustration, but travel soon became part of the argument surrounding the announcement of Daguerre's 1839 invention. His method of mechanically capturing an image of the world, one proponent claimed, was predicted to become "an object of continual and indispensible use" to the traveler, enabling "every author ... to compose the geographical part of his own work" (quoted in Goldberg 1988: 22). And, indeed, very soon travelers equipped themselves with daguerreotype outfits and stereoscopic cameras "to take on itineraries established by historical tradition and the parameters of their country's influence" (Hambourg 1996: 33; see also Schwartz 1996). It is a very short step from the mid-nineteenth-century daguerreotype or stereoscopic view to the mid-twentieth-century *National Geographic*: both served as a surrogate for travel for primarily middle-class audiences.

Thus, while George Rodger might have been the first photographer to record some portions of Africa during his epic travels across the continent in 1948, in fact, he was working in the long shadow of others documenting "unknown" geographies. He began his long career as "a photographic voyageur," as someone belonging to "the great tradition of explorers and adventurers," when he enlisted in the Merchant Navy as a teenager. He then became famous as a British freelance photographer who purportedly traveled 75,000 miles covering the remote perimeter of the war in Africa and Asia before documenting the Allied invasion of Europe (Naggar 2003).[9] He famously gave up war photography, for which he had acquired such a sterling reputation, when he reflected on his way of taking pictures at the liberation of the Bergen-Belsen concentration camp. Rodger was appalled that he treated "this pitiful human flotsam as if it were a gigantic still-life," he later recalled. "It wasn't even a matter of what I was photographing as what had happened to me in the process. When I discovered that I could look at the horror of Belsen ... and think only of a nice photographic composition, I knew something had happened to me and I had to stop. I said this is where I quit." Photography, Rodgers seemed to be saying, could not only link people to places, but also drive them away. While this has been most commonly interpreted as Rodger's response to the brutality and dehumanizing effect of war, it may also be surmised that the dehumanization that he opposed came from his camera – or, the specific photographic response to atrocity (Boot 2004: 402).

Africa became the place where Rodger (1999: ii) hoped to find respite – "some spot in the world that was clean and untrammeled" – from those horrors. Months after Magnum's founding, he began a two-year, 28,000-mile journey across Africa, from Johannesburg to the Mediterranean. Along the way, he photographed South Africa, Uganda, Swaziland, Zaire, Tanzania, Egypt, and Sudan, sending his images to the Magnum office in Paris for distribution to magazines across Europe and the United States. Perhaps more than most photographers, writing served as an equal partner in "composing the geographical part" of his travels, at least initially. Rodger was a leader in developing the "package story," which combined text with images; thus, in place after place, he took detailed fieldnotes that became the basis for extensive captions and narratives to accompany his photographs.

His detailed package story on the Nuba of Kordofan is arguably his best example. For two weeks, in February and March 1949, Rodger photographed and wrote about a place that he believed embodied the peace and idyllic repose he was searching for. While Africa, including Sudan, was undergoing massive political and social upheavals associated with postcolonial transformation, Rodger instead focused on a region as far removed as possible from those struggles. "I traveled thousands of miles to see if somewhere, in some remote corner, there was not still a little of the old Africa that had been seen by men like Brazza and Livingstone," he wrote in the text to accompany his photographs. "I found it at last in Kordofan" (Rodger 1949: ii).

What Rodger found both dazzled and perplexed him. The mountainous landscape that made the region so inaccessible to outsiders, the exotic ceremonies and traditions, the bewildering interactions among individuals and groups: Rodger struggled to make sense of what he encountered during his travels. Most puzzling of all were the wrestling matches and the bracelet fighting ceremony. As Rodger's biographer notes, he was "thrown into the heart of a ceremony he did not understand, performed by a people he knew little about" (Naggar 2003: 181). Rodger's photographs alternatively reflect that disorientation and his attempt to make sense of what he was seeing on his own, Western terms. One striking example is his picture from the interior of a Nuba house (Figure 1.6).

In this photograph, a man is captured, midstride, walking through the dwelling's entrance. Unlike other captions that Rodger wrote to accompany his photographs – captions that provide considerable ethnographic detail to the layout of a house, the kitchen utensils, the physical appearance of people, and their exotic customs – this one was originally

9 Rodger's June 29, 1995, obituary in the *New York Times* went by the title "Death of an Adventurer." See also 75,000 miles (1942).

Figure 1.6 George Rodger, *The Keyhole Entrance to a Nuba House in the Korongo Jebels Mountains*, Kordofan, Sudan, 1949
Source: Magnum Photos

described in the briefest terms: "A man of the Mesakin Qusar Nuba returns through his keyhole doorway in the evening, carrying a gourd." For a man who determinedly refused to consider himself an artist, Rodger did much more with this picture than simply make a visual record of his travels: the photograph's superb interplay of light and dark, shadow and reflection, geometric shape and symmetry suggest someone who had not abandoned photographic composition at the gates of Bergen-Belsen.

These photographs thus depict a place simultaneously isolated – a geography "around which nature has built a protective wall against Western invasion," as Rodger put it – and, from today's perspective, anachronistic and a little naïve. Several decades after his first photographs of the Nuba brought world attention to the region, photographic safaris were organized as part of a global tourism infrastructure. And when Magnum photographers document Sudan today they picture a very different place, one marked by the violence of ethnic and civil wars, and where the reverberations of postcolonial life are felt through and through. By contrast, Rodger's Kordofan region of Sudan is peaceful, insulated, and tranquil. It is a place that seems to have vanished from the earth.

Gone as well is the kind of explorer that Rodger worked so hard to be. Magnum photographers remain inveterate travelers, skimming the globe at ever increasing rates and taking pictures of the world as it is. But they can no longer leave home for weeks, or months, and maintain only minimal contact with the home office. Increasingly, the nature of travel itself has become the subject of their photography, none more so than in the work of Martin Parr, someone more likely to focus on the safaris of camera-touting tourists in Africa than either its endangered traditional cultures or the military forces that have wracked the continent.

Parr is interested in the absurdities and incongruities of the modern world, and the ways that ordinary people try to navigate it. The tourism industry is central to that navigation, and in it Parr finds much that is simultaneously amusing and poignant. One of his first major projects, "The Last Resort" (1983–1986), satirically documented the tourist destination of New Brighton, a dilapidated seaside resort, which had seen better days. With his now trademark style of saturated color and uncompromising directness, he pictured the English working class trying to sneak a few hours of leisure time by sunbathing under looming construction equipment, waiting among the perspiring hordes at grubby lunch counters, and dipping their feet into trash-strewn water.

The work was controversial – some critics found it "aggressive" and "cynical" – but also groundbreaking, and helped Parr gain entry into Magnum (Williams 2002). At this time, partly as a result of the increased travel for commercial assignments that the agency made possible, Parr expanded his work from the local to the global, and eventually to a large-scale project on global tourism, "Small World," of the early 1990s. Whether photographing souvenir vendors at the Giza pyramids in Egypt or rain-soaked Japanese tourists in a Hawaii visitor-center boat, Parr's greatest interest seems to be the disjunction between geographical expectation and reality that is endemic to the modern traveler experience. There are the guidebooks and Web sites that promise one version of Athens, and then there is the modern Greek capital, flooded with travelers of all varieties, who invariably change the experience of visiting the place.

Some might be disappointed by that disjunction, but, for Parr, the gap between myth and reality functions as a central element of the modern world and is therefore worth documenting. When he was recently asked by *American Photo* magazine to choose the "Ten Places You Must Photograph," Parr picked Rome "because of the quality of its tourists." He says that "when most travel photographers go to some destination the last thing they want to see are tourists, but that's usually the first thing I want to see." And what better destination than Rome?

> *Here you have the Eternal City, which is fundamentally one of the most magical cities, exquisitely beautiful, and what you notice are all the people who have come to be part of it. To me, people are much more interesting than ruins. People move around and change. Ruins just sit there and do nothing.* (Parr 2008: 62–63)

With his flash-on camera and its resulting combination of garish color, and raw, off-kilter framing, Parr presents Rome with both affection and skepticism (Figure 1.7). His 1993 photograph of the Spanish Steps really is not about the famous landscape, but instead about the people who travel there see it, how they react to it, and (by implication) how they experience it. It's more about a distinct sense of place than about landscape – an experience of place that treats the site itself as if it were something to be viewed rather than lived in. And in this case, not even something to be viewed, but passed through. Sometimes, as the picture's focal point suggests, tourists spend as much time planning where to go next on their itinerary, reading guidebooks and maps, with a back to the destination, and checking off places from their "must see" lists.

Upon seeing this and other photographs from his 1995 "Small World" exhibition, Henri Cartier-Bresson famously told Parr, "I have only one thing to say to you. You are from a completely different planet" (quoted in Miller 1997: 297). Part of the intergalactic difference, of course, concerned style, especially the distinction between color and black-and-white photography. Part also is the playful irony that consistently runs through Parr's travel photographs. But perhaps the Magnum founder meant something more literal as well; after all, no less than Cartier-Bresson, Parr uses surrealist techniques of juxtaposition and

Figure 1.7 Martin Parr, *The Spanish Steps*, Rome, Italy, 1993
Source: Magnum Photos

dislocation, which then often raise questions about what is normal in a given place. It is just that those places had changed beyond recognition, with mass tourism as a leading force in those transformations. Photography, through the lens of Martin Parr, incessantly challenges preconceived assumptions, as it concurrently reinforces a sense that we, as viewers, are there. Never merely a "record of simple truth and precision" – although it is that – a photograph is also the product of imagination as it shapes perceptions of place (Schwartz 2000).

Inside/Outside

A second geographic lens was recently articulated by Bruce Davidson (2009: 9) when, reflecting on his 50-year career, he said that "I often find myself an outsider on the inside discovering beauty and meaning in the most desperate of situations." Magnum's members frequently document places across the chasms of gender, race, class, and national origins. Nowhere, however, is the sense of an "inside" and an "outside" – of intimacy and exposure, of private life and public space, of being in place and out of place – better seen than in Davidson's landmark *East 100th Street*.

"What you call a ghetto, I call my home," Davidson (1970: n.p.) recalls hearing from residents of the East Harlem neighborhood that became his photographic subject during the mid-1960s. The sense of essential difference – between himself as a white, middle-class professional photographer and his photographic subjects, the black and Hispanic people who lived in what was then known as New York's "worst slum" – remained throughout the two-year personal project, but it was a difference that he strived to overcome (Klein 1968: 32). Occasionally compared to Jacob Riis and his photographs of New York's "ghettos," Davidson purposively eschewed his predecessor's sensationalistic voyeurism (Sontag 1977: 56). He furthermore abandoned the small, handheld camera that had become the Magnum trademark, choosing, instead, to work with a large view camera on tripod, which delivered images of a sharpness, depth of field, and precision superior to those produced with 35 mm film.

More importantly, it also meant that Davidson recast himself from street photographer working in the reportage tradition into the role of neighborhood photographer, a recognizable and trusted person who was allowed access to households, streets, and business that his outsider status would have otherwise denied. Less important than dramatic narrative was a concern for the ability of photography to "evoke an indefinable sense of place" – at least according to the Museum of Modern Art, which exhibited 43 photographs in 1970 (MoMA 1970). This is how Davidson (1970: n.p.) described his intentions:

> *The presence of a large format camera on a tripod, with its bellows and black focusing cloth, gave a sense of dignity to the act of taking pictures. I didn't want to be the unobserved observer. I wanted to be with my subjects face to face and for them to collaborate in my taking the picture.*

Such collaboration would only be possible with community participation and support, an ethnographic basic that Davidson had learned from his earlier work with Brooklyn gangs, and with the Freedom Rides and Civil Rights movement. He worked with local religious leaders and the members of the neighborhood citizens' committee, who agreed that he could take a few pictures and then present them for review. After receiving approval from both the committee and the families of the first photographs, Davidson began going to the block every day, carrying an album of sample photographs that he showed to people he hoped to photograph. He eventually gave away several thousand prints to residents, and invited community members to MoMA's opening.

Some community members were coming to see themselves. A few of the published photographs were of the cityscape: alleys strewn with garbage, distant vistas of the block from a rooftop, the interior courtyard of a tenement building. Most, however, were "environmental portraits": people across the age spectrum, in their personal space, whether outdoors, on the street, or on front stoop, or indoors, in a bedroom or kitchen or basement. "During the two years I photographed East 100th Street, NASA was sending probes into outer space," Davidson (1970: n.p.) wrote years later. "I wanted to see instead into the inner space of the city."

That inner space might have been terra incognita for the majority of the city's white residents, who knew only of the block's sordid reputation, but for its residents, the block of East 100th Street, between First and Second Avenues, was something much more complex. The range of environmental portraits articulates a heightened sense of that complexity, individuality, and ambiguity, and refrains from the objectification that came so easily to photographers documenting the lives of "others." Some photographs show people worn out by the incessant struggle of living in poverty, while others appear more rebellious and proud in difficult circumstances; some people seem vulnerable, but others suggest resistance. In each case, Davidson sought to portray what had been previously treated as an abstract concept (namely, urban poverty) into a geography of clearly delineated worlds.

In this photograph, two young girls sit on one end of a blanket-covered couch in the family's sparse living room (Figure 1.8). Wearing lovely, Sunday-best dresses they look directly at the camera lens. Behind the girls, a window offers a view of the city beyond. The girls and their parents may have played an active role in defining their pose, but the point of view was the photographer's. Windows, with their tenuous yet impervious borders between public and private, are a central feature of Davidson's series. Sometimes the view is from outside looking in, but more common, as in this photograph, is the interior view showing the world beyond. Davidson put it this way: "I wanted to explore not only the rooms, but what you saw out the window, across the courtyard and into infinity. Not only the room, but what the room saw" (quoted in Vanderbilt 2003: 9). It was a view that he had never seen before and the result is an awkwardness and tension that appears in many of the photographs. Davidson certainly achieved his goal of earning the trust of many in the community, and he was able to create a documentary record of a neighborhood in transition. Nevertheless, an unbridgeable barrier remained and helped create the tension that runs through such images.

For many viewers, it is precisely this tension that gives the East 100th Street photographs their power – and their controversy. The collaborative process, for Carl A. Kramer (1971), endows Davidson's project with its "total honesty" and its evocation of a "real piece of the world," while for the *New Yorker*'s reviewer, it made for a "fatal loss of spontaneity." A.D. Coleman's review comes to a rather different conclusion. While applauding Davidson for his "sincerity of motives [and] his commitment" to those he pictured, Coleman (1970) finds that "something is being kept back by the subjects" and by Davidson himself: "there is a caution in his eyes as well as in those of his subjects." Paradoxically, the unarticulated, but nonetheless very real tension generated by photographing across lines of sociogeographical separation, bestow the photographs with their most damning quality: beauty. "Davidson has transmuted a truth which is not beautiful into an art which is." For Coleman, better models for such a project are the "strong, simple, artless" reform photographs of Lewis Hine and Jacob Riis (see also Reinhart et al. 2007).

Davidson is clearly aware of such criticism, but to him it is beside the point. He notes that when he lent cameras to some of the local residents, they "don't photograph the slums. They photograph their friends … all sort of possibilities, without sentimentality. They photograph the life they know, not its horrors." And it was not uncommon for Davidson to see his own "beautiful" photographs hanging on the walls of the homes of

Figure 1.8 Bruce Davidson, *East 100th Street*, New York City, 1966
Source: Magnum Photos

people he had pictured. His photographs neither glorify the neighborhood nor dwell on its very real social problems – though its scars and pain are evident. Instead, by simultaneously acknowledging and collaborating across the socioracial divide that inevitably separated himself from the residents of this community, he produced a photographic record of a place thick with texture, individuality, and dignity.

Visual images, no less than language, can assume a critical role in the creation of place – in this case, a new place that most New Yorkers had never seen before. Photography alone cannot mold the natural world. But it can direct attention to things formerly overlooked – invisible and seemingly nonexistent – as it also organizes apparently insignificant entities into significant composite wholes (Tuan 1991). Although not a professional geographer, Davidson clearly understood something about the complex, constitutive relationship between photography and place.

Conclusion

Photographs by Bruce Davidson, and all his colleagues at Magnum, suggest a very particular way of seeing that has two, distinct components. First they exhibit a sense of place that is an open and progressive force in the world. A sense of place – that deeply personal way that people think and feel about the world they live in – will obviously vary from individual to individual, including Magnum's photographers. But what many share is *a progressive sense of place* that, by its very definition, links to places beyond, all the while maintaining its distinctiveness. Christopher Anderson (2012) captures this progressive sense of place when he describes his work as an exploration of the "relationship between politics, economics, consumption, and the earth. I approach the topic ... by looking at how consumption in the developed world creates the conditions for further destruction of the earth in the developing world, specifically Latin America" (see also Massey 1994: 146–56).

Second, and more broadly, they demonstrate an ambitious engagement with the therereness of photography. One of the photo agency's most recent members, Peter van Agtmael (2012), put it this way: "For me, reality is inevitably more interesting, more strange, than anything created purely by the imagination." In many ways, he was echoing a deep tradition within documentary photography, with roots in the work of Lange and Cartier-Bresson that seeks to document "things as they are." But the paradox, of course, is that such work "creatively interpret[s] and translate[s] the chaos of life into a product that can be distributed to readers" (Panzer 2005: 10). And, as sophisticated photographers like Agtmael would immediately acknowledge, the business of representing reality is very much about imagination or, as his Magnum colleague Philip Jones Griffiths once said, it's about "making caustic comments" about what you see (quoted in Miller 1997: 211).

Such a perspective has clear resonance with those who also want to explore the relationship between people and the world around them, and it behooves geographers to pay close attention to creators of this important visual medium. As I have tried to argue (and hopefully demonstrate) in this chapter, the very ubiquity of photography and its unique relationship with the observable world demand an approach that favors depth over surface. Such an approach embraces and interrogates the thereness of photography, rather than backing away from the troublesome nature of representation. It recognizes that photographs are not just things to be looked and used for evidence, but should be the source of questions. They can function as puzzles to decode, sites of performance, and embodiments of emotion.

This is not always easy to do, especially living in a world awash with photographs that multiply at an ever-accelerated rate – by some estimates, more than 100 million photographs are uploaded to Facebook every day. Photographs are so omnipresent, so multifaceted, so powerful that the medium changes everything: from where we go, what we want, and what we do, to what we see, what we remember, and who we are (Heiferman 2012). And yet, as Abigail Solomon-Godeau (1994: xxi) notes, photography is "a medium whose very ubiquity may well have fostered its invisibility as an object of study." This is regrettable, given the profound ability of photographs to shape perceptions and understandings of place. Sometimes it's best simply to slow down, look closely at the images that envelope us, think about the social conditions and effects of visual objects, and consider what each of us brings to the bus stop. Developing a critical, geographical methodology for studying photography is as simple – and complex – as that (Rose 2012: 16–17).

References

Abel, E. 2012. Skin, flesh, and the affective wrinkles of civil rights photography. *Qui Parle: Critical Humanities and Social Sciences* 20(2): 35–69.

Agtmael, P.V. 2012. Interview with the author. Arles, France. July 1.

Anderson, C. 2012. Artist's statement for the global award in photography and sustainability, Prix Pictet. Available at: www.prixpictet.com/portfolios/earth-shortlist/christopher-anderson/statement [accessed September 23, 2013].

Badger, G. 2010. *The Pleasures of Good Photographs*. New York: Aperture.
Barthes, R. 1972. *Mythologies*. New York: Hill and Wang.
Barthes, R. 1981. *Camera Lucida: Reflections on Photography*. New York: Hill and Wang.
Batchen, G. 1997. *Photography's Objects*. Albuquerque: University of New Mexico Art Museum.
Boot, C. 2004. *Magnum Stories*. London: Phaidon.
Cartier-Bresson, H. 1952. *The Decisive Moment*. New York: Simon and Schuster.
Coleman, A.D. 1970. Two critics look at Davidson's East 100th Street. *New York Times*, October 11.
Davidson, B. 1970. *East 100th Street*. Cambridge, MA: Harvard University Press.
Davidson, B. 2009. *Outside, Inside*. Göttingen: Steidl.
Driver, F. 2003. On geography as a visual discipline. *Antipode* 35(2): 227–31.
Edwards, E. and J. Hart. 2004. *Photographs Objects Histories: On the Materiality of Images*. New York: Routledge.
Evans, W. 1974. Snapshot. *Aperture* 19(1): 94–95.
Galassi, P. 2010. *Henri Cartier-Bresson: The Modern Century*. New York: Museum of Modern Art.
Gelder, H.v. and H. Westgeest. 2011. *Photography Theory in Historical Perspective: Case Studies from Contemporary Art*. Malden, MA: Wiley-Blackwell.
Goldberg, V. 1988. *Photography in Print: Writings from 1816 to the Present*. Albuquerque: University of New Mexico Press.
Hambourg, M.M. 1996. Extending the grand tour. In *Illuminations: Women Writing on Photography from the 1850s to the Present*. Edited by L. Heron and V. Williams. Durham, NC: Duke University Press, 32–36.
Harvey, D. 2005. The sociological and geographical imaginations. *International Journal of Politics, Culture & Society* 18(3/4): 211–55.
Heiferman, M. 2012. *Photography Changes Everything*. New York: Aperture.
Hill, P. and T. Cooper (eds). 1979. *Dialogue with Photography*. New York: Farrar, Straus and Giroux.
Hoelscher, S. 2012. Dresden, a camera accuses: Rubble photography and the politics of memory in a divided Germany. *History of Photography* 36(3): 288–305.
Hoelscher, S. 2013. Magnum's geographies: toward a progressive sense of place. In *Reading Magnum: A Visual Archive of the Modern World*. Edited by S. Hoelscher. Austin: University of Texas Press, 139–65.
Ignatieff, M. 2003. *Magnum Degrees*. London: Phaidon Press.
Klein, W. 1968. Why one of the worst slums in New York hasn't been torn down. *New York Times Magazine*, May 6: 22.
Kozloff, M. 1994. *Lone Visions, Crowded Frames: Essays on Photography*. Albuquerque: University of New Mexico Press.
Kramer, C.A. 1971. Posting proud. *Washington Post*, January 7: C1.
Lutz, C. and J.L.Collins. 1993. *Reading National Geographic*. Chicago: University of Chicago Press.
Massey, D. *Space, Place, and Gender*. Minneapolis: University of Minnesota Press, 1994.
Matless, D. 2003. Gestures around the visual. *Antipode* 35(2): 222–26.
Miller, R. 1997. *Magnum: Fifty Years at the Front Line of History*. New York: Grove Press.
Misrach, R. 2010a. Oral history interview with Richard Misrach by Steven Hoelscher, August 11–12. Archives of American Art, Smithsonian Institution. Available at www.aaa.si.edu/collections/interviews/oral-history-interview-richard-misrach-15883 [accessed: September 23, 2013].
Misrach, R. 2010b. *Destroy This Memory*. New York: Aperture Foundation.
Morris, J. 1948. People Are People the World Over. *Ladies Home Journal*, May: 42–43.

Morris, J.G. 1998. *Get the Picture: A Personal History of Photojournalism*. New York: Random House.
Murphy, M. 2010. *Magnum Unique Numbering Guide*. Magnum Photos Archive Collection: Harry Ransom Center, the University of Texas at Austin.
Museum of Modern Art. 1970. Press Release. No. 97, September 23, MoMA Press Archives.
Naggar, C. 2003. *George Rodger: An Adventure in Photography, 1908–1995*. Syracuse, NY: Syracuse University Press.
Paglen, T. 2010. *Invisible: Covert Operations and Classified Landscapes*. New York: Aperture.
Panzer, M. and C. Caujolle. 2005. *Things as They Are*. New York: Aperture Foundation/World Press Photo.
Parr, M. 2008. Rome. *American Photo* 19(3), 62–63.
Price, L. [1858] 1973. *A Manual of Photographic Manipulation*. New York: Arno Press.
Reinhart, M., H. Edwards, and E. Duganne. 2007. *Beautiful Suffering: Photography and the Traffic of Pain*. Chicago: University of Chicago Press.
Rodger, G. 1949. Kordofan captions. G. Rodger Caption Notebooks, New York Magnum Office Archives.
Rodger, G. [1955] 1999. *Village of the Nubas*. London: Phaidon.
Rose, G. 2003. On the need to ask how, exactly, is geography "Visual"? *Antipode* 35(2): 212–21.
Rose, G. 2012. *Visual Methodologies: An Introduction to Researching with Visual Materials*. Thousand Oaks, CA: Sage.
Ryan, J.R. 2003. Who's afraid of visual culture? *Antipode* 35(2): 232–37.
Sandeen, E.J. 1995. *Picturing an Exhibition: The Family of Man and 1950s America*. Albuquerque: University of New Mexico Press.
Sanghvi, D. 1981. Ernst Haas. MA thesis, Syracuse University.
Schwartz, J.M. 1996. The geography lesson: Photographs and the construction of imaginative geographies. *Journal of Historical Geography* 22(1): 16–45.
Schwartz, J.M. 2000. "Records of simple truth and precision": Photography, archives, and the illusion of control. *Archivaria* 50: 1–40.
Schwartz, J.M. and J.R. Ryan. 2003. *Picturing Place: Photography and the Geographical Imagination*. London: I.B. Tauris.
75,000 miles: In his own pictures and words: George Rodger tells of his travels as *Life* war photographer. *Life Magazine*, August 10: 61–67.
Solomon-Godeau, A. 1994. *Photography at the Doc: Essays on Photographic History, Institutions, and Practices*. Minneapolis: University of Minnesota Press.
Sontag, S. 1977. *On Photography*. New York: Anchor Books.
Spirn, A.W. 2009. *Daring to Look: Dorothea Lange's Photographs and Reports from the Field*. Chicago: University of Chicago Press.
Stallabrass, J. 2011. Negative dialectics in the Google era: A conversation with Trevor Paglen. *October* 138: 3–14.
Sturken, M. and Cartwright, L. 2001. *Practices of Looking: An Introduction to Visual Culture*. New York: Oxford University Press.
Subotzky, M. 2013. Magnum Photos Photographer Profile. Available at www.magnumphotos.com/mikhaelsubotzky [accessed: 23 September 2013].
Towell, L. 2013. Magnum Photos Photographer Profile. Available at www.magnumphotos.com/larrytowell [accessed: 23 September 2013].
Tuan, Y.-F. 1979. Sight and pictures. *Geographical Review* 69(4): 413–22.
Tuan, Y.-F. 1991. Language and the making of place: A narrative-descriptive approach. *Annals of the Association of American Geographers* 81(4): 684–96.
Vanderbilt, T. 2003. The picture man. *New York Times*, 19 January, 9.
Williams, V. 2002. *Martin Parr*. London: Phaidon.

Film

Deborah Dixon

Introduction

Scholars in disciplines such as media and film studies have time and again invoked a "geography of cinema," by which is largely meant the political economic settings within which film is sponsored and produced, and the differential scales of activity exhibited by the entertainment industry, as well as the re-presentation of specific locations on screen, and the role of such scenes in setting the emotional tone for a character, culture, or plot device. Research emerging from geography, however, is arguably distinctive by virtue of the fact that "space" and "place" are at the forefront of their analyses, and, moreover, that film becomes a means of nuancing these terms, and of exploring new "spatial turns." Certainly, and in concert with scholars outside of the discipline, geographers have looked to film as a case study, a metaphor, an analogy, a symptom, and a causal factor. But also, geographers have looked to cinematic film as a site for exploratory and innovative thought and practice around some of the discipline's key terms, or "primitives."

In large part, this disciplinary interest is driven by a recognition of and desire to understand the "extent and reach" of cinema industries, its "globalizing" effects, and its role in "subject formation." Whilst cinematic film as an object of analysis boasts numerous characteristics, there is no doubt that the primacy of the visual in all of these issues and more has also captured attention. Accordingly, whilst commentators have long bemoaned that for a quintessentially visual enterprise, geography is remarkably uncritical in regard to their own and others' deployment of the image, at least one area of human geography has consistently addressed this very issue: cinematic geographies. This "minor" subfield has turned time and again on the question of how, where, and with what effect the image has helped to constitute, and confound, our own and others' spatiotemporal imaginaries and materialities.

It is none too surprising, then, to find that some of the most contentious, as well as productive, conceptual lines of inquiry to emerge in geography have been played out within cinematic geographies. Some of these will be outlined below. It must also be recognised, however, that as with many topics considered to help comprise "popular culture," there has also been a tendency within the discipline to eschew cinematic geographies as both marginal and ephemeral in comparison with the "real" terrain of (especially) economic and urban processes and practices (Aitken and Zonn 1994). Indeed, film itself has often been referred to as the "reel" counterpart to the "real" (e.g. Lukinbeal 1998; Zonn 1984; 1985). In arguing the case for the dissolution of such a distinction, numerous geographers have taken the opportunity to make a variety of conceptual points in regard to the mediated character of the "real" and the extratextual character of the "reel" (Benton 1995; Dixon and Grimes 2004; Gold 2002; Hanna 1996).

In this chapter, I provide an overview of the emergence of the cinematic geography subfield, noting a significant shift from film as a real-world mimetic, and hence useful teaching medium, to film as a complex social construct and material assemblage that "does work" on a variety of levels, from the ideological to the affective. Whilst providing a sense of the relevant literatures available, I also stress at key moments individual essays that speak to a conceptual, as well as methodological, engagement with space especially. I conclude the chapter by turning to current lines of inquiry that, whilst using film as an exemplar and symptom, promise to speak to broadscale debates across the geographic discipline.

An Emerging "Cinematic Geography"

Whilst film as a complex and important object of analysis became a feature of social theoretical writings early in the twentieth century – indeed, the early reach of the industry, and the societal impacts of film-watching, were taken by some as helping to define a "modern condition" (see Clarke 1997) – there is no doubt that within geography film was to become instrumentalized as a minor element in practitioners' teaching strategies. The earliest disciplinary writings on film, for example, produced for the *Geographical Magazine* in the 1950s, were explicitly concerned with their utility as teaching aids, insofar as selected clips could re-present for students the "earth and its people" (Cons 1959; though see Sherman 1967). Indeed, film was superior to photographs in this regard, insofar as their capturing of movement as well as scenery would allow for an even more faithful experience of "being in the field" (Griffith 1953; Koval 1954; Manvell 1953; 1956a; Wright 1956; Knight, 1957). Some subsequent film analyses have echoed this concern over the fidelity of such representations, with a tendency to bemoan the "subjective" input provided by filmmakers, such that images are "distorted" and "misleading" (Liverman and Sherman 1985; Godfrey 1993). Whilst recognizing the pioneering work of Gold (1984; 1985), it is only since the 1990s – and in particular the publication of Aitken and Zonn's (1994) genre-building, edited collection – that sufficient quantities of critically engaged research articles and books on this popular medium have been produced to allow for a disciplinary subfield to emerge.

Such efforts were very much influenced by broadscale debates within and without the discipline on the complex, socially constructed character of "popular culture" per se, and looked to interrogate film in terms of its content, form, and distribution, but also its efficacy as a particular medium of expression. Such efforts can be very loosely grouped into two bodies of literature and methodological practice. First, geographers already interested in ideological apparatuses turned to the work of the Frankfurt School, emerging in 1930s Germany, to understand the particular role of screened people and places, as well as the relationship established between the screen and the audience. The shooting as well as the content of such films, it was argued, more often than not served to divert attention away from the broader effects of the global capitalist system, such as a pervasive neoliberal discourse, toward viscerally exciting scenes of sex and violence, or a more benign concern with the melodramatic plight of the individual (Dixon 2008). What is more, it was argued, as people and place become part of cinematic production and screening, their individuality and uniqueness are subsumed. In response, some geographers were to urge the critical analysis of film as a consciousness-raising exercise (for example, Alderman and Popke 2002; Algeo 2007; Cresswell 2000; Lukinbeal 2002; Mains 2004; Youngs and Martin 1984). And yet, as Scott was to caution, with specific reference to the film industry, any analysis of culture as a matter of identity and power must take into account the potential for a heightened cultural differentiation, as well as a sustained resistance to a homogenized "cultural osmosis." He writes,

> *Alongside the grim analyses of the Frankfurt School about the leveling and stupefying effects of capitalist culture we must set not only the resilient and creative reception that it encounters in many sorts of traditional cultures, but also the enlightening and progressive cultural forces constantly unleashed by capitalism. (1997: 15)*

This more avowedly dialectical approach to screen-audience encounters certainly animated Harvey's (1989) now iconic analysis of *Blade Runner* (1982), as well as Natter and Jones's (1993) innovative analysis of Michael Moore's *Roger and Me* (1989), which takes to task the role of General Motors in building, and then breaking, the town of Flint, Michigan. For Natter and Jones cinematic form as well as content is crucial, insofar as a documentary-style montage presentation does not sum up the tensions inherent in contemporary capitalism: instead,

> *It juxtaposes past and present, class perspectives of the rich and poor, views of capital as both a private and social power, and the seemingly impersonal laws of the economy against their personalized effects. The trope of irony which organizes the film's stylistic juxtapositions does not permit a reconciliation of these differences, but instead exposes them as unresolved contradictions. It is between the positions thus revealed as unreconcilable that the viewer is forced to choose. (1993: 142)*

Importantly, such a line of analysis can also burrow deep into the mythology of the film industry to uncover the embodied, labored production of filmmaking itself. Writing on the shooting of Walt Disney Studios' live-action version of *Rudyard Kipling's: The Jungle Book* in the city of Jodhpur, India, in the spring of 1994, for example, Robbins (2002: 160) observes how, "it is here, at the location of filming, where the industry acts in its economic and social moment, that the practices of colonialism, later encoded in film, are actually constituted." Drawing on his own experiences as an extra on the set, Robbins describes the contempt for local people and place by imported US workers, and the broiling tensions emerging amongst the extras themselves, culminating in an attempted "strike." In the following, we gain a sense of the banal bodily performances that enable such filming to take place, but also something of how the on-screen geographies of people and place that pop up on TVs across the globe, and in so doing appear to exist unto themselves, can be tracked back to a site-specific geography riven by all manner of tensions:

> *I suppose we should have all seen this coming. The extras had been meeting in the dining tent and planning a strike all night. The thought of all of those upper middle-class tourists going on the picket line for the first time, in India of all places, made me laugh. They complained about long hours and little respect. They go to all those movies and don't seem to have any sense about Hollywood hierarchy. I must admit it is frightful seen in close-up. They were looking for a volunteer to represent them but I stayed well clear of that. Most vocal of all was this thick-necked, sort of dim, bully-boy with a strained cockney accent who had "had enough of these American bastards" pushing him around. He sprang on the guy between shots, while they were clearing the floor. His target was a belligerent big guy with a bellowing American voice and a pony-tail. When he wrapped himself around the guy's neck, he was hollering "come on London boys!" trying to rally some kind of mass attack, but no one budged. The two of them were just spinning around in the middle of the courtyard, in a sweaty violent dance. By the time it happened we were all too exhausted to do anything, anyway.*

> *We just sat back, lounging in a wide circle. It seemed to go on forever. I suppose we all hoped they'd just kill one another. Some of the larger gaffers eventually pulled the two apart and then hauled the insurgent from the set. Someone turned on that Strauss Waltz, the one we've have been hearing all week and I was getting pretty sick of by this point, and the crew set up for the next shot, as if nothing had happened. (2002: 171)*

Such a tracking back and forth between the on-screen and the offscreen, as well as the emphasis upon "revealing" such linkages, can be contrasted with the second body of literature to emerge. The increasing prevalence of post-structural theories in the 1990s had significant repercussions for how some geographers approached film as a site wherein meanings were articulated and disseminated. Largely concerned with debunking the truth-status underlying key philosophical and scientific framings of the world, such efforts sought to bring to light the manner in which seemingly fixed and inviolate foundational terms – presence, essence, existence, cause, origin, substance, subject, truth, God, and "man," – were necessarily related to a host of other discursive referents that gave them shape and import. Whilst geographers were also concerned with the relation between the on-screen and the offscreen, these boundaries were to be subsumed within a broader analysis of how particular objects, from bodies to landscapes, were highly complex, polycentric entities. Not only is their meaning and valence constructed via a range of discourses, but these discourses are themselves brought to bear though a range of mediums, from the eye to the camera. As Aitken and Dixon summarize these efforts,

> *To be sure, the camera records mass and motion, but the nature of those objects that appear off the screen is firmly located in the world of meaning. Similarly, the nature of those objects that appear on screen are just as embedded in social meaning. Accordingly, film geographers … look at: (1) how particular meanings are indeed ascribed to people and place as they appear on screen. This requires an appraisal of how cinematic techniques are used to present action, narrative and emotion. And (2), how the meanings of those people and places on-screen interconnect with meanings established through other mediums, including actually being 'in' a particular place. (2006: 327)*

Whilst such an approach is predicated upon the differentially constructed character of objects, it must be acknowledged, however, that geographers have tended to focus on one such medium – the film camera – to the isolation of others. The motivation here is very much a matter of deconstructing how the film camera works to produce a particular spatiality on screen, by which is meant the relations between people and things, as well as between components of each such that particular meanings and emotions are evoked. Certainly, a slew of analyses have emerged that seek to interpret how various meanings are indeed evoked by particular filmic contents and techniques, such as jump-cuts that fracture space (Aitken and Lukinbeal 1997; 1998; Lukinbeal and Aitken 1998; Kirsch 2002), the juxtaposition of protagonists and landscapes (Bain 2003; Eriksson 2010; Fish 2007; Jansson 2005; May 2010; Selby and Dixon 1998), and even the invocations of racial othering and social distance afforded by lighting effects (Farish 2005; Natter 2002). Clearly, the space of a shot, or how the frame holds the action, is of great import to film narrative, sequence, and rhythm. In addition, camera techniques such as panning, tilting, and tracking define not only the space of the image but also perceptual position and perspective.

A prime example is Brigham and Marston's (2002) "reading" of two Los Angeles–based films, *Mi Vida Loca* (1993) and *Terminator 2* (1991) as expressing a millennial (post)modernity, including "the access, negotiation and endangerment of places: perceptions of placelessness and dislocation, and the fundamental importance of gender, race, ethnicity, and class to the construction of landscapes" (2002: 226). The task becomes one of decoding the iconography of each film in terms of camera shots, use of lighting and color, sound, and so on. These are firmly tied to an evocation of meaning, as the following quote, wherein the opening shots of each film are discussed, illustrates:

> *Terminator 2's first image is of a L.A. freeway, overwhelmed by a sea of cars, with the passengers all trapped, exposed, and, perhaps most significantly, cut off from any perceptible destination or direction. The image cuts to one of "L.A. 2029 A.D." where the landscape stretches into a vast wasteland, devoid of life. These aerial long shots of the freeway and the apocalyptic future landscape minimize human presence, figuring L.A. as an alienating space, reduced to the blue-black of ruin and the red of perpetual fire. Its particular condition is an outcome of global war, suggesting that this landscape is representative of a universal condition. Conversely, Mi Vida Loca's opening sequence registers a different use of scale. The shot selection consists of close ups and medium shots that pan the landscape from within the city. The camera tracks the Echo Park barrio from ground level starting at the level of a car's tires moving from the street to the cemetery to a string of stores with signs in Spanish and English. The camera gives us a vivid pastiche of the particular places that codify and coordinate this very specific landscape. Unlike Terminator 2, the pace is quick, indicating there is activity and life. The different shot angles are at a different scale, a "local" scale, emphasized even by the disorientating effect that could be caused by this cluster of shots." (2002: 232)*

Underpinning much of this work is an interest in querying the power relations behind the production of such meaning, wherein it is argued that some notions of what people and place are like have become much more "taken for granted" than others. The pervasive characterization of Nature as feminine and an encroaching society as masculine, for example, has been the subject of research in film geography (Lukinbeal 2005), as has the scripting of particular landscapes with a geopolitical edge (Crampton and Power 2005). The argument is made that these meanings are much more complex than prevailing cinematic representations of them; but also, that because films are read over and against other forms of representation, these are open to continual transformation such that "dominant" and "marginal" representations are in continual flux (Aitken 1994; Craine and Aitken 2004). Akin to Scott's argument, noted earlier, on the dialectic nature of film, such representations can even be read as temporary resolutions that, when subject to critical scrutiny, reveal their fraught construction. And so Mains (2004b: 253), for example, in interrogating the discursive construction of the US-Mexico border, looks to how,

> *the creation of border narratives in cinema is interwoven with efforts to define space, place, and identity ... ['border films' are] a means by which mainstream tropes of 'Southern' US regional identities are represented through anxieties over boundaries, tensions that at times provide challenges to dominant representations, particularly within more recent filmic renderings. (e.g. Lone Star [1996])*

More recently, this line of inquiry has opened out into a discussion of how the meanings of those diverse places within which film-watching occurs – the cinema, the home, the car, and even the bus/train via the mobile phone – are themselves transformed though the practice of film-watching, a practice that is just as much about hearing, tasting, touching, and smelling as it is about spectatorship (Crang 2002; di Palma 2009; Hubbard 2003; Nicholson 2002; 2006;

Tranter and Sharpe 2011). An excellent "harbinger" of this line of inquiry is provided by Smith's (2002) exploration of the manner in which Robert Flaherty's classic documentary *Nanook of the North* was exhibited in diverse venues in the decades following its 1922 release. In addition to the screening of various combinations of footage and voice-over narration, these exhibitions demonstrated considerable ingenuity in their efforts to engage the cinematic audience in a full-on sensory experience. Asserting the importance of "other Nanooks" circulating outside of the screened image, Smith details how,

> *Pathé Pictures produced a Nanook of the North to be shown in the theater, and a pre-packaged "campaign book" featuring posters and window displays, suggestions for press releases, and recommendations for local "tie-in" activities. To encourage local businesses to publicize Nanook of the North, the campaign book promoted "shop tie-ups" such as Nanook mannequins and igloos in shop windows, in addition to hiring someone to dress "like an Eskimo" and stroll about town with a sled on wheels. Movie exhibitors were encouraged to decorate their lobbies with arctic-like artifacts; it was suggested they "get the Eskimo atmosphere." (2002: 112)*

What is more, each exhibition was received in a differential, critical context. Whilst 1922 reviewers hailed the arrival of a new cinematic phenomenon – "the unfolding of the reality of a 'natural man' locked in a tragic struggle with the environment," as Smith (2002: 101) puts it, a view echoed by Manvell (1956b) – by the late 1970s and the early 1980s the "innocent" filmmaker was firmly implicated within the context of the fur industry as well as the image-crafting traditions of Hollywood.

Taken together, a readily observable feature of this line of inquiry is the tendency to mark a distinction between the terms *re-presentation* and *representation*, thereby critiquing a traditional tendency for the former to indicate the impossible, namely, capturing and reflecting – as in confining and mirroring – a real world referent in thought, language, and visual media. Yet, what was arguably brushed over in such work was an accompanying post-structural emphasis upon how such foundational terms also performed as pivots for an apparently all-pervasive discourse that sought to "name" all there was to the world. Whilst scholars interpreted the term *discourse* far beyond speech to include the inscription of social relations (and thereby the exercise of power) on and through the body itself, for example, this was very much a matter of assuming bodily behaviors and routines to be both intelligible and subject to interpretation, as with any other semiotic system. It is no small wonder, then, that for some film geographers the various concepts and ideas brought together under the rubric of "non-representational geographies" were an opportunity to rework film not so much as an object of analysis but as a complex site of assemblage, wherein various affects were engineered (Clarke 2010; Clarke and Doel 2005; 2007) and mobilized (Aitken 2009; Curti 2008; 2009; Lorimer 2010; Olund 2012).

To a large extent, this work has been inspired by a Deleuzian ontology that describes, not a world of similarities shared by static objects, but rather one in which all of materiality is continuously moving, mutating, and transforming, differentiating even from itself in a constant process of becoming. Aitken (2006: 494) provides a summary of Deleuze's key points on cinema, which is dominated by a "moving-image" comprising,

> *(i) the perception-image that focuses on moving me from indistinguishable knowledge at the periphery of my universe to a central subjective perception, (ii) the action-image that is part of me perceiving things here at the center of my universe and then grasping the 'virtual action' that they have on me … and (iii) the affection-image … [The latter is a] movement of expression that carries stories between different levels*

> *of articulation; for example, between the embodied and the visceral, the moral and the valued, the mythic and actual.*

For Aitken (2006), it is the visceral experience of watching scenes of masculine heroics, and in particular the tortured masculine face of Mel Gibson in *Braveheart* (1995), that is of interest insofar as it is this affect that allows for particular moral messages concerning the nature of good and evil to be proffered.

An extended example of this line of inquiry is provided by Aitken and Dixon's (2011) exploration of the violent, oil-rich Western *There Will Be Blood* (2007), a film that has often been described as an incisive indictment of capitalist exploitation of both land and labor. They suggest that whilst it is tempting to consider how the screened image is "deterritorialized through the camera lens only to be reterritorialized with ideological intent through a variety of film-making techniques, from juxtaposition and 'point-of-view' and 'establishing' shots to lighting, sound, and narrative," that this practice glosses over the shifting, mobile affect of such spectacles. Hence,

> *Films, buildings, plans, and other geovisual data are always representations, but they are also more than representation. And it is with this in mind-from the affective-that subversive feminist cartographies enable an opening of the political that is also and at the same time intimate and personal. With the movie over, we reflect on connections, rewind the moments that pulled us into new spaces of intimacy and appreciation. We discuss the anger, the fear, the love; we embrace the affective localities and reinvent the moving landscapes into something we use. We create a mapping of our own moving pictures: an intimate geography, a fragile landscape with political muscle. (2011: 203–4)*

Here, then, is a geography encountered from the perspectives of movement and force relations: rather than structured, whole objects (the human, the screen, the film, the camera, and so on), there are continuously interconnecting multitudes of partial objects affecting and being affected by other partial objects, constituting – if only for a moment – assemblages that appear to cohere by working together, or initiating processes that are specific to that relation. Emotions, such as fear, excitement, boredom, and so on, are not the properties of individuals, but emerge from this process, and can be more usefully described as that part of affect that is recognised viscerally as well as intellectually. And so for Carter and McCormack (2006), for example, the visceral upheaval encountered by watching war movies such as *Black Hawk Down* (2001) does some form of work, principally, they argue, in regard to decontextualizing and downsizing war to (now nongeopolitical) individual heroics and terrors.

Future Directions

Whilst cinematic geographies remains a minor subfield, there is no doubt that film as an object of inquiry strikes a chord with geographers interested in all manner of economic, political, and cultural topics, insofar as film becomes a vehicle for the representation of these to a wide-ranging audience. Hence, while there are relatively few who would claim to be "film geographers" first and foremost, there are many who have written on film at some point in their career. Having said that, one can still discern an interest in film as a means of "pushing" broader-scale thinking on the nature of space. As a means of concluding this chapter, then, I want to identify two such lines of inquiry that have recently emerged, and that look set to provide food for thought for future efforts within but also beyond the subfield.

First, it is possible to discern the description of filmmaking, distributing, and viewing as a complex "site," a term that has been recently deployed by some geographers as a means of denoting the composition of a flat, rather than scalar, ontology. Again inspired by a largely Deleuzian philosophy, work here seeks to portray sites as immanent (that is, self-organizing) event-spaces dynamically composed of bodies, doings, and sayings. These sites are differentiated and differentiating, unfolding singularities that "hang together" through the congealments and blockages of force relations, affording a distinct assemblage to emerge and reemerge. For Marston et al. (2007), Nollywood – in spite of its nickname – is usefully understood as just such a singularity, insofar as,

> *Unlike Hollywood, video films in Nollywood are made quickly, recorded on video equipment, and marketed directly to the consumer, initially on videocassettes and more recently in digital format. From the moment the camera begins to produce footage, a very different product is being created that possesses a visuality significantly different from more mainstream cinematic products. In addition, the representations of their content, the action and stories they record, derive from a range of video practices that are particular to Nollywood … . There are no national tours where stars hawk their new video films. But there are magazines, billboards, radio and television advertisements, as well as Lagos television shows devoted entirely to publicizing the video films and movie posters plastered throughout the city to advertise their upcoming releases. (2007: 54)*

Other than emphasize the ontological diversity underpinning contingency, however, it is unclear at the moment as to what this particular empirical example adds to prior geographic analyses of emerging film economies (see also Featherstone's critique, 2011). Nevertheless, film, perhaps because of its highly complex architecture of vision, once again provides the grounding for debates around geography as the study of relations between things; in this case, how we might theorize how noncompossible yet highly significant fragments are placed over and against each other.

An alternate discussion of site that does move beyond film as an extended example, however, is provided by Shaw (2010), who infuses the term with the notion of "event," as outlined by Badiou. Here, film is a specific yet thoroughly intertextual component of popular culture capable of presenting the "cinematic idea"; this is the articulation of a paradox – namely the simultaneous *appearance* of the finite, which promises closure, and the infinity of *being*, which promises excess. Using the animated film *WALL-E* (2008) as an analogy, Shaw draws out the shock of encounter as, first, the singular hero's lonely world of terrestrial reclamation is made anew by the discovery of a growing plant and the arrival of an EVE (or, "Extraterrestrial Vegetation Evaluator"), and then, second, as the scruffy WALL-E (or, "Waste Allocation Load Lifter Earth-Class") inserts himself into the clean, cosmic environment of Axiom, a spaceship that has allowed humanity to escape the polluted consequence of its actions. Each encounter draws attention to the beingness of a site that,

> *is "autonomous". Unlike other multiples in a world that are indexed against the transcendental – indeed require the transcendental for their own worldy appearance – the site indexes itself, and is therefore autonomous and singular with respect to the world it finds itself placed within … . because the site is autonomous, it follows that it is inexistent with respect to the world: it is invisible to the transcendental … . the appearance of the site causes a world to reconstitute its transcendental because it is*

> *unable to absorb the ontological excess of the site. That is to say, the appearance of the site is the eventual subversion of appearing by being. The dialectic between appearing and being, or world and site, is the source of political torsion for Badiou, and in the movie WALL-E it is our metallic hero's encounter with the world of the Axiom that animates this dialectic. (2010: 398)*

For Shaw, if philosophy be a form of cinema for Badiou, then this is because philosophy itself "can only be understood as splayed across lived geographies Real and representational, and its ideas; as impure travellers in uncertain animations" (2010: 395). Moreover, this splayed geography makes us aware of the "*topological relations* that cinema feeds upon, distorts, and distributes" (ibid.), a point that takes us to a second line of recent inquiry.

> *The term "topology" has come to denote, for geographers, a "stretching" and "folding" of space that brings points into proximity, thereby allowing connections to be made between people and things. The "bodies" that constitute ontology are not contained within rigid time spaces, nor are they constituted as self-sufficient, self-reproducing entities. Rather, bodies are 'stretched' across space and time as they incorporate and shed energy and materials, and as they are affected in diverse ways by the environments they inhabit and traverse. There is no one set of connections, or network, along which this stretching occurs. Rather, and by virtue of its many re-assemblings, bodies are embedded in diverse networks, each constituted from other organisms and technologies, and each with its particular velocity, or speed, in relation to others. These networks cross over each other, fold and 'scrumple' as each constituent part is similarly stretched out.*

Grounding their discussion via the "hyperlink cinema" of Steven Soderbergh, as well as a "haptics" of cinema viewing (Crang 2002) and the "intimate" philosophy of Luce Irigaray, Dixon and Jones (2012) observe that what is missing from such accounts is an "ontology of touch" that might account for and simultaneously "ground" topological geographies, lest they become one more imaginary spatiality. By its very name, an ontology of touch would focus on the material connections among mobile bodies; that is, the manner in which various materials and forces rub up against each other, interpenetrate, and reassemble at various speeds and intensities, such that diverse proximities and distances, contacts and connections are made and remade. Watching *Contagion* (2011), they note that,

> *There is a strong yet flat emphasis on networks throughout the narrative, during which the virus enters an already thoroughly interconnected socio-environmental-technological space, moves rapidly across transportation routes and the hosts and things that traverse them, and produces more networks as it stretches across space and time … . This stretched and scrumpled space is confirmed by a particular, visual repertoire. On-screen shots of computer-generated maps, with their emerging epicentres and lines of flow, appear intermittently; more often, we see footage of objects being touched by fingers, or people being coughed upon. To be sure, scenes show the 'global' spread of disease as a set of rapid flows – primarily as hosts move within and between cities – but these are constantly being interrupted, exceeded, overwhelmed by other points of connection, each of which becomes yet another epicentre. Slick surfaces are crucial points of passage, as the virus spreads from mouth to hand to object and back again. Contagion thus maps a viral topology that stretches and folds back on itself time and again.*

In similar vein, Secor dwells on the feel as well as the imagery of *The Adjustment Bureau* (2011), *Midnight in Paris* (2011), and *Inception* (2010), insofar as "These films [can] be said to tap into our experience of the city as topological" (2013: 431). For Secor, however, it is the "topological subject," following Lacan, rather than Deleuzian multiplicities, that is of interest; here, topological figures exhibit a twisting that constantly interiorizes the exteriors of subjects and exteriorize their interiors. And so *Inception*, for example, hinges upon the making "real" of a dream space, wherein,

> *Ariadne is the architect; that is, she is the one who designed the dream space, and so she experiments with her power by folding the city in two. The city that she appears, in the scene, to inhabit is thus inhabiting her; it is both interior and exterior to her. And given that Cobb is there with her (and his presence is not merely apparent – like the apparition of his dead wife that stalks his unconscious – but actual), this inside-out city exceeds Ariadne's subjectivity. Indeed, it is both exterior and interior to Cobb as well … . Given this division of labor, one could argue that despite the blatant topology of the folded city, in fact absolute space – space as abstractable from that which it contains – resurfaces in this strange fantasy of inhabitable dream space … . [Thus] the city, with all of its historical and geographical specificity, can be understood as the field within which power and desire are constituted. To be clear, the city in this argument is not simply "subjective," something that each person has her own version of. It is not simply a projection of the subject – any more than the subject is merely an introjection of the city. The city and the subject instead are, one could say, distributed, splayed out, a Mobius surface that encircles its own limit.*

It is appropriate, I think, to end the chapter by reference to this splayed out Mobius strip, insofar as geographers concerned with cinema, and the grounding of spatial thinking, continue to turn inside out not only the notion of on-screen and offscreen, viewer and viewed, spectacle and spectator, subject and object but also the narrative devices of previous cohorts of film geographers. As Secor notes, however, such a figure proceeds to encircle its own limit. And, perhaps, it is time for geographers to think more carefully about the conceptual thresholds of their field, and to consider what lies not beyond but outside of this surface.

References

Aitken, S.C. 1994. I'd rather watch the movie than read the book. *Journal of Geography in Higher Education* 18: 291–306.

Aitken, S.C. 1997. Analysis of texts: Armchair theory and couch-potato geography. In *Methods in Human Geography*. Edited by R. Flowerdew and D. Martin. Harlow: Longman, 197–292.

Aitken, S.C. 2006. Leading men to violence and creating spaces for their emotions. *Gender, Place and Culture* 13(5): 491–507.

Aitken, S.C. and D.P. Dixon. 2006. Imagining geographies of film. *Erdkunde: Archiv Fur Wissenschaftliche Geographie* 60: 326–36.

Aitken, S.C. and D.P. Dixon. 2011. Avarice and tenderness in cinematic landscapes of the American West. In *Geohumanities: Art, History, Text at the Edge of Place*. Edited by M. Dear, J. Ketchum, S. Luria, and D. Richardson. London and New York: Routledge, 196–205.

Aitken, S.C. and C. Lukinbeal. 1997. Disassociated masculinities and geographies of the road. In *The Road Movie Book*. Edited by I. Hark and S. Cohan. London: Routledge, 349–70.

Aitken, S.C. and C. Lukinbeal. 1998. Of heroes, fools and Fisher Kings: Cinematic representations of street myths and hysterical males in the films of Terry Gilliam. In *Images of the Streets: Planning, Identity and Control in Public Space*. Edited by N. Fyfe. New York: Routledge, 141–59.

Aitken, S.C. and L.E. Zonn (eds). 1994. *Place, Power, Situation and Spectacle: A Geography of Film*. Lanham, MD: Rowman and Littlefield.

Alderman, D.H. and E.J. Popke. 2002. Humor and film in the geography classroom: Learning from Michael Moore's *TV Nation*. *Journal of Geography* 101: 228–39.

Allen, S. 1997. *The Cultural Economy of Cities: Essays on the Geography of Image-Producing Industries*. Thousand Oaks and London: Sage.

Algeo, K. 2007. Teaching cultural geography with *Bend It Like Beckham*. *Journal of Geography* 106(3): 133–43.

Bain, A. 2003. White Western teenage girls and urban space: Challenging Hollywood's representations. *Gender, Place and Culture* 10(3): 197–213.

Benton, L. 1995. Will the Real/Reel Los Angeles please stand up? *Urban Geography* 16(2): 144–64.

Brigham, A. and S.M. Marston. 2002. On location: Pedagogy and the production of the western American landscape in *Mi Vida Loca* and *Terminator 2*. In *Engaging Film: Geographies of Mobility and Identity*. Edited by T. Cresswell and D. Dixon. Lanham, MD: Rowman and Littlefield, 226–45.

Carter, S. and D.P. McCormack. 2006. Film, geopolitics and the affective logics of intervention. *Political Geography* 25(2): 228–45.

Clarke, D.B. (ed.). 1997. *The Cinematic City*. Routledge: New York.

Clarke, D.B. 2010. Dreams rise in the darkness: The white magic of cinema. *Film-Philosophy* 14(2): 21–40.

Clarke, D.B and M.A. Doel. 2005. Engineering space and time: Moving pictures and motionless trips. *Journal of Historical Geography* 31(1): 41–60.

Cons, G. 1959. The geographical film in education. *Geographical Magazine* 32: 456–66.

Craine, J. and S.C. Aitken. 2004. Street fighting: Placing the crisis of masculinity in David Fincher's *Fight Club*. *GeoJournal* 59(4): 289–96.

Crampton, A. and M. Power. 2005. Frames of reference on the geopolitical stage: *Saving Private Ryan* and the Second World War/Second Gulf War intertext. *Geopolitics* 10(2): 244–65.

Crang, M. 2002. Rethinking the observer: Film, mobility, and the construction of the subject. In *Engaging Film Geographies of Mobility and Identity*. Edited by T. Cresswell and D. Dixon. Lanham, MD: Rowman and Littlefield, 13–31.

Cresswell, T. 2000. Falling down: Resistance as diagnostic. In *Entanglements of Power: Geographies of Domination/Resistance*. Edited by J. Sharpe, P. Routledge, C. Philo, and R. Paddison. New York and London: Routledge, 256–68.

Cresswell, T. and D. Dixon (eds). 2002. *Engaging Film: Geographies of Mobility and Identity*. Lanham, MD: Rowman and Littlefield.

Curti, G. 2008. The ghost in the city and a landscape of life: A reading of difference in Shirow and Oshii's *Ghost in the Shell*. *Environment and Planning D: Society and Space* 26(1): 87–106.

Curti, G. 2009. Beating words to life: Subtitles, assemblage(s)capes, expression. *GeoJournal* 74(3): 201–8.

Di Palma, M. 2009. Teaching geography using films: A proposal. *Journal of Geography* 108(2): 47–56.

Dixon, D.P. 2006. *Film, Geography and, in Encyclopedia of Human Geography*. Edited by B. Warf. Thousand Oaks and London: SAGE, 165–67.

Dixon, D.P. 2008. Independent cinema in the US: The politics of personal passions. In *A Geography of Cinema – A Cinematic World*. Edited by C. Lukinbeal and S. Zimmermann. Stuttgart: Franz Steiner Verlag, 65–83.

Dixon, D.P. and J. Grimes. 2004. On capitalism, masculinity and whiteness in a dialectical landscape: The case of Tarzan and the tycoon. *GeoJournal* 59(4): 265–75.

Dixon, D.P. and J.P. Jones. 2012. Touch: Ontologies and pathologies of the micro in Soderbergh's *Contagion*. Paper presented at the Association of American Geographers, New York, February.

Doel, M. and D.B. Clarke. 2007. Afterimages. *Environment and Planning D: Society and Space* 25(5): 890–910.

Eriksson, M. 2010. "People in Stockholm are smarter than countryside folks" – Reproducing urban and rural imaginaries in film and life. *Journal of Rural Studies* 26(2): 95–104.

Farish, M. 2005. Cities in shade: Urban geography and the uses of noir. *Environment and Planning D: Society and Space* 23(1): 95–118.

Featherstone, D. 2011. On assemblage and articulation. *Area* 43(2): 139–42.

Fish, R. (ed.). 2007. *Cinematic Countrysides*. Manchester: Manchester University Press.

Godfrey, B. 1993. Regional depiction in contemporary film. *Geographical Review* 83(4): 428–40.

Gold, J. 1984. *The city in film: A bibliography*. Monticello, IL: Vance Bibliographies.

Gold, J. 1985: From "metropolis" to "the city": Film visions of the future city, 1919–39. In *Geography, the Media and Popular Culture*. Edited by J. Burgess and J. Gold. New York: St. Martin's Press, 123–43.

Gold, J. 2002. The real thing? Contesting the myth of documentary realism through classroom analysis of films on planning and reconstruction. In *Engaging Film: Geographies of Mobility and Identity*. Edited by T. Cresswell and D. Dixon. Lanham, MD: Rowman and Littlefield, 209–25.

Griffith, R. 1953: America on the screen. *Geographical Magazine* 26: 443–54.

Hanna, S. 1996. Is it Roslyn or is it Cicely? Representation and the ambiguity of place. *Urban Geography* 17(7): 633–49.

Harvey, D. 1989. *The Condition of Postmodernity*. Blackwell: Oxford.

Hubbard, P. 2003. A good night out? Multiplex cinemas as sites of embodied leisure. *Leisure Studies* 22(3): 255–72.

Jansson, D.R. 2005. "A Geography of Racism": Internal orientalism and the construction of American national identity in the film *Mississippi Burning*. *National Identities* 7(3): 265–85.

Kirsch, S. 2002. Spectacular violence, hypergeography, and the question of alienation in *Pulp Fiction*. In *Engaging Film: Geographies of Mobility and Identity*. Edited by T. Cresswell and D. Dixon. Lanham, MD: Rowman and Littlefield, 32–46.

Knight, A. 1957. Geography and the documentary film: The United States. *Geographical Magazine* 30: 290–301.

Koval, F. 1954. The rise and fall of German film-making. *Geographical Magazine* 26: 575–84.

Liverman, D. and D. Sherman. 1985. Natural hazards in novels and films: Implications for hazard perception and behaviour. In *Geography, the Media and Popular Culture*. Edited by J. Burgess and J. Gold. New York: St. Martin's Press, 86–95.

Lorimer, J. 2010. Moving image methodologies for more-than-human geographies. *Cultural Geographies* 17(2): 237–58.

Lukinbeal, C. 1998. Reel-to-real urban geographies: The top five cinematic cities in North America, *California Geographer* 38: 64–77.

Lukinbeal, C. and S.C. Aitken. 1998. Sex, violence and the weather: Male hysteria, scale and the fractal geographies of patriarchy. In *Places Through the Body*. Edited by H. Nast and S. Pile. New York: Routledge, 356–80.

Lukinbeal, C. and S. Zimmermann (eds). 2008. *The Geography of Cinema – A Cinematic World*. Stuttgart: Franz Steiner Verlag.

Mains, S.P. 2004a. Teaching transnationalism in the Caribbean: Toward an understanding of representation and neo-colonialism in human geography. *Journal of Geography in Higher Education* 28(2): 317–32.

Mains, S.P. 2004b. Imagining the border and Southern spaces: Cinematic explorations of race and gender. *GeoJournal* 59(4): 253–64.

Manvell, R. 1953. The geography of film-making. *Geographical Magazine* 25: 640–50.

Manvell, R. 1956a. Geography and the documentary film. *Geographical Magazine* 29: 417–22.

Manvell, R. 1956b. Robert Flaherty, geographer. *Geographical Magazine* 29: 491–500.

Marston, S.M., K. Woodward, and J.P. Jones. 2007. Flattening ontologies of globalization: The Nollywood case. *Globalisations* 4(1): 45–63.

May, J. 2010. Zombie geographies and the undead city. *Social and Cultural Geography* 11(3): 285–98.

Natter, W. 2002. "We just gotta eliminate 'em": On whiteness and film in *Matewan, Avalon* and *Bulworth*. In *Engaging Film: Geographies of Mobility and Identity.* Edited by T. Creswell and D. Dixon. Lanham, MD: Rowman and Littlefield, 246–70.

Natter, W. and J.P. Jones. 1993. Pets or meat: Class, ideology, and space, in *Roger and Me. Antipode* 25(2): 140–58.

Nicholson, H.N. 2002. Telling travelers' tales: The world through home movies. In *Engaging film: Geographies of mobility and identity.* Edited by T. Cresswell and D. Dixon. Lanham, MD: Rowman and Littlefield, 47–66.

Nicholson, H.N. 2006. Through the Balkan states: Home movies as travel texts and tourism histories in the Mediterranean, c. 1923–39. *Tourist Studies* 6(1): 13–36.

Olund, E. 2012. Geography written in lightning: Race, sexuality, and regulatory aesthetics in *The Birth of a Nation. Annals of the Association of American Geographers* 103(4): 925–43.

Robbins, P. 2002. Pax Disney: The annotated diary of a film extra in India. In *Engaging Film: Identity, Mobility and Pedagogy.* Edited by D. Dixon and T. Cresswell. Lanham, MD: Rowman and Littlefield, 159–73.

Secor, A. 2013. Topological City. *Urban Geography,* 34(4), 430–44.

Selby, E. and D.P. Dixon. 1998. Between worlds: Considering Celtic, feminine identities in *The Secret of Roan Inish. Gender, Place, and Culture* 5(1): 5–24.

Shaw, I.G.R. 2010. WALL-E's world: Animating Badiou's philosophy. *Cultural Geographies* 17(3): 391–405.

Sherman, S. 1967: How the movies see the city. *Landscape* 16(1): 25–6.

Smith, L. 2002. Chips off the old ice block: Nanook of the North and the relocation of cultural identity. In *Engaging Film: Identity, Mobility and Pedagogy.* Edited by T. Cresswell and D. Dixon. Lanham, MD: Rowman and Littlefield, 94–122.

Tranter, P. and S. Sharpe. 2011. Disney-Pixar to the rescue: Harnessing positive affect for enhancing children's active mobility. *Journal of Transport Geography* 20(1): 34–40.

Wright, B. 1956. Geography and the documentary film: Britain since 1945. *Geographical Magazine* 29: 586–95.

Youngs, M. and A. Jenkins. 1984. Shell-shocked: Critical film analysis and teaching strategies. *Geography* 69(1): 46–53.

Zonn, L. 1984. Landscape depiction and perception: A transactional approach. *Landscape Journal* 3(2): 144–50.

Zonn, L. 1985. Images of place: A geography of the media. *Proceedings of the Royal Geographical Society of South Australia* 84: 35–45.

Radio

Alasdair Pinkerton

Radio is an inherently spatial medium. From the birth of radio waves as a mechanism for transmitting messages during the late nineteenth century, their capacity to traverse space and to bring people and places into close contact has been harnessed and celebrated. Guglielmo Marconi, widely acknowledged as the father of long-distance radio communications, was particularly sensitive to, and indeed motivated by, the geographical and spatial consequences of these burgeoning technologies. As well as seeking commercial opportunities in improving maritime safety through enhanced ship-to-ship and ship-to-shore communications, Marconi demonstrated an almost missionary zeal in the quest to "annihilate" space and time, and to defeat the strictures of distance. Reflecting on the first successful transmission of radio signals across the North Atlantic in December 1901, Marconi proclaimed that "the electric waves sent out into space from Poldhu had traversed the Atlantic – the distance, enormous as it seemed then, of 1700 miles – unimpeded by the curvature of the Earth." "I now felt," he continued, "for the first time absolutely certain that the day would come when mankind would be able to send messages without wire not only across the Atlantic but between the farthermost ends of the earth" (Marconi 1901: n.p.). Radio thus resounded with modernist ambition. Marconi, in particular, invested radio with a rhetorical power to control "the elements and forces of nature" and to collapse the physical dimensions of geography. But radio's allusion to "power" was more than simply a rhetorical device. It was Marconi's obsession with the bridging of oceans by electromagnetic means that drove both the development of ever more powerful transmitting stations (such as those at Poldhu in Cornwall and Caernarvon in west Wales) as well as establishing an early iconography of an immense radio "power" both in terms of the scale of its global broadcasting ambition and in the scale of its technological and engineering achievement. As the media historian David Hendy (2010) has also argued, radio played a part in "rewiring" the modern mind, in turning attention toward the sky and the "air" (often interjected with the rhetorical metaphor of "the ether") as a medium with a near-utopian capacity to unite and secure peace. But, even from the earliest days, radio's strategic capacities were recognized.

Radio's fortunes were intimately linked with wartime investments and priorities between 1914–18 and, alongside other airborne technologies (such as poison gas, aircraft, and aerial reconnaissance, etc.) seemed to be part of a movement to increasingly "weaponize" the air. Radio thus occupied an unsettling space somewhere between "science" and "national service" and was all the more sinister and or seductive for its invisibility from human detection. As a mass communications technology, and instrument of statecraft, radio was able for the first time in history to "extend cultural practices, symbols and narratives to millions of people simultaneously across great distances" (Hayes 2000: xiii). It was implicated in building national unity through the dissemination of shared sounds and symbols and the performance of collective rituals. Radio was equally embraced as a tool of imperial consolidation as Britain, France, Italy, and other European powers used radio to connect their metropolitan capitals with the furthest outposts of their respective imperial territories. On the "home" front, radio is often described as being instrumental in the transformation of domestic space. As Simon Frith (2002) has noted, with specific reference to the United Kingdom and the BBC as a national broadcaster:

> *I believe that radio was the most significant twentieth-century mass medium. It was radio which transformed the use of domestic space, blurring the boundary between the public and the private, idealising the family hearth as the site of ease and entertainment, establishing the rhythm of everydayness: the Children's Hour, Breakfast Time, Friday Night is Music Night! It was radio which shaped the new voice of public intimacy, which created the nation as a mediated collectivity, which gave ordinary people a public platform (creating the concept of "ordinary people" in the first place). It was radio which made sport a national symbol, which created the very idea of "light entertainment". Where radio led, television simply followed. And it was radio (rather than film, as Adorno and Bottum suggest) that established the possibility of music as an ever-playing soundtrack to our lives. (41)*

Radio has had a transformative effect at multiple scales of human experience with profoundly spatial consequences, and yet, radio as a medium has been remarkably little studied by geographers. If Pauliina Raento (2006) can claim that it is surprising postage stamps have been neglected as sources of popular geographical and geopolitical representations, then radio must fall into a similar category of surprising lacunae. Like stamps, radio is globally ubiquitous, highly symbolic, and is involved in the production of everyday engagements between citizens and "the state" (and is therefore an expression of "banal geopolitics"). It has, as this chapter demonstrates, played a critical role in shaping the geographical "imaginations" of citizens and at times challenging domestic and international regimes. Even with the rise of "media geography" and "communications geography" as active areas of interest within the discipline, radio has received comparatively little attention, albeit with some notable exceptions (Jones 2005a; 2005b; MacDonald 2006; and Pinkerton 2008a; 2008b; 2009). It may be possible to speculate that this has something to do with geography's sustained disciplinary interests in "the visual," but radio's comparative silence within the academy is not limited to geography. In media studies and media history there has been a comparatively limited scholarly engagement with radio by comparison with film, television, and the Internet. It is often argued that radio's very success, as measured by its omnipresence in our lives, has contributed to it being almost hidden in plain sight (for want of a more appropriate aural metaphor). As Martin Shingler and Cindy Wierniga (1998) suggest,

> *Radio is one of the world's most pervasive mass media, reaching the most far-flung corners of the planet (even beyond it) and is heard by millions of people every minute of every day. It is such an everyday and familiar aspect of modern life that most of us take it entirely for granted and, in so doing, underestimate its power. Yet radio is a powerful cultural influence in the modern world and has an important role to play in the lives of millions of people. (ix)*

All this is not to suggest that radio, or its geographies/spatialities, have been entirely neglected; only that scholarly attention has been fleeting and fragmented. Radio-related scholarship has traditionally emerged from two different intellectual trajectories and has coalesced around two dominant facets of radio. On the one hand, a range of political scientists and historians have sought to examine radio's implication in "official" (and, indeed, "unofficial") propaganda during the twentieth century's "hot" and "cold" conflicts (see, for example, Hale 1976). On the other, media scholars have performed institutional and commercial analyses of radio programming, schedules, and broadcasting conventions, with a particular attentiveness toward the "developed" radio markets of the United States and "global North" (see Hendy 2007; Shingler and Wierniga 1998). These approaches conceptualize radio in markedly different, but nonetheless spatially important, ways. The former considers issues of "radio power," conflict and radio's international dimensions. The latter seeks to decipher the codes, conventions, formats, and practices of radio programming and its reception in contemporary and place-specific contexts. Sitting adjacent to these themes (although with clear points of contact) is interest within international relations and critical geopolitics in radio as a channel for "soft power," "public diplomacy," and the phenomenon of "cultural relations." This has been driven by scholars of public diplomacy, such as Nick Cull (2008; 2012), and include includes some of my own work on radio and its interface with critical and popular geopolitics.

This chapter, then, draws upon a number of interdisciplinary engagements with radio broadcasting and traces the geographical facets of radio in terms of the places and spaces of "broadcasting" and "reception." Equally, this chapter examines how radio constitutes and produces senses of place at a range of different scales, and how radio as a "blind" medium constructs and constitutes space through its transmissions. In so doing, the chapter is also a stepping-stone for a more detailed engagement with the popular geopolitics and the geographical dimensions of radio broadcasting. The chapter is structured with a nod to Paul Adams's (2011) taxonomy of media geography by examining, initially, geographical literature that has considered the role of radio in producing and giving meaning to place(s). In the second section, I juxtapose claims to radio's ubiquity with my own research into the spatially situated nature of radio's reception in the context of the BBC World Service (what Adams might call "media in place"). This is followed by a geopolitically informed examination of the "physical geography" of international radio networks, platforms, and infrastructures ("media in space"). The third section briefly considers academic literature that has attempted to conceptualize the sensory and psychological production of space within and between the listener and the radio ("space in media"). The final and concluding section sets out three possible future research agendas for geographical engagement with radio by calling for increased attention to institutional practices, radio audiences, and, more conceptually, radio as an assemblage of geographically situated components.

Placing Radio

In 1964, the media theorist Marshall McLuhan declared that radio was a "hot" medium, that television was "cool," and that all other forms of media existed somewhere on an always shifting metaphorical hot-cold spectrum. To be "hot," in the McLuhan sense, involved extending or challenging one single sense in "high definition," where "high definition" referred to a state of being "well filled" with data. Hot media are, McLuhan argued, "low in [audience] participation," while cool media required the audience to "complete" the information supplied to them. Radio audiences were, therefore, rendered *passive* whereas audiences of television were considered *active* (McLuhan 1964: 36). Many of these distinctions found spatial formation and were wrapped in McLuhan's particular brand of metaphorical allusion. Indeed it was *space, according to* Cavell (1999; 2002), that represented the single most consistent conceptual category running through McLuhan's work and this is certainly evidenced by his interests in spatial inequalities and cultures/spaces of media production, as well as his conceptual (and metaphorical) work on "the global village" and "visual" and "acoustic" spaces. Radio was similarly subject to spatialized interpretation and was variously conceptualized as "the tribal drum" and "the kit of the global villager" in recognition that it "contracts the world to village size and creates village tastes for gossip, rumor and personal malice" (McLuhan 1964: 143). As well as contracting global space, McLuhan also recognized that radio was productive of new and alternative kinds of places and spatial experiences. Somewhat sinisterly, McLuhan posited that radio might be conceptualized as "the architect of lebensraum":

> *The concept of territoriality that comes into the study of the social life of in general has much to do with the radio phenomenon. The scientist now explains bird song, not as a lyric impulse or emotional expression, but as the form and precise effort of a creature to create and define its lebensraum. Applied to the use of the transistor radio by the young, this concept yields some startling events. The idea that each object makes its own space is not new to the painter or to the physicist. In a highly visual culture such as our own, we are less accustomed to the fact that each sound creates its own space. Sounds in general have an unrivalled power to shape and pattern their own unique spaces. (McLuhan 1964: 134. See also Elden 2010 for a review of territorial "thinking")*

Writing in 1964, it is inconceivable that McLuhan could have been unaware of the problematic associations between the concept of "lebensraum" and the geopolitical priorities of Nazi Germany (which had been partly enacted through the deployment of "radio power") before and during World War II, and yet these are neither acknowledged nor dismissed. It is perhaps for this reason that the editor of *AV Communication Review*, the volume in which McLuhan's article was published, provides a covering note acknowledging, "the discomforting characteristics of Mr. McLuhan's writings" (Hoban, 1964: 133). Hoban was probably not the first, and certainly not the last, person to make this kind of observation. Much of McLuhan's oeuvre has been subject to sustained criticism and derision, although many of his ideas and ambitions (including the hot-cold spectrum) continue to echo in media studies literature and elsewhere. McLuhan's more spatial concepts have, however, been somewhat less resonant despite his acknowledgment of radio's spatial and cultural situatedness, and his identification (above) of radio's power to *shape* and *pattern* unique spaces and places of transmission and reception. This is beginning to change (see Cavell 1999; 2003; Gow 2001). My own work on the BBC World Service and other broadcasting organizations – which has drawn upon and contributed to geopolitical scholarship in a rather different way than Marshall McLuhan – has similarly sought to understand and conceptualize radio's capacity to produce and structure different kinds of places and spaces at a range of different scales (Pinkerton 2008a; 2008b; 2009), albeit without explicit attention to radio's radio function as an electromagnetic "lebensraum."

A number of other geographers have also acknowledged radio's production and reassertion of place. Keith Jones (2005), for example, has critiqued radio's "affective power" in the geographical and psychological assemblage of wartime industrial workplaces. Using the example of the BBC's *Music While You Work* program, Jones examines how industrial psychologists and the BBC sought to "engineer" the industrial productivity of workers while acoustically reflecting and reproducing the "sonic landscape" of British factories. If "lyrics" and "the voice" were considered distracting (and therefore unproductive) for British industrial workers, Fraser MacDonald's work on the rocky Atlantic outcrop of Rockall points to their appeal to the national geographical imagination. MacDonald observes that while the UK's legal claim to Rockall can be traced to a very particular moment of imperial possessiveness in September 1955, Rockall's place within British culture (and the UK's maritime zone) has been constructed through the repetition of "everyday citations," including a series of peculiar meteorological observations broadcast nightly on UK national radio:

> *Broadcast at the end of BBC Radio 4's daily schedule, the cadences and rhythms of the UK shipping forecast have a soporific effect. This is true, at least, for those on land who have the liberty of receiving it as poetry rather than as information. For such a disengaged listener, the shipping forecast constitutes a nightly tour of the extent of the British Isles and its surrounds: a familiar and comforting register of sea areas and coastal stations that have come to define the symbolic boundary of a nation. (MacDonald 2006: 628)*

Radio also has a powerful appeal to the ritualized aspects of place (see Cresswell 1996). As MacDonald suggests in his description of the shipping forecast, radio listening was (and, for many, remains) a highly ritualized performance that not only structures daily life for individual listeners but also allows those listeners to dramatize their shared values through the embodied practice of "tuning in." Franklin Roosevelt's *Fireside Chats* performed a similar function in the United States during and after the Great Depression of the 1930s (Ryfe 1999). The media historian Emma Robertson has similarly noted, in the context of the BBC's Empire Service programming during the 1930s, that the extraordinary popularity of hearing Big Ben chiming simultaneously revealed a sentimental connection with "home" (i.e. Britain) and a means for listeners to participate in (and regulate) the rhythms of colonial life (Robertson 2008).

The symbolic, rhetorical, and acoustic reproduction of the United Kingdom and its maritime waters is echoed through critiques of radio as a vehicle for nation building. As Clive Barnett (1999) and Joy Elizabeth Hayes (2000) have recognized in the contexts of South Africa and Mexico respectively, radio's function as an acoustic map of national boundaries must be considered alongside radio's implication in the cultural construction and articulation of "the national" as an identifiable cultural container (Hayes 2000: xv) and its facility as a tool of open, democratic communication and reconciliation (Barnett, 1999). In India, British instincts for political consolidation (pre–1947) and the government of India's nation-building ambitions (post–1947) were both served by the highly controlled deployment of radio broadcasting and were reflected in the naming practices and visual identity of the state broadcaster, All India Radio, which has gone unchanged since 1935 (Pinkerton 2008b). This also serves as a powerful reminder that radio exists beyond "the aural." It resonates through institutional archives (both textual and aural), cartoons and photographs, the pages of listings magazines and the visual branding of radio networks.

Tamar Liebes has critiqued radio's role in national building in the context of Mandatory Palestine and Israel post–1947 (Liebes 2006). Liebes notes that the *Voice of Israel*, as the only official "national" media in the new state of Israel, became the de facto narrator of unfolding national events, the mediator of an evolving national culture, the distributor of a Eurocentric cultural Zionism, and the encoder of an Israeli collective identity and memory. While riven by cultural politics, the Voice of Israel has nonetheless been conceptualized as "accoutrement of sovereignty" and a component in the social and psychological "normalization" of the Zionist project (Penslar 2003: 23). "In the decades when it reigned alone," Liebes argues, "radio was truly the point of focus. It acted as a virtual town hall in crisis, gathering Israelis (at home, often the streets and town squares) to live through the collective experience in real time" (Liebes 2006: 74). Understood in this way, radio might be considered not only as symbolically productive of geopolitical spaces and places (i.e. states, regions, cities) but, equally, to have emerged as a distinctive site – even a *place* – of collective refuge.

Individual listeners could, through the positioning of a needle on a dial, be brought into contact via the shared experience of listening to unfolding events live and "all at once."

As this section demonstrates, radio's role in the production of place (at a range of scales) has been subject to academic scrutiny within and beyond geography. However, As Benny Morris and Erskine Childers have noted, Israeli radio was also implicated in the unsettling, undermining, and destruction of place, as was the case during the 1947–48 Palestinian exodus when Haganah radio broadcasts, in Arabic, announced the arrival of "the day of judgement" and called upon Arab Palestinians to "move away from every house and street, from every neighbourhood, occupied by the foreign criminals" (Morris 2004: 191). Radio thus has a complex and contested relationship with place. In the next section, this complexity is further demonstrated through a consideration of how the codes, conventions, and meanings of "ubiquitous medium" are, nonetheless, spatially situated and rooted "in place."

Locating the Everywhere Medium

Radio's diversity in format, geographical range, modes of broadcast (from FM to shortwave), and places/spaces of consumption are suggestive of a medium that is perhaps better characterized by its differences than points of similarity. Nonetheless, radio scholars have sought to examine what makes radio identifiably unique among other media; deciphering its codes, conventions, and formats in order to reveal how the "medium" is spatially and temporally structured and negotiated by audiences (see, for example, Hilliard 1985). Many of these efforts have been conditioned by the domination of television in popular and scholarly discourse and the perception, born in the 1960s, that radio's future may be precarious. Writing in 1985, Hilliard noted, "[t]oday, some twenty years later, radio has not only survived, but has grown to almost twice as many stations earning almost three times as much revenue" (xi). Although rooted in US broadcasting data, these trends do have more widespread application.

Important here is the issue of *ubiquity* – that is to say radio's seeming capacity to traverse vast geographical spaces (and be heard "in the middle of vast oceans or on the top of remote mountain peaks") and its ability to penetrate, accompany, and narrate every moment of modern life (Shingler and Wierniga 1998: ix). "For many of us," note Shingler and Wierniga, "[radio] is the first thing we hear in the morning and the last thing we hear before we fall asleep" (ix–x). Radio, for many, is *the* everywhere medium. It is in our bedrooms and bathrooms and at our breakfast tables, in our cars, on buses and trains, at our desks and on the factory floor, in our gyms and waiting rooms and supermarkets. Its speeches and rhythms drift out from open car windows and shop doors momentarily fading into, and out of, our consciousnesses. Broadcasters have responded to the new listening spaces made possible by technological and lifestyle changes. "Drive-time" programs and "phone-in" shows (now augmented with social networking) have evolved to become a staple of radio stations' output and have, themselves, created new spatialities of broadcaster-listener interactivity. As Jody Berland (1990) has recognized in the Canadian broadcasting context, these mobilities and interactivities imbue radio with certain kinds of authority and instrumental power. "Clearly evident," Berland suggests, "is radio's management of urban space, perhaps its chief accomplishment, in its promotion of local business, its management of traffic, time and temperament in relation to rhythms of the working week" (114). It is important, however, not to universalize these kinds of claims. Radio takes on different meanings in different contexts. For many people it is far from being ubiquitous or, as much of this might imply, taken for granted.

The transistor revolution and the wider availability of cheap radio receivers from the 1960s onwards transformed the radio medium in the contexts of both the developed and "developing" worlds. The portability of new radio technologies ensured that it would be open to new kinds of mobilities, through radio's incorporation into battery-powered (and wind-up) personal stereos and into the vast majority of motor vehicles produced around the world (Hendy 2000: 2). Internet streaming of radio has further internationalized the transmission and reception patterns of radio programming. And yet radio's ubiquity in the global North must be viewed alongside regional and local scarcity in much of the developing world where topography makes radio broadcasting, technically or economically challenging; where political suppression restricts access to radio through the prohibition of receiver equipment or the jamming of external broadcasts; where poverty limits the ownership of, or access to, even the most basic radio equipment; or where, held in captivity, individuals or groups of individuals are able only to hear intermittent reports from makeshift wireless tuners. For people in such situations, listening to the radio is far from mundane: it is often dangerous, frustrating, and unreliable and yet, when it is heard, radio is cherished as a source of information and entertainment throughout periods of conflict, famine, and political change, but also as a source of companionship and support during stretches in isolation (Walker 1992). As David Hendy (2000) notes, radio is perhaps the "most adaptable" medium at locating its audience:

> *We are ... defined at different times and simultaneously by our membership of a nation-state, a local community, an ethnic group and a set of musical tastes. Radio almost, but not quite entirely, matches this range. While being the local medium par excellence, radio is also able to reach across large spaces, potentially threatening place-specific cultures with its homogenized content, potentially forging new delocalised communities of interest; it has a history in which nation states often led the way in establishing services, but its oral code of communication allows it to tie itself to communities of language which ignore official borders; it betrays a commercial imperative to reach large, high spending audiences, but it also has a cost structure which creates at least the possibility of a community station surviving on the tiniest of audiences. (215)*

For these and other reasons, radio is often lauded for its inclusivity and democratizing capacities. Even terms like radio *station* are analyzed for their air of accessibility and complicate notions of radio's unidirectional flow of knowledge from broadcaster to listener. As Hendy suggests, communities may be forged through the empowerment of listeners to *transmit* as well as to *receive*, transforming the role of the listener from the passive *consumer* of broadcasts into an active contributor and, in some cases, the *producer* of programming. Talk radio exemplifies this kind of listener interactivity on local and national scales. On an international scale, the BBC World Service has been particularly adept in embracing interactivity with its audiences through format changes to its radio programming (allowing phone ins, the exchange of e-mails, and SMS messages) and the development of supporting online environments, including messages boards, which operate currently in 27 languages. This has prompted renewed academic interest in the BBC World Service, and international broadcasting, as a "trans-cultural contact zone" (Gillespie et al. 2010a) and an expression of Web-enabled "digital diasporas" (Gillespie et al. 2010b).

It would be wrong to think that this kind of active listener engagement with radio is entirely a product of electronic communications technologies. This is neatly illustrated by a phenomenon experienced daily by the BBC World Service since it commenced international broadcasting during the 1930s; the sending and receiving of letters by the BBC from its worldwide listenership (Pinkerton 2008a). This correspondence – often words of "thanks" for broadcasts during periods of difficulty or political crisis, anecdotes and stories explaining the importance of radio to particular families and communities – can be conceptualized within a broader process of social and cultural exchange, connecting broadcasters and listeners into a transnational "imagined community" (see Anderson 1983). However, letters also reveal that radio broadcasts that appear innocent and unproblematic at the site of radio transmission (Bush House in London in the case of the BBC World Service) can have very different meanings and implications at sites of radio reception.

The diplomatic implications of place-specific interpretations of radio have been illustrated in my own work on the BBC's international and foreign-language services (see Pinkerton 2008b, 2008c). At the most basic level, striking geographical variations can be observed in the reputation and cultural meaning ascribed to the BBC as an institution. Whereas in the Falkland Islands, the BBC and its *Calling the Falklands* program have long been considered a palpable connection with "home" and a reassuring voice during moments of anxiety and conflict (see Pinkerton 2008c), in Iran the BBC Persian Service has a long-held reputation for being a perfidious manifestation of the British state (Sreberny and Torfeh 2008). In these and other ways, the BBC's global reputation – often described as being imbued with values of "impartiality" and "trustworthiness" – is subject to significant geographical and geopolitical variability.

Letters received from listeners to the BBC's Urdu Services in Pakistan and Northern India (and now archived in the BBC's Written Archive Centre) reveal similar spatial variations in the reception of specific BBC broadcasts. During the Indo-Pakistan conflicts of 1965 and 1971, for example, listeners' letters from both India and Pakistan criticized the BBC for "one-sided" and "inflammatory" reports of the fighting (Pinkerton 2008b). This kind of correspondence has a long history in the BBC's relationship with its South Asian listenership. Soon after the outbreak of the Second World War, an Indian Army brigadier reported hearing a BBC broadcast destined for Australia in which the Australian Prime Minister John Curtin proclaimed, "We are fighting to obtain a white Australia." While some in Australia might have considered Curtin's speech a rousing call to arms in defence of Australia and the Empire, in India the racist overtones were condemned along with the BBC broadcast as a serious "insult to Asiatic people" (Gillespie et al. 2010: 8). The India Office in London recorded other such criticisms of BBC broadcasts. The chronic mispronunciations of Indian place names by the BBC's metropolitan announcers, for example, were noted as having a "corrosive effect" on listeners in India. Attempts to pronounce Peshawar, Rawalpindi, Deccan, Deolali, Mhow, and Delhi were thought "absurd" and "creating a bad impression here." It was further reported,

> *Good effect of publicity being given by BBC to exploits of Indian troops in Africa is somewhat marred by mistakes in announcing. For instance two occurred in 9.30 IST, news bulletin on 6th March. The first syllable of Punjab rhymes with "gun" and "Dogra" is not name of place in Africa but of an Indian martial tribe. (Quoted in Gillespie et al. 2010: 8)*

As well as revealing something of the spatialized interpretation of radio transmissions as texts (in which broadcasts are read), these incidents also reveal something of the institutional geopolitics of international radio broadcasting. "The relationship between the BBC and Indian listeners has," as K.C. Sharma (1994) observes, "been one of love and hate. Love for the professional competence and hate as it represented the voice of a colonial empire" (82). At the root of this duality was a striking contradiction at the heart of the BBC's wartime broadcasts that called upon European and South-East Asian populations to overthrow their oppressors while, in India, preaching the need for loyalty to a British Raj that had violently suppressed the campaign for India's independence.

Importantly, this also acts as a powerful indicator and reminder that radio listening (far from being a singularly benign, passive experience that is "taken for granted") has to be given greater nuance, particularly with regards to issues of geographical, social, cultural contexts. Additionally, and as the next section demonstrates, the spatialities of radio listening "in place" cannot be divorced from a critical – and geopolitical – sensitivity to the spatial configuration of radio as a communications network and infrastructure.

Spaces of Radio Transmission

Radio is – today – both a global medium and a globalized industry. Estimates suggest that there may be upwards of 40,000 radio stations in active operation around the world (although this is necessarily a rough estimate due to the operations of "illegal" and informal stations). The worldwide commercial radio industry – which is dominated by fewer and larger media conglomerates (and their national subdivisions) integrated by the commercial trade in radio program formats – is projected to be worth US$62.08 billion by 2015, with most significant growth anticipated in Asia-Pacific, and Latin America (GIA 2009). Shrugging off the threat of television and the Internet, radio can now be consumed via a raft of new listening platforms and delivery technologies, such as digital audio broadcasting (DAB), digital satellite radio services, and via Internet streaming. It is also not unusual now to "watch," somewhat counter intuitively, radio programs live on digital televisions, often animated with webcams of the broadcasting studios. Radio's embrace of broadcast and production technologies has led to the emergence of more specialist, interest-driven networks while simultaneously homogenizing "the mainstream" through the commercialization of "formats" and globalization of popular music (see Hendy 2000).

While these commercial developments have extraordinary implications in terms of how global "radio space" is configured, this section pays particular attention to an alternative and rather more geopolitical expression of radio's international scale. Radio's capacity to communicate internationally is not, of course, a modern phenomenon having developed out of the political turbulence that predominated in interwar Europe (during the late-1920s). For much of the near-century that followed international broadcasting (i.e. broadcasting across borders of sovereign states) has been dominated by state and pseudo-state broadcasters. As Hale (1976) noted,

> *Radio is the only unstoppable medium of mass communication. It is the only medium which reaches across the entire globe instantaneously and can convey a message from any country to any other. Combined, these qualities of radio ensure that it plays an indispensable role in international communications, and keeps its place as the most powerful weapon of international propaganda. (Hale 1976: ix)*

Writing in 1976, in the midst of the Cold War and in an era before the development and proliferation of satellite television and Internet technologies, it would be easy to read Julian Hale's praise for radio's communicative capacities as a last flourish of the "Cinderella medium." After all, with the notable exception of the Falklands conflict in 1982, when radio broadcasting came to the fore in the absence of television relays from the apparently remote South Atlantic (see Pinkerton 2008b), radio's primacy as a source of news reporting and political communication has, seemingly, been diminished by the rise of international television and phenomena such as the "CNN effect." Even the BBC World Service – which had been dedicated solely to radio broadcasting since 1932 – appeared to acknowledge this trend during the early 1990s when World Service Television launched on Asia's STAR TV network; a move that the then Director of World Services, John Tusa, described as both "natural" and "essential" in maintaining global audiences (Tusa 1992: 14). However, if radio had proven its "unstoppability" over almost 60 years of international broadcasting, World Service Television would fare rather less well. By 1994, STAR TV (and the AsiaSat satellite) had been subsumed into Rupert Murdoch's News Corporation, and BBC's World Service Television was shortly thereafter removed from the China-oriented transmission in order to appease the Chinese government (Nye 2008). Murdoch, who was looking to access China's satellite television market, only later acknowledged that "The BBC was driving them [the Chinese regime] nuts. It wasn't worth it" (Varadarajan 2001). The Internet has shown itself to be equally vulnerable to such direct and indirect government interference. In recent years, Chinese and Iranian authorities have sought to control information flows by systematically blocking public access to major news and information Web sites and social networking platforms, leading some commentators to reflect on the construction of China's "great firewall."

While radio is not without its own 'firewalls' (China, Iran, North Korea, and Ethiopia have all engaged recently in radio jamming), its ability to traverse international borders and reach deep into foreign territories, connecting with people in their own homes, has reinvigorated radio as a space for public/cultural diplomacy. The emergence of the US-funded Radio Farda (the Iranian branch of Radio Free Europe/Radio Liberty) as a 24-hour news and cultural programming station in 2002 is but one example of a much broader recognition of radio's continuing relevance and "potential" in a post–Cold War, post–9/11 geopolitical context. Voice of America has received targeted funding increases from the US administration, via the BBG (Broadcasting Board of Governors), to boost programming for Afghanistan and the Middle East, with Iran frequently highlighted for particular attention. The British government, too, after years of cutbacks during the 1980s and early 1990s, increased BBC World Service funding each year between 1998–2009 allowing for long-term strategic investments in infrastructure and improvements in audibility through more powerful transmitter technologies and networks.

The issue of international broadcasting's "physical geography" is an important one and needs to be considered in conjunction with discussions of the "ethereal networks" that they create. As I have shown elsewhere in the South Asian context (when, for example, the BBC/VoA proposed the construction of a 1000kW station in Bengal – capable of broadcasting far into Southeast Asia – during 1963; see Pinkerton 2008a), radio transmitters, their geographical situation, their power, and their broadcast range all carry considerable geopolitical meaning and can provoke powerful emotions. The location, orientation, and strength of transmitting stations also reveal lingering geographical and political traces of imperial legacies, and, at the same time, the most contemporary of broadcasting strategies. As James Wood recognized in the mid-1990s, "Anyone examining its [the BBC World Service's] relay network, which is strategically located at key points around the world, might be forgiven for thinking that Britain had never lost its Empire" (168–9).

World Service audiences in the Mediterranean region are served by transmitters on Cyprus, the Middle East by facilities in Oman (which has strong military/geopolitical relations with the United Kingdom), South Asia by transmitters in Singapore and, until 1997, by a broadcasting station in Hong Kong. Since then, to avoid the possibility of political interference from the incoming Chinese authorities (following the British handover in 1997), the BBC relocated its SW broadcasting station – which largely serves audiences in mainland

China – to the strategically valuable Nakhon Sawan province in Thailand where new aerial arrays were constructed to deliver BBC services into both China (northwards) and South Asia (west), including Burma, Bangladesh, and India. A powerful relay station on Ascension Island in the mid-Atlantic provides an equally strategic position for BBC broadcasting to Africa and Latin America. This was visually demonstrated in 1982 with the publication of a set of Ascension Island stamps to commemorate the fiftieth anniversary of BBC external broadcasting, and locating Ascension at the heart of the BBC's South Atlantic network. This has been repeated on two further occasions to mark the twenty-fifth and thirtieth anniversaries of the Atlantic Relay station in 1991 and 1996 respectively.

Such representations are significant. As Pauliina Raento (2006) has recently highlighted, stamps (not unlike radio) have considerable "communicative power" and, importantly, have been implicated in the creation not only of imagined communities but, equally, in the establishment, or destruction of, "imperial rule, territorial claims, and sources of national pride" (602). For an island, such as Ascension, these are not inconsiderable issues and may help to explain repeated appeals to its "strategic" capacities (see Royle 2004) and its symbolic production as a central space in the configuration of international broadcasting. As the next section goes on to consider, however, radio's "spaces" are not solely physical or geopolitical – they might also be considered to be social, mediated, and fictional.

Spaces of the Ear and the Mind's Eye

Given that perceptions of "space" have been so intimately connected with the act of "seeing," of "visualizing" and, therefore, the eye as a sensory organ, it is perhaps unsurprising that space has been somewhat less than overt in configurations of the sound medium. Indeed, radio has often been considered not only a sonic/aural medium par excellence but also a medium deprived of sight:

> *What strikes everyone, broadcasters and listeners alike, as significant about radio is that it is a blind medium. We cannot see its messages, they consist only of noise and silence, and it is from the sole fact of its blindness that all radio's other distinctive qualities – the nature of its language, its jokes, the way in which its audiences use it – ultimately derive. (Crisell 1994: 3. Emphasis added)*

For Crisell, then, it is the "blindness" of radio that conditions the codes, conventions, and the modes of consumption of the radio medium by its listenership. Significant to this interpretation is Crisell's belief that people – both broadcasters and listeners – are "struck" by the absence of visual cues available from radio. The suggestion is that audiences are somehow surprised by, or at very least conscious of, radio's singularly aural message; radio's sound being less complete and less satisfactory than the combined sounds and pictures generated by television or film. In this way, radio's status as a medium is forged in terms of impairment or disability, invoking a sense that something is essentially lacking from its broadcast capacity. Such an interpretation does not appear to credit radio's positive attributes, power, and even "magic" (Shingler & Wierniga, 1998: 74). Indeed, far from being a disability, radio's supposed "nonvisual" character might be recognized as the definition of radio's advantage over television and film and even constitutive of a certain kind of "visuality" composed from listeners' experiences and memories – the "minds eye" (see Beck 1999).

Rejecting the "deficiency of sound" approach to radio, Beck (2009) conceptualizes radio messages as productive of two spatializing and visually attuned concepts. First, the "extra-radio world": this is the world that is assembled through the interaction of radio apparatus – including the recording microphone, sound equalizers, transmitters, and the radio receiver – and which is represented to listeners through the process of broadcast and reception. The second is radio's *mise en scène* (stagecraft), composed of the locations, spaces, and perspectives invoked in radio's "sound pictures" and animated by radio's "performers." This goes beyond the "sound scenery" of radio dramas and hints at a more inclusive conceptualization of radio's sound*spaces* that responds to, and is co-constituted with, "listener space" and radio's "fictional time-space" (Beck 1998). Echoing Nitsche's "planes of space" in computer games, radio might be understood through social, mediated and fictional spaces, and so on. As Ash has noted in this volume, computer games also have a powerful appeal to the imagination and, indeed, the "mind's eye," a connection further emphasized in Douglas's (2004: 75) account of "exploratory radio listening" in the United States during the 1920s:

> *Radio provided out-of-body experiences, by which you could travel through space and time mentally while remaining physically safe and comfortable in your own house. Time and again the historian finds comments like "I can travel over the United States and yet remain at home" or "With that magic knob I can command the musical programs from a dozen broadcasting stations."*

Notwithstanding the productive connections that can be drawn between radio and other media, this kind of conceptual work on radio remains in the margins of the academy. There is a continuing risk of privileging what we see over what we hear (see Sui 2000). While this may very well be a continuing legacy of Enlightenment culture that places primacy on written evidence in the negotiation of credibility, it is important to recall that prior to the development of textual communication, human experience of space was largely conditioned through shared oral traditions. Radio, according to McLuhan, represents a reverberation of that "tribal drum" with all of the opportunities this affords, but equally, all of the attendant dangers (McLuhan 1964).

Radio Futures

Notwithstanding the relative inattentiveness of geographers to the spatial configurations and implications of radio, there are signs, as this review demonstrates, that this may be changing. Within the subdisciplines of cultural and political geography, in particular, it is possible to discern a growing interest in radio's capacities to produce, reinforce or, indeed, to unsettle and undermine different kinds of sociocultural and political formations and at a range of different scales. There are number of areas that may prove to be productive for future investigation.

First, more work needs to be undertaken to address a lacunae in geographical scholarship concerning the technologies, technical operations, and institutional practices that determine, for instance, the production and circulation of media and, in this case, radio programming. In so doing, it may be possible to address dominant media narratives that marginalize parts of the world where radio is still the most important medium for many communities, especially in the global South. If we want to understand how hegemonic powers such as the United States attempt to communicate with these communities, then we need to better understand the institutional and broadcasting practices of Voice of America, Radio Saw,

Radio Farda as well those of CNN and filmmaking practices of Hollywood. Likewise, in the case of the United Kingdom, the BBC World Service should be acknowledged as a powerful instrument of public diplomacy, as should less well-known broadcasters such as the Voice of Tibet (based in Norway).

Second, the issue of radio's audiences might be more squarely addressed both in order to better understand the relationship between listeners and radio broadcasts, broadcasters and broadcasting institutions, and also as a means of exploring radio's production of place- and space-based subjectivities via the sound medium.

Finally, if we hope to develop a genuinely rich and nuanced understanding of how radio (as a medium) and radio stations (as institutions) are constituted and configured, then it would be productive to think in terms of radio as an assemblage of geographically situated components; of producers and presenters, studios and radio cars, transmitters, relay stations, receivers and, of course, listeners. Guattari's own interest in "popular free radio" is suggestive here and points to radio's capacities for "short-circuiting" media representations by generating a "collective assemblage of enunciation" – that is, a forum, or as Guattari put it, a "meeting place," for self-expression (Guattari, quoted in Goddard 2011: 12). Put simply, the interaction between radio's component parts is, itself, productive of particular kinds of interactive spaces that need to be better understood within and beyond notions of "transnational contact zones" and "digital diasporas" (Gillespie 2010).

References

Anderson, B. 1983. *Imagined Communities: Reflections on the Origin and Spread of Nationalism.* London: Verso.

Barnett, C. 1999. Broadcasting the Rainbow Nation: Media, democracy, and nation-building in South Africa. *Antipode* 31(3): 274–303.

Beck, A. 1998. Point-of-listening in radio plays. *Sound Journal* [Online]. Available at: www.kent.ac.uk/arts/sound-journal/beck981.html [accessed: August 22, 2013].

Beck, A. 1999. Is radio blind or invisible? A call for a wider debate on listening-in. *World Forum for Acoustic Ecology* (WFAE) [Online]. Available at: www.wfae.proscenia.net/library/articles/beck_blindness.pdf [accessed: August 22, 2013].

Berland, J. 1993. Radio space and industrial time: The case of music formats. In *Rock and Popular Music: Politics, Policies, Institutions*. Edited by T. Bennett, T., S. Frith, L. Grossberg, J. Shepherd, and G. Turner. London: Routledge, 179–92.

Brecht, B. 1993. The radio as an apparatus of communication. In *Radiotext(E)*. Edited by N. Strauss and D. Mandl. New York: Semiotext[e], 15–17.

Cavell, R. 1999. McLuhan and spatial communication. *Western Journal of Communication* 63(3): 348–63.

Cavell, R. 2002. *McLuhan in Space: A Cultural Geography*. Toronto: University of Toronto Press.

Cresswell, T. 1996. *In Place/out of Place: Geography, Ideology, and Transgression*. Minneapolis: University of Minnesota Press.

Crisell, A. 1994. *Understanding Radio*. 2nd edition. London: Routledge.

Cull, N.J. 2008. *The Cold War and the United States Information Agency: American Propaganda and Public Diplomacy, 1945–1989*. Cambridge: Cambridge University Press.

Cull, N.J. 2012. *The Decline and Fall of the United States Information Agency: American Public Diplomacy, 1989–2001*. New York: Palgrave Macmillan.

Dodds, K. 2006. Popular geopolitics and audience dispositions: James Bond and the Internet movie database (IMDB). *Transactions of the Institute of British Geographers* 31(2): 116–30.

Douglas, S.J. 2004. *Listening In: Radio and the American Imagination*. Minneapolis: University of Minnesota Press.

Frith, S. 2002. Music and everyday life. *Critical Quarterly* 44(1): 35–48.

Gillespie, M., D. Herbert, and M. Andersson. 2010. The Mumbai attacks and diasporic nationalism: BBC World Service Online forums as conflict, contact and comfort zones. *South Asian Diaspora* 2 (1): 109–29.

Gillespie, M., A. Pinkerton, G. Baumann, and S. Thiranagama. 2010. Introduction – South Asian diasporas and the BBC World Service: Contacts, conflicts, and contestations. *South Asian Diaspora* 2(1): 3–23.

Goddard, M.N. 2010. Towards an archaeology of media ecologies: The case of Italian Free Radios. *FibreCulture Journal* 17: 6–17.

Gow, G. 2001. Spatial metaphor in the work of Marshall Mcluhan. *Canadian Journal of Communication* [Online] 26(4). Available at: www.cjc-online.ca/index.php/journal/article/view/1254/1251 [accessed: 22 August 2013].

Hale, J.A.S. 1975. *Radio Power: Propaganda and International Broadcasting*. Philadelphia: Temple University Press.

Hayes, J.E. 2000. *Radio Nation: Communication, Popular Culture, and Nationalism in Mexico, 1920–1950*. Tucson: University of Arizona Press.

Hendy, D. 2010. *The Essay: Rewiring the Mind* [radio programme], BBC Radio 3, UK, 14–18 June 2010.

Hendy, D. 2000. *Radio in the Global Age*. Cambridge: Polity Press.

Hendy, D. 2007. *Life on Air: A History of Radio Four*. Oxford: Oxford University Press.

Hilliard, R.L. 1985. *Radio Broadcasting: An Introduction to the Sound Medium*. 3rd ed. New York: Longman.

Jones, K. 2005. Music in factories: A twentieth-century technique for control of the productive self. *Social & Cultural Geography* 6(5): 723–44.

Liebes, T. 2006. Acoustic space: The role of radio in Israeli collective history. *Jewish History* 20(1): 69–90.

MacDonald, F. 2006. The last outpost of empire: Rockall and the Cold War. *Journal of Historical Geography* 32(3): 627–47.

Marconi, G. 1901. Marconi's vision for wireless. *Marconi Calling* [Online]. Available at: www.marconicalling.co.uk/museum/html/objects/sounds/objects-i=1010.005-t=5-n=0.html [accessed online: August 22, 2013].

McLuhan, M. 1964. Radio: The tribal drum. *AV Communication Review* 12(2): 133–45.

Morley, D. 1992. *Television, Audiences, and Cultural Studies*. London: Routledge.

Nye, J.S. 2008. Public diplomacy and soft power. *Annals of the American Academy of Political and Social Science* 616: 94–109.

Penslar, D.J. 2003. Transmitting Jewish culture: Radio in Israel. *Jewish Social Studies* 10(1): 1–29.

Pinkerton, A. 2008a. A new kind of imperialism? The BBC, Cold War broadcasting and the contested geopolitics of South Asia. *Historical Journal of Film, Radio and Television* 28(4): 537–55.

Pinkerton, A. 2008b. Radio and the Raj: Broadcasting in British India (1920–1940). *Journal of the Royal Asiatic Society* 18(2): 167–91.

Pinkerton, A. 2008c. "Strangers in the Night": The Falklands conflict as a radio war. *Twentieth Century British History* 19(3): 344–75.

Pinkerton, A. and K. Dodds. 2009. Radio geopolitics: Broadcasting, listening and the struggle for acoustic spaces. *Progress in Human Geography* 33 (1): 10–27.

Raento, P. 2006. Communicating geopolitics through postage stamps: The case of Finland. *Geopolitics* 11(4): 601–29.

Robertson, E. 2008. "I get a real kick out of Big Ben": BBC versions of Britishness on the Empire and General Overseas Service, 1932–1948. *Historical Journal of Film, Radio and Television* 28(4): 459–73.
Royle, S.A. 2004. "The island has been handed over to me": Ascension Island as a company colony, 1922–42. *Singapore Journal of Tropical Geography* 25(1): 109–26.
Ryfe, D.M. 1999. Franklin Roosevelt and the fireside chats. *Journal of Communication* 49(4): 80–103.
Shingler, M. and C. Wieringa. 1998. *On Air: Methods and Meanings of Radio*. London: Arnold.
Sreberny, A., and M. Torfeh. 2008. The BBC Persian Service 1941–1979. *Historical Journal of Film, Radio and Television* 28(4): 515–35.
Sui, D.Z. 2000. Visuality, aurality, and shifting metaphors of geographical thought in the late twentieth century. *Annals of the Association of American Geographers* 90(2): 322–43.
Tusa, J. 1992. *BBC World Service: A World in Your Ear*. London: Broadside Books.
Varadarajan, T. 2001. Editorial: Bad company. *Wall Street Journal*, March 26, 2001.
Wood, J. 1992. *History of International Broadcasting*. London: P. Peregrinus, Ltd.

Comic Books

Jason Dittmer

Introduction

Comic books are a relatively recent topic within geography; however, their appearance in the literature has quickly sparked an efflorescence of papers, if not approaches (Dittmer 2014). While there are precedents within the geographic literature, such as the study of literature (Hones 2008) and political cartoons (Dodds 1996), this review is self-consciously limited to the world of graphic narrative, whether in "comic book" or "graphic novel" format ("graphic narrative" and "comics"/"comic books" will be used interchangeably through the remainder of this chapter). Graphic narrative can be understood as the juxtaposition of images, usually with text overlaying or within the images, to produce a story (there is an extensive debate about the definition of comics, see Varnum and Gibbons 2001b; Holbo 2011). If comic books are only recently a feature of the geographic literature, it does not hold that they are unimportant, or tacked onto an already full roster of media to be studied. Rather, comics may be understood as the spatial medium par excellence.

In this chapter, I will trace some of the geographies inherent to, and produced through, comic books by adopting Adams's taxonomy of media geography (2011). I begin by reviewing the literature, largely from within the tradition of popular geopolitics, on representation and narrative in comics ("place in media"). This is followed by brief attention to the limited work that has been done on comics as consumed in particular contexts ("media in place"). The chapter then moves to a more extensive discussion, drawing both from the geography literature and more broadly, on how spaces have been reconfigured within the comics industry ("media in space"). After this the chapter shifts to a discussion of the role of space within comics, enunciating two different relations between space and time in graphic narrative ("space in media"). Finally, the chapter concludes with a discussion of the possible futures for comic book geographies.

Representations and Narratives

Popular Geopolitics

Arguably, the largest emphasis in the literature on comics within geography has occurred within the frame of popular geopolitics. Popular geopolitics refers to a tradition within critical geopolitics of examining the representations and narratives of place and space that circulate through everyday life, constructing the field in which foreign policy decisions are made and legitimated. Within this frame, comic books have generally been critiqued as offering simplistic, moralizing tales that are aimed at younger audiences, although as we shall see there are important exceptions. My work on nationalist superheroes began with just such a framing, considering these heroes, such as Captain America, as key "rescaling icons" that allow the vast, horizontal community of the nation to be embodied in a single, knowable figure whom young readers can aspire to become (Dittmer 2005; 2007a; 2007b; 2009). This rescaling of the nation has important implications for the way in which the relationship between power, authority, and legitimacy are imagined by readers. That is, the genre of the nationalist superhero has become increasingly popular as a way of understanding the realm of international relations and geopolitics, not only reproducing the nation (and its political cognate, the state) but also projecting the conditions of superpowered conflict into the international system (Dittmer 2013).

Geopolitical critique is not limited to the discourses associated with American hegemony. Oliver Dunnett (2009) argues that a parallel critique can be made of comics within the Franco-Belgian tradition of *bandes dessinées.* In particular he turns his attention to the Adventures of Tintin, arguing that they reflect a Eurocentric worldview. Intriguingly, while visual analysis of Captain America and his ilk has emphasized the dense semiotics of the superhero physique and costume, Dunnett (2009: 586) argues that what makes Tintin a potent symbol is his under-coding:

> *[H]ere we have a character that is essentially iconic in its form, a facet which allows some readers to relate to Tintin as a generic "everyman" figure, albeit clearly a young, male, European everyman. … This basic depiction of Tintin contrasts effectively with the surrounding landscapes and settings of the stories, and Hergé went to a great deal of effort to research into the minutiae of real objects such as automobiles and buildings.*

A similar critique of visual representation in *bandes dessinées* is made by Juliet Fall. Her analysis of *La Frontière Invisible,* by Schuiten and Peeters, highlights the story's critique of the gaze as an instrument of power "by examining maps as tools of power, control, and colonization, illustrated by the story of Roland de Cremer, a young cartographer" (2006: 653). This subversive critique, Fall argues, is undercut by the substitution of the female body for the territorial map (de Cremer becomes obsessed with a woman whose body bears a map of the country), a naturalism that obviously has gendered political implications: "Faced with the ever-tempting idea of natural boundaries, literally inscribed and incarnated in the flesh, the critique of the geopolitical eye is lost" (Fall 2006: 666).

Visuality and Mapping

These critiques hint at the wide realm of possibility that comic books have beyond textual representation. Indeed, it is in the visual dimension that comics distinguish themselves from the vast literature on textualism in geography. In contrast to the respectful criticism offered by earlier scholars in popular geopolitics, Ted Holland (2012) highlights the emancipatory potential of comics. Tracing a counter-history of nonfiction documentaries and journalism produced through graphic narrative, Holland highlights the potential of the anti-geopolitical eye to emerge through the creative framing of comics' panels.

Beyond popular geopolitics, comics have come to be of interest to cartographers as another way of representing space that shares certain formal characteristics with maps but which offers new possibilities. Moore (2009) argues that maps often feature in comics, often as a device to drive a narrative forward but equally because comics are themselves exercises in world-building. Further, the ability of comics to represent time through the juxtaposition of images is understood as something that might be more fully incorporated into cartographic practice (Moore et al. 2011). The ability of comics to represent in unique ways has been taken up by several cartographers and other geographers (Jones and Evans 2011; Han 2008; Krygier and Wood 2009), but in general these efforts are attempts to produce reader-friendly accounts of how place unfolds as a process (e.g. mapping, research administration) rather than attempts to tell stories that are distinctively graphic narrative. However, as Holland noted, the ability of comics to represent places in unique ways, to see differently, is a central feature of the medium.

From the above it is clear that place-in-comics is a fairly well-developed research of theme in geography, with a particular emphasis on geopolitics and mapping. In the next section, this chapter approaches comics-in-place, that is to say the way in which comics take on different meanings in a range of places.

Contextualizing the Comic

The dematerializing instinct of analysts considering place-in-comics is inverted when considering comics-in-place. Rather, the fact that comic books are objects, originating in some places and circulating to others, becomes salient. What does it mean for comics books to be located in specific sites, and how does that change the meanings attached to them?

Cultural Value

Comics take on different meanings in different contexts. Martin de la Iglesia (2007: 333) argues that

> *A geographical approach to comics is anything but far-fetched, since comics have nearly always been closely associated with geographical terms. For a long time, in some countries comics were almost exclusively imported from the U.S. ... which led to comics being seen by the public as purely an American phenomenon. In some non-Anglophone countries even the term for the genre, like the Spanish "cómic" or the German "Comic," stems directly from the English language spoken in the U.S.*

Despite this, in the United States comics have traditionally been a denigrated medium, seen as escapist, puerile, and as a drag on literacy uptake by children (Lopes 2009). This low status is in part because the comic book, in the United States, has long been associated with the superhero genre. However, this low cultural status is not matched elsewhere; there are two other major hearths for graphic narratives: the already mentioned Franco-Belgian comics region and Japan (perhaps with South Korea added in). In France, graphic narrative is referred to as the ninth art, alongside other major forms such as cinema, architecture, dance, and poetry. Each region has its own history of production and canon of important moments, authors, and comics. Still, the globalization of publishing has meant that the Franco-Belgian industry began to gain global stature from the 1960s onward (Beaty 2007), with Japanese *manga* exploding onto the scene in the 1990s. Hence, we can see an uneven geography emerging in relation to both the associations and statuses of various comic book traditions and in relation to the general status and cultural meaning of the form itself. "Generally speaking, comics are a global phenomenon. The dynamics, though, of their production and reception, has [*sic*] developed differently in different countries" (Iglesia 2007: 334). Place, in this formulation, is produced through the relational valuation of comics readers and aficionados around the world. Such a formulation necessarily draws attention to these readers and aficionados, who are themselves geographically rooted in place.

Meaning Making

Reading can be understood as a performative event (Hones 2008), in which the circulating popular culture object intersects with the reader, who is spatiotemporally embedded within particular places (marked by commonalities of language, social structures, etc. – Livingstone 2005). Producers' attempts to convey a desired message on the comics page are complicated by differences in the cultural capital possessed by readers located in various places. This section will outline some of the research that has tried to take into account this context of reading.

One method has remained popular over the past several decades in considering audience response to the image-text of American comics: analysis of readers' letters to the editor (Matton 2000). Letters to the editor, in comics, have their origins in the early twentieth-century pulp science fiction fan community, which corresponded with one another regarding the stories they were reading and writing (Jones 2004). This transferred into the superhero comics as there was a significant carryover of generic content and readership. In the 1960s, Marvel Comics's Stan Lee realized this offered an excellent opportunity to establish a dialogue with the audience, not only conducting market research about what fans considered good or bad storytelling but also making them feel like part of a community rather than just a consumer (Wright 2001). These letters to the editor continued as a tradition until fairly recently, when the advent of the Internet undercut the basis for the slow mail-and-publication based system. While it must always be remembered that these letters were selected by editors for publication, they nevertheless provide a useful window into how comics were understood by their readers at the time of publication. Further, the problem of editorial selection diminishes (but does not disappear) when we remember that the editors often liked to highlight controversy to make their comics seem edgy.

The importance of this place-based context in readers' interpretive processes can be witnessed in research I conducted on nationalist superheroes in Canada and the United Kingdom (Dittmer 2011; Dittmer and Larsen 2007; 2010). In these countries, new superheroes such as Captain Canuck and Captain Britain were introduced to their respective national audiences, but not as entirely fresh enterprises. Both had to deal with the archetype of the genre, Captain America, as a character that was both understood as the Platonic ideal of the nationalist superhero (note the similarities in name and flag-based costume) and yet was so identifiably American that he had to be avoided. Tiptoeing down this threshold between slavish adoption of American generic conventions and enacting an obscure, unidentifiable heroism required constant modulation of the stories in response to letters to the editor.

For instance, Captain Canuck was initially given no superpowers whatsoever; rather, his skills and strength stemmed entirely from clean, moral living. This made for a nice contrast with the drug-augmented Captain America. One letter to the editor from a Canadian said that the emphases on morality and good living "indicate a humaneness and profoundness that puts your comic in a class by itself. It is this, I believe, that makes it distinctively Canadian." Similarly, another reader wrote "I like the idea of a Canadian hero not using sorcery or something phoney like that" (quoted in Dittmer and Larsen 2007: 742). However, as the comic struggled to stay afloat, the creative staff was forced to broaden the appeal of the comic to American comics readers. Therefore, by 1979 Captain Canuck's origin story was changed to give him supernatural powers. This was angrily rejected in at least one letter to the editor: "As for Captain Canuck, I was sorry to see that his strength is not all 'good clean living,' as you stated in one of your earlier issues. To me, this makes him seem phony. It lowers him to the level of the American superheroes, and he becomes just another of the horrid mess of ridiculous characters with impossible powers" (quoted in Dittmer and Larsen 2007: 743). Considering the act of reading as an event that occurs in place, and which is shaped by that place, helps to show schisms of meaning emerge and how various place-based subjectivities figure in them.

Spaces of Production, Distribution, and Consumption

Of course, there are a great many comic book industries, both divided among countries and within countries (as in the distinction between corporate-promoted comics and independent comics). Given the impossibility of covering all of these in the available space, this section on media-in-space will trace the changing spaces of the US corporate-owned comic book industry, originally the "Big Two" (Marvel and DC) but now widening out to include producers such as Dark Horse. The US comic book industry is an interesting case study because it can be understood as an assemblage composed of geographically situated components: writers, artists, newsstands, comic book shops, printing technologies, and so on. The changing relations among those components are themselves productive of new spaces.

Changes in Creative Production

Comics production during the Depression and World War II drew on a Fordist model, emphasizing assembly line production and formulaic writing. One person would write plots and design characters, which would then be drawn by an artist, which would then be colored in by a third worker. Finally, a fourth worker would insert the text. This method of production encouraged geographic centralization, as New York art school graduates took on freelance work on the assembly line to tide them over during the Depression until their "real" careers took off with something more respectable (Wright 2001). Comics icon Stan Lee adopted his pseudonym (his real name is Stan Lieber) in hopes of a forthcoming career in journalism. Thus, both the assembly line production process and the stigma associated with the industry led to a lack of creative credit for individuals. Further, this system of freelance workers left the publishers with all the rights to the characters they published, which would have tremendous implications for the men toiling away in these early years as their creations later reached the status of global icons (Ro 2004).

The decline of the assembly-line system resulted from the decline of sales in the 1950s. Bringing production in-house enabled the publishers to dictate the kinds of stories being produced, away from superheroes and on to new horizons. Following the example of Dell Publishing, which, with its license to publish Disney and Warner Brothers characters, had previously adapted its art and writing to mesh with those products, publishers created "house styles" that would function as a type of publicly recognizable branding, forcing creative staff to accommodate themselves to corporate artistic and writing styles (Wright 2001). House styles remained even after superheroes returned to dominance in the 1960s, with DC and Marvel emerging in the period as the dominant players in the market. J.M. DeMatteis, a writer for *Captain America* in the 1980s, described the "Marvel method" of production this way: "In those days, we worked "Marvel Style" —which meant that I wrote a detailed plot outline, the penciler drew from that and then I dialogue from the pencils. It's done less and less these days but it's a wonderful way to work" (DeMatteis 2009: n.p.) Subsequently, Marvel abandoned this in-house production method in favor of the style in place at DC. Steve Engelhart, who wrote *Captain America* in the 1970s and then worked for DC Comics in the 1970s and 1980s, describes the later system this way:

> *The alternative, now firmly in place by both DC and Marvel, is the old "script in advance" way, wherein I describe each panel and write the dialogue without seeing how the artist will render anything, and the artist is reduced to following my directions. I did DARK DETECTIVE, JLA [Justice League of America], and other DC stuff like that, and it does put me more firmly in control which, with a tense strip like Batman, made for a more tightly-controlled result, which was a good thing – but I still like the now anachronistically-named Marvel style better because it gives everybody involved more freedom. (Englehart 2009: n.p.)*

During the so-called Golden and Silver Ages, the "bullpen" (where assembly-line production took place) existed not only because of the need for workers to hand paper back and forth to each other as it was produced but also because it provided a site of surveillance and intervention by the editor/publisher (see Figure 4.1).

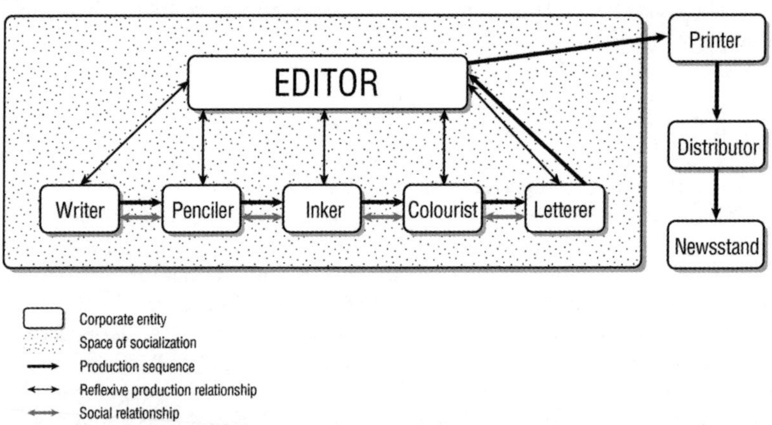

Figure 4.1 Comic book production and social relations with the bullpen model (pre–1980)
Source: Norcliffe and Rendace 2003

However, changes to both corporate strategy and distribution in the 1980s and 1990s toward subculture marketing (more on this later) has weakened the control of the publishers. Englehart (2009: n.p.) argues that "in the 70s, the writers were top dogs. Artists became ascendant in the late 80s." Indeed, as individual artists (and their styles) became the object of fans' cultlike followings, sales followed artists as they changed from one title or publisher to another. This "star system" enabled a fundamental reworking of the power relationships within the industry, with creators gaining leverage in negotiations with publishers. This allowed for the geographic fragmentation of the production process. As Glen Norcliffe and Olivero Rendace argue (2003: 247),

> *When comics were mass-produced, sales were, for the most part, market driven, and work was supervised within vertically integrated firms. Since then, comics have been increasingly addressed to specific submarkets, with artists using know-how, specialized skills, and their own contact networks to assess the interests of readers. In this latter interpersonal world, a great deal of reflexivity is found between producers and consumers who are in frequent communication, especially during the comic convention season. Comic production is now vertically disintegrated with networks of subcontractors who are often geographically dispersed.*

This geographic dispersion reflects a reworking of the comic book assemblage, enabled by the incorporation of new technologies that carry with them the quasi-agency that Latour emphasizes. Norcliffe and Rendace (2003: 248) elaborate, "[Comic book writers and artists] may work in teams that change by the project, bounce ideas and sketches around the Web, surf for hours looking for inspiration and ideas, and frequently pick up on the most current trends that they may satirize or incorporate recursively into the comics' story lines."

In short, processes of creative production within the comic book industry between the 1930s and the present have gone from Fordist to post–Fordist, with creative control following an uneven trajectory from the anonymous production line to a dispersed technology-dependent system in which comics producers no longer need to work in the same location as their employers and colleagues, and indeed can work for multiple employers (Figure 4.2)

While comic book creators currently work freelance much like their Depression-era predecessors, their production systems, and their consequent empowerment within those systems, are not comparable.

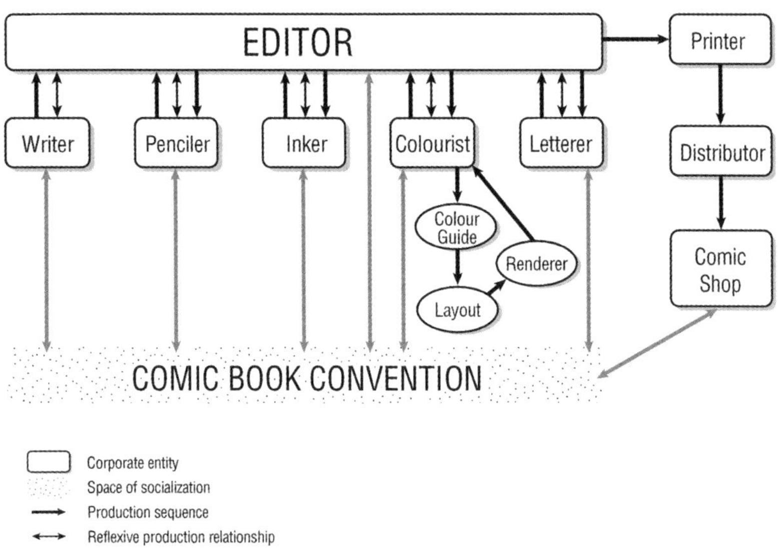

Figure 4.2 Comic book production and social relations with the distanced model (post–1990)
Source: Norcliffe and Rendace 2003

Changes in Distribution/Consumption

Another key shift in the spaces of mainstream comics in the United States is the transition from newsstand distribution to direct marketing. While subscriptions have always remained one way of getting comics delivered to your door, they have remained a small portion of overall sales. In the first half century of comics, a range of comics could normally be found at newsstands and other commercial spaces such as a rack by the cash register in a supermarket. In this era, newsstands and other retail markets were allowed to return unsold merchandise for a credit. Retailers typically only sold one comic out of every three that publishers printed (Wright 2001). Collecting these comics had long been a pastime for fans, but direct marketing changed the basis for this market. With the introduction of direct marketing, comic book stores emerged as the primary site for purchasing comics, and comics at newsstands evaporated. Comic book stores bought comics from the publishers at a discount but forfeited their opportunity to return unsold merchandise, meaning that supply could better reflect actual demand. The remaining unsold comic books then were fed into the market for "back issues," where they either went up in value as collectibles or stagnated if deemed unimportant by collectors. Publishers liked this system because it cut costs and saved them money but, crucially, it also reduced the chances of new readers finding their way to comics.

The move to direct marketing changed the relationship between comics fans and the object of their affection. Given the older, and overwhelmingly male, demographics of fandom, direct marketing was not just a change in *where* you could buy comics, but also in *who* was buying them. By eliminating the casual buyer, comics producers increasingly bent to the desire of fandom for darker, more sophisticated, violent storylines. The 1980s were marked by the dominance of vigilante heroes like Wolverine and the Punisher, while 1990 saw the emergence of Ghost Rider, a demon from hell on a motorcycle intent on exacting justice for those wronged. The complicated stories and ambiguous morality finished off whatever casual readers might have picked up a comic book out of curiosity, and the comic book increasingly began to cater more and more to the most vocal, amping fans up with crossover events and promises of mayhem (Wright 2001).

The shift to direct marketing coincided with the implementation of new graphic design software that enabled publishers to easily print comics with special "collector's edition" covers that helped to inflate the collector's market, with fans purchasing multiple copies of the same comic with no intention of reading them, but instead sealing them up in plastic collectors' bags to maintain value. With buzz building around the comics industry throughout the early 1990s, Marvel made a bid for preeminence, attempting to vertically integrate their product line by buying out a distributor in 1994. This led to the collapse of other distributors, as Marvel's missing market share undercut their profitability. One distributor, Diamond Distributors, led the creation of a bloc to counter Marvel by signing the other major comic producers to an exclusive distribution agreement. However, Marvel's ambition ran aground when fans decided that the comics had become shallow and inferior; the common view was that Marvel's comics had become all show and little substance, intended solely to dupe collectors into purchasing multiple copies. In short, the comic collection bubble burst. Marvel's sales plummeted and the company was forced to declare bankruptcy in 1996. Marvel's bid to distribute their own comics was a failure, but had effectively created a monopoly under Diamond (Marvel was itself forced to sign with Diamond during its corporate restructuring, leaving Diamond the only game in town). This drove up cover prices (as Diamond charges monopoly rates to distribute) just when the industry was perceived as cynical by its consumers. Overall sales plummeted from $850 million in 1993 to $225 million in 2001 (Norcliffe and Rendace 2003).

Marvel recovered subsequently with a smaller slate of comics, and the industry overall has worked hard to recover from the excesses of the 1990s. With this rebuilding project in mind, the major comic book companies have tried to cater to an increasingly pluralistic set of fan cultures revolving around comics. Marvel and DC each set up boutique imprints under which they could print comics for more mature audiences without sullying their child-friendly brand names. Conversely, both companies also have a selection of superhero comics for children that tone down the violence and complicated storylines that had emerged since the turn to direct marketing. In short, the boom and bust of the 1990s has forced comic book companies to be more attentive to multiple audiences. Taken with the changes in production, it is now "not unusual for a comic book to be written in Scotland, penciled in Canada, readily produced ... in the USA and distributed to hundreds of thousands of places throughout the world" (Iglesia 2007: 332).

Over the history of the comic book the relationship between consumers and their comic books has been intimately linked to the type of distribution available. Newsstand and other forms of retail distribution (linked with the creation of the Comics Code in the 1950s) led to a modernist generic homogeneity, which forced companies to produce for a mass market (with all the inefficiencies inherent to that production), thereby shaping the kinds of stories that could be told. However, the shifting assemblage of the comic book industry (e.g. the incorporation of direct marketing) reworked the boundaries of the possible, enabling the turn to the amorality and antiheroism of the late 1980s and 1990s, also allowing the collectors' bubble of the mid-1990s to devastate the industry. The comic book has itself been reworked through these processes, from a disposable object to a collectible, and also from a modern Fordist product to a plural, niche-marketed one. While the present-day comic book maintains all of these traces, the emphasis has shifted from one to the other over the past 80 years.

Spaces and Times in Graphic Narrative

Turning our attention to space-in-comics directs our attention to the two distinct ways of considering space in graphic narrative. They differ primarily with regard to how space is related (or not) to time. As both of these spatialities are informed by comics literacy, it is worth first considering the way in which comics are read. As Elisabeth El Refaie (2009: 199) points out regarding single-frame political cartoons, "the reading of individual newspaper cartoons poses quite a challenge and requires a whole range of literacies, including a broad knowledge of current events, an excellent grasp of idioms and other linguistic phenomena, a cast repertoire of cultural symbols, a familiarity with cartoon conventions, and a capacity for lateral thinking." Adding in the complexity of sequential art – through which longer narratives are created through the juxtaposition of images (usually supplemented by text) – ensures that reading a comic book requires a learned literacy. There is nothing obvious or natural about linking sequential images together to produce narrative; it is a way of communicating with a specific history and therefore reading sequential art is a learned skill (Kunzle 2001; Couch 2001). Indeed, it is the belief of the reader that sequential art is meant to be understood together as a narrative that leads the reader to attempt to produce a coherent story from the montage in front of them. "[Images] convey ideas and values, and reading them requires sophistication and skill" (Varnum and Gibbons 2001a: xii).

Any analysis of comic book form has to begin with the foundational unit of a comics page – the panel. The panel is identifiable by its form, area, and site; that is to say that every panel has a shape, a size, and a location vis-à-vis other panels on the page. It is separated from other panels by a space (real, or metaphorical) called the gutter. All together, the composition of panels on a page (or across two facing pages) is called the layout (sometimes known as the breakdown).

Einsteinian Space

The first form of spatiality found in comics can be broadly described as Einsteinian, in that it considers time and space to be interlinked. In graphic narrative, space is translated into time, such that displacement on the page can be understood as displacement in time (Dittmer 2010). Typically, readers are expected to make their way through the layout from top-left to bottom-right, although this is not always true (Groensteen 2007). This conventional reading pattern is of course drawing on cultural practices of reading; in countries where reading occurs from right-to-left (like Japan), comics' panels are ordered on that principle. When the conventional pattern is not to be used, there are usually visual clues (sometimes arrows, but usually more subtle) as to the order to be followed.

The layout of panels on the page (and their intended order) has implications for the readers' engagement with the material form of the comic book. For instance, *Tintin* creator Hergé explains how his expectation of readers' engagement with the comic book structured the way he drew his stories:

> *When I show a character who is running, he generally goes from the left to the right … ; and then, that corresponds to a habit of eye, which follows the movement and which I accentuate: from left to right, the speed appears faster than from right to left. I use the other direction when a character returns on his footsteps. If I always make him run from right to left, he will have the air, in each drawing, of returning, of chasing himself. (quoted in Groensteen 2007: 48)*

Further, given the spatial limitations of the page itself, panels tend to be quadrilaterals of various types in order to maximize the blank page (as round or other panel shapes would not abut each other). The tendency (unless of course maximizing space takes a back seat to other creative concerns) then is for panels to stack like bricks, allowing the readers' eyes to sweep across a strip before they lift and move down to the next strip (Groensteen 2007). This disjuncture at the end of a strip is often used to introduce a change of scene, or some other form of narrative break, mirroring the disconnect that is physically manifested in the act of reading. Similarly, the bottom-right panel of a "traditional" layout provides an even bigger disjuncture as the eyes must lift to the top of the next page. The bottom-right panel of a right-hand page provides an even bigger disjuncture, as the narrative is broken until the page can be turned. Many comics producers will embed cliffhanger moments in the comic book so that they "hang" across a turning of the page for just that reason. The language of music has seemingly become the metaphor of choice for theorists and comic book producers to describe the embodied rhythm of reading a comic book. Theorist Thierry Groensteen (2007: 60–61) describes reading practice as "a natural rhythm, a breathing aroused by its discrete apparatus of enunciation, which, discontinuous, is laid out in strips and tabular," while cartoonist Chris Ware describes reading practice thus: "In comics you can make the beat come alive by reading it, by experiencing it beat by beat as you would playing music" (quoted in Raeburn 2004: 25).

Bergsonian Space

Therefore, it can be seen that the process of reading a comic book, the comic's material form (size and shape of pages), and the narrative/visual content of the comic are all intertwined. It is impossible to locate an origin point for this relationship; instead of efficient causation the assemblage of graphic narrative *emerges* in this particular formation (Gallacher 2011 refers to this process as "alchemy"). This leads us to the second form of space found in comics: Bergsonian space. Henri Bergson famously debated Einstein about the nature of time, claiming that time ran only in one direction (unlike Einstein, whose equations rendered time relative). Bergson was widely regarded as losing the debate, but his views are making a comeback both in the physical and social sciences (Guerlac 2006). With regard to comics, Bergsonian space refers to a disconnect between space and time, with the experience of time (as intensive and durational) linked to the topological space of the page in multiple, overlapping ways.

Space in graphic narrative is topological because, rather than emphasizing sequence or authorial intent, we can imagine a web of relations tying together the panels of the comic, or indeed of many comics. That is to say that there is a multitude of possible relationships linking panels together across the nonrepresentational space of the gutter. For instance, every panel in a given comic can be understood to be in relation, given their material links (on paper that is stapled or bound together). Similarly, those panels can be understood as in relation to every other panel published under that title. Of course, relationships can be understood to be of differing intensity; most would argue that random panels in *Action Comics* #1 and *Action Comics* #654 are only loosely linked (barring some artistic homage). Whereas, the panels in the same comic that the writer and artist wanted to be read one after the other are strongly related. What is unique in this topological reading of comics is that those relations are not actualized by semiotic clues left by the creative team, but by the act of reading itself. If a reader does not instantiate a relation between two panels, for that unique reading event there *is* no relation.

Therefore, the spatiality of the comic book is always unstable; this occasionally leads to a breakdown in the relationship between the people and objects in the assemblage. Complicating matters for both producers and readers is that while reading conventions are generally well understood, these conventions are often unmet, either as a result of producers' misjudging readership practices or because the producers wish to disrupt the continuity of reading to generate affect or slow down the reading process (notice here time is disconnected from in-story time, but rather is subjective). An example of the former can be found in this blog entry by Jim Tierney (2007: n.p.), a cartoonist:

> *For the longest time, I've been hung up with rendering. I always thought the most important thing was how well something was drawn. I would always compulsively "fill the space" whenever making any cartoon, and I'd draw everything in the cartoon with equal care to make it look as good as possible. This led to some nice looking comics, some nice looking, utterly incomprehensible comics. People would look and my comics, and say "they look good", followed with, "I don't get it." I often found myself explaining things. It's because you could look at a single panel, and have no idea what was important, or what I was trying to communicate (but they looked sharp).*

Tierney's post illustrates how artists need to guide their readers through topological space, but this is only true if the artist wants to foster the Einsteinian notion of space, in which space passes as beats and measures. Disrupting that spatial rhythm, disorienting the subject, can be the intent just as much as facilitating the production of smooth narrative.

An example of an artist intentionally playing with the layout in order to disorient the reader and break the rhythm of reading can be found in Figure 4.3. Here, the layout gives an impression of fragmentation and disorientation, with five "real" panels in a quite traditional layout (only one strip is divided into two panels, so the reading pattern is primarily top-to-bottom), but the images are mostly tilted on a diagonal, with "false" frames cutting through the panels. This layout expresses the sense of unreality being experienced by Captain America, who is presently existing in a false reality imposed by his nemesis, the Red Skull (note the shading of the frames and the light bursting through the hole through which he escapes in the final panel). Hence, the layout is not entirely about easing the reading process, but is also about creatively expressing content within the material constraints of the comic book itself. Rather than a single extensive relationship between space and time (as in Einsteinian readings of space in graphic narrative), there are multiple, overlapping temporalities that connect to both the spaces-in-comics and the spaces out of them.

The Future of Comic Book Geographies

Given the relative paucity of sources from geography journals in this review, it could be seen as silly to be speculating about the future of comic book geographies. Perhaps a better question is, does this constellation of work even really have a past? Still, given the relative novelty of the topic in geography and the speed with which it has been taken up, there are reasons to be optimistic about the future. But what will such a future look like?

I would like to suggest that there are two particularly intriguing ways forward. The first is to address a number of the lacunae that are readily apparent upon reading this chapter's review. For instance, in the anglophone geography literature there is a fair amount of research on North American/British representations, audiences, and comic book industries. There is far less work that has considered non-anglophone traditions (but see Gallacher 2010), "independent" producers and their comics, and casual readership. Of course, the list of lacunae could be an infinite set, but those three are glaring absences waiting for scholarly attention. Future scholars would do well to consider them.

The second way forward is to consider the interstices and overlaps between these places and spaces of comics. These places and spaces are not disconnected, but instead intersect with one another and even co-constitute each other. For example, geographer Shaun Huston's documentary *Comic Book City, Portland, Oregon USA* (2012) is about Portland, a center of comic book creativity (both corporate and independent) that forms a key node in the networks of production discussed in the section of this chapter covering comics-in-space. However, it is also an experimental film, shot to incorporate some of the spaces-in-comics, such as panels and the gutters between them, within the cinematic visuality. Huston's attempt to overlay comic book spatiality onto other phenomena is potentially very fruitful.

The notion of comics as assemblages with a topological spatiality opens up many such possibilities, as assemblages (and other network ontologies) are at present very much on the avant-garde of social science. That comics mirror that ontology implies that comics may be particularly effective in narrating social processes, if only academics can develop the tools to produce these narratives. Other examples of this kind of interstitial work are Jörn Ahrens and Arno Meteling's edited collection (2010) and Marcus Doel and David Clarke's chapter on urban space and the aesthetics of comics (2009). Both address the intertwining of urban spaces and spaces of comics: from the metropolitan city as hearth of twentieth-century comics production to the connections between Marvel Comics's New York and the "real" Big Apple, and from the role of Alan Moore's comics in the production of London as a place to the idea of the city *as* a comic. By thematically linking across the divides between

Figure 4.3 Creative use of layout to illustrate the unreality of the world that Captain America is experiencing within the narrative

Source: *Captain America: Reborn* #5. © 2013 Marvel Characters, Inc. Used with permission comics-in-media, media-in-comics, comics-in-space, and space-in-comics, the book itself serves as the topological bridge across the gutter of comic book geographies. We could do worse than to turn to such a model for future work.

References

Adams, P.C. 2011. A taxonomy for communication geography. *Progress in Human Geography* 35(1): 37–57.

Ahrens, J., and A. Meteling (eds). 2010. *Comics and the City: Urban Space in Print, Picture and Sequence*. New York and London: Continuum.

Beaty, B. 2007. *Unpopular Culture: Transforming the European Comic Book in the 1990s*. Toronto: University of Toronto Press.

Couch, C. 2001. *The Yellow Kid* and the Comic Page. In *The Language of Comics: Word and Image*. Edited by R. Varnum and C. Gibbons. Jackson: University Press of Mississippi, 60–74.

De la Iglesia, M. 2007. Geographical classification in comics. *International Journal of Comic Art* 9(2): 330–39.

DeMatteis, J. M. 2009. E-mail interview with author.

Dittmer, J. 2005. Captain America's empire: Reflections on identity, popular culture, and post–9/11 geopolitics. *Annals of the Association of American Geographers* 95(3): 626–43.

Dittmer, J. 2007a. "America is safe while its boys and girls believe in its creeds!" Captain America and American identity prior to World War 2. *Environment and Planning D, Society & Space* 25(3): 401–23.

Dittmer, J. 2007b. Retconning America: Captain America in the wake of WWII and the McCarthy hearings. In *The Amazing Transforming Superhero! Essays on the Revision of Characters in Comic Books, Film and Television*. Edited by T. Wandtke. Jefferson, NC, and London: McFarland and Co., 33–51.

Dittmer, J. 2009. Fighting for home: Masculinity and the constitution of the domestic in the pages of *Tales of Suspense* and *Captain America*. In *Heroes of Film, Comics and American Culture: Essays on Real and Fictional Defenders of Home*. Edited by L. DeTora. Jefferson, NC, and London: McFarland and Co., 96–115.

Dittmer, J. 2010. Comic book visualities: A methodological manifesto on geography, montage, and narration. *Transactions of the Institute of British Geographers* 35(2): 222–36.

Dittmer, J. 2011. Captain Britain and the narration of nation. *Geographical Review* 101(1): 71–87.

Dittmer, J. (ed.). 2014. *Comic Book Geographies*. Stuttgart: Franz Steiner Verlag.

Dittmer, J. 2013. *Captain America and the Nationalist Superhero: Metaphors, Narratives, and Geopolitics*. Philadelphia, PA: Temple University Press.

Dittmer, J., and S. Larsen. 2007. Captain Canuck, audience response, and the project of Canadian nationalism. *Social and Cultural Geography* 8(5): 735–53.

Dittmer, J., and S. Larsen. 2010. Aboriginality and the Arctic North in Canadian nationalist superhero comics, 1940–2004. *Historical Geography* 38: 52–69.

Dodds, K. 1996. The 1982 Falklands War and a critical geopolitical eye: Steve Bell and the *If …* cartoons. *Political Geography* 15(6–7): 571–92.

Doel, M.A. and D.B. Clarke. 2009. The artistry of cities: Chris Ware's comic strips. In *Parcitypate: Art and Urban Space*. Edited by T. Beyes, S.-T. Krempl, and A. Deuflhard. Zurich: Verlag Niggli AG, 27 pages [unpaginated].

Dunnett, O. 2009. Identity and geopolitics in Hergé's *Adventures of Tintin*. *Social and Cultural Geography* 10(5): 583–98.

El Refaie, E. 2009. Multiliteracies: How readers interpret political cartoons. *Visual Communication* 8(2): 181–205.

Englehart, S. 2009. E-mail interview with author.
Fall, J. 2006. Embodied geographies, naturalised boundaries, and uncritical geopolitics in *La Frontière Invisible*. *Environment and Planning D: Society & Space* 24(5): 653–69.
Gallacher, L.-A. 2010. Sleep of reason? The practices of reading *shōnen manga*. PhD thesis, Institute of Geography, University of Edinburgh.
Gallacher, L.-A. 2011. (Fullmetal) alchemy: The monstrosity of reading words and pictures in *shōnen manga*. *Cultural Geographies* 18(4): 457–73.
Groensteen, T. 2007. *The System of Comics*. Jackson: University Press of Mississippi.
Guerlac, S. 2006. *Thinking in Time: An Introduction to Henri Bergson*. Ithaca and London: Cornell University Press.
Han, J.H.J. 2008. Missionary. *Aether: The Journal of Media Geography* 3: 58–83.
Holbo, J. 2011. Redefining comics. In *The Art of Comics: A philosophical approach*. Edited by A. Meskin and R. Cook. Malden, MA, and Oxford: Wiley-Blackwell, 3–30.
Holland, E. 2012. "To think and imagine and see differently": Popular geopolitics, graphic narrative, and Joe Sacco's "Chechen War, Chechen Women." *Geopolitics* 17(1): 105–29.
Hones, S. 2008. Text as it happens: Literary geography. *Geography Compass* 2(5): 1301–17.
Huston, S. 2012. *Comic Book City, Portland, Oregon USA*. Documentary film. 58 minutes. USA.
Jones, G. 2004. *Men of Tomorrow: Geeks, Gangsters, and the Birth of the Comic Book*. New York City: Basic Books.
Jones, P., and J. Evans. 2011. Creativity and project management: A comic. *ACME: An International E-Journal for Critical Geographies* 10(3): 585–632.
Krygier, J., and D. Wood. 2009. Ce n'est pas le monde. In *Re-thinking Maps*. Edited by M. Dodge, R. Kitchin, and C. Perkins. Abingdon: Routledge, 189–219.
Kunzle, D. 2001. The voices of silence: Willette, Steinlen and the introduction of the silent strip in the *Chat Noir*, with a German coda. In *The Language of Comics: Word and Image*. Edited by R. Varnum and C. Gibbons. Jackson: University Press of Mississippi, 3–18.
Livingstone, D.N. 2005. Science, text and space: Thoughts on the geography of reading. *Transactions of the Institute of British Geographers* 30(4): 391–401.
Lopes, P. 2009. *Demanding Respect: The Evolution of the American Comic Book*. Philadelphia: Temple University Press.
Matton, A. 2000. Reader responses to Doug Murray's *The 'Nam*. *International Journal of Comic Art* 2(1): 33–44.
Moore, A. 2009. Maps as comics, comics as maps. Paper read at 24th International Cartography Conference (ICC 2009), November 15–21, 2009, at Santiago, Chile.
Moore, A., D. Marinescu, and R. Tenzer. 2011. A visual art interface to an embedded sequence of maps. *Cartography and Geographic Information Science* 38(2): 184–91.
Norcliffe, G., and O. Rendace. 2003. New geographies of comic book production in North America: The new artisan, distancing, and the periodic social economy. *Economic Geography* 79(3): 241–63.
Raeburn, D. 2004. *Chris Ware*. New Haven, CT: Yale University Press.
Ro, R. 2004. *Tales to Astonish: Jack Kirby, Stan Lee, and the American Comic Book Revolution*. New York and London: Bloomsbury.
Tierney, J. 2009. *Visual Language* 2007 [cited February 9, 2009]. Available from www.jtyranny.com/2007/04/visual-language.html.
Varnum, R., and C. Gibbons. 2001a. Introduction. In *The Language of Comics: Word and Image*. Edited by R. Varnum and C. Gibbons. Jackson: University Press of Mississippi, ix–xix.
Varnum, R., and C. Gibbons (eds). 2001b. *The Language of Comics: Word and Image*. Jackson: University Press of Mississippi.
Wright, B. 2001. *Comic Book Nation: The Transformation of Youth Culture in America*. Baltimore, MD: Johns Hopkins University Press.

Stamps and the Postal System

Pauliina Raento

Media and communication technologies play a critical role in the evolution of states and empires. They form and maintain territorial networks by facilitating exchange of information, ideas, and experiences. They support efficient administration and help build nations through narratives about place and identity. But power is inherent in all communication, and the same media and technologies can be used to contest and resist the existing rule. These processes are generally applicable because media, communication, society, and space are inherently interconnected. Simultaneously, however, they are unique because of particular circumstances in particular places (Adams 2009).

Power is also inherent in social capital and trust, which shape the contents, channels, and styles of communication. They therefore deserve more attention in media and communication studies. Social capital refers to structural resources embedded in interpersonal and cultural organizations and networks. Trust is a prerequisite for these resources to form and endure. Ideally, social capital and trust help people act, work, and prosper together (e.g. Putnam 1995). More often, and more critically, however, they are "unevenly distributed resources" and one's fortunes may vary depending on status or perspective (e.g. Bourdieu 1985; Portes 1998). This directs attention to the spatial aspects of structures and institutions, in addition to regional differences in economic development and performance (see Hudson 1998; Mohan and Mohan 2002; Huber 2009). Social capital and trust thus add to the study of cultural, political, and urban spaces (e.g. Entrikin 2003; Häkli and Minca 2009; Raento 2010), which could benefit from insight in media and communication geographies.

This chapter argues for disciplinary cross-pollination by shedding light on the interconnected mechanisms of social capital and trust, state territoriality, and narration of nation. The case is made by following the evolution of one particular medium and surrounding structures – the postage stamp and the post – in one country, Finland. This approach is useful because of their multidimensionality as sites of power: the postage stamp and the post are simultaneously global and local, standardized and unique, public and private, and collective and personal. The post has had a prominent role in defining Finland, and the postage stamp has been a contested site of national pride, unity, and resistance. Because of the country's historical geopolitical and cultural location between two empires, Russia to the east and Sweden to the west, and because of sharp internal contrasts, this stamp imagery highlights the fluidity of identity in changing geopolitical and social circumstances. Detailed attention has been paid to the design of this imagery as part of the Finnish state's strong tradition in visual communication (Raento and Brunn 2005; 2008; Raento 2006; 2009). The assessment emphasizes everyday nationalism, varying popular engagement and experience, and their evolving contexts in response to recent critical views about the study of "banal nationalism" (Billig 1995; Dodds 2006; Dittmer and Dodds 2008; Jones and Merriman 2009; Benwell and Dodds 2011; Penrose 2011; Jokela and Linkola 2013).

The chapter has three chronological parts, which illustrate the interconnections between space, place, and media (see Adams 2009: 1–3). First, Finland's postal affairs complement the ongoing research discussion about the role of institutions and networks, and social capital and trust, in the making of empires, nations, and places that matter to the politics of identity. The second part continues recent examinations of nationalism in geography. In the third part, the transformations of Finland's post and stamp imagery since the 1990s further exemplify the impact of context-driven change on national narration, its audiences, and their responses.

Space, Place, and the Post in the Making of Finland

A Local Empire

Systematic measurement of land started in Sweden in 1628. The kingdom had become a Baltic superpower in the late sixteenth century and needed a tighter hold of its resources. The development of other state institutions, including roads, population statistics, schooling, the military, the justice system, and medical care followed, as Stockholm sought to be a "territorialized and informed government" (Häkli 2008: 10). New laws and administration supported territorial control and maintenance, understanding of boundaries, efficient taxation – and the development of a shared identity (Paasi 1996).

The standardization of the Crown's institutions relied on effective communication over distance and at least some territorial control in support of this exchange. The growth of administrative mail was accommodated by creating regular postal routes and post offices in 1636. The postal system replaced Crown couriers, which in the kingdom's eastern buffer zone against Russia – Finland – had operated between castle-fortresses at least since the 1580s (Finland's Postal Museum 2006).

Imperial power is evident in the fast communication of ideas and implementation of reforms in distant lands (Ogborn 2007; 2008). In Finland land surveys and mapping started five years later than in the colonial center, and the first postal routes and standard rates were in effect in two years. Like any media innovation, these "techno-territorial networks" affected power balance and social relations at multiple scales, and facilitated new contacts (Adams 2009: 14–15). The opening of mail service to private citizens erased boundaries of access, even if this penetration was still limited to the wealthiest literati. The new networks also began to craft the "material" and "conceptual borders" for, and "situated knowledge" about, "Finland" in a globalizing world (O'Tuathail and Dalby 1998: 2–7). That the eastern periphery had its own institutions and some of the Crown's instructions were written in the vernacular (Finnish) greatly aided these processes.

The institutionalization also highlights the geostrategic importance of Finland to Sweden as a buffer zone against Russia and in Baltic trade. In Finland, the network expanded from the coast to the country's interior in about one hundred years, following urbanization, industrialization, and economic activity. The location of post offices – nodes of the network – reveals the strategic motives behind the development: in addition to the capital city Turku (Åbo, on the southwestern coast), offices were opened in the second-largest city Vyborg (in the east), in the centers of provincial administration, in coastal trade ports, and at the Russian border. The new system also toned down complaints from farmers about the high cost and abuse of the transportation, food, and lodging they were obliged to offer to the Crown couriers. National security, social order, economic development, and government image were all considered in this network design, which brought together institutions, norms, and trust. The Crown's subjects still had obligations but participation was becoming increasingly beneficial.

The periphery was connected to globally expanding networks, flows of exchange, technologies, and influential ideals of preferable world order. Mail was a "globalizing technology" that promoted standardization, homogeneity, and shrinking of distances by facilitating the efficient distribution of the written word – and the control and opportunities that traveled with it (Ogborn 2007; 2008). But Finland was also becoming a particular place, which had a sense of its boundaries and unique cultural, social, and identity-political characteristics. The world was increasingly formed by "mutually exclusive spatial entities," but flexible and fluid networks that ignored this "modern cartographic reason" were active in the same space at the same time (Häkli 2008). Instead of being competitive or mutually exclusive, the postal experience suggests that these were interdependent and supportive of each other from the onset (see Hudson 1998). Here, too, the material and immaterial aspects of communication and media networks were intimately intertwined (Adams 2009).

Very importantly, the post built the state, social capital, and trust from two directions. Postal routes were initiated by a royal order from Stockholm, from the top down and from the center to the periphery. But their implementation progressed from the bottom up, from individual and local interests (see Sahlins 1989). In Finland's postal network, farm houses located at regular intervals offered the state men and horses for the delivery of mail. The "sworn-in and, preferably, literate peasant mail carriers" recruited for the job received tax and other reliefs in compensation, including exemption from military service (Finland's Postal Museum 2006). In urban centers, "trustworthy citizens" were charged with the responsibility of organizing postal services. This boosted the named individuals' social status and visibility in the surrounding community. Participation in the emerging national network was in the rational interest of the individuals, whose calculation helped to justify the state at the local level. Participation also strengthened the idea of worthy citizenship and interdependency of the state and its subjects in the minds of individuals and their communities. This participation, normative obedience, and positive experiences accumulated social capital and trust (Newton 2004) in particular geopolitical and local circumstances (Mohan and Mohan 2002; Huber 2009).

That "[t]he system was the only one of its kind in the world" – in the view of Finland's Postal Museum (2006) – further highlights the particularity of Finland as a (postal) place within global networks. The local construction of the empire's worldwide communication network with the help of ordinary people challenges the assumptions that globalization is something "big" and individual or local scale is affectively intimate whereas global scale is faceless and driven by calculation of profit (Flusty 2007; Ogborn 2007; 2008). In postal matters "all empire is local" (Wilson 2003: 213), and the "trust that is necessary for social and governmental institutions to function properly" draws from individual participation (Entrikin 2003: 270).

The system was in place well into the nineteenth century, which in a dynamic state shows that it worked for all parties. At this time national aspirations were on the rise in Finland, making even clearer that measurable territorial space could not exist without flexible interdependent networks that helped to perform this territory (Häkli 2008; Adams 2009).

Ground-Breaking Innovations

Imperial Russia took over Finland in 1809 but kept intact its institutions and laws. A mail treaty in 1810, one of the first postwar agreements between Sweden and Russia, secured access to strategically and economically critical communication networks. The Czar, however, drew

Finland closer to the orbit of St. Petersburg by moving the capital city eastward from Turku to Helsinki and by centralizing postal administration. Censorship and inspection of mail for reasons of national security tightened the empire's hold over its subjects, creating suspicion and increasing social distance between center and periphery (Buchan and Croson 2004).

The institutionalization also responded to the growing volume of mail. It grew because of new industries and trade, and the expansion of the schooling system and the print media. They all benefited from improvements in printing technology. International political unrest, emigration, and concentration of population in urban centers had the same impact because they increased people's need for information and communication over distance. Rate standardization and new delivery solutions speeded up delivery. Innovations in transportation technology made delivery more regular and homogenized people's sense of time, which ran faster thanks to a better transportation network. By the mid-nineteenth century nationwide schedules and home delivery replaced local schedules and the picking up of mail from the post office. Practices became uniform, temporal distances shortened, and the state strengthened its territorial control. Regularity made the state more predictable and therefore more trustworthy, as good experiences accumulated (Newton 2004: 22). By the end of the nineteenth century, the Finnish countryside was within the sphere of influence of urban centers and the central government (Figure 5.1). The hiring of rural landless people for mail delivery continued the participatory practices of state-making and state-maintaining networks – and tied them to place through employment in the context of emigration.

The postage stamp was a critical innovation for global networking and national particularity. The novelty, introduced in Britain in 1840, was soon adopted in Finland. The autonomous Senate authorized the first Finnish domestic and foreign stamps in 1856. One proof of the interest in new postal (and other) technologies is that Finland was the second country in the world to introduce postal stationaries (in 1845), at which time postal rates were standardized in anticipation of the postage stamp. The prompt implementation of novel ideas and technologies introduced in the centers of world power was one way to demonstrate the progressive outlook and modernity of the emerging nation to the international community of nation-states and acquire credibility needed in the aspirations of national particularity. The investment paid off soon, as Finland was invited to join the international postal union UPU in its founding year 1874. The membership was seen as a signal of international trust toward "Finland" as a separate entity from Russia (see Hudson 1998), and it aided the country's international relations and standardization. The autonomous state was acquiring agency and integrating its people in cross-national networks and norms.

The postage stamp also highlighted Finnish identity at home. The first Finnish stamps depicted the Lion of Finland (the country's heraldic symbol from the Swedish period) and the name of the territory in Finnish and Swedish (Raento 2006: Figure 1A). The first denominations in Finnish currency were issued in 1866, one year after the introduction of this currency. In this way Finland's stamp issues further shaped the idea of "Finland" by marking territorial boundaries (the area within which the stamps could be purchased) and by semiotic visualization (Raento 2006: 604). Stamps and currency were tools of exchange and positive institutions typical of independent nations. This made them symbolically very important to the nation-aspiring and internationally networking Finns.

Visual Resistance

In February 1899 a letter from Czar Nicholas II to Finland reduced the autonomous parliament to an advisory position. For the Finns this "February Manifesto" was a coup that violated their privileges defined in 1809, when Sweden ceded Finland to Russia.

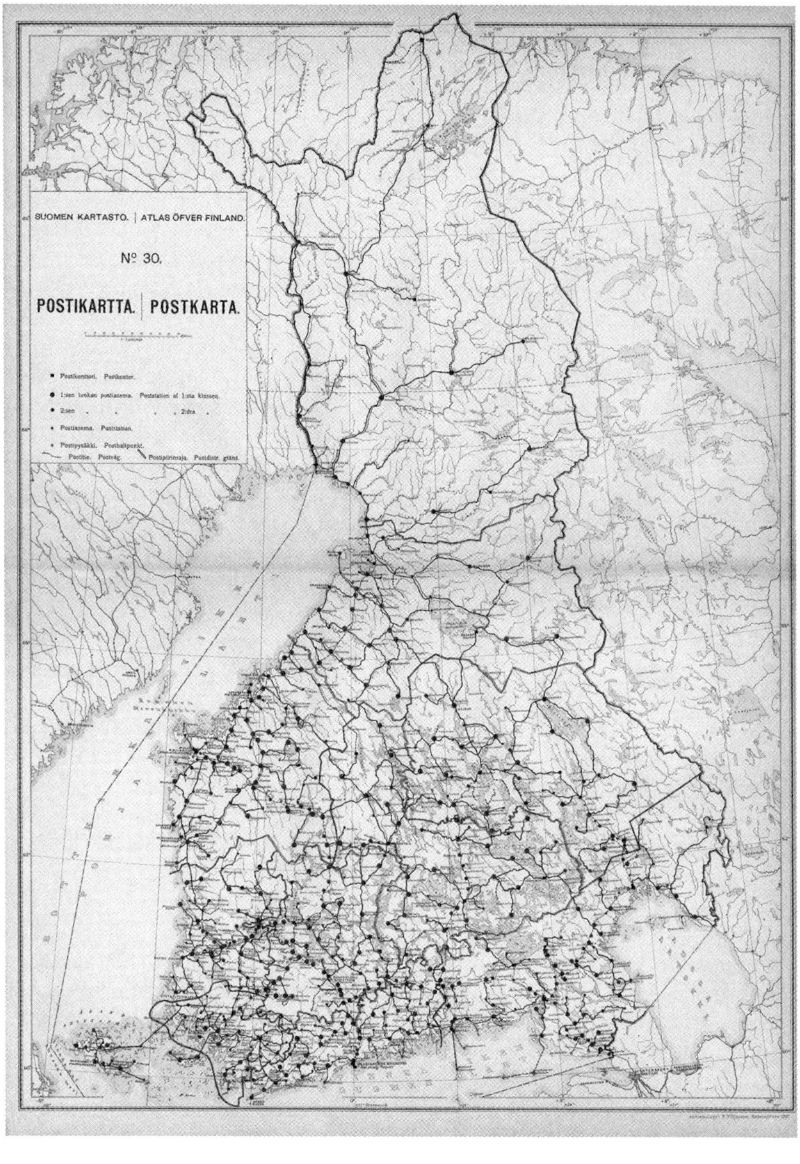

Figure 5.1 **Finland's postal network at the end of the nineteenth century. The 1899 Atlas of Finland, introduced to international audiences at the Paris World Fair of 1900, portrayed Finland as a separate sovereign territory despite its formal status as an autonomous Grand Duchy of Russia (1809–1917). This map, together with similar depictions of schools, telegraph, telephone, and road networks, communicated that a sovereign place called Finland existed, modern communication technologies were used there, and its territory and population were within easy reach.**

Source: Map #30, depicting Finland's postal network. Published in the Atlas of Finland [Suomen Kartasto / Atlas öfver Finland] in 1899

The Czar wanted to open Finland's key administration to Russian employees, integrate the autonomous military in the empire's armed forces, and enhance the position of the Russian language in this Finnish- and Swedish-speaking borderland.

The Russification was contested at home and abroad. Ordinary Finns dressed in black to express their grief, and the statue of Czar Alexander II, favorer of Finland, was covered in flowers in Helsinki. Students skied from village to village to collect signatures for a popular petition against the manifesto, gathering over half a million names in a few weeks – in a country of 2.5 million people. Over the summer Finnish cultural notables residing abroad mobilized their foreign contacts for another petition. The emperor's refusal to receive the two delegations in St. Petersburg provoked further resistance (Poutvaara 1973: 37–38). In Finland this shortened the social distance between the primarily Swedish-speaking elite of cultural notables, businessmen, politicians, scholars, and landowners and the Finnish-speaking masses. International announcements of sympathy supported the building of national identity and boosted ideals of independence by further confirming to the Finns that their country and its institutions were internationally trusted actors (see Hudson 1998).

The resistance relied on visualization in its communication about the Finnishness of Finland. The nation was narrated through cartography, political cartoons, paintings, landscape photography, postcards, and postage stamps (Poutvaara 1973). One explanation to this emphasis is the power of images to cross linguistic and ideological boundaries. The same message was understood at home and abroad. Another, preceding explanation is the strong tradition of visual communication in Finland. The emerging national education system and the autonomous military had advanced literacy and map-reading skills, which the state had cultivated since the Swedish period. Because of this literacy, Finland had a sizable print media, which favored popular cartography and political cartoons in its communication across socioeconomic boundaries and contributed to the understanding of national boundaries and particularity (Paasi 1996; Kosonen 2008). Cultural and business life was busy and well connected, enabling the prompt adoption of technological innovations especially in southern cities. National-romanticist painters and photographers, many of whom were prominent in the resistance, quickly employed these innovations in their construction of national identity.

Finland's own post and postage stamps were major resources for the visually and internationally oriented resistance. For centuries the post in Finland had involved citizens in its networks and, thanks to the mobilization of people for the popular petition against the 1899 February Manifesto, the resistance had established access to a large number of sympathizers. Very importantly, attention had centered on the post already in 1890 when a Postal Manifesto subjected Finland's postal administration to Russia's Ministry of the Interior. The most visible result of this maneuver was the changing appearance of Finnish postage stamps. Cyrillic script and the empire's double-headed eagle gradually replaced the Finnish- and Swedish-language text and the Lion of Finland, which had become important symbols of nationhood (Raento 2006: Figure 1D). These pieces of paper thus became a significant site of power, where opposing views about the appropriate contents of this medium were expressed and challenged. The right to control communication and media in the autonomous territory was one stake in the Finns' struggle for national self-determination.

When Russian eagle stamps replaced Finnish stamps in 1901, secret leaflets encouraged people to respond by sending letters without the Russified stamps. The largely domestic postal employees ignored the lack of paid postage. Cultural notables in Helsinki protested by designing and printing a Mourning Stamp that depicted the lion coat of arms on a black grief-indicating surface. Their public announcement confirmed that the stamp marked the Finnishness of Finnish mail, and the sales were launched by newspaper advertisements and circular letters when the ban of Finnish stamps began. Once the Mourning Stamp became illegal, letters decorated with this protest issue were hauled to postal ships docked in the harbor to escape confiscation and destruction of mail. The stamps were sent abroad in bulk and back to Finland on regular mail to guarantee their local visibility. Double envelopes were used: one transparent on top carried the required Russian postage, and the other underneath made the protest issue visible but difficult to remove. This stamp was positioned above the Russian stamp on envelopes, and the latter was often placed upside down. Finnish postal workers expressed their support by letting through these signals of hierarchy and thus keeping the stamp in circulation long after its prohibition by Russian authorities (Poutvaara 1973: 50, 54–57, 59, 61; Raento 2006: 605–6; Raento and Brunn 2008: 51–52).

The social capital and trust within Finland now drew from attachment, emotion, and collective national identity across social boundaries rather than individual calculation and self-interest in relation to the state. The distrust in "political leaders and the institutions of government" in St. Petersburg clearly reduced the effectiveness of imperial government in Finland and drew Finns closer to one another against an external enemy (Newton 2004: 16, 23).

The audience response to the Mourning Stamp convinced the organizers of the resistance about the efficiency of personal networks and everyday visual messages in national mobilization. Ad hoc media innovations emerged in response to the emperor's orders: Finnish stamps and other national symbols were soon depicted on candy wrappers, matchboxes, jewelry, greeting cards, and other inexpensive everyday items, which were impossible to control. Among the people, they communicated efficiently but in a moderate tone about a common cause, generating feelings of togetherness (Poutvaara 1973; Raento and Brunn 2008: 51–52). The post and the stamps were popular-geopolitical media that spoke effectively to "leaders, masses, and enemies" (Raento 2009: 125), generating "an agreement" about Finland as a place (Hudson 1998: 917) and popularizing the centuries-old lion as its political symbol. This nationalism was "hot" in a sense that it was consciously proactive, but it used mundane artifacts and engaged ordinary people in their daily life in a way that exemplifies "the *everyday* reproduction of nationalism" (Jones and Merriman 2009: 166; emphasis in original, cf. Billig 1995).

Social trust empowered the resistance and its communication in multiple ways: it "enable[d] cooperative behavior; promote[d] adaptive organizational forms, such as network relations; reduce[d] harmful conflict" between social groups within Finland, "decrease[d] transaction costs; facilitate[d] rapid formulation of ad hoc work groups; and promote[d] effective responses to crisis" (Rousseau et al. 1998: 394). But whereas the process lowered social boundaries in favor of Finland, it simultaneously hardened its boundary against Russia (see again Figure 5.1). From the empire's perspective social capital and trust in Finland were negative and destabilizing forces. The experience confirms that limiting a group's access to media does not necessarily render it powerless and the increase of social capital is not automatically positive to a society as a whole (Portes 1998: 15–18; Häkli and Minca 2009; cf. Bourdieu 1985: 248–49; Putnam 1995).

Shifting Identity in Independent Finland

Expanding the View on Postage Stamps

The discussion above summarizes the identity-political media qualities of the postage stamp. It matters to the state, even if it is not always produced or authorized by the state (Penrose 2011). Technically, stamps are receipts of paid postage, but they carry rich persuasive images about particular places, reflecting the views and operative environments of the issuer at that time (Raento and Brunn 2005). The stamps thus communicate situated knowledge and "a structured field of power," which makes them "significant sites for cultural [and identity-political] analysis" (Fürsich 2002: 205, 220; Raento 2009: 125).

The "material and representational" function of the stamps serves citizenship education and thus spreads a particular "visual order" across a territory. This pedagogy and the "optical consistency" of stamps highlight the above-described connection to territory-managing practices, because stamps, like maps, are simultaneously "*fixed* as a representational form and *movable* across territory as inscribed on paper" (Ó Tuathail and Dalby 1998: 2–7; Raento 2006: 603). They confirm – with an example that well precedes the Internet and WikiLeaks – that in communication (or other spatial) networks, significant actors do not need to reside within a national territory but, instead, they can be mobile in international networks and still enhance that territory (Häkli 2008). Stamps thus direct attention to "both what happened in particular sites and settings and to what moved between them" (Ogborn 2007: 5), stressing the cumulative, long-term nature of media innovation (Adams 2009). Stamps "saturate the everyday life of states and nations" by being present in people's daily life and by celebrating "our" possessions and sources of pride. Popular participation in the making of Finland's international networks and resistance against Russia show how stamps visualize both "elitist and popular" worldviews and how their meaning cuts across society (Ó Tuathail and Dalby 1998: 2–7; Raento 2006: 603). They exemplify how visual media and their messages themselves are meaningful sites for identity politics.

It is no wonder then that the study of postal media as a form of "banal nationalism" (Billig 1995) centers on representation, and content and discourse analyses of the postage stamp imagery (e.g. Raento and Brunn 2005; 2008; Raento 2006; 2009). Some scholars, however, have rightly stressed the need to investigate power structures behind the production of iconography (Dobson 2005; Brunn 2011; Penrose 2011; Jokela and Linkola 2013), audience response to popular-geopolitical communication (Dodds 2006; Dittmer and Dodds 2008), and everyday mechanisms of nationalism (Jones and Merriman 2009; Benwell and Dodds 2011).

Considerable changes in the style and contents of Finnish nationalism and participation in nation making during independence (since 1917) steer attention to social capital and trust as useful tools in this research. This direction is encouraged by Häkli's (2008: 15) observation that even if "Finnish identity has mostly been expressed in a very structured and consistent manner through core symbols, narratives and a set of propositions about what it means to be a Finn, the actual experience of Finnishness has always varied greatly depending on context." Accordingly, Finnish postal history reveals important variation in nationalism, audience response, and geopolitical communication in particular geopolitical circumstances (see Adams 2009; Raento 2010; Benwell and Dodds 2011).

The Changing Tone of Finnish Nationalism

Experiences during the Russian rule (1809–1917) made the postage stamp an important identity-political medium in independent Finland. Architect Eliel Saarinen was invited to design its first stamps, when the Postal Manifesto had been overruled in March 1917 and when the provisional government of revolutionary Russia had expressed its support for Finland's aspirations. That the Senate launched the stamp design process and then accepted the new denominations and colors in June offers evidence about the smallness of the decision-making elite and the status of stamps in Finnish nation building (Penrose 2011). The first stamps, carrying the Lion of Finland, Finnish- and Swedish-language texts, and the stamp's value in Finnish currency, were released in October 1917, two months before independence (Raento 2006: Figure 1E).

A civil war in 1918 between the Finnish government's supporters (Whites) and opponents (Reds) followed the collapse of the Russian Empire and general political unrest in Europe (Alapuro 1988). After the war, deep distrust along ideological and economic dividers prevailed (Newton 2004: 23–24) and almost 37,000 people were dead (Suomen sotasurmat 2004). The victorious government had to reconstruct the country and legitimize itself in the eyes of the people and other nation-states. The White elite closed ranks against the enemy within, drawing a strict "boundary of trust" between good citizens (trustworthy sympathizers) and bad citizens (untrustworthy opponents) (Fukuyama 1995; Buchan and Croson 2004; Raento 2010).

The postal imagery was tightly controlled by the country's top politicians and their ideological partners among the cultural notables. The new issues, some of which were based on sketches by individual cabinet members, were executed by the artists of the Printing Works of the Bank of Finland, some of whom were influential in the cultural circles of Helsinki (Raento and Brunn 2008: 53). Also influential in the design process was the national-romanticist painter Akseli Gallén-Kallela, who was a White activist, designer of the 1900 Mourning Stamp, personal assistant to the regent of state Gustav Mannerheim (later president and marshall of Finland), and the designer of Finland's official orders and military uniforms. In this transitional era, the national elites and the postal service of a small country were closely interconnected, the participants knew each other, and the stamps were indeed fairly "straightforward products of the state, elite [and] government control" (Penrose 2011: 431; cf. Jokela and Linkola 2013).

The lack of "adequate trust" in Finnish society (Rousseau et al. 1998: 398) and, therefore, insecurity and weakness of the young state materialized in the stamp imagery as a demand for uniformity. Little space was left for alternative interpretations about what was "Finnish" and worthy of recognition. From independence to the end of World War II (1917–1945), Finnish nationalism was defined and performed by a small state-controlling group and its ideological sympathizers. Their nationalism was highly masculine in its military, institutional, and religious outlook. The emphasis was on law, order, and strong leadership, the tone was pompous and sublime, and the scale was that of the state (Brunn and Raento 2008: 57–58). The Lion of Finland still stood for unity, but this message was now imposed from the top down. The style of communication was formal, responses were rigid, and trust was limited because of suspicion. Social capital thus drew from deterrence rather than reciprocity (Rousseau et al. 1998: 398–400). The same bonding that benefited White Finland made it possible to exclude the Red losers from national networks of social capital and restrict individual freedoms. This efficiently impeded bridging between these sociopolitical groups. The social capital in place was thus negative for Finnish society and nation as a whole (Portes 1998: 15–16; Larsen et al. 2004; Häkli and Minca 2009), and the same imagery had two "radically different" audiences and responses (Dodds 2006: 120; Dittmer and Dodds 2008; Benwell and Dodds 2011).

An external enemy and economic necessity changed this situation. A review of Finnish stamp imagery shows how postal imagery was redefined to foster trust within Finnish society already during and especially after World War II (Raento and Brunn 2005; 2008). Euphoric warrior propaganda gave way to sharing and caring especially in the moments of despair (Raento 2006: 612–13). Reconstruction deviated from the dominant masculinity by associating allegorical females and children with the shared interest of care, continuity, and brighter future (see Raento and Brunn 2008: Figure 5). The Lion of Finland opposed the enemy so that this heraldic cat again became a shared symbol of sovereign Finland and its popular defense. The war showed that the functionality of the state depended on universal participation rather than on imposed, ideologically narrow male leadership.

Figure 5.2 The new friendly, future-oriented face of Finnish nationalism after World War II. President Paasikivi's spouse Alli held a child in her arms on a Finnish postage stamp in 1947. The stamp collected a voluntary tax for the national tuberculosis campaign, serving as one vehicle for national reconciliation and trust formation.

By the 1950s the official interpretation of the foundations of Finnish national identity had become more accommodating. The postage stamps now depicted a place of social well-being and Nature (Figure 5.2), which were generally appreciated in the sparsely settled, war-ridden country. Technology, institutions, and sports communicated about progress and international achievements (Raento and Brunn 2008: 62–63). In an economically difficult situation the stamps were harnessed to collect a voluntary tax, as optional surcharge stamps were issued to fund health and social work (such as the national anti-tuberculosis campaign) and major events (such as the 1952 Summer Olympics in Helsinki). Citizens were thus invited to participate in nation building and construction of "common good," but they could choose how much, if any, they wanted to invest in each cause. Participation was flexible, voluntary, and inexpensive, which made these stamps sites of national reconciliation and construction of social capital. The charity stamps were "structural holes" (Burt 1992) through which one could participate equally anywhere and communicate with the state and fellow citizens directly, yet anonymously. This exemplifies the social capital and trust-building qualities of free choice and egalitarianism identified in research (Portes 1998: 6; Newton 2004: 30). It is fair to argue that the primary audience of these stamps was domestic, even if their semiotics simultaneously defined Finland to foreigners.

The first Finnish charity stamp issued in support of the Finnish Red Cross in 1922 highlights the shift in style and ideology. That stamp failed in the atmosphere of deep distrust, perhaps partially because a proportion of its audience refused to purchase a stamp depicting the White hero Mannerheim (also head of the Finnish Red Cross) together with the Lion of Finland. It is possible that they objected to the victorious government's use of the symbol and saw the Finnish Red Cross as a White organization in the aftermath of the civil war and in the context of miserable prison camps. This, however, is speculative at best, for the circumstances were economically and socially complex, and individual thoughts about the matter are unavailable (Raento and Brunn 2008: 58, 63). However, the reading echoes the views of urban planner Larissa Larsen and others (2004: 67) that people are unlikely to engage in civic action if they feel their community is overburdened by problems and they lack power to change it. It also finds support in the view that one image can be "understood in radically different ways" by very "different audiences" (Dodds 2006: 120; Jones and Merriman 2009: 167). In this light there was a clear mismatch between the proposed White narrative and the experience of the Red audience (Dittmer and Dodds 2008: 452–53).

In stamp charity social and economic capital correlated only after the imagery shifted toward neutrality, the bases of national unification and the welfare state had been laid, and the economic situation of the population had improved. The conditions for social capital and national trust building – and the emergence of one national narrative – in Finnish society were generally favorable after World War II, including accumulating wealth, modernization, and external geopolitical concerns. The country was small, ethnically quite uniform, and Protestant, and it had a long history of functional government. All these characteristics are known to have "a strong, direct, and positive effect on trust" (Newton 2004: 29–30). The development was now toward "affective" and "identity-based" trust and "bounded solidarity" type of social capital (Portes 1998: 7–8; Rousseau et al. 1998: 399).

Postage Stamps as Geopolitical Signs

After World War II Finland was obliged to take into account the wishes of its powerful eastern neighbor. In a delicate global situation obedience was beneficial (Portes 1998: 7). On the postage stamps open propaganda turned to persuasion, resorting to people's visual literacy. The desired Western identity and related international events had to be celebrated discretely by using cartographic and other visual conventions, including direction, colors, and light. Pointed uses of silence and the timing of breaking it spoke loudly, too (Raento 2006: 613–15; Raento and Brunn 2008: 64–65). In contrast, the postal celebration of UNESCO's Lenin Symposium and the anniversary of the Friendship and Collaboration Treaty between Finland and the Soviet Union in the 1970s can be interpreted as signs of Finlandization (Raento and Brunn 2008: 66) – the reduction of social distance and boundaries of trust between Helsinki and Moscow (Fukuyama 1995; Buchan and Croson 2004) – and the power of Leftism in Finland, especially because Soviet references were absent before this time. An examination of the historical continuum gives grounds to argue that the imagery was a "largely self-conscious" medium between the national elite, the people, and their international partners (Cohen 1995: 411) and their reception in daily life was active rather than "mindless" in the context of "little internal challenge" (Billig 1995: 41).

The development of the welfare state and comprehensive school system, and international emancipation of women and minorities, fostered egalitarianism in Finland. The Nordic welfare state and Protestant tradition, both "associated with equal rights and duties of citizenship" (Newton 2004: 30, see 25, 29), held a strong ideological stand that all citizens should have the same value and rights, and income disparity should be discouraged. In addition to women, children and the disabled were now "actors in their own right" on postage stamps, and the existence of some religious minorities and regional linguistic differences in Finland was acknowledged. On the one hand, this can be interpreted as a sign of improved self-confidence among the nation's leaders, increased social capital and trust in Finnish society, and a more inclusive definition of the nation. On the other hand, the narrative of equality was enforced so that no space was left for deviance from the official representation. Much of Finland's ethno-cultural diversity therefore continued to stay invisible, and some of the homogeneity was imagined (Raento and Brunn 2005: 156; see also Dittmer and Dodds 2008: 450).

Audience Responses to Commercialization

Finland after the Cold War grew to be an affluent, modern nation characterized by social insecurity, risk talk, and the functional importance of trust in daily exchanges, many of which were global in character (Giddens 1990; Beck 1992). Finland's membership in the European Union (1995) confirmed the nation's Western identity (Moisio 2008) and boosted consumer culture and individual freedom of choice. "Formal state involvement in considerations of iconography" was deemed less important under these circumstances (Penrose 2011: 431), even if the postal authorities still had the last word in stamp design. Most importantly, the newly commercialized post must now compete in a diverse media environment. Like many of the state's central administrative offices, the post had been disconnected from the centrally steered structures of the state economy and market developments now guided its activities, following international trends. The change of scale and commercial pressures emphasized revenue generation over citizenship education and directed attention to global networks of collectors and national image making within these networks. The number of audiences and possible interpretations of the Finnish national narrative multiplied. The social distance between the producers and consumers of this narrative was increasingly flexible and context-dependent (Hudson 1998; Entrikin 2003; Raento 2010).

In response, the stamp imagery moved closer to the daily life of ordinary people (Raento and Brunn 2005; 2008). Popular culture, regions, and individuals took space from formal celebrations of global and national events, as "the satisfaction of the consuming public was vital for revenue" (Raento 2006: 616). The Lion of Finland, which had ruled supreme on the definitive stamp series since 1856, gave way to provincial flowers. No-value-indicator stamps, introduced in 1992, further reduced the role of the state in the imagery by replacing national currency indicators with a generic reference to delivery type and rate (first or second class) and thus further standardizing stamps internationally. This standardization supported the easy legibility of these place-specific representations and the functioning of the postage stamp as a place advertisement and branding tool in international postal traffic. Imagery on the postage stamps and on the national tourism authorities' advertisements was strikingly similar, courted multiple audiences, and exemplified new commercial collaboration. National tourism promotion was one important popular and "informal arena" in this process (Raento 2009: 125–26; Häkli and Minca 2009; Jokela 2011).

New Level of Participation

The harnessing of postal services to the service of place promotion was nothing new, however, because the State Department had collaborated with tourism promotion authorities through the twentieth century (Jokela 2011). It was well understood that the postage stamp worked like any other "standard communication tool within the tourism and hospitality industry" (Jenkins 2003: 312; Raento 2009). But in the 1990s, Finland's post elevated people's participation to a whole new level in its efforts to please the citizen-consumer. The post expanded its selection of merchandise and presence online and in major events. Popular voting for the most beautiful stamps and open design contests became more common and diverse, even if the authorities kept the emphasis on themes relevant to identity politics (e.g. a child's drawing about homeland; Raento and Brunn 2008: Figure 8). Six thousand photographs were mailed to stamp designers for consideration in response to a public invitation to send in representations of "Finnishness" for the ninetieth anniversary of independence in December 2007. Forty thousand votes were cast to determine the final selection for eight stamps. The process also resulted in a book and an exhibition, all of which were very popular

(Raento 2009: 125). Finnish nationalism was again more popular in a sense that it sprung up from bottom up, from the people themselves, from multiple sources, and it was spontaneous and ordinary in character (Sahlins 1989; Raento 2010). Informal audience response guided formal nation building. The positive response communicated that the postal authorities were doing it right, that there was "an agreement" about "Finland" (Hudson 1998), and that the writers of the national narrative were multiple indeed (Penrose 2011; Benwell and Dodds 2011: 443; Jokela and Linkola 2013).

The number of these writers rose and the image of a people's post was promoted further with the introduction of tailor-made personalized stamps. Those wishing to use their own pictures for a special-purpose postage stamp could now have it made for a fee, if the image met the regulations designed for the service (Omakuvapostimerkki 2012). Against this blooming of social trust as nation-building capital between national decision makers and ordinary citizens, it is most striking that

> *the [official] imagery remained selective, consistently favouring the Finnish-speaking, white, Lutheran Christian, heterosexual, and middle-class majority population. This observation suggests that the state-promoted myth of Finland's cultural uniformity and social equality had managed to grow deep, largely unquestioned roots by the end of the century. It was now the participating citizens' own choices that clung on to this representation of Finland. (Raento and Brunn 2008: 71–72)*

On the one hand, this suggests that the state had succeeded in its citizenship education and that the social distance and boundary of trust between the elite and the people had largely disappeared. On the other hand, this can be seen as a sign of increased insecurity in Finnish society. Trust issues were now less about the state than fellow citizens, and popular or "informal arenas" were increasingly important for social capital and trust formation (Häkli and Minca 2009).

Own Stamps – But Contested Narrative

Both interpretations find empirical support in a strongly worded exchange of letters to the editor in *Helsingin Sanomat*, Finland's largest Finnish-language daily newspaper, in the summer of 2004. The first letter, titled "Own Stamps a Destructive Idea," criticized the new personalized stamp service offered by Finland's post (HS 4 Aug. 2004: A5). For the author, this "Own Life – Own Stamp" campaign was a disgrace and sign of "the trends of our era: extreme individualism and narcissism, the denial of all communality, and even the gradual dissolution of the Finnish nation-state." In his view people were now trusted "too much," and their disengagement from voluntary community life would undermine important institutions (Newton 2004: 16). Harm to collective participation and therefore to "trust, reciprocity, co-operation, empathy for others, and an understanding of the common interest and common good" (Newton 2004: 19–20) would erode social capital to the detriment of Finnish society and nation, because generalized trust and spontaneous sociability were clearly on the decline (Fukuyama 1995; Putnam 1995). Actions of strangers were unpredictable and difficult to monitor, which in the author aroused a need for centralized fostering of nationwide communality as a guarantee for social order (Entrikin 2003: 260, 264). In his view, structural normativity would keep people integrated in the collective and the responsibility would lie with a state institution. For this man, social capital, trust, and nation building were "fundamentally a moral matter" (Newton 2004: 26).

Expressing historical suspicion toward the east (Moisio 2008), the author also worried about the international image of Finland, for which stamps were of paramount importance. In his view Finland's reputation would be tarnished by "fuzzy" images of silly individuals or events, leading to "the image of a poor and confused, perhaps East European country" in the eyes of outside observers and collectors. Therefore "[t]he much-talked-about image of Finland [was] about to receive a really hard and destructive blow." In his opinion, "the postage stamp is a valuable window to the nation-state, one that should not be rendered to be a playground of private fantasies," based on which he defended the state's sole authority in the design of the postal imagery. He stated that "the importance of symbolism in political and state-related life should not be underestimated," pointing out the historically significant role of postage stamps in Finnish nation building. This underestimation would likewise "lead to the dissolution of the Finnish state" and even precede general turmoil in Finnish society. This concern about order reflects the "highly formalized and institutionalized" tradition of social trust and capital in Finland (Häkli and Minca 2009: 2).

Two responses to the outburst were published, both in favor of individual freedom of choice. The first letter, from a fellow citizen, titled "Own Stamps Are Not Related to a Revolution," shot down the "accusations" as exaggerated (HS 6 Aug. 2004: A5). The respondent admitted of being "proudly" guilty as charged, because he had had a family stamp made of his daughter's photograph and believed that "most of the new service users only want a nice personalized stamp" and "are not preparing a revolution."

The other defense for individualism came from a representative of the Stamp Center, who in his letter titled "Own Stamps Build Image of Finland" acknowledged the role of the state in stamp design, but highlighted the post's interest in serving its customers who had "requested" this service (HS 7 Aug. 2004: A5). Finland's international image would not be harmed because of the small edition of each personalized issue. The official also pointed out the internationally pioneering role of Finland's post in developing personalized services, simultaneously with "Austria, Holland, and Canada." His response was loyal to the commercial outlook and the national traditions in postal innovation and international image building. On the one hand, the author was pleasing the paying customers – and managed to flatter them by suggesting that the initiative came from enlightened citizen-consumers. On the other hand, typical of Finnish authorities, he used other countries' activities to justify domestic choices and stressed that Finland was a progressive actor in international networks (Moisio 2008; Raento 2010). It seemed to matter that the other "pioneers" were from the Western cultural sphere and Finland's post was again among the first adopters of innovations. Little had changed in this regard since the nineteenth-century introduction of postal stationeries and postage stamps in Finland and the country's membership in the international postal union UPU.

The exchange confirmed that the understanding of the role of nation and state had become diverse and flexible, and self-interest and collective affection were equal and perhaps competing motives for participation. The iconography had multiple keen audiences and responses which made separation between hot and banal nationalism very difficult in its everyday forms.

Conclusion

Finland's postal affairs illustrate how "nation-state territories, as socially meaningful regional spaces, are produced by means of networks" (Häkli 2008: 13) where media and communication are in a central role. This production has been a complex interplay between "the exertion of imperial power over people and places" (Ogborn 2007: 2) and individual participation and audience response (Sahlins 1989; Raento 2010). The case thus adds strength to the claim that the seemingly static nation-states and fluid networks should be examined discursively together at multiple scales (Ogborn 2007; 2008; Häkli 2008) – not least because the fluidity of networks stabilizes individual places in global space (Hudson 1998). The claim complements the basic view of media and communication geographies that the interdependent relationship between space, place, and communication should be treated as a whole in reflection of particular social processes (Adams 2009). The observations also agree with the view that the Swedish empire deserves more attention in the investigation of Finnish state structures and nation building (Häkli 2008).

The case study confirms that recent criticism of the study of "banal nationalism" (Billig 1995) and identity-political iconography is on the right track. Attention to mechanisms of, and individual engagement in, "everyday nationalism" helps in overcoming the emphasis on representation and the misleading division between hot and banal nationalism. It also helps in understanding why and how the relationships between the writers (producers) and audiences (consumers) of national narratives are multiple, interconnected, and dependent on geopolitical and social circumstances in particular places and times (Jones and Merriman 2009; Penrose 2011; Benwell and Dodds 2011; Jokela and Linkola 2013). The case shows that "little things" still matter (Dittmer and Dodds 2008: 444–45) but more research is needed about the mechanisms and processes of everyday nationalism. Finnish postal affairs suggest also that people may be more conscious about nationalist communication and media channels in their regular life than students of banal nationalism have assumed. This chapter has argued that mixing social capital and trust with media and communication geographies could be a valuable asset in future research along these lines.

It is relevant to geography scholarship that social capital and trust are multi-scalar concepts that integrate "microlevel psychological processes and group dynamics with macrolevel institutional arrangements" and "institutional mechanisms can play a critical role in shaping the mix of trust and distrust" in a particular place (Rousseau et al. 1998: 393, 401). Here, too, motives for participation and the degree of emotional attachment to both territorial stability and fluid networks vary per social and geopolitical circumstances – which always include particular media and communication environments. This repeats the view that more society-level research is needed about the mechanisms of social capital and trust formation, which may have both positive and negative consequences and depend on available options for communication (Bourdieu 1985; Häkli and Minca 2009; Huber 2009). From the perspective of Finland's postal affairs, it therefore seems that the study of everyday nationalism, the study of popular geopolitics, and the study of social capital and trust have plenty of unexplored synergy that can advance communication and media studies.

Acknowledgments

I wish to thank Jouni Häkli for his help with the social capital and trust literature. The feedback from Jason Dittmer and Paul Adams was most useful. The chapter is related to the Academy of Finland research project "Landscape, Icons, and Images" (2008–2012) and to my writing grant from the Alfred Kordelin Foundation.

References

Adams, P.C. 2009. *Geographies of Media and Communication*. Chichester: Wiley-Blackwell.

Alapuro, R. 1988. *State and Revolution in Finland*. Berkeley: University of California Press.

Atlas of Finland 1899. Helsinki: Geographical Society of Finland and Otava.

Beck, U. 1992. *Risk Society*. London: SAGE.

Benwell, M. and K. Dodds. 2011. Argentine territorial nationalism revisited: The Malvinas/Falklands dispute and geographies of everyday nationalism. *Political Geography* 30(8): 429–40.

Billig, M. 1995. *Banal Nationalism*. London: SAGE.

Bourdieu, P. 1985. The forms of capital. In *Handbook of Theory and Research for the Sociology of Education*. Edited by J.G. Richardson. New York: Greenwood, 241–58.

Brunn, S.D. 2011. Stamps as messengers of political transition. *Geographical Review* 101(1): 19–36.

Buchan, N. and R. Croson. 2004. The boundaries of trust: Own and others' actions in the US and China. *Journal of Economic Behavior and Organizations* 55(4): 485–504.

Burt, R.S. 1992. *Structural Holes*. Cambridge: Harvard University Press.

Cohen, C. 1995. Marketing paradise, making nation. *Annals of Tourism Research* 22(2): 404–21.

Dittmer, J. and K. Dodds. 2008. Popular geopolitics past and future: Fandom, identities and audiences. *Geopolitics* 13(3): 437–57.

Dobson, H. 2005. The stamp of approval: Decision-making processes and policies in Japan and the UK. *East Asia* 22(2): 56–76.

Dodds, K. 2006. Popular geopolitics and audience dispositions: James Bond and the Internet movie database (IMDb). *Transactions of the Institute of British Geographers* 31(2): 116–30.

Entrikin, J.N. 2003. Placing trust. *Ethics, Place, and Environment* 6(3): 259–71.

Finland's Postal Museum. 2006. Basic and *150 years of Finnish Stamps* exhibitions. Helsinki.

Flusty, S. 2007. *De-Coca-Colonization*. London: Routledge.

Fukuyama, F. 1995. *Trust*. New York: Free Press.

Fürsich, E. 2002. Packaging culture: The potential and limitations of travel programs on global television. *Communication Quarterly* 50(2): 204–26.

Giddens, A. 1990. *Consequences of Modernity*. Cambridge, UK: Polity.

Häkli, J. 2008. Regions, networks, and fluidity in the Finnish nation-state. *National Identities* 10(1): 5–20.

Häkli, J. and C. Minca (eds). 2009. *Social Capital and Urban Networks of Trust*. Aldershot: Ashgate.

Huber, F. 2009. Social capital of economic clusters: Toward a network-based conception of social resources. *Tijdschrift voor economische en sociale geografie* 100(2): 160–70.

Hudson, A.C. 1998. Placing trust, trusting place: On the social construction of offshore financial centres. *Political Geography* 17(8): 915–37.

Jenkins, O. 2003. Photography and travel brochures: The circle of representation. *Tourism Geographies* 5(3): 305–28.

Jokela, S. 2011. Building a façade for Finland: Helsinki in tourism imagery. *Geographical Review* 101(1): 53–70.

Jokela, S. and H. Linkola. 2013. 'State idea' in the photographs of geography and tourism in Finland in the 1920s. *National Identities* 15(3): 257–75.

Jones, R. and P. Merriman. 2009. Hot, banal, and everyday nationalism: Bilingual road signs in Wales. *Political Geography* 28(3): 164–73.

Kosonen, K. 2008. Making maps and mental images: Finnish press cartography in nation-building, 1899–1942. *National Identities* 10(1): 21–47.

Larsen, L., S.L. Harlan, B. Bolin, E.J. Hackett, D. Hope, A. Kirby, A. Nelson, T.R. Rex, and S. Wolf. 2004. Bonding and bridging: Understanding the relationship between social capital and civic action. *Journal of Planning Education and Research* 24(1): 64–77.

Mohan, G. and J. Mohan. 2002. Placing social capital. *Progress in Human Geography* 26(2): 191–210.
Moisio, S. 2008. Finlandisation versus Westernization: Political recognition and Finland's European Union membership debate. *National Identities* 10(1): 77–93.
Newton, K. 2004. Social trust: Individual and cross-national approaches. *Portuguese Journal of Social Sciences* 3(1): 15–35.
Ó Tuathail, G. and S. Dalby. 1998. Introduction. Rethinking geopolitics: Towards a critical geopolitics. In *Rethinking Geopolitics*. Edited by S. Dalby and G. Ó Tuathail. London: Routledge, 1–15.
Ogborn, M. 2007. *Indian Ink*. Chicago: University of Chicago Press.
Ogborn, M. 2008. *Global Lives*. Cambridge: Cambridge University Press.
Omakuvapostimerkki: tuotteen perustiedot. 2012. Finland's Post. www.posti.fi/kortitjakirjeet/postimerkit/omakuvapostimerkki/ [accessed September 27, 2012].
Paasi, A. 1996. *Territories, Boundaries, and Consciousness*. Chichester: Wiley.
Penrose, J. 2011. Designing the nation: Banknotes, banal nationalism and alternative conceptions of the state. *Political Geography* 30(8): 429–40.
Portes, A. 1998. Social capital: Its origins and applications in modern sociology. *Annual Review of Sociology* 24: 1–24.
Poutvaara, M. 1973. *Postia sortokaudelta*. Jyväskylä: Gummerus.
Putnam, R. 1995. Bowling alone: America's declining social capital. *Journal of Democracy* 6(1): 65–78.
Raento, P. 2006. Communicating geopolitics through postage stamps: The case of Finland. *Geopolitics* 11(4): 601–29.
Raento, P. 2009. Tourism, nation, and the postage stamp: Examples from Finland. *Annals of Tourism Research* 36(1): 124–48.
Raento, P. 2010. Stomaching change: Finns, food and boundaries in the European Union. *Geografiska Annaler Series B* 92(4): 297–310.
Raento, P. and S.D. Brunn. 2005. Visualizing Finland: Postage stamps as political messengers. *Geografiska Annaler Series B* 87(2): 145–63.
Raento, P. and S.D. Brunn. 2008. Picturing a nation: Finland on postage stamps, 1917–2000. *National Identities* 10(1): 49–75.
Rousseau, D.M., S.B. Sitkin, R.S. Burt, and C. Camerer. 1998. Not so different after all: A cross-discipline view of trust. *Academy of Management Review* 23(3): 393–404.
Sahlins, P. 1989. *Boundaries*. Berkeley: University of California Press.
Suomen sotasurmat 1914–1922. (2004). National Archives of Finland. Available at http://vesta.narc.fi/cgi-bin/db2www/sotasurmaetusivu/stat2 [accessed August 23, 2012].
Wilson, K. 2003. *The Island Race*. London: Routledge.

Dance

Derek McCormack

Introduction

When we think of the relation between dance and media, one of the first things that might spring to mind is the depiction of dancing bodies in cinema, on TV, and, more recently, on the Internet. Many of us follow dance-based competition shows on TV, and find ourselves unable to resist watching amusing dance clips on YouTube. And yet, while dance is portrayed and depicted in a range of popular media practices, it is also frequently affirmed, particularly by professional dancers, choreographers, and those who write about dance, as an activity that in some sense has an existence prior to and independent of its incorporation by media practices. In other words, dance is characterized by a kind of raw, affective, and kinesthetic physicality to which the term *media* stands in a derivative relation. Consequently, if we think of media as ecologies of technologies and practices that are primarily representational, then we might be forgiven for thinking that dance is badly served by considering it in relation to these ecologies, for it reduces a concern with an activity often taken to be "unmediated" to the question of how that activity is mediated representationally in either analog or digital form. Indeed, we might be forgiven for thinking that the very mediatization of moving bodies runs the risk of undermining the authenticity and immediacy of the lived experience of the space times of dance – whether by dancers or audiences, a concern that is often voiced more widely in relation to the growing incorporation, for instance, of video and digital technologies into the staging and choreographing of live performances (Gieseken 2007). Even if we don't share or subscribe fully to these concerns or to their theoretical, aesthetic, or political motivation, we must still acknowledge that media technologies and practices transform the space time of dance in interesting ways. And even if we start with the deceptively straightforward proposition that dance "takes place at a particular location and in a particular space" (Hagendoorn 2012: 69), then we have to accept that dance's mediation transforms these locations and spaces in ways worth investigating.

Clearly, then, there is already something at stake here – the question of how moving bodies should be understood in relation to media practices and technologies, and with what consequences for our understanding and appreciation of the space times of both. As is clear from the contributions to this book, pursuing answers to these questions involves going far beyond understanding media or bodies in representational terms to embrace the distributed materiality of affect and sensation as they flow across bodies, screens, and technologies (see Simpson, this volume). Equally, writing and thinking about dance is increasingly attentive to how moving bodies are generative participants in the production and distribution of spaces of experience in ways that cannot be grasped unless we have a sophisticated understanding of their imbrication in an expanded conception of media. Drawing upon work across a range of disciplines and practices, my point of departure in this chapter is the claim that while thinking about the relation between dance and media in representational terms gives us purchase on some instantiations of this relation, it is insufficient to the task of thinking through the complex and compelling ways in which dance participates and circulates in contemporary "media ecologies" (Fuller 2005), composed as these ecologies are of shifting configurations of technologies, practices, percepts, and affects. My discussion is developed as follows. I first provide a brief overview of how geographers have thought and written about dance, doing so with the aid of various autobiographical details. I then turn to the relation between dancing bodies and media, considering efforts to think through the sensory capacities of moving bodies as themselves prosthetic technologies for inhabiting affectively mediated worlds. I then consider how the relation between moving bodies and moving images might be grasped, highlighting how thinking about dancing bodies can aid understandings of the distribution and circulation of affect across and between bodies. In the penultimate section, I examine how the relation between dance and media offers opportunities for exploring possibilities for experimenting with space times of experience.

Geography and Dance

I would like to begin, if I may, by indulging in a little autobiographical detail that foregrounds the geography of the emergence of my own interest in the space times of moving, dancing bodies. In 1995 I moved from Ireland to the United States to pursue graduate studies in Geography at Virginia Tech. During my time there, I became interested in the relation between bodies and technologies and, more specifically, in how this relation is articulated through ideals and practices of fitness. I was interested in how fitness came to matter, and became meaningful, through particular configurations of bodies and technologies. Looking back at this now, what is interesting is the kind of theoretical and methodological approach that framed my research and, equally, what this says about the kind of cultural geography that was relatively dominant in Anglo-American Geography at the time. Revealingly, my emphasis was on the critical analysis of representations of fitness as a way of thinking about broader issues of technology and bodies. And I took it to be sufficient to examine images and texts about fitness that appeared in magazines, on television, and to a limited extent (at that point) on the Internet, in order to understand how bodies and their relation with fitness technologies were shaped and reshaped within particular discursive contexts. Influenced by the thinking of Foucault, Haraway, and Butler, my key aim was to examine the material-semiotic shaping of potentially inhabitable worlds composed of bodies and technologies (see McCormack 1999).

To some extent this approach to fitness also framed my initial, tentative ideas about the cultural geographies of dance, and how these geographies were sustained and shaped by popular representations. Such nascent ideas were, in turn, shaped by various encounters that threw into sharp relief how certain styles of dancing were transformed, and became more mobile, through their exposure in popular media events. For instance, during my time at Virginia Tech a good friend brought me to see an amateur staging of some scenes from the dance production *Riverdance* at a neighboring university. As is now well known, *Riverdance* began its public life as a seven-minute filler between the songs and voting sections of the 1994 Eurovision song contest staged in Dublin, before being produced as a full-length stage show that subsequently toured around the world. That amateur performance prompted me to think about how *Riverdance* worked as a cultural and media event in which a certain image of Irish dancing bodies had come to circulate within particular circuits and sites of global popular culture in ways that for better or worse, transformed the meaning of Irish dance. Certainly, the bodies lined up on stage either in Dublin or Virginia could be read in a rather different ways to traditional Irish dance, at least as I had been familiar with it – gone were the gaudy multicolor costumes and wigs, and in their place was what seemed to be an altogether more confident, and more contemporary style of embodiment. In some ways, then, one could understand the embodied style of *Riverdance* as capturing a wider transformation in Irish cultural and social life, a kind of choreography of transition that countered, while also reproducing, elements of the narrative about the intertwined relation between diaspora, dance, and identity (see, for example Morrison 2001).

This brief autobiographical narrative foregrounds one way in which the geography of dance can be understood in relation to different media practices and technologies – we can explore how representations of dance produce, reproduce, and challenge different culturally specific meanings of the space times of moving bodies. And we can do this by engaging in the kind of critical reading of bodies and images as texts that informed much cultural geographical thinking during the 1980s and 1990s. And yet, in retrospect, it is not difficult to see how certain important aspects of the relation between dance and media are absent from this critical-analytical approach. There is little, for instance, about the affective qualities of mediatized encounters with moving bodies. Indeed, in an Irish context, *Riverdance* might be taken as an occasion for the embodied amplification of the emergence of the kind of structure of feeling that, beginning in the mid-1990s, gave an affective tone to a small, open, globalizing economy. Equally, there is little about the affective surge that moved visibly through the audience in the auditorium as they watched that first seven-minute performance of *Riverdance* in 1994, and, almost at the same time, flowed through those thousands of TV viewers, including myself, as we watched the performance and the response by the audience. Moreover, there is also little about the spatio-temporal experience of the dancers themselves, experience that, while shaped by socially embedded practices of corporeal discipline and training, cannot be reduced to the constitutive effect of discourses of Irish identity, however important these may be (although see Leonard 2005).

Somewhere between the end of that MSc in Virginia Tech and the beginning of my PhD in Bristol, I read a chapter by Nigel Thrift (1997) about dance, embodiment, and resistance. In that chapter, Thrift sets out to show how dance, as an embodied practice, has a certain expressive quality that exceeds efforts to incorporate it within an epistemology and politics of representation. Reading this chapter was also, in some respects, my first introduction to some of the tenets of nonrepresentational theory – a set of ideas that has been profoundly influential across and within the discipline (see Thrift 2008) during the intervening period. Clearly, nonrepresentational theory is not just about dance, but dance has figured in the writing and thinking of Thrift (2000) and related scholars within and beyond geography as a vehicle through which to develop and exemplify nonrepresentational styles of thinking (e.g. McCormack 2002, 2003; Dewsbury, 2010). While here is not the place to review all of this work, a number of initial points about the nonrepresentational dimensions of dance are worth mentioning at this juncture insofar as they serve to orient a discussion of the relation between dance and media. First, and most basically, dance may be said to be nonrepresentational insofar as its enactment does not necessarily depend upon the deliberate interpretation of external representations in the form of signs or symbols – although it certainly does not preclude this process, and indeed it can do so as part of experiments that go beyond representational thinking. Consider, for instance, a rather romantic example – a young child beginning to dance without ever learning to interpret a visual or schematic representation of choreographic steps or routines. This simple example suggests there is something important about dance as an expressive activity that involves the capacity to be moved and to move in ways that are prior to the practices of meaning-making upon which much of the cultural geographical work outlined above was based, while also being shaped by processes of imitation embedded in the corporeal tissue of forms of social life.

Second, and relatedly, dance can be said to be nonrepresentational insofar as its enactment challenges the claim that human intelligence is defined solely in terms of a cognitivist representationalism involving the manipulation of internal codes or symbols. Instead, for Thrift and others, dance foregrounds how much of this intelligence is better grasped as a kind of embodied knowing in action that takes place too quickly for representational processes. That is not to say that dance is defined against thinking but, rather, that the cognitivist model of thinking that informs much work in the social sciences is inadequate to the task of grasping the styles of knowing and moving that dance, and indeed a range of other activities, involves. Third, dance is nonrepresentational insofar as it foregrounds the importance of processes and powers that challenge a representational model of ethics and politics. Affect is especially important here, a point on which I will elaborate below. Perhaps most significantly here, dancing bodies foreground the force of affect as a power to move bodies through different registers of feeling. Finally, dance is nonrepresentational because it requires the cultivation of styles of scholarship and research that challenge the epistemological and methodological orientations of much social science research. That is not to say one needs to abandon entirely certain methodological approaches and techniques, but that they can be made to dance a little (Latham 2003).

These claims about dance have not, of course, been uncontroversial, and have attracted various critical responses. For some commentators, early nonrepresentational approaches to dance appeared to affirm a kind of precultural view of embodiment that too easily elided the social and cultural politics of the discursive formations within which bodies move. Notable here, for instance, were interventions by figures such as Catherine Nash (2000) and Tim Cresswell (2006; 2011) for whom, in slightly different ways, Thrift's work was not sufficiently attentive to the social constraints that shape the lived experience of different kinds of dance. And yet, while Thrift himself has acknowledged some of the problems with aspects of his earlier thinking about nonrepresentational theory, particularly the tendency to emphasize intentional action at the expense of differentiated assemblages of movement and stillness (2008), his writing on dance, performance, and moving bodies has also developed to include ways of thinking about society and culture that elaborate further an affirmative critique of representational modes of thought as part of the effort to understand how moving bodies generatively participate in contemporary forms of mediated life. Put another way, the outcome of this work has not so much been a form of thinking about the body in which it is desocialized through a critique of representation, but one in which dance becomes one of many conceptual-empirical vehicles through which the whole question of what counts as social life is opened up to an affirmative critique (Anderson and Harrison 2010). And in this respect, thinking about the mediated worlds in which dancing bodies move is a valuable contribution to this project.

In what follows I want therefore to show that when considered alongside other scholarship both within and beyond geography, nonrepresentational approaches broadly conceived offer interesting ways of thinking about the relation between dance, media, and geography. Clearly, nonrepresentational approaches are not the only way of thinking about this relation. Moreover, there is a growing range of work by geographers and others in which dance figures prominently in ways that overlap with some elements of nonrepresentational theories, without necessarily being reducible to it. We can point here to work in anthropology and cultural studies that seeks to temper an emphasis on representation with an investigation of the structures of kinesthetic experience that shape participation in particular styles and genres of dance (for examples, see Sanchez Gonzalez 1999; Sklar 2001; Downey 2005). However, the following discussion is perhaps inevitably framed by my own interests and approaches, which have been influenced to no small degree by nonrepresentational styles of thinking, an indulgence for which I hope readers will forgive me. In the process I want to develop three key points. My first point is a broad one, and revolves around the claim that affirming the nonrepresentational qualities of bodies does not mean abandoning any conceptual or empirical concern with those phenomena and processes we might traditionally group under the heading of media including, notably, images and image making. My second point is that such approaches, broadly defined, can actually sharpen our understanding of how moving bodies participate in the generation of mediated environments. Third, and finally, I also want to suggest that these approaches might also encourage us to engage in distinctive forms of empirical experiment within these environments.

Mediating Bodies

In beginning to think about these questions, it is first necessary to dwell a little on the details of the relation between dancing bodies and media, where both terms obviously designate phenomenon that are always already multiple. In the previous section, we considered briefly one way in which to imagine this relation – namely, in terms of how certain media practices represent bodies. While this can tell us something about how media representations contribute to shaping the meaning of moving bodies, it tells us little, however, about how the experience of dance is shaped and transformed through media events and technologies. And there remains a kind of gap between the body and media technology that can only really be grasped through the transmission and incorporation of a kind of dematerialized representation. In these terms, the relation between moving bodies and media is largely an epistemological one defined in terms of the promise or the failure of representation. Arguably, however, this relation is better grasped in ontological terms, through a more materialist account of the distributed energies and powers in which moving bodies are generatively implicated. This, indeed, is one of the key directions in thinking about "media" more generally, one involving a move toward a more fully materialist account of media as practices and technologies woven into the space times of everyday life (see Fuller 2006; Parikka 2011).

One way to begin developing this account is by understanding media technologies as a kind of prosthetics for the sensory capacities of bodies: that is, as technologies for drawing out these capacities as part of the relational phenomenology of embodiment in the world. In this view, media are not technologies of separation in which a subject is alienated from the world in the act of perception. Instead, they are the very means by which bodies and selves become extended throughout a wider sensorium of experience (see also Adams 2005). One way to illustrate this claim is, for instance, to think of the relation between dance and drawing. While we could think of drawing as a technology of alienation or distancing, it can also be a technique for drawing out the affects of kinetic experience (see Reason 2010). Similarly, painterly experiments by Dadaists and Futurists, in addition to those by Klee and Kandinsky, can also be understood as efforts to draw out the space of perception through a kind of graphic choreography. Developing this further, we can point to choreographic experiments that use technologies, both analog and digital, in order to stretch the space times of kinesthetic expression, without always assuming that this expression is necessarily motivated by some inner phenomenological impulse. Examples of this include the choreographic scaffoldings developed by Rudolf Laban, or, more recently, and for very different reasons, the use of digital choreographic technologies such as *LifeForms* by Merce Cunningham and *Improvisation Technologies* (1999) by William Forsythe (for a discussion, see Birringer 1998).

In some ways, what these technologies do is expand the space of attention, and in the case of Cunningham, media and digital-based technologies are put to use to pose the very question of how and to what we should attend when moving bodies and choreographic forms unfold multiply and simultaneously (see Copeland 2004). Indeed, by foregrounding this question of multiple objects of attention, Cunningham is also encouraging the wider cultivation of particular habits of attention and inattention. For instance, as Roger Copeland writes, a piece called "Tango" (1978) can be understood "among other things – as a model for this sort of selective inattention. Here Cunningham danced alongside a television set broadcasting a live image, but with the sound turned alternately on and off. By contrast, in a work such as *Variations V* (which incorporates multiple film and video projections), we need to divide our attention so as to simultaneously apprehended two or more unrelated phenomenon" (2004: 285). Clearly, the use of various screen-based media in choreographing moving bodies is not only a feature of performance-based, professional dance: in various ways it is also an element of more popular practices and forms of dance-based entertainment that employ a degree of interactivity to generate different movement experiences. These include arcade-style games such as Konami's *Dance, Dance, Revolution*, and a host of other games sold to individuals for use on home-based and mobile devices. As Behrenshausen claims (2007; see also Chien 2006), in the context of a critique of the ocularcentrism of games studies, such games are interesting because they rely on the active mobilization of moving bodies in ways that generate a space of kinesthetic interactivity, a line of argument that has been developed further by geographers interested in the affective dimensions of video gaming (see, for example Ash 2009; 2010; Simpson, this volume).

And yet, perhaps this does not go far enough insofar as it still frames media technology as prosthetic to the body. Perhaps we can think of the senses themselves as prosthetic, prior to their coupling with technologies. This is the claim made by thinkers such as Brian Massumi (2011) and Erin Manning (2009), for whom the senses are not mediated, but are, in effect, media themselves. In this view, mediation is not a process that separates a form of authentic embodied perception from an object of experience. Instead, if we think of bodies as "relational matrices" (Manning 2009) of capacities to sense and be sensed, then mediation is always part of the immediacy of sensing rather than something added to it from outside. An important aspect of this approach is that it helps us avoid the tendency to think of the relation between dance and media as really only beginning with the emergence of digital technologies or, relatedly, to think of the virtual solely in relation to the digital. This approach also forces us to revisit and revise understandings of the relation between moving bodies and technologies. If we think of technology as prosthetic to bodies, then it is also external to bodies. However, as thinkers such as Erin Manning (2009) have argued, it is more helpful to think of the technicity of the body in relation to the ongoing composition of relational movement. This approach conceives of the body in technogenetic terms. As Manning puts it, "technogenesis defines bodies as nodes of potential that qualitatively alter the interrelations of the rhizomatic networks of spacetime in which they themselves are ephemerally housed. Sensing bodies in movement are not discrete entities but open systems that reach toward one another" (2007: 3).

The upshot of this work is that the relation between dance and media does not begin when we consider technologies, representations, or practices that are added to and transform the body from without. Instead, we can think of dance as always already a sort of multimedia system (Birringer 2002), and dance-spaces as the emergent quality of processes that are always already mediated. What becomes interesting, therefore, is how different technologies and practices transform these systems in ways that modulate the affective and perceptual capacities of moving bodies, generating distinct space times of experience in the process.

Moving Images of Moving Bodies

Conceptualizing the relation between moving bodies and media in these terms does not, of course, mean that we should no longer think about questions that might be more conventionally considered media-related. Rather, it suggests that we should extend our understanding of this relation to attend more closely to the kinesthetic play of moving bodies in the affective materiality of media experiences. One way to do this might be to examine the relation between dance, sound, and music as part of the generation of rich sensory experiences and often rhythmically collective atmospheres. Here, however, I want to take a different tack and give my discussion focus by considering the relation between dance and visual images as part of a broader concern with how embodiment is shaped in contemporary moving-image cultures (see Sochack 2004). As Sherill Dodds argues, "dance is embedded within the visual fabric of media technologies," in a reciprocal relation, whereby visual images are often participants in dance performances and experiences of different kinds, at the same time as dance routines are designed and produced for particular visual media events and genres (2004: 1; see also Mitoma et al. 2003; Brannigan 2011). This relation was clear from the early days of film, a claim that is hardly surprising given that the "natural subject of moving pictures is movement" (Carroll 2001: 46). Indeed, we can see this relationship, albeit in very different ways, in the pre-cinematic experiments of Muybridge's and Marey's time and motion studies (for a discussion of the differences between their work, see Manning 2009). Beyond this, early filmmakers, among them Louis Lumière, documented various genres of dance, while dancers such as Loïe Fuller experimented with film (Dodds 2004). More generally, the physical qualities of the acting featured in early commercial films of the silent era owed much to the music hall dance training received by stars such as Charlie Chaplin. Later, of course, an entire genre of film dance-musicals emerged featuring actors like Fred Astaire, Ginger Rogers, and Gene Kelly. Paralleling these commercial genres were important avant-garde developments, such as Maya Deren's exploration of the relation between film and choreography. This is not the place to explore further the details of this relation. However, it is worth remarking that important overlaps and differences exist between the techniques that underpin choreography, and those that developed as part of the emergence of film. Both involve concerns with the positioning and movement of bodies and their relations – to each other and to the space times they inhabit. As such, both also involve not only the manipulation but also the generation of space times. But choreographing dance for screen differs from other contexts insofar as different space times of the body can be generated (see Rosenberg 2012). As Emshwiller writes,

> *When the dancer is used in filmic terms, rather than dance terms, space, and time are flexible. The images projected on the screen may seem to move forward and backward in time, may be discontinuous, in fast motion, slow motion, frozen repetitious, or simultaneous. The dance can appear to shift instantaneously from one location to another, can be compressed, elongated, distorted, or seen from widely varying perspectives. (Cited in Carroll 2001)*

A further point germane to an understanding of the relation between visual images and dance concerns their shared implication in the emergence of a kinesthetic structure of feeling in which rhythm is a crucial concept for understanding and organizing a range of activities, practices, and technologies across different domains of life. In the late nineteenth and early twentieth centuries in particular, the idea of rhythm seemed to provide a way of grasping the dynamic becoming and vital energy of life conceived in terms of movement. Rhythm had an obvious appeal to dancers, as it seemed to affirm the sense that aesthetic and harmonious movement was essentially organic and continuous. Equally, for early filmmakers, rhythm provided a way of grasping the visual and spatio-temporal continuity of this emerging technology (see Cowan 2007). And yet both dance and film depend upon a series of techniques that choreograph bodies and images to give the effect of rhythmic continuity. As Yvette Bìro puts it, "the physical movements of a film's actors, together with alternation of light and shadow, the vitality of the camera, and, moreover, the elements of sound and silence, the accents and the beats, all express content and emotion, and these devices stand in a complex, dialectical relationship with each other" (2008: 232). This emerging relation between the rhythm of moving images and moving bodies was also something upon which philosophers such as Henri Bergson reflected. As is well known, Bergson was was critical of cinema as analogy for perception insofar as it seemed to disguise the underlying continuity of duration as a kind of continuity of perception – it was based on the movement of individual frames per second and therefore reproduced the kind of snapshot-like habits of perception that he was so eager to challenge (see Bergson 2007). Bergson's critique of cinema needs revision, however – a point made by Deleuze (2005), for whom cinema is Bergsonist in a way that Bergson himself failed to recognize. This claim allows Deleuze to develop an understanding of images as moving blocks of space time in ways that nevertheless also recall Bergson's own claim, in *Matter and Memory* (1991), that images have an existence somewhere between representation and thing. For Deleuze, then, Bergson seems to forget that cinema does not produce images to which movement is added. Rather, it produces images as blocks, or sections, of movement that themselves are mobile – hence the term "movement-image." As part of this writing on cinema, Deleuze also points to the fact that these blocks of space time have an affective quality, and this affective quality is critical to the way in which moving images relate to other kinds of images, including those of which the moving body might be said to be an aggregate. Images, as blocks of space time, have a mobile materialism that relates to the body in terms of the blocks of space time of which the latter is composed, or, more accurately, the blocks of space time it is composing.

Such ideas have figured in efforts to develop a kind of materialist energetics through which to grasp moving images of moving bodies in relational rather than representational terms, a task which is made even more challenging with the emergence of digital images. There are various ways in which this can be pursued. First, we can use film as a kind of site for exploring the kinds of space times generated by moving bodies of different kinds. For instance, in *Politics of Touch*, Erin Manning (2006: 20) presents a discussion of Wong Kar Wai's *Happy Together* (1997) in order to explore the moving body not as "a point on the grid of experience, but as an experience, a sensation that *creates*" the space times through which it navigates. In other words, by examining such films in ways that are not defined primarily by how the action of these films rehearses or challenges particular discursive scripts, it becomes possible to use film as a thinking-space for exploring relations of affective movement within and between bodies.

Then, and second, we can explore how moving images, as blocks of space time, participate in the distribution and circulation of affect across and within bodies. Feature-length films still have a role to play here – we might think, for instance, about 1970s and 1980s feature-length films such as *Saturday Night Fever*, *Flashdance*, *Dirty Dancing*, and *Footloose*, each of which participated in the popularization and visibility of certain genres of dance, notably disco. In the contemporary juncture, arguably more influential however are various kinds of short film clips that are not produced in relation to, or dependent upon, a longer narrative. The emergence of the music video is obviously important here, many examples of which involve carefully choreographed bodies in routines that themselves are imitated as part of the transmission of styles of affective embodiment across cultures – we might think here (if we can bear it) of everything from Black Lace's *Agadoo* to Los Del Rio's *La Macarena*.

Perhaps more palatable, and arguably more inventive, are the kinds of video-choreography in music videos such as Fatboy Slim's *Praise You* and Grace Jones's *Slave to the Rhythm*. Similarly, there are a range of advertisements that also trade on the appeal of moving bodies, including the *Gap* ad about which political theorist Jane Bennett (2001) has written.

Clearly, the emergence of digital images has not only transformed the conditions of production of these video-clips but also offers new possibilities for their distribution and circulation. The rise of digital file-sharing has allowed these blocks of space time to circulate more widely and far more quickly as part of the emergence of what cultural theorist and philosopher Steven Shaviro (2010) calls "post-cinematic affect" (see also Rodowick 2007). Shaviro employs this term to grasp the affective quality of a contemporary structure of feeling no longer defined primarily in terms of the narrative and emotional structure of feature-film-length images: it is defined instead by movement-images of variable duration whose qualities reside much more in their ability to generate affects across screens and within bodies. For some commentators in the humanities, this development encourages renewed emphasis on the phenomenon of "screendance," a term that rehearses themes captured by earlier categories such as film dance and cine-dance (see Rosenberg 2012). As Reason and Reynolds (2010: iii) put it, the importance of screendance emerges from a sense that "internet and social media [are] transforming how audiences relate to and interact with dance while also vastly multiplying audience and participant numbers." Indeed, a new journal – the *International Journal of Screendance* – has recently been established to explore the "intersection of dance and the moving image" (ibid.). As an aside, we might also note that dancers' bodies are also used as screens onto which images are projected (Barnett 2009).

We should be interested in the relation between dance and screens for more than philosophical or aesthetic reasons, however. The circulation of moving images of moving bodies is also a matter of the generation of value via the production of interest and enthusiasm through the kinds of processes of invention and imitation about which Gabriel Tarde (1903) wrote at the beginning of the twentieth century. One of the most notable recent efforts to mobilize moving images of moving bodies in these terms is the T-Mobile advertisement, featuring a flash-mob mobile disco in Liverpool Street Station, London, filmed in 2009. As Paul Grainge argues, the T-Mobile ad was interesting to some degree because its "affective power was a function of dance choreography" and also because it seemed to exemplify the possibility of a spontaneous, collective urban culture that transcends the routine and habits of everyday urban life. But as he continues, the dance ad was also designed to "capture attention within the television schedule and to appeal in ways that encouraged audiences to seek out and watch the performance again." Doing this included the distribution of "online teasers about the coming live event, making-of documentaries showing the auditioning and filming process, and bonus material featuring off-screen interviews and performance. Fostering fan re-enactment, T-Mobile also posted branded 'how to' videos breaking down the moves of the dance routine. These instructional videos formed the basis of several amateur re-enactments of the flash mob in shopping malls, demonstrating the strategic potential of dance to engage the productive potential of ordinary consumers" (2011: 173). Beyond the generation of brand-spaces as affectively and kinesthetically inhabitable worlds, there are also emerging developments that focus on how dance-based "exergaming" might generate enthusiasm within individuals for exercise and obesity-reduction practices (for an example, see Thin et al. 2011; for a critique, see Millington 2009).

All this is not to suggest that ads or marketing campaigns effortlessly mobilize bodies to particular ends. But it does raise questions about the processes through which kinesthetic affects travel between and through bodies via screens in ways that are generative of shared and value-adding enthusiasms. This, of course, is a question raised by Tarde (1903). The process by which this might take place within bodies is, of course, an interesting one, and certainly one subject to much debate. For instance, the role of mirror neurons has been suggested as one way of explaining the kind of affective-kinetic imitation through which styles of moving flow across and between bodies, a thesis that rehearses earlier theories of meta-kinesis advanced by figures such as John Martin (for a critical overview, see Rubidge 2010b; Sheets-Johnstone 2011). Regardless of how this imitation takes place, it raises interesting questions about how audiences view screen-based images of moving bodies, and how bodies respond to this process (see Wood 2010).

None of the foregoing discussion necessarily means we need to dispense with concerns about spaces and forms of belonging that have animated the work of geographers. Instead, however, we need to point to the constitutive role that images play in this process. The writing of Charles Stivale points to the direction in which such work might be taken, describing as it does how "different forms of the visual medium – commercial films, documentaries, instructional tapes – contribute to the development of a collective feeling, both of identity and community, in the Cajun dance and music arena" (2003: 108). On one level for Stivale, "these films and videos accomplish this both by facilitating the self-definition of this identity and community and by attracting non-Cajuns to participate in versions of this community's cultural practices." At the same time, "the commercial products such as the dance tapes also constitute important elements in the creation of the spaces of affects that relate to the Cajun dance and music arena" (2003: 108). There is plenty of scope to examine further how moving images participate in the reproduction and transformation of other dance styles and genres (see also David 2010; Kavoori and Joseph 2011). More recently, Carroll (2008) has described the impact that new digital video file-sharing platforms have had on the revival and reproduction of styles of swing dancing in African American communities, particularly through the production and circulation of dance clips that can be exchanged, and their moves learned, before being reproduced both at home and in shared dance-spaces. As such, YouTube offers a "fascinating example of the ways in which swing dancers combine embodied dance practice and knowledge – always the most valued and most privileged – with their mediated cultural practices" (Carroll 2008: 196). In the process, dance-spaces become distributed across real and digital sites (see also Peters and Seier 2009).

Space, Dance, Experiment

Foregrounding the relation between dance and media not only provides new objects of analysis and investigation for geographers. It also offers opportunities for pursuing empirical experiment with the relations between moving bodies, technologies, and space times. On one level, this can involve direct collaboration between geographers, dancers, and performers working in a range of different fields. Here, long-standing geographical concerns with cartography can inform choreographic experiment. We can point for instance, to the involvement of geographers at Ohio in the development of choreographic experiments by William Forsythe using digital technologies and dancers to generate new kinds of choreographic objects (see also Neff et al. 2012). Elsewhere, in a remarkable discussion of *Dance Your PhD* contests, Natasha Myers (2012: 16) has explored how the bodies of scientific practitioners and their circulation in digital file-shared videos "become effective media for articulating the forms, forces, and energetics of molecular worlds, and for propagating these insights among students and colleagues."

In turn, such experiments direct our attention to the qualities of the spaces and sites that facilitate or are generated in the process. While the emergence of digital technologies has, of course, generated claims about virtual worlds and of new forms of reality, we also need to temper some of these claims – reality has not just become "mixed" with the advent of digital technologies. This necessary qualification notwithstanding, there are nevertheless interesting questions about the qualities of the spaces generated by efforts to experiment with dance and digital technologies, not least the degree to which they generate possibilities for remote collaboration (Birringer 2002). Equally, experiments with digital technology can offer ways of developing a more expansive sense of how images participate in the movement of thinking. For instance, researcher and choreographer Sarah Rubidge (2007; 2010b) has written about how choreographic experiments with bodies remind us of the importance of thinking of images in ways that are expressive without necessarily being representational. This, in turn raises questions about how dance can facilitate forms of learning and expression that allow participants to think in the multimedia spaces between and across different registers of experience in ways that amplify elements of nonrepresentational theory (see Rubidge 2010). Equally, in this context the role of the choreographers becomes an interesting one – characterized by a kind of learned improvization leaning into an emergent situation. As Birringer puts it, when dance and information technology are used together, "choreography more closely resembles the 'live mix' experienced in techno culture when DJs create a situation, a combinatory sound continuum, and use filter devices to modify the parameters in response to energy that is transferred between dancers and musical stream. … the composition process is like an 'emergent system', symbiotic improvisation with invisible sensor 'lines' or dynamic fields in space" (2002: 87).

However the relation between dance, media, and spaces of experimentation is not confined to digital media, but also extends to analog practices and sites (see also Merriman 2010). Consider, for example, a site about which I have previously written – Hellerau, near Dresden. In the second decade of the twentieth century, the performance space there became the setting for a range of collaborations between theater-designer Adolphe Appia and the composer and pedagogue Emile Jaques-Dalcroze. Central to these collaborations were shared efforts to develop spaces that would be responsive to, and in some sense would facilitate experiment with, the rhythms of the moving body. Such spaces can justifiably be called multimedia environments – they attempted to mix movement, light, and sound to produce immersive performance experiences (McCormack 2005; Beacham 2006).

But there is arguably a more mundane and accessible way in which the relation between dance, media, and spaces of experiment can be understood. More specifically, everyday encounters with moving images of dancing bodies can become occasions for reworking the ethical and political sensibilities through which thinking takes place. This is the argument that figures such as William Connolly and Jane Bennett make. For these thinkers, minor encounters with moving bodies can draw out the affective dimensions of taken-for-granted dispositions to respond and act into situations in particular ways. Similarly, J.K. Gibson-Graham (2006) has also used the example of moving images of moving bodies to exemplify a kind of affirmative critique that takes seriously the affective basis of thinking and resistance as part of the articulation of different economies of value. The force of these encounters is not necessarily about subverting representational meaning, but about reworking and in some case generating new sources of affective attachment to different forms of life. This might involve, for instance, deliberate efforts to revisit particular video clips of moving bodies in order to explore how their kinesthetic affects continue to circulate within your body, and how, in doing so, they reproduce certain values (see Blanco Borelli 2012). In the process, the repetitions and rhythms of replay, rewind, pause, fast-forward, and so on, offer ways of holding open the process through which movement-images participate in the multiple durations of our own habits of thinking and dispositions (Corrieri 2012).

Conclusion

I began this discussion by foregrounding how concerns about the relation between dance and media are focused on how the "liveness" of the former is somehow diminished by the increasing intrusion of the latter into the performance and experience of dance. Admittedly, it remains the view for many that the "liveness of the dancer is a ghost that haunts" understandings of how bodies are mediated, and especially so in relation to screen-based processes (Reason and Reynolds 2010: iv). This is not to suggest that there are no significant differences between and difficulties with, for instance, video documentation of dance performances that may in time come to be seen as equivalent to the performance itself and to all the versions of that performance that may have been (see Phelan 1993). And yet, as Ann Dils argues with respect to screendance, "we need to move past the dichotomy of immediate live presence versus denatured representation and begin to think about how screendance impacts our perceptions of bodies, movement, and space" (2012: 24; see also Jones 1997). As I have tried to show in this chapter, such a dichotomy is far too simplified for a variety of reasons. In the first place, it ignores the fact that dance, as a kind of technicity of relational movement, is always already mediated at the level of our sensory prosthesis: there is no pure, unmediated form of spatio-temporal experience that exists prior to relational and generative involvement within the world. Second, even if we privilege liveness in dance performance, we cannot assume that liveness is a form of unmediated presence. Liveness is already a creation, the outcome of processes geared toward the production of the present moment. Third, the privileging of liveness and presence against "media" holds to a rather narrow sense of the space times of moving bodies. Rather than undermining the authenticity of the space time of the moving body, we are better off trying to grasp the generation and distribution of lively space times composed of bodies in movement across the rhythmic intensities of different screens (see, for instance, Portanova 2005). This helps us temper claims about the essential ephemerality of dance, or of the fact that its disappearance is an essential aspect of its ontology. As dance scholar André Lepecki (2006) has written, this understanding of dance is heavily imbued with a melancholic affect based upon the primacy of a particular space time – the present. And yet, as he continues, equally important are the multiple presents, pasts, and futures of dance, all of which are unthinkable without an expanded sense of the mediated immediacies of the spaces of moving bodies.

References

Adams, P. 2005. *The Boundless Self: Communication in Physical and Virtual Spaces*. Syracuse, NY: Syracuse University Press.

Anderson, B. and P. Harrison (eds). 2010. *Taking Place: Nonrepresentational Theories and Geography*. Farnham, Surrey: Ashgate.

Ash, J. 2009. Emerging spatialities of the screen: Video games and the reconfiguration of spatial awareness. *Environment and Planning A* 41: 2105–24.

Ash, J. 2010. Architectures of affect: Anticipating and manipulating the event in practices of videogame design and testing. *Environment and Planning D: Society and Space* 28: 653–71.

Barnett, A. 2009. The dancing body as screen: Synchronizing projected motion graphics onto the human form in contemporary dance. *ACM Computers in Entertainment* 7(1): 5–32.

Beacham, R. 2006. "Bearers of the flame": Music, dance, design, and lighting, real and virtual – the enlightened and still luminous legacies of Hellerau and Dartington. *Performance Research* 11(4): 81–94.

Behrenshausen, B.G. 2007. Toward a (kin)aesthetic of video gaming. *Games and Culture* 2(4): 335–54.
Bennett, J. 2001. Commodity fetishism and commodity enchantment. *Theory and Event* 5(1): no pagination.
Bergson, H. 1991. *Matter and Memory*. Translated by N. Paul and W. Palmer. New York: Zone Books.
Bergson, H. 2007. *The Creative Mind: An Introduction to Metaphysics*. Translated by M. Andison. Mineola, NY: Dover Publications.
Bìro, Y. 2008. *Turbulence and Flow in Film: The Rhythmic Design*. Bloomington: Indiana University Press.
Birringer, J. 1998. *Media and Performance along the Border*. Baltimore, MD, and London: Johns Hopkins University Press.
Birringer, J. 2002. Dance and media technologies. *Performance Art Journal* 70: 84–93.
Blanco Borelli, M. 2012. Dancing in music videos, or how I learned to dance like Janet … Miss Jackson. *International Journal of ScreenDance* 2: 52–55.
Brannigan, E. 2011. *Dancefilm: Choreography and the Moving Image*. Oxford: Oxford University Press.
Carroll, N. 2001. Toward a definition of moving-picture dance. *Dance Research Journal* 33(1): 46–61.
Carroll, S. 2008. The practical politics of step-stealing and textual poaching: YouTube, audio-visual media and contemporary swing dancers online. *Convergence: The International Journal of Research into New Media Technologies* 14(2): 183–204.
Chien, I. 2006. This is not a dance. *Film Quarterly* 59(3): 22–34.
Corrieri, A. 2012. Giving up the world for an image. *International Journal of Screendance* 2: 78–80.
Cowan, M. 2007. The heart machine: "Rhythm" and body in Weimar film and Fritz Lang's Metropolis. *Modernism/Modernity* 14(2): 225–48.
Cresswell, T. 2006. *On the Move: Mobility in the Modern Western World*. London and New York: Routledge.
Cresswell, T. 2012. Review essay. Nonrepresentational theory and me: Notes of an interested sceptic. *Environment and Planning D: Society and Space* 30(1): 96–105.
Cunningham, M. 2004. *Merce Cunningham: The Modernizing of Modern Dance*. New York: Routledge.
David, A. 2010. Dancing the diasporic dream? Embodied desires and the changing audiences for Bollywood film dance. *Participations* 7(2): 215–35.
Deleuze, G. 2005. *Cinema 1: The Movement-Image*. Translated by H. Tomlinson and B. Habberjam. London and New York: Continuum.
Dewsbury, J-D. 2000. Performativity and the event: Enacting a philosophy of difference. *Environment and Planning D: Society and Space* 18 (4): 473–96.
Dils, A. 2012. Moving across time with words: Toward an etymology of screendance. *International Journal of Screendance* 2: 24–26.
Dodds, S. 2004. *Dance on Screen: Genres and Media from Hollywood to Experimental Art*. New York and Basingstoke: Palgrave Macmillan.
Downey, G. 2005. *Learning Capoeira: Lessons in Cunning from an Afro-Brazilian Art*. Oxford: Oxford University Press.
Fuller, M. 2005. *Media Ecologies*. Cambridge, MA: MIT Press.
Forsythe, W. 1999. *Improvisation Technologies: A tool for the analytical dance eye*. CD-ROM. Karlsruhe: Centre for Art and Mediatechnology.
Gibson-Graham, J-K. 2006. *A Post-Capitalist Politics*. Minneapolis: University of Minnesota Press.

Giesekam, G. 2007. *Staging the Screen: The Use of Film and Video in Theatre.* London: Palgrave Macmillan.
Grainge, P. 2012. A song and dance: Branded entertainment and mobile promotion. *International Journal of Cultural Studies* 15(2): 156–80.
Hagendoorn, I. 2012. Inscribing the body, excribing space. *Phenomenology in the Cognitive Sciences* 11: 69–78.
Jones, A. 1997. "Presence in absentia": Experiencing performance as documentation. *Art Journal* 56 (4): 11–18.
Kavoori, A. and Joseph, C. 2011. Bollyculture: Ethnography of identity, media and performance. *Global Media and Communication* 7(1): 17–32.
Latham, A. 2003. Research, performance, and doing human geography: some reflections on the diary-photograph, diary-interview method. *Environment and Planning A* 35(11): 1993–2017.
Lepecki, A. 2006. *Exhausting Dance: Performance and the Politics of Movement.* New York: Routledge.
Leonard, M. 2005. Performing identities: Music and dance in the Irish communities of Coventry and Liverpool. *Social and Cultural Geography* 6(4): 515–29.
Manning, E. 2006. Prosthetics making sense: Dancing the technogenetic body. *Fibreculture* 9: no pagination. Available at *journal.fibreculture.org/issue9/issue9_manning_print.html.*
Manning, E. 2007. *Politics of Touch: Sense, Movement, Sovereignty.* Minneapolis: University of Minnesota Press.
Manning, E. 2009. *Relationscapes: Movement, Art, Philosophy.* Cambridge, MA: MIT Press.
Massumi, B. 2011. *Semblance and Event: Activist Philosophy and the Occurrent Arts.* Cambridge, MA: MIT Press.
McCormack, D.P. 1999. Body-shopping: Reconfiguring geographies of fitness. *Gender, Place and Culture* 6(2): 155–77.
McCormack, D.P. 2002. A paper with an interest in rhythm. *Geoforum* 33(3): 469–85.
McCormack, D.P. 2003. An event of geographical ethics in spaces of affect. *Transactions of the Institute of British Geographers* 28(4): 488–507.
Merriman, P. 2010. Architecture/dance: Choreographing and inhabiting spaces with Anna and Lawrence Halprin. *Cultural Geographies* 17(4): 427–49.
Millington, B. 2009. Wii has never been modern: "Active" video games and the "conduct of conduct." *New Media and Society* 11(4): 621–40.
Mitoma, J., E. Zimmer, and D. Stieber (eds). 2003. *Envisioning Dance on Film and Video: Dance for the Camera.* London: Routledge.
Morrison, J. 2001. Dancing between decks: Choreographies of transition during Irish migrations to America. *Eire-Ireland* 36(1–2): 82–97.
Myers, N. 2012. *Dance Your PhD*: Embodied animations, body experiments, and the affective entanglements of life science research. *Body and Society* 18(1): 151–89.
Nash, C. 2000. Performativity in practice: Recent work in cultural geography. *Progress in Human Geography* 24(4): 653–64.
Neff, M., D. Sumner, G. Bawden, E. Bromberg, J. Crutchfield, D. Davidson, S. Gilbride, L. Kellogg, and O. Kreylos. 2010. Blending art and science: Collapse (suddenly falling down). *Leonardo* 43(3): 274–81.
Parikka, J. 2012. New materialism as media theory: Medianatures and dirty matter. *Communication and Critical Studies* 9(1): 95–100.
Peters, K. and A. Seier. 2009. Home dance: Mediacy and aesthetics of self on YouTube. In *The YouTube Reader*. Edited by P. Snickars and P. Vonderau. Stockholm: National Library of Sweden, 187–203.
Phelan, P. 1997. *Unmarked: The Politics of Performance.* New York: Routledge.

Portanova, S. 2005. The intensity of dance: Body, movement and sensation across the screen. *Extensions: The Online Journal of Embodied Technology* 2. Available at www.wac.ucla.edu/extensionsjournal/.

Reason, M. and D. Reynolds. 2010. Special issue editorial: Screen dance audiences – why now? *Participants: Journal of Audience and Reception Studies* 7(2): iii–vii.

Rodowick, D. 2007. *The Virtual Life of Film*. Cambridge, MA: Harvard University Press.

Rosenberg, D. 2012. *Screendance: Inscribing the Ephemeral Image*. New York: Oxford University Press.

Rubidge, S. 2007. Sensuous geographies and other installations: The interface of body and technology. In *Performance and Technology: Practices of Virtual Embodiment and Interactivity*. Edited by S. Broadhurst and J. Machon. Basingstoke: Palgrave.

Rubidge, S. 2010a. Nomadic diagrams: Choreographic topologies. *Choreographic Practices* 1: 43–56.

Rubidge, S. 2010b. Understanding in our bodies: Nonrepresentational imagery and dance. In *Degrés: Revue de Synthèse à orientation sémiologique: Dance Research and Transmedia Practice*, 141.

Sanchez Gonzalez, L. 1999. Reclaiming salsa. *Cultural Studies* 13(2): 237–50.

Shaviro, S. 2010. *Post-cinematic affect*. Winchester: Zero Books.

Sheets-Johnstone, M. 2011. Movement and mirror neurons: A challenging and choice conversation. *Phenomenology in the Cognitive Sciences*: 1–17.

Sklar, D. 2001. *Dancing with the Virgin: Body and Faith in the Fiesta of Tortugas, New Mexico*. Berkeley and Los Angeles: University of California Press.

Sobchack, V. 2004. *Carnal Thoughts: Embodiment and Moving Image Culture*. Berkeley: University of California Press.

Somdahl-Sands, K. 2006. Triptych: Dancing in thirdspace. *Cultural Geographies* 13(4): 610–16.

Stivale, C. 2003. *Disenchanting Les Bon Temps: Identity and Authenticity in Cajun Music and Dance*. Durham, NC: Duke University Press.

De Tarde, G. 1903. *The Laws of Imitation*. New York: Henry Holt and Company.

Thin, A., L. Hansen, and D. McEachen. 2011. Flow experience and mood states while playing body movement-controlled video games. *Games and Culture* 6(4): 414–28.

Thrift, N. 1997. The still point: Expressive embodiment and dance. In *Geographies of Resistance*. Edited by S. Pile and M. Keith. London: Routledge, 124–51.

Thrift, N. 2000. Afterwords. *Environment and Planning D: Society and Space* 18(2): 213–55.

Thrift, N. 2008. *Nonrepresentational Theory: Spaces, Politics, Affect*. London: Routledge.

Wood, K. 2010. An investigation into audiences' televisual experience of *Strictly Come Dancing*. *Participations* 7(2): 262–91.

Video Games

James Ash

Introduction

Video games are a fundamentally spatial medium. Whether playing a puzzle game on an iPhone or a Strategy game on a PC, upon picking up a controller one manipulates objects or moves through predesigned locations and spaces of some sort. However, little work has been undertaken that seriously considers space as a basic element of what video games are (exceptions include Nitsche 2009 and Borries et al. 2007). While the terms *space* and *place* are often used when discussing different games, there is almost no explicit reflection on what these terms might mean, or how video-game spaces are different or similar to other technological or mediated spaces. This is strange given the broad variety of disciplines that have studied games. As Malaby and Burke (2009) point out, video games have been studied by writers from a range of perspectives, including new media (Dovey and Kennedy 2006; Hjorth 2011), English literature (Aitkins 2003; 2007), game studies (Calleja 2011; Juul 2004), and cultural studies (Egenfeldt-Nielsen et al. 2008), using a range of theoretical perspectives such as psychoanalysis (Spittle 2011), phenomenology (Crick 2011), and postcolonial theory (Allen 2011). These perspectives have been complimented through a variety of qualitative and quantitative research methods including ethnography (Nardi 2010), video ethnography (Giddings 2009; Ash 2010), questionnaires (Quandt et al. 2011), and interviews (Kelly 2004).

One possible reason for a marked absence of work on space and place in video games is the abstract and difficult nature of these concepts themselves. While geographers have long grappled with ideas of space and place, Malpas argues that "spatial ideas and images are constantly in play, and yet what is at issue in the very idea of space and the spatial is almost never directly addressed" (2012: 1; for more on geographers concerns with space and place, see the introduction to this volume and Harvey 2006; Massey 2005; Tuan 2001; Cresswell 2004). Within work on video games, this difficulty is further compounded by the broad range of technologies that are gathered under the umbrella term *video games*. Indeed when using the term *video game* one has to be aware that games can be played on a large array of different platforms including cell phones, dedicated video-game consoles, personal computers, and arcade cabinets. On top of the fact that a broad variety of technologies can be called video games, there is also a difficulty in clarifying how these technologies differ from other media. As Bolter and Grusin (1999) argue, video games actively "remediate" older forms of media, drawing upon narrative techniques, event direction, and camera framing from other media such as television and cinema (Poremba 2006; Ip 2008; Kirkland 2009).

Rather than offering a formal definition of what video games are, for the purpose of this chapter, I argue that what is consistent among different games and platforms is that they form particular "possibility spaces" of one kind or another. Following Bogost (2008), by possibility space I mean that part of what makes games unique are the ways in which they generate a space between the rules of the game set by the designers of the game and the contingency of player action as they explore and play within this space. These possibility spaces are therefore relative to and dependent on the hardware and software upon which games are created and played. An open world sandbox game such as *Grand Theft Auto IV*, which allows players to explore a whole city, has a very different possibility space from *Plants vs. Zombies*, a puzzle game where users control the movement of plants on tiled squares in a single screen, for example. In turn these possibility spaces are what makes video games different from other media such as television where the possibility for what takes place on the screen is completely predetermined by the production team. To understand space and place in video games, one has to be sensitive to the ways in which factors such as game genre, age of hardware, and game engine shape the possible spaces and places produced by and experienced in video games.

Taking the idea of possibility space as its basis, this chapter examines video games as a geographical form of media in order to provide a starting point for further theorization and exploration of the spaces and places in video games. Through a review of current literature on games from the disciplines of new media, cultural studies, games studies, and geography, the chapter argues that space in video games can be conceptualized in three main ways: a space internal to the screen, a space of the body, or as an assemblage of body and screen. The chapter then discusses how video games represent other places as well as producing fantasy places that serve as the site for new forms of social relationships and communities. In conclusion, the chapter looks to four currently neglected areas that offer future research opportunities for media geographers interested in video games.

Space and Video Games

Spaces of the Screen

Within literatures on gaming, space has been understood in a number of ways. Accounts of space often invoke a distinction between the screen space of the image and the offscreen space of the player and the player's body. A number of writers explicitly generate typologies to understand the different forms of screen space and the relation between them. Such forms of typology could be understood as part of a broader "game ontology project" developed for "describing, analyzing, and studying games by defining a hierarchy of concepts abstracted from an analysis of many specific games" (Zagal 2008: 176; also see Zagal and Mateas 2010).

Typologies of video-game screen space concentrate on the different "spatial structures" (Wolf 1997: 53) and geometries possible within the on-screen space of the game. Calleja (2011) likens video game screen space to a form of rollercoaster ride in which the player is channeled through pathways and spatial structures. In "the medium of the videogame," Wolf (1997) identifies 11 basic geometries in games, including, to name a few, no visual space; all text based (exhibited in early text adventure games); one screen contained (such as the early game *Space Wars*); one screen contained with wrap around (such as *Pac Man*, where leaving the edge of one screen would result in Pac Man appearing from the opposite edge of the screen); scrolling on one axis (such as horizontally from left to right in the game *Super Mario Bros*); scrolling on two axes (such as an isometric perspective allowing movement up and down, left and right in the game *Gauntlet*); adjacent spaces displayed one at a time (meaning each screen acts as a separate room as in the game *Spy vs. Spy*); layers of independently moving planes (meaning action scrolls on one axis while other planes appear to scroll in the background as in the game *Thunderforce IV*), and interactive three-dimensional environments (such as *Super Mario Galaxy*). Today the majority of console video games use three-dimensional interactive environments, although many casual and puzzle games use one screen or scrolling on one axis structures. In any case, a geometric understanding of screen space assumes that space is a property of the screen and that different forms of space are dependent on how geometry and graphical lines are presented on the screen. Space is therefore a bounded property of the distance between the lines and polygons that delimit the edges of the game environment and serves to separate and partition how and where the player can move within this space through the joining of straight lines and polygons.

How these partitions are generated fundamentally affects the possibility for action within the game itself. As I have argued elsewhere (Ash 2010), the various aspects of video-game environments operate as inhibitors and disinhibitors for movement and action. In doing so these environments also work to inhibit and disinhibit capacities for creative and critical thought. In this case the specific architectural structures of games do not just operate as a container for action but also shape the narrative and temporal flow in which games play out. As Jenkins (2004) argues, games can be understood as kinds of "narrative architecture" in which the players' actions are driven by the space itself (on narrative structure in video games, see Ip 2011; 2011b). In many games, reaching certain points in space triggers events, narrative cut scenes, and "focalizations": "*Prince of Persia: The Sands of Time* can automatically enforce certain camera positions when the system considers such adjustments necessary; *God of War* adjusts the camera only to the position of the avatar and even excludes any player influence except for sharpshooting segments" (Nitsche 2009: 151).

As well as aiding and directing narrative, the very act of exploring and overcoming obstacles in the environment also creates a sense of reward for the player in and of itself. As Gazzard suggests in relation to the game *Limbo*: "the reward of overcoming an obstacle along the path results in both rewards of environment and exploration being granted. The player is now able to continue exploring along the new paths of the game, and further obstacles are put in the way of the player-character to be overcome" (2011 no pagination).

The capacity of game environments to produce spatially complex structures as well as respond to players' location within them helps to generate what Calleja (2011) calls "spatial involvement" in the space of the image, whereby movement and navigation require effort and skill. This effort and skill then produce a sense of exploration: "when a player plots a route through a geographical expanse and then navigates it, it is more likely that she will feel a sense of habitation within the game environment" (2011: 75).

What is interesting about these accounts is the way that the space of the image is framed as primarily Euclidian – understood as a distance between particular points and the ways in which this distance is sensed and experienced visually. Indeed, as Ken Hillis puts it, video games are "world[s] composed of light" (1999: xxvi). As Hillis goes on to argue, there is a long history in the Western world of thinking and conceptualizing space as primarily a visual phenomenon in which space extends outwards and beyond us: "visual space is the farthest removed from our bodily sense and covers the largest area experienced by a sense" (ibid.: 92). Typological accounts of video game image space are so appealing precisely because they reiterate a (Western) historical narrative that links the phenomenon of space with the sense of sight. Video games use the sense of sight to construct space using techniques of perspective, creating the appearance of a three-dimensional world that extends beyond the confines of the frame of the screen and beyond the vanishing point of the image. Of course, such a conceptualization of space is not the only one. As Ong (1982) argues, before the advent of writing, space was primarily experienced as acoustic, based upon the sharing and circulation of oral history. Thinking about video-game space as a bodily experience, using all of the bodily senses, opens up other ways for conceptualizing the space of the video game itself.

Spaces of the Body

Alongside enquiries into the screen space of video games, a number of writers concern themselves with the nondiagetic space of the body that players inhabit while playing games. This is especially the case with the development of gesture-based interfaces such as the Nintendo Wii, Microsoft Kinect, and Playstation Move, all of which map extended bodily movement onto what is happening on the screen space of the image. A turn toward the body as central to the experience of video-game space could be considered a response to, and critique of, accounts of video-game space as part of an ephemeral virtual sphere or realm. As Lehdonvirta argues,

> *even at the core of virtual space, physical space cannot be ignored. Guilds in World of Warcraft (Blizzard, 2004; from hereon, WoW) and corporations in EVE Online (CCP Games, 2003; from hereon, EVE) recruit members based on the continent and time zone in which they reside in. For WoW raiding guilds it is important that members can be online simultaneously for extended periods of time. For EVE alliances engaged in war over territory, it is vital that members are available to keep guard at all hours. (2010: n.p.)*

Simply put, a dichotomy between virtual and real is unhelpful. Players need their bodies to experience and control the spaces and places of video games, and these spaces and places are already tied into particular geographical and material infrastructures, systems, and contexts. However, as Behrenshausen argues, until recently academics have "exhibit[ed] a near-exclusive preoccupation with video games' relation to players' embodied sense of sight at the expense of exploring other powerfully carnal modes of player–game engagement" (2007: 335–36). Turning toward the other bodily senses involved in game play, Crick argues for a phenomenological understanding of games:

> *When I "enter" the virtual world of a FPS [first-person shooter] such as Call of Duty 4, my experience is not one of disembodied perception nor can my body be reducible to a mere set of eyeballs. For example, sometimes my heartbeat races or my body feels rushes of excitement and jolts during moments of intense combat with NPCs [non-player combatants]. (2011: 266)*

From a phenomenological perspective, senses such as touch and hearing are as important as sight in understanding how players engage with video games. However, as Kirkpatrick points out, these senses are under-discussed: "[it is] … curious that the details of … what each game feels like in the hand, so to speak – is so rarely a matter for reflection" (2008: 130). Thinking about the corporeal aspect of video games is important as it opens new ways to think about the spatiality of video games as a spatiality produced through the body. As Grodal argues, "video game experience is very much similar to such an everyday experience of learning and controlling by … [embodied] … repetitive rehearsal" (2000: 148). Examples of such experience include learning the route through a new building or how to ride a bike. In video games, the control pad or interface device acts as the condition of possibility for this learning process. The space of the image is actively felt through the combinations of button presses and the sensitivity of directional sticks that are unique to this or that game, which in turn are necessary to engage with the game itself. The space of the image is experienced in the body through the emotional and affective resonances the player has as they control their character or avatar on screen. Grodal suggests that such resonances can be stronger in video games than other media because of the two-way feedback loop between player and game, in which the player can respond to what is happening on-screen. Whereas one can be scared by the actions of a character they see in a film, in a video game this fear manifests itself in a direct response to what is happening in the game. For example, in *Uncharted* the player encounters a series of cursed humans that have become monsters. These monsters leap toward the player's avatar and swipe with claws that can quickly kill them, requiring the section of the game to be replayed. The player may experience fear here and this fear is linked to whether the avatar lives or dies and the sensorimotor effort required to beat the cursed enemies. This is qualitatively different in a film, where the outcome is out of the player's control. Taking this phenomenological perspective seriously allows us to recognize the key role all the bodily senses play in constructing an experience of space. It is only through the bodily senses that the flat image on-screen is experienced as a space rather than an image (also see Gee 2008).

Space as Assemblage of Screen and Body

Drawing upon ideas of the space of image and body, Nitsche argues that video-game play involves an assemblage of five different "planes" of space:

> *rule based space as defined by the mathematical rules that set, for example, physics, sounds AI and game-level architecture ... mediated space as defined by the presentation, which is the space of the image plane and the use of this image including the cinematic form of presentation ... fictional space that lives in the imagination, in other words, the space 'imagined' by players from their comprehension of the available images ... play space meaning space of the play, which includes the player and the video game hardware; and ... social space defined by interaction with others, meaning the game space of other players affected (e.g., in a multiplayer title). (Nitsche 2009: 16, emphasis in original)*

For Nitsche, these five different planes of space are not separate but work together to generate the overall space of the video game. What is interesting about Nitsche's account is the way in which different types of space are invoked within his five-plane model. From Nitsche's account at least four types of space are invoked: extended, metaphorical, visual, and relational. For example, the rule-based space could be understood as contained within the hardware of the video-game console and the software that runs on this hardware. In this case, the "space" of the rules is an extended space, understood as the shape and size of the physical hardware and its capacity to execute code-based operations. The fictional space "imagined by players" is a metaphorical space generated by the mind's eye and mediated space is linked to a visual image of space that is itself linked to particular understandings of vision. In contrast to this, the social and play space of the video game are relational; emerging from the particular arrangement and location of different players' bodies. Developing Nitsche's perspective, one could understand the experiential space of video games as an emergent assemblage of body and screen. As Taylor puts it,

> *Games, and their play, are constituted by the interrelations between (to name just a few) technological systems and software (including the imagined player embedded in them), the material world (including our bodies at the keyboard), the online space of the game (if any), game genre, and its histories, the social worlds that infuse the game and situate us outside of it. (2009: 332)*

In this case, space is not "in" or "behind" the screen and neither is it "in" the body or mind. Rather it emerges from the relationship between body and screen, between the geometries that limit player action and how players corporeally and skillfully respond to these limitations using their embodied knowledge and sensorimotor skill. Arguments that point to the necessary assemblage of body and game are now being made by a variety of writers in different ways. Calleja suggests that players become "incorporated" into the game environment: "Incorporation … operates on a double axis: the player incorporates (in the sense of internalizing or assimilating) the game environment into consciousness while simultaneously being incorporated through the avatar into that environment" (2011: 169). Rush, using different language, points toward the "embodied metaphor" of play in which

> *the player is … sensitized to how the physical act of game playing crosses an order of reality to be expressed through its successful representation on-screen; this is sometimes experienced as a double consciousness, a sensation of both moving through game space while at the same time directing this movement from the outside. (2011: 246)*

In my own work (Ash 2009), I have developed the theme of assemblage to argue that the conjunction of body and screen creates worlds in which experiences of space and place are conceivable and possible for the player. Developing a post-phenomenological account of body, brain, screen, and interface, I argue that the space of the image and the capacity of the user to control this image generate a sense of locatedness in time and space through the activities and possibilities for movement that the user negotiates as they play. From this perspective there is no "imaginative" space in the mind's eye created from available images. Instead, space emerges directly from the players concerned, embodied engagement as they are involved in a particular task in the game. In this case, images are not interpreted or analyzed purely through their representational content but also resonate through the apparatus of the screen onto the body of the player, fleshing out and placing the player's body in relation to the events on screen.

As such, video-game "space" can be understood as multiple and transitory, constantly being shifted and translated between different states and locations. When stored on a disk or server, such worlds remain as numbers, code, and operations, largely inaccessible to players. It is only when activated on the appropriate hardware that such worlds become experiential in a way that corresponds to the visual aspects of space that players may be familiar with. In this case, such experiential worlds do not preexist their technical and bodily performance. However, this is not to say that the content of these worlds is unimportant. Such content raises a number of issues regarding the politics and communal possibility of games that are addressed in the next section.

Place and Video Games

The Politics of Video-game Place

If space in video games is understood as meeting point of body and screen, then place can be understood as the content of the image on-screen that organizes and shapes the tasks and activities of the user as the play. In other words, place refers to the specific location and sites that are created by designers in which action takes place. Just as the architectural layout of these sites is not just accidental, neither are the way these sites draw upon and create representations of people and places. As a number of writers are now highlighting, there is a clear representational politics to video-game images and how they shape the geographical imagination of users. This politics has two clearly identifiable strands: representations of conflict and militarism and representations of human identity.

Video games have a long historical relationship with military technology and simulation. Patrick Crogan (2011) argues that video games originate in computerized war gaming and planning and that military logics continue to underpin the development of video games. As Der Derian (2009) suggests, the relationship between the military industrial complex and the video-game industry is not simply historical. Today this relationship is actively cultivated and encouraged by both parties, leading to what Der Derian (ibid.) has dubbed "the military-entertainment industrial complex" (also see Halter 2006; Witheford 2009). This complex manifests itself both explicitly and implicitly in how video games represent other people and places.

For example, Power (2007) argues that the US Army–backed *America's Army* is a clear instance of the ways in which video games are used to attempt to manufacture consent for military intervention and encourage recruitment into the army. Shaw suggests that many video games produce an "oriental aesthetics" that depict the Orient as a "simplified Islamic world, in which cultural and ethical differences are flattened … [whereby] … [t]he 'Middle East' becomes an anonymous topography of floating signifiers" (2011: 796). According to Shaw, the very places of these games help reinforce this otherness: "the military entertainment complex depicts Middle Eastern cities as in a state perpetual war. More than just maze-like and mystical, the Middle Eastern city is a site of conflict that must be brought under Western democratic order" (ibid.: 796).

Brock (2011) develops this problematic link between representation, place, and identity in her work on *Resident Evil 5* (RE5), an action game set in Africa. She discusses the role of Sheva, a female sidekick who guides and backs the main character, Chris, through the game's environments. As Brock puts it, "Sheva is the videogame equivalent of Pocahontas: a woman of color coerced into 'guiding' White explorers across a foreign land that she is presumed to be familiar with because of her ethnic heritage … and in doing so serves to embody a logic of White control over the 'Other' in the game" (2011: 440). Here the relationship between the identity and representation of characters and the places in which those characters inhabit become mixed:

> *For RE5, the switch to the African continent … works as a setting to be cleansed and civilized, a role Africa has symbolized to the West for centuries. At no point are the Africans allowed to be anything other than savage; they are never seen within familiar Western contexts such as high-rise buildings, shopping centers, or at leisure. (ibid.: 443)*

Other games such as *Grand Theft Auto* have been read in a similar way. Leonard (2009) argues that the city of San Andreas in *Grand Theft Auto* offers a ghettocentric account of urban life that "deploys reactionary visions of communities of color through its narrative and virtual representations … [in which] … the ghetto … [is] … a war zone inhabited by Black gangstas that not only prey on Black residents but also on those White families living outside its virtual ghetto center" (2009: 266). Such visions, he argues, help rearticulate a politics of division, partition, and separation based on racial difference.

But as Allen has argued, video games do not have to generate representations of particular landscapes in order to be problematic. Rather than producing representations of a particular place, games like *America's Army 3* create a fictional anyplace, which attempts to play down any relation to a real landscape or location. As Allen points out, the environments of *America's Army* are stripped of any identifiable cultural markers and signage in the game displays an invented language that cannot be related to a particular country or nation. Such abstraction is very powerful because it enables a mind-set in which any nationality, race, or nation could potentially be an enemy and primes the cultural imaginary of players with such assumptions. As Allen puts it,

> *Nameless, elusive, and always just around the corner, the unreal enemy is not confined to any singular game or moment. He influences and precedes the production of real enemies of the United States Army; comprehending how this production of a cultural imaginary occurs is crucial in achieving any sort of knowledge regarding the real consequences of war and conflict. (2011: 55–56)*

In this case, representations of place in video games can have powerful effects in two ways. Firstly, through what and how they present the world based upon existing stereotypes and, secondly, through creating anonymous places that are scrubbed of these stereotypes.

Recent work is starting to paint a more complex picture of the implicit ways in which the places represented in video games shape players' understanding of the world, as well as recognizing that players do not necessarily accept these representations. Working with players of *Grand Theft Auto 4*, DeVane and Squire (2008) contest a narrative in which the game's transmission of negative racial stereotypes encourages players to develop their own negative stereotypes. As DeVane and Squire put it, "Far from simply reproducing discriminatory discourses regarding young Black men, Gamer 1 [a participant in the study] explicitly recognizes and identifies or 'calls out' the negative stereotypes present in the game: the notion of a Black man joining a gang and the gang members having certain character archetypes" (2008: 276).

Huntemann (2010) has conducted audience reception research with military-war game players and argues that these games do not "inhibit critical engagement" (2010: 249) and "players ... retained their skepticism about current military actions, questioning the motives, strategies, purported goals and likely success of US foreign policy and military intervention" (ibid.). For both DeVane and Huntemann, there is a recognition that place in video games is

> *not a blank slate onto which players can reinscribe their cultural models at will. It is a designed artifact with affordances and constraints as well as possibilities and limitations. The player makes meaning in concert with the ideological world of the game through play, and play entails some form of acceptance of the semiotics of the game space, if only temporarily. (DeVane 2008: 281)*

Taking into account the designed nature of video games, alongside the multiple ways in which this space is interpreted, complicates simple accounts of games as sites of "othering." While games such as *Grand Theft Auto* and *Resident Evil 5* certainly have many flaws, this is not to say that the way they represent people and places is just accepted by those that play them.

Indeed, while the negative aspects of representation in video games have been emphasized, a growing body of work is also pointing toward the ways in which the representations of video-game places can be actively utilized to challenge and complicate such negative narratives. Video games can be actively used to question and interrogate how representations about people and places are constructed, rather than just utilized as a medium for disseminating and multiplying negative representations of particular states, regions, or ethnics groups.

A number of games such as *Bioshock, Mass Effect,* and *Fallout 3* include morality systems that actively encourage players to weigh up how their actions will affect different groups or individuals within particular game worlds. While these may be fantasy worlds, Sicart (2005) argues that the complexity and ambiguity of the choices available to players, and the tangible impacts these choices have on the game world, encourages sustained ethical thought (also see Sicart 2009; Simkins and Steinkuehler 2008). In games like *Fallout 3* for example, players' moral actions in the game directly affect the places they can safely visit: "evil NPCs like slavers and raiders welcome the player if one is evil enough while those who oppose these factions respond by attacking and barring entry to their locations" (Schulzke 2009: no pagination). In this case, the environments of the games act as a moral landscape. Moral decision-making literally shapes player's access to and relationship with particular places in game.

The encouragement of such reflection points to the capacity of video games to cultivate a variety of critical-thinking skills. A whole genre of so-called serious games capitalize on this capacity in order to encourage players to reflect on real-world issues and problems. In *Darfur Is Dying,* a Web-based browser game, the player controls a child traveling to a local well to collect water for their family, while trying to avoid being captured by the local Janjaweed militia. Bogost argues that games like *Darfur Is Dying* "invite us to step into the smaller, more uncomfortable shoes of the downtrodden rather than the larger, more well-heeled shoes of the powerful" (2011: 19). The main gameplay mechanic in *Darfur Is Dying* revolve around the player trying to hide from passing militia vehicles behind rocks and foliage. In stark contrast with many other video games, the player has no weapons or skills to fight back with. The barren nature of the landscape and the dispersal of foliage to hide behind in the environment, alongside the lack of abilities the player is given, actively work to create empathy between the player and those suffering in Darfur (also see Flanagan 2009).

As well as encouraging emotional states such as empathy, serious games can also work to inform and encourage resistance in players. For example, the game *Vagmundo: A Migrant's Tale* serves to both critique the ways in which America positions illegal immigrants from Mexico within US society as well as inform players about how they can help real-world immigrants who have recently entered the United States. Across a series of levels, the player has to sneak across the border from Mexico and work as an unskilled laborer. Upon completing the last level of the game and gaining acceptance into American society, the player is then given a choice to either shun or help new immigrants. Choosing to help the new immigrants links the player to online information from immigrant charities. Shunning the immigrants results in a level where the player now sits on the US- Mexican border and shoots other immigrants as they attempt to enter. Taylor argues that in giving the player this choice, "the boundaries of the computer game are opened up, and the user is encouraged to break beyond the confines of the gaming world with its circular logic and reinforcement of the system, to enter into real-life activism" (2011: 314).

These examples demonstrate that the places of video games and the representations they draw upon and reiterate are not inherently negative. Video games are a medium that can be powerfully used to critique existing representations of other people and places around the world. However, it must be said that for now at least, such games are in the minority. While games like *Call of Duty* and *Grand Theft Auto* generate millions of sales, games such as *Darfur Is Dying* and *Vagmundo* are played by much smaller numbers of people and receive far less mainstream attention. These games also have very low production values and gameplay that is not as sophisticated or engaging as games made by large game-design studios. These technical and budgetary limitations arguably inhibit the power of the messages they attempt to communicate. The possibilities of such titles should be celebrated, while recognizing their limited impact on mass culture.

The Communities of Video-game Place

As well as reiterating or challenging existing representations of place, video games also produce forms of community that are shaped by, and local to, the places of particular games and game environments. This form of place-based community is most obvious in massively multiplayer online role-playing games (MMORPGs). In successful MMORPGs, hundreds of thousands of players log on to a persistent online world, undertaking quests and communicating with other players through text and voice-based interfaces. A variety of writers argue that MMORPGS such as *World of Warcraft* signal the generation of new forms of sociality and community (Fields and Kafai 2009; Lastowka 2009; 2009b; Pearce 2009; Bainbridge 2010; Williams 2007; Hemminger 2010). These forms of sociality and community are shaped by the mechanics and goals of the game as well as the fantasy places they represent (Humphreys 2009; Ruch 2009). For example, Chen (2008) explores practices of "raiding" in *World of Warcraft*, where groups of players develop strong forms of camaraderie through meeting to battle high-level monsters and complete difficult quests. Yee (2009) argues that the communal possibilities of these groups, and the kinds of relationships that are developed within these groups, are actively shaped by the affordances and restrictions of the game's rules, which he terms their "social architecture." Raiding groups require players to closely coordinate their actions and use characters with varying abilities to complete their goals. The often intense and frantic nature of raiding also involves the development of shared technical vocabularies and slang that are local to the group in question. The example of raiding points to the ways in which the particular places of video games enable and cultivate forms of community novel to the medium.

The places in which these raids take place also shape and generate a sense of coherence and history for the user. Klastrup (2009) suggests that MMORPGs should be understood as generating fictional worlds, that emerge from the relationship between their spatial structure and the history and lore that is communicated through the design and embellishment of these environments. For example, *World of Warcraft* makes extensive use of ruins in its environments. As Krzywinska argues, the "cultural use of ruins … cast an aura of mystery and nostalgia. The ruins of once splendid temples and cities act within the game (as in real life) as in memoriam signifiers of passed glory, representing in romanticized terms a lost object of desire" (2006: 389). Creating the appearance of a world stooped in history helps cement the coherence of MMORPGs as places with their own past, which can encourage players to role-play as the avatars and characters they control (Nardi 2010; Williams et al. 2011; Corneliussen et al. 2008). MMORPGs encourage this form of role-play through the way in which players interact with the places in game. For example, specific high-value items are only available in certain regions in games and quests are only available from specific characters that reside in particular locations (Ducheneaut et al. 2006).

While the social and spatial architecture of these games can encourage forms of altruism and teamwork, the same architecture can be used to discipline and govern players' actions. Developing more pointed language than Yee (2009), Kucklich argues that rather than simply operating as a form of social architecture, MMORPGS are "social factories" in which players are laborers. These social factories "appear … to fulfill primarily an economic function but which also create … social and cultural capital, as well as forms of political organization, which in turn feed back into the business models of the providers of virtual worlds" (2009: 344).

In other words, the social architecture that Yee describes as central to generating relationships with others in MMORPGs is actually a form of emotional labor used to keep players engaged in the game and thus willing to continue to pay a subscription fee in order to play. Silverman and Simon (2009) develop this theme of governance, in examining practices of "power gaming" among a self professed elite core of players in MMORPGs. These power gamers created "Dragon Kill points" (DKP), a social system that exists outside of the actual game software, designed to fairly distribute rewards to groups who worked together to destroy difficult enemies (also see Malone 2009). Silverman and Simon argue that the development of these systems operate as a further form of self-discipline, on top of the rules of the game, that attempt to engineer social relationships. As Silverman and Simon put it, "DKP is, in fact … a disciplinary technology for producing gameplay as a form of rationalized labor" (2009: 364; also see Malaby 2006).

The communal potentials generated by the places of particular video games should be understood as a double-edged sword. As the example of MMORPGs show, creating coherent places enables players to generate strong connections to the games they play and facilitates a variety of productive social and communal encounters. At the same time, these encounters are always actively shaped by the companies that design these games in order to maximize player engagement, which in turn is motivated by a desire to generate profit. While it is too simplistic to think about MMORPGs as inherently "good" or "bad" (on the construction of debates around the positive and negative aspects of MMORPGs, see Kelly 2009; Golub and Lingley 2008; Lange 2011), recognizing how place is used in these games to help cultivate social and communal interaction is a good point from which to ask critical questions about control and power in these worlds.

Future Media Geographies of Video Games

This chapter has examined various ways of conceptualizing video-game space and place. It has argued that what makes video-game spaces and places unique is that, as digital simulations, video games are possibility spaces – spaces of potential opened up between the rules that limit players' actions and the freedom that is available within these spaces. Ontologically the chapter has made the claim that "space" itself in video games emerges from the relationship between body, hardware, software, and screen, which in turn creates a world in which space and place are conceivable. As such, space and place in video games don't preexist their technical and bodily performance. The chapter has also suggested that video games are productive of particular spaces and places through the ways in which environments are designed within this possibility space and the representations they draw upon to visually realize these spaces. Rather than a passive backdrop, these representations actively shape players experience and understanding of the world. In this concluding section, I want to point to four areas that may be of interest for future study by media geographers interested in the spaces and places of video games.

First is to think more carefully and explicitly about the role of affect in video games and particularly the ways in which video games can be understood as forms of affective design (Ash 2010, 2012). As the chapter has argued, what makes video games a unique medium is the ways in which space is used to inhibit and enable movement and action by the player. Rather than just containers for action, video-game spaces and places are actively designed to anticipate, shape, and respond to players' actions in increasingly sophisticated and context-dependent ways. How this is achieved is of great interest to those thinking about the broader bodily politics of games. In particular, the ways in which logics of movement are generated and emphasized by games may have possible governmental effects on broader processes of spatial awareness and decision-making for those that use them. One has to recognize that these systems and environments do not simply translate, transport, or hold affect within them. Instead, affects emerge from the contingent relations between player and game. To get at these relations one needs to understand how the potential for affect is created as well as the technical systems that are used to transport this potential for affect to other times and places (see Barnett 2008; Pile 2012).

Second is to deal more explicitly with the complex relationships between the representational content of games and the nonrepresentational forces and affects that shape player experience. This chapter has examined a variety of work from postcolonial perspectives on military- and war-based games that argue such games produce militarized subjectivities and racialized forms of otherness. However, many of these studies do not actually ask how people experience and interpret these representations. There seems to be an assumption that if an image contains a specific representational content with a dominant meaning, then this dominant meaning is the only possible meaning that can be experienced. Thinking more closely about the relationship between the representational content of images and the forces and rules that govern and shape how these images are experienced in video games may bring more subtle and interesting understandings to the foreground.

Third is to think more explicitly about the complexities of interfaces. Just as maps, compasses, and other instruments have been studied by geographers to think about the ways in which geographical knowledge is constructed, we can use interfaces to think more explicitly about the ways in which space and place in video games is encountered, navigated, and explored. Interfaces such as the graphical user interface on-screen and the control pad used to play games are not just neutral mediums that are used to access some specific piece of information or content. Instead, we can begin to think about the ways in which these interfaces shape players' experiences and capacities to sense space and time.

Fourth is to think about the emergence of mobile and augmented reality games in relation to broader arguments around "gamification" (Wark 2007) and space (on mobile gaming, see Chan 2008; Hijorth 2010; Souza e Silva 2009). In augmented reality devices, information is added to, and augments, users' experience of the world. For example, in the Nintendo 3DS console, players can look at paper cards and see three-dimensional characters standing on those cards when observing through the system's screen. In smartphone apps such as *ZipRealty,* users can look through the screen and see information about houses available for sale, overlaid on top of the environment through which they are traveling. In these examples, the interface logics of game environments bleed into extended spaces of the world through such devices. Here augmented reality devices bridge the divide between screen space and extended space. In doing so, the spatial logics that drive video-game design and play may shape users' experiences of extended space in cities, malls, and other locations. Returning to the issue of affective design, one could think through the ways in which such devices could bring new forms of affective value into existence. The same logics of accumulation used in games to reward achievement could be used in AR devices to reward users of these apps to purchase goods from affiliated stores and so on. In this case, the media geographies of games become opened into much broader debates around the relationship between technology and space. As an emerging field of study, media geography is well placed to examine and report upon these processes at work.

References

Aitkins, B. 2003. *More than a Game: The Computer Game as Fictional Form*. Manchester: Manchester University Press.

Aitkins, B. and T. Krzywinska. 2007. *Videogame, Player, Text*. Manchester: University of Manchester Press.

Allen, R. 2011. The unreal enemy of America's army. *Games and Culture* 6(1): 38–60.

America's Army. 2002. Video game. Produced by the U.S. Army.

America's Army 3. 2009. Video game. Produced by the U.S. Army.

Ash, James. (2009). Emerging spatialities of the screen: video games and the reconfiguration of spatial awareness. *Environment and Planning A*, 41(9), 2105–124.

Ash, James. (2010). Teleplastic technologies: charting practices of orientation and navigation in videogaming. *Transactions of the Institute of British Geographers*, 35(3), 414–30.

Ash, James. (2012). Attention, Videogames and the Retentional Economies of Affective Amplification. *Theory, Culture & Society*, 29(6), 3–26. doi: 10.1177/0263276412438595.

Bainbridge, W.S. 2010. *Online Worlds: Convergence of the Real and the Virtual*. New York: Springer Publishing.

Barnett, C. 2008. Political affects in public space: Normative blind-spots in non-representational ontologies. *Transactions of the Institute of British Geographers* 33(2): 186–200.

Behrenshausen, B. 2007. Towards a (kin)aesthetic of video gaming: The case of *Dance Dance Revolution*. *Games and Culture* 2(4): 335–54.

Bioshock. 2007. Video game. Produced by 2K Boston.

Bogost, I. 2010. *Newsgames: Journalism at Play*. Cambridge, MA: MIT Press.

Bogost, I. 2011. *How to Do Things with Videogames*. Minneapolis: University of Minnesota Press.

Borries, F.V., S.P. Walz, and M. Böttger. 2007. *Space, Time, Play*. Basel: Birkhäuser Press.

Brock, A. 2011. When keeping it real goes wrong: Resident Evil 5, racial representation and gamers. *Games and Culture* 6(5): 429–52.

Call of Duty 4: Modern Warfare. 2007. Video game produced by Infinity Ward.

Calleja, G. 2010. Digital games and escapism. *Games and Culture* 5(4): 335–53.

Calleja, G. 2011. *In-Game: From Immersion to Incorporation*. Cambridge, MA: MIT Press.

Chan, D. 2008. Convergence, connectivity and the case of Japanese mobile gaming. *Games and Culture* 3(1): 13–25.

Chen, M.G. 2008. Communication, coordination and camaraderie in World of Warcraft. *Games and Culture* 4(1): 47–73.

Corneliussen, H. and J.W. Walker Rettberg. 2008. *Digital Culture, Play and Identity: A World of Warcraft Reader*. Cambridge, MA: MIT Press.

Cresswell, T. 2004. *Place: A Short Introduction*. London: Wiley-Blackwell.

Crick, T. 2011. The game body: Toward a phenomenology of contemporary video gaming. *Games and Culture* 6(3): 259–69.

Crogan, P. 2011. *Gameplay Mode: War, Simulation and Technoculture*. Minneapolis: University of Minnesota Press.

Darfur Is Dying. 2006. Video game. Produced by InterFUEL.

Deen, P.D. 2011. Interactivity, inhabitation and pragmatist aesthetics. *Game Studies* 11(2). Available at www.gamestudies.org/1102/articles/deen [accessed March 1, 2012].

De Schutter, B. 2011. Never too old to play: The appeal of digital games to an older audience. *Games and Culture* 6(2): 155–70.

Der Derian, J. 2009. *Virtuous War: The Military-Industrial-Media-Entertainment Network*. New York: Routledge Publishing.

DeVane, B. and K.D. Squire. 2008. The meaning of race and violence in Grand Theft Auto: San Andreas. *Games and Culture* 3(3–4): 264–85.

Dovey, J. and H.W. Kennedy. 2006. *Game Cultures: Computer Games as New Media*. New York: Open University Press.

Ducheneaut, N., N. Yee, E. Nickell, and R.J. Moore. 2006. Building an MMO with mass appeal: A look at gameplay in *World of Warcraft*. *Games and Culture* 1(4): 281–317.

Egenfeldt-Nielsen, J. Heide Smith, and S.P. Toscan. 2008. *Understanding Videogames: The Essential Introduction*. London: Routledge Publishing.

Eve Online. 2003. Video game. Produced by CCP Games.

Fallout 3. 2008. Video game. Produced by Bethesda.

Fields, D. and Y.B. Kafai. 2009. Knowing and throwing mudballs, hearts, pies and flowers: A connective ethnography of gaming practices. *Games and Culture* 5(1): 88–115.

Flanagan, M. 2009. *Critical Play: Radical Game Design*. Cambridge, MA: MIT Press.

Gazzard, A. 2011. Unlocking the gameworld: The rewards of space and time in videogames. *Games Studies* 11(1). Available at www.gamestudies.org/1101/articles/gazzard_alison [accessed March 1, 2012].

Gauntlet. 1985. Video game. Produced by Atari.

Gee, J.P. 2008. Video games and embodiment. *Games and Culture* 3(3–4): 253–63.

Giddings, S. 2009. Events and collusions: A glossary for the microethnography of videogame play. *Games and Culture* 4(2): 144–57.

Gosling, V.K. and G. Crawford. 2011. Game scenes: Theorizing digital game audiences. *Games and Culture* 6(2): 135–54.

Golub, A. and K. Lingley. 2008. Just like the Qing Empire: Internet addictions, MMOGs and moral crisis in contemporary China. *Games and Culture* 3(1): 59–75.

Grand Theft Auto 4. 2008. Video game. Produced by Rockstar Games.

Halter, E. 2006. *From Sun Tzu to Xbox: War and Video Games*. New York: Thunder's Mouth Press.

Harvey, D. 2006. *Spaces of Global Capitalism: Towards a Theory of Uneven Geographical Development*. London: Verso Books.

Hayot, E. and E. Wesp. 2009. Towards a critical aesthetic of virtual-world geographies. *Games Studies*. Available at: www.gamestudies.org/0901/articles/hayot_wesp_space [accessed March 3, 2012].

Heeter C., R. Egidio, P. Mishra, B. Winn, and J. Winn. 2008. Alien games: Do girls prefer games designer by girls? *Games and Culture* 4(1): 74–100.

Hemminger, E. 2010. *The Mergence of Spaces: Experiences of Reality in Digital Role-Playing Games*. Berlin: Edition Sigma Publishing.

Higgin, T. 2009. Blackless fantasy: The disappearance of race in massively multiplayer online role playing games. *Games and Culture* 4(1): 3–26.

Hjorth, L. 2011. *Games and Gaming: An Introduction to New Media*. Oxford: Berg Publishing.

Holin, L. and C.T. Sun. 2011. Cash trade in free-to-play online games. *Games and Culture* 6(3): 270–87.

Humphreys, S. 2009. Norrath: New forms, old institutions. *Games Studies* [Online], 9(1). Available at: www.gamestudies.org/0901/articles/humphreys [accessed March 1, 2012].

Huntemann, N. 2009. *Joystick Soldiers: The Politics of Play in Military Videogames*. New York: Routledge Publishing.

Ip, B. 2008. Technological, content and market convergence in the games industry. *Games and Culture* 3(2): 199–224.

Ip, B. 2011. Narrative structures in computer and videogames, Part 1: Context, definitions, and initial findings. *Games and Culture* 6(2): 103–34.

Ip, B. 2011b. Narrative structures in computer and videogames, Part 2: Emotions, structures and archetypes. *Games and Culture* 6(3): 203–44.

Jenkins, H. 2004. Game design as narrative architecture. In *First Person: New Media as Story, Performance, and Game*. Edited by N. Wardrip-Fruin and P. Harrigan. Cambridge, MA: MIT Press.

Juul, J. 2010. *A Casual Revolution: Reinventing Video Games and Their Players*. Cambridge: MIT Press.

Kallio, K.P., F. Mayra, and K. Kaipainen. 2011. At least nine ways to play: Approaching gamer mentalities. *Games and Culture* 6(4): 327–53.

Kelly, R.V. 2004. *Massively Multiplayer Online Role-Playing Games*. Jefferson, NC: McFarland Publishing.

Kirkland, E. 2009. *Resident Evil*'s typewriter: Survival horror and its remediations. *Games and Culture* 4(2): 115–26.

Kirkpatrick, G. 2009. Controller, hand, screen: Aesthetic form in the computer game. *Games and Culture* 4(2): 127–43.

Klastrup, L. 2009. The worldness of Everquest: Exploring a 21st century fiction. *Games Studies* [Online] 9 (1). Available at: www.gamestudies.org/0901/articles/klastrup [accessed March 1, 2012].

Krzywinska, T. 2006. Blood scythes, festivals, quests, and backstories: World creation and rhetorics of myth in *World of Warcraft*. *Games and Culture* 1: 383–96.

Kucklich, J.R. 2009. Virtual worlds and their discontents: Precarious sovereignty, governmentality and the ideology of play. *Games and Culture* 4(4): 340–52.

Lange, P.G. 2011. Learning real-life lessons from online games. *Games and Culture* 6(1): 17–37.

Lankoski, P. 2011. Player character engagement in computer games. *Games and Culture* 6(4): 291–311.

Lastowka, G. 2009. Rules of play. *Games and Culture* 4(4): 379–95.

Lastowka, G. 2009b. Planes of power: *Everquest* as text, game and community. *Game studies* [Online]. Available at: www.gamestudies.org/0901/articles/lastowka [accessed March 1, 2012].

Lehdonvirta, V. 2010. Virtual worlds don't exist: Questioning the dichotomous approach in MMO studies. *Game Studies* [Online] 10(1). Available at: www.gamestudies.org/1001/articles/lehdonvirta [accessed March 1, 2012].

Leonard, D. 2009. Young, black (& brown) and don't give a fuck: Virtual gangstas in the era of state violence. *Cultural Studies Critical Methodologies* 9: 248–72.

Limbo. 2010. Video game. Produced by Playdead Games.

Malaby, T. 2006. Parlaying value: Capital in and beyond virtual worlds. *Games and Culture* 1(2): 141–62.

Malaby, T.M. and T. Burke. 2009. The short and happy life of interdisciplinarity in game studies. *Games and Culture* 4(4): 323–30.

Malone, K.L. 2009. Dragon kill points: The economics of power gamers. *Games and Culture* 4(3): 296–316.

Malpas, G. 2012. Putting space in place: Philosophical topography and relational geography. *Environment and Planning D: Society and Space*, 30(2): 226–242.

Martey, R.M. and J. Stromer-Galley. 2007. The digital dollhouse: Context and social norms in *The Sims Online*. *Games and Culture* 2(4): 314–34.

Mass Effect. 2007. Video game. Produced by Bioware.

Massey, D.B. 2005. *For Space*. Thousand Oaks, CA: SAGE.

Nardi, BA. 2010. *My Life as a Night Elf Priest: An Anthropological Account of World of Warcraft*. Ann Arbor: University of Michigan Publishing.

Nitsche, M. 2009. *Video Game Spaces*. Cambridge, MA: MIT Press.

Ong, W. 1982. *Orality and Literacy*. New York: Routledge Publishing.
Pacman. 1980. Video game. Produced by Namco.
Pearce, C. 2008. The truth about baby boomer gamers: A study of over-forty computer game players. *Games and Culture* 3(2): 142–74.
Pearce, C. and T. Boellstorff. 2009. *Communities of Play: Emergent Cultures in Multiplayer Games and Virtual Worlds*. Cambridge, MA: MIT Press.
Pile, S. 2012. Distant feelings: Telepathy and the problem of affect transfer over distance. *Transactions of the Institute of British Geographers* 37(1): 44–59.
Plants vs. Zombies. 2009. Video game. Produced by Popcap Games.
Poremba, C. 2006. Point and shoot: Remediating photography in gamespace. *Games and Culture* 2(1): 49–58.
Prince of Persia: Sands of Time. 2003. Video game. Produced by Ubisoft.
Quandt, T., H. Grueninger, and J. Wimmer. 2009. The gray haired gaming generation: Findings from an explorative interview study on older computer gamers. *Games and Culture* 4(1): 27–46.
Resident Evil 5. 2009. Video game. Produced by Capcom.
Ruch, A. 2009. *World of Warcraft*: Service or Space? *Games Studies* [Online] 9(2). Available at: www.gamestudies.org/0902/articles/ruch [accessed March 1, 2012].
Rush, J. 2011. Embodied metaphors: Exposing informatic control through first-person shooters. *Games and Culture* 6(3): 245–58.
Schulzke, M. 2009. Moral decision making in *Fallout*. *Games Studies* [Online] 9(2). Available at: www.gamestudies.org/0902/articles/schulzke [accessed March 1, 2012].
Schulzke, M. 2011. How games support associational life: Using Tocqueville to understand the connection. *Games and Culture* 6(4): 354–72.
Shaw, IGR. 2011. Playing war. *Social and Cultural Geography* 11(8): 789–803.
Spacewar! 1961. Video game. Produced by Russell.
Spittle, S. 2011. Did this game scare you? Because it sure as hell scared me! Fear, the abject and the uncanny. *Games and Culture* 6(4): 312–26.
Spy vs. Spy. 1984. Video game. Produced by First Star Software.
Silverman, M. and B. Simon. 2009. Discipline and dragon kill points in the online power game. *Games and Culture* 4(4): 353–78.
Silva, S.E.A and L. Hjorth. 2009. Playful urban spaces: A historical approach to mobile games. *Simulation and Gaming* 40(5): 602–25.
Siva, S.E.A. 2009. Hybrid reality and location-based gaming: Redefining mobility and game spaces in urban environments. *Simulation and Gaming* 40(3): 404–24.
Simkins, D.W. and C. Steinkuehler. 2008. Critical ethical reasoning and role-play. *Games and Culture* 3(3–4): 333–55.
Stuart, K. 2011. *Modern Warfare 3* smashes records: $775m in five days. *The Guardian* [Online]. Available at: www.guardian.co.uk/technology/2011/nov/18/modern-warfare-2-records-775m [accessed March 1, 2012].
Super Mario Bros. 1985. Video game. Produced by Nintendo.
Super Mario Galaxy. 2007. Video game. Produced by Nintendo.
Taylor, C. 2011. Resistant gaming and resignifying the border online: Ricardo Miranda Zuniga's *Vagamundo, A Migrant's Tale*. *Journal of Latin American Cultural Studies* 20(3): 303–21.
Taylor, T.L. 2006. Does WoW change everything? How a PvP server, multinational player base and surveillance mod scene caused me pause. *Games and Culture* 1(4): 318–37.
Taylor, T.L. 2009. The assemblage of play. *Games and Culture* 4(4): 331–39.
Thunderforce IV. Video game. Produced by Technosoft.
Tuan, Y.-F. 2001. *Space and Place*. Minneapolis: University of Minnesota Press.
Vagmundo: A Migrant's Tale. 2002. Video game. Produced by Ricardo Mirando Zuniga.

Uncharted. 2007. Video game. Produced by Naughty Dog.
Wark, M. 2007. *Gamer Theory*. Cambridge, MA: Harvard University Press.
Williams D., N. Ducheneaut, L. Xiong, Y. Zhang, N. Yee, and E. Nickell. 2006. From tree house to barracks: The social life of guilds in *World of Warcraft*. *Games and Culture* 1(4): 338–61.
Williams D., T.L.M. Kennedy, and R.J. Moore. 2011. Behind the avatar: The patterns, practices and functions of role playing in MMOs. *Games and Culture* 6(2): 171–200.
Williams, J.P., and J. Heide Smith. 2007. *The Players' Realm: Studies on the Culture of Video Games and Gaming*. Jefferson, NC: McFarland Publishing.
Witheford 2009, N. and G. Peuter. 2009. *Games of Empire: Global Capitalism and Video Games.* Minneapolis: University of Minnesota Press.
Wolf, M.J.P. 1997. *The Medium of the Video Game*. Austin: University Texas Press.
World of Warcraft. 2004. Video Game. Produced by Blizzard Entertainment.
Yee, N. 2009. Befriending ogres and wood-elves: Relationship formation and the social architecture of Norrath. *Games Studies* [Online] 9(1). Available at: www.gamestudies.org/0901/articles/yee [accessed March 1, 2012].
Zagal, J.P., C. Fernandez-Vara, and M. Mateas. 2008. Rounds, levels and waves: The early evolution of gameplay segmentation. *Games and Culture* 3(2): 175–98.
Zagal, J.P. and M. Mateas. 2010. Time in videogames: A survey and analysis. *Simulation and Gaming* 41(6): 844–68.
ZipRealty. Video Game. Produced by ZipRealty.

The Internet

Darren Purcell

> "'The Internet means we don't need libraries anymore.' HAHAHAHAHAHA."
> Croft 2012: n.p.

> "It's a chapter about the Internet? Just plagiarize the remaining pages as a kind of academic meta-joke."
> Champion 2012: n.p.

Perhaps it is appropriate for a chapter on the geographies of the Internet to start with responses to a complaint about writer's block posted (by the author) to Facebook. The "help" provided by both comments reflect two views that appropriation of the Internet has helped to foster over time. The first was that information would be free and at the user's fingertips, easily recalled at a moment's notice, while the power to access said information would be diffused across space and time. Concomitantly, the need for filters and gatekeepers would decline. This delinking of places as the stores of information in favor of easily accessible, free-floating data and information across space was not likely in the minds of the Internet's earliest developers, but nevertheless it has become the dominant mode of thinking about the Internet. The continual development of technologies enabling both mobility and dispersed data access has produced a pendulum-like swing in "where" information is stored and subsequently accessed.

The first stage of computer usage saw users interacting with data and processing power at the mainframe computer (and its gatekeeping handlers feeding in punch cards). Access to mainframes was then distributed, via physical networks to dumb terminals as the Internet diffused and grew rhizome-like into more social practices. The 1970s, '80s, and '90s saw a series of changes that impacted where computers were located, and where data access and storage processes occurred. The development of personal computers (PCs) and modems, along with the rapid diffusion of these machines in schools and universities (a result of marketing discourses playing on parents' and educators' of fears of students being technologically left behind) enabled greater access to become a norm. Declines in the costs expanded the possibilities of home use. This diffusion of access begot needs for the portability of programs and data, which the computer industry addressed with the development of a succession of devices such as the early floppy disks, then compact discs, and subsequently flash drives, enabling ease of movement to fixed computers. The development of laptop computers only enhanced the norm of mobility, facilitated by the greater provision of Wi-Fi Internet in homes, shops, and other forms of public space. Today, in the 2010s, the emphasis has again returned to the idea of accessing data and processing power stored elsewhere but this is combined with a demand for personalized, near-complete mobility, signaling a decided shift in the importance of "where" when using the Internet.

The second comment focuses on plagiarism, which could be considered a shorthand for a larger issue, data ownership. Plagiarism not only in classrooms but by politicians (Bailey 2008a; 2008b) and pundits (Haughny 2012) demonstrates changes in how information is viewed and shared. Flows of information that challenge borders as well as social norms (Bilton 2013) in their creation and dissemination call into question many of the spaces and places taken for granted as stable and unchanging. Concepts such as borders, social boundaries, public spaces, private spaces, identities, and the notion of privacy, as well as plagiarism, are simultaneously under pressure as technology and the data it can carry are appropriated for a myriad of purposes.

These are but two of several changes that Internet technologies have facilitated in terms of where and why activities occur, the spaces and places they occur, and the spaces and places that are produced through Internet usage. Many people assume these trends are new but one should question an assumption that is trumpeted by marketers and "visionaries." For example, while the number of people working from home has changed, the idea of flexible, mobile working spaces has existed in previous eras, and has even been called into question by the CEO of an Internet company, whom you would expect to trumpet it (Goudreau 2012). When working from home for textile firms, piecemeal production was the norm in advance of the Industrial Revolution. Internet technologies have facilitated changes in the scale of spatially flexible work, meaning that where value is created in an information-based service economy is not limited to the office or the shop floor, but the free Wi-Fi coffee shop or the breakfast table bathed in a home network. This also reflects a change in the ability to extend control into other spaces and places. These examples underscore the flows of information and human responses to these flows. Much of that response is found in our conceptions of space and place, which are being altered through highly varied appropriations of the Internet. The remainder of this chapter addresses four themes. The first section provides an overview of the claims and intent behind the Internet with a specific focus on the realities and rhetoric that undergird its diffusion, including its uneven nature. The following section focuses on the constraints on Internet networks and the barriers to the diffusion and appropriation of the technologies. The third section explores how network infrastructure facilitates changes in spaces and places, and what social processes in technology use create the changing world we inhabit. The conclusion poses questions about methods for studying the new forms of space and place that geographers are concerned with, while suggesting that some things that are new should be firmly linked to earlier works. Taken in its entirety, this chapter argues that the Internet is indeed new and actors are using it to rework space and place in ways scholars and pundits are still grappling with, yet there are processes that constrain its usage and transformative potential, reflecting ties to older media experiences. These are processes that geographers are cognizant of and to which we bring a unique perspective to potential changes.

Rethinking the New and Recovering the Old: Tendencies of Internet Diffusion

Techno-optimists have articulated sweeping generalizations about the impacts of the Internet. Thinkers and political leaders envisioned a space of freedom and democratic action (Bremmer 2010), a public sphere where the various ideas of humanity could be debated and then implemented without the interference of states (see Barlow's Declaration of the Independence of Cyberspace 1996). Some ideals of the early Internet designers and users have been realized, but in other ways the technology has replicated the worst tendencies of individuals in terms of their interaction with ideas that challenge their own (Sunstein 2001; 2009), facilitating the development of spaces resembling echo chambers and information cocoons that undercut the possibilities of a robust public sphere where engagement across ideological lines is the norm. Additionally, those predicting the demise of authoritarian states did not foresee the development of state apparatuses aimed at monitoring and suppressing democratic activities online (Bremmer 2010; Wu 2010.)

One of the keys to the Internet is that it was designed as an open platform, capable of being changed by end users. As Zittrain (2008) described the possibility of user development, the Internet was designed to be a generative network, one open to growth through development of capacities by those who would add to it through an ethos of improving the system. A simple platform itself, the key was about connection.

> *From its start, the Internet was oriented differently from the proprietary networks and their ethos of bundling and control. Its goals were in some ways more modest. The point of building the networks was not to offer a particular set of information or services like news or weather to customers, for which the network was necessary but incidental. Rather, it was to connect anyone on the network to anyone else. It was up to the people connected to figure out why they wanted to be in touch in the first place; the network would simply carry data between the two points. (Zittrain 2008: 27)*

The Internet as a social space reflects the norms imbued in the technology by its designers; the network was designed to connect and serve as a conduit for data. Centralized hubs, or spaces to control consumption of the services and content, were not envisioned, and in fact ran counter to the very advantage in flexibility that the Internet provided. Connection to users, wherever they were, was central to the Internet's function. How people interact with the network and the resultant space(s) is a function of the software chosen and used, which reflects individual needs for appropriating the technology. What is used is a function of locality, dominant culture and norms, availability, and the diffusion of skills, among other variables that vary spatially. This is the stage where actual Internet usage and capabilities are determined and reworked. Software packages and platforms are open to appropriation in ways that the designers never intended. Real people, embedded in real places, use a variety of communication technologies, not just the Internet, to reproduce the places they live in and import characteristics of other places if they so choose. When we consider the global pattern of these processes, it is vital to consider that the relative location in the world system will influence these processes greatly, as well as what patterns the Internet is used to reinforce.

When one considers the geographies of economic and political power in terms of world systems analysis (Wallerstein 1979; Taylor 1992), the great advantage for core regions has been the ability for entities to shape and dominate global flows, thus exacerbating inequalities. It is no surprise that geographies of the Internet's networks reflect the accrued technological advantages that core states have enjoyed for several centuries. These advantages are only enhanced by each new wave of technological developments. With uneven development as part and parcel of capitalism, that the Internet's origins and the diffusion should reflect these patterns is unsurprising and is similar to previous rounds of communications developments. As several observers have noted (Castells 1996; Sassen 2006), the reinforcement of certain advantages is to be expected and core-periphery tensions exacerbated and heightened (see Florida 2005).

If the Internet enables the core at the global scale, it is also no surprise that the urban nature of the Internet network's backbone was predictable. Graham (1998) points out that the very institutions key to the development of cities and their character were expected to be present in electronic spaces as well as material spaces, partly due to processes and interactions that are resistant to substitution in an electronically mediated environment. The fact that cities are ranked in terms of Internet speed and connectivity underscores the point that the growth of cities is linked to the provision of Internet services that need material geographies while maximizing the extensibility of the people and firms using Internet technologies (Adams 1995). Internet technologies further enhance the advantages of urban areas in their command and control function and in general, have served to only accentuate the comparative advantages of cities in terms of their information infrastructure while simultaneously allowing for enhanced diffusion of lower-level economic activities through core-periphery relationships at a global scale (Hargittai 1998).

This unevenness in the diffusion of what is argued to be the fastest-spreading communications technology in history is a concern to many policymakers and scholars, who term this state of affairs the digital divide, or even more pointedly when noting the racial and ethnic imbalances, digital apartheid (Powell 1999: n.d.). The term *digital divide* has been subject to debate as scholars work to refine the concept and calculate its impact. Digital divides are often framed in terms of mere access to information technologies. If this were the case, then simple provision of hardware and services would close the divide. However, efforts to address perceived divides require greater sensitivity to context. Hargittai argues for a more nuanced understanding "of the 'digital divide' to include a discussion of different dimensions of the divide focusing on such details as quality of equipment, autonomy of use, the presence of social support networks, experience and online skill" (Hargittai 2003: n.p.).

The diffusion of the Internet from the core regions to the rest of the globe has been shown to be related to several variables such as relative wealth and levels of urbanization; even the level of English usage in a country served as a barrier (Warf 2007; 2009). These variables reinforce the notion that Internet diffusion has followed the relative position of a country in the world system. Perkins and Neumayer (2011) point out through their analysis of variables influencing the uptake of earlier technologies, such as income, educational levels, and measures of international trade, that the impact of material geographies on the diffusion of the Internet mirrors the diffusion patterns of other communication technologies, thus underlining the similarities in patterns. This is not to say that inequalities did not exist with other technologies but to acknowledge that more localized divides will likely persist as they have with previous communications technologies. Phone service is not universal nor is its quality. Cable television is not always available in rural areas and cell-phone diffusion is leading many to bypass the telephone landline in Africa (Worstall 2011). The diffusion of telecommunications technologies such as the Internet simply mirrors the paths of previous technologies in terms of network development, initial uses, and the material condition barriers their developers faced. This layering of another coat of advantage (access to information flows along with the presence of the social and material infrastructure to handle flows of bits) overlays extant economic geographies, adding even more protection to the urban core's privileged position.

However, despite this seeming urban bias, the Internet and the software used to access it were framed in a particular spatial discourse that reflected the ideas of moving into a new space that transcends physical distance. As with any new technology, the language used to describe the processes borrows from what humans know and can conceptualize, both enabling and constraining initial appropriation. The tropes and geographical metaphors used to explain the complexities of Internet activities oversimplify reality. It was no accident that the early Internet browsers employed the names of Netscape Navigator and Internet Explorer in regards to making use of "cyberspace," a trend that continues with Apple's Safari browser. The vocabulary that fueled the hype and hyperbole around the need to have access to the transformative powers of technology and the global world that was just beyond the screen, are just that, hype and hyperbole, and yet these rhetorics have power to them, specifically spatial metaphors such as "cyberspace," which is argued to have negative, unintended effects on societal conceptions of the Internet. Graham's survey of the situation in the mid-1990s, found that

> *Too often, then, the pervasive reliance on spatial and technological metaphors actually serves to obfuscate the complex relations between new communications and information technologies and space, place and society. In the simple, binary allegations that new technologies help us to access a new 'electronic space' or 'place', which somehow parallels the lived material spaces of human territoriality, little conscious thought is put to thinking conceptually about how new information technologies actually relate to the spaces and places bound up with human territorial life. (Graham 1998: 167)*

However, these simplistic conceptions of the Internet have impacted policymakers. As M. Graham (2011b) points out, perceptions of the need for a country to address disparities in access to the Internet and computers in general have generated many projects around the globe attempting to address the issue as promulgated by those with a stake in the digital divide's elimination. These efforts often articulate dire consequences for those unable to access technology, rightfully raising issues of social justice. M. Graham (2011a: 219) argues, "Those without access to the 'global village' are therefore seen to be segregated from the contemporary socio-economic revolution taking place." Whether this view is hyperbole is irrelevant in the face of increasing public pressure to provide access to technologies either through market-based solutions or the state; it is no longer a questionable point for policymakers concerned about digital divides in terms of class or apartheid between ethnicities. Several states, most notably South Korea and Estonia, have been particularly eager to promote the Internet as an economic development tool. The perception that a country or region is being left behind creates pressures to roll out technology access at multiple scales. Consider efforts to get low-cost computers into Africa such as the One Laptop per Child, WorldReader, and other efforts to reuse secondhand computers (www.appropedia.org 2013). Driven by the idea that Internet access is the key to addressing education and economic development gaps, these efforts run into the very cultural, educational, and economic constraints highlighted earlier. Despite these difficulties, technocrats still envision space and place as eminently connectable and yet do not directly address the underlying causes of the social distances they wish to bridge. This view is not unique to the Internet as hyperbolic claims were made about the telephone, and while change was facilitated, it was not utopian. Even in core regions, gaps between rural and urban usage of the Internet persist despite the diffusion of the technology. As Malecki (2003) demonstrates, the rural development literature is too optimistic and there are clear barriers to the Internet being the driver of rural growth. Thus, the diffusion of the Internet may be considered to closely mirror the rollout of previous telecommunications technologies. However, as will be explored in the next section, the networks produced function in ways not always appreciated by users, with reworkings of space and place that are not always clear.

The Limitations of Networks and Their Impacts on Space and Place

The size and scope of networks matter in all communication technologies, adding value to the seller of network services and the user in terms of potential reach with increasing size. Observers of cloud computing imply that the cloud is everywhere, and yet bracket out the immense infrastructure necessary to access the cloud "everywhere." As Kitchin and Dodge phrase it, the infrastructures that support the Internet are "taken for granted because, unlike roads or railways, they are often invisible – buried underground, snaking across ocean floors, hidden inside wall conduits, or floating unseen in orbit above us" (Dodge and Kitchin 2001: 10). This invisibility fuels the rhetoric of being connected at all times through various Wi-Fi and cellular data networks, perhaps giving some credence to the idea, and yet the infrastructure supporting constant connection is quite mappable. Access is certainly mappable as cell-phone and data providers show the areas they cover, ensuring the map has few gaps and yet never showing how the coverage is actually achieved. Thus, the idea of being potentially connected constantly *and* globally has fueled powerful metaphors that are the flip side of the digital divide debates.

However, each communications technology has specific limits in enabling the reworking of space. Space-biased communication technologies (those that facilitate the extension of information over space), Innis (1950) argued, annihilated space and rendered it less of a barrier to trade, commerce, and the diffusion of ideas and innovations, whereas time-biased communications were firmly rooted in the era and in the locale. He considered technologies such as clay tablets and speech as seen in an oral culture as time-biased (those technologies that facilitated the development of social hierarchies in societies based on tradition and were relatively localized). The adoption of space-biased communication (relatively light and easily transported writings on paper, dashes and dots tapped out on the telegraph, and voice via the phone) facilitated rapid changes in the size of territory that could be managed through enhanced communication speeds, thus effectively annihilating time, and expanding space from the perspective of those seeking greater reach (Massey 2005: 91).

The Internet is clearly a space-biased medium enabling users to experience near instantaneous communications in several forms, over great distances. Developments in Internet networks have facilitated changed expectations of its users. Today the expectations of rapid downloads, seamless Skype calls, and the smooth operation of streaming feeds that link places in terms of bandwidth (a form of relative location) have reworked what is possible in terms of command, control, interaction, and by extension, the ways in which space and place could be conceived.

One example stands out from the early days of the mass diffusion of the Internet. IBM launched an advertising campaign in 1997 invoking the hype over the Internet. The scene shows one man pointing to a newspaper, "Says here, 'the Internet is the future of business'.... We have to be on the Internet." When his junior colleague asks, "Why?" the senior executive replies, "Doesn't say." The end of the advertisement displays the IBM logo with the tagline, "Solutions for a small planet" (International Business Machines 1997). Rooted in the idea of Internet access as a necessity, IBM's services would allow a firm to become capable of exploiting the small planet. The metaphors that decry the digital divide support the idea that the Internet is the new normal and one must be on it, lest economic consequences occur if one is not. The ad also articulates the idea of time-space compression as applied to the entire planet, shrinking it to a manageable size.

Despite the various claims about the transformative powers of Internet technology, perhaps the one thing that is argued that makes it unique when compared to previous communication technologies is that unlike any other space-annihilating technology, the potential to create a "flat world" celebrated by pundits like Thomas Friedman (2005), if rolled out universally, is quite possible in theory. The flat world metaphor stands for enhanced creative and economic connections between people based on their skills, interests, and talents, essentially a level playing field unhindered by the friction of distance. Removing this barrier of distance to economic activity is seen as a positive, allowing for the fostering of global chains of innovation and as the IBM ad hinted at, the ability to exploit localized comparative advantages and reach expanded markets.

However, the idealized vision of the flat world runs counter to the history of communication technologies. As humanity adopts the technology, people will use it to do what the species has done with every other telecommunications technology of the past five centuries, deploy it to provide greater command, control, and coordination so that the world becomes flat for those in the centers of power (see Deibert 1997). However, it is the potential of the Internet to extend so much farther in ways that span the globe that make it unique in the eyes of many societal observers, especially the techno-optimists such as Friedman and Cairncross, the latter noting that "the death of distance" was upon the globe, for those who were connected (Cairncross 1997), and with good reason. Once a user paid for infrastructure and basic access (which varies in price spatially), users were not billed for the *distance* data packets traveled. A new flat-space in terms of data transfer costs was created. Various Internet pricing models emphasize the amount of data sent to a mobile device, others pay flat rates for generous data plans and most users of Wi-Fi at home and work never notice anything more than prices based on projected download and upload speeds. In this mode, distance does not matter in terms of cost.

However, this reduction of cost-distance as a barrier has facilitated changes in the spatial patterns of friendships for only a small minority of Internet users. Observers have demonstrated that the spatial patterns of social tie formation have not expanded with the adoption of new communication technologies. Despite the potential, most social ties remain relatively localized (Takhteyev et al. 2012; Mok et al. 2010), and like the telephone, Internet technologies are used primarily to reinforce localized social ties. Thus for most people, their flat world is a small plain they may know very well, surrounded by a ring of hills and even mountains, depending on where one lives and their technology access.

The ability to move files and the development of browsers that were capable of carrying multiple forms of content were a major breakthrough for the Internet's ability to uniquely facilitate transformations of space. Early versions of the Internet based on simple file swapping and perusing e-mails on monochromatic displays seem quaint today when the hardware norm is tablet devices and smartphones. The development of capabilities to handle video and sound through MPEG formats, pictures with JPEG compression algorithms, and even the development of animated GIFs and JAVA, combined with technical developments and infrastructure upgrades that increased bandwidth, allow the potential richness of the medium to be fully utilized. Some will argue that the Internet simply allowed various media to be aggregated into one site of consumption, which would be correct. However, the medium is important, and one does not have to resort to a McLuhanesque aphorism such as the "medium is the message" to see that the distribution potential for a broader spectrum of media was reconfigured in a way not seen before. The Internet and the increasing capacity of the network allowed for representations of places to change in the geographies of their creation and distribution. Challenges to official representations and broader diffusion of "authoritative" worldviews are increasingly possible, though not on an even playing field, as efforts to rein in information flows are common across the globe. Government efforts to censor Internet flows are well known (Warf 2011) and include states such as China, Saudi Arabia, and Iran, but also include lesser-known examples such as Vietnam, Pakistan, Russia, and Belarus.

As with previous communication technologies, the tension between the control of information and data and the ability to resist those efforts creates very different spaces, particularly those facilitating resistance. As Castells (1999) points out, if domination exists, resistance to the dominators is also present, and the communication media of the era will be deployed in such efforts (see Deibert 1997 for the impact of the printing press on the Roman Catholic Church's power). However, with Internet technologies the scope and scales are different. Qualitatively, the sources of resistance are different with the Internet facilitating broader aggregate potential for resistance to specific geographies, with networks linking across the globe in specific nodes. Quantitatively, the potential number of people participating is higher as well. These latter aspects of the Internet, with their tremendous potential reach and the ability to be multimedia in nature, stand out in unique ways. This technology facilitated the exploitation of several facets of the medium. The use of the Internet to facilitate resistance to powerful movements is readily chronicled in various literatures (e.g. Ho et al. 2002; Aouragh 2008; Pal and Dutta 2012). The specific ability to expand the scale of protest is demonstrated in studies of the Zapatista movement (Froehling 1997) and deployed to place political pressure on governments to free political prisoners (de Socio 2010).

This section has asked the reader to consider the Internet's potential for facilitating networks. However, what is unique is the potential capabilities. Efforts to roll out the Internet by states and firms are underway with the convergence of technologies and declining costs of bandwidth and infrastructure facilitating connections that the telegraph and telephone could not deliver.

This section has asked the reader to consider the Internet's potential for facilitating the development of networks across space. It is clear that barriers have been removed and these developments exploited for several causes. However, the majority of Internet usage often reinforces more localized social ties and concentrates power in places that have dominated historically due to previous dominance of transportation and communication technologies. The next section moves to considering the processes and resulting characteristics of potential spaces and places fostered by users of the Internet, particularly the idea of augmented realities shaped by our usage of the Internet and the process of mediatization of our worlds.

Making the Internet's Spaces and Places

> *Without a thorough and critical consideration of space and place, and how new information technologies relate to, and are embedded in them, reflections on cyberspace, and the economic, social and cultural dynamics of the shift to growing 'telemediation', seem likely to be reductionist, deterministic, oversimplistic and stale. (Graham 1998: 167)*

The importance of space and place in networks is underscored by an advertising campaign for London's Heathrow Airport, owned by BAA Limited. As seen in Figure 8.1, one notes a poster displaying a map of connections to Heathrow Airport that then connect to other nodes or places. The value of the air network, as with any network, is in the number of potential connections. However, in asking for the British government to pour resources into Heathrow Airport, the campaign argues that if certain place-specific characteristics are not invested in, the role and the importance (with the attendant impacts upon the British economy) of Heathrow as a node will decline (www.hub.heathrowairport.com 2012). In trying to enhance the connections by improving the ability to connect to the air network through a particular node, BAA's effort remakes place in order to make the purported

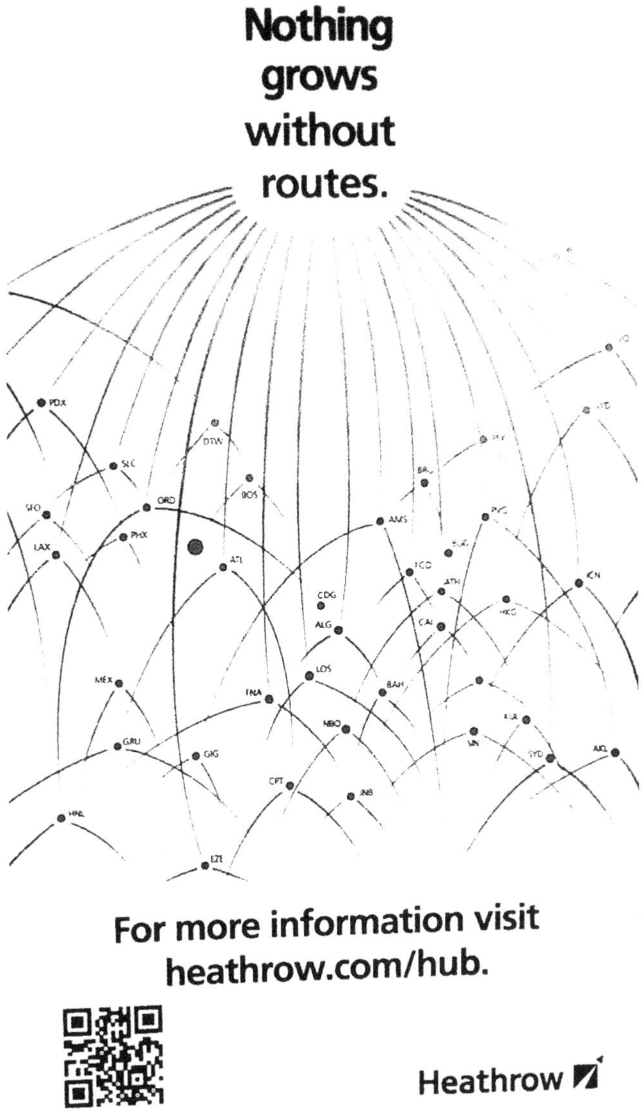

Figure 8.1 Network lobbying at Heathrow International Airport, May 2012
Source: Image provided by the author.

annihilation of space that much easier, but only for those on, or in close proximity to, the network. Plans to add a runway (which was subsequently rejected), the improvement of train lines to the airport, and the renovation of terminals are intended to enhance Heathrow's attractiveness as a global airline hub. Reducing the barriers to entering the air network through this particular node aims to recreate Heathrow as a special place, providing fliers a range of comparative advantages. However, it is not one singular place, but the product of multiple spaces and places (with their own unique local characteristics) that coalesce in Heathrow. The value of Heathrow is a function of the ease of extensibility for the air traveler through this particular node.

The same applies to those using the Internet network to achieve specific goals, be it economic development, political mobilization, the attraction of hipsters to coffee shops, or the maintenance of family connections. Spaces and places are reworked by those who argue that networks must be developed, which of course changes their relative position and even the positionality of those using Internet technology, and by those users who appropriate Internet-based technologies to achieve their own goals.

The relatively rapid growth of the Internet gave rise to rhetorical concepts such as the death of distance (Cairncross 1997) and flat world (Friedman 2005) to describe changes facilitated by communication technologies. These now permeate many aspects of modern life, in particular, the rhetoric of governments and firms positioned to exploit the advantages that accrue to these entities with the capability to compete in global markets. Other popular pundits argue conversely that the world is still "spiky" (Florida 2005) and resistant to the evening out of inequality, highlighting that urban areas continue to dominate economic flows and are increasingly important nodes in the networks.

These views are rooted in the overarching idea of globalization that can be seen as the penetration of networks into new spaces and places. For Cairncross and Friedman, the evening out of differences and the connections across space are to be celebrated while Florida argues that the same processes produce concentrations of talent, innovation, and capital that reinforce existing geographies (but note, the attraction of capital and talent occurs at a global scale). All three share the view that as Internet technologies diffuse, the globalization of the planet is inevitable, despite their very different conclusions as to the impacts.

Optimists about the Internet argued that technology would remove the idea of space as a barrier. Geography, conceptualized as a "burden" to be overcome, was presented as a limiting variable and prevented the development of networks that would enable people to rise above the factors of local context (see Robins 1997). Yet the efforts highlighted in the first section of remaking space underscores a geographer's view that space is not a burden but a set of possibilities fostered by relative connection to other spaces and places. Perhaps a trite example is the plethora of Internet memes exploding across areas of well-networked continents, consumed in places that see greater usage of English or sharing some aspects of culture that allows the memes to resonate (the ubiquitous memes involving kittens comes to mind), while creating a common space globally for understanding and comprehending a particular meme.

The spaces and places that are produced via the Internet are multiple. At one level, the potential of colliding cultures, as in the meme example, gives credence to McLuhan's global village in which new knowledge is exchanged and the potential for convergence is present. McLuhan discussed the issue of tribalism, the idea that news events from around the globe would diffuse and serve to unify as a common experience. What he did not foresee was the idea of building the walls that would enable tribalism at smaller scales in response to the challenges global flows of data might generate. Today there is very little global about most digital networks at a personal scale. What the Internet has allowed individuals to do is digitally cordon themselves off from opposing perspectives and facilitate a preference for echo chambers replete with Web sites and data flows that never call into question one's worldviews (Sunstein 2009).

Internet technologies' capabilities, in theory, allow individuals to filter out the multiplicities in our world, thereby privileging interaction with those nodes on a social network that agree with the user. As Massey points out in setting up her critique of this form of thinking, if one wishes, the reworking of social interactions begins to privilege the distant "sites" that reinforce positions and allow a challenge to the notion that spatial proximity is the basis of how individuals prioritize their relationships and commitments, with declining salience to their lives with increasing distance (Massey 2005: 95).

However, the idea that one can create their own, virtual, gated communities via the Internet, no matter how beguiling for liberals and conservatives alike, is a pipedream. The idea of creating a purified space, devoid of the previously distant and culturally and politically challenging, simply cannot exist. Massey argues that

> *"space" won't allow you to do it. Space can never be definitively purified. If space is the sphere of multiplicity, the product of social relations, and the relations are real material practices, and always ongoing, then space can never be closed, there will always be loose ends, always relations with the beyond, always potential elements of chance. (Massey 2005: 95)*

Thus, the Internet does not set up technological borders impervious to global flows, but allows for the best of all possibilities: the multiplicities become mashups on one's Facebook feed, memes are shared that reflect the global collision of cultures and connections reforged to schoolmates who are completely opposite to you in political leanings. The spaces produced are multiple within one's mind as the flows of data are processed. The multiplicities we interact with define us as multiple as well, allowing online personas to exist that reflect our interests, passions, and beliefs with differences being highlighted by the Internet forum we contribute to.

The discussion above yields a question, that if spaces that are Internet connected allow individuals to experience space in many of its multiplicities, what about places, the sites for our actions? Transformed by the pervasiveness of Internet technology, one can refer the changes in our places as an augmented reality (Graham et al. 2013), one that realizes the extensibility of many authors to influence perceptions of place. As with Massey, the idea is the meshing of the multiple. Graham et al. use the term *augmented realities* "in reference to the indeterminate, unstable, context dependent and multiple reality brought to into being through the subjective coming together in time and space of material and virtual experience" (2013: 2). Such augmentation of reality depends on the role maps play in our lives and the politics of code. Augmented reality is argued at its most basic to be nothing new, as people have used geographic data in the past in many forms. Two older, analog examples of augmented reality stand out. First, the use of road maps that privilege the role of automobiles over pedestrian or bicycle routes is well known for older readers. Secondly, the ubiquitous travel guides that normatively define what tourist should see and steer them toward specific sites, hotels, and restaurants clearly framed experiences. However, current Internet technologies offer the means to qualitatively and quantitatively intensify and shape the forms of information we draw upon to understand the places that we inhabit and navigate. Trends such as mobile Internet usage, the expansion of the author pool for Web content about places, and the role of the geospatial Web reliant on volunteered, crowd-sourced, geocoded data have transformed the capabilities of multiple people to define place, and for individuals to navigate and grapple with the competing meanings, or more precisely, find ways to deal with the information that is coming to their screens. What do these new realities look like? They arrive as apps for smartphones that provide local information about restaurants (and reviews), Flicker photos of famous sites that demonstrate the sharing party's framing of the site, and Panoramio photo layers on Google Earth's virtual globe. Issues such as the distribution of the power to create content (highly uneven globally), the power to communicate across languages and cultures (to disseminate and even defend what one creates and makes available), the oft-invisible role of various code that shapes the flows of data we consume, and the power of images to be stripped of their time context; all contribute to formations of places that are based on multiple geographic content and the various codes used to present them, connecting the multiplicities of space.

One issue raised above is the issue of interactivity through the mobile Web. Adams and Jansson (2012: 303) remark that interactivity allows the replacement of "fixed and predefined texts" with dynamic relationships as texts "move" from platform to platform. Additionally, as with Graham et al. (2013), time is also a key concern, but for different reasons. It is the interactivity that challenges the stability of any text. Web sites, blogs, and social media interfaces are being added to, deleted, and edited by a myriad of users. Internet-based texts are malleable and open to reworking, and these texts may address the same place but be totally different in their approach and tone, based on the geographic perspective of the authors (See Graham et al. 2013: 9–12).

Mobility in combination with mediatization (Hjarvard 2008) has also changed our perceptions of space and place. The increasing dependence on media in daily life reflects a duality, with mediatization reflecting the increased integration into the operations of social institutions as well as being treated as "social institutions in their own right" (Hjarvard 2008: 113). For example, analysis of mediatization of tourism (Jansson 2002) highlights the perceived need to share immediately, the changing expectations of tourists, and their social networks when on holiday. The ability to challenge official tourism representations and shape the experiences of other tourists, and by extension, potential tourists, creates multiplicities that are at first glance, equally powerful if one naively considers the Internet a neutral conduit.

Regardless of the type of text or its relative ephemerality, the context of consumption is vital to consider as well. The well-known aphorism, the medium is the message, is perhaps cliché, but does the medium make a difference if it is a smartphone, a tablet device, a laptop, or a desktop? One should conclude yes, as the proliferation of media devices that are increasingly incorporated into daily life have facilitated reworking of space and place. Adams and Jansson (2012: 303) highlight this technological convergence, arguing that the relationship between media fundamentally changes when devices can carry multiple media (albeit in forms congruent with the platform's limitations). Further, it is argued that convergence via Web 2.0 allows for problematization of the author-text relationship, opening these processes up to the public. This represents the active incorporation of the multiplicities of spaces and places, the contexts of content creation. However, this is not the only change. Interactivity produces texts of ephemeral nature (as Wikipedia's rules on editing demonstrate), a facet that is promoted on many news sites, blogs, and of course social networking sites that encourage the sharing of views and opinions.

What does increased mediatization mean for space and place? One must consider that despite the ephemerality of various texts due to increased ability to author in a shared manner, the increasing use of new social network technologies have provided affordances that have an impact on communication between individuals, such as persistence through archiving and recording of information, replicability through the cutting and pasting of content or the design of digital architecture designed to facilitate sharing, scalability through the mass distribution of content across various social barriers (borders as but one example) and searchability through various archives and search engines (Boyd 2011). This view of social media, which underpins much of what is reviewed in this section, does not undercut the idea of ephemerality of texts. Space and places will remain unstable and open to contestation as authors vie for the power to edit and be authoritative in defining space and place and challenge hegemonic representations of both. However, the structure of social networking platforms will mean that the works of multiple authors will live on in all likelihood, stored and accessible for years to come, serving as a resource for future contestations. The next section explores the ramifications of these spaces and places on how the Internet and the social changes it facilitates will be studied.

How Will We Come to Know These Spaces Going Forward?

If, as argued above, there are unique, qualitative differences in the way that the Internet helps to shape place and space that reproduce extant power relationships while simultaneously providing some measure of hope for mounting a challenge, the issue for scholars will be in how to conceptualize space and place in digital form. We have seen the reproduction of advantages accrued to those in the global core, mostly exercised by global elites (though with over 2.4 billion Internet users in 2012, the continued diffusion of the Internet may obviate the issue for the most part [Internet World Stats 2013]). We have seen efforts to challenge state monopolies over media communication and state claims to "Internet Sovereignty" (Wu 2010: 182) that have had varying success most recently in states such as Algeria, Egypt, and Libya during the mediatized Arab Spring. Additionally, the efforts of Edward Snowden to pull back the curtain on the US National Security Agency's efforts to monitor digital communications remind us that the power of the state to create, monitor, and even shut down these platforms has not disappeared. Barlow's declaration was clearly ignored (*Guardian* 2013: www.theguardian.com/world/the-nsa-files).

Yet much of what we study are heightened versions of old media processes. The difference that makes the Internet unique is the capacity for network creation due to declining costs that may bridge multiple divides in media consumption. Additionally, the similar declines in cost of access also portend declining costs of production. The power of an aggregator such as the Drudge Report, or any influential blogger, and efforts by mainstream media to encourage citizen journalists to contribute to content underscores the potential for shifts in power to author and comment. The spaces and places produced through these processes will confound our methods. How do we map these multiplicities? Are current maps and conceptions of space adequate? Data at what constructed scale? Will scale even matter in studies of the texts and networks of communication (see Marston et al. 2005)? The shifting landscape of social media and other forms of digital text creation, a terrain made further unstable by media convergence, presents major challenges to scholars. Wider appropriation of the Internet has facilitated changes in what media geography scholars focus upon, as well as the epistemological concerns that arise. The scraping of a Twitter feed is not a survey of a representative sample, the scraping of a Facebook page is not equal to a focus group, and the positionality issues involved in a Skype interview are myriad, yet all are deployed by scholars seeking to understand and map mediatized processes. The future will mean taking on methods resembling marketing research and present ethical quandaries in terms of protecting human subjects (issues most institutional review boards are underprepared to address). The challenges of how we will come to understand the mediatized processes of space and place in the future is not quite old wine in new bottles, but the grapes used harken back to older vintages of scholarship, producing new flavors in the hands of vintners with new techniques.

References

Adams, P. 1995. A reconsideration of personal boundaries in space-time. *Annals of the Association of American Geographers* 85 (2): 267–85.

Adams, P. and A. Jansson. 2012. Communication geography: A bridge between disciplines. *Communication Theory* 22 (3): 299–318.

Aouragh, M. 2008. Everyday resistance on the Internet: The Palestinian context. *Journal of Arab and Muslim Media Research* 1(2): 109–30, doi: 10.1386/jammr.1.2.109/1.

Appropedia.org. n.d. Low cost computer guide [Online]. www.appropedia.org/Low_cost_computer_guide [accessed January 26, 2013].

Bailey, J. 2008a. The Obama plagiarism scandal. *Plagiarism Today* [Online]. Available at: www.plagiarismtoday.com/2008/02/20/the-obama-plagiarism-scandal/ [accessed January 20, 2013].

Bailey, J. 2008b. The McCain plagiarism scandal. *Plagiarism Today* [Online]. Available at: www.plagiarismtoday.com/2008/08/13/the-mccain-plagiarism-scandal/ [accessed 20 January 2013].

Barlow, J.P. 1996. *A Declaration of the Independence of Cyberspace* [Online February 8]. Available at: www.projects.eff.org/~barlow/Declaration-Final.html [accessed May 27, 2012].

Bilton, N. 2013. At Google conference, cameras even in the bathroom [Online 17 May]. Available at: www.bits.blogs.nytimes.com/2013/05/17/at-google-conference-even-cameras-in-the-bathroom/ [accessed May 19, 2013].

Boyd, D. 2011. Social network sites as networked publics: Affordances, dynamics and implications. In *A Networked Self: Identity, Community, and Culture on Social Network Sites*. Edited by Z. Papacharissi. New York and London: Routledge, 39–58.

Bremmer, I. 2010. Democracy in cyberspace: What information technology can and cannot do. *Foreign Affairs* [Online]. November/December. Available at: www.foreignaffairs.com/articles/66803/ian-bremmer/democracy-in-cyberspace [accessed January 5, 2013].

Cairncross, F. 1997. *The Death of Distance: How the Communication Revolution Will Change Our Lives*. London: Orion Publishing Group Limited.

Castells, M. 1996. *The Rise of the Network Society*. Cambridge, MA: Blackwell.

Castells, M. 1999. Grassrooting the space of flows. *Urban Geography* 20(4): 294–302.

Champion, A. 2012. Comment on Facebook post [Online]. Available at: www.facebook.com/profpurcell, May 24, 2012 [accessed May 26, 2012].

Croft, J.B. 2012. Comment on Facebook post [Online]. Available at: www.facebook.com/profpurcell, May 24, 2012 [accessed May 26, 2012].

De Socio, M. 2010. Geographers mobilize: A network-diffusion analysis of the campaign to free Ghazi-Walid Falah. *Antipode* 42(2): 310–35.

Deibert, R. 1997. *Parchment, Printing and Hypermedia: Communication in World Order Transformation*. New York: Columbia University Press.

Dodge, M. and R. Kitchin. 2001. *Atlas of Cyberspace*. Harlow, UK: Addison-Wesley.

Florida, R. 2005. The world is spiky: Globalization has changed the economic playing field, but hasn't leveled it. *Atlantic* 296(3): 48–51.

Friedman, T. 2005. *The World Is Flat: A Brief History of the Twenty-First Century*. New York: Farrar, Straus, and Giroux.

Froehling, O. 1997. The cyberspace "war of ink and Internet" in Chiapas, Mexico. *Geographical Review* 87(2): 291–307.

Goudreau, J. 2013. Back to the Stone Age? New Yahoo CEO Marissa Mayer bans working from home [Online]. www.forbes.com/sites/jennagoudreau/2013/02/25/back-to-the-stone-age-new-yahoo-ceo-marissa-mayer-bans-working-from-home/ [accessed July 27, 2013].

Graham, M. 2011a. Time machines and virtual portals: The spatialities of the digital divide. *Progress in Development Studies* 11(3): 211–27.

Graham, M. 2011b. Cyberspace [Online]. Available at: www.zerogeography.net/2011/11/cyberspace.html [accessed July 27, 2013].

Graham, M., M. Zook, and A. Boulton. 2013. Augmented reality in urban places: Contested content and the duplicity of code. *Transactions of the Institute of British Geographers* 38(3): 464–79.

Graham, S. 1998. The end of geography of the explosion of place? Conceptualizing space, place and information technology. *Progress in Human Geography* 22(2): 165–85.

The Guardian (n.d). The NSA Files [Online]. Available at: www.guardian.co.uk/world/the-nsa-files [accessed July 16, 2013].

Hargittai, E. 1998. Holes in the Net: The Internet and international stratification. Presentation at Internet Society, Geneva, Switzerland [Online]. Available at: www.isoc.org/inet98/proceedings/5d/5d_1.htm [accessed February 13, 2013].

Hargittai, E. 2003. The digital divide and what to do about it [Online].Available at: www.eszter.com/research/pubs/hargittai-digitaldivide.pdf [accessed October 12, 2012].

Haughny, C. 2012. CNN and Time suspend journalist after admission of plagiarism [Online]. Available at: www.mediadecoder.blogs.nytimes.com/2012/08/10/time-magazine-to-examine-plagiarism-accusation-against-zakaria/ [accessed May 19, 2013].

Hjarvard, S. 2008. The mediatization of society: A theory of the media as agents of social and cultural change. *Nordicom Review* 29(2): 105–34.

Ho, K.C., Z. Baber, and H. Khondker. 2002. "Sites" of resistance: Alternative websites and state-society relations. *British Journal of Sociology* 53(1): 127–48.

Hub.Heathrowairport.com. 2012 [accessed 12 November 2012].

Innis, H.A. 1950. *Empire and Communications* [Online]. Available at: www.gutenberg.ca/ebooks/innis-empire/innis-empire-00-h.html [accessed February 1, 2013].

International Business Machines. 1997. Hype [Online]. Available at: www.youtube.com/watch?v=IvDCk3pY4qo [accessed July 27, 2013].

Internet World Stats. 2013. Internet users in the world, distribution by world regions – 2102 Q2 [Online]. Available at: www.Internetworldstats.com/stats.htm [accessed February 1, 2013].

Jansson, A. 2002. Spatial phantasmagoria: The mediatization of tourism experience. *European Journal of Communication* 17(4): 429–43.

Malecki, E.J. 2003. Digital development in rural areas: Potentials and pitfalls. *Journal of Rural Studies* 19(2): 201–14.

Marston, S.A., J.P. Jones III, and K. Woodward. 2005. Human geography without scale. *Transactions of the Institute of British Geographers* 30(4): 416–32.

Massey, D. 2005. *For Space*. London: SAGE.

Mok, D., B. Wellman, and J. Carrasco. 2010. Does distance matter in the age of the Internet? *Urban Studies* 47(13): 2747–83.

Pal, M. and M.J. Dutta. 2012. Organizing resistance on the Internet: The case of the international campaign for justice in Bhopal. *Communication, Culture & Critique* 5(2): 230–51.

Perkins, R. and E. Neumayer. 2011. Is the Internet really new after all? The determinants of telecommunications diffusion in historical perspective. *Professional Geographer* 63(1): 55–72

Powell, C. n.d. A special message from General Colin L. Powell, U.S.A. (ret.) [Online]. Available at: www.businessweek.com/adsections/digital/powell.htm [accessed July 27, 2013].

Powell, C. 1999. Powell encourages students [Online]. Available at: www.vanderbilt.edu/News/register/Mar15_99/powell.htm [accessed January 20, 2013].

Robins, K. 1997. The new communications geography and the politics of optimism. *Soundings* 5: 191–202.

Sassen, S. 2006. Electronic networks, power, and democracy. *Tailoring Biotechnologies* 2(2): 21–48.

Sunstein, C.R. 2001. *Republic.com*. Princeton, NJ: Princeton University Press.

Sunstein, C.R. 2009. *Republic.com 2.0*. Princeton, NJ: Princeton University Press.

Takhteyev, Y., A. Gruzd, and B. Wellman. 2012. Geography of Twitter networks. *Social Networks* 34(1): 73–81.

Taylor, P.J. 1992. Understanding global inequalities: A world systems approach. *Geography* 77(1): 10–21.

Warf, B. 2007. Geographies of the tropical Internet. *Singapore Journal of Tropical Geography* 28(2): 219–38.

Warf, B. 2009 . The rapidly evolving geographies of the Eurasian Internet. *Eurasian Geography and Economics* 50(5): 564–80.

Warf, B. 2011. Geographies of global Internet censorship. *GeoJournal* 76(1): 1–23.

Worstall, T. 2011. Africa might just skip the entire PC revolution. Forbes.com [Online]. www.forbes.com/sites/timworstall/2011/08/17/africa-might-just-skip-the-entire-pc-revolution/ [accessed October 20, 2012].

Wu, T. 2010. Is Internet exceptionalism dead? In *The Next Digital Decade – Essays on the Future of the Internet*. Edited by B. Szoka and A. Marcus, 179–88. Washington, DC: TechFreedom [Online]. Available at: www.ssrn.com/abstract=1752415 [accessed February 1, 2013].

Zittrain, J. 2008. *The Future of the Internet and How to Stop It*. New Haven, CT, and London: Yale University Press.

PART II
Places

Places of Mediated Nature

David Lulka

Befitting the times, I want to begin this consideration of nature media by utilizing a specific technology – namely, Google's Ngram Viewer. This technology allows one to chart the prevalence of particular words or phrases published in books over the last few hundred years. Thus, for example, from 1750–2008, it can be seen that the notion of "pestilence" had its heyday before 1900, whereas "pollution" only garnered a moderate presence until it spiked in the late 1960s and rebounded once again in the 1990s (Figure 9.1). Or, it is possible to observe that discussion of "wilderness" peaked in the mid-1800s before its representation gradually declined amid other modern concerns. In the meantime, the idea of "sustainability" emerged in the 1980s as a powerful dogma, its presence eventually statistically eclipsing that of wilderness. With these examples in mind, the main goal of this chapter is to reconsider the cause of these changes: in short, does narrative play a determinate role or do nonhuman forces also have a substantial impact?

The texts quantified by Google's Ngrams, of course, have a variable relation to the public, as many of them were (and are) read in private spaces, a fact that conflicts with the notion of media as a public enterprise. Nonetheless, it must be recalled that Anderson (1991) referenced the printing press as one of the mechanisms that led to the development of an "imagined community" in the modern era. And so we see that modern public discourse immediately encounters nonhuman force. This slippage from the private to the public (via the middle ground of technology) is but one crease creating the historical change emphasized here. Adding another element, Dawkins (2009) refers to a "scripto-visual matrix," in which the words used to describe nature impact (and are influenced by) the visual imagery that accompanies those words. As Dunaway (2005) showed, this scripto-visual dynamic became politically and culturally influential in the Sierra Club's production of weighty coffee-table books. Dawkins's matrix, however, is unfortunately bounded by contemporaneity, image, and word being situated in the same time-space. That is unproblematic for some analyses, but to gather a properly transmutational view of nature media, it is necessary to elongate this matrix so that it extends (like Ngrams) over a lengthy period of time, a period that does not simply include the past and present but also looks to the future.

It is crucial to recall, despite the current dominance of television and cinematic media, that visual depictions of nature did not always predominate. As Neuzil and Kovarik (1996) show, during the early twentieth century, information about the environment and environmental risks were largely transmitted to the public through words published in newspapers, journals, and other texts. Over extended time, however, heterogeneous avenues of information formed, creating patterns of media coexistence and succession. And while popular conceptions of nature are now driven by cinematic images – a situation implied by Cracknell's (1993) reference to nature as "mediagenic" and Morey's (2009) identification of notable animals as "econs" – nature in the computer and Internet world is emerging.

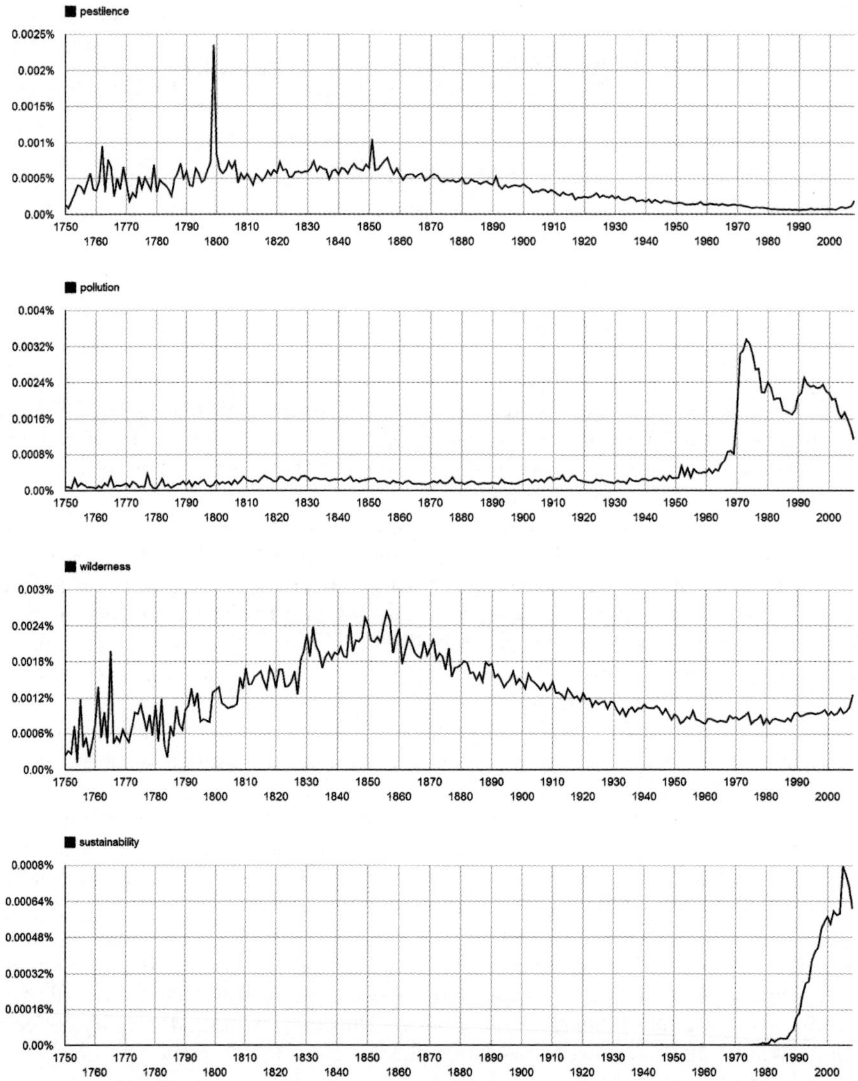

Figure 9.1 Historical prevalence of environmental terms as shown by Google Ngrams for *pestilence, pollution, wilderness, and sustainability*

Source: Google Inc.

Any compartmentalization of this trajectory is problematic, as it fosters discrete modes of analysis that obscure the evolving nature of media itself.

Thus, here, I approach media broadly, not so much to be comprehensive, but rather as a methodology designed to expose the limitations of current analyses. Specifically, and perhaps heretically, I seek to tame the behemoth that is narrative that is predominant in studies of film and television, a situation that Brereton (2005: 12) refers to as a "preoccupation with narratology." I do not so much deny narrative's import but rather contest the notion that narrative courses through technology undisturbed and that narrative somehow outpaces material events with a prescient foresight wholly opposed to the synchronicity of medium and message. My contention is that changing media formats, in and of themselves, can be informative about the place known as nature. In this kneecapping of narrative, I will further argue that nature itself plays a pivotal role in media productions, for it is also part of the medium.

Currently, the specter of narrative touches everything, even bringing the status of nature documentaries into question. Bousé (2000), in referencing Baudrillard and his articulation of simulacra, is unequivocal in saying that nature films, including those of the highest scientific stature, are not documentaries, but rather creations of narrative. In rejecting the reality of nature films, Bousé (2000: 19) seemingly naturalizes narrative, lending it a Promethean quality by stating, "In the recorded history of representation there is little evidence to suggest there was ever a time when the will to narrative was not present in some degree." In contrast, Cubitt (2005) offers an alternate perspective that does not nullify nature so resolutely. In examining the BBC nature film *The Blue Planet*, Cubitt addresses the romantic notion of the sublime and places it in contradistinction to narrative. For him, "Sexuality, like mortality is a temporal phenomenon, structured by the yes and the no. Always negotiated, it has its narratives, its direction through time, its goals and its regrets. But the sublime knows nothing of that, denies and annihilates it in the vast emptiness of obscene completion" (46). This incompatibility between the sublime (embodied in the faceless ocean and landscapes without knowable origin or end) and narrative may explain why the public's early fascination with wave movies passed, and why animals – who are born, have sex, and die – assumed a primary role in depictions of nature.

In the following two sections, I illustrate how narratives and critiques (mostly in the dominant film genre) distort distance between humans and the nonhuman, effectively erasing the middle ground of socionatural engagement and diminishing the avenues through which nature, and our conceptions of nature, change. This penchant for distorting distance is illustrated firstly through global visions of humanity's place on Earth, and then secondly (at a smaller scale) via reactions to romanticism, anthropomorphism, and ecoporn. As a corrective, the final section emphasizes technology and materiality to establish a means for breaking out of this narratological cul-de-sac and provide new ways of analyzing nature media. By virtue of their evolutionary propensities, these nonhuman forces mitigate the limiting effects of the narrative approach, an approach that has become largely prefigured through incessant schematization over the last few decades.

Global Distance – Home, Alienation, Extinction

A primary pattern narratives of nature exhibit is ambivalence regarding the relation between humans and the nonhuman world – namely, how they come together, if at all. The meaning attributed to NASA photographs, the work of Werner Herzog, and the prospect of human extinction exemplify this ambivalence. Respectively, they play with distance in divergent ways to express the proper or unavoidable ontological relation between humans and the world.

During the Apollo space missions of the late 1960s and early 1970s, NASA took photographs of Earth, most notably those entitled Earthrise (1968) and 22727 (1972). These images of the Blue Planet placed Earth within a context of seeming isolation, one in which Earth was portrayed as limited and fragile, yet necessary for human existence. As Cosgrove (1994) notes, the black gaps of space surrounding Earth placed humanity within a vulnerable unified context, one that impacted the culture and politics of the day, as this wholly contiguous imagery of Earth fed into and amplified the egalitarian ethos of that era, instigating the first Earth Day. Far from being forgotten, decades later these exact images resurfaced in *An Inconvenient Truth*, a film about global warming. Indeed, near the end, the film amplifies this imagery by using a more distant image of the planet to heighten perceptions of Earth's precarious environment. Paradoxically, the tangible distance displayed in these NASA images fostered the conception of Earth as home. In the wider cosmos, it is *the* place of humanity. The insertion of Al Gore's personal biography into the film's narrative accentuated this underlying theme (Minster 2010). Unfortunately, the holistic message of NASA photographs and Gore's film subsumes many of the material antagonisms that typify earthly life, and thus obscure the realities produced in the middle ground of existence.

In contrast, the works of Werner Herzog, far from portraying Earth as home, instantiate a chasm between humanity and the planet. As with NASA photographs, Herzog's films provide a unifying humanistic framework, but it is one with a much darker mood grounded in phenomenological perceptions of existential separation (Ames 2009). *Fata Morgana* – which was filmed, fittingly, in 1969 (the era of the Apollo program and Earth Day's origin) – was initially intended to be a science-fiction film representing Earth as it might look to extraterrestrials. Herzog's narrative plan failed, but what remnants remained comprised a flatly depicted film of vistas, creatures, and rusted machinery, conveying the strange nature of earthly existence. Thus, Prager (2007: 83–84) states,

> *[Herzog] says that these images should not resemble images that one would find on the Discovery Channel ...; the sequence is only supposed to wash over the viewer, making the same strange and sensual impression that it would on a visitor from outer space who is seeing Earth for the first time, one who has no categories with which to comprehend the colours and shapes of the planet.*

Vogel (1986: 45) appropriately described its landscape as a "shimmering opacity," something, I would suggest, which fascinates but remains (for humans as much as extraterrestrials) utterly unbridgeable. The result is a sense of Earth that is "amoral" (Peucker 1984: 181) or "indifferent" (Prager 2010). As with Gore, for Herzog Earth generates intense interest that speaks to humanism, yet it is not home. Contra NASA images, Herzog's close examination of Earth's substance only generates alienated distance.

Lodged somewhere between Gore's and Herzog's narratives are a spate of recent productions that imagine the extinction of humanity. As Jendrysik (2011) notes, these productions present a twist on utopian visions, one in which we are "consoled" by the persistence of nature in spite of humanity's rapaciousness. Garrard (2012) refers to this imagined disappearance as "disanthropy," whereby humanity is extracted from the planet that was formerly its home. Distance is not the result of perception, but rather the literal demise of the species. Fostered by apocalyptic visions (which are ignored here because they are derivative of holistic representations), these portrayals of extinction enact a curious mixture of longing and alienation. Ultimately, they suggest the middle ground of material relations has no place for humanity, and thus humanity is doomed to be cast out.

Narrative, Oscillating Distance, and the Middle Ground

These pancultural narratives – alternately of earthly inclusion and exclusion – provide a context for examining smaller articulations of nature and humanity's place within it. Here, the concepts of romanticism, anthropomorphism, and ecoporn are used to exhibit our tendency to navigate – as above, in a wildly oscillatory fashion – between creaturely communion and nonhuman difference. These oscillations exhibit society's inability (or unwillingness) to accede to our messy entanglement with nature, wherein human-nonhuman similarity and difference coexist. Instead of grasping the middle ground that romanticism, anthropomorphism, and ecoporn offer, narratives and critiques launch these notions back and forth like a shuttlecock, purifying relations by erasing difference – spatially and corporeally – or transforming it into an insuperable abyss.

Romanticism, perhaps the most pervasive yet contentious influence on nature imagery, emerged amid the confluence of the Enlightenment and the Industrial Revolution, when exploration, rationalization, and mechanization simultaneously generated awe and detachment (Holmes 2008). Thus, the romantic era arose when disparate materialities – in the "wilderness" of distant colonial spaces and the museums and laboratories of Europe – were coming together. In their response, some romantics unduly subsumed materiality underneath symbolism, yet material heterogeneity (encapsulating human and nonhuman) was a fundamental prerequisite for romantic productions. Indeed, this heterogeneity explains romanticism's riven quality, wherein romantics simultaneously expressed a desire to commune with nature and (in a manner more nostalgic and less bitter than Herzog) a fundamental inability to achieve that union. Distance oscillated – the human extended outward and retracted.

Undoubtedly, romanticism is problematic because it commonly evacuates humanity from the landscapes it depicts. Not unlike the vast spaces exhibited in NASA photographs, geographic scale is important in romantic renderings, as the desire for reunification is manifest in the grandness of nature and the smallness (perhaps absence) of humanity. Yet the critique of romanticism has created its own distortions. Critiques of romanticism typically emphasize the role of class, gender, and race in the manufacture of pristine images, essentially condemning romantic portrayals as illicit consequences of social power. Berila's (2010) examination of *A River Runs Through It* and *The Horse Whisperer* exhibits this penchant in averring these films' privileging of white masculinity. While partly valid, these sociological approaches, being grounded in narrative analysis, essentially erase the materiality that was always necessary for romanticism. Ironically, the rejected symbolism of romanticism is only replaced by another set of categorizations. In substituting the social for the subjective, the pendulum of insight does not so much swing away from humanity as it finds a new place to settle upon it. In such analyses, no reintegration, no middle ground between the human and nonhuman, is established. Conversely, Hamilton (1999: 23) suggests an alternate response to romanticism, stating "postmodernist interpretations of the Romantic sublime allow it to include a sheer particularity usually thought to be inimical to its symbolic discourse."

Romanticism, I would argue, looks quite different if we take our lead from new schools of thought that focus on affect. From this perspective, the notion of the sublime is not a cultural mirage, but instead a bodily disposition that need be acknowledged. If MacDonald (2001: 7) is not entirely correct in saying that our reliance upon plot has made us "virtually blind to imagery," narrative techniques have nonetheless allowed us to run roughshod over the material realities that constitute and disturb daily life. It is for such reasons that Ingram (2000) warned against a general condemnation of the gaze – which is often the handmaiden of narrative critique – because such condemnations often ignore substantive particularities and the specific character of any relation. Though inadequately, the affections articulated in romanticism should be used to legitimize the middle ground and trouble the distanced objectivity of sociological critique.

The polarization of relations only becomes more intense when narratives and critiques broach anthropomorphism, presumably because anthropomorphism not only proffers a questionable vision of external nature but also a vision that impinges directly on human nature. Nonetheless, despite reservations, narrative is more intimately linked with anthropomorphism than romanticism, for animals (as Cubitt suggested) typically serve as vectors that facilitate the production of narrative timelines (through the telling of single lives or cycles of regeneration). The extent of this polarization is exemplified in two films. According to Ladino (2009), the dominant theme in *March of the Penguins* is love. To her, the frigid (romantic) Antarctic generates penguin bonding, leading to a depiction of penguins as "capable of love" (56). Conversely, in *Grizzly Man*, Herzog rejects Timothy Treadwell's romantic anthropomorphizing fascination with bears in favor of cold modernity; for him, the separation of species is hard reality, not something to be mourned. Herzog's dubbed narrative accentuates the inhumanity of bears, painting the animals as inexhaustibly and insurmountably indifferent (Lulka 2009). In these two representations there is thus a simultaneous yet inconclusive movement toward and away from nonhuman animals – alternately, distance is obliterated and affirmed in narrative and critique.

While the affections outlined by Ladino may hold their own in popular culture, Herzog's views predominate in cynical analytical circles. In response to anthropomorphism's reduction of difference, skeptics have established distance in two ways: desubstantialization and mechanization. Indicative of the first, King (1996: 62, original italics) states, "This is nature, but of a very special kind: not an ecosystem, but an *ego-system* – one viewed through a self-referential human lens: anthropomorphized, sentimentalized, and moralized." In this critique, the animal is nothing more than a symbol that represents something other than the animal, and consequently, as in critiques of romanticism, the nonhuman and its agency is absented. Animal studies literature has increasingly moved away from this representational perspective by accentuating nonhuman agency (e.g. McFarland and Hediger 2009), but in media scholarship the tendency to dissipate nonhumans still predominates.

As for mechanization, Bousé (2000) reverts unreservedly to a rigid view of wildlife, noting more than once the role of random events (like a falling rock) in evolution rather than the flexibility of animals themselves. It must be recalled that, since Descartes, the machine has been used as a pivot for differentiating human from nonhuman. These pervasive mechanical expositions suggest the surge of anthropomorphism (alternately insightful and askance) is really just a small temporal wave amid a larger sea of mechanism. Far from an impartial check against irrationality, critiques of anthropomorphism are a reaffirmation of a long-standing mechanical orthodoxy that – in line with modern objectivity – reestablishes species' distance. Such critiques do not recognize that many scientists have changed their attitude toward anthropomorphism, seeing it now as a valid method of understanding (Griffin 1977; Daston and Mitman 2005; Rees 2007). While anthropomorphism should be interrogated theoretically, the experiential world of science and popular culture suggests the rabble of human-nonhuman relations is not merely mechanical.

While anthropomorphism has a long history and pervades a wide array of productions (confer to Mitman [1999] on the "nature fakers" and Pierson [2005] on the Discovery Channel), Disney and Disney-related productions – ranging from early animated features to the True-Life Adventures of the 1940s and 1950s to the more recent Pixar offerings – garner most critical attention due to their popularity in mainstream culture. In line with the general argument offered here, rather than catalog Disney examples (which, for better or worse, are well known), I want to briefly suggest these anthropomorphisms are deeply entwined with materiality, technology, and humanity in such a way that negates the dissolution and distance offered in narratives and critiques. On the production side, it has been noted that nature documentaries and Disney productions influenced one another, whereby the metaphoric and the real became inhered to one another without extinguishing all credibility. As to consumption, the contradictory impacts of these anthropomorphic renderings is exhibited most clearly in reactions to *Bambi*, which was seen as blurring the boundaries between reality and fiction despite its obvious anthropomorphism. Lutts (1992), for one, argued *Bambi* generated negative reactions from hunters and ecologists, a point echoed by Hastings (1996) in mentioning a person who would not allow his children to watch *Bambi* because it expressed an antihunting philosophy. Alternately, Whitley (2008) finds much positive environmental information in Disney productions (despite the anthropomorphism), noting additionally that many ecologists of the postwar era were initially motivated by creations such as *Bambi*. Years later, blurred boundaries and ethical concerns emerged again with *Finding Nemo*, as some children flushed their fish down the toilet to free them (Henry 2010). Most relevant here, these involuted and contradictory outcomes suggest anthropomorphism – in production or as product – has never been completely successful in distancing itself from material reality. Rather, anthropomorphism is persistently intervened upon. Nevertheless, whether as symbol or animal, sufficient attention has not been given to the material affect nonhumans have on the world and the visceral affect they have on humans.

The notions of romanticism and anthropomorphism comingle with the newer critical notion of ecoporn. Ecoporn recalls the visuality of romanticism while alluding to some of the biological activities that ground anthropomorphism. Distance is once again enlarged and contracted simultaneously. Of the images that fall within this category, Millet (2004) says their silence is "nothing short of submissive" (146) and states these "Tarted up" images "offer to the viewer the illusions of control, ownership, subjugation; they tell us to take comfort: they will always be there, ideal, unblemished, available" (147). Knighton (2002) discusses it in more poetic fashion, relating ecoporn initially to landscape images in calendars. In equating such images with pornography, he notes the use of "provocative lighting" (168), and contends pornographic and nature images are "equally manipulative and exploiting" (167). Welling (2009: 57–58) goes into more detail, noting initially that ecoporn is defined by its reiteration of the "land-as-woman" (approximating Berila) and the placement of the viewer in the position of "the all-seeing male subject to Nature's unseeing, aestheticized female object." Only in his third definition of ecoporn does he mention nature media's relatively recent incorporation of violent and sexual scenes. Bousé (2000: 182), though not using the term, moves this imagery explicitly toward the biological, stating "the scene of the big kill can be compared to the obligatory 'cum-shot' in XXX-rated films; each serves as a guarantor of authenticity."

Interestingly, Knighton (2002: 167) states, "Unfortunately, once they are coined, metaphors, portentous or vacuous, tend to circulate," without realizing critiques of ecoporn simply restate prevailing views of pornography and nature. These critiques work with a conventional depiction of pornography, one that is resolutely heterosexual. That both Knighton and Welling mention *Playboy* is indicative. They fail to recognize that pornography has become incredibly diversified over the years, the heterosexual increasingly sharing space with the homosexual, bisexual, and beyond, with the increasingly differentiated means of broadcasting performing a central role in this queering. To the extent that this critique is grounded in a rather puritanical (i.e. conventional) notion of pornography, its efficacy as critique becomes diluted by the shifting (some might say liberatory because self-broadcast) character of sexuality within pornography. Although Welling observes the meaning of ecopornography has itself changed (being initially used to criticize corporate attempts to greenwash economic practices), by overrelying upon heterosexuality, he effectively halts any further redefinition of the term that might enable a reconceptualization of nature.

Instead of delving into the messiness that porn and nature necessarily enact, voyeuristic distance is oddly reified while being rejected.

Overall, the critiques of romanticism, anthropomorphism, and ecoporn – while occasionally warranted – produce polarized narratives that obscure nature's involutions. Importantly, these critiques also resonate with the orthodoxy of mechanism, for they strike predictability into existence. (Gore's *Inconvenient Truth* is also steeped in a mechanistic view of Earth processes, validating as it does mechanism's authority via a barrage of charts and statistics.) To the contrary, the turmoil of romanticism helpfully bespeaks an uncertainty that is not entirely distinct from the postmodern dismantling of language. Anthropomorphism alludes to the evolutionary slippage between species (including humans) and the undetermined change it necessarily brings. Ecoporn elides a sexuality that was never puritanical in the first place and has become less so with the incorporation of more technology. These terms suggest a middle ground that is ripe.

An Inconvenient Nature

The primary shortcoming of these narrative critiques is their tendency to distance and dissolve nature in the process of examining it. This is not an objection to narration (which is perhaps now ineradicable from human being), for narration is of the moment, ad hoc, and provisional. Narrative, however, is not the same as narration, for it is unjustifiably prefigured; the architecture of its telling is overdetermined. There is some irony here in that the narrative tools employed to open up analyses of nature have created their own rigidity. Thus, Cameron (2012) notes, many geographers have shifted from narrative to stories, as the latter incorporates the affective, material, and performative aspects of living. Although "stories" insufficiently differentiates her notion from narrative, in her framework stories ingest, exhibit, and affirm the nonhuman agency (Philo and Wilbert 2000), immanence (Lulka 2012), and "lively biogegraphies" (Lorimer 2010) that manifest the world. Although Haraway (2008) only uses the notion of messmates to describe relations with companion animals, we can literalize and extend this to the general spate of relations we find ourselves amid. Here, I argue this earthly tide of events, coming as it does in many forms, has moved the Google Ngrams as much as, if not more than, narrative.

As a corrective, this analysis began with the presentation of Ngrams, not so much as a criticism of any particular narrative but a critique of narrative as a metaconcept. The ultimate objective, which can now be more explicitly stated, was not to paint a narrative of pollution or wilderness (which could be done), nor to critique the society of any respective time, but to suggest that the tools of critique are just as susceptible to periodization as the common worldview of any given time. In short, I am suggesting that narrative analysis, though a mode of thinking one step further removed from events, is no less susceptible, say, than "pestilence" to becoming an inadequate, partial, and, at times, blinding notion that signifies and stigmatizes a particular era.

It is necessary to reassess the general relation between materiality and narrative, something that proponents of actor-network theory and the growing literature on hybridity have addressed. The differing views on this relation were succinctly crystallized in a debate between Bloor (1999) and Latour (1999) some years ago. Without rehearsing the entire debate, their antagonistic positions ultimately arose from disagreement as to whether or not language circumscribes the materiality it encounters. Answering in the affirmative instantiates a perspective of oversight, an asymmetry, and a distance that is crucial to the functioning of narrative. In rejecting this view, I have chosen to validate narration rather than narrative, for the concept of narration – as one factor among many – reestablishes symmetry. In short, contrary to its designated character, narrative is always susceptible to forces.

At a more fundamental level, the focus on narrative requires a belief in, and an adherence to, rationality. By this, I do not mean the analysis of narrative is troubled by ill-conceived storylines, for it has surely addressed those. Rather, what I am suggesting is merely that to have a narrative one must have a sequential order of events. In many respects, this sequentiality is bare mathematics, and yet it reflects a humanism because it suggests a resolve (or duration) of thought that is sufficiently impervious to worldly events and technological change. Increasingly, however, the rigor of this rationality has been called into question as writers delve into the boundary that supposedly separates humans from other species (Fudge 2002; Armstrong 2008; Rohman 2009). This new relation is complex, one in which nonhumans are more rational than previously conceded, and humans less so.

Such irrationality – which is defined by a certain inability to remain consistent over time – is riddled with conceptual and sequential gaps that are more receptive to the contingencies occurring around and within us. As such, irrationality fosters a certain symmetry too that undoubtedly provides avenues for transforming our thoughts about nature, yet one unhinged from a legacy of trenchant narratives. In contrast, by holding onto the notion that narrative is essentially autonomous (if albeit distorted), we lose this agentially heterogeneous foundation for place-making. What is being suggested is that a move away from narrative and toward incomplete rationality provides a new vista for producing and perceiving nature. Thus, while Heisse (2008) helpfully appropriated the multiscalar dynamics of Google Earth usage to highlight the deficiencies of "local" and "global" environmental orthodoxies, here I suggest Google Earth is informative because the spatialities it generates are not completely rational, as view selections are inflected by ignorance, the limits of visual acuity, and tactile insensitivities (arising from movements of a mouse) that bring about a degree of randomness. The agency of human users, technology, and earthly elements comingle.

Despite the real insights brought about by narrative analysis, what is being suggested here is that, in a profound respect, analysis of nature in the media has been led into a cul-de-sac. Understandably, this has occurred in large part due to an overreliance upon movies and television, which were the dominant forms of communication in the twentieth century. Mitman (1999) notes two modes of nature representation were available in the early twentieth century: the diorama and film. The former fell into the dustbin of history presumably because the taxidermied animals stood forever rigid, while the latter blossomed into a multibillion dollar industry in part because it was able to capture movement in new and more exacting ways. (The economics of productions, entangled in various materialities, is not to be forgotten as a concurrent intervening force on narrative [Cottle 2004; Horak 2006]). That the opening up of narrative within film coincided with this technological elaboration of movement ensured that narrative never comprised film's totality.

As such, the dominance of narrative (and of film) is in no way inevitable or transcendent. Indeed, it is very likely the opposite, for the "extra-cinematic" world in which filmic (and other) productions take place is endlessly generating change. More insidiously, the extra-cinematic world is in no way extra-cinematic, for it becomes an element of cinematic constructions. The concerns mentioned here revolve around the belief that narrative analysis has not adequately accounted for this large process of material and technological change and has thus become taxidermied itself by its unwillingness to inhale the world.

Helpfully, Cubitt (2005) emphasizes the notion of communication rather than narrative, a theoretical move that allows "information" to emanate from a number of nonhuman sources. This shift in thinking is helpful, but seemingly remains constrained within the orbit of signs and symbols. A better way to indicate the approach advocated here is to recall McLuhan's (1967) contention that the "medium is the massage." McLuhan's phrase suggests that we do not simply partake of a message, but rather that we are worked over by it because we are in the midst of the medium itself (see Tyler [2009] for a more detailed exposition). McLuhan's maneuver effectively eliminates the distance necessary for the articulation of authoritative narratives and thereby dilutes any narrative's power to fully determine the response. Neither the recipient amid the medium of the day nor the "nature" partially conveyed is rigidly cast within this matrix, but instead they are massaged in a way that disrupts taxidermic tendencies of narrative. That said, McLuhan's framework is still too narrow, as it is ultimately hinged to the electric transmissions of his era. The massage needs to go deeper.

Gershon and Malitsky (2010) offer an additional avenue for reconsideration, one in which they employ actor-network theory. Specifically, they note the role microphones played in documentaries of Fidel Castro, wherein Castro's engagements with microphones modulated the filmic stories being told. This repositioning of agency (to the idiosyncrasies of microphones and the difficulties they pose) modestly suggests the impact of the nonhuman world on narrative. Drawing on a different set of sources, Ivakhiv (2011) broadens the scope of these nonhuman and extra-filmic influences by articulating his notion of the "anthrobiogeomorphic machine." For him, cinema is a machine that simultaneously produces the human, other biological happenings, and the regions we come to know as a particular landscape. In this perspective, cinema is an incomplete collaboration because reality is continually in motion. Accordingly, Ivakhiv claims that "cinema 'stalks' the real world, and that our appreciation of its potentials should similarly involve a kind of 'stalking' of its effects in the material, social, and perceptual dimensions of the world from which cinema emerges and to which it returns" (119). There are some commonalities with Cubitt, McLuhan, and Gershon and Malitsky, but the lines of influence have become more diffuse. What needs to be stated more explicitly here is that nature is part of the medium, and we (and other species) are massaged by it.

The import of this contention cannot be overstated. The passivity or rigidity of nature is often assumed, thereby paradoxically excluding nature's impact on nature media. In his New Deal film, *The Plow That Broke the Plains*, Pare Lorentz sought to explain society's role in the creation of the Dust Bowl, but also present a vision of the grassland region that he subsequently characterized as "Nature minding its own knitting" (cited in Dunaway [2005: 47]), a holistic vision, but now on a regional rather than global scale. Similarly, in prioritizing sustainability over the romantic notion of unpeopled wilderness (paralleling trends exhibited in Figure 1), Berilla presumes nature does not create its own unsustainability, evolutionary or otherwise. For her, sustainability is primary because nature is home (echoing Gore), yet her depiction is as idealistic as romantic portrayals of nature in that it assumes nature has no agency other than the rote processes schematized in modern science. Bousé expresses this perspective in an alternate way, differentiating the role of "courtship rituals, mating displays, nest-building, and other social or reproductive behavior" in nature and society, respectively, by stating that "in animals these are *fixed* behavior patterns, while in humans they are culturally shaped and constantly subject to changing circumstances" (170, original italics). All of these convey the belief that nature is quiescent and that humanity is the agent that brings about history.

Cubitt (2005) alters this critical configuration by defining the ocean's motions as "an endlessly differentiating repetition" (49), whereby "nature too has a history" that suggests "absolute conservation is not an option" (51). Generally, media has not adopted this stance. In referencing the media images of polar bears and the Arctic that inform conceptions of global warming, Cosgrove (2008: 1878) states,

> *neither physical nature (landscape) nor biological nature (fauna) is represented as a active participant in the processes of environmental change (although they may have become actants in the semiological sense of playing a role in the construction of a specific narrative by the fact of being represented in the image itself). They are intended to be read as passive victims of anthropogenic processes underway in far distant locations – those of the viewer.*

While such portrayals are understandable given current conditions, they fundamentally skew perceptions of nature in a way that not only disempowers nature but undermines important rationales for its protection. It is not simply that polar bears live in the Arctic but also how they live agentially in the Arctic that is in need of conveyance. Yet another example from Herzog indicates the importance of nonhuman agency to narrative. In *La Soufrière*, Herzog documents an impending volcanic explosion on the island of Guadaloupe. The volcano, however, never erupts and thus ruins the projected narrative (as Herzog notes). The volcano may be construed as passive, a nonentity failing to produce an event, but in reality it speaks to the noncompliant, incompletely known character of nature that never aligns perfectly with narrative.

These contentions can be pushed in other directions wherein technology has a profound influence. Petterson (2011) notes that the moviegoing experience was vastly different during the early 1900s. In addition to lacking sound, movies were very short, often accompanied by lectures and the use of material objects, and were displayed in halls originally designed for other purposes. Today, a different technological arrangement is emerging, but one in which time is also frequently compressed. Examining new platforms, Best (2004) argues that portable, digitized imagery "fracture and layer visual consumption" (68), their proliferation "refracting and redirecting" interactions (72) in a way that amplifies and distracts consumption. DeLuca (1999) refers to the notion of distraction as well, suggesting that it is not opposed to perception, but a different type of perception. Crucially, distinct formats not only have unique heritages but also distinct capacities. On the Internet, file size, upload and download time, and Web site restrictions undoubtedly hinder narrative and its reception.

Yet even before one arrives at a particular image of nature on the information superhighway, there are other factors. Search engines – those incredibly sterile artifacts – are now a primary means of image acquisition. The search process is complex. As Pan et al. (2007) note, users place a substantial amount of trust in search engines, meaning algorithms play a driving role in the conceptions of nature produced in consumers. On some sites, such as Netflix, StumbleUpon, or Amazon, the search is guided by the preferences of the user. Even in these cases, however, seemingly odd associations are frequently generated. Significantly, while these computational interactions do not construct space themselves, they increasingly form the basis (in collaboration with a host of other factors) for the reception of nature. In fundamental ways, algorithms provide the context in which narratives are encountered.

The interplay of all these forces can be illustrated in a few contexts. The Sundance Channel, for one, created a series of vignettes entitled *Green Porno*. Each film was of short duration and starred Isabella Rossellini in abstract settings. In each of these videos, Rossellini portrayed a different type of animal (commonly an insect), specifically enacting its method of copulation. The sparse yet brightly colored settings thus became the arena for hermaphroditic sex (snail) and violence (praying mantis). In addition to noting the queer nature of these videos and how they subvert heteronormative orthodoxies, Sinwell (2010) accentuated the role technology and public personality plays in the videos' distribution. Thus she cites the codirector of the project as saying, "What do people mostly go online for, but to look at porn? ... So we put 'Porno' in, and when people Google it, maybe we'll get lucky and *Green Porno* will come up. We might as well take advantage of the delivery system" (cited in Sinwell [2010: 125]). This comment helpfully interlaces the dynamics of the Internet, the power of personality (as with Gore's *An Inconvenient Truth*), and sex (long displayed in other representations). This is queer serendipity as much as narrative.

Or, as another example, we might look to yet a third species of bear, the panda bear, to relocate our thinking about the impact of media. Pandas are well known for being poor reproducers, and consequently managers have used videos of mating pandas to induce mating among captive pandas (Gray 2006). Managers believe this inducement works (though perhaps by virtue of the videos' sounds rather than sights), a conclusion that again must reshape what we think of nature, one in which passivity and rigidity does not rule the day. Affect is relevant here too, not in terms of how pandas affect us or the world, but in how pandas are susceptible to affect. In both the case of *Green Porno* and pandas, ecoporn is reconstituted.

There are undoubtedly many venues in which a recalibration of nature takes place and is not wholly shrouded by narrative. Even though news events can be assimilated into dominant narratives, they are also capable of disturbing convention or complacence (DeLuca 1999). Such is the case when a video showing a panda bear eating a deer carcass is displayed on a news Web site (MSNBC 2011), or when a herd of cape buffalo is shown on YouTube unexpectedly returning en masse from a distance to rescue (at least temporarily) a young calf from the grasp of lions when the herd could have more easily done otherwise (Jason Schlosberg 2007). Yet again it might be the case when an asteroid passes near Earth, the seeming randomness generating a conceptual flux about all that we know (Revkin 2011). In such instances, there is no illusion that nature is passive. Even in the latter instance, the holistic view of Earth, which accentuated isolation, is replaced by Earth's placement within a larger concatenation. We may thus extend Heise's (2008) "cosmopolitanism" – in which the local and global are interconnected – to include interstellar space and the jarring effects it might bring from abroad, thereby fracturing any sense of local or global holism. And yet, while these agencies are pervasive and potentially revolutionary, they do not retrace the divergent destructive path established by apocalyptic narratives, which are merely the obverse of holistic, harmonious visions of nature. Rather, they suggest a final resolution with our messmates is not in the offing.

None of this is to say that narrative is inconsequential or that technology determines narrative in toto. As a case in point, one may look at video games, another media technology. As Chang (2011) notes, video games generally relegate the environment to the background, use stereotypical settings, and view nature as a source of resource extraction. This pattern follows the history of neglect and depletion. In the case of the video game *Spore*, which could conceivably allow gamers to see how innumerable life forms develop and interact, the potential of the spore is locked within a game format defined by stereotypical stages of development: cell, creature, tribal, civilization, and space. These game stages entirely subvert the undetermined essence signified by a spore. Nevertheless, the argument put forth here is that narrative is always in actuality a form of weak narration – administered in the moment – and no more linguistic than the material capacities that bring it temporarily into being. And importantly, since this chapter is ultimately about nature as a place, it must be emphasized that these technological advancements are not separate from nature but an indication of nature's own recombinatory tendencies. Moving forward, research in this area must account for this fundamentally heterogeneous aspect of, and active property within, nature. Such an approach allows us to examine the forces that trouble narrative as well as the assumptions of narrative.

References

Ames, E. 2009. Herzog, landscape, and documentary. *Cinema Journal* 48(2): 46–69.
Anderson, B. 1991. *Imagined Communities: Reflections on the Origin and Spread of Nationalism*. London: Verso.
Armstrong, P. 2008. *What Animals Mean in the Fiction of Modernity*. London: Routledge.
Berila, B. 2010. Engaging the land/positioning the spectator: Environmental justice documentaries and Robert Redford's *The Horse Whisperer* and *A River Runs Through It*. In *Framing the World: Explorations in Ecocriticism and Film*. Edited by P. Willoquet-Maricondi. Charlottesville: University of Virginia Press, 116–32.
Best, K. 2004. Interfacing the environment: Networked screens and the ethics of visual consumption. *Ethics & The Environment* 9(2): 65–85.
Bloor, D. 1999. Anti-Latour. *Studies in History and Philosophy of Science* 30(1): 81–112.
Brereton, P. 2005. *Hollywood Utopias: Ecology in Contemporary American Cinema*. Bristol: Intellect.
Cameron, E. 2012. New geographies of story and storytelling. *Progress in Human Geography* 36(5): 573–92.
Chang, A.Y. 2011. Games as environmental texts. *Qui Parle* 19(2) : 56–84.
Cosgrove, D. 1994. Contested global visions: *One-world, Whole-Earth*, and the Apollo space photographs. *Annals of the Association of American Geographers* 84(2): 270–94.
Cosgrove, D. 2008. Images and imagination in 20th-century environmentalism: From the Sierras to the Poles. *Environment and Planning A* 40(8): 1862–80.
Cottle, S. 2004. Producing nature(s): On the changing production ecology of natural history TV. *Media, Culture, & Society* 26(1): 81–101.
Cracknell, J. 1993. Issue arenas, pressure groups and environmental agendas. In *Mass Media and Environmental Issues*. Edited by A. Hansen. Leicester: Leicester University Press, 3–21.
Cubitt, S. 2005. *Eco Media*. Amsterdam: Rodopi.
Daston, L., and Mitman, G. 2005. *Thinking with Animals: New Perspectives on Anthropomorphism*. New York: Columbia University Press.
Dawkins, H. 2009. Ecology, images, and scripto-visual rhetoric. In *Ecosee: Image, Rhetoric, Nature*. Edited by S. I. Dobrin and S. Morey. Albany: SUNY Press, 79–94.
DeLuca, K.M. 1999. *Image Politics: The New Rhetoric of Environmental Activism*. New York: Guilford Press.
Dunaway, F. 2005. *Natural Visions: The Power of Images in American Environmental Reform*. Chicago: University of Chicago Press.
Fudge, E. 2002. *Animal*. London: Reaktion Books.
Garrard, G. 2012. Worlds without us: Some types of disanthropy. *SubStance* 41(1): 40–60.
Gershon, I. and J. Malitsky. 2010. Actor-network theory and documentary studies. *Studies in Documentary Film* 4(1): 65–78.
Gray, D.D. 2006. Pandas getting new view of mating ritual. *Washington Post* [Online, November 23]. Available at www.washingtonpost.com/wp-dyn/content/article/2006/11/22/AR2006112202039.html [accessed May 31, 2013].
Griffin, D.R. 1977. Anthropomorphism. *BioScience* 27(7): 445–46.
Hamilton, P. 1999. From sublimity to indeterminacy: New world order or aftermath of romantic ideology. In *Romanticism and Postmodernism*. Edited by E. Larrissy. Cambridge: Cambridge University Press, 13–28.
Haraway, D.J. 2008. *When Species Meet*. Minneapolis: University of Minnesota Press.
Hastings, A.W. 1996. Bambi and the hunting ethos. *Journal of Popular Film & Television* 24(2): 53–59.
Heise, U.K. 2008. *Sense of Place and Sense of Planet: The Environmental Imagination of the Global*. Oxford: Oxford University Press.

Henry, E. 2010. Bambi and Finding Nemo: A sense of wonder in the wonderful world of Disney? In *Framing the World: Explorations in Ecocriticism and Film*. Edited by P. Willoquet-Maricondi. Charlottesville: University of Virginia Press, 170–86.
Holmes, R. 2008. *The Age of Wonder*. New York: Pantheon.
Horak, J-C. 2006. Wildlife documentaries: From classical forms to reality TV. *Film History* 18(4): 459–75.
Ingram, D. 2000. *Green Screen: Environmentalism and Hollywood Cinema*. Exeter: University of Exeter Press.
Ivakhiv, A.J. 2011. The anthrobiogeomorphic machine: Stalking the zone of cinema. *Film Philosophy* 15(1): 118–39.
Jason Schlosberg (YouTube username). 2007. *Battle at Kruger* [Video online]. Available at www.youtube.com/watch?v=LU8DDYz68kM [accessed May 1, 2012].
Jendrysik, M.S. 2011. Back to the garden: New visions of posthuman futures. *Utopian Studies* 22(1): 34–51.
King, M.J. 1996. The audience in the wilderness: The Disney nature films. *Journal of Popular Film and Television* 24(2): 60–68.
Knighton, J. 2002. Ecoporn and the manipulation of desire. In *Wild Earth: Wild Ideas for a World Out of Balance*. Edited by T. Butler. Minneapolis: Milkweed Editions, 165–71.
Ladino, J.K. 2009. For the love of nature: Documenting life, death, and animality in *Grizzly Man* and *March of the Penguins*. *Interdisciplinary Studies in Literature and Environment* 16(1): 53–90.
Latour, B. 1999. For David Bloor … and beyond: A reply to David Bloor's "Anti-Latour." *Studies in History and Philosophy of Science* 30(1): 113–29.
Lorimer, J. 2010. Elephants as companions species: The lively biogeographies of Asian elephant conservation in Sri Lanka. *Transactions of the Institute of British Geographers* 35 (4): 491–506.
Lulka, D. 2009. Consuming Timothy Treadwell: Redefining nonhuman agency in light of Herzog's *Grizzly Man*. In *Animals and Agency*. Edited by S.E. McFarland and R. Hediger. Leiden: Brill, 67–87.
Lulka, D. 2012. The lawn; or On becoming a killer. *Environment and Planning D: Society and Space* 30(2): 207–25.
Lutts, R.H. 1992. The trouble with Bambi: Walt Disney's *Bambi* and the American vision of nature. *Forest and Conservation History* 36(October): 160–71.
MacDonald, S. 2001. *The Garden in the Machine*. Berkeley: University of California Press.
McFarland, S., and R. Hediger. 2009. *Animals and Agency: An Interdisciplinary Exploration*. Leiden: Brill.
McLuhan, M. 1967. *The Medium Is the Massage*. New York: Bantam.
Millet, L. 2004. Die, baby harp seal! In *Naked: Writers Uncover the Way We Live on Earth*. Edited by S. Zakin. New York: Four Walls Eight Windows, 146–50.
Minster, M. 2010. The rhetoric of ascent in *An Inconvenient Truth* and *Everything's Cool*. In *Framing the World: Explorations in Ecocriticism and Film*. Edited by P. Willoquet-Maricondi. Charlottesville: University of Virginia Press, 25–42.
Mitman, G. 1999. *Reel Nature: America's Romance with Wildlife on Film*. Cambridge, MA: Harvard University Press.
Morey, S. 2009. A rhetorical look at ecosee. In *Ecosee: Image, Rhetoric, Nature*. Edited by S. I. Dobrin and S. Morey. Albany: SUNY Press, 23–52.
MSNBC. 2011. Meat-eating panda caught on tape [Online, December 30]. Available at www.msnbc.msn.com/id/45825843/ns/technology_and_science-science/t/meat-eating-panda-caught-camera/#.T6C6RvlxHuh [accessed May 31, 2013].

Neuzil, M., and Kovarik, B. 1996. *Mass Media & Environmental Conflict: America's Green Crusades*. London: SAGE.
Pan, B., H. Hembrooke, T. Joachims, L. Lorigo, G. Gay, and L. Granka. 2007. In Google we trust: Users' decisions on rank, position, and relevance. *Journal of Computer-mediated Communication* 12(3): 801–23.
Petterson, P.B. 2011. *Cameras into the Wild: A History of Early Wildlife and Expedition Filmmaking, 1895–1928*. Jefferson, NC: McFarland.
Peucker, B. 1984. Werner Herzog: In quest of the sublime. In *New German Filmmakers*. Edited by K. Phillips. New York: Frederick Unger, 168–94.
Philo, C., and C. Wilbert. 2000. Animal spaces, beastly places: An introduction. In *Animal Spaces, Beastly Places: New Geographies of Human-animal Relations*. Edited by C. Philo and C. Wilbert. London: Routledge, 1–34.
Pierson, D.P. 2005. "Hey they're just like us!" Representations of the animal world in the Discovery Channel's nature programming. *Journal of Popular Culture* 38(4): 698–712.
Prager, B. 2007. *The Cinema of Werner Herzog: Aesthetic Ecstasy and Truth*. London: Wallflower.
Prager, B. 2010. Landscape of the mind: The indifferent earth in Werner Herzog's Films. In *Cinema and Landscape*. Edited by G. Harper and J. Rayner. Bristol: Intellect, 89–102.
Rees, A. 2007. Reflections on the field: Primatology, popular science and the politics of personhood. *Social Studies of Science* 37(6): 881–907.
Revkin, A. 2011. Close encounters of the rocky kind. *New York Times* [Online, November 8]. Available at www.dotearth.blogs.nytimes.com/2011/11/08/close-encounters-of-the-rocky-kind/ [accessed May 31, 2013].
Rohman, C. 2009. *Stalking the Subject: Modernism and the Animal*. New York: Columbia University Press.
Sinwell, S.E.S. 2010. Sex, bugs, and Isabella Rossellini: The making and marketing of *Green Porno*. *Women's Studies Quarterly* 38(3–4): 118–37.
Tyler, T. 2009. The test of time: McLuhan, space, and the rise of *Civilization*. In *Ecosee: Image, Rhetoric, Nature*. Edited by S.I. Dobrin and S. Morey. Albany: SUNY Press, 257–77.
Vogel, A. 1986. On seeing a mirage. In *The Films of Werner Herzog*. Edited by T. Corrigan. New York: Methuen, 45–49.
Welling, B.H. 2009. Ecoporn: On the limits of visualizing the nonhuman. In *Ecosee: Image, Rhetoric, Nature*. Edited by S.I. Dobrin and S. Morey. Albany: SUNY Press, 53–77.
Whitley, D. 2008. *The Idea of Nature in Disney Animation*. Aldershot: Ashgate.

Bodies

Julie Cupples

Introduction

Bodies are ubiquitous in media. Slim and fit bodies, obese and carnivalesque bodies, young and old bodies, murdered and mutilated bodies, alien and machinic bodies appear constantly on our television and computer screens, producing diverse modes of entertainment, engagement, and contestation. Media are also ubiquitous in bodies. Media technologies such as personal computers, cell phones, and gaming consoles transform and extend our bodies in all kinds of ways, often leading to cyborgian materialities and subjectivities. Even though people often think of media technologies as producing "virtual" as opposed to "physical" environments, the body is never absent in media. Bodies can be transcended or reconfigured in online environments, in the sense that children can become adults and vice versa, men can become women and vice versa, bodies can be differently abled, but the body is never absent. Being online often means being seated in front of a computer screen or at the very least having a smartphone in one's hand or pocket. People have sex in Second Life and have of course been having "phone sex" for decades (Stone 1995). As Mark Hansen (2006: xvi) puts it, the contemporary moment is one in which we are seeing "the exteriorization of the human into a convergent media platform and the massive infiltration of technics into the body." So while our bodies are never absent, the use of media technologies does transform the ways in which we are embodied.

The mutual constitution of bodies and media, while welcomed and celebrated by some, is viewed by many as a serious cause for concern. Publications on New Zealand teenagers' use of cell phones (Thompson and Cupples 2008; Cupples and Thompson 2010) attracted substantial attention from local and national media and this attention was clearly driven by a sense of moral panic about the dangers of media technologies to young people. Children and young people are frequently seen as vulnerable in the face of new technologies, and television, gaming, and Internet use are blamed for creating couch potatoes or mouse potatoes. Media use is often associated with obesity epidemics and perceived declines in sociality as conventionally understood. In our case, we discovered that such moral panic leads to inaccurate reporting by journalists and inappropriate uptake by school authorities.[1]

[1] In a 2008 paper, we argued that teenagers were adopting cyborgian subjectivities and positionalities in ways that were positive for friendships and other forms of sociality and in ways that smoothed the transition to high school (Thompson and Cupples 2008). We were building on prior research such as that by Holloway and Valentine (2003) that asserted through empirical research that many children were very competent and responsible users of media technologies. Yet *The Press* reported with alarm that New Zealand teenagers were becoming cyborgs, with an article placed on the Web site of a local high school, Papanui High School, with the headline – Teens too attached to mobiles: Study – presumably to justify their restrictive approach to cell phone use in school, a move not supported by the

Even well-established media scholars such as Sherry Turkle (2011) have expressed concern about the social and cultural dynamics of being or needing to be online all the time, displacing optimism in her earlier work about the positive opportunities that online worlds provide users (Turkle 1995). Media use does not of course *cause* obesity or antisocial behavior, and watching television or surfing the Internet is no more or less passive than reading and it is interesting to note that concerns about inactivity or obesity are rarely directed at "bookworms."

The body-media interface has been studied from a range of theoretical approaches, including psychoanalysis, phenomenology, posthumanism, cultural studies, and feminism and gender studies. It has drawn on and contributed to a growing interest in the body as an object of analysis that began in the 1980s and exploded in the 1990s across the social sciences and humanities (for discussions in geography, see Bell and Valentine 1995; Cream 1995; Longhurst 2001; Pile and Nast 1998). There has been a substantial amount of scholarship within geography on the body-media interface, focused on a range of topics including the embodied geographies of cyberspace, pregnancy and birth, pornography, and cell phones (see inter alia Batty 1997; Crang, Crang, and May 1999; Cupples and Thompson 2010; England 2011; Featherstone and Burrows 1995; Hillis 1999; 2009; Graham 1998; Kitchin 1998; Longhurst 2001; 2006; Thompson and Cupples 2008). As geospatial, locative, and convergent media forms develop new technological capacities and become more accessible and commonplace, the body-media interface will provide ripe avenues of enquiry for geographers. We are, as Nigel Thrift (2011) writes, "swimming in a sea of data" and living in a world in which ontologies are proliferating. These developments mean that "new forms of the body and mindfulness are being produced via technologies which have concentrated on amplifying just a few means of bodily extension as surrogates for communication" (Thrift 2011: 10).

This chapter focuses on the geographic dimensions of the body-media interface and outlines the spaces, knowledges, discourses, and relations that bring mediated bodies into being and that are brought into being by mediated bodies. It is divided into three main sections: the first explores the representation of bodies in the media, the second focuses on the ways in which bodies are extended or redistributed in space, and the final section discusses the making over of bodies in the media and their cultural politics.

Representing Bodies

The media is often blamed for creating an obsession with body image and an unobtainable desire among ordinary women and girls to be unrealistically thin. Many media commentators, psychologists, and feminists have asserted that there is a direct causal relationship between media images of the thin body and serious eating disorders such as anorexia and bulimia. Advertisers, editors of glossy magazines, and organizers of fashion shows are frequently called upon to behave in a more responsible manner and provide more realistic images of "real" women. For example, Cyndi Tebbel (2000) asserts that media imagery of extremely thin women leads to self-loathing and low self-esteem among ordinary women and brainwashes them into starving themselves, wasting time and money on diet programs, and feeling guilty about food. Emily Fox-Kales (2011: 73) believes that Hollywood "chick flicks" "are so compelling that they can inspire particularly susceptible moviegoers to shape

research findings and one that we had never advocated. (See Wilson 2006 and www.intranet.papanui.school.nz/CommunicationsTeenstooattachedtomobiles.doc.)

their own bodies at *any* cost" (emphasis added). Similarly, in 2012, the *Sydney Morning Herald*, reporting on a documented rise in eating disorders among middle-aged women, blamed the tendency on what they referred to as "Desperate Housewives Syndrome," suggesting that it was driven by the desire to look thin like the stars on comedy drama *Desperate Housewives* (Smith 2012). This assertion comes despite that such an association has not been empirically demonstrated and that one could equally argue that the dysfunctional lives of the suburban housewives are hardly successful role models for the rest of us. This approach is consistent with a "media effects" model, also found in the simplistic causal relations assumed between on-screen violent and offscreen violent behavior that has been heavily criticized by scholars in media and cultural studies but somehow seems to persist (see Gauntlett 1998; Jenkins 2000). As Maggie Wykes and Barrie Gunter (2005: 3) write, "[b]laming the media for reproducing and extolling representations of unrealistic female bodies that influence young women to starve themselves has almost become a popular truism." They point out, however, that very little scholarship has addressed what viewers do with the body images in the media. They argue that the role of the media can only be understood in broader social and cultural contexts. Glossy magazines containing images of super-thin models would not sell unless they resonated with dominant understandings of gender identity. A cultural studies–oriented approach, on the other hand, understands the media as terrain of discursive struggle in which active audiences, including those who are socially subordinated, make sense of media texts in complex and heterogeneous and frequently oppositional or progressive ways (see, for example, Fiske 1987; Hartley 1999; Morley 1992; Jenkins 1992).

The media is also blamed for commodifying and objectifying women's bodies, turning them into objects ready for the male gaze. In a highly influential and much-critiqued essay in film studies, Laura Mulvey (1973) argued that in mainstream cinema women were victims of a male gaze, constructed as objects of sexual desire by a male spectator and protagonist. This argument, which Mulvey herself would revise and nuance in later work, simplifies the role of desire in media consumption as well as the act of looking, ignoring how both straight and gay women also gain pleasure from looking at the female body as well as how men's bodies are also gazed at by both men and women. It also relies on a fairly one-dimensional static view of power as something held by the powerful male to the detriment of the female victim. As Jeff Lewis's (2002) discussion of dancers who work in the sex industry illustrates, a structuralist view of power tends to see such women as victims of a patriarchal system. If, however, we adopt a Foucauldian view of power as something that circulates, a more much complex and less stable picture of the relationship between the viewer and the viewed emerges. It becomes apparent that there is no settling or definitive locating of power as "the dancer may have a higher income than her patron but is still subject to a range of demeaning social attitudes. Even so, the youth, beauty, vigour and athleticism of the performer may place her 'condition' above that of the overweight salacious patron" (Lewis 2002: 310; see also Rowe 1994: 205).

While associations between media consumption and bodily disorders such as anorexia cannot be completely ruled out, it is important not to essentialize either bodies or media, as neither have fixed properties and consequently their association does not have predictable outcomes. Rather than seeing the strong, slim, or sexy female body on-screen as an antifeminist icon that dupes women into acting against their own interests, alternative views rooted in performativity theory and third-wave feminism present a more sophisticated understanding. While much mainstream media space of the 1980s was taken up by muscular masculine bodies such as that of Sylvester Stallone and Arnold Schwarzenegger, which could be read as a backlash to the feminist gains of the 1970s and early 1980s (Tasker 1993), the 1990s and the start of the new millennium gave way to a diversity of interesting gendered on-screen bodies. We began to see many female protagonists and performers in both popular music and prime-time television who were young, sexy, and attractive, indeed in many ways hyperfeminine, but who were also strong, independent, and liberated. Instead of manipulating ordinary women and girls to act against their own gender interests, they were read instead as empowering role models for ordinary women and girls, a trend that has continued until now and that is often referred to as postfeminism or third-wave feminism. In popular music, the Spice Girls, Madonna, Destiny's Child, and more recently Lady Gaga have used their bodies to present gender-bending and gender-ambiguous modes of being in the world as well as articulating narratives of survival or sexual liberation. Lady Gaga identifies as bisexual, she is openly pro LGBT struggles, she performs in drag, and she refused to refute an accusation of intersexuality (Halberstam 2012). In much 1990s and early millennium television, we began to see the emergence of strong confident female and postfeminist protagonists, from detectives to vampire slayers. Buffy Summers (*Buffy the Vampire Slayer* 1997–2003) is often considered to be the quintessential postfeminist or third-wave icon (Pender 2004), while even Lisa Simpson, a cartoon schoolgirl character with a yellow face (*The Simpsons* 1989–present), embodies a model of femininity that is about speaking up against injustice or environmental degradation and not about to conforming to a normative model of slimness or beauty. In more recent years, Hermione Granger, protagonist of the *Harry Potter* films, has also emerged as a postfeminist icon. For Katrin Berndt (2011), Hermione presents an empowering model of growing self-confidence that enables her to skillfully promote humanist values while rejecting misogyny and challenging disabling gender stereotypes.

Scholars who have analyzed contemporary media texts through the lens of third-wave feminism have tended to underscore both its liberatory potential as well as its more confining, oppressive, or contradictory dimensions (see Lotz 2001 and essays in Johnson 2007). As with most media texts, both feminist and antifeminist (and other) readings are discursively available, readings are negotiated and the text, the production values of the text, the social location of the viewer, and the society in which the text is consumed are all significant.

While there is no doubt that unrealistically thin women are common in mainstream media, the contemporary mediasphere is also replete with women who inhabit nonnormative and carnivalesque bodies and who challenge dominant models of femininity. For example, Roseanne Barr played an overweight working-class protagonist, struggling to maintain her family (*Roseanne* 1988–97). *Roseanne* was an immensely popular show and at the end of the second season, Roseanne was voted favorite female television star by the readers of *People's Weekly* (Rowe 1994). In many ways, Roseanne's popularity can be attributed to the ways in which she transgresses normative gender and class identities. For Kathleen Rowe (1994), Roseanne embodies the unruly disruptive woman who endorses social disobedience, takes up space, is comfortable in/with her large body, and repeatedly violates dominant codes of social and corporeal acceptability. For this reason, she is reviled by some (those who benefit from the dominant class-gender order) while adored by others and as a result she is laden with feminist potential. Britain's sketch comedy show *Little Britain* (2003–2006) features many grotesque and unruly female bodies, played by male actors, including Marjorie Dawes and her weight-loss group Fat Fighters (a parody of groups such as Weight Watchers) and Vicky Pollard, a single working-class teenage mother or "chav" whose grotesque body is expressed through her weight, her pink track suit, and excessive sexuality. In a context of growing social and economic inequalities, the "chav" figure has become the target of widespread middle-class disapproval and disgust (Tyler 2008). But as Sharon Lockyer (2010) notes, Vicky Pollard is an ambivalent and contradictory character that at once seems to ridicule working-class culture and bodies for their lack of discipline and decorum but also mocks middle-class pretensions and their notions of social order. She writes,

> *Her ambivalence facilitates an interpretation that places Vicky Pollard as a contemporary "unruly woman" who rebels against, and is resistant to, cultural demands to restrain, restrict and define her working-class body and behaviour so it reflects middle-class discipline and governance. Further, the anti-pretension critique evident in some sketches, such as the Babysitter sketch, serves to highlight negative aspects of middle-class identities and cultures and exposes the hypocrisy that underpins middle-class resentment of chavs.* (Lockyer 2010: 133)

Multiple interpretations of the classed and gendered body are also available to audiences of Australian sitcom *Kath and Kim* (2002–2007), in which the protagonists, Kath Day-Knight and Kim Craig, and Kim's second-best friend, Sharon Strzelecki, project what Ann-Marie Cook (2010) refers to as "monstrous femininity." This is a rebellious mode of projection achieved largely through the body through gluttony and the breach of middle-class fashion conventions. Sharon, for example, only ever wears netball uniforms, while Kim is usually dressed in cheap, revealing, and ill-fitting tween clothing. While such representations could be understood as offensive to upwardly mobile working-class Australians as they underscore their lack of taste and cultural capital, they are also potentially liberating and subversive because they take "irreverent swipes at the values and policies that structured Australian society" at a time when a right-wing coalition led by John Howard was rolling back rights for women, workers, indigenous peoples, and sexual minorities that had been put in place under the previous government (Cook 2010: 71). Scholars that have studied shows such as *Roseanne* and *Kath and Kim* frequently turn to Russian philosopher Mikhail Bakhtin's concept of the carnivalesque to locate their subversive potential (Rowe 1994; Cook 2004). For Bakhtin, carnival was a time when authority could be mocked and subverted by the subordinated. Cross-dressing was also common in carnival, so men got to experience being a woman and women got to behave like men. Even when carnival was over and life returned to "normal," affective memories of alternative ways of being remained, potentially ready to resurface. Shows that feature excessive, grotesque, or carnivalesque bodies are often as popular as those that feature women who have unrealistically thin supermodel-style figures and that appear to encourage ordinary women to go to extreme measures as a route to self-esteem. So while in many ways, as an overweight protagonist in prime time, Roseanne is unique, what we find in the media are diverse and heterogeneous representations of body cultures.

Indeed, shows such as *Little Britain*, *Kath and Kim*, and *Roseanne* draw our attention to the constructedness and instability of the body and its relations with class, racial, and gender identities (Creed 2005). So while it is common to think of the body as a natural entity determined by gender, race, and sexuality, it is more useful to think of it as a performative entity that brings gender, race, and sexuality into being. In other words, the mediation of the body is a performative process. As Judith Butler (1990: 33) writes, "Gender is the repeated stylization of the body, a set of repeated acts within a highly rigid regulatory frame that congeal over time to produce the appearance of substance, of a natural sort of being." Butler's work has revealed how such repeated acts result in two contradictory effects. On the one hand, they reify gender and sexuality and make them appear natural and prior to their enactment. On the other hand, however, they also interrogate them and call them into question, often through subtle changes in the ways in which they are enacted. Butler (1990: 25) argues that there is "no gender identity behind the expressions of gender; that identity is performatively constituted by the very 'expressions' that are said to be its results." Such an approach means that a woman does not wear lipstick because she is a woman, but rather that the act of wearing lipstick brings an identity as woman into being. But in our everyday repeated enactments of gender and sexuality (applying lipstick, choosing clothes, shaving and waxing, working out, restricting what we eat, flirting), we both reproduce *and* potentially subvert these identity constructs. This is because there is always the possibility of performing our bodies and therefore our gender and sexuality differently, as witnessed for example in butch-femme lesbian or transboi gender performances as well as in the more subtle ways in which women appropriate male privilege in public space and in which gays and lesbians resist the heterosexing of space or recode heterosexist spaces in liberating ways (see Browne 2004; Bell and Valentine 1995). Such parodic performances of heterosexual gender "expose heterosexuality as an incessant and *panicked* imitation of its own naturalized idealization" (Butler 1991: 22–23). These recodings happen outside of the media all the time, but there is no doubt that the media is a key site for their repeated destabilization, both in terms of the content of what we consume but also because media consumption provides a space for people to both take pleasure in and reflect upon corporeal performances and representations in the context of their own social, economic, and cultural lifeworlds. As Barbara Creed (2005: 486), drawing on Butler, writes,

> *The media, however, specifically television programmes such as soap operas and sitcoms, frequently use performance to expose the performative nature of sexuality and, by extension, the everyday. ... Television and other organs of the cultural imaginary ... are frequently given some latitude in representing unfamiliar sexual roles and in giving voice to unconventional, often bizarre, forms of sexual behaviour—although if these are too threatening censorship bodies have the power to curtail discursive practices. This latitude is central to the success of markedly diverse programmes, which focus on sexuality, from The L Word to Little Britain and Kath & Kim. What many of these programmes do is point to the constructedness of gender, and by extension, the everyday.*

There is therefore an urgent need to nuance and question much of the work that sees the media as having a causal effect on actual bodies and actual men and women. Indeed, what we find in the media is a diversity of representations and performances of the body. Then if we add to that the diversity of readings available, including the ways in which for example "straight" texts are often queered by gay and lesbian viewers (see Tulloch and Jenkins 1995; Lewis 2002; Berger 2010; Gregg 2010), it means we cannot generalize about what the media does to the body. Indeed, media and bodies are entangled in so many ways that the material outcomes of this entanglement can only ever be understood in context. The context is produced by the conditions of production of the media text, the conditions of its reception, and the ways in which both production and consumption are embedded in societies in which discursive tensions surrounding gender, race, class, and sexuality are mobilized by diversely positioned social actors.

Extending Bodies

Performativity theory is not the only scholarship to disrupt the focus on representationalism. Other scholarship in both cultural studies and cultural geography has emphasized the body's materiality in ways that has implications for our understandings of bodies in media and media in bodies. In 1985, Donna Haraway released her antiessentialist and anticapitalist cyborg manifesto, which urged a rethinking of the boundary crossings between the natural and the artificial, human and machine, and human and animal. She urges us to embrace these boundary crossings because of the radical political potential that a nonhumanist ontology can help to facilitate. In the 1990s, much work on the body and new media technologies discussed the ways in which virtual environments enabled users to transcend their bodies in ways that were empowering or exhilarating, including online cross-dressing (Stone 1991; see also Batty 1997; Robins 1995; Wark 1994). Rosanne Allucquère Stone (1991) recounts the story of Julie, a severely disabled older woman who formed part of an online computer conference in the 1980s. Julie operated her computer with a headstick and attracted a massive online following of admirers, supporters, and people who turned to her for advice. It transpired later that Julie was actually a middle-aged, able-bodied male psychiatrist who developed "Julie" upon learning that people online talked to him differently when they thought he was a woman. But even the early theorists in cybercultural studies recognized the diffuseness of the boundary between the "real" body and the avatar or "virtual" body. Sex in a virtual environment can still produce orgasm in the real body and one's avatar must be paused if its user needs to go to the toilet. Being immersed in a virtual reality environment has tended to involve the wearing of a cumbersome helmet and goggle and even walking on a treadmill. It is an intensely embodied experience. Rather than thinking about virtual environments as enabling the displacement or transcendence of the body, it is productive to recognize that embodied motor activity and the movement of the physical body through space is the fundamental mode of access to and experience of alternative virtual or mixed reality realms (Hansen 2006).

While the cyborg appears as a figure of science fiction, media technologies have always reconfigured bodies. Media use places the body in a relationship to technology in a manner in which both are mutually transformed. Even the early landline telephones created new modes of embodiment and therefore new embodied geographies as did the early live radio broadcasts. As Stone (1991) notes, using Franklin D. Roosevelt's radio broadcasts as an example, radio enabled the body to be in two places at once. FDR could address US citizens directly rather than through delegates. His body was inserted in their living rooms as their bodies were inserted into his. Consequently, the notion of bodily presence did not begin to shift with the development of information technology in the late twentieth century but much earlier. Even mundane and everyday forms of media consumption from watching live sport to catching up on the latest episode of a soap opera produces active and diverse modes of bodily response, including excitement, tension, concentration, and relaxation. Live broadcast can produce an adrenaline rush in those participating as presenters or spectators (Kuritsky-Fox 2008). So media use and consumption produce an entanglement and merging of bodies, media content, and devices that are often pleasurable and that can have diverse and sometimes unpredictable outcomes for viewers or users. Since the turn of the millennium, bodies have become increasingly connected, wired, and networked, or tethered (Turkle 2008b). People report checking their smartphones hundreds of times a day and keeping them on and close whilst sleeping; exercise cannot be imagined without one's iPod; television viewing or updating one's Facebook status no longer must be postponed until one gets home after work but can be done during the commute on public transport; and people lead detailed and complex parallel lives in Second Life. Media devices are now smaller, individually rather than collectively owned, and are increasingly physically attached to the body during use. Cell phones in particular have become ordinary media devices, always attached to or in close proximity to the body. For Leopoldina Fortunati (2002: 48), "of all the mobile technologies, the mobile phone is the one most intimately close to the body," shaping the ways in which we negotiate proximity and distance. Cell phones extend our bodies, enabling us to be in two or more places at once. A recent news article described cell phones as resembling phantom limbs in the sense that we have become so reliant on them that if they fail or are absent, it will be as if we have lost a limb (Hom 2011). For Gathman (2008: 48), her cell phone functions as a protective device; talking into it in public spaces shields her body from "panhandling and unwelcome advances." Teenagers in particular display impressive cyborgian tendencies with respect to cell phone use, with their ability to text rapidly without needing to look at the keypad and often without being seen by teachers or parents (Thompson and Cupples 2008).

The rapidity and miniaturization of contemporary technological development have complicated what it means to be human, creating a posthuman condition (Hayles 1999). The mutual constitution of humans and technology is not however a new phenomenon and it could be argued we have always been posthuman, and as Hayles (1999: 3) argues, the body is "the original prosthesis we all learn to manipulate so that extending or replacing the body with other prostheses becomes a continuation of a process that began before we were born." Just as "an online avatar can come to feel continuous with the self" (Turkle 2008a), it is worth bearing in mind the totally unremarkable ways in which things and objects are extensions of bodies and selves. We routinely rely on prostheses such as spectacles or walking sticks; we make holes in our body in order to wear pieces of jewellery and leave traces of our bodies in texts, including letters, diaries, photographs, and notes on the fridge; we rely on a machine to wake us up in the morning, and our daily social and economic reproduction would quickly become unfathomable if the electricity system failed. Everyday media technologies are just additional and often thoroughly mundane ways in which our bodies get extended and additional sites in which our bodies leave their traces, including the text or voice-mail message sent to announce our late arrival, the need to get up to the next level on the latest Playstation game before leaving for school, programming the DVD-R to watch a television program after its initial broadcast to bring our media and bodies into more comfortable alignment and to prevent us having to remove our bodies from other places (work, social events, family activities) prematurely. Being human means being posthuman (Halberstam and Livingston 1995: 8) and we are all cyborgs to some extent (Gray 2002).

While many dystopian and apocalyptic understandings about the merging of humans and technology abound both in science fiction and everyday discourse and many people struggle with the concept of posthumanism and the challenge it poses to the imagined coherence of the human body (Halberstam and Livingston 1995), the merging of humans and technologies is ordinary. So unless we grapple with the concept of the cyborg or of being posthuman, we risk failing to properly grasp the risks and opportunities that our everyday bodily interfaces with media technologies pose as they unfold, and we might fail to notice the outcomes, good, bad, and contradictory, that are already here.

Scholarship in science and technology studies and related fields that has focused on the blurring of machines and humans has also involved a recognition that media technologies are agentic, lively, and have human properties and people frequently think of them in that way (Stone 1991; Thompson and Cupples 2008). People fall in love with their prosthesis (Stone 1995) or develop an eroticized attachment to their cell phone (Gathman 2008). Use of media technologies contributes to bodily sense-making as well as bodily extension. For example, Ash and Gallacher (2011: 362) describe video games as "as contributing to a (micro)politics of practice in which technologies structure the ways in which people make sense of their own bodies, particularly in relation to societally sensitive issues of weight, size and obesity."

Technological developments associated with the Web 2.0 environment are enabling new mediations, extensions, and redistributions of the body. Increasingly, ordinary people are filming and uploading their own bodies to social media sites such as YouTube and Vimeo. You can find hundreds of personal videos of ordinary people giving birth, getting a bikini wax or a nipple piercing, having an IUD inserted or working out at the gym. People use smartphone apps such as *runkeeper.com* to measure their speed, distance, and calories burned, which they then share with their friends on Facebook. People photograph or film and then, often using timelapsed images, upload their weight-loss progress, their hair growth, or their own ageing. Traceurs and skateboarders upload their bodily skill to YouTube to bring new forms of engagement with urban environments into being and new ways of making and knowing the city (Glynn 2009; Mould 2009). According to Francis Barker (1984, see discussion in Turkle 1991), in the premodern era the body was constituted through public spectacle, but then retreated from the public sphere in the seventeenth century to become increasingly privatized and hidden. It appears that in the Web 2.0 environment, the body is increasingly a public spectacle. While online videos of skateboarding and parkour could be seen to contribute to a progressive anticapitalist aesthetic, the progressive potential of other mediated bodies is less readily apparent. Robyn Longhurst (2006) reviewed hundreds of YouTube videos of births and although she acknowledges their potential for democratizing the birthing experience, most videos seemed to reproduce the dominance of the heterosexual nuclear family and discourses of "good" mothering.

Making Over Bodies

New social media is not the only site in which the body is constructed as a public spectacle. Mainstream commercial television also uses spectacular constructions, imaginings, and transformations of the body to attract viewers and drive up ratings. One of the most salient media phenomena of the new millennium has been the dramatic growth and proliferation of reality television and within that of the makeover genre. In many prime-time shows, contestants deemed to be overweight, unhealthy, or badly dressed are provided with advice and assistance to help them lose weight, eat more healthfully, or dress in a more appealing manner. Self-appointed or qualified experts in exercise and fitness, nutrition management, and fashion are brought in to enable the contestants to make over their bodies in the course of a single episode or season. Some shows such as *America's Next Top Model* attempt to turn already beautiful women into models through competition. The recreation of the body and the positive consequences of such a makeover for the individual's life opportunities are central to the appeal of such shows. Some shows such as *The Biggest Loser, The Swan,* and *Extreme Makeover* are focused on beauty and/or weight loss using exercise, nutrition, and sometimes cosmetic surgery. Others such as *What Not to Wear, Trinny and Susannah Undress,* and *Queer Eye for the Straight Guy* deal largely with clothing, helping people to dress in more flattering or fashionable ways. In *Trinny and Susannah Undress,* the show's experts, advisors Trinny Woodall and Susannah Constantine, visit couples who are experiencing relationship difficulties. To overcome these difficulties, they are encouraged to undress behind a screen (viewers get to see a silhouette of the naked bodies) and are taken clothes shopping by the experts. Some shows deal with children's or teenagers' bodies, focusing either on nutrition management as in *Honey We're Killing the Kids* (which uses computer-generated images to show what children will look like when they grow up should they continue on such an unhealthy path) or on unruly behavior as in *Super Nanny, Little Angels,* or *My Teen's a Nightmare.* The carnivalesque unruly body appears in *My Big Fat Obnoxious Fiancé* (2003–2004), a reality show in which a woman wins $500,000 for herself and her family if she can dupe her family to attend her imminent wedding with an obnoxious and ill-behaved man who is actually an actor. There are other reality television shows that are not part of the makeover genre in which the body features in alternative ways. Shows such as *Survivor* or *Fear Factor* are in part about pushing bodies to limits of endurance. *Black.White,* which screened in 2006, involved a black family from Atlanta and a white family from Los Angeles that through innovative makeup trade "races," giving the black family access to white culture and the white family the experience of being black in the United States.

Reality television shows often do well in the ratings and can be relatively cheap to make. They are therefore appealing to commercial television broadcasters. The makeover genre attracts much criticism from scholars and other commentators with many people believing that they lack quality or are cruel and humiliating to participants. Health professionals have criticized shows such as *The Biggest Loser* for encouraging participants to undergo dramatic calorie-cutting diets, punishing exercise routines, and even dehydration in order to lose abnormally large amounts of weight in a short space of time (Wyatt 2009). Laurie Ouellette and James Hay (2008) and Katherine Sender (2006) understand reality television as a key modality of governmentality in neoliberal post-welfare states in the sense that these shows aim to empower and encourage citizens to act as self-governing responsible citizens. The shows target viewers as well as contestants. As noted by Ouellette and Hay (2008), as the (overweight) contestant who is put through a highly mediated spectacle of grueling exercise, healthful-eating advice, and dramatic weigh-ins, viewers are encouraged to focus on their own (overweight) bodies and incorporate the techniques covered in the show into their own lives. The shows therefore play a role in creating the kind of citizens that the neoliberal state requires, citizens that take responsibility for their own health and well-being rather than relying on state bodies.

There is no doubt that much reality television can be seen as politically conservative, but the ways in which such shows mediate the body means their progressive potential cannot be overlooked. Indeed, the makeover genre draws explicit attention to the constructedness of bodies and in particular how the normative body is classed. In other words, overweight, unhealthy, or unprepossessing working-class bodies can become "beautiful" with access to a personal trainer, cosmetic surgery, and/or designer clothing. Just like Haraway's cyborg, the naturalization of class, race, gender, or sex is destabilized and opened to critical reflection. Of course, the denaturalization of such categories can be both disempowering and empowering, as it emphasizes that beauty (and access to the life opportunities that it brings) is out of reach to the majority of people. It does however also show that beauty is made and is not naturally given, so people deprived of opportunities are so deprived because of their location in a class structure. Some reality shows do not so much reproduce neoliberalism but draw attention to the negative consequences of neoliberalism for ordinary people. As John McMurria (2008: 306) writes of home makeover television,

> *Many of these families have suffered severe health issues, such as a child with brittle bone disease, a parent recently diagnosed with adult epilepsy, a baby that required a heart transplant, and perhaps most heartrending, a deaf couple with a blind, autistic child. Other families have lost loved ones from car accidents or gun shootings, and some have suffered property damage from floods and fires. While many of these problems seem exceptional, these Sunday evening glimpses into the lives of struggling families expose the daily situations many Americans face as neoliberal policies have reduced social safety nets.*

Conclusions

Its undeniable materiality notwithstanding, the gendered, racialized, and sexed body is always in the process of becoming and so there is no static model of womanhood, manhood, or sexuality that is reinforced in the mediation of bodies. Cultural understandings about bodies, those of men, women, children, and adults are in a constant state of flux. Many discourses of the body are in cultural circulation. Feminist critiques of thinness circulate alongside adorations of supermodels. In turn, these circulate alongside public health concerns about obesity epidemics as well as alongside the resistant celebration of excess. All of these coexist with advertising for both fast food and aids to weight loss. The KFC Double Down[2] competes for media space with the African Mango supplement, just as Vicky Pollard competes for media attention with Eva Longoria, and both are popular with consumers and audiences. Even sexy, fit female performers whose body size and shape could not be attained by the vast majority of women are open to both feminist and counter-feminist readings. As well as being thin, they might also articulate an oppositional politics that can be harnessed by larger and less fit women. They are of course never just their bodies, and as media texts they are open to a variety of interpretations, and as analysts we might be able to identify how they both reproduce oppressive understandings of gender and sexuality or open such understandings to destabilization or interrogation. The media is as much a site for the contestation of dominant body politics as it is for its reaffirmation. And both contestation and reaffirmation can occur simultaneously. The body on-screen can never act in a direct way upon a viewer nor does the decision or desire to watch emerge in isolation from the broader social, cultural, and economic contexts in which viewers, media texts, and media devices are immersed.

References

Ash, J. and L.A. Gallacher. 2011. Cultural geography and videogames. *Geography Compass* 596: 351–68.

Barker, F. 1984. *The Tremulous Private Body: Essays on Subjection.* London: Methuen.

Batty, M. 1997. Virtual geography. *Futures* 29(4–5): 337–52.

Bell, D. and G. Valentine. 1995a. Introductions: Orientations. In *Mapping Desire: Geographies of Sexualities.* Edited by D. Bell and G. Valentine. London: Routledge, 1–24.

Bell, D. and G. Valentine. 1995b. *Mapping Desire: Geographies of Sexualities.* London: Routledge.

Berger, R. 2010. Out and about: Slash fic, re-imagined texts and queer commentaries. In *LGBT Identity and Online New Media.* Edited by C. Pullen and M. Cooper. London: Routledge, 173–84.

Berndt, K. 2011. Hermione Granger, or, A vindication of the rights of girl. In *Heroism in the Harry Potter Series.* Edited by K. Berndt and L. Steveker. Farnham: Ashgate, 159–76.

Browne, K. 2004. Genderism and the bathroom problem: (Re)materialising sexed sites, (re) creating sexed bodies. *Gender, Place and Culture* 11(3): 331–46.

Butler, J. 1990. *Gender Trouble: Feminism and the Subversion of Identity.* London: Routledge.

Butler, J. 1991. Imitation and gender subordination. In *Inside/Outside: Lesbian Theories, Gay Theories.* Edited by D. Fuss. New York: Routledge, 13–31.

Cook, A. 2010. "Look at moiye!" Monstrous feminine as social rebellion in *Kath & Kim.* In *Illuminating the Dark Side: Evil Women and the Feminine.* Edited by A. Ruthven and G. Mádlo. Oxford: Inter-Disciplinary Press, 71–78.

Crang, M., P. Crang, and J. May. 1999. *Virtual Geographies: Bodies, Space and Relations.* London: Routledge.

Cream, J. 1995. Re-solving riddles: The sexed body. In *Mapping Desire: Geographies of Sexualities.* Edited by D. Bell and G. Valentine. London: Routledge, 28–36.

[2] A chicken, bacon, and cheese bunless sandwich sold by KFC heavily criticized by nutritionists for its high calorie and fat content.

Creed, B. 2005. The end of the everyday: Transformation, sexuality and the uncanny. *Continuum: Journal of Media and Cultural Studies* 19(4): 483–94.

Cupples, J. and L. Thompson. 2010. Heterotextuality and digital foreplay: Cell phones and the culture of teenage romance. *Feminist Media Studies* 10(1): 1–17.

England, M. 2011. Suicide girls: Bodies, beauty and cyberspace. *Aether: The Journal of Media Geography* 8: 8–24.

Fiske, J. 1987. *Television Culture.* London: Routledge.

Fortunati, L. 2002. Italy: Stereotypes, true and false. In *Perpetual Contact: Mobile Communications, Private Talk, Public Performance*. Edited by J.E. Katz and M.A. Aakhus. Cambridge: Cambridge University Press, 42–62.

Fox-Kales, E. 2011. *Body Shots: Hollywood and the Culture of Eating Disorders.* New York: SUNY Press.

Gathman, E.C.H. 2008. Cell phones. In *The Inner History of Devices*. Edited by S. Turkle. Cambridge, MA: MIT Press, 41–48.

Gauntlett, D. 1998. Ten things wrong with the "effects model." In *Approaches to Audiences: A Reader*. Edited by R. Dickinson, R. Harindranath, and O. Linné. London: Arnold, 120–30.

Glynn, K. 2009. Contested land and mediascapes: The visuality of the postcolonial city. *New Zealand Geographer* 65(1): 6–22.

Graham, S. 1998. The end of geography or the explosion of place? Conceptualizing space, place and information technology. *Progress in Human Geography* 22(2): 165–85.

Gray, C.H. 2002. *Cyborg Citizen: Politics in the Posthuman Age.* New York: Routledge.

Gregg, R. 2010. Queering Brad Pitt: The struggle between gay fans and the Hollywood machine to control star discourse and image on the Web. In *LGBT Identity and Online New Media.* Edited by C. Pullen and M. Cooper. London: Routledge, 139–46.

Halberstam, J. 2012. Pregnant men, heteroflexible women and gaga feminism. Public lecture delivered at the University of Birmingham, April 19.

Halberstam, J. and I. Livingston. 1995. Introduction: Posthuman bodies. In *Posthuman Bodies.* Edited by J. Halberstam and I. Livingston. Bloomington: Indiana University Press, 1–19.

Hansen, M.B.N. 2006. *Bodies in Code: Interfaces with Digital Media.* London: Routledge.

Haraway, D. 1991. *Simians, Cyborgs and Women: The Reinvention of Nature.* New York: Routledge.

Hartley, J. 1999. *The Uses of Television.* London: Routledge.

Hayles, K.N. 1999. *How We Became Posthuman: Virtual Bodies in Cybernetics, Literature and Informatics.* Chicago: University of Chicago Press.

Hillis, K. 1999. *Digital Sensations: Space, Identity and Embodiment in Virtual Reality*. Minneapolis: University of Minnesota Press.

Hillis, K. 2009. *Online a Lot of the Time.* Durham: Duke University Press.

Holloway, S.L. and G. Valentine. 2003. *Cyberkids: Children in the Information Age.* London: Routledge-Falmer.

Hom, A. 2011. How mobile phones are turning into phantom limbs. *Telegraph* [Online, April 18]. Available at: www.blogs.telegraph.co.uk/technology/adrianhon/100006561/how-mobile-phones-are-turning-into-phantom-limbs/ [accessed June 22, 2012].

Jenkins, H. 1992. *Textual Poachers: Television Fans and Participatory Culture.* London: Routledge.

Jenkins, H. 2000. Lessons from Littleton: What Congress doesn't want to hear about youth and media. *Independent School Magazine* 59(2) [Online]. Available at: www.nais.org/publications/ismagazinearticle.cfm?Itemnumber=144264&sn.ItemNumber=145956 [accessed 22 June 2012].

Johnson, M.L. 2007. *Third Wave Feminism and Television: Jane Puts It in a Box.* London: I.B. Tauris.

Kitchin, R. 1998. Towards geographies of cyberspace. *Progress in Human Geography* 22(3): 385–406.

Kuritsky-Fox, O. 2008. Television. In *The Inner History of Devices*. Edited by S. Turkle. Cambridge, MA: MIT Press, 55–61.

Lewis, J. 2002. *Cultural Studies: The Basics.* London: SAGE.
Lockyer, S. 2010. Dynamics of social class contempt in contemporary British television comedy. *Social Semiotics* 20(2): 121–38.
Longhurst, R. 2000. Corporeographies of pregnancy: 'Bikini babes." *Environment and Planning D: Society and Space* 18: 453–72.
Longhurst, R. 2001. *Bodies: Exploring Fluid Boundaries.* London: Routledge.
Longhurst, R. 2006. YouTube: A new space for birth? *Feminist Review* 93(1): 46–63.
Lotz, A. 2001. Postfeminist television criticism: Rehabilitating critical terms and identifying postfeminist attitudes. *Feminist Media Studies* 1(1): 105–21.
McMurria, J. 2008. Desperate citizens and good Samaritans: Neoliberalism and makeover reality TV. *Television and New Media* 9(4): 305–32.
Morley, D. 1992. *Television, Audiences and Cultural Studies.* London: Routledge.
Mould, O. 2009. Parkour, the city, the event. *Environment and Planning D: Society and Space* 27: 738–50.
Mulvey, L. 1973. Visual pleasure and narrative cinema. *Screen* 16(3): 6–18.
Nast, H. and S. Pile. 1998. *Places Through the Body.* London: Routledge.
Ouellette, L. and J. Hay. 2008. *Better Living Through Reality TV.* Malden, MA: Blackwell.
Pender, P. 2004. "Kicking ass is comfort food": Buffy as third wave feminist icon. In *Third Wave Feminism: A Critical Exploration.* Edited by S. Gillis, G. Howe, and R. Munsford. New York: Palgrave, 164–74.
Robins, K. 1995. Cyberspace and the world we live in. In *Cyberspace/Cyberbodies/Cyberpunk: Cultures of Technological Embodiment.* Edited by M. Featherstone and R. Burrows. London: SAGE, 135–55.
Rowe, K.K. 1994. Roseanne: Unruly woman as domestic goddess. In *Television: The Critical View.* 5th ed. Edited by H. Newcombe. New York: Oxford University Press, 202–11.
Sender, K. 2006. Queens for a day: "Queer Eye for the Straight Guy" and the neoliberal project. *Critical Studies in Media Communication* 23(2): 131–51.
Smith, S. 2012. "Desperate Housewives" syndrome. *Sydney Morning Herald* [Online, May 30]. Available at: www.smh.com.au/lifestyle/beauty/desperate-housewives-syndrome-20120529-1zgoa.html [accessed June 7, 2012].
Stone, R.A. 1991. Will the real body please stand up? In *Cyberspace: First Steps.* Edited by M. Benedikt. Cambridge, MA: MIT Press, 81–118.
Stone, R.A. 1995. *The War of Desire and Technology at the Close of the Mechanical Age.* Cambridge, MA: MIT Press.
Tasker, Y. 1993. *Spectacular Bodies: Gender, Genre and the Action Cinema.* London: Routledge.
Thompson, L. and J. Cupples. 2008. Seen and not heard? Text messaging and digital sociality. *Social and Cultural Geography* 9(1): 95–108.
Thrift, N. 2011. Lifeworld Inc. – And what to do about it. *Environment and Planning D: Society and Space* 29: 5–26.
Tulloch, J. and H. Henry Jenkins. 1995. *Science Fiction Audiences: Watching* Doctor Who *and* Star Trek. London: Routledge.
Turkle, S. 1995. *Life on the Screen: Identity in the Age of the Internet.* Cambridge, MA: MIT Press.
Turkle, S. 2008a. Inner history. In *The Inner History of Devices.* Edited by S. Turkle. Cambridge, MA: MIT Press, 2–29.
Turkle, S. 2008b. Always-on/Always-on-you: The tethered self. In *Handbook of Mobile Communication Studies.* Edited by J.E. Katz. Cambridge, MA: MIT Press, 121–37.
Turkle, S. 2011. *Alone Together: Why We Expect More from Technology and Less from Each Other.* New York: Basic Books.
Tyler, I. 2008. Chav mum chav scum. *Feminist Media Studies* 8(1): 17–34.
Wilson, E. 2006. Texters called cyborgs. *The Press,* June 7, A2.

Wyatt, E. 2009. On "The Biggest Loser," health can take a back seat. *New York Times* [Online, November 24]. Available at: www.nytimes.com/2009/11/25/business/media/25loser.html?_r=2&partner=rss&emc=rss&pagewanted=all [accessed June 25, 2012].
Wark, M. 1994. *Virtual Geography.* Indianapolis: Indiana University Press.
Wykes, M. and Gunter, B. 2005. *The Media and Body Image: If Looks Could Kill.* London: SAGE.

Places of Interiority

Stuart C. Aitken

> *[Packer] wasn't sure whether he was watching a computerized mapping of his heart or a picture of the thing itself. It throbbed forcefully on-screen. The image was only a foot away but the heart assumed another context, one of distance and immensity, beating in the blood plum raptures of a galaxy in formation … He felt the passion of the body, its adaptive drive over geologic time, the poetry and chemistry of its origins in the dust of old exploding stars. How dwarfed he felt by his own heart. There it was and it awed him, to see his life beneath his breastbone in image-forming units, hammering on outside him.*
>
> *DeLillo 2003: 44*

Ostensibly driving across Manhattan to get a haircut, 28-year-old Eric Michael Packer ambulates through a series of moments that become increasingly surreal and dangerous. Packer is a successful Wall Street executive who attained galactic heights in the financial universe through his ability to predict nuanced changes in the market. Packer's world, on this particular day, is circumscribed by a stretch-limousine that guides him through Manhattan streets clogged in anticipation of a presidential cavalcade. The drive to the haircut is a series of fits and starts through which we learn a little more about Packer's world with each pause. From within the limousine's sumptuous but cramped space, Packer conducts the quirky meetings that comprise his craft. The pulsating, mobile interior space of the limousine provides a perfect *mise en abyme* for Canadian filmmaker David Cronenberg. The limousine is decked out with computers connected to global markets and, in the extraordinary scene described in the epigram, it connects Packer to essential organs inside his body. For Cronenberg, *Cosmopolis* (2012, based on Don DeLillo's 2003 novel) is the apex of a 35-year auteuristic journey that seeks to elaborate the affects of interiority. In his earlier work, Cronenberg focuses on the ways interiority shows up on the outside: squeezed out of orifices, erupting through evisceration (e.g. *They Came from Within* aka *Shivers* 1975) or more subtly uncovered by psychoanalytic processes (e.g. *Dead Ringers* 1988; *A Dangerous Method* 2011). With *Cosmopolis*, much like his early cult classic *Videodrome* (1983), Cronenberg explicitly connects places of interiority, *en abyme*, to larger global movements. It is the media connection between places of interiority and worldwide forces that I want to explore in this chapter, using Cronenberg's work as a particularly poignant example.

Sonia Front and Katarzyna Nowak (2010: xiii) argue that it is through the body that we distinguish exteriors and interiors. The body acts as the geography closest in, providing the scope and limits of touch, smell and vision, and hence a point of reference that is a litmus test for drawing borders between the interior versus the exterior. Of course, the distinctions between what we chose to include and exclude are always political, raising lasting questions of ethical and moral value. How do we distinguish between interiors and exteriors?

Should we? The contemporary feminist and some post-structural critique of binaries[1] suggest that we should not make those distinctions anymore, but if we don't where does that leave us? If we are left with multiple readings and a plurality of spaces, what are the political complications of an expanding relativism? What are the political ramifications of dismissing representational categories? How do representational categories affect existential political crises? If these representations come from the inside out, whose insides are of most concern?

In what follows, I spend some time thinking about how we have theorized about places of interiority, and conclude that past musings are of little worth unless they make explicit connections with relations beyond what is inside. These relations are woven in, through and beyond media that are always more than the message; they define spaces of culture and suggest places of belonging. I then open up these relations by considering exterior and endogenous affectations before returning to Cronenberg's cinematic oeuvre that, I argue, points to a way of understanding interior life-spaces in a more politicized, radical, and far-reaching context of openness and becoming. Although I speak of Cronenberg's movies in toto as a collective that opens up interiorities, I focus on *Cosmopolis* as a particular poignant example that communicates from an intense place deep within while simultaneously reaching out cosmographically, to a seeming universal polity.

Thinking Inwardly

A media chapter entitled "places of interiority" may be of concern to those who remember the rise of psychogeography in the 1980s, and some overreaching battles between Freudian, Lacanian, and feminist theory. Freud's focus on the development of self through the Oedipal-stage was challenged by Lacan's mirror-stage and a linguistic turn in how we understood the development of consciousness and the evolution of unconscious drives. Feminism challenged the patriarchal basis of the Oedipal- and mirror-stages as being too rigorously structured around a white, male European model of human development. By so doing, feminism obviously also challenged the patriarchal structure of society. Taking this further as part of their influential *Anti-Oedipus*, Deleuze and Guattari (1983) famously connected the focus of psychoanalysis on pathologies and developmental normalization to the apparati of capitalism and the state. They take Freud beyond the family, seeing individuals as the heterogeneous aggregate of parts of social and natural machines. They reposition desire as positive, productive, and more than libidinal, and the unconscious as indifferent to personal and political identity. Deleuze and Guattari empty out the Oedipus, dissipating its power into a multiplicity of "desiring machines." The subject eviscerates, turns inside out, and continuously reconstructs itself as a temporary "body without organs" along lines of desire. Deleuze and Guattari evoke the breast-mouth as a body without organs that comes together as a temporary assemblage, which may not be part of other wholes but a working body with its own purpose. Unlike Freudian and Lacanian theory, desire is positive. There is no lack or unconscious desire left unfulfilled.

Deleuze and Guattari position Marxian thought as a libidinal exercise, seeing the social and political as immediately invested with desire. The entire notion of a complete monadic "subject" with political and personal interests of its own becomes meaningless unless understood relationally, in terms of its recombinatorial power. For Deleuze and Guattari, analytic possibilities cannot reside in a space already occupied by objects precipitated out

[1] Deleuzean post-structuralism notes that language presents to us a field of binaries but they are produced by nonbinary processes from a multiplicity of virtual spatiotemporal levels (Massumi 1992: 46).

of the state's binary machine, like man/woman or inside/outside (Kirby 1996: 115). The ideal state of a body without organs is most often relational and recombinatorial, temporary, lacking restraints, moving in excess of the boundaries between subjects and objects, insides and outsides.

From a Deleuzean perspective, it may be useful to think in terms of intensity as a movement toward the internal and extension as a movement toward the external. And, brilliantly, Delouse sidesteps the issue of ontological binaries because actual intensity has form and substance, or extension, which may be thought of as an exteriority. This not to say that virtual or pure intension is undifferentiated, only that it is an indeterminate part of our spatiality (Massumi 1992: 66).

Kathy Kirby (1996: 117) argues that a focus on Deleuze and Guattari – as well as other post-structural perspectives that reorder the space of the subject, "can lead subjects to disrespect the bounds of others, or to cede too much of the social territory and lose the capacity to maintain their own self-interests." The danger here, she argues, is that we change the space of the subject – the mental landscape – instead of affecting some politically constructed external world. For some, the development of Deleuzian post-structural critiques lose the interpretative power of a Freudian and Lacanian analysis that is pointed at the political construction of the external. As a counter, Paul Ricoeur (1981) argues that psychoanalysis is a hermeneutics of suspicion that searches for deception and thereby destabilizes reliance on reason, rationality, and seemingly clear meanings. Heidi Nast (2000), for example, uses a Lacanian focus on linguistic and representational power to argue that police strategies and procedures in Chicago during the mid-twentieth century problematically racialized landscapes around the Oedipal and the bestial. For Nast, Ricoeur, and others, it is reasonable to laud psychoanalysis for its interpretative qualities in that it can get us behind the curtain to where the autocratic patriarch is revealed in all his insecurity. The epistemological question raised by Nast's work relates to how far a focus on interiorities resonates with outward affects and, if we are interested in media, is it possible and desirable to imbricate the representational power of those relations? If we agree that within capitalist modes of production, representation simply functions as a means of coordinating flows of power that are hierarchically arranged then perhaps a new politics of creativity (e.g. Deleuze and Guattari's (1988) schizo-politics) is possible, one that can create new patterns of expression and being (e.g. Marston, Jones, and Woodward's (1994) flat ontologies).

Some geographers, like Steve Pile (1996; 2010), embraced Freudian perspectives to help uncover interesting proportions about how material landscapes resonate with embodied political identities. As a stalwart defender of Freud, Pile (2010: 5) argues that psychoanalytic perspectives offer relief from "conceptual blind-spots" in how geographers come to understand desire, affect, and emotion. Curti and his colleagues (2011: 1475) challenge this standpoint by suggesting that when focusing on affect and emotion, psychogeographers like Pile fail to confront the diverse political and geographical implications that underpin questions about identity and difference. For Curti and his collaborators, understanding differences and wholes through heterogeneous aggregates is more rewarding than positioning individuals and their distinctions within what they see as some larger normalizing or universalizing set of theories. Liz Bondi, another early proponent of psychogeography, embraced larger contexts of scholarship on emotions, but tempered her enthusiasm for Freud and Lacan with feminist admonitions that move in a direction of geographies of care (Bondi 1993; Davidson et al. 2005). To the extent that a combination of psychoanalytic and feminist theories of care move our thinking of places and landscapes in a direction that embraces larger understandings of affect, emotion, desire, and the unconscious, for Bondi it is clearly important to question the relations between interiority and exteriority. And to the extent that Deleuzian concepts of deterritorialization, reterritorialization, folds, striations, and smoothings suggest a series of crowded polarities, it is still important to understand the valence of relations between what we feel inside (interior/intensive) and what we perceive as outside (exterior/extensive).

My beginning assumption, then, is that it is worthwhile contextualizing interiority and intensive sexual/political identities through emotional and affectual geographies that are not encumbered by the ontological partitioning of mind and body that often underpins Freudian and Lacanian theory (Curti et al. 2011). What the psychoanalytic turn in geography does that remains germane to what I want to discuss in this chapter relates to the ways it weaves together landscapes of interiority around contexts of suspicion and desire, and points to the outward affects of those contexts on difference and larger existent, extensive materialities.

Of course, the notion of interiority precedes psychogeography and in terms of media and place studies can perhaps be traced to Walter Benjamin's prematurely truncated *Arcades Project* (2004). With this project, Benjamin described the ways middle- and upper-class Parisians walked through their city, voyeuristically penetrating its depths through perambulations and window shopping. For Benjamin, the city was a place of profane illumination and, as such, he was perhaps the first to link subconscious desires with places. Benjamin's work later propelled media theorists to highlighted connections to the globalized other. Victorian fascinations with the phantasmagoria of dioramas depicting ancient tribal and contemporary anthropological discoveries suggests intrinsic desire through spectacles of the other (Friedberg 1993). It is no coincidence that early twentieth-century geographers – with their colonial connections – were wrapped up in these depictions and media contrivances of the other (Aitken 2010). For Benjamin, this was the birth of the modern, a bourgeoisie world that was shallow and hollow inside, waiting to be filled with commodities and fetishes. What the work on desire, place, and media does well is make connections between landscapes, bodies, and psyches through a focus on the politics of representation. Benjamin's contribution connects all of these affects to larger economic and class forces. For him, desires and fetishes are reified in the urban landscape, which in time becomes a place valuing only the interiority of those who control the mode of production and the processes of reproduction. Working people are reified as their labor is commodified within market capitalism. The ruling classes prosper from this reification and the workers (and women) become submissive, unable to grasp their political identities and the real conditions of their lived experience. Reification permeates the whole of Benjamin's social life, flourishing in politics and culture, and reinforced through popular media (Merrifield 2002: 57). The connection of the arcades and street-walking to prostitution, by contrast, highlights a different class of voyeurism and a different production of space, leading Giuliana Bruno (1992) to argue important connections with film that counter the reification of sex, and the objectification of women as commodities. Bruno uses Italian urban film to highlight women's views of love, poverty, desire, violence, and death. Her filmic critique ranges from the city's exteriors to the body's interiors, reclaiming an alternative history of women's filmmaking, which forcefully articulates a spatial, interior/exterior and corporeal interpretation of film language.

Since Benjamin's work in the first half of the twentieth century, focus on interiorities continues as a vibrant part of literary and cultural studies (Front and Nowak 2010). The importance of interior spaces and the ways that it molds and disturbs protagonists shows up in a vast array of Western literary work from Charles Dicken's *The Old Curiosity Shop* (1841) to Mervyn Peake's Gormenghast trilogy (1968) (Punter 2010). For some, this is a liminal transformation through doorways and portals, or it may be the changing form and function of rooms, venals, and passageways and how those changes affect characters and their views of the world.

A large part of the psycho-feminist underpinnings of this media work derives from Julia Kristeva's object relation theories, which magnificently tie together bodies and subjectivities in *Power of Horror* (1982). Theoretically, this work revolves around the notion of the abject, which Kristeva defines in terms of horror, repulsion, and excretion. Abjection is a broad concept that threatens the subject's identity; something we do not like but from which we cannot divorce ourselves. Kristeva argues, for example, that bodily excretions are metaphorically and linguistically linked to symbolic aversions to the bestial other embodied in racism and sexism. It is the dissolution of the internal and external; body and surroundings, self and other. Barbara Creed (1986: 69) draws on Kristeva to suggest that the notion of the monstrous feminine is enacted as a "primal fantasy" again and again in science-fiction horror movies, where "the alien is more than a phallus; it is also coded as toothed vagina, the monstrous feminine as the cannabilistic mother."

In his elaboration of Kristeva's abject, Wolciech Kalaga (2010: 3) argues for focus on encounters of the same and the other that create indeterminate spaces of in-between. This is similar to object relations theorist Donald Winnicott's transitional space of becoming (1971; see Aitken and Herman 1997). Kalaga argues that otherness – a key concept of contemporary discourses in the humanities – relies on the principle of *tertium not datur*, the excluded middle, which precludes a consideration of anything beyond the boundary. This exclusion finds its origins in rational positioning from Descartes through Darwin to the structuralism found in Freud and Lacan. And despite concerns over structuralism and binary thinking, the *tertium not datur* may be found in post-structuralist ideas that permeate Kristeva's prelinguistic semiotics, in Bakhtin's *chronotopos* (space/time), in Bhabha's ideas on postcolonial hybridity, and in Deleuze's notion of the fold (cf. Aitken 2012). Kalaga's work relates to that of Kirby and Kristeva to the extent that his excluded middle is not an ontological but a political exclusion. Further, he argues for understanding undefined spaces of in-between in terms of internalization and externalization as political processes rather than focusing on interior and exterior as stable ontological categories. Following from Kristeva, Kalaga's (2011: 5) externalization always retains an element of sameness with the body and his internalization retains a moment of otherness. In moving this thinking forward, he notes an ontological inadequacy and a political expediency in trying to embraced the *tertium*. There is hope, however, in understanding the bodies (and rescuing them from biological determinism) as continually becoming, and it is in the service of this hope that Kalaga evokes the Deleuzian principle of difference in repetition. To the extent that externalization always retains aspects of sameness and internalization retains aspects of otherness, then they resonate with Deleuze's notions of difference in degree and difference in kind. Rather than a body, Kalaga (2011: 19) evokes – again from Deleuze – the concept of an ever active and interactive assemblage: "a molecular heterogeneity in a state of permanent flow effected by internalization and externalization." As satisfying as Kalaga's conclusions may appear, they do not help with the politics of interiority that I want to use to elaborate the radical cinematography of Cronenberg. To do so, I use Kalaga as a conduit between Kristeva's Freudian inspired object relations and the Deleuzian inspired "new" feminism evoked by the recent work of Elizabeth Grosz and Kaja Silverman.

Insideness and Outsideness

Luce Irigaray (1977) was one of the first feminists to highlight the exclusion of women from Freudian and Lancanian theories through a critique of the masculine subject. This critique was taken up by Silverman (1992) and Grosz (1994), who elaborated feminist contexts of sexuality with an agenda focused on overturning the Cartesian mind/body split and concomitantly problematizing interior/exterior dichotomies and boundaries. Grosz and Silverman have written copiously about overcoming the boundaries of insideness and outsideness. Early on, Grosz (1994: 3) argued for "rethinking the relations between the inside and the outside of the subject … by showing … the torsion of one into another, the passage vector of uncontrollable drift of the inside into the outside and the outside into the inside." Silverman (1992) evokes the image of the Möbius strip to illustrate this torsion; as you move around the strip, you simultaneously move from outside to inside the circle. At that time, Grosz (1990: 269) was concerned about "reclaim[ing] the body from the realms of immanence and biology in order to see it as a psycho-social product" and Silverman (1990) uses Deleuzian-inspired notions of libidinal politics and the films of Fassbinder to argue there are important aspects of maleness that fall outside of the phallic pale. In her essays on space, time, and perversion, Grosz (1995) began her consideration of the importance of space and place continuously from the outside in and the inside out as politically intertwined with bodies and selves.

Grosz and Silverman are at the forefront of a new feminism that is rethinking biological determinism and the contexts of dichotomous thinking. Silverman (2009), for example, reframes classic feminist questions about how men and women relate to each other. She notes that art and literature have increasingly valorized uniqueness and self-sufficiency; and that contemporary theoreticians tend to privilege difference over similarity. Silverman reminds us that this is only half the story, "and a dangerous half at that, for if we are all individuals, we are doomed to be rivals and enemies" (2009: xi). Silverman asks if our yearning for "wholeness" refers to something real, and if it does, what is it, and why do we feel so estranged from it? To answer these questions, she raises a much older story, one that prevailed through the early modern era, that suggests likeness or resemblance is what organizes the universe, and that everything emerges out of the same flesh. Silverman shows that ideas of analogy, equivalence, and sameness, seemingly discredited by much of twentieth-century science, art, and thought, offer a promising view of human relations.

Questions about interiority and exteriority deserve consideration from what Grosz (2011) describes as a new kind of feminism that disturbs ideas of difference and identity through a Bergsonian understanding of affect and emotion. Henri Bergson's *Introduction to Metaphysics* (1999) is a beginning plea for a coherent focus on interiority, which he calls intuition (as opposed to analysis) in the world of thought. Arguing against the Newtonian and Cartesian extraction of metaphysics from science, Bergson offers intuition as a way of placing more metaphysics in science and more science in metaphysics. Through his notion of intuition, he was one of the first to look carefully at what Grosz (2011: 1) calls "imperceptible movements, modes of becoming, forms of change, and evolutionary transformations that make up natural, cultural and political life." Bergson was primarily interested in science and his point was that static positions for viewing the world are absolute and do not represent well the relationality of the material world. Psychology, for Bergson, proceeds like all the other sciences through analysis. It resolves the subject – which is given to it initially through intuition – into ideas, perception, cognition, and a host of mental states that arrive as abstract and motionless, and perhaps no longer recognizable as parts of the whole. Every feeling and emotion, however fleeting, contains within it the whole past and present of the being experiencing it. This is an important crux for how I want to understand interiority. Bergson's point is that rather than looking at something from the outside and trying to represent it in absolute but fragmented terms, we can look at it from the inside and get in motion with it and, to this extent, he was the first to elaborate a philosophy of mobility and relationality, but also interiority.

Bergson's project to conceptualize life so that it comes to include the material universe in its undivided complexity converges with Silverman's project to attain wholeness through analogy. Grosz (2011: 1) is particularly interested in movement rather than what things become because "movement pre-exists the thing and is the process of differentiation that distinguished one object from another." Movement does not attach to a stable object, putting it in motion; and so for Bergson it is the movement that defines the ways objects are differentiated. The process of movement makes and unmakes objects, including people, animals, and institutions. What Grosz is interested in are the ways that material and living things overcome themselves and become something different. It is a context of difference that is about the relations between things. The importance of interiority is that the forces of change emerge from within and then meet other forces that surround, embroil, and entangle.

With this balance of this chapter, I want to take the preceding discussion about bridging psychoanalytic and post-structural theory joined with the corpus of work that defines contemporary understanding of mobile, affectual, and emotional geographies to say something about the relations of interiority to global processes and freedoms. I use the work of Cronenberg to say something meaningful about mobile landscapes of interiority, resting my arguments most heavily on his last movie, *Cosmopolis*. I then return in conclusion to Bergson and Grosz to say something about difference, freedom, and the ways media objects are complicit in the production of space and scale.

Outwardly Mobile

Auteurism is a particularly useful term to describe Cronenberg's work, which always tries to create cinematically, a landscape of interiority that broaches boundaries (flesh, tattoos, computers, televisions) in both subtle and in-your-face horrific ways. Auteur theory holds that a director's film reflects his or her personal creative vision that transcends the collective process of filmmaking and studio interference. The idea came under significant criticism in the 1990s, at a time when critics were smitten by postmodern depthlessness and fragmentation, the crisis of representation, and the death of the author. The concept was justifiably criticized by feminists as exemplifying male-dominated Anglo-American film directorship, which lauded the auteur as primary artist and creator while dismissing the behind-the-scenes work of women and minorities. That Cronenberg's last several movies were taken from already published books suggests a dilution of his auteur status, but there is, I argue, a very clear trajectory in all of his movies that finds its apex in *Cosmopolis*. If we are not willing to distinguish Cronenberg as an auteur, then I think that it is reasonable to consign his works to a larger oeuvre: it is the dissolution of the internal and external (body and surroundings, self and other, psyche and society) that Cronenberg's work repeatedly enacts.

Cronenberg's first commercial movie, *Shivers* (1975, aka *They Came From Within*), is the story of an apartment complex in Toronto that descends into an orgiastic hell when an epidemic of sexual parasites develop and grow from the insides of infected hosts. The parasites enter the body through any opportune orifice; coitus is taken to new dizzying heights for a while but ultimately the host is destroyed as the parasite feeds. Cronenberg's depiction of the parasites as simultaneously phallic and excremental suggests a Kristevian double articulation of desire and horror. This is something Cronenberg seeks in all his early moves. In *Rabid* (1977), an accident victim awakens from experimental grafting surgery with a penis-like syringe under her armpit and an insatiable desire for blood. In *The Brood* (1979), Cronenberg experiments with externalized emotions, as a patient under the care of a "psychoplasmic" doctor (played beautifully by Oliver Reed) literally gives birth to her anger in the form of a brood of demented fetuses that grow into malignant objects of torture and murder. These movies provide a backdrop for Cronenberg's fourth movie, *Scanners* (1981), which propelled him to cult status in North America and Europe. To suggest that the graphic depiction of an exploding head was the main attraction of this movie does not detract from other subtle influences about the ways the things from the outside get in, and things from the inside get out. With this movie, Cronenberg takes his interest in externalizing emotions and the positive and negative effects of experimental medical treatments to new levels with the story of telepaths (scanners) who exercise their power for good by empathizing with, and healing, people or for ill, by exploding the brains of people with whom they disagree. The telepaths derive their power from mothers who were given the experimental drugs diethylstilbestrol and thalidomide when they were pregnant. In maturity, these children develop the capacity to scan and download the central nervous systems of other people and computers. With *Scanners*, Cronenberg brings together the embryonic ideas in his past projects to create a movie that indulges the co-mingling of pleasure and pathology, desire and horror, insides and outsides, bodies and technology.

Scanners was followed by *Videodrome* (1983), which also supplanted it as Cronenberg's most critically acclaimed movie to date. In the movie, Videodrome Syndrome is realized through druglike psychotic illusions perpetrated by watching indistinct, disturbing, and yet tantalizing sadomasochistic images on a pirate TV channel. After watching the images, protagonist Max (James Woods) begins to have alarming hallucinations. In a disturbingly graphic Freudian moment, his gun is consumed by an oozing vaginal-opening in his stomach to return later as a phallic, cancerous techno-appendage at the end of his arm. Once more, Cronenberg's narratives and images work at a subtle cerebral and visceral level to confound and disturb our hold of reality. His idea is to co-mingle horror and desire into a monstrously abject rendering of the subject For Cronenberg, the monster is never comfortably external, nor is it totally from within. Cronenberg's monster resides *tertium not datur* in the spaces *between* us, our culture, our society, and our relations of want and desire.

As Jim Craine, Giorgio Curti, and I (2011: 215–17) argue, *Videodrome* is "like a Deleuzian dream of Bergsonian virtuality." On the surface, the movie is about the power of images and video representations, but what we are conscripted into is a cocreation of technology, flesh, sex, murder, horror, and desire: "*Videodrome* presages our cosmopolitan intrigue with spectacle and the commodification of desire, and it highlights the dystopian underbelly of an enlightened cosmopolitanism through addiction and horror, technology and corporeality, sex and death." *Videodrome* plays out internal and external complications through a kind of cosmopolitan conspiracy that resonates with Kristeva's (1982) abject in the sense that it examines the choices made around desire for horror, castration, marginalization, and exile. The abject is situated outside of the symbolic order of things to which we are simultaneously drawn and repelled; the horror is external but so too is it part of our own intensive embodiments. *Videodrome* takes tantalization to its most horrific extremes and, in so doing, shows us the heart of corporate cosmopolitanism (Craine et al. 2012: 218). *Videodrome* anticipated Cronenberg's later films *The Fly* (1986), *Dead Ringers* (1988), *Naked Lunch* (1991), *Crash* (1996), and *Spider* (2002) to the extent that pathology is indistinguishable from pleasure and each finds solace in the body. In noting this, *Village Voice* film critic Carrie Rickie (1983) points out that while riddled with these kinds of paradoxes, Cronenberg's films are nonetheless manifestos of how attempts at corporate control inevitably dissolve into corporate anarchy.

In *Cosmopolis*, the anarchy is almost always external to the stretch limousine that Packer – played by Robert Pattison – uses to move through increasingly frenzied and unruly Manhattan streets. It is not until we near the end of the movie that we learn about the catastrophic collapse of world financial markets around Packer's mind, body, and mobility. That the body affecting the markets is traveling across the New York landscape in search of a haircut and that this pretext is perhaps a foil for recovering childhood security lands *Cosmopolis* squarely in Freudian and Lacanian territory. But this is not a psychodrama like Cronenberg's *Dead Ringers* or *A Dangerous Method* (2011). Nor is it about how the interior disrupts the exterior, or the whole. Rather, *Cosmopolis* is about a slow movement into ruin, and we are present inside the limousine, inside Packer's body, as it interacts with itself and forms new assemblages with things around it. In many ways, Packer's interior is more animated than his exterior, which remains supercool and immobile – almost robotic – as the normally well-ordered streets of Manhattan dissolve into chaos. Packer likes the splendor of the echocardiogram depicting his pounding heart and wonders if it could command a beauty contest. In the scene depicted in the epigram, a doctor conducts his daily medical checkup inside the limousine while Packer talks to Jane Melman, his chief of finance, who has just dropped in from a jog around Central Park. In a deliciously uncomfortable scene, Packer's face is only a few inches from Jane as the doctor checks his prostate (DeLillo 2003: 43–44).[2]

> *"So you do what. Same routine every day," she asks.*
> *"Varies … depending." Packer's retort is jarring as the doctor's finger penetrates his rectum.*
> *As the doctor probes, the conversation and the eye contact between Packer and Jane becomes more suggestive.*
> *"So he comes to your house, nice, on weekends."*
> *"We die, Jane on weekends. People. It happens."*
> *"I thought we were moving. But we're not anymore," she says.*
> *"The president's in town," he says.*
> *"You're right. I forgot. I thought I saw him when I ran out of the park. There was an entourage of limousines going down Fifth, with a motorcycle escort. I thought all these limos for the president I can understand. But it was somebody famous's funeral."*
> *"We die every day," he tells her.*
> *At this point Packer notices a suspicious mark on his lower abdomen, a blackhead.*
> *"What do we do about this?" he asks the doctor.*
> *"Let it express itself."*
> *"What. Do nothing."*
> *"Let it express itself."*

In the context of the movie – and in particular, its conclusion – the idea of a blackhead expressing itself resonates with the idea of a body without organs focusing on realizing a specific desire. The conclusion of the movie, that I'll get to in a moment, suggests a more ominous bodily desire, which rests fitfully with a Deleuzian interpretation of affect.

The coupling of Packer with his advisors and his limousine is punctuated by detours; breakfast with his wife, sex with his bodyguard. Painfully slowly, the limousine wends its way through the chaos of Manhattan. At lunch with his wife, two protestors burst into the diner – Packer motions that his bodyguard should not intervene – and throw two rats at the patrons before dashing out the back. Quoting Polish poet Zbigniew Herbert, near the beginning of the movie Packer speaks to his currency analyst of the possibility of a time when "a rat became the unit of currency." Packer's words presage the protest that is about to erupt over the current global fiscal crisis: people in rat costumes and effigies of rats show

2 At the time of writing, the DVD of *Cosmopolis* is unavailable. The text here and in what follows is excerpted from DeLillo's book, which Cronenberg follows with little change.

up all around the limousine. And still the streets of Manhattan unravel outside as if they had no consequence to Packer.

> *He slid open the sunroof and thrust his head into the reeling scene. The bank towers loomed just beyond the avenue … They looked empty from here. He liked that idea. They were made to be the last tall things, made empty, designed to hasten the future. They were the end of the outside world. They weren't here, exactly. They were in the future, a time beyond geography and touchable money and the people who stack and count it. (DeLillo 2008: 36)*

As a back-projection seen through the limousine's glass, the protest seems unreal but also, perhaps, a deliberate affect emanating from Packer's body like the blackhead on his abdomen expressing itself.

The riot continues and in one of the most powerful scenes in the movie, Packer listens to Vija Kinski – a theoretician on his payroll – talk about the protesters and global corporate capitalism as the limousine is spray-painted, rocked, and beaten (DeLillo 2003: 90–100):

> *"You know what capitalism produces, according to Marx and Engels?"*
> *"Its own grave-diggers," he said.*
> *"But these are not grave-diggers. This is the free market itself. These people are a fantasy generated by the market. They don't exist outside the market. There is nowhere they can go to be on the outside. There is no outside."*

The camera in the limousine tracks a cop chasing a young man through the crowd, an image that seems to exist at some drifting distance from the moment.

> *"The market culture is total. It breeds these men and women. They are necessary to the system they despise. They give it energy and definition. They are market driven. They are traded on the markets of the world. This is why they exist, to invigorate and perpetuate the system."*
> *Kinski tightens her seatbelt as protestors bang on the hood and the roof.*
> *"You have to understand?"*
> *"What?"*
> *"The more visionary the idea, the more people it leaves behind. That is what the protest is all about. Visions of technology and wealth. The force of cyber-capital that will send people into the gutter to retch and die. What is the flaw of human rationality?"*
> *"What?"*
> *"It pretends not to see the horror and death at the ends of the schemes it builds. This is a protest against the future. They want to hold off the future. They want to normalize it, keep it from overwhelming the present … The future is always a wholeness, a sameness. We're all tall and happy there. This is why the future fails. It always fails. It can never be the cruel happy place we want to make it."*

During this monolog, Packer listens raptly and Kinski barely flinches as violence after violence is perpetrated on the limousine.

> *"How will we know when the global era officially ends?" He asks and then answers: "When the stretch limousines begin to disappear from the streets of Manhattan."*
> *"This is the thing about genius," she says. "Genius alters the terms of its habitat."*

Packer waits, listening to her, he clearly likes what he hears and wants more.

> *"Think of it this way. There are rare minds operating, a few, here and there, the polymath, the true futurist. A consciousness such as yours, hyper-maniacal, may have contact points beyond the general perception."*
> *He waits.*
> *"Technology is crucial to civilization ... But it is also crouched and undecidable. It can go either way."*
> *He says, "you've been talking about the future being impatient. Pressing upon us."*
> *She retorts, "that was theory. I deal in theory."*

The scene shifts to the ticker's in Time Square, now outside the limousine. A SPECTER IS HAUNTING THE WORLD – THE SPECTER OF CAPITALISM reads one, followed by A RAT BECAME THE UNIT OF CURRENCY on another. Packer opens the sunroof and stands up, exhilarated by the scene of struggle, ruin, and transformation.

Packer sits down, picks up the Web-phone and starts buying an unprecedented amount of yen. At this point a man sits cross-legged on the sidewalk and sets himself on fire. Whereas the riot had a veneer of artifice – Kinski's fantasy market – this was different, it changes everything for Packer. The market, he realizes, is not total: it cannot claim the man or assimilate his act. Kinski opines that the immolation is not original, that it is appropriated from Vietnamese and Tibetan monks.

> *"To say something. To make people think," he says.*
> *"It's not original," she repeats.*
> *"Does he have to be a Buddhist to be taken seriously? He did a serious thing. He took his life. Isn't that what you have to do to show them that you're serious?"*

To this point in the movie, Cronenberg has focused his characteristic interest in transgression and taboo with something more discursive and cerebral. To this point everything is cramped, confined, and yet connected globally. As Peter Bradshaw (2012), movie critic for the *Guardian* observes, "It's a movie about danger in which nothing is credibly at stake." Now, as we get close to the haircut, the movie transforms into a conventional narrative and gets serious. Packer kills his bodyguard through tricking him to give up and then voice-activate his weapon. He and his driver arrive at a deserted backstreet somewhere in lower Manhattan late at night. The barbershop and its barber are a throwback to his childhood and a time before he was obscenely rich. Packer gets half a haircut before leaving abruptly to take the limousine to the garage district where all limousines go at night. With the limousine gone, Packer loses his mobility.

Bergson points out that there is a multiplicity of successive states of consciousness, which are synthesized through one single duration as apprehended by the self. He considers duration under the simple aspect of a movement accomplishing itself through space. We are placed in this movement through intuition. Duration may be viewed as a single thread connecting pearls in a necklace, where the pearls are moments. There may be as many moments as we care to apprehend depending on whether we conceive them as small or large. Duration and the moments that make up its timeline are unsustainable when subjected to analysis (for Bergson, the opposite of intuition), which requires that the movement is stopped and laid out for inspection. The movement (duration and moments) is emptied of the mobility that gave it life. Bergson calls this an "eternity of death."

Without mobility, Cronenberg directs Packer into the movie's tense and cerebral final scene. It is a scene laced with notions of eternity, death, and what really constitutes life.

Packer is shot at in the street and then drawn into a derelict tenement to be confronted by Richard Sheets, a former employee of Packer Capital. Played superbly by Paul Giamatti, Sheets is nervous, tormented, and more than a little bit disgruntled while Packer maintains his demeanor of focused analysis on the moment but with Bergsonian peripheral engagement.

Framed as opposites, Sheets and Packer have one startling thing in common: asymmetrical prostates (DeLillo 2003: 199–200):

> *"What does it mean?" asks Packer.*
> *"Nothing. It means nothing," says Sheets. "It's harmless. A harmless variation. Nothing to worry about. Your age, why worry?"*
> *After a moment, Sheets continues, "You should have listened to your prostrate."*
> *"What?"*
> *"You tried to predict movements in the yen by drawing on patterns from nature. Yes, of course. The mathematical properties of tree rings, sunflower seeds, the limbs of galactic spirals … The way signals from a pulsar in deepest space follow classical number sequences, which in turn can describe the fluctuations of a given stock or currency. You showed me this. How market cycles can be interchangeable with the time cycles of a grasshopper breeding, wheat harvesting. You made this form of analysis horribly and sadistically precise. But you forgot something along the way."*
> *"What?"*
> *"The importance of the lopsided, the thing that's skewed a little. You were looking for balance, beautiful balance, equal parts, equal sides. I know this. I know you. But you should have been tracking the yen in its tics and quirks. The little quirk. The misshape."*
> *"The misweave."*
> *"That's where the answer was, in your body, in your prostate."*

Sheets wants Packer to save him, but Packer has already failed this friendless, raging man once and would fail him again and again, ad nauseam. So Sheets has to shoot him; we do not know if this actually happens because the movie ends abruptly before the shot.

For the robotic, supercool financial wizard that is Packer, the death of the material body seems like a logical continuation of his experience as long as he can "live outside the given limits, in a chip, on a disk, as data, in whirl, in radiant spin, a consciousness saved from void" (DeLillo 2010: 206). What Cronenberg deftly portrays – through closing credits presented against a backdrop of abstract-expressionist paintings by Mark Rothko – is the impossibility of this kind of extension of life. The Rothko paintings harken back to a scene in the movie in which Packer says he'd rather buy the whole Rothko chapel in Houston, walls and all, than just the one painting he is offered. Packer is told that the chapel owners won't sell, and so Cronenberg leaves us with the distinct impression that there are things – perhaps of a spiritual nature – that cannot be bought and that even although the technology to extend human experience beyond death may be imminent, such a feat is impossible. In a classic Cronenberg scene, Packer shoots a hole through his hand and experiences excruciating pain that connects him in important ways to his body. He recognizes its duration, its lopsidedness, and its global affects. He realizes the unfathomable connections between insides and outsides, and the complexity that is bound by, in, and through life. And again, in a classic Cronenberg moment, the pain interferes with his ideas of immortality and brings Packer back to some form of real, some form of truth, some kind of wholeness:

> *It was crucial to his distinctiveness, too vital to be bypassed and not susceptible, he didn't think, to computer emulation. The things that made him who he was could hardly be identified much less converted to data, the things that milled in his body, everywhere, random, riotous, billions of trillions, in neurons and peptides, the throbbing temple vein, in the veer of his libidinous intellect. So much come and gone, this is who he was, the lost taste of milk licked from his mother's breast, the stuff he sneezes when he sneezes, this is him, and how a person becomes the reflection he sees in a dusty window when he walks by. He'd come to know himself, untranslatably, through his pain. (DeLillo 2012: 207)*

At this point, whether Sheets murders Packer or not is of little consequence.

Becoming Undone

Bergson's project is to transform our understanding of being from a static, immobile concept to an intuitively mobile idea of becoming. Becomings are differentiated, open-ended elaborations of tendencies and virtualities, and the movements of these tendencies. The movements form relations with other tendencies and virtualities to form, from moment to moment, Deleuzian desiring machines that have some demarcation but are fundamentally unpredictable. A person or subject does not become; rather, it is the tendencies and virtualities that move toward a multiplicity of becomings (Grosz 2011: 51). Life is not a subject or a material object but is, as Grosz (2011: 52) points out, "inserted into the world of material objects only to the extent that it partakes of them and can use them for its own purposes."

Cosmopolis ends with Packer contemplating a Bergsonian eternity of death. Although his wealth may buy the possibility of transcendence through data chips and stored experiences this does not constitute life because it is static, contained, and limited. Media objects reify and stultify, and by so doing they provide only the illusion of immortality. And this is the hope that comes out of a Benjaminian project, which recognizes that reification through media spectacles is not only a bourgeoisie project, it is doomed to failure because it is static, contained, and limited. Packer recognizes that his being, his life, is wound up in distinctiveness, difference and movement. He finally understands that life for bodies – whether his own, Packer Capital, or the global market – cannot be analyzed, taken apart, and projected through a variety of media toward outcomes. Rather, they comprises a myriad a relating, connecting, and reconstituting employees, peptides, ideas, neurons, transactions, molecules, and a host of other things that have come and gone as desiring machines, as bodies without organs, all wrapped within, through, and beyond his libidinous intellect. For Bergson (2004: 276), life relates to the material world only in terms of movements and vibrations, and when our consciousness is removed, "matter ... resolves itself into numberless vibrations, all linked together in uninterrupted continuity, all bound up with each other, and travelling in every direction like shivers in an immense body." It is only through his immense pain at the close of *Cosmopolis* that Packer – the cool, composed architect of global financial analyses – gets to know himself, gets turned inwards, and finally gains Bergsonian intuition toward, possibly, his last movement.

This chapter is a rethinking of interior places and their relations to the whole through Cronenberg's oeuvre. I brood on *Cosmopolis* not only because it is his latest film at the time of writing or even his best but because it elaborates a number of Bergsonian contexts of life and its connections to matter and media. Whether the asymmetry of Packer's prostate could ultimately have prevented the collapse of world financial markets is of less concern than how it helps constitute his own transformation. Throughout the movie, the mobility and recombinatoral power of his limousine is of less concern to Packer than its analytic power through computational patterns and media landscapes that connect him intimately to global markets, and his inner body. But throughout the movie – and this is the power of Cronenberg's cinematography – the limousine is in motion and its only when it stops (disappears from the streets of Manhattan) that Packer realizes the limits of his analytic prowess. Through the windows of his limousine, he witnesses the outcome of his flawed analysis. And when it stops and he is confronted by Sheets, those consequences are brought into sharp relief. Rather than seeing a technological image of his insides, he realizes the complex, recombinatorial moments that make him who he is; fixing his attention on these movements, he is able to abstract from the divisible space that underlies them and consider only their mobility. And this is precisely what Cronenberg has been doing for us, the audience, throughout the movie; using the slow perambulation of the limousine to connect Packer to the people in his life and its affects as a multiplicity of recombinatorial and unpredictable desiring machines.

Grosz (2011) uses Bergsonian theory to advocate a new feminism that focuses on "freedom to" rather than "freedom from." While not dismissing the importance of removing the limitations that constrain individual freedoms (from oppression, tyranny, patriarchy), she argues that this is partially a story linked to autonomy and choice. Grosz (2010: 71–72) points out that although Bergson's ideas predate the notion of sexual difference posed by Irigaray, his conception of freedom links actions to a form of self-making that parallels Irigaray's understanding of difference as something that is virtual, in the process of becoming. Bergson's ideas of freedom link not to choice and autonomy but to innovation and invention. Freedom, for Grosz, is about action; it is positive and imminent, and not contained in anything that is predictable from the present:

> *It is not a state one is in or a quality that one has, for it resides in the activities one undertakes that transform oneself and (a part of) the world. It is not a property or right bestowed on or removed from an individual by others but a capacity, a potentiality, to act both in accordance with one's past, as well as "out of character," in a manner that surprises. (Grosz 2011: 72)*

Cosmopolis is a cautionary tale. Packer is a sorry character. His cool objective analytic frame, financial wizardry, and obscene wealth seemingly give him freedom from everything, but he is constrained by looking at things as static. Packer requires constant monitoring and analysis of things internal (his body) and external (the market), while Cronenberg uses the movement that drives the movie (the limousine) to indicate precisely where Packer can find absolution; a freedom that resides in Bergsonian intuition.

References

Aitken, S.C. 2010. Throwntogetherness: Encounters with difference and diversity. In *The Handbook for Qualitative Methods in Geography*. Edited by D. DeLyser et al. Thousand Oaks, CA, and New Delhi: SAGE, 46–68.

Aitken, S.C. 2012. Young men's violence and spaces of addiction: Opening up the locker room. *Social and Cultural Geography* 13(2): 117–33.

Aitken, S.C. and T. Herman. 1997. Gender, power and crib geography: Transitional spaces and potential places. *Gender, Place and Culture: A Journal of Feminist Geography* 4 (1): 63–88.

Benjamin, W. 2004. *The Arcades Project*. Translated by H. Eiland and K. McLaughlin. Paris: Belknap Press.
Bergson, H. 1999. *An Introduction to Metaphysics*. Translated by T.E. Hulme. Indianapolis, IN, and Cambridge: Hackett Publishing Company.
Bergson, H. 2004. *Matter and Memory*. London and New York: Dover Publishing.
Bondi, L. 1993. Locating identity politics. In *Place and the Politics of Identity*. Edited by M. Keith and S. Pile. New York and London: Routledge, 84–101.
Bruno, G. 1992. *Streetwalking on a Ruined Map*. Princeton, NJ: Princeton University Press.
Craine, J.W., G.H. Curti, and S.C. Aitken. 2012. Cosmopolitan sex, monstrous violence and networks of blood. In *The Fight to Stay Put: Social Lessons through Media Imaginings of Urban Transformation and Change*. Edited by G. Curti, J.W. Craine, and S.C. Aitken. Stuttgart, Germany: Verlag Publishing, 215–29.
Creed, B. 1986. Horror and the monstrous feminine: An imaginary abjection. *Screen* 27(1): 44–70.
Curti, G.H., S.C. Aitken, F.J. Bosco, and D.D. Goerisch. 2011. For not limiting emotional and affectual geographies: A collective critique of Steve Pile's "Emotions and affect in recent human geography." *Transactions of the Institute of British Geographers* 36(4): 590–91.
Davidson, J., L. Bondi, and M. Smith. 2005. *Emotional Geographies*. Aldershot: Ashgate.
DeLillo, D. 2003. *Cosmopolis*. New York: Simon and Schuster.
Deleuze, G. and F. Guattari. 1983. *Anti-Oedipus: Capitalism and Schizophrenia.* Minneapols: University of Minnesota Press.
Deleuze, G. and F. Guattari. 1988. *A Thousand Plateaus: Capitalism and Schizophrenia*. London: Athlone Press.
Friedberg, A. 1993. *Window Shopping: Cinema and the Postmodern*. Berkeley: University of California Press.
Front, S. and K. Nowak. 2010. *Interiors: Interiority/Exteriority in Literary and Cultural Discourse.* Newcastle-Upon-Tyne: Cambridge Scholars Publishing.
Grosz, E. 1994. *Volatile Bodies: Towards a Corporeal Feminism*. St. Leonard: Allen and Unwin.
Grosz, E. 1995. *Space, Time and Perversion*. London and New York: Routledge.
Grosz, E. 1999. Psychoanalysis and the body. In *Feminist Theory and the Body*. Edited by J. Price and M. Shildrick. New York and London: Routledge, 267–71.
Grosz, E. 2008. *Chaos, Territory, Art: Deleuze and the Framing of the Earth*. New York: Columbia University Press.
Grosz, E. 2011. *Becoming Undone: Darwinian Reflections on Life, Politics and Art*. Durham: Duke University Press.
Irigaray, L.1977/1985. *This Sex Which Is Not One*. Translated by C. Porter. Ithaca, NY: Cornell University Press.
Kalaga, W. 2010. In/exteriors: The third of the body. In *Interiors: Interiority/Exteriority in Literary and Cultural Discourse*. Edited by S. Front and K. Nowak. Newcastle-Upon-Tyne: Cambridge Scholars Publishing, 3–21.
Kirby, K.M. 1996. *Indifferent Boundaries*. New York: Guilford Press.
Kristeva, J.1982. *Power of Horror*. New York: Columbia University Press.
Marston, S., J.P. Jones, and K. Woodward. 2005. Human geographies without scale. *Transactions of the Institute of British Geographers* 30(4): 416–32.
Massumi, B. 1992. *A User's Guide To Capitalism and Schizophrenia: Deviations from Deleuze and Guattari.* Cambridge, MA: MIT Press.
Merrifield, A. 2002. *Metromarxism*. New York and London: Routledge.
Nast, H. 2000. Mapping the "unconscious": Racism and the Oedipal family. *Annals of the Association of American Geographers* 90(2): 215–55.
Pile, S. 1996. *The Body and the City*. New York and London: Routledge.

Pile, S. 2010. Emotions and affect in recent human geography. *Transactions of the Institute of British Geographers* 35: 5–20.

Punter, D. 2010. Gothic interiors: Questions of design and perspective. In *Interiors: Interiority/ Exteriority in Literary and Cultural Discourse*. Edited by S. Front and K. Nowak. Newcastle-Upon-Tyne: Cambridge Scholars Publishing, 175–90.

Ricoeur, P. 1981. *Hermeneutics and the Human Sciences: Essays on Language, Action and Interpretation*. Translated by J.B. Thompson. Cambridge: Cambridge University Press.

Rickie, C. 1983. Make mine Cronenberg. *Village Voice*, February1, 62–65.

Silverman, K. 1992. *Male Subjectivity at the Margins*. New York and London: Routledge.

Silverman, K. 2009. *Flesh of My Flesh*. Stanford, CA: Stanford University Press.

Winnicott, D.W. 1971. *Playing and Reality*. London: Tavistoc.

Syncretic (S)p[l]aces

Giorgio Hadi Curti and Tamara M. Johnson

Introduction

What is the syncretic? How does it come to us? What does it do? These are all questions eminently – if not immanently – geographical. Yet, they are little explored or even discussed within the well-trodden chambers of the geographical annals and disciplinary halls. Perhaps a lack of geographical engagement with the syncretic is an effect of its contemporary conventional usage as "the amalgamation or attempted amalgamation of different religions, cultures, or schools of thought" (www.oxforddictionaries.com 2012). By speaking simply of syncretic amalgamations (or assemblages, combinatorials, coalescings, emergences, etc.) in terms of beliefs, cultures, and philosophies, their amorphous mo(ve)ments that find extension only in and through the membranous relations between bodies and spaces becomes a necessary field of encounter – the very concrete production of geography that has embarrassingly only relatively recently became a matter of investigation and concern to the discipline through long-needed feminist, humanist, and post-structuralist correctives and critiques.

Like the syncretic, related conceptual pursuits – such as the creole and the hybrid – have been dominated by cognate fields of study and similarly inadequately underdeveloped in geography's long-drawn and diverse disciplinary explorations; in practice, the former largely closed into and onto a particular location of racialized and linguistic "mixture" and sedentation and the latter only gaining explicit intellectual geographical embrace with Whatmore's (2002) working through the "de-centering of social agency" and "de-coupling … [of] the subject/object binary" of *hybrid geographies* to travel "closely-textured journeys that follow various social-material imbroglios as they are caught up in, and convene, the spatial practices of science, law and everyday life" (2002: 4). Central to these hybrid journeys (and vital for our discussion here of the syncretic) is an approach to difference that works before and after after fixed identities, forms, and meanings; an approach that understands difference as *difference–production* – a sensibility "requiring us," as Whatmore (2003: 119) explains of hybrid geographies, "to distinguish between bodies in ways that appreciate their specificities and respect the affects and affordances that flow between them."

Sensibilities informing hybrid geographies, thus, certainly find amity in our engagements here of the syncretic. Our interests, however, meander from hybrid journeys in three interrelated ways. First, our concerns around difference-production are drawn particularly to *place*, and what particular media and performative expressions articulate to us about the syncretic nature of place(s) as chemically activated "roiling maelstroms of affect[s]" (Thrift 2007: 171). Secondly (and relatedly), we wish to move away from hybridity's entanglements in "sedentary images of thought" (Doel 1999: 7) and "that which already is" (Stafford 2008: 11) to point to how the syncretic can inform place as an always emerging "verbal rather than nounal, a becoming rather than a being" (Doel 1999: 7).

In this, we diverge from hybridity's collapsing and mixing of difference into captured and capturable genealogical variation to, instead, explore the always partial, non-soluble, and overflowing ways the syncretic transversally becomes[1] through a "deterritorialized dance of the most disparate things" (Ansell-Pearson 1999: 143).[2] Finally, we stray from the biological and racialized underpinnings ensnared in notions of hybridization (Stewart 1999) to unpack a different kind of politics of difference as illustrated (and, perhaps, can best be illustrated) through imaginative media and performative movement as they connect to place and place production.

We begin by exploring the genesis of the concept of the syncretic in order to rescue an affirmative and productive expression flowing within that offers insights into the strengthening nature of collective difference and difference-production. We then touch on the importance of media and performance for understanding how the syncretic is always entangled with(in) place and place production. We follow this by moving through three interrelated elements – syncretic scapes, syncretic space, and syncretic politics – that are vital for understanding the always-syncretic nature of place. We work with Michael Arias's Japanese animated (*anime*) film *Tekkonkinkreet* (2006; based on Taiyō Matsumoto's *manga* [1993–1994]) and the social, political, and corporeal mo(ve)ments of Salsa dancing as manifold ways to illustrate the dynamic nature and multiple becomings that syncretic places unhinge, unfold, and unleash – in the process pointing to how all places are syncretic and that all that is syncretic *takes* and *makes* place. We finish with considerations of what syncretic places do and how artistic performances such as dance and media are always at the heart of a (difference-producing) geography of place.

The Syncretic

The history of syncretism dawns its earliest conceptual light in the writings of the Greek philosopher Plutarch, who mined the word *synkretismos* (συγκρητισμός) to explain how a divergent Cretan multitude assembled together to confront the shared threats of oncoming enemies (Kraidy 2005: 49; Willets 1977: 180). The "Prince of the Humanists," Desiderius Erasmus, later excavated the concept to discuss how fluxes of different ideas come together in kaleidoscopic union. He drew upon Plutarch's understanding of the power of the uniting difference of the Cretans to affirmatively conclude that "[c]oncord is a mighty rampart" (Bamaiyi n.d.: 3) – a truth recognizing and underscoring the false dichotomies of idea and practice, thought and action. In the seventeenth century, the ideational trajectory of syncretic analysis gained steam in explorations of becoming religious assemblages created through interreligious "borrowing" and "fusion." The affirmative connotations of syncretism's early conceptual usages were soon usurped by orders of Christian religious hierarchy and hegemony, malforming the emerging combinatorial differences and powers the concept sought to explain into negations because of the syncretic process's supposed tainting of orthodox "purity" and devotional piety (Kraidy 2005: 49–50).

1 Deleuze and Guattari (1987) describe the transversal as "a line of deterritorialization" (1987:196) and "communication" that "scramble[s] the genealogical trees" (1987:11) and explain that "a transversal movement [is] that [which] sweeps one and the other away, a stream without beginning or end that undermines its banks and picks up speed in the middle" (1987: 25).

2 As may be apparent to some, our understanding of both the differences and relations between the syncretic and the hybrid conceptually parallel in some ways Massumi's (2002) explanation of the differences and relations between affect and emotion.

Framing the syncretic as a negative merely served and still today serves political ends upholding standing relations and imbalanced geometries of power. The overwhelming irony of course is that the life of the majority of the world's Christianity is itself an oversaturated syncretic stew cooked on a boiler plate of European intellectual misappropriation and contextual bastardization over a burning flame of myopic Orientalizing confabulations. In this context, geographical inattention to the syncretic should come as little surprise. As the right-hand tool of colonialism and a royal science, the geographical discipline has been a (still largely ongoing) futile exercise of attempting to achieve some sort of "purity" – of spaces, of identities, of "races," of classes, of bodies, of organisms, of scales, of places (see Whatmore 2002; Doel 1999; and Gibson-Graham 1996). A consequence of geography's misguided attempts to artificially bound and tame that which is motile and pulsating coupled with its long refusal to sincerely engage the messy, membranous relations between bodies and spaces has been that interests in the syncretic have been largely dominated by fields such as anthropology and cultural studies. This has not only been a loss for geographical insights into difference and difference-production, but a deprivation for understanding the power of the syncretic as a conceptual spatial tool.

Stewart and Ernst (2003: 586) explain that modern-day uses of the syncretic can be typed according to four general "models of interaction and encounter: [1] influence and borrowing; [2] the 'cultural veneer'; [3] alchemy; and [4] organic or biological reproduction." The first two models are bound up in a representational condition of stasis, where processes of complex syncretic emergence are subsumed by "mechanistic vagueness" (Stewart and Ernst 2003: 587) or disregarded altogether. The latter two models, though they attempt to account for the conditions of the syncretic and the processes of its emergence, both have their own conceptual and pragmatic deficiencies. The first (alchemy) allows for combinatorials of difference and emergence, but its trajectories remain atomistic insofar that the component parts producing shared difference themselves can never be transformed: "The result [of a syncretic alchemy] is a temporary mixture that will invariably separate over time, because the component parts are unalterable and must forever remain distinct and apart" (Stewart and Ernst 2003: 587). The second (organic or biological reproduction), while holding a unique, creative, hybridized internal difference, is itself not capable of contributing to difference-(re)production as it can only and always end in sterility and disaggregation (Stewart and Ernst 2003: 587).

The problems underlying all four models, Stewart and Ernst state (2003: 586), are tendencies of ahistoricism, essentializing, and seeming inadequacy in explaining anything particularly interesting – or, to be more specific, interestingly explaining anything about the particular. But such negative critique is to miss the very point – the very *power* – of an *affirmative* concept of the syncretic: it is about difference *as* difference, not as opposition, not simply as measurable or categorical degrees, but as internal differences of capacity and intensity; a difference in kind that always overflows, to be only momentarily slowed and clumsily snatched under the guise of representations and identities until it breaks out once again to show the ridiculousness of any attempt at holistic "purity," genealogical consistency, or totalistic structure or origination. This is not to be ahistoric, but more than historic, to find more interesting how the past is becoming the future than how a still slice of the present came to be. And herein lies the diabolical disruption of engaging the syncretic: it is never finished, never stopped; it is less a syn-thesis than a sin-thesis: a subversive countermove to the closure, hierarchy, transcendence, and authority of what is and what has been for what is becoming and what can be. Approaching the syncretic in this way renders it a verbal, never a nounal – an expression of the constant deterritorializing of any territorialization and a recognition of what the *Diné* (Navajo) have long known: that "space and time are so inextricably interwoven that one cannot be discussed without the other" and that the universe is a dynamic becoming, "made up of processes rather than objects and situations" (Ascher 2008: 901).

What syncretism forces us to confront in its most affirmative sense, then, is that *real* differences are not based on or tied to *representation(s)* or the *representational*. Rather, they are attracting manifold assemblages produced by and through transversal eruptions of the universe's difference-making processes unleashed in all of their e/affects. This also forces us to confront that *real* differences do not and cannot stand alone or apart as if isolated points in metric space; syncretism demands transversal sensibilities nourished through the life processes of disjunctive (comm)union that immanence and affect continually bring (Curti 2008a) – the ongoing productions of experimentation that compose maps, never tracings. Deleuze and Guattari (1987: 12) explain:

> *What distinguishes the map from the tracing is that it is entirely oriented toward an experimentation in contact with the real. The map does not reproduce an unconscious closed in upon itself; it constructs the unconscious. [...] The map is open and connectable in all of its dimensions; it is detachable, reversible, susceptible to constant modification.*

Affirmative syncretism can, thus, perhaps best be explained as an artistic event of origamic mapping, as it is expressive of the very processes (re)creating the world:

> *The world can be (un)folded in countless ways, with innumerable folds over folds, and folds within folds, but such a disfiguration never permits one (or more) of those folds to become redundant, nor for one (or more) of them to seize power as a master-fold. Every fold plays its part in lending consistency to the thing that is folded, and since every fold participates in the lending of consistency to "something = x" without ever belonging to it ..., folds cannot be distinguished in terms of the essential and the inessential, the necessary and the contingent, or the structural and the ornamental. Every fold plays its part: ever fold splays "it" apart. The event of origami is the (un)folding, just as the gift is in the wrapping: not as content, but as process. (Doel 1999: 18)*

Approaching the world in this way requires an accounting for both the coming-together – *the syncretic amalgamated* – and breaking-apart – *the emergent migrating* – of the very living processes continually (re)composing the zones of variable intensities and integrities that are place and places: geography as life (even if it is a life inorganic) and all life as geographical (even if this life seemingly never leaves a geographical place). Difference-production, origamic construction, syncretic amalgamation, emergent migrations: all involve the forces and flows, speeds and intensities by and through which differences concretely and corporeally (be)come and accrue, fold and unfold, together.

The Event of Media and Place

It is for these reasons that media is so important for exploring the syncretic natures of place, as different media objects and performances continually challenge through different experiential encounters and their ever-changing *scapes* that which is measured, weighed, categorized, set, fixed, and bounded. So, too, are "pointallistic" (Doel 1999) notions of place subverted by media expressions, as they necessarily put place "out of joint" through their narratives, visuals, vibrations, and trajectories while drawing together new coherent relations of difference across constructions of scale as well as before or after any of its notions (Marston et al. 2005). In these ways, media experiences are, in their own ways, *events*, in the

Deleuzo-Guattarian (1994: 56) sense of that "virtuality that has become consistent"; and dance becomes as much a media object as film or music as identity and form become secondary to the amalgamating capacities of bodies[3] and their transversal modes of becoming.

Speaking specifically on the "event of place," Massey (2005: 141) explains that it is expressive of "the coming together of the previously unrelated, a constellation of processes rather than a thing. This is place as open and as internally multiple. Not capturable as a slice through time in the sense of an essential section. Not intrinsically coherent." Understanding place as an event in this way, thus, requires two parallel movements: (1) an approach to place as *difference* and the *(be)coming-together of difference* and (2) a corralling and drawing differences together in a way that render their relations knowable (even if only partially) through the product of an *encounter*. Indeed, it is only by engaging both of these movements together that we can be brought to the *syncreticity* of place. Massey's language characterizing the "event of place" as a "constellation of processes" is very telling here, as the Deleuzian notion of the event and Walter Benjamin's notion of constellations recall each other in interesting ways. For Deleuze (1993: 76–78).

> *Events are produced in a chaos, in a chaotic multiplicity, but only under the condition that a sort of screen intervenes.*
> *Chaos does not exist; it is an abstraction because it is inseparable from a screen that makes something – something rather than nothing – emerge from it. Chaos would be a pure Many, a purely disjunctive diversity, while the something is a One, not a pregiven unity, but instead the indefinite article that designates a certain singularity. How can the Many become the One? A great screen has to be placed in between them. Like a formless elastic membrane, an electromagnetic field, or the receptacle of the Timaeus, the screen makes something issue from chaos, and even if this something differs only slightly … .*
> *… [T]he event … [is] "a nexus of prehensions." Each new prehension becomes a datum. It becomes public, but for other prehensions that objectify it; the event is inseparably the objectification of one prehension and the subjectification of another; it is at once public and private, potential and real, participating in the becoming of another event and the subject of its own becoming.*

This is paralleled by Benjamin, who brings us a similar sensibility related to historical *time*:

> *The constellation links past events among themselves, or else links past to present; its formation stimulates a flash of recognition, a quantum leap in historical understanding … Benjamin writes: "what has been comes together in a flash with the now to form a constellation", and again: "the concern is to find the constellation of awakening the dissolution of 'mythology' into the space of history the awakening of a not-yet-conscious knowledge of what has been". The constellar image marks the transition from "mythology", or illusion, into an authentic understanding of history. The task of the critical historian is, Benjamin argues, positioning himself against the ideology of "progress", "to root out every trace of 'development' from the image of history and to represent becoming … as a constellation in being."* (Rollason 2002)

The Deleuzian *event* and the Benjaminian *constellation*: even in their differences, both work together to explain how creatively drawn-together elemental divergences of space

[3] Important to remember here is that "[a] body can be anything" (Deleuze 1988: 127).

and time (be)come together in assemblages of images, movements, transformations, revolutions, and difference-productions to counter any hegemonic or bourgeois notions of linear origins, closed arrangements, or fixed essences; through the Deleuzian event, in the Benjaminian constellation, truths are never facts or states of affairs, but *a/effective (re)actions* (un)folding (in) time-space. By understanding media as experientially intervening screenic elements lending both affective and awakening actions to becoming, they, too, are indelible constituents of constellations/events impacting and illuminating the very syncretic nature of place; they de-territorialize what is to re-territorialize (with) what may (be)come (see Curti 2008b) – through *scapes*, by *space*, as *politics*.

Syncretic Scapes/Syncretic Space/Syncretic Politics

Writing on current global conditions and their "fundamental disjunctures between economy, culture and politics," anthropologist and cultural theorist Arjun Appadurai (1999) presents five dimensions of global cultural flows he terms (a) ethnoscapes, (b) mediascapes, (c) technoscapes, (d) finanscapes, and (e) ideoscapes. What is relevant for our purposes here are not the meanings of these typologies or what they describe, but what they tell us about the very syncretic qualities of *scapes*. Appadurai (1999: 221–2) explains, "the common suffix scape ... indicate[s] first of all that these [sets of landscapes] are not objectively given relations which look the same from every angle of vision, but rather that they are deeply perspectival constructs, inflected very much by the historical, linguistic and political situatedness of different sorts of actors" and "[t]he suffix scape also allows us to point to the fluid, irregular shapes of these landscapes, shapes which characterize international capital as deeply as they do international clothing styles." By pointing to the fluidity, irregularity, and perspectival qualities bound up in the term scapes, Appadurai underscores the very syncretic nature of their varying assemblings as well as the fact that these assemblings are always entangled in and dependant on the affective natures and capacities of singular and collective bodies. He continues: "These landscapes thus, are the building blocks of what, extending Benedict Anderson, I would like to call 'imagined worlds', that is, the multiple worlds which are constituted by the historically situated imaginations of persons and groups spread around the globe." These perspectival landscapes of global cultural flows, then, as entangled in imaginations as they are, are always horizontally emerging out of sensory bodies caught up in the sounds, lights, texts, colors, textures, vibrations, intensities, etc., of screenic "assemblage(s)capes" (Curti 2009; Curti and Craine 2011). We explain elsewhere,

> *Assemblage(s)capes have no origins or ends. Neither do they privilege one element or component over another. Instead, they are horizontal entanglements of expression and creation which enfold and are enfolded by bundling capes of sensory bodies, regardless of status(es), form(s) or identity(s). Assemblage(s) capes are orgies of expression(s) and desire(s); (pro)creations of something new; continually manifolding aggregation(s) and condensation(s) of melodic and rhythmic difference ... Assemblage(s)capes are a simultaneous coming-together and breaking-apart, an exchanging of fluids, a becoming-different ... (Curti and Craine 2011: 138–9)*

Salsa, as its very name implies, has always been a pulsating assemblage(s)cape of sensations (re)created by and through a complex intertwining and intermingling of bodily patterns, sounds, speeds, motions, visuals, rhythms, and intensities; and its developments and continual transformations cannot be separated from a syncretic history of the global flows,

Figure 12.1 A still slice of Salsa movement
Source: © Kevin Riddle Photography

movements, and migrations of people nor the syncretic amalgamations of their geographies that point to life always being a meeting place and story of the *middle* – a "simultaneity of stories-so-far" (Massey 2005: 9). Rhythms of sound, sight, movement, performance, and sharing that mingled and merged after arriving at their Caribbean destinations from desperate departure points across the Atlantic Ocean have syncretically entangled to become a middle known as Salsa; from its intensive zones of Cuban ballrooms and backyards to the hottest dance halls in Harlem and through the polyrhythmic complexity of the Afro-Cuban rumba punctuated by rapid steps of Brazilian samba, a constellation of Salsa has emerged through a simultaneous coming-together and breaking-apart of rhythmatic difference(s); a global circulation of a dance movement and performance that, when it arrives, moves; and when it moves, develops specificities that constantly erupt and transform. Today, Salsa brings all of its history and geography to travel shared *journeys* of hip-hop's sharp and smooth energy, flamenco's dramatic and statuesque poses and intricate hand stylings, the sensual hip, abdomen, and chest isolations of belly dancing, and dramatic tango leg flares – differences of Salsa syncretically amalgamating: a return of difference once again in a different way.

Portraits

The astute ear can distinguish Salsa's syncretic time-spaces in the steady, hollow, clack-clack, clack-clack-clack of the clave and in the deep tones and slaps of the conga drum that form the underbelly of Salsa's (heart) beat(s). The brassy trumpet and piano's light energy drive melodic mo(ve)ments that explode in passion and energy. Bodies react to Salsa's syncretic rhythmic ebbs and flows, creating a constellation of motion, sound and sight on the dance floor – it, itself, a multiplicitous event of place, or space: a *splacing* (Doel 1999) – moving notions of self beyond subjectivities and objectivities to the transversal relationalities of difference becoming and self beyond self. The micro-movements of singular bodies (be)come-together in motion – spinning, snapping, rolling, twirling, and twisting in communion; the event of the dance floor – functioning as a screen – collects the chaos and circulates it like a broken kaleidoscope that now knows only the infinite speeds of sound, color, rhythm, and sensation: thought is not lost – but becoming: "for the skin is faster than the word" (Massumi 2002: 25).

Through all of this, the Salsa dance floor becomes a place of becoming, of difference *becoming* difference, of the syncretic amalgamating through the becoming–West African of the New Yorker, the becoming-Cuban of the South African, the becoming-Brazilian of the Korean, the becoming-Spaniard of the Canadian; and while Salsa may be momentarily arrested by "schools" or "styles" – vain attempts of creeds at capturing and colonizing "purity" that life proves to be nothing more than photograph stills (re)presenting "a functional blockage, a neutralization of experimental desire – the untouchable, unkissable, forbidden, enframed photo that can only take pleasure (*jouir*) from its own sight, a submissive desire that can only take pleasure from its own submission … the desire that imposes submission, propagates it; a desire that judges and condemns" (Deleuze and Guattari 1986: 5) – Salsa's continuous performative (pro)creation joyfully and experimentally betrays any sense of appropriate convention or orthodoxy through the moving fluidity and inevitability of the experiential affections of the syncretic. As with any functionality or blockage, such attempts at closure may have their politics and purposes, but we must then ask: for whom? And, perhaps just as importantly, how are they creating a "who(m)"?

Tekkonkinkreet asks these questions of a place called Treasure Town – the third ward of an unnamed Japanese city that greets us most forcefully through its syncretic constellation of narrative, theme, affections, and sights – where we are presented with a seemingly simple story of gentrification and displacement taking place through a complex combination of historical, religious, mystical, and mythological conjunctions. Emerging from a different middle than Salsa – yet materially and spiritually intersecting it in a *someplace* and *sometime* that is the very (un)folding of this paper – *Tekkonkinkreet* weaves its narrative together through the beautiful violence of science-fiction and the schizophrenic voices of magical realism syncretically coupled with allusions to the Babylonian historical personae of Hammurabi and Nebuchadnezzar II; Zoroastrian and Biblical stories of the *Serpent* and the fight between good and evil; the mythical battle between Theseus and the Minotaur in the founding of Athens; and the loving actions and care of Johnny Appleseed. The central protagonists, *Kuro* (Black) and *Shiro* (White), are the very embodiments of the forces of *yin* and *yang* – Taoist principles of the complimentary relations of becoming. Orphaned and calling a small broken-down hatchback under a bridge by a river home, Kuro and Shiro together form a gang known as *Neko* ("The Cats") and their biggest challenge comes when foreign and local interests embodying the impersonal coldness of neo-liberal capital and the universalizing dogmatic ideologies of urban planning and "economic religiosity" (Nelson 2001) band together to displace, destroy, and reproduce Treasure Town into a "Kiddle Kastle" amusement park – an attempt to transform the town's syncretically formed material realities and capacities into a distilled and homogenized container of pure consumption. Like the Cretans before them, the Cats ultimately (be)come-together through affective encounters with a Treasure Town multitude composed of once-rival gang members, police officers, and *yakuza* to collectively resist and repel the oncoming violent displacements and cruel impositions of this unadulterated capitalism (see Curti 2013).

Paralleling this affirmative syncretic narrative is Treasure Town itself, a metropolitan mélange architecturally and aesthetically draw(i)n(g) from and emerging out of the Islamic calligraphy of Southwest Asia, the divine iconography of Hindu India, the cityscapes of French graphic-novels, and the streetscapes of contemporary Japan. Its capacities for affective encounters are found most intensively in the syncretic spaces of its streets, its squares, its rooftops, its allies – the most intensive zones of "the chance of space" wherein "otherwise unconnected narratives may be brought into contact, or previously connected ones may be wrenched apart" (Massey 2005: 111); spaces where even the phantasmagorias of commodity culture and the powers that seek to protect its hegemony through the suppression and homogenization of any and all difference in its way cannot purify space from the desynchronized temporalities and subversive seepages of the syncretic. It is in and through these syncretic spaces that Treasure Town does not ask what difference is – for, it is collectively all around in matrimonies of sight and sound – but what it does; and whatever it does, it asks who it is doing it for.

The constellations that Salsa and *Tekkonkinkreet* (re)present on paper, in the streets, at the dance clubs, and as membranous screens to ask these questions are, themselves, political and decolonizing acts as the syncretic themes, sights, sounds, and rhythms composing both Treasure Town and Salsa dance floors are saturated with difference-producing capacitational validities all their own – pushing us to question our own historical syncretic becomings by fantastically illustrating the self beyond self, the outside inside, the margins within; being becoming. Writing about the political potentialities of syncretistic (re)presentation in the context of stage performance, Balme (1999: 2) explains,

> *In contrast to religious syncretism, which is usually an extended process brought about by friction and interchange between cultures, theatrical syncretism is in most cases a conscious, programmatic strategy to fashion a new form of theatre in the light of colonial or post-colonial experience. It is very often written and performed in a europhone language, but almost always manifests varying degrees of bi- or multilingualism. Syncretic theatre is one of the most effective means of decolonizing the stage, because it utilizes the performance forms of both European and indigenous cultures in a creative recombination of their respective elements, without slavish adherence to one tradition or the other.*

While Balme identifies the decolonizing and political power of syncretic theater in its uneasy linguistic combinatorials as they creatively emerge on the stage to represent difference, the lives of both Salsa and *Tekkonkinkreet* politically move before and after the verbal to non-representationally act through affects and effects of assemblage(s)capes origamically mapping dance-floor and cinematic events. It is the very creative power of these events that forces us to recognize that place – every place – is a syncretically stewing "maelstrom of affect[s]" (Thrift 2007: 171) that becomes, and can only become, before and after the fixities, closures, and blockages of identity.

Let us take here, for instance, something central to *Tekkonkinkreet*'s affirmative narrative of the syncretic nature of place: gentrification as an (un)folding process of affective entanglements. The focus of critical gentrification research, and definitions of gentrification in general, have largely centered on notions of identity – especially that of "class" – as explanatory mechanisms. In fact, at many times and in many ways gentrification as a process is virtually reduced to it.[4] As such, class relations are introduced as the most fundamental components of the most personal mo(ve)ments of place transformation. In the course of this, the very syncretic processes continually entangling and (trans)forming such relations are effectively blocked off (see Gibson-Graham 1996). This is similar to the Salsa scene, where apologists and proselytizers of "schools" and "styles" often unwittingly work to erode affirmative syncretic processes through Inquisitions seeking to homogenize or cleanse real difference. Many Salsa practitioners and scholars promulgate it as a unifying force where a coming-together of difference on the dance floor creates places of "belonging" (see Johnson 2011). Salsa dancers, for example, often mention Salsa's capacities to bring people together from different backgrounds through dance to participate in a shared, affective experience. They suggest that it is the harmonious social inclusivity of the performance that makes it a relatively unique scene. Much like critical interrogations of gentrification, however, difference in these Salsa narratives are almost exclusively attached to closed and fixed categories of class, race, age, and/or gender.

Such perspectives problematically draw on notions of identity (e.g. class and race) that are based on *social groupings* rather than *social processes* (see Gibson-Graham 1996, especially 46–71; and Gibson-Graham 2006; Saldanha 2006). The harm here is twofold: by approaching social groupings of identity (e.g. class, gender, race, age, sexuality, etc.) as foundational principles in discussions of social belonging and/or gentrification and displacement, affective and horizontal relationships that (re)constitute and (trans)form place are bypassed in favor of top-down categories, essentialized differences, and/or predesignated conflicts, in the process simplifying the complex, emergent, and syncretic natures of place and place negotiations as well as their always socially produced and producing affective relations. This is both limiting in terms of conceptualizations of place as a material medium capacitating a *(be)coming-together* of difference(s) because difference itself is fixed along lines of ideology and identity, and politically incapacitating in its effects because an affirmative politics of place is lost: that of (the) syncretic *becoming*.

Doel (1999: 46) tells us that in geography, "[d]ifference has been taken as a given – by context, for example – when in fact difference is what *takes place*. [...] If difference is *in* place, it is not in place in the same way that something could be said to be *in* a box. Difference is in place only to the extent that it puts place *out of joint*. Difference is what splays out." As a combinatorial, a coalescing, an assemblage that is always emerging as the creative and the new, the syncretic as the (be)coming together of difference *micro-politically* challenges any closure, weighing, measuring, categorizing, delimiting, ossifying, fixing, or essentializing of singular bodies, social relations, or productions of space. Marston et al. (2005: 427) draw attention to the fact that it is particularly the "small areas," the "site ontology" (see also Schatzki 2002; 2003; 2005), "the *milieu* or site actualized out of a complex number of connective, potential processes ... [where] we have the place – the only place – where social things happen, things that are contingent, fragmented and changeable." What takes place – and, more importantly, what *takes* place – in *Tekkonkinkreet* and on Salsa's dance floors is a return to syncretism in its most affirmative and earliest micro-political forms: the

[4] For example, Slater (2006:745) states, "[t]he middle classes are the gentri- part of the word, and they are moving into new-build residential developments – built on formerly working-class industrial space – which are off limits to the working classes." According to Neil Smith (2008:197), "the class etching of the urban landscape that gave rise to the language of gentrification is, if anything, more intense today, and this should be a central part of our inquiries and analyses," and Loïc Wacquant (2008:199) argues, "Any rigorous study of gentrification would seem ex definitionis to hold together the trajectories of the lower-class old timers and of the higher-class newcomers battling over the fate of the revamped district, since this class nexus forms the very heart of the phenomenon."

(be)coming-together of a multitude of difference(s) working before and after any notions of (fixed class or racial) identity to confront the contingent, the fragmented, and the changeable processes of a milieu (Treasure Town, the dance floor) to create new collective capacities and spaces of and for action.

The implications of this on first look, we recognize, may bring to some certain levels of pause and consternation. J.K. Gibson-Graham (1996: 48) points to discursive practices surrounding "economic development 'beyond' class" that have "produce[d] a vision of the decline of class politics as a potent social force." Such a disempowering narrative and its implications for place politics, however, are far from what *Tekkonkinkreet* or Salsa present to us. Rather, like Gibson-Graham (1996, 2006; see also Saldanha 2006), their syncretic amalgamations provide "different political insights that may accompany a reconceptualization of class [and race]" (Gibson-Graham (1996: 48) that highlight their joint and multiplicitous, emergent, and becoming natures with place, while simultaneously illustrating that by approaching place as a relational *capacity to act*, different nuances of a potent (class and racial) politics can horizontally cut across (and, as a result, transform) different identities while remaining sensitive to and able to confront wider processes of capital accumulation, current strategies of neoliberal urban governance, and historical and geographical legacies of social and spatial privilege and marginalization. As this suggests, *Tekkonkinkreet*'s and Salsa's affirmative syncretics do not dismiss or neglect the social and spatial materialities of class or race relations or their entanglements in (trans)formations of place, but move away from vertical and structural explanatory mechanisms to recognize that "horizontality provides more entry points – conceived as both open multi-directionally and unfolding non-linearity – for progressive politics, offering the possibility of enhanced connections across social sites" (Marston et al. 2005: 427). To engage the syncretic nature of place in this way is, therefore, not only to embrace the fundamental validity and value of difference, but that difference *makes* a difference – and that difference is an (un)folding that never *sits in* or *out of place*. In this, place loses any sense of fixity as it is continually recomposed through mo(ve)ments of "throwntogetherness" and the "negotiating [of] the here-and-now" (Massey 2005: 140), demonstrating that "there is nothing but *splace*, taking splace – [a] *splacing*" that is "always already … disjointed, disadjusted, and unhinged; both place and space … effects of splacement's inaugural duplicity" (Doel 1999: 9).

Considerations

Our play here with the syncretic has been far more than simply a wish to (re)present *place as mixture*. Rather, it has been an affirmative wading through how complex connections and couplings of place move with (all of our and their) differences as artistic expressions of dance and media help to creatively weave them together. Neglect of the syncretic in geography has been both to the loss of the discipline as well as to the concept as an understanding of how difference as difference affirmatively moves together to continually (re)produce place; a matter by-and-large avoided in "the diabolical art of spatial science" (Doel 1999). Why has this been? We suspect because as much as some geographers may like to talk about difference and thinking difference, most are met with discomfort whenever the "impurity" of *difference without identity* begins to seep in. Despite possible protestations otherwise, an invisible "teleology of whiteness"(Stewart 1999: 48) limiting creativity and thought to a prescribed rationalization and representational understanding of expression still widely envelopes and dominates the discipline, its acceptable forms of communication and its conventional understandings of people and places; To put it another way: geographical art(istry) has not (yet) become diabolical enough.

Elizabeth Grosz (2011: 188–89; see also Grosz 2008) explains that

> *If living bodies make art, it is also true that bodies are transformed by art. No longer reflective or contemplative bodies, far from action, surveying at a distance the events that don't touch one but are available for one's observations, bodies are now touched directly by the same forces that the art object invokes. Bodies, living bodies, the bodies of objects, bodies of land and of water, become the objects of art, what art depicts and transforms. Art affects bodies, bringing them into touch with the forces of the past and future, with the forces of the universe, with the force of other animals with which one shares a history and geography, and with the force of one's ancestors, which enable us to exist as we currently do and yet to differ from them. Art is an agent of change in life, a force that harnesses potentially all other forces of the earth, not to make sense of them, not to be useful, but to generate affects and to be affected, to affect subjects, but also objects and matter itself. Art is the excess of matter that is extracted from it to resonate for living beings.*

Art is thus not only a geographical force, but "an ethical imperative, because it involves a kind of moving beyond the already familiar ..., precisely a kind of self overcoming" (O'Sullivan 2001: 129); art is difference *as* difference: the heartbeat of the syncretic. General artistic mo(ve)ments such as dance and media, and the specific types of challenges presented to us by Salsa and *Tekkonkinkreet* – if we are willing and worthy of them – are, then, fundamental to both living and gaining any glimpses into syncretic processes as those which continually *take* and *make* place. As much of disciplinary geography has been born out of a duplicitous folly set on the closures, purities, and beginnings and ends of identity that have littered it with fear of anything that is different, creative, subversive, or new, media geography and its syncretic encounters offer an emerging promise for those who do not fit so comfortably into the confines of the prescripted, the conventional, the acceptable, or the "appropriate."

Stadon and Grasset (2011) relay that "[a]s art is fundamentally an articulation of the human condition it can therefore be said that syncretism is also a valid method for analysing identity within the post-biological discourse. If we are indeed post-biological then we must exist in syncretic mixed reality state." It is precisely here where the syncretic differs most fundamentally from the hybrid: it is not biological growth, it is not genealogical organism, and any analysis of its identities will be fleeting as it can never represent or be represented; instead, the syncretic exists before and after hybrid convenings in waves of affections and seepages of affect, as the non-capturable harbinger of difference that floods and overflows through the ventricles of *difference-production*, where marriages and their offspring always are and can only be products of post-biological polyandrous and polygamous (comm) unions: the simultaneously singular and multiple that helps us "[a]rrive at the magic formula we all seek – PLURALISM = MONISM" (Deleuze and Guattari 1987: 20). Rhythmic drumbeats, shimmering projector lights, glistening sequins, animations of animation: they are the transversal forces of (e)art(h) pushing body(s) and thought(s) to once again (re)create the world as a syncretic universe of amalgamating differences; artistic media and dance performance(s) becoming the diabolically worthy content and expression of origamic *earth-writing(s)*.

Acknowledgments

We would like to thank Julie Cupples, Jim Craine, and Leticia Garcia for their helpful questions, comments, and critiques. We would also like to thank Jim Craine for providing us a space with/in which to experiment and be creative.

References

Appadurai, A. 1999. Disjuncture and Difference in the Global Cultural Economy, in *The Cultural Studies Reader*, second edition, edited by S. During, pp. 220–30. New York: Routledge.

Ansell-Pearson, K. 1999. *Germinal Life: The Difference and Repetition of Deleuze*. London, Routledge.

Ascher, M. 2008. Ethnomathematics, in *Encyclopaedia of the History of Science, Technology, and Medicine in Non-Western Cultures* Vol. 1, edited by Helaine Selin, pp. 899–903. Berlin: Springer-Verlag.

Balme, C.B. 1999. *Decolonizing the Stage: Theatrical Syncretism and Post-Colonial Drama: Theatrical Syncretism and Post-Colonial Drama*. Oxford: Oxford University Press.

Bamaiyi, P.H. n.d. The Effect of Syncretism on Christian Spirituality (A Seminar Paper) [Online]. Available at: https://docs.google.com/viewer?a=v&pid=gmail&attid=0.1&thid=13af246408581ba8&mt=application/pdf&url=https://mail.google.com/mail/?ui%3D2%26ik%3D80bd1dc131%26view%3Datt%26th%3D13af246408581ba8%26attid%3D0.1%26disp%3Dsafe%26zw&sig=AHIEtbSl7IYyEAh9V4292PD-IqwXh1tJtg [accessed 11 November 2012].

Curti, G.H. 2008a. From a Wall of Bodies to a Body of Walls: politics of affect| politics of memory| politics of war. *Emotion, Space and Society* 1(2), 106–18.

Curti, G. H. 2008b. The Ghost in the City and a Landscape of Life: A Reading of Difference in Shirow and Oshii's *Ghost in the Shell. Society and Space*, 26(1), 87–106.

Curti, G. H. 2009. Beating Words to Life: Subtitles, Assemblage(s)capes, Expression. *GeoJournal* ,74 (3), 201–8.

Curti, G.H. 2013. "This is my Town" – Exploring the Affective Life of Urban Transformation and Change via Taiyo Matsumoto's and Michael Arias' Tekkonkinkreet, in *The Fight to Stay Put: Social Lessons through Media Imaginings of Urban Transformation and Change*, edited by G.H. Curti, J.W. Craine, and S.C. Aitken, pp. 19–55. Stuttgart: Franz Steiner Verlag.

Curti, G.H., and Craine, J.W. 2011. Lark's Tongue in Aspect: Progressing the Scapes. *Aether: The Journal of Media Geography*, 7, 137–40.

Deleuze, G. 1988. *Spinoza: Practical Philosophy*. San Francisco: City Light Books.

Deleuze, G. 1993. *The Fold: Leibniz and the Baroque*. Minneapolis: University of Minnesota Press.

Deleuze, G., and Guattari, F. 1986. *Kafka: Toward a Minor Literature*. Minneapolis: University of Minnesota Press.

Deleuze, G., and Guattari, F. 1987. *A Thousand Plateaus: Capitalism and Schizophrenia*. Minneapolis: University of Minnesota Press.

Deleuze, G., and Guattari, F. 1994. *What is Philosophy?* New York: Columbia University Press.

Doel, M. 1999. *Poststructuralist Geographies: The Diabolical Art of Spatial Science*. Edinburgh: Edinburgh University Press.

Gibson-Graham, J.K. 1996. *The End of Capitalism (as We Knew It): A Feminist Critique of Political Economy*. Oxford: Blackwell.

Gibson-Graham, J.K. 2006. *A Postcapitalist Politics*. Minneapolis: University of Minnesota Press.

Grosz, E. 2008. *Chaos, Territory, Art: Deleuze and the Framing of the Earth*. New York: Columbia University Press.

Grosz, E. 2011. *Becoming Undone: Darwinian Reflections on Life, Politics, and Art*. Durham: Duke University Press.

Johnson, T. 2011. Salsa Politics: Desirability, Marginality, and Mobility in North Carolina's Salsa Nightclubs. *Aether: The Journal of Media Geography*, 7, 97–118.

Kraidy, M.M. 2005. *Hybridity, or the Cultural Logic of Globalization*. Delhi: Dorling Kindersley.

Marston, S. A., Jones III, J. P., and Woodward, K. 2005. Human Geography without Scale. *Transactions of the Institute of British Geographers*, 30, 416–32.

Massey, D. 2005. *For Space*. London: Sage.

Massumi, B. 2002. *Parables for the Virtual: Movement, Affect, Sensation*. Durham: Duke University Press.

O'Sullivan, S. 2001. The Aesthetics of Affect: Thinking Art Beyond Representation. Angelaki: *Journal of the theoretical humanities*, 6(3), 125–35.

oxforddictionaries.com. 2012. Syncretic [Online]. Available at: http://oxforddictionaries.com/definition/american_english/syncretism?region=us&q=syncretic#syncretism__3 [accessed 16 May 2012].

Rollason, C. 2002. The Passageways of Paris: Walter Benjamin's *Arcades Project* and Contemporary Cultural Debate in the West [Online]. Available at: http://www.wbenjamin.org/passageways.html [accessed 12 October 2012].

Saldanha, A. 2006. Reontologising Race: The Machinic Geography of Phenotype. *Environment and Planning D: Society and Space*, 24, 9–24.

Schatzki, T.R. 2002. *The Site of the Social: A Philosophical Account of the Constitution of Social Life and Change*. University Park: The Pennsylvania State University.

Schatzki, T.R. 2003. A New Societist Social Ontology. *Philosophy of the Social Sciences*, 33(2), 174–202.

Schatzki, T.R. 2005. Peripheral Vision: The Sites of Organizations. *Organization Studies*, 26(3), 465–84.

Slater, T. 2006. The Eviction of Critical Perspectives from Gentrification Research. *International Journal of Urban and Regional Research*, 30(4), 737–57.

Smith, N. 2008. On 'The Eviction of Critical Perspectives'. *International Journal of Urban and Regional Research*, 32(1), 195–7.

Stadon, J., and Grasset, R. 2011. A Syncretic Approach to Artistic Research in Mixed Reality Data Transfer. 2011 *IEEE International Symposium on Mixed and Augmented Reality--Arts, Media, and Humanities* [Online]. Available at: http://www.computer.org/csdl/proceedings/ismar-amh/2011/0057/00/06093659-abs.html [accessed 2 October 2012].

Stewart, C. 1999. Syncretism and its Synonyms: Reflections on Cultural Mixture. *Diacritics*, 29(3), 40–62.

Stewart, T.K., and Ernst, C.W. 2003. "Syncretism" [Online]. Available at: http://www.unc.edu/~cernst/pdf/Syncretism.pdf [accessed 11 November 2012].

Tekkonkinkreet. (dir. Michael Arias, 2006). DVD. [United States]: Sony Pictures Home Entertainment, 2007.

Thrift, N. 2007. *Non-representational Theory: Space, Politics, Affect*. London: Routledge.

Wacquant, L. 2008. Relocating Gentrification: The Working Class, Science and the State in Recent Urban Research. *International Journal of Urban and Regional Research*, 32(1), 198–205.

Whatmore, S. 2002. *Hybrid Geographies*. London: Sage.

Willets, R.F. 1977. *The Civilization of Ancient Crete*. Berkeley: University of California Press.

Haunted Places

Colin Gardner

Introduction

In a key series of projected installation works completed during the mid-1990s – most notably *Der Sandmann* (1995) and *Nu•tka•* (1996) – the Canadian artist/theorist Stan Douglas redefined the distinction between place and space through a process of temporal deterritorialization, transforming both the individual and the historical subject into a spectral absence. Through a number of self-reflexive filmic and video mechanisms that deconstructed the enunciative properties of the apparatus itself (largely through split screen and a questioning of the historical or subjective authority of voice-over narration), Douglas used his camera to define a specific place – Nootka Sound on Vancouver Island; the studio reproduction of a fictional *Schrebergärtenkolonie* in Postdam, East Germany – all the better to fracture its dynamic connections to otherwise contiguous spaces through dislocations of time and memory. As a result, traditionally repressed or marginalized forces such as the territorial rights of indigenous peoples and schizoid childhood traumas – defined as "other" in relation to the dominant colonial power or patriarchal Oedipal authority respectively – were effectively activated as a willful disruptor of linear time as a "return of the repressed." This paranoia-inducing haunting creates a new kind of rhizomatic, and by extension, political space that is always in process, for as Douglas argues (1998a: 29), "Almost all of the works, especially the ones that look at specific historical events, address moments when history could have gone one way or another. We live in the residue of such moments, and for better or worse their potential is not yet spent."

In this respect, Douglas's investment in a kind of "forked" historical time is heavily indebted to Gilles Deleuze's two groundbreaking works on cinema – *Cinema 1: The Movement-Image* (1986) and *Cinema 2: The Time Image* (1989) – in particular the postwar transition in European cinema to a direct time-image epitomized by Italian neorealism and the French New Wave, as well as their literary counterparts in the form of the nouveau roman (Alain Robbe-Grillet, Marguerite Duras) and the film/TV work of Samuel Beckett. According to Deleuze (1989: xi), as the movement-image gives way to a direct time-image, "What tends to collapse, or at least to lose its position, is the sensory-motor schema which constituted the action-image of the old cinema. And thanks to this loosening of the sensory-motor linkage, it is time, 'a little time in the pure state', which rises up to the surface of the screen."

Until recently, such an overt focus on the time-image – itself heavily inspired by Henri Bergson's 1896 work, *Matter and Memory* – would have been dismissed as incompatible with traditional geographies of space and place. As Foucault (1980: 70) famously put it in his attempt to rehabilitate space contra the philosophical prioritization of *durée* over spatiality, "A critique could be carried out of this devaluation of space that has prevailed for generations. Did it start with Bergson, or before? Space was treated as the dead, the fixed, the undialectical, the immobile. Time, on the contrary, was richness, fecundity, life, dialectic." Massey concurs (2005: 17), "Over and again space is conceptualized as (or, rather, assumed to be) simply the negative opposite of time." Within this reductive binary, space is seen negatively as the lack of movement and duration because Bergson reduces it to a dimension of quantitative divisibility, cutting up time into instantaneous sections. As a result, he finds it impossible to "make" time out of space. As Massey argues (2005: 30),

> *Thus the supposedly weaker term of a dualism obliterates the positive characteristics of the stronger one, the privileged signifier. And it does this through the conflation of the spatial with representation. Space conquers time by being set up as the representation of history/life/the real world. On this reading space is an order imposed upon the inherent life of the real. (Spatial) order obliterates (temporal) dislocation. Spatial immobility quietens temporal becoming. It is, though, the most dismal of pyrrhic victories. For in the very moment of its conquering triumph 'space' is reduced to stasis. The very life, and certainly the politics, are taken out of it.*

Part of Massey's project is to reimagine both place *and* space less as exclusivist representations than as *processes* that are imbued with the same qualities of movement and transformation, posing the obvious question: "Why can we not imbue these instantaneous sections with their own vital quality of duration? A dynamic simultaneity would be a conception quite different from a frozen instant" (2005: 23).

By introducing the third factor of time, Massey is also able to deconstruct the traditional binary between space and place, allowing for a far more dynamic interchange. Thus space is no longer something to be traversed and colonized (itself pertinent to Douglas's *Nu•tka•*):

> *Conceiving of space as in the voyages of discovery, as something to be crossed and maybe conquered, has particular ramifications. Implicitly, it equates space with the land and the sea, with the earth which stretches out around us. It also makes space seem like a surface; continuous and given. It differentiates. ... So easily this way of imaging space can lead us to conceive of other places, peoples, cultures simply as phenomena 'on' this surface. It is not an innocent manoeuvre, for by this means they are deprived of histories. ... They lie there, on space, in place, without their own trajectories. (2005: 4)*

Against this invasive trajectory, place necessarily becomes defensive – closed off, a coherent bulwark of the meaningful and real against the alien and inauthentic, a secure retreat or domicile designed to guarantee a regional purity. But, Massey posits (2005: 6), "What if we refuse that distinction, all too appealing it seems, between place (as meaningful, lived and everyday) and space (as what? the outside? the abstract? the meaningless?)."

Marcus Doel agrees with Massey's assertion, arguing that,

> *one must also be incredulous about the polarization of place and space, which hinges on the glaciation of events in perpetual process. If it were not such an inelegant neologism, I would be tempted to say that there is nothing but splace, taking splace – splacing. And there would be nothing negative about this: no possibility of a catastrophic or negatory displacement insofar as splacement would always already be disjoined, disadjusted, and unhinged; both place and space would be special – illusory? – effects of spacement's inaugural duplicity. (Doel 1999: 9)*

Importantly for our purposes, which are as much psychological as geographic and historical, the same principles apply with schizoanalysis: "Not dis-placement. Just di-splacement: the prefix 'di-' signifying the double register in which the spacement takes splace; or else the prefix 'di-' or 'dis-' signifying the intensification and thoroughgoingness of the splacement" (1999: 9). For Doel, place is also what *takes place* – a case of both producing *and* the product itself, a threshold occupying the position between noun and verb. In short, "place is an event: it is verbal rather than nounal, a becoming rather than a being" (1999: 7).

By infusing both space and place with the vicissitudes of becoming and time, space ceases to be a mere "surface" and place loses its hold as a point of authenticity. Instead of the old "chain of meaning" – space-representation-stasis – we get a meeting-up of different histories as a deterritorialized form of dynamic multiplicity: "It is what I am calling space as the dimension of multiple trajectories," notes Massey (2005: 24), "a simultaneity of stories-so-far. Space as the dimension of multiplicity of durations." Massey thereby proposes that we see space as the product of a series of heterogeneous interrelations and interactions, "from the immensity of the global to the intimately tiny" (2005: 9). In short, there can be no multiplicity without space, no space without multiplicity for they are co-constituting forces. Moreover, because they are always in process, they are never complete, always open to a repoliticization by the intervention of a future agency. Similarly, place can never be fixed in either space or time. There is no concrete here and now separate from there and then (or indeed a future projection), only a series of contesting narratives that constantly reform in new configurations, each with their own temporality and cycle of return. As Massey notes (2005: 140), "What is special about place is not some romance of a pre-given collective identity or of the eternity of the hills. Rather, what is special about place is precisely that throwntogetherness, the unavoidable challenge of negotiating a here-and-now (itself drawing on a history and a geography of thens and theres); and a negotiation which must take place within and between both human and nonhuman."

We can now see that the Bergsonian time-image is no longer incompatible with theories of space and place as multiplicitous processes but indeed may act as a catalyst for making visible the latent relationships of different temporalities and false continuities (the time-image precludes a simple past-present-future reductionism) that had hitherto been hidden in the represented landscape or object. Equally important is that the time-image is directly associated with thought and affect rather than motor action. This is crucial to understanding both *Der Sandmann* and *Nu•tka•* because both are as much mental images – psychological hauntings – as they are places and spaces *en acte*. Secondly, affect is manifested in the qualities and powers of a new kind of space, what Deleuze calls "any-space-whatever." Far from being a universal abstraction – that is, a multiplicitous space located in all times and all places – the any-space-whatever is actually a specifically singular space. It has simply lost its homogeneity and a clear understanding of its own internal connections and relations. As a result, linkages can be made in an infinite number of ways, a rhizomatic line of flight without limit or boundary. In short, notes Deleuze (1986: 109), "It is a space of virtual conjunction, grasped as pure locus of the possible." Once again, this is fully compatible with Massey's assertion that space cannot be a closed system, for "In this open interactional space there are always connections yet to be made, juxtapositions yet to flower into interaction (or not, for not all potential connections have to be established), relations which may or may not be accomplished" (2005: 11). In addition, this consequently sets up a new set of political questions, for "There can be no assumption of pre-given coherence, or of community or collective identity. Rather the throwntogetherness of place demands negotiation" (2005: 141).

This essay will explore these multiplicitous contestations through an extended discussion of the complementary interaction and interpenetration between time, place, and space via two very different kinds of haunting in Douglas's *Der Sandmann* and *Nu•tka•*, tracing a trajectory from the return of the repressed in relation to Freud's uncanny to a more postcolonial reading of historical empowerment, whereby the very absence or suppression of the other in regard to a specific time and place allows it to act as a virtual catalyst for the idea of a people yet to come, a collective in the very act of formation (Deleuze 1989: 221–22). As Derrida (1994: 196) reminds us, "Given that a *revenant* is always called upon to come and to come back, the thinking of the specter, contrary to what good sense leads us to believe, signals toward the future. It is a thinking of the past, a legacy that can come only from that which has not yet arrived – from the *arrivant* itself." In this sense, Walter Benjamin's *Theses on the Philosophy of History* takes on a very specific geographic resonance given Massey's multiplicitous reading of the relationship between here/now and there/then as a throwntogetherness of historical time, producing what Benjamin (1968: 263) would call a *constellation*, "a conception of the present as the 'time of the now' which is shot through with chips of Messianic time."

Der Sandmann: The Uncanny and the Throwntogetherness of (S)place

Douglas's *Der Sandmann* is a particularly complex example of spatiotemporal return because it references (and subsequently deterritorializes) at least nine different constructs of place, spanning both psychological and historical time from the early nineteenth-century to the fall of the Berlin Wall in 1989 (aka *Die Wende* or "The Turn"). Firstly, as the title suggests, the work is very loosely based on E.T.A. Hoffmann's 1817 epistolary short story, which uses three different letters to relate the story of a childhood trauma before the omniscient narrator brings the story to its tragic close. In the first epistle, the adult protagonist Nathanael writes to Lothar, the brother of his fiancée Clara, recalling his childhood terror of the notorious Sandman, who was believed to throw sand in the eyes of children who refused to turn in at their allotted bedtime. He would then pluck out their eyes and feed them to his own owl-beaked children who lived on the moon. More importantly, Nathanael came to associate this fantasy figure with the lawyer Coppelius, a mysterious nightly visitor to his father, who was in the process of conducting alchemical experiments. Determined to confirm his suspicions, one night Nathanael hides in his father's study to see the Sandman in person. Sure enough, it's Coppelius, who is spotted removing glowing coals from the fire with red hot tongs. He hammers them into the shape of human faces but, most significantly for Nathanael's impressionable mind, they lack eyes. Then, as Coppelius shouts, "Eyes here – eyes!" Nathanael shrieks in horror and is promptly discovered. The evil lawyer flings him to the hearth, threatening to burn out his eyes with the embers. When his father pleads for mercy, Coppelius instead removes Nathanael's hands and feet, causing the boy to pass out. Hoffmann deliberately blurs the line between fantasy and reality so that we are never sure as to the accuracy of Nathanael's nightmarish account. The trauma is further exacerbated when a year later, Coppelius returns for another evening's experiments and the father is mysteriously killed by an unexplained explosion. Coppelius disappears without trace, but the psychic damage is done. Nathanael's childhood trauma recycles into his adult life when a recently arrived optician and barometer salesman, Giuseppe Coppola, turns out to be the hated Coppelius. Nathanael swears vengeance for his father's death.

Replying on behalf of herself and her brother, Clara assures Nathanael that the terrors are of his own imagining and urges him to put Coppelius/Coppola from his mind. In the third and final letter, Nathanael confirms to Lothar that Coppola is not in fact Coppelius and has been vouched for by the optician's long-time friend, the newly arrived physics professor,

Spalanzani, who has moved in across the street from Nathanael's lodgings. This revised truth is reinforced by Nathanael's attraction to Spalanzani's daughter, Olimpia, whom he has briefly glimpsed sitting in the window. Although he is determined to propose to Olimpia, the strangely stiff and mechanical young woman turns out to be an automaton. Nathanael arrives just in time to see her inventors, Spalanzani and Coppola, arguing over who fabricated the eyes and who constructed the clockwork of the doll-like body. Coppola – now horrifyingly revealed as Coppelius himself – overcomes Spalanzani in the ensuing struggle and takes off with the eyeless Olimpia. Alas for Nathanael, when he sees his beloved's eyeballs lying on the ground, the childhood conflation with his fear of the Sandman and the death of his father is complete. Although he appears to recover and is eventually reconciled with Clara, the story ends in tragedy as Coppelius reappears some time later shouting his familiar refrain – "pretty eyes, pretty eyes" – and Nathanael, overcome with madness, leaps to his death.

While Hoffmann's story constructs two initial psychological places – the trauma of Nathanael's childhood and its inexorable return into his adulthood – it is also spatially aligned with Freud's theory of the uncanny, explicated in his 1919 paper of the same name (Freud 1990). The uncanny – a translation of the German word *unheimlich* (literally "unhomely," the opposite of what is homely and familiar) – is both a dialectical term and also inexorably tied up with repetition and the return of the repressed: "Thus *heimlich* is a word the meaning of which develops in the direction of ambivalence, until it finally coincides with its opposite, *unheimlich*. *Unheimlich* is in some way or other a subspecies of *heimlich*" (Freud 1990: 347). Moreover (1990: 340), "the uncanny is that class of the frightening which leads back to what is known of old and long familiar." However, this isn't just a question of the unfamiliar being something new: "Something has to be added to what is novel and unfamiliar in order to make it uncanny" (1990: 341). In other words, the trauma is long-established in the mind but has become alienated from it through a process of repression. What ought to have remained hidden has since come to light through a process of repetition and coincidence – a case of chance becoming pure destiny.

In this respect, *Der Sandmann* is a perfect case study for Freud's argument because it not only fulfills most of the characteristics of the *unheimlich* but also allows him to fold Nathanael's condition into a primary Oedipal economy. Thus there is the uncertainty of whether a figure in the story – in this case Olimpia – is a human being or automaton. Freud associates her appearance with Nathaniel's childhood fear of his feminine attitude toward his father. He overcomes this by doubling himself as Olimpia and also falling in love with her, so that he is able to both divide and conflate his role as controller and controlled, much like the child's manipulation of the reel of string in Freud's *Fort-Da* game. By extension, the Sandman himself as a robber of eyes is a convenient substitute for Nathanael's dread of being castrated by his father. Like the fetish, the double acts as an insurance against castration as well as a sign of its inevitability: thus its uncanniness operates on the level of both dread and reassurance simultaneously. "And finally," notes Freud (1990: 356), "there is the constant recurrence of the same thing – the repetition of the same features or character-traits or vicissitudes, of the same crimes, or even the same names through several consecutive generations." The eternal return of the uncanny – Coppola as Coppelius as the Sandman – acts as a parallel to the eternal return of the repressed from childhood, for "When all is said and done, the quality of uncanniness can only come from the fact of the 'double' being a creation dating back to a very early mental stage, long since surmounted" (Freud 1990: 358). All these elements are bound together by an overriding characteristic, the omnipotence of thoughts over actions. In this respect, the *unheimlich* house is a *haunted* house, for "Animism, magic and sorcery, the omnipotence of thoughts, man's attitude to death, involuntary repetition and the castration complex comprise practically all the factors which turn something frightening into something uncanny" (Freud 1990: 365).

Paradoxically, Douglas eschews attaching such a reductive psychoanalytical reading to his retelling of the Hoffmann story by displacing it onto another of Freud's case studies, that of Daniel Paul Schreber (1842–1911), the subject of his 1911 essay, "Psychoanalytic Notes on an Autobiographical Account of a Case of Paranoia (Dementia Paranoides)" (1979: 129–223). The Schreber case also serves a double duty of retemporalizing place-as-process as it allows Douglas to reference both the father, Moritz Schreber (1808–61) and the son (the presiding judge over the Saxon Supreme Court from 1893) and to suggest that the illness of the latter – described in his 1903 memoirs, *Denkwürdigkeiten eines Nervenkranken* – was symptomatic of the remedial methods of the former. Instead of filming Nathanael's story in its original 1817 context, Douglas updates it both spatially and temporally by resetting it in a studio reconstruction of a *Schrebergarten* (thereby indirectly associating it with the later Freud study), which, as we shall see, is itself split into two time frames: a fully functioning garden on the outskirts of Potsdam in the early 1970s (i.e. pre-*Wende*) and its contemporary, redeveloped state after the plot was razed for new construction (i.e. the post-*Wende* of the mid-1990s).

According to Douglas (1999: 7–10), *Schrebergärten* evolved out of working class *Armengärten* (poor gardens) that were first established in Kiel in 1805. They were leased to rural workers who had migrated to the city during the early nineteenth-century urbanization of Germany as a means of supplementing their poor wages. Under strict state supervision – administrators determined what was to be grown, the date of harvest, and so on – these allotments slowly expanded throughout the century so that by 1880 Berlin alone could boast almost 2,800 gardens. After the entire system was shut down in 1897, the Federal Social Security chairman, Alwin Bielefeld set up short-lived *Arbeitergärten* under the aegis of the Red Cross until these too were terminated by the outbreak of World War I. *Schrebergärten* – which consisted of a rectangle of grass plus a small resting house-cum-hut (aka Lauben) – were a middle-class equivalent of these gardens designed for the physical education of young people. They were initially formulated in Leipzig by the educator Ernst Hausschildt, who in 1864 established the first Schreberverein (Schreber Association), named after his colleague, Moritz Schreber, who had died three years earlier.

By 1907 the *Schrebergärten* were so well established that most people had lost track of their original objectives. Never popular with the nation's youth, adults instead adopted them for relaxation and pleasure. Their function changed yet again in the aftermath of World War I when, under the Weimar Republic, they were converted to allotments at a time of increasing food shortages. During this period, the gardens took on the political stripes of both the Left and the Right, a factor that Douglas exploits fully in his own filmic setting. Thus, the Kühle Wampe garden in Northwest Berlin was the setting for Bertolt Brecht and Slatan Dudow's pro-Communist 1932 film *Kuhle Wampe, oder: Wem gehört die Welt?* (*Kuhle Wampe, or: Who Owns the World?*). Alternatively, the gardens were also adopted by the Nazis, for as Douglas explains (1999: 10), "Under National Socialism, the socialist origins of many of the allotment associations were obscured by imposed militaristic and ideological objectives of self-sufficiency and 'attachment to the soil.'" After World War II, the allotments were again used to alleviate food shortages while also providing spaces for middle-class recreation. Under the newly formed D.D.R. [German Democratic Republic], members of the *Kleingartenverein* now had a weekend retreat and a supplementary food source that they were able to sell at market. Douglas's pre-*Wende* setting of one-half of *Der Sandmann* represents this socialist "golden age," while the other reflects new laws established in 1989 designed to "synchronize" governance.

This is an excellent example of the historical intersection of the double trajectories of Massey's (1995: 139) concepts of throwntogetherness (place) and stories-so-far (space), for this new "here" of the pre- and post-*Wende*

> *is where spatial narratives meet up or form configurations, conjunctures of trajectories which have their own temporalities (so "now" is as problematic as "here"). But where the successions of meetings, the accumulation of weavings and encounters build up a history. It's the returns ... and the very differentiation of temporalities that lend continuity. But the returns are always to a place that has moved on, the layers of our meeting intersecting and affecting each other; weaving a process of space-time.*

Thus in post-*Wende* Potsdam, where the other half of the film is set, small amounts of produce could no longer be sold to vendors, while gardeners were forbidden from sleeping in their Lauben (which now lacked plumbing and electricity). Under the aegis of a reunited Germany, the city was now prime real estate: over half its thousands of *Schrebergärten* were being razed and replaced by hotels, luxury housing, and light industry and it is this discrepancy between the socialist past and capitalist future that the film is designed to express both historically and psychologically.

In terms of the latter, the elder Schreber himself was a fervent advocate of athletic activity in green space to alleviate the detrimental psychological effects of industrialization on children and adolescents. This runs parallel to his development of prosthetic devices and restraints designed to correct children's posture while sleeping, as well as the infamous *Geradehalter*, a confining brace designed to keep them sitting upright at the dinner table. As Scott Watson argues (1998: 32), "One imagines that there is some connection between the elder Schreber's experimentation with corrective devices for children's posture and the later mental collapse of his son who had been fitted with them as a child. In a sense Daniel Paul was himself a product of the *Schrebergärten* and Freud's account of paranoia one of the garden's earliest harvests." The son's early symptoms of insomnia and anxiety quickly developed into a paranoid system that entailed the depopulation of the world and its repopulation by walking corpses ("improvised men"), talking birds, as well as rays of light transmitting "nerve language" directly into his consciousness. Exhibiting obvious identification with the "Wandering Jew" and, like Nathanael in *Der Sandmann*, the feminine, young Schreber's ultimate objective was to facilitate his gradual transformation into a woman so that he could bear God's children and repopulate the earth.

As in the case of Freud's reading of *Der Sandmann*, this is obvious material for a reductive Oedipal analysis, yet once again Douglas complicates both the psychological and historical sense of place/space by looking to a more schizophrenic theorization rooted in noncontiguous becoming. In *A Thousand Plateaus* (1987: 293), Deleuze and Guattari argue that becoming "constitutes a zone of proximity and indiscernibility, a no-man's land, a nonlocalizable relation sweeping up the two distant or contiguous points, carrying one into the proximity of the other – and the border-proximity is indifferent to both contiguity and to distance." Extending this principle to Freud's psychoanalytic model, they criticize the latter as an example of a disjunctive synthesis that works through "exclusive disjunctions" such as "either/or," whereby difference or otherness can only be applied from the outside, as a difference in degree. Thus for Freud, Schreber's illness is conveniently explained through the structure of an Oedipal economy, as a patriarchal relation between father and son, castrator and castrated, masculine and feminine.

In contrast, Deleuze and Guattari reinterpret the Schreber case through schizoanalysis – difference in kind – seeing Schreber's transformation into a child-bearing woman as an "Other" form of relation, what they call "the inclusive disjunction," a process of "either ... or ... or ... ." Like Doel's contrast between *dis*-placement and *di*-splacement in his discussion of *splace*, the extra "or" radically changes the configuration, leaving the inclusive disjunction suspended, with Schreber caught *between* sexes as a third sex of paradox:

> *Schizophrenia teaches us a singular extra-Oedipal lesson, and reveals to us an unknown force of the disjunctive synthesis, an immanent use that would no longer be exclusive or restrictive, but fully affirmative, non restrictive, inclusive. A disjunction that remains disjunctive, and that still affirms the disjoined terms, that affirms them throughout their entire distance, without restricting one by the other or excluding the other from the one, is perhaps the greatest paradox. "Either ... or ... or." Instead of "either/or." (Deleuze and Guattari 1983: 76)*

If we apply the same paradoxical logic when discussing the cross-gendered Judge Schreber, he becomes schizophrenic in the form of a body-without-organs: "he does not abolish disjunction by identifying the contradictory elements by means of elaboration; instead, he affirms it through a continuous overflight spanning an indivisible distance. He is not simply bisexual, or between the two, or intersectional. He is transsexual" (1983: 76–77). It is this preference for the inclusive disjunction – "either ... or ... or" – that Douglas uses throughout both *Der Sandmann* and *Nu•tka•*, creating a form of psychohistorical delirium that links all his characters' paranoid delusions via the realm of the political and social, a disjunction that threatens to run all the way to infinity. For as Deleuze and Guattari remind us (1983: 274), "every delirium is first of all the investment of a field that is social, economic, political, cultural, racial and racist, pedagogical, and religious: the delirious person applies a delirium to his family and his son that overreaches them on all sides."

The inclusive disjunction is built into the very form of the film itself. Filmed during a residency in Berlin, Douglas utilized the close proximity of the old DOKFILM Ufa film studios in Babelsberg, just outside Potsdam. Ufa – with its rich history of silent filmmaking including *The Cabinet of Dr. Caligari* and most of the 1920s film output of F.W. Murnau and Fritz Lang – is synonymous with German expressionism and the horror/fantasy genre. Douglas's main inspiration was the use of a split screen device in Henrik Galeen's 1926 remake of *The Student of Prague* with its strong *doppelgänger* motif. In this film, the confrontation between the student and his double was shot by blocking half the lens and then reshooting with the other half of the stock. Filming in black and white on a continuous loop for twin 16mm film projection, Douglas reproduces this technique in *Der Sandmann* – thus allying his own film to an earlier incarnation of German cinema – in order to suture (or does it?) the gap between two historical manifestations of the *Schrebergarten*. On one side of the central gutter is time past – the 1970s garden functioning as a working allotment – on the other time present (the razed garden filled with rubble, bric-a-brac, scaffolding, and chain-link fencing). As Douglas explains (1998b: 127), "The latter set was built upon the former, as in a palimpsest, but one abiding feature is the old man – the Sandman – toiling away at some mysterious contraption that, after two decades, is still not quite working." Each set was filmed twice (for a total of approximately 9.50 minutes duration) in a continuous 360-degree sweep using a motion-control system. The shots are identical in terms of camera angle and motion as they reveal the details of the gardens. The two films were then projected onto the same screen. Half of each was blocked out and the missing half appears to be "completed" by the other.

Douglas's script makes significant changes to the Hoffmann story. Firstly, only the letters are featured, omitting the appearance of Coppola, Spalanzani, and Nathanael's ill-fated romance with Olimpia. Secondly, only Nathanael is featured on-screen (played by Frank Odjidja) and is depicted as a young, black German man (thereby reinforcing the historical shift in the racial makeup of postwar Germany from its Nazi past). In contrast, Clara and Lothar's responses are read as voice-overs. Thirdly, as befitting the scenario's relocation to a *Schrebergarten*, Nathanael's nemesis is no longer a nefarious lawyer but, as Clara explains, "nothing more evil than the old gardener Coppelius who thought he could grow spargel out of season by covering our sandy Brandenburg soil with boiled loam and heating it all with his crazy plumbing. Maybe the fear he inspired in you came from his suspicion of people in general and of children in particular." Finally, Clara's new, sisterly role is largely to remind her brother of Coppelius's connection with the saddest moment of their childhood: "The same night you snuck out with Lothar, mother was called from home. She came back very late. We were asleep. She woke us up to tell us father had been killed. Now I understand why you cried so desperately, '*It's my fault! It's my fault!* It was the *Sandman*!'"

Significantly, the film begins and ends each rotation inside the garden Laube, which is also littered with film equipment, thereby meta-communicating the film's own formal methods as a designator (but also producer) of place-as-space, akin to Doel's *splace*. At this point the two spatiotemporal halves of the film seem to be in synch, but as Nathanael first appears in the right frame reading his letter to Lothar, we notice that his words – "Something's wrong here" – are out of synch with his lips. His face wobbles slightly as it crosses the gutter between the two images and suddenly his words come into full synchronization. As the 360-degree pan continues, we gradually realize that the left half of the screen – with its functioning garden – is set in the socialist past, while the right side – littered with rubble and building materials – represents the post-*Wende* present. In that case, Nathanael is only in visual synch with his words in historical time past (which may well represent his diegetic, subjective sense of the present). His disjunction from his own words in historical time present may then represent his alienated subjective sense of the future, so that he is never temporally or psychologically coincident with himself as a subjective whole. Watson agrees (1998: 36), noting that "From the beginning of his career, Douglas has been concerned with how the imagination of history – or the repression of this imagination – determines the possibility of a self-articulating subject. He has centered increasingly complex projects on the notion of the absence of such a subject. The problem of alienation is through structural displacements in the works. These reveal how the history of techniques of modern representation is also the history of social relations."

This reading is fully confirmed on the second circuit, where the past and present images switch sides, for Nathanael's words desynchronize as he crosses the frame into time present (his subjective future). We also notice that the repeat pan of the studio is not exactly the same as the first, as the images have moved slightly out of register. As Douglas explains (1998: 127),

> *They are out of phase with each other by one complete rotation of the studio ... The effect created is that of a temporal wipe. Left and right halves meet at the centre of the screen in a vertical seam that pans with little effect over Nathanael and the studio; however, as the camera passes the set, the old garden is wiped away by the new one and, later, the new is wiped away by the old; without resolution, endlessly.*

In this respect both psychological and historical time are caught in a cycle of eternal return, creating a fateful displacement of the past by the present and an even more disturbing displacement of the present by the past, suggesting a conflation of Nathanael's trauma with that of post-*Wende* Germany as a (fractured) whole.

This spatiotemporal *aporia* is best expressed by the persistent presence of the Sandman in both halves of the split screen. Significantly, Douglas keeps him spatially apart from Nathanael, for although we see the young man standing outside the set in the studio/Laube, Coppelius the Sandman is placed at a 180-degree angle on the opposite side of the set, puttering aimlessly amid the vegetables (past) and rubble (present). The lack of direct confrontation between them would suggest that the Sandman is a manifestation of the always deferred return of the revenant, the figure that haunts all future becoming. This is reinforced by his relationship to the central seam or gutter that dissects the middle of the screen, for he appears to move in and out of view with equal facility in both past and present. As the physical manifestation of the uncanny, the seam acts as a divider of historical time – Deleuze's time-image as an interstice rather than the conventional splice of montage – acting as both a dehiscence of past trauma and also a devouring and disgorging mechanism that sucks objects and bodies into its abyss before they once again reemerge. As Watson puts it (1998: 77), "*Der Sandmann*'s seam brings the wound to the surface … the minute the seam appears, the fiction of plenitude and coherence falls apart. To the extent that our viewing 'work' becomes an anxious effort to put things together again, or to figure out the trick, we are struggling to create the suture we want and need and that classical cinema is designed to provide." This denial of suture is crucial to an understanding of Douglas's work as a whole. Initially developed by *Cahiers* critics Jean-Pierre Oudart, Jacques-Alain Miller, and Daniel Dayan, suture was originally conceived as a critique of bourgeois/Hollywood film's attempt to enfold character, camera, and spectatorial "viewing-views" into a unified field of vision. The objective was to erase multiple and conflicting points of view by telling a story as coherently as possible. Epitomized by realist cinema, suture encourages the spectator to identify with an omniscient eye and a unified subjectivity. In contrast, like the return of the repressed in *Der Sandmann*, the seam literally puts the filmic cut front and center and forces us to look at cinema's absences despite its traditional insistence on an enunciatory coherence.

It is here where Douglas's conflation of throwntogetherness and stories-so-far pays its richest historical dividends. Many critics have commented that *Der Sandmann* alludes to the fall of communism in Eastern Europe via the symbol of *Die Wende*, for as Daina Augaitis rightly argues (1994: 34),

> *This collapse is the background from which Der Sandmann emerges, and through the work's simultaneous representation of the old and new, it offers reflections on changes in politics, urban economics and the psyche of the German people. The narration of this work … delves into states of uncertainty, loss, innuendo, even madness. It serves as a suggestive commentary on both old and new memories regarding the changing state of Berlin, the Second World War, and the communist experiment itself.*

In this respect, Nathanael's trauma and paranoia becomes that of the collective history of the twentieth century, as well as its spatiotemporal corollary, the spectral critical history epitomized by Walter Benjamin's *Angelus Novus*. Inspired by Paul Klee's 1920 print of the same name, Benjamin opined (1968: 257–58),

> *This is how one pictures the angel of history. His face is turned toward the past. Where we perceive a chain of events, he sees one single catastrophe which keeps piling wreckage upon wreckage and hurls it in front of his feet. The angel would like to stay, awaken the dead, and make whole what has been smashed. But a storm is blowing from Paradise; it has got caught in his wings with such violence that the angel can no longer close them. This storm irresistibly propels him into the future to which his back is turned, while the pile of debris before him grows skyward. This storm is what we call progress.*

… and perhaps what Douglas would call Der Sandmann.

Nu•tka•: Stories-so-far and the Conjoining of Discordant Histories

Set in July 1789 in the community of Yuquot or "Friendly Cove" on Vancouver Island's Nootka Sound, Douglas' room-sized 1996 video installation, *Nu•tka•*, employs a strategy of apparatus-based bifurcation within and between sound and image to set up a disembodied, paranoid narrative utilizing the conflicting tales of the region's two chief colonial powers: that of the Commandant of Yuquot's first Spanish occupation, José Estéban Martinez, envoy of the Spanish crown, and that of his captive, the English Captain James Colnett. Each of the two rivals claimed imperial and mercantile rights to land already occupied by a notably "absent" third party, Chief Maquinna and the indigenous people of the Mowachaht Confederacy.

Douglas uses two different angles of the Sound shot hours apart from a location on San Miguel Island, the original Spanish garrison site at Yuquot where Martinez had arrested Colnett. These are interlaced on alternating odd and even raster lines within the projected video image. Recycled every seven minutes on a continuous loop, the lines split asunder in synch with the overlapping and conflicting voice-overs of the two antagonists as the camera pans and tilts in continuous motion. Derived from historical documents and personal journals, these monologues express the increasing paranoid delirium of the tormented Colnett as, agonized by his failed mission and convinced he was about to be hanged, he fantasizes about the possibility of escape; and the growing paranoia of Martinez as he becomes increasingly aware of his uncertain hold on the region. Martinez's authority is shaken after Callicum, the pro-English chief of the neighboring Clayoquot Sound, is accidentally shot by one of Martínez's crew. As a result, Maquinna ceases all relations with the Spaniards and Martínez loses the trust of his own government.

On six occasions the camera ceases its movement and the image and soundtrack come into rough synchronization as we focus temporarily on a single stretch of landscape. One should point out that the seemingly synched images are not in exact registration as they are also composed of two different shots, depicting the effects of different winds and tides, creating what Douglas calls an "uncanny apparition." During these sequences, Colnett and Martinez concurrently quote excerpts from the Gothic and colonial literatures of Edgar Allan Poe, Cervantes, Jonathan Swift, Captain James Cook, and the Marquis de Sade. These extracts, enhanced by the quadraphonic mix, resemble a looped musical composition, wrapping around the gallery spectator like aural sculpture. Excluded from these Western-centric texts is the suppressed voice of the Nootka people themselves. Significantly, even the name Nootka derives from a Western-devised misunderstanding. In 1776, two years after the first Europeans landed on Vancouver Island, when Captain Cook asked Chief Maquinna the name of his land, he replied "Nootka!" which roughly translates as "go" or "turn-around." Instead of being granted their own rights to speech and discourse, the natives are thus identified directly with the iterative presence of the natural landscape, ripe for conquest. However, Douglas reasserts the autonomy of the people in the interstices between sound and image, between conflicting and ultimately unintelligible colonial discourses. In this way, the innate unfixedness of place – and its corollaries of contested/contesting power and identity – is constructed exclusively in and through mediation at the very point where direct communication breaks down. As Watson (1998: 66) argues, "Here and elsewhere, Douglas explores what he calls the 'idiomatic languages' of media as if they constituted evacuated sites where the main actor has been absented."

Douglas himself sees *Nu•tka•* as a Canadian Gothic romance which, as he notes (1998c: 132),

> *was typically characterized by a return of the repressed: some past transgression haunts, then destroys the culpable person, family or social order. It is no surprise that these narratives flourished during the era of high imperialism – when remote and exotic areas of the world were being drawn into the European orbit and providing, if not the mise-en-scène, then at least the sublimated object of Gothic anxiety.*

Thus although the Western discovery and appropriation of the "foreign" – with its concomitant commingling of previously discrete cultural tropes into new racial and linguistic hybridities – was invariably accompanied by its willful oppression and abjection, the repressed other always threatened to return through a variety of sublimated manifestations such as the uncanny, the monstrous, or the ineffable. Thus in Gothic tales we discover a ready taxonomy of narrative devices: "a decrepit clan wallows in decadence awaiting its final annihilation (*Fall of the House of Usher*); a monster appears, threatening to infect the whole of the social and natural order (*Frankenstein*); the bourgeois individual himself might become infected and begin to display mortally morbid symptoms (*Dracula*)" (Douglas 1998c: 132).

Certainly, both rival captains begin to exhibit such morbidity as they begin to lose their mental grip, reciting their stories simultaneously until they effectively negate each other through an overdetermined *heteroglossia*. However, despite the dialectical confrontation between them mirroring the conflicting colonial ambitions of Spain and England, Martinez and Colnett's accounts are still firmly entrenched within the master narrative of colonial discourse and its corollary, the Gothic romance. This is, of course, both an ideological strength *and* a weakness. A strength because their accounts are mutually reinforced by their shared implication with, and imbrication by, the jointly quoted excerpts from Poe, Cervantes, de Sade, and so on, which create a hegemonic discourse that effectively Orientalizes the other as inferior. Mission accomplished! However, it's also a weakness because Martinez and Colnett's ephemeral clarity of vision, in both image and soundtrack, only occurs within a textual diegesis of madness, a madness imbued with the abject presence of the natives themselves, which is all the more latent because of their absence as representations (which reinforces the colonialist's need for space-as-stasis) and as descriptive text. As Douglas confirms (1998a: 9), "In *Nu•tka•* the whole question of unrepresentability has been dramatized in the relationship between these two European colonists. They are in a situation they can hardly stand: they have contempt for the landscape around them, they have contempt for the people who live there, the natives, and they have contempt for each other. But that contempt, combined with their faith in the law of their respective kings, gives them their greatest comfort and sense of identity."

We see this ambivalence in Douglas's use of two abridged quotations from Poe's *Fall of the House of Usher* whereby the poet's description of the monumentality of the House of Usher becomes analogous to the monumentality and conceptual and affective impenetrability of the landscape of the New World: "during the whole of a dull, dark, and soundless day … when the clouds hung oppressively low in the heavens … as the shades of the evening drew on … a sense of insufferable gloom pervaded my spirit … an unredeemed dreariness of thought which no goading of the imagination could torture into aught of the sublime." Then, a minute or so later, Poe conjures up an uncanny sense of being enveloped by feelings of bodily incapacity and dread: "I had so worked upon my imagination as really to believe that about the whole … domain there hung an atmosphere peculiar to [itself] … and … vicinity – an atmosphere which had … reeked up from the decayed trees, and the grey [horizon] wall, and the silent tarn – a pestilent and mystic vapour, dull, sluggish, faintly discernible, and leaden-hued." This sense of foreboding is reinforced by the slightly off-kilter registration of the video images, for as Watson perceptively observes (1998: 66),

> *There is something odd about them, for the sea and sky, shot at different times of the day, are stirred by different winds and tides. This alienated landscape parodies a local "touristic" tradition of coastal landscape motifs that suggest a kind of lordship over the terrain, with its mountain ranges, islands, rain forests and inlets. This derives from the European tradition by which property and national values are always the subtext of what is surveyed.*

However, as Watson continues (1998: 66), "The view of the surveyor, topographer or colonist, evoking the panorama, and the centrality of an observing eye, is deconstructed. Instead of a mapping of the landscape there is a disintegration and coalescence that imitates nature." In this way, the raster lines act as both an opaque material screen that reflect hegemonic pictorial values – depth of field, horizon line, vanishing point – but also a fractured scrim through which they can be called into question as an instrumental device of power/knowledge.

It's also significant that Douglas draws upon the writings of the Marquis de Sade, specifically an extract from the introduction to *The 120 Days of Sodom* in which the narrator, after cataloging the various sleeping quarters of the libertines, the brothel keepers, their aides and victims, proceeds to tell of another, almost unspeakable place in the bowels of a neighboring Christian temple, a place "in the depths of an uninhabitable forest, [which] ... only the birds of the air could approach, ... a hundred times woe to the unlucky creature who in the midst of such abandonment were to find himself at the mercy of a villain lawless and without religion, whom crime amused, and whose only interest lay in his passions, who heeded naught, had nothing to obey but the imperious decrees of his perfidious lusts." This quote is important given Douglas's critical investment in Deleuze, specifically the latter's account of the overdetermination of text in de Sade and Sacher-Masoch in his essay on masochism, "Coldness and Cruelty" (Deleuze: 1991). In this case, the Gothic, uncanny elements – and their connection to unrepresentable desires – lie less in the image than in the mercilessly descriptive nature of the texts themselves. "Both of the writers discussed by Deleuze are masters of speaking around whatever they're talking about," notes Douglas (1998a: 15–16):

> *With Sade you have exhaustive lists and descriptions, and with Sacher-Masoch you have different kinds of descriptions, which have reference to detail – the real object is never really described. The 'big' object is always something that is not there. And absence is often the focus of my work. Even if I am resurrecting these obsolete forms of representation, I'm always indicating their inability to represent the real subject of the work. It is always something that is outside the system.*

In other words, something that lies in the cracks between the component parts of the image (in this case the raster lines), between image and sound, between place and the sensory mode of communication, between *Nu•tka•* and its audience.

As in *Der Sandmann*, Douglas expresses this terrifying sublimity as a form of paranoid space. While in the earlier film this is expressed through the vertical seam or gutter between two separate yet abutting projections which never quite cohere into a seamless spatiotemporal whole, *Nu•tka•* adopts a similar formal strategy but works horizontally instead of vertically, using the raster lines of the video image to represent conflicting historical but complementary hysterical accounts of the colonial experience. In this respect, *Nu•tka•* is about the material structure of video itself, implicating the apparatus in a critique of colonial power structures and their hegemonic voices, while at the same time setting up a third space through which the subaltern can speak through the cracks in the audiovisual template.

As Douglas confirms (1998a: 16), "The hugest absence in *Nu•tka•* is the natives. They were the trading partners, they were the people who were residing on the land before the Europeans got there, but they are completely out of the discussion that goes on between the two characters. Except that the Spanish Commandant is paranoid about them coming and playing tricks on him and his crew, and the Englishman fantasizes about becoming one of their mythic characters." As in all Gothic tales, that which isn't shown or described takes on a far more incommensurable affect when the anchor of meaning is taken away. Deleuze reiterates this point in *Cinema 1* (1986: 57–58) when he argues that

> *The cinema can, with impunity, bring us close to things or take us away from them and revolve around them, it suppresses both the anchoring of the subject and the horizon of the world. Hence it substitutes an implicit knowledge and a second intentionality for the condition of natural perception … Instead of going from the acentred state of things to centred perception, it could go back up towards the acentred state of things, and get closer to it.*

Nu•tka• is thus highly paradigmatic of Douglas's work in general because it uses the innate characteristics of the cinematic apparatus to show us how new centers and connecting spaces can be formed through deterritorializing film's inherent focalization.

This liminality opens up what Homi Bhabha calls a "Third Space" (another form of "Either … or … or …" and *splacing*) that deconstructs the opposition between the "I" (Colnett and Martinez) and the "You" (the *Nu•tka•* natives) constructed through the colonial/Gothic enunciation. As Bhabha shows us (1989: 129–30),

> *The production of meaning requires that these two places be mobilized in the passage through a Third space, which represents both the general conditions of language and the specific implication of the utterance in a performative and institutional strategy of which it cannot 'in itself' be conscious. What this unconscious relation introduces is an ambivalence in the act of interpretation. […] It is that Third Space, though unrepresentable in itself, which constitutes the discursive conditions of enunciation that ensure that the meaning and symbols of culture have no primordial unity or fixity; that even the same signs can be appropriated, translated, rehistoricized, and read anew.*

It is this refusal to succumb to the performative spatial hybridity innate to foreign landscapes that causes the return of the repressed in Martinez and Colnett's respective accounts, notably their fear of the natives' otherness as well as their own atavistic desire to transgress the laws of reason while acting as the colonial ambassadors of their respective crowns. In *Nu•tka•*, it is the discordant relationship (as inclusive disjunction) between landscape-as-place and apparatus, between soundtrack and mise-en-scène that reflects a divided Western soul, inextricably torn between manifest destiny and a desire for the abject, between representation and the ineffable, where, to quote Pascal, "The eternal silence of these infinite spaces frightens me."

Conclusion: Space, Place, and a People to Come

Just as Massey's notions of throwntogetherness and stories-so-far are central to both *Der Sandmann* and *Nu•tka•* through their different forms of haunting, one might also add that the two films also harness their respective processes of both place and space as an incommensurable event whose forces are spread out across a multiplicity of trajectories. In this sense, they are innately political, even though there is no preestablished or pre-given sense of community or popular identity. The latter is always in the process of formation, a becoming-collective, a people yet to come. However, from our perspective this latency – whether spread across psychological or historical time – is the very powder keg of historical change, for as Benjamin states, "The historical materialist leaves it to others to be drained by the whore called 'Once upon a time' in historicism's bordello. He remains in control of his powers, man enough to blast open the continuum of history" (1968: 262). In this sense, Massey's here/now, there/then displacement contains the seed of a future becoming, whereby Douglas's work is concerned not with "addressing a people, which is presupposed already there, but on contributing to the invention of a people" (Deleuze 1989: 217).

This raises an obvious question of agency. Who exactly constitutes the historical subject(s) who enunciate the stories-so-far and cobble together the ephemeral component parts of place-as-multiplicity? Judging from our analysis of both *Der Sandmann* and *Nu•tka•*, the hopelessly split subjectivities of Nathanael and the Schrebers seem to be incapable of playing such a role, as are the paranoid colonial emissaries Martinez and Colnett. How might the future manifestations of *splace* be incarnated as collective utterances? Surprisingly, Deleuze argues that all forces of narration – in this case both within and without Douglas's filmic diegeses – are capable of such an act. Thus Douglas, Freud, the Schrebers, Hoffmann, Martinez, and Colnett may successfully act as catalysts for potential forces or incommensurable events that give rise to the idea of a people still in formation: "The author can be marginalized or separate from his more or less illiterate community as much as you like; this condition puts him all the more in a position to express potential forces and, in his very solitude, to be a true collective agent, a collective leaven, a catalyst" (Deleuze 1989, 221–22).

References

Augaitis, D. 1999. Casting doubt: The narratives of Stan Douglas. In *Stan Douglas*. Edited by D. Augaitis, G. Wagner, and W. Wood. Vancouver: Vancouver Art Gallery, 33–38.

Benjamin, W. 1968. Theses on the philosophy of history. In *Illuminations*. Translated by H. Zohn. London: Fontana/Collins, 253–64.

Bergson, H. 1991. *Matter and Memory*. Translated by N.M. Paul and W. Scott Palmer. New York: Zone Books.

Bhabha, H.K. 1989. The commitment to theory. In *Questions of Third Cinema*. Edited by J. Pines and P. Willemen. London: BFI Publishing, 111–32.

Deleuze, G. 1986. *Cinema 1: The Movement Image*. Translated by H. Tomlinson and B. Habberjam. Minneapolis: University of Minnesota Press.

Deleuze, G. 1989. *Cinema 2: The Time Image*. Translated by H. Tomlinson and R. Galeta. Minneapolis: University of Minnesota Press.

Deleuze, G. 1991. Coldness and cruelty. In *Masochism*. New York: Zone Books, 7–138.

Deleuze, G. and Guattari, F. 1983. *Anti-Oedipus: Capitalism and Schizophrenia*. Translated by R. Hurley, M. Seem, and H.R. Lane. Minneapolis: University of Minnesota Press.

Deleuze, G. and F. Guattari. 1987. *A Thousand Plateaus: Capitalism and Schizophrenia*. Translated by B. Massumi. Minneapolis: University of Minnesota Press.
Derrida, J. 1994. *Specters of Marx: The State of the Debt, the Work of Mourning, and the New International*. Translated by P. Kamuf. New York and London: Routledge.
Doel, M. 1999. *Poststructuralist Geographies: The Diabolical Art of Spatial Science*. Lanham, MD, Boulder, CO, and New York: Rowman and Littlefield.
Douglas, S. 1997. *Stan Douglas*. Cologne: Museum Haus Lange, Museum Haus Esters, Krefeld/Oktagon Verlag, 22.
Douglas, S. 1998a. Diana Thater in conversation with Stan Douglas. In *Stan Douglas*. Edited by S. Watson, D. Thater, and C.J. Clover. London: Phaidon, 6–29.
Douglas, S. 1998b. Der Sandmann. In *Stan Douglas*. Edited by S. Watson, D. Thater, and C.J. Clover. London: Phaidon, 124–27.
Douglas, S. 1998c. *Nu•tka•*. In *Stan Douglas*. Edited by S. Watson, D. Thater, and C.J. Clover. London: Phaidon, 132–36.
Douglas, S. 1999. Potsdamer Schrebergärten: Historical background. In *Stan Douglas*. Edited by D. Augaitis, G. Wagner, and W. Wood. Vancouver: Vancouver Art Gallery, 7–10.
Foucault, M. 1980. *Power/Knowledge: Selected Interviews and Other Writings, 1972–1977*. Translated by C. Gordon, L. Marshall, J. Mepham, and K. Soper. New York: Pantheon Books.
Freud, S. 1979. Psychoanalytic notes on an autobiographical account of a case of paranoia (Dementia Paranoides) (Schreber). In *The Penguin Freud Library, Vol. 9: Case Histories II*. Translated by A. and J. Strachey. London and New York: Penguin Books, 129–223.
Freud, S. 1990. The uncanny (1919). In *The Penguin Freud Library, Vol. 14: Art and Literature*. Translated by A. Strachey. London and New York: Penguin Books, 335–76.
Massey, D. 2005. *For Space*. London, Thousand Oaks, CA, and New Delhi: SAGE.
Watson, S. 1998. Against the habitual. In *Stan Douglas*. Edited by S. Watson, D. Thater, and C.J. Clover. London: Phaidon, 32–67.

Advertising Place

Jim Craine, Chris Dando and Ron Davidson

In 1869, after traveling across the continent to California as part of an Interior Department survey team, Albert Bierstadt completed *The Oregon Trail*, perhaps the most celebrated image of frontier expansion and the heroic achievement of "manifest destiny" in the annals of American art. That same year, the driving of the golden spike through the rails at Promontory, Utah, marked the completion of the nation's first transcontinental railroad. The railroad's completion underscored how Bierstadt's painting was one of rousing nostalgia rather than of history in the making. A more contemporary rendering of the American West, published that same year, came in the form of a travelogue, George A. Crofutt's *Great Trans-Continental Railroad*, that described more than 500 places to see in the newly opened West. The contemporaneous appearance of *The Oregon Trail*, the spike, and the travelogue illustrates how romantic imagery of manifest destiny overlapped with the rise of national tourism in the post–Civil War West. Indeed, this chapter adopts the perspective that manifest destiny, as a cultural institution, national identity project, and set of spatial representational practices, became inseparable from the colonization of the West as a tourist space starting in the late nineteenth century. Moreover, the cultural meanings and associated spatial representations of manifest destiny evolved as the tourist industry itself adapted to wider social, economic, and political forces.

We do not aim here to trace the intricacies of this evolution from its beginnings but rather focus on a pivotal moment along the way, the immediate post–World War II years. On one level, this period parallels the late 1860s and early 1870s, for in both times the West held meaning as a fresh field of adventure for suddenly expanded populations of American travelers. The completion of the transcontinental railroad in 1869, which enabled (primarily affluent) Americans to visit Western resorts in the relative luxury of Pullman cars, was paralleled in the 1940s by the nascent expansions of both the middle class and leisure time. The deluge of postwar travel was also facilitated by technology, notably the steady improvement of thousands of miles of the nation's roads and highways (a fairly steady project since the 'teens halted only briefly during the war years) and the production of increasingly reliable and comfortable automobiles and roadside accommodations (Jackle 1985). The postwar years also saw the end of a 15-year period of grudging sedentariness enforced by economic hardship and, as brought most tangibly to bear on domestic travel possibilities by rubber and fuel shortages, World War II. Despite the parallel, the late 1940s must also be seen as a unique moment in the history of tourism. They mark the beginning of a 15-year run of unprecedented American confidence, affluence, and leisure that would ultimately transform the West. Most importantly for our purposes, the democratization of postwar mobility was also expressed in spatial representations of manifest destiny-as-tourism within the postwar travel boom.

To illustrate how this is so, we focus on the "See Your West" advertising program tested by Standard Oil of California in 1938 but fully launched in 1940. The advertising was in the form of a series of collectable high-quality photographic prints of, as the collectible album stated, "scenic views of the West prepared for your enjoyment: to recall to memory certain favorite spots you visited in the past, and to help you visualize the beauties of those regions you have yet to see." Like nineteenth-century images of manifest destiny, the Standard Oil series linked images and ideas with specific places in the western United States, defining the meanings of western landscapes and then reifying those definitions by inscribing them onto landscapes. However, the conventions that governed the spatial representations of the West in the Standard Oil series deviate from those that Bierstadt and his contemporaries employed. The "See Your West" conventions imparted a thoroughly modern, self-conscious reflexivity to the series, transforming its "tourist gaze" into a meta-gaze.

Advertising and Consumption

How is this meta-gaze created? Mobility is a rich metaphor: the cornerstone concept of the frontier, manifest destiny, westward expansion, even the American dream, all depend upon the pairing of freedom and movement, and all were exploited by outdoor advertisers in their endless quest to sell, and thereby improve their own mobility as well (Gudis 2004). The development of advertising and changing patterns of consumption are intricately connected to both technology and geography. As technological advances provided new products, these products changed Americans' relationship with their landscape. With each new product, especially transportation, their geographies shifted. Advertising was central to both the new product and its sales but also communicating information about their new geographies.

Since there has been a "market," there has been advertising. In preliterate cultures, a variety of methods were used to get the word out about products and services. Strolling peddlers would call or sing-out about their wares, be it knife-sharpening, produce, or baked goods. Carved shapes and signs were used to indicate shops, for example a shoe or boot for a shoemaker or a striped pole for a barber. With the advent of the printing press and increasing levels of literacy, advertisements could circulate farther and reach a broader audience in the form of handbills, posters, and eventually newspapers (Sivulka 1998: 4–5). Advertisements were not just for manufactured goods: beginning in the early 1600s, books, brochures, and posters were used to promote America and its opportunities (Sivulka 2003: 749). The American colonies were set up as business ventures and required both capital investment and settlers, such as the Massachusetts Bay Company. Advertising was used to promote investment and immigration, reaching two very different populations.

With the Industrial Revolution, advertising was a means of stimulating demand for goods and this growth in manufacturing also contributed to the development of a national infrastructure of railroads, canals, roads, and communication. Railroads represented multiple advertising fronts. While associated with transportation of people and goods, the development of the transcontinental railway network also meant that railroad builders were in the land business. In exchange for the construction of the transcontinental railway, the Union Pacific and the Central Pacific railways were given land as part of the agreement to undertake the task. Most of the land was sold, with land in towns along the rail lines retained to construct depots and lease to elevator companies. Railroads produced millions of flyers, pamphlets, posters, and other materials to advertise this land, distributing them extensively in the eastern United States and in northern Europe. With this new railway network came an active promotion of tourism. With the railroad, parts of the American landscape that had been largely inaccessible now came within reach of those with the financial means. Early guides for "transcontinental travelers" were first published in the late 1860s and detailed not just how to go but also what was worth seeing (Shaffer 2001: 7–18). Realizing the market that was opening for tourism, the railroads quickly began to publish their own guides for travel that were a combination of advertising and information and, in 1883, the Northern Pacific completed a spur to Yellowstone, making America's first park accessible to the public (Shaffer 2001: 26).

While the railroad provided access to a previously uninhabited West (at least in terms of white Europeans), there was still a need to create the desire needed to entice a large-scale population movement to undertake such a dangerous relocation. Nineteenth-century paintings of western conquest and migration comprise their own subgenre of American landscape art known by John L. O'Sullivan's famous phrase, "Manifest Destiny." The conventions exhibited what art historian Roger Aikin characterizes as a directional national sensibility – a "compass consciousness" unique to the United States in the nineteenth century (Aikin 2000). Such consciousness derived from the importance of westward migration in national identity and the prominent role played by latitude and longitude in national history. Latitude and longitude, for example, defined the Mason-Dixon Line and the Missouri Compromise, and gave meaning to the heroic portrayals of surveyors and explorers such as John C. Fremont. Artists expressed "compass consciousness" on canvas by producing images that combined aesthetic beauty with directionality in scenes depicting movement toward the left (by convention, the west) side of the canvas. Such compositions "invited the viewer physically into the picture to the divinely inspired completion of the American destiny" (Aikin 2000: 84). In the manner of picturesque art, paintings of manifest destiny therefore presented landscape in the context of a visual linear narrative, a sequence of two-dimensional images to be encountered by the viewer. The distinct feature of the manifest-destiny genre was its insistence on geographic literalness, on the sequence moving always West.

Concurrent with the emerging business of railroad tourism came advances in technology related to printing and photography leading to the increased use of images in advertisements. In 1906, a group of boosters created the "See America First" campaign, designed to promote commercial development and tourism in the West, their logo "See Europe if you will, but see America first" (Gudis 2004: 52, Shaffer 2001: 26–39). In what is termed "national tourism," Americans explored their nation:

> *As national transportation systems and communication networks spread a metropolitan corridor across America, as methods of mass production and mass distribution created a national market, as corporate capitalism begot an expanding middle class with time and money to spend on leisure, tourism emerged as a form of geographical consumption that centered on the sights and scenes of the American nation. … In teaching tourists what to see and how to see it, promoters invented and mapped an idealized American history and tradition across the American landscape, defining an organic nationalism that linked national identity to a shared territory and history. (Shaffer 2001: 3–4)*

This exploration of the landscape was transformed by an ever-expanding car ownership facilitated by Henry Ford's production of the cost-effective Model T. Automobiles are a product that requires a great deal of other products to maintain their continuing performance, ensuring "an endless chain of consumption" (Gudis 2004: 48). Automobiles required fuel and oil, and this increasing need contributed to the expansion of the petroleum industry. While the petroleum industry had existed prior to the automobile, producing kerosene and other petroleum products, the advent of the automobile led to vast growth. Jakle and Sculle state, "gasoline consumption soared from 25 percent of the petroleum market in 1909 to 85 percent only ten years later" (1994: 50). Gas stations provided not only fuel but also assistance in keeping the machines running (thus came the "service station"). Further, additional industries sprang up to support the automobile, such as tires and other auto parts. Drivers traveling long distances looked for food and shelter: restaurants and hotels were developed. As competition increased, major producers consolidated and coordinated their logos, colors, designs, even architecture so consumers could just glance at a service station or restaurant and "see" if this was a recognizable brand or not, in what is termed place-product-packaging (Jakle and Sculle 1994: 19). This resulting landscape, oriented toward "automobility," was a "corridor of consumption" (Gudis 2004: 49).

As competition between oil company-owned service stations grew, new methods were sought to set them apart and draw in customers. The first free roadmaps offered by a service/gas station were by Gulf Oil in 1913. Road maps tied consumers to the companies in two ways: the need for maps took them to the stations and the company logos on the maps reminded them where to buy their auto-related products (Jakle and Sculle 1994: 59). Some stations offered "Green Stamps" that could be redeemed for a variety of goods, others offered china or other promotional items free with a fill-up. Standard Oil's "See Your West" images were one of the latter.

"See Your West" and the Continuation of Manifest Destiny

Like an early chapter in a book that informs how we interpret and respond to all subsequent chapters, the manifest-destiny period of US history still reverberates within and conditions American experience. It still shapes political and economic practices to produce tangible outcomes. To give but one example, Laura Barraclough has shown how suburban whites in the San Fernando Valley, California, have fabricated links between the area's old Western movie ranches and the "actual" Old West as Americans' "collective heritage" to help them win zoning augmentations (permitting horse-raising) and obtain public funds to create large open spaces in their part of town. Settling into a house with a stable out back in Chatsworth or Shadow Hills is represented in local narratives as the grand achievement of manifest destiny – as "the ultimate objective of westward expansion and the signpost of imperial conquest" (Barraclough 2011: 90). Manifest destiny is not something closed off in the increasingly remote past, but remains an active framework within which western Americans understand and organize their world.

The post–World War II years provide a particularly interesting time to observe the reverberations of manifest destiny in US culture. A deluge of tourism promotions encouraged the nation to go. One notable example was Standard Oil's "See Your West" campaign that consisted of 25 9"x12" Kodachrome prints distributed free of charge to motorists at Standard and Chevron gas stations and garages and other distribution sites in 15 western states, British Columbia, and Hawaii. Each year a new set of 25 prints was distributed. Information about each location was presented in accompanying text. The use of famous photographers (e.g. Ansel Adams) and writers (e.g. Ernie Pyle, Erle Stanley Gardner) increased the desirability of these prints enabling Standard Oil, in their effort to sell more products to our new and highly mobile society, to take advantage of the postwar travel boom and the burgeoning westward movement of the population.

The program originated in the mid-1930s when Oliver Applegate, a Standard Oil employee who worked in the company's Sales Development Department (SDD), secured some of the first Kodachrome film released to the public. During a vacation trip, he took some color photographs of western landscape scenes. Back from vacation, Applegate brought his pictures to the SDD office and projected them on the wall for viewing by other members of his staff. SDD was so impressed by the clarity and beauty of the pictures that they formulated an idea to use reproductions of the pictures as sales-stimulating giveaways at the service stations. This creative effort culminated in Standard Oil's first Scenic View Program, and the first in the petroleum industry, under which many thousands of colorful prints were distributed to customers at stations throughout Oregon. The immediate popularity enjoyed by these first views resulted in a total of eight different series of scenic views. By the end of the 1955 program, more than 130 million full-color prints, featuring more than 200 different scenes, had been distributed to customers.

The Scenic View Program began in the Oregon market in 1938 under the title "See Your West" and ran approximately 10 to 12 years between 1938 and 1961 (see Table 14.1). Different prints were available at each service station. Customers could get a free print at participating stations when they filled up with gasoline.

Table 14.1 The "See Your West" program

Program year	Region	Number in series	Number printed	Reference
1938	Oregon	5 Prints	Unknown	*Selling Standard*, 08/38, p. 6
1939	Arizona	Unknown	Unknown	*Standard Oil Bulletin*, 06/1940, p. 6
1940	16 areas in the western US and Hawaii	43 Prints	9,000,000	*Standard Oil Bulletin*, 06/1940, p. 6
1941	91 zones 7 western states	60 Prints	12,000,000	*Standard Oil Bulletin*, 06/1941, p. 10 *Standard Oiler*, 06/1941, p. 6
1942	Note about 25 prints different format (*Standard Oiler*, 04/1946, p. 11, notes that the 1942 program was started then stopped by the war).			
1943–45	Program suspended during World War II			
1946	100 zones 15 states, BC, and Hawaii	25 Prints	20,000,000	*Standard Oil Bulletin*, spring 1946 *Standard Oiler*, 04/1946, p. 10
1947	15 western states, BC, Hawaii and Alaska	54 Prints	27,000,000	*Standard Oiler*, 04/1947, p. 6 *Standard Oiler*, 07/1947, p. 16 *Standard Oil Bulletin*, spring 1947, p. 16
1948–54	None according to Standard Oiler, 04/1955			
1955		32 Prints	25,000,000	*Standard Oiler*, 04/1955
1959	Border areas of the West – targeting eastern visitors. 147 stations only	6 prints	Unknown	Management Newsletter, 07/1959, p. 3
1960	Arizona only	Unknown	Unknown	Winter month campaign for just Arizona – Management newsletter, 06/1960, p. 2
1961	Central and Western US, BC	12 Prints	Unknown	*Chevron News*, 06/1961, p. 6 *Management News*, 04/1961, p. 1 Note: "more than 200-million prints have been given away in nine scenic view programs since 1938" *Marketing News*, 04/1961, p. 4
1969	California Bicentennial celebration prints – 21 California Missions and 21 other historical sites, *Marketing News*, 05/1969, p. 1.			

Source: Peder Hash, Chevron Archives

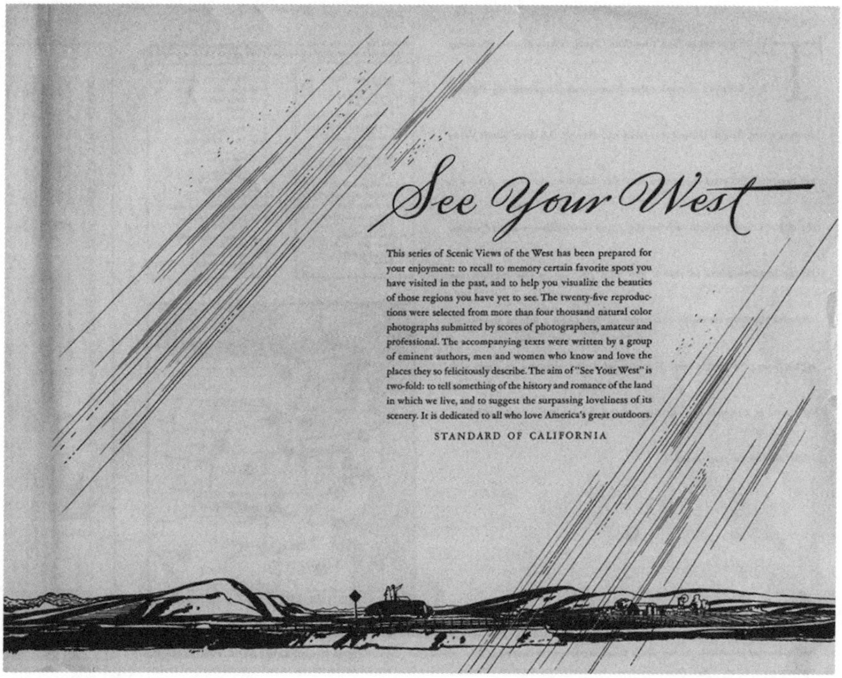

Figure 14.1 A scan of the first page (or title page) that was included in the "See Your West" collector's album, most likely from a 1946 album. Albums also included an index of all the prints that could be collected each year.
Source: Courtesy of Chevron Corporation

Albums were also available to collect the new prints that were distributed each week during the summer months (see Figure 14.1). Prints were also designed so they could be framed, if the customer desired. In 1939, the program was brought to the Arizona market and in 1940, the program was expanded throughout the West and into Hawaii. In 1941, 60 prints were being distributed but the program was then suspended between 1942 and 1945 because of World War II. The images were chosen from 7,000 submitted by photographers from all over the West. While many of the finest professional photographers are responsible for the majority of the pictures, not all the selections were the work of professionals. A Seattle housewife, a Denver dental goods manufacturer, and a Royal Canadian Air Force Flying Officer also contributed to the series. Ivan Dmitri, staff color photographer of the *Saturday Evening Post* is represented, along with John Kabel, dean of American scenic photographers, and Ansel Adams, perhaps the most distinguished American landscape photographic artist.

Like nineteenth-century images of manifest destiny, "See Your West" depicted the wilderness in pristine form, offering on one level a familiarly romantic, nostalgic vision of nature. It did so with great specificity, singling out places to go and objects to admire, even angles from which to view them. In this way it reified those places and objects. The photographs are captioned in small cursive letters with the depicted subject's name. The captions' factual brevity gives them the force of revelation: the solar flare launching out of the earth to become a billowing cumulonimbus *is* "Old Faithful." The snow-clad, almost ethereally shining volcano framed by yellowing leaves in the foreground *is* "Mt. Hood." One presumes that a different composition, extracting a different mood from the landscape, would require a modifier such as "Mt. Hood at Dusk." "See Your West" does not digress into permutations; it reveals *the* West. To object that some places (such as Mt. Hood) reappear in different guises in different annual series (though still framed by autumnal leaves) is merely to nit-pick. Also, like nineteenth-century images of manifest destiny, "See Your West" conveys a tone of palpable pride as Americans encounter the West. The source of this pride is not Anglo-capitalist civilization per se, however. As an advertising campaign, "See Your West" attends mainly to the image of Standard Oil. The company is the "expanding and technologically advanced" object of admiration this time around. That it could launch a promotion as epic as "See Your West" already makes the point. Only a great corporation could marshal high-caliber talent to "conquer" the West with an annually replenished series of photos and written descriptions that capture the region's essence in handsome, collectible form – *and* provide the gasoline for Americans to motor to the region en masse themselves. The boilerplate on the envelopes provided to sheathe the photos portrays Standard Oil stations almost like imperial outposts, havens of confident masculinity where the lost or confused traveler can stop to gather intelligence about the region: "In every way, the Standard Service Man is *the* man to see on the road – for information about local accommodations, points of interest, roads or maps. Also see him before you start – he can arrange through Standard Travel Information Service for a complete tour plan including special routings," states the text (italics in original). It is only a slight exaggeration to say that the Standard serviceman has replaced the goddess Columbia in John Gast's 1872 painting *Spirit of the Frontier*, an omnipresent figure casting light and bringing technology into the western wilderness.

If "See Your West" revives themes of the manifest destiny paintings of the 1860s–1870s, it diverges from them in one key respect. Beneath its surface romanticism, "See Your West" hints at a less dualistic vision of nature and civilization. The illusion of nature as pristine is presented, but thinly; the wilderness has lost much of its remoteness and autonomous power. A technologically optimistic, triumphant postwar American culture as refracted through an oil company's advertising campaign seems to have viewed nature as less pure and "other."

Consider the photograph of "White Sands, New Mexico" (in some series the state name appears in the caption). In the image, two women wearing bright, summery outfits stroll toward camera on the crest of a sand dune as if they have come from the brooding mountains in the distance. Clearly, the two figures must be completing a loop from their (off-camera) car on the shoulder of a(n off-camera) highway onto the dunes and back. The image's playful contrary suggestion, that the women have crossed a great dune sea from the distant mountains, like Bedouins, transforms the landscape into mise-en-scène. The superordinate reality of highway and automobile renders the wilderness fantastic and unreal. It can be hopped into for a brief stroll in a cocktail dress, and posed against playfully. And, of course, it can be materially appropriated, sealed in an envelope, and brought home as a "See Your West" collectible.

Perhaps as Americans traveled within increasingly thick and comfortable shells of technology, they became removed from the landscape and experienced it as less substantial and real. Earl Pomeroy made the point that the automobiles and highways that made the West accessible to American motorists also cut them off from it. The car, he wrote, facilitated "velocity rather than appreciation" (Pomeroy 1957: 210). Even some "See Your West" photographs that strain to portray a wilderness transcendent render artifice instead. "Chimney Rock, Nebraska," for example, appears almost as an overwrought religious icon. The photograph shows a rock pinnacle pointing dramatically heavenward atop a

Figure 14.2 A print of White Sands National Monument, New Mexico, from the 1941 collection. Interestingly, none of the 1941 prints have a photographer attribution; instead, they are attributed to regional companies, in this case Standard Oil Company of California.

Source: Courtesy of Chevron Corporation

rotunda-like hillside saturated with warm yellow and green hues. But what defines the image is the tiny figure of a man, standing on a ledge at the base of the rotunda, paused in apparent veneration of the scene. Like the women in the White Sands photo, this speck of a figure seems improbable, and gives the landscape the air of a special effect. Indeed, the figure looks suspiciously "pasted in" to the image. His feet are centered rather too perfectly in an eyebrow-raising patch of bare ground in an otherwise boulder-strewn, rough landscape. The mountain – or pinnacle – as cathedral is a common-enough romantic trope. However, the unreal quality of the Chimney Rock photograph – its too-conspicuous attempt at landscape veneration – makes kitsch of what it aims to glorify.

Not all of "See Your West" reduces landscape to kitsch or mise-en-scène, or advocates superficial, fleeting engagements with it, however. In particular, some of the written descriptions aim to coax travelers out of their cars into deeper, peripatetic encounters with the West. Yet even in some of these cases, the landscape lapses into artifice. For example, in the text accompanying his photograph of Half Dome in Yosemite, Ansel Adams portrays the road as smoothly integrated with the wilderness even as he exhorts departure from it. "You must thank the highways and the automobile for lifting you deftly out of the lowlands and into the high temples of the mountains, but to get the most intense and stimulating experience you must park your car and walk along the river banks, follow the trails through the quiet forest, and venture those steeper paths to which your energy and time are adapted."

Even the most emphatic literary efforts to depict nature in romantic terms fall at times strangely short. In the text about Sequoia National Park, California, Erle Stanley Gardner, the popular detective writer and inventor of the television lawyer Perry Mason, invites the reader to imagine setting up camp in the mountains: "People huddling around a cheerful camp fire somehow knit new and closer bonds of friendship. The roar and noise of cities, the hot reek of exhaust gases are but the nightmare of another existence." The wilderness experience is an encounter with people, not nature – it is social, a making of deep friendships. Moreover, the campfire invokes the "hot reek of exhaust gases" in the "nightmare" city that hovers over the scene as its hellish "other." In Gardner's prose, the wilderness invokes the city rather than provides escape from it.

Perhaps the most interesting sense in which landscape becomes artifice lies in the medium of representation itself. "See Your West" consists of photographs and text, not oil paintings like nineteenth-century images of manifest destiny. Photographs wield great potential to reify their subjects. This power derives, writes Steven Hoelscher, from the medium's "factuality" as an apparently transparent window into its subject. This transparency renders photography "a superb vehicle for cultural mythology": "As it presents a thoroughly convincing illusion of factuality while providing a repertoire of techniques that enable a photographer to make a powerful statement, the medium is uniquely positioned to naturalize cultural constructions" (Hoelscher 1998: 551).

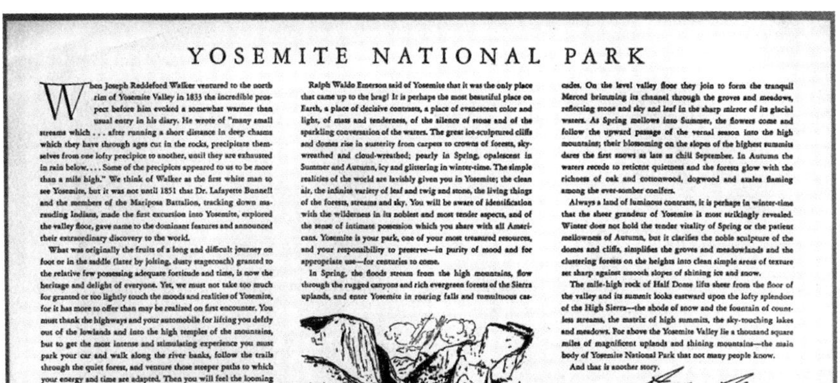

YOSEMITE NATIONAL PARK

When Joseph Reddeford Walker ventured to the north rim of Yosemite Valley in 1833 the incredible prospect before him evoked a somewhat warmer than usual entry in his diary. He wrote of "many small streams which . . . after running a short distance in deep chasms which they have through ages cut in the rocks, precipitate themselves from one lofty precipice to another, until they are exhausted in rain below. . . . Some of the precipices appeared to us to be more than a mile high." We think of Walker as the first white man to see Yosemite, but it was not until 1851 that Dr. Lafayette Bunnell and the members of the Mariposa Battalion, tracking down marauding Indians, made the first excursion into Yosemite, explored the valley floor, gave name to the dominant features and announced their extraordinary discovery to the world.

What was originally the fruits of a long and difficult journey on foot or in the saddle (later by jolting, dusty stagecoach) granted to the relative few possessing adequate fortitude and time, is now the heritage and delight of everyone. Yet, we must not take too much for granted or too lightly touch the moods and realities of Yosemite, for it has more to offer than may be realized on first encounter. You must thank the highways and your automobile for lifting you deftly out of the lowlands and into the high temples of the mountains, but to get the most intense and stimulating experience you must park your car and walk along the river banks, follow the trails through the quiet forest, and venture those steeper paths to which your energy and time are adapted. Then you will feel the looming grandeur of thousands of feet of clean granite rising above you and thrill at the white thunder of the waterfalls pouring out of the sky.

Ralph Waldo Emerson said of Yosemite that it was the only place that came up to the brag! It is perhaps the most beautiful place on Earth, a place of decisive contrasts, a place of evanescent color and light, of mass and tenderness, of the silence of stone and of the sparkling conversation of the waters. The great ice-sculptured cliffs and domes rise in austerity from carpets to crowns of forests, sky-wreathed and cloud-wreathed; pearly in Spring, opalescent in Summer and Autumn, icy and glittering in winter-time. The simple realities of the world are lavishly given you in Yosemite; the clean air, the infinite variety of leaf and twig and stone, the living things of the forests, streams and sky. You will be aware of identification with the wilderness in its noblest and most tender aspects, and of the sense of intimate possession which you share with all Americans. Yosemite is your park, one of your most treasured resources, and your responsibility to preserve—in purity of mood and for appropriate use—for centuries to come.

In Spring, the floods stream from the high mountains, flow through the rugged canyons and rich evergreen forests of the Sierra uplands, and enter Yosemite in roaring falls and tumultuous cascades. On the level valley floor they join to form the tranquil Merced brimming its channel through the groves and meadows, reflecting stone and sky and leaf in the sharp mirror of its glacial waters. As Spring mellows into Summer, the flowers come and follow the upward passage of the vernal season into the high mountains; their blossoming on the slopes of the highest summits dares the first snows as late as chill September. In Autumn the waters recede to reticent quietness and the forests glow with the richness of oak and cottonwood, dogwood and azalea flaming among the ever-somber conifers.

Always a land of luminous contrasts, it is perhaps in winter-time that the sheer grandeur of Yosemite is most strikingly revealed. Winter does not hold the tender vitality of Spring or the patient mellowness of Autumn, but it clarifies the noble sculpture of the domes and cliffs, simplifies the groves and meadowlands and the clustering forests on the heights into clean simple areas of texture set sharp against smooth slopes of shining ice and snow.

The mile-high rock of Half Dome lifts sheer from the floor of the valley and its summit looks eastward upon the lofty splendors of the High Sierra—the abode of snow and the fountain of countless streams, the matrix of high summits, the sky-touching lakes and meadows. For above the Yosemite Valley lie a thousand square miles of magnificent uplands and shining mountains—the main body of Yosemite National Park that not many people know.

And that is another story.

Ansel Adams

• *Written especially for See Your West program by Ansel Adams.*

Facts about Yosemite National Park

Yosemite National Park lies on the western slope of the Sierra Nevada in east-central California, about 85 miles northeast of Merced, 200 miles from San Francisco, 310 miles from Los Angeles. The park covers 1,189 square miles, approximately the size of the State of Rhode Island. Over 700 miles of trail and roads make it possible to explore and appreciate the less known areas. Park is open all year. Accommodations are available to fit every taste or purse. Summer season is from May 1 to October 1. Winter sports are enjoyed, usually, from December 15 through April.

Many visitors are of the opinion that Yosemite Valley constitutes the entire park, but actually it is less than one-hundredth of the total area. The floor of Yosemite Valley lies at an elevation of about 4,000 feet and is surrounded by cliffs and pinnacles towering 3,000 to 5,000 feet higher. Half Dome (seen in our natural color photograph on the opposite side) stands 4,892 feet above the valley. It is about 4 times as high as the world's tallest man-made structure, the Empire State building. The top of the Dome can be reached via trail.

El Capitan, largest exposed monolith of granite in the world, rises 3,604 feet above the valley floor. An impression of El Capitan's height and overpowering bulk may be gained from a tree which grows in a niche on the sheer granite cliff. From the valley floor this tree appears to be a shrub so tiny it is difficult to see. Actually it is 80 feet tall.

Glacier Point is one of the finest observation points in the park. It overlooks Yosemite Valley, 3,254 feet below. Each evening, during the park season, a bonfire is built atop Glacier Point. Promptly at 9 o'clock embers are pushed over the precipice to become the widely known Fire Fall.

Five great waterfalls are features of Yosemite: Yosemite Falls consists of three falls in one almost continuous drop of 2,425 feet—nearly a half mile.

Bridalveil Fall, perhaps the most beautiful of all Yosemite waterfalls, drops 620 feet. It becomes a roaring cataract during high water season, with great clouds of mist drifting from its base.

Nevada Fall is considered by many to be the most graceful waterfall in the park. It is 594 feet high and can easily be reached via trail.

Vernal Fall is formed by the Merced River dropping a sheer 317 feet. It is easily accessible by trail.

Ribbon Fall, during the full water season, is the highest of all Yosemite waterfalls, with a drop of 1,612 feet . . . ten times as high as Niagara.

Yosemite National Park has three big-tree groves. Largest and most popular is the Mariposa Grove located near the southern entrance of the park, 35 miles from Yosemite Valley over paved highway. The often pictured Wawona tree is in this grove. In 1881 a tunnel 8 feet wide and 26 feet long was cut through this tree. An auto road runs through the Wawona tree today. Tuolumne Grove is 17 miles from the valley on the Big Oak Flat Road. The Merced Grove is about 8 miles west of Crane Flat in a secluded corner of the park.

Photographic data: Kodachrome by Ansel Adams, San Francisco. 8 x 10 Ansco Commercial View camera; 14-inch Ektar lens, coated; CC 14 filter; daylight type film; 1/10 sec. @ f:16; slight pre-exposure of film to grey card to enhance shadow values; spring season, June, 1946.

STANDARD OF CALIFORNIA

Figure 14.3 Ansel Adams's commentary about Yosemite National Park from the 1947 "Scenic View" collection
Source: Courtesy of Chevron Corporation

See Your West

This is one of a series of Natural-Color Scenic Art Prints of the West being distributed in this vicinity. Other prints are available in other areas.

Free at Standard

LAKE TAHOE

That great American, Mark Twain, wrote from the shores of world-famous Lake Como in Italy:

"How dull Como's waters are, compared with the wonderful transparence of Lake Tahoe! I have fished for trout in Tahoe, and at a measured depth of 84 feet I have seen them put their noses to the bait and I could see their gills open and shut. I could hardly have seen the trout themselves at that distance in the open air.

"As I go back in spirit and recall that noble sea, reposing among the snow peaks 6,000 feet above the ocean, the conviction comes strong upon me again that Como would only seem a bedizened little courier in that august presence."

Twenty-three miles long—13 miles wide—rimmed by snow-covered peaks—Lake Tahoe is circled by a shoreline boulevard, each mile revealing new colorings in its blue waters, incredibly gorgeous from the east shore at sunset, equally spectacular in the moonlight.

Few, if any, scenic areas in the world offer to motorists, trail-riders and hikers alike so many tempting and accessible lakes, streams and mountains—or so many ways of having a good time. Spend a part or all of your vacation at Tahoe—and you will understand why so many thousands keep returning year after year. Mark Twain was right!

Note: For an interesting, permanent souvenir, frame this Art Print for your home—and paste the above description and map on the back of frame.

GET EACH OF THESE BEAUTIFUL SCENIC ART PRINTS . . . READY FOR FRAMING

For the encouragement of travel through wider knowledge and appreciation of the many famous natural wonders and beauty-spots of the West, we are distributing to motorists this summer, at three-week intervals, Full-Color Art Prints of Western Scenes. Other delightful pictures like the one enclosed are offered free in other localities.

These Scenic Art Prints are available only at Standard Stations, Inc., Authorized Distributors and Standard Oil Dealers. (At Calso Gasoline Dealers in Rocky Mountain states.) Drive in and get them—for they're *all beautiful!*

So wherever you travel this summer, make a special point of collecting your Scenic Prints from Standard Service Men. In every way, the Standard Service Man is *the* man to see on the road—for information about local accommodations, points of interest, roads or maps. Also see him before you start—he can arrange through Standard Travel Information Service for a complete tour plan including special routings.

STANDARD OIL COMPANY OF CALIFORNIA

© THE H. M. GOUSHA COMPANY

DRIVE TO THE WORLD'S FAIR OF THE WEST
Bigger and Better . . . on Treasure Island

M-296-39 Printed in U.S.A.

Figure 14.4 "They're *all beautiful*" – the envelope that held the 1946 Lake Tahoe print
Source: Courtesy of Chevron Corporation

Hence the photographs in each annual "See Your West" series present a more "objective" visual record of the West than a gallery's worth of nineteenth-century landscapes could have. Moreover, the collectability of "See Your West" prints ("they're *all beautiful*," the envelope states) unleashes their reifying power on an imperial scale. To visit each of the sites featured in "See Your West," as the series invites one to aspire to do, one would have to conquer thousands of miles of highway.

By celebrating the marriage of automobile and camera in the postwar travel boom, the Standard Oil series embraced and contributed to the democratization of the technological conquest of the West. It is sequel, perhaps, to the story of the surveyors who mapped and named western landscapes the century before (Trachtenberg 1989). A third spatial trope complicates matters, however, by rendering the celebration reflexive and self-conscious, transforming the tourist's gaze into a meta-gaze. This trope is the insertion of front and back regions in each photograph (Goffman 1959). In discussions of tourism, the "back region" usually refers to the locals' places of repose and preparation for future appearances before tourists. In our context, however, "back region" refers to a paragraph of fine print, appearing on the mounting paper behind each photograph, which provides "Photographic data." The paragraph lists the type of film, camera, lens, and filter used to take the photo, plus the shutter speed and any other steps taken such as preexposure of the film to capture light effects or the erection of a scaffold to get a certain view. This section uncloaks, in other words, the very "repertoire of techniques" used to produce these reifying images of the West, inviting the viewer to admire or emulate them. The inclusion of the "Photographic data" foregrounds the technical procedures by which western landscapes become scripted and reified. We do not imply that its inclusion is intended to raise critical awareness about the unique power of photography to "naturalize cultural constructions." The point is that in the highly confident postwar years, a broad stratum of American tourists could, vicariously or in fact, reflexively engage in the project of making and reaffirming the West through photography.

Up to now, the critique we have offered of the "See Your West" images has been that is has occasionally "unmasked" the romantic wilderness, presenting what appears as artifice rather than nature. The theme of wilderness as civilization's "other" – which is reflected in the manifest destiny paintings of Bierstadt and others – has become wilderness as "us." However, things take a different turn in "See Your West." Just as "wilderness" loses its remoteness and authority in some of the images, the ethos of technological mastery embedded in the photographs becomes subverted in them as well.

The "photographic data" reveal the meticulous work and fussy attention to detail of the photographer. By drawing attention to the effort and skill that went into capturing the images, the data state plainly that the West in the images was created rather than found. At the same time, in conjuring an image of the photographer sweating over the untidy mechanics of taking a worthy picture, it reveals the contingency of the technological frame itself. The masterful accomplishment of the entire "See Your West" series, and by extension the corporation that produced it and hovered over the West like a godlike Standard serviceman, can be glimpsed as through a curtain as human beings working fussily at so many levers.

References

Aikin, R. 2000. Paintings of Manifest Destiny: Mapping the nation. *American Art*, 14: 79–89.

Barraclough, L. 2011. *Making the San Fernando Valley: Rural Landscapes, Urban Development, and White Privilege*. Athens, GA: University of Georgia Press.

Goffman, E. 1959. *The Presentation of Self in Everyday Life*. Garden City, NY: Doubleday.

Gudis, C. 2004. *Buyways, Billboards, Automobiles, and the American Landscape*. New York: Routledge.

Hoelscher, S. 1998. The photographic construction of tourist space in Victorian America. *The Geographical Review*, 88:, 548–70.

Jakle, J. 1985. *The Tourist: Travel in Twentieth-Century North America*. Lincoln, NE: University of Nebraska Press.

Jakle, J. and K. Sculle., K. 1994. *The Gas Station in America*. Baltimore, MD: Johns Hopkins University Press.

Pomeroy, E. 1957. *In Search of the Golden West: The Tourist in Western America*. New York: Alfred Knopf.

Shaffer, M. 2001. *See American First: Tourism and National Identity, 1880–1940*. Washington, DC: Smithsonian Institution Press.

Silvulka, J. 2003. History: Pre 19th century. In *The Advertising Age Encyclopedia of Advertising*. Edited by, eds. J. McDonough and K. Egolf, 745–50. New York: Fitzroy Dearborn, 745–50.

Silvulka, J. 1998. *Soap, Sex, and Cigarettes: A Cultural History of American Advertising*. Belmont, CA: Wadsworth Publishing. "The Scenic View Program 1946," *The Standard Oiler*, June 1946: 10.

Trachtenberg, A. 1989. *Reading American Photographs: Images as History*. New York: Hill and Want.

Places of Graffiti

John Finn

Introduction

In the summer of 2009, I was invited to give a talk at a research seminar organized by a research group affiliated with the Federal University of Bahia in Salvador, Brazil. The topic of the seminar – "representations of Bahian[1] society" – posed a challenge for me: as an outsider who had been living and working in Brazil for less than a year, how should I approach this presentation to an audience that would be dominated by local scholars, students, and the public? I opted to put together a talk that merged a central aspect of my own research in Brazil – race – with the idea using the urban landscape as a visual medium to understand the racial and identity struggles taking place in Bahian society. Indeed, there had been something about the visual urban landscape that had been nagging at me since I had landed in Bahia the year before: if everyone in the city suddenly disappeared, and we were forced to understand the city in terms of images of people in advertising throughout the city, what would we see? If we were to judge Salvador's human geography based on this capitalist representational landscape, how would our perspective of the city change?

The city that is depicted through advertising is a white city. This happens everywhere, from upscale shopping centers to working-class markets, from the historic – and historically marginalized – neighborhood of *Pelourinho* to the elite high rises of the *Corredor da Vitória* sporting names like *Edifício Yacht Privilege*. In this context of whiteness dominating nearly all visual representations of race in advertising, the graffiti prevalent throughout the city is a pervasive way that representations of race in the urban landscape are reappropriated, through which dominant representations of whiteness in a black city are contested. In the words of Don Mitchell (2000: 100), while "one of the chief functions of landscape is precisely to *control* meaning and to channel it in particular directions … it is also certainly the case that landscape meaning is contested every step of the way." Mitch Rose (2002) agrees: "Social subjects are not the passive recipients of representation or its inscriptive powers … landscape is a terrain of struggle where various agents continually attempt to impose and/or resist differing representational constructs." In Salvador, graffiti becomes a tool of those marginalized from view via mainstream commercial advertising for taking back the vertical spaces throughout the city. Graffiti acts to democratize the visual messages sent and reasserts control of race representations in the Bahian capital.

With this chapter, based loosely on that original 2009 talk at the Federal University of Bahia and a short photo essay published a year later (Finn 2010), I further aim to explore the idea of landscape as media. It is widely documented that landscapes are much more

1 *Bahian* refers to a person from Bahia, a state in northeastern Brazil. The term is often deployed, however, not as simply a geographical marker, but as a cultural and social one, too.

than the result of mixing culture and nature (Sauer 1963 [orig. 1925]), or that landscape is, in the words of Lewis (1979: 12), "our unwitting autobiography." Rather, any landscape is the ephemeral but very real material product of infinite social processes occurring in place, and it itself is implicated in its own reproduction, normalization, and naturalization. Landscape, in other words, is a powerful communicative medium. It brings the past into the present (Schein 2006: 8), and it pushes the present into the future. As I aim to show in this chapter, the urban landscape itself, and visual representations of race in the landscape, become unique visual modalities of communication by simultaneously reflecting, perpetuating, and naturalizing societal attitudes and constructions of race in the urban form. In the end, my goals are quite simple: (1) to critique and deconstruct racialized/racist visual representations of people in the advertising landscape of Salvador, and (2) to explore the power of alternatives via the Afro-graffiti movement and one individual street artist's efforts to re-represent race in a way that challenges discourses of white supremacy infused in the fully racialized landscape. To do so, it is first necessary to explore recent theoretical developments at the intersection of race, representation, and landscape.

Race, Representation, and Landscape

Opening her 1992 book *Black Looks: Race and Representation*, bell hooks commented,

> *If we compare the relative progress African Americans have made in education and employment to the struggle to gain control over how we are represented, particularly in the mass media, we see that there has been little change in the area of representation. Opening a magazine or book, turning on the television set, watching a film, or looking at photographs in public spaces, we are most likely to see images of black people that reinforce and reinscribe white supremacy. (hooks 1992: 1)*

In a Brazilian context, reinforcing and reinscribing white supremacy has more often tended to erase representations of blackness altogether from the popular media. In an essay titled "Where Are the Blacks?," actor and former Rio de Janeiro city council member Antônio Pitanga once remarked that

> *a foreign observer [in Rio de Janeiro] … with even the slightest concern with understanding race relations in the country would immediately ask this question: where are the blacks? Starting in the airplane, this observer would probably not be surrounded by black Brazilian men and women … On arriving at the airport in Rio de Janeiro, it is unlikely that the hypothetical observer would be waited on by a black attendant, except the baggage carrier or perhaps the taxi driver … Picking up a magazine to read in his room, the observer will look for a photograph of a black model, but will not find one. The obstinate observer will flip through more and more magazines and will find a photograph of a black person only if there is an article about crime. (Pitanga 1999: 31–32)*

Pitanga goes on in this way, arguing that this imaginary observer would only start to see the black Brazil on the street, away from the elite sections of the city. Yet still, were this observer to stop at a newsstand, "the photos he sees are almost all of European men and women" (Pitanga 1999: 32).

The absence of representations of blackness is not restricted to print media. In terms of television, at the end of Brazil's 2008 prime-time television season, out of 150 characters cast in the top three shows, only 10 were of African descent. In a country that is 51 percent white according to the 2010 Brazilian census, the fact that 93 percent of the faces in Brazil's most powerful visual cultural conduit are white is significant. bell hooks (1992: 2–3) once again directly addresses this issue, arguing that "when we critically examine contemporary representations of blackness and black people … the field of representation remains a place of struggle." In a Brazilian context, the field of media representation is a central place of struggle indeed.

In the northeastern Brazil state capital of Salvador, one of those places of struggle over racial representation is in the very real materiality of the city's vibrant and colorful vertical landscapes manifest largely through two visual mediums: advertising and graffiti. Representations of blackness in advertising are rare, and where they do appear are most often "token" representations. Granted, any single advertisement or billboard may reflect the individual narrow-mindedness of the person responsible for that display. Collectively, however, the near exclusive use of whiteness to denote beauty and seductiveness, to attract the eyes of the public, to sell products, projects, quite literally, a "discursive formation" of racial prejudice onto the vertical advertising spaces of the city (Foucault 1973; 1982; Hall et al. 1997; see also Schein 1997; 2006) and a racial preference for whiteness, is naturalized into the urban landscape (see Duncan and Duncan 1988; Robertson and Richards 2003; Schein 2006).

Before going any further, it is worth taking a step back to consider landscape in more general terms, and racialized landscapes specifically. The literature on landscape in cultural geography is diverse, the contours of which have recently been outlined in various recent articles and chapters (e.g. Schein 1997; Mitchell 2001; 2002; Rose 2002; Mitchell 2003; Schein 2006). Thus rather than rehearsing the broader discussions and debates revolving around the place of landscape in geography, I'll focus on recent literature at the intersection of race and the material landscape.

The material landscape has long been a central interest in the discipline of geography. The oft-cited quote from Peirce Lewis's *Axioms for Reading the Landscape* captures this early approach to landscape:

> *Our human landscape is our unwitting autobiography, reflecting our tastes, our values, our aspirations, and even our fears, in tangible, visible form. We rarely think of landscape that way, and so the cultural record we have "written" in the landscape is liable to be more truthful than most autobiographies because we are less self-conscious about how we describe ourselves. Grady Clay has said it well: "There are no secrets in the landscape." All our cultural warts and blemishes are there, and our glories too; but above all, our ordinary day-to-day qualities are exhibited for anybody who wants to find them and knows how to look for them. (Lewis 1979, citing Clay 1973)*

In this configuration, the landscape is an innocently open book, waiting to be read and interpreted by an observant passerby – a job made easier with Lewis's *Axioms*.

While this notion of landscape is rather romantic and antiquated, there is still an important area in critical cultural geography that focuses explicitly on the production of the material landscapes. The vital difference, however, is that where earlier landscape geographers saw landscapes as surfaces without secrets, the ensuing generations of scholars interested in material landscapes have come to a quite different conclusion: rather than "existing in obscurity … the landscape *obscures*" (Mitchell 2008: 33). Or, in the words of W.J.T. Mitchell (1994: 5, cited in D. Mitchell 2008: 33), "Like money, landscape is a social hieroglyph that conceals the actual basis of its value. It does so by naturalizing its conventions, and conventionalizing its nature." Landscape is produced, but both the fact that it is produced, and the social forces that produce it, are naturalized in it. And since the social forces are naturalized into the landscape, the landscape itself becomes implicated in the reproduction of social and cultural life (cf. Massey 1984; Soja 1989; Lefebvre 1989; Schein 1997).

As a result, Mitchell (2003) has argued that landscapes are much more than the "dreamwork of empire" (W.J.T. Mitchell 1994: 10, quoted in Cosgrove 2003: 264): they are also the very "groundwork of empire" (D. Mitchell 2003: 787). The struggle over landscape, therefore, is a struggle for justice. Building on Henderson (2003), Mitchell (2003) remarks that studying landscape not only demands a theory of landscape but also theorizations of social processes that are materialized in the landscape, of "capital circulation and crisis, of race and gender, and of geopolitics and power" (D. Mitchell 2003: 790). Rather than focusing on reading a landscape as a passive reflection of the "culture" that produced it, the object of landscape research should be the processes that give rise to the landscape, and the ways that those processes effectively hide themselves in a naturalized landscape.

In this context, one of the most compelling ways that landscape has been conceptualized is as the materialization – the physical manifestation – of multiple intersecting and interacting social discourses (Schein 1997; 2009). The cultural landscapes of, for instance, the United States, are, quite literally, the materializations of discourses of American individualism, free-market economic ideology, private property rights, democracy, and so on (Schein 1997). Indeed, "most landscapes in the U.S. are the result of countless individual, independent, self-interested decisions that create, alter, and maintain landscapes, their meaning, and their symbolism" (Schein 1997: 663). But while those individual decisions are often self-interested, any action that contributes to the production of a landscape takes place within a discourse (Schein 1997). Schein elaborates that examples of these discourses include zoning regulations, trends in architecture and design, and consumption patterns, among others: "As a material component of a particular discourse or set of discourses, 'the cultural landscape' at once captures the intent and ideology of the discourse as a whole and is a constitutive part of its ongoing development and reinforcement" (Schein 1997: 663).

However, while critical geographers have long since dispensed with the notion of landscape as an innocent reflection of an ontologically secure notion of the "culture" that produced it, once again in the words of Pierce Lewis, "for most Americans, cultural landscape just *is*" (Lewis 1979: 12). It is this ease with which the social forces that produce the landscape are naturalized in it for the majority of observers that delivers to the landscape its most powerful disciplinary capacity (Schein 1997).

One area where the concept of landscape as materialized discourse has been particularly informative is in the area of racialized landscapes. The focus of much of Schein's work over the years has been to attempt to uncover and denaturalize seemingly "normal" American landscapes, seeing them rather as both the product of racial/racist structures present throughout society *and* an active part in the perpetuation of these racial/racist structures through the naturalization of landscapes (Schein 1999; 2006). Indeed, racialized lines of belonging are inscribed and naturalized in everyday landscapes across the country. And where Schein has focused especially on race and everyday landscapes, others have focused on more overt representations of race in the symbolic landscapes. Since power over symbolic landscapes has historically been held by white citizens, the American *symbolic* landscape is, not surprisingly, utterly racialized (Foote 1997; Leib 2004): the Confederate flag in South Carolina (Webster and Leib 2001); the muralization of Robert E. Lee in a public park in Richmond, Virgina (Leib 2004); the inclusion of a statue of Arthur Ashe alongside Robert E. Lee, Jefferson Davis, and Stonewall Jackson on Richmond, Virginia's Monument Avenue (Leib 2002; 2006). In all cases, from the everyday to the symbolic, the landscape as materialized discourse possesses a disciplining power. It reproduces, naturalizes, and in naturalizing further perpetuates society's racialized/racist structures. It has the ability to, quite literally, delineate, in the physical landscape, lines of belonging. And while most Americans "would honestly deny a racist intent in our daily activities ... the very structures of the world that we live in can make us unconsciously complicit in perpetuating processes of racialization through our interaction with and through the landscape" (Schein 2006: 9). Landscape is indeed implicated in questions of social justice (Mitchell 2003).

Salvador's Urban Landscape

In Salvador, the question of race is brought even more directly to the surface as the urban landscape is full of racialized photographic representations of people, especially through outdoor advertising on storefronts, signs, and, most strikingly, billboards. This visual representational landscape, as I noted before, is one where whiteness is normalized into the vertical surfaces of the urban expanse. So, as the landscape naturalizes the social forces that produce it, in this particular landscape it is the social processes that gave rise to the racialized/racist representations embedded in the landscape that are obfuscated and naturalized. The landscape becomes a medium through which white supremacy is reinforced and naturalized in society. This happens at all scales. Larger-than-life images of white women covering entire sides of buildings fix their gaze on society below as these images of whiteness fade into the "naturalized," "nonracial" landscape. The eyes of white models stare out through the glasses that images are being harnessed to sell, further normalizing whiteness in the landscape. White babies look down from signs, advertisements, and storefronts; white brides model dresses, tiaras, and flower arrangements; and even the mannequins used to display dresses, shirts, and swimwear are racialized as white, with light "skin," blue eyes, and straight hair. Through these images of race, whiteness – even in an Afro-descendant majority city – become seen as nonracial/racialized, which are naturalized both in the realm of landscape and the realm of discourse.

Throughout the landscape, though, nothing caught my attention more than the multitude of advertisements for housing – whether apartments, condos, hotels, or beach houses. These provide perhaps the most startling sign of the pervasiveness of white representation in a black city. In this context, the disciplining power of landscape as materialized discourse has reach far beyond the actual billboards displaying naturalized, supposedly "nonracial" images of whiteness. In this materialized discourse, images of whiteness connected to the marketing of housing are so insidious that eventually, when a billboard appears that doesn't depict any people at all, the line between white and black has already been discursively fixed in the Foucauldian "regime of truth" and etched into the social subconsciousness (Foucault 1980). The landscape is not simply the seemingly naturalized product of multiple underlying forces; it goes to work. These advertisements become agents in determining the lines between white neighborhoods and black, and all of Salvador knows very well that the new residents of this upscale building will not be the slum-dwellers in the *favela* in the background of the picture that are losing their ocean view as a result of its construction.

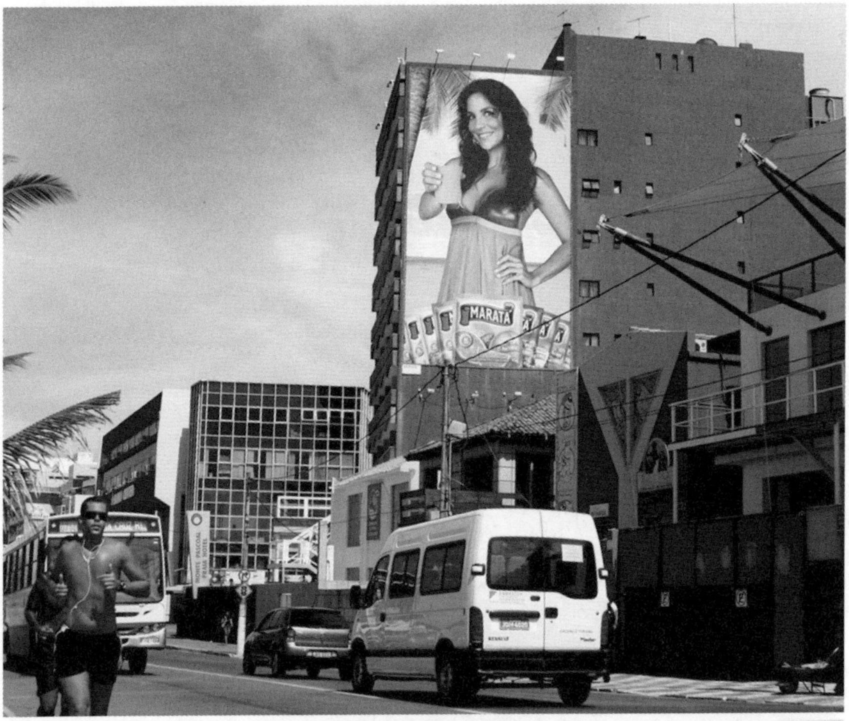

Figures 15.1 (above) and 15.2 (facing page) Representations of whiteness in advertising in Salvador, Brazil

Source: Photos by author

PREVI
A 4785

25 Reais
20 Reais

Visibility, Contestation, and Belonging through Landscape

Throughout the previous sections of this chapter I have tried to demonstrate the ways in which representations of race through capitalist media form a part of broader discourses of white supremacy in Brazil, and how those discourses are manifested in the physical, visual landscapes of the city through advertising. In this section I turn my attention to the ways that hegemonic discourses about race in Brazil are being challenged in the same way: through the visual landscape. Richard Schein (2009: 811) writes that it is too easy a task to simply "unmask the ideological undergirdings of land and landscape." Rather, he sets out to show the ways in which land and landscape can become a "stage upon and through which citizenship and community can be practiced." While it is true that the landscape is the physical manifestation of the discourses of society, so too is the landscape a place of struggle (Mitchell 2000), a place where hegemonic discourses of white supremacy can be challenged. In Salvador, where the vast majority of the city's population has been written out of a racialized/racist visual urban landscape that naturalizes whiteness, the *afro-grafite* (Afro-graffiti) prevalent throughout the city creates what Schein (2009: 824) refers to as "points of intervention [that] allow for an oppositional politics aimed at claiming belonging and exerting citizenship." *Afro-grafite* challenges the racialized and racializing visual landscapes of the city, and in doing so challenges the broader societal discourses that are manifested in that landscape. At this point it is worth considering graffiti in a broader context before returning to explore the specifics of graffiti in Salvador.

A basic definition of *graffiti* is that it is "a pictorial and written inscription on a publically accessible surface" (Hanauer 2004: 29; see also Kostka 1974; Blume 1985; Gross and Gross 1993; Scheibel 1994; Ferrell 1995). Graffiti is a communicative but transgressive act of appropriating public surfaces that do not belong to the artist for unauthorized visual interventions. Through graffiti, the physical landscape of a place becomes a platform from which people and groups can claim a voice in the public domain (Peteet 1996; Hanauer 2004). Through graffiti, the urban landscape provides a route to visibility, a surface for contesting marginality, and a place to attempt to carve out a place of belonging. As I will show, though, in all times and in all places, landscape is a site of struggle – a struggle with outcomes and implications that reach far beyond the landscape and into the societies that produce it.

Perhaps one of the most basic functions of graffiti is that it provides a route to visibility for marginalized people and groups. In a North American context, graffiti-as-visibility exploded in New York City in the 1970s and 1980s through what is known as tagging, where a "writer" would, quite literally, pen his or her own name (or at least street name) on surfaces throughout the city. While all visible places in the city were considered fair game for taggers, the city's subway train cars became the maximum object of desire for the writer's spray can:

> *Through their painting, writers 'made a place' for themselves in the city's public network, claiming a 'right to the city' as a valuable and necessary part of its social and cultural life ... Writers saw themselves as embodying an (illegal) urban beautification and education program for a fading city bent on denying its own magnificent cultural dynamics and destroying its own 'local color,' both figuratively and literally. In taking the trains, writers created a new mass media, and in that media they 'wrote back' to the city. (Austin 2001: 4)*

Visibility in writing was key (Snyder 2009). When the Metropolitan Transit Authority changed its policy and stopped circulating train cars with graffiti until they could be "cleaned," the train cars no longer provided this route to visibility, and the writers stopped tagging train cars (Snyder 2009). Similarly poor, marginalized areas in the urban periphery don't attract the writer's spray can, nor do rich areas known for rapid graffiti-removal for the same reason: writers are after visibility. As one New York City tagger of the era explained, "I think people write graffiti to fill some sort of void in their lives or their psyche where they are like, 'Do I really exist?' And one of the ways to prove it to themselves is if they write graffiti and they can say, 'Look, I actually am here. I did that. I exist" (graffiti artist Claw, quoted in Murray and Murray 2006: 159). Through tagging, the spray can provides a method for an otherwise invisible, marginalized youth to shout back at a society that has left them behind, saying essentially, *Fuck You, I Exist*. These visual transgressions thus provide a method for the marginalized to force their ideas and viewpoints, their complaints, their voices, into the public sphere, and into dialogue with the very forces of marginalization. Graffiti becomes a discursive tool to challenge the disciplining forces of dominant discourses as they are materialized in the landscape and to carve out spaces of belonging in society by carving out spaces of representation in the physical landscape.

Contesting Whiteness in a Black City

While São Paulo and Rio de Janeiro receive the lion's share of attention with respect to graffiti in Brazil, Salvador has a young but burgeoning graffiti scene in its own right. A much smaller city than either São Paulo or Rio, Salvador is a microcosm of the economic disparity that plagues Brazil as a whole, and in Salvador the added social dimension of race is brought to the fore. In Brazil, geography, economic inequality, and race correlate very tightly. Nationally, the richest 10 percent of the population controls nearly half the country's wealth, while the poorest 50 percent control just 10 percent. This broad national measure, however, can't illustrate the geographic dimension to economic disparity: Salvador's GDP per capita is less than half of that of Rio and São Paulo. Further, while the populations of São Paulo and Rio de Janeiro are 60 percent and 50 percent white, respectively, Salvador's population is overwhelmingly black or mixed race (80 percent between those two categories, according to the 2010 census). At the scale of the city, whites of all education levels command salaries that nearly triple the salaries of Afro-Bahians, and illiteracy among Afro-Bahians is 60 percent higher than it is among Bahia's white population. Given all this, it should come as no surprise that the city's white population has long wielded political power citywide (Nascimento and Nascimento 1992; Butler 1998).

It is in this economic and racial context that *afro-grafite* is becoming an increasingly dominant visual intervention into a racialized advertising landscape citywide that is both a product of and naturalizing force for those racialized/racist discourses of whiteness in the landscape. Starting in 2007, I have had the opportunity to get to know Marcos Costa, one of the most visible graffiti artists painting an alternative vision of race onto the vertical surfaces of the city. Costa was born in 1983, grew up in the urban periphery of Salvador, and is a product of the notoriously poor public school system. At the age of 10, Costa got involved with tagging, and a few years later with graffiti. Through this engagement with visual mediums, he developed a broader interest in art and design and entered the Federal University of Bahia to pursue a degree in fine arts. His story, as much as his art, aim to denaturalize the normalized dominance of whiteness throughout the city and illustrates the idea that landscape as materialized discourse is not simply a disciplining medium but can also be a medium of radical possibility. In May 2012, standing in an alley near his home in central Salvador just before starting a new work, Costa told me,

> *I do graffiti because I believe that art can bring positive messages to others. [...] I place at the center of my work my roots, ancestry, identity, African and Afro-Brazilian messages, though African-inspired design, symbols, and other graphics. [...] The work that I developed at the university is just such a dialogue between graffiti and traditional African and Afro-Brazilian art, through candomblé,[2] through capoeira, through sculpture, painting, graphics, through the universe of African and Afro-Brazilian art. This is the center of my research, and this is what I take to the streets through graffiti ... Our art is not just to beautify a place. I seek to make an art to make people think, to make people reflect, to make people believe in who they are, in what they live. So my art is an art of construction, of the constructions of concepts, of assertion, an art of resistance.*

In an earlier interview with Costa in 2009, he expressed a similar approach to his art:

> *I paint our people, I paint our ancestral black values, those of the orixás [African gods]. I paint messages for workers, for students, messages like "have respect for your place", messages criticizing society, but also affirming. Messages like "Tio, me da um respeito" [My uncle, give me a little respect (see Figure 15.5)]. The kid is not asking for money, only respect ... I think that where there is inequality, graffiti has to denounce it. Where there is exploitation, graffiti has to denounce it ... . Even while graffiti could simply be aesthetically pleasing, it also has to have a social message. I try to bring meaning out of that wall, to create a dialogue between pedestrians and my art, so that they not only see it with their eyes, but also read the messages that are there shouting out at them.*

His work is not coincidental or ad hoc. It is not purely embodied, as scholars have sometimes seemed to want to characterize the actions of "primitive" peoples in "primitive" places. Rather, his work is calculated, researched, thought out, considered. Costa consciously sets out to use his art to legitimize Afro-Brazilian identity through Afrocentric graffiti in the streets of Salvador.

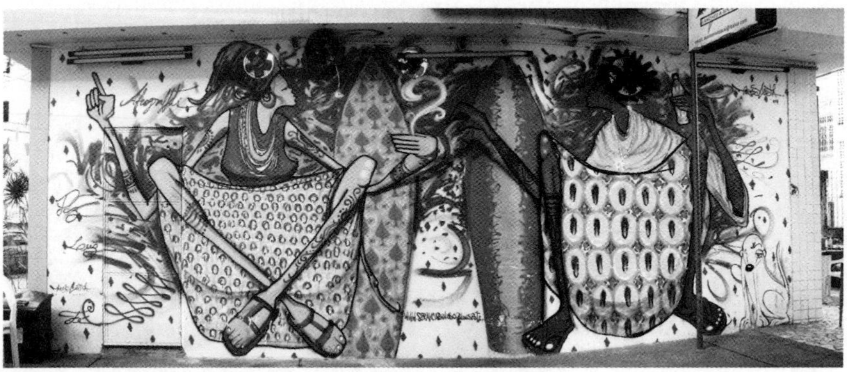

Figure 15.4 Afro-graffiti by graffiti artist Marcos Costa
Source: Photo by author

2 Candomblé is the syncretic Afro-Brazilian religion that mixes elements of Catholicism with elements of different animist sub-Saharan African religions, especially those originating in Nigeria and Angola.

Figure 15.5 *Art of Resistance* **and** *My Uncle, Give Me a Little Respect* **by graffiti artist Marcos Costa**
Source: Photo by author

Costa understands very well the marginalizing force of a landscape that is the materialization of a racialized/racist social structure embedded throughout society. But he also knows that interventions in the landscape have effects far beyond the visual/representational realm:

> *A lot of young people have died. I am here with the names of three friends of mine who died. Two were killed, another committed suicide because of depression caused by police violence, caused by unemployment, caused by lack of social assistance, lack of education, public health quality. There are many problems that affect the youth of Bahia. And I, as an artist, I seek to represent.*

The Spray Can vs. the Sword

Reflecting on a massive mural/graffiti project on the Separation Wall between Israel and the occupied West Bank, William Parry asks, "Is the spray can mightier than the sword" (Parry 2011: 9). The answer to that question remains to be seen. At the time of this writing in the winter of 2012, Israel has just concluded yet another weeklong bombardment of Gaza and has announced new plans for settlement expansion in East Jerusalem and the West Bank. *Is the spray can mightier than the sword*? It is, in the end, a rather utopian vision: artistic intervention in the landscape to affect concrete social change throughout broader society. Writing about the same mural/graffiti project as Parry (2011), renowned graffiti artist Ron English commented,

> *Maybe it seems preposterous that art can change the world, but it can give a voice to silenced and oppressed citizens on the dark side of any wall. Think about it. If you had a choice between these two powerful vehicles of communication – a spectacular act of destruction, or a spectacular creation of art that spoke eloquently of your anger and alienation – which would you choose? Which speaks louder and longer? Violent resistance? A mural? Don't laugh. Little boys are making these decisions every day. (English 2011: 7)*

In Salvador, Brazil, and elsewhere, while graffiti may not upend completely the unequal distribution of wealth and power, the racialized and racist social structures, the forces of marginalization, it does provide a method to contesting these dominating forces in the realm of landscape. And these contestations, through graffiti interventions, are not trapped in the visual/representational medium of landscape, but become forces of contestation throughout society's web of intersecting and colliding discourses. In the words of Julie Peteet, they become "critical component[s] of a complex and diffuse attempt to overthrow hierarchy" (Peteet 1996: 140). The urban landscapes of cities and towns throughout northeast Brazil become, quite literally, a prime communicative medium in the battle over racialized/racist representations in that landscape, and racialized/racist formations throughout society.

References

Austin, J. 2001. *Taking the Train: How Graffiti Art Became an Urban Crisis in New York City*. New York: Columbia University Press.

Blume, R. 1985. Graffiti. In *Discourse and literature: New Approaches to the Analysis of Literary Genres*. Edited by T.A. van Dijk. Amsterdam: John Benjamins Publishing Company, 137–48.

Butler, K.D. 1998. *Freedoms Given, Freedoms Won: Afro-Brazilians in Post-abolition São Paulo and Salvador*. New Brunswick, NJ: Rutgers University Press.

Clay, G. 1973. *Close Up: How to Read the American City*. Chicago: University of Chicago Press.

Cosgrove, D. 2003. Landscape and the European sense of space – Eying nature. In *Handbook of Cultural Geography*. Edited by K. Anderson, M. Domosh, S. Pile, and N. Thrift. London: SAGE, 249–68.

Duncan, J. and N. Duncan. 1988. (Re)reading the landscape. *Environment and Planning D: Society and Space* 6: 117–26.

English, R. 2011. Forward. In *Against the Wall: The Art of Resistance in Palestine*. Edited by W. Parry. Chicago: Lawrence Hill Books, 6–7.

Ferrell, J. 1995. Urban graffiti: Crime, control and resistance. *Youth & Society* 27(1): 73–92.

Finn, J. 2010. Propaganda, grafite e as representações de uma cidade negra. *Educação Temática Digital* 11(2): 75–101.

Foucault, M. 1973. *The Order of Things: An Archeology of the Human Sciences*. New York: Vintage Books.

Foucault, M. 1980. *Power/Knowledge: Selected Interviews and Other Writings, 1972–1977*. New York: Pantheon Books.

Foucault, M. 1982. *The Archeology of Knowledge*. New York: Pantheon Books.

Foote, K.E. 1997. *Shadowed Ground: America's Landscapes of Violence and Tragedy*. Austin: University of Texas Press.

Gross, D. and T. Gross. 1993. Tagging: Changing visual patterns and the rhetorical implications of a new form of graffiti. *ETC: A Review of General Semantics* 50(3): 251–64.

Hall, S., J. Evans, and S. Nixon. 1997. *Representation: Cultural Representations and Signifying Practices*. London: SAGE.

Hanauer, D.I. 2004. Silence, voice and erasure: Psychological embodiment in graffiti at the site of Prime Minister Rabin's assassination. *Arts in Psychotherapy* 31: 29–35.

Kostka, R. 1974. Aspects of graffiti. *Visible Language* 8: 369–75.

Henderson, G. 2003. What (else) we talk about when we talk about landscape: For a return to the social imagination. In *Everyday America: Cultural Landscape Studies after J.B. Jackson*. Edited by C. Wilson and P. Groth. Berkeley: University of California Press, 178–98.

Hooks, B. 1992. *Black Looks: Race and Representation*. Boston: South End Press.

Lefebvre, H. 1991. *The Production of Space*. Cambridge, MA: Blackwell.

Leib, J.I. 2002. Separate times, shared spaces: Arthur Ashe, Monument Avenue and the politics of Richmond, Virginia's symbolic landscape. *Cultural Geographies* 9: 286–312.

Leib, J.I. 2004. Robert E. Lee, "race," representation and redevelopment along Richmond, Virginia's Canal Walk. *Southeastern Geographer* 44(2): 236–62.

Leib, J.I. 2006. The Witting autobiography of Richmond, Virginia: Arthur Ashe, the Civil War, and Monument Avenue's racialized landscape. In *Landscape and Race in the United States*. Edited by R.H. Schein. New York: Routledge, 187–212.

Lewis, P. 1979. Axioms for reading the landscape. In *The Interpretation of Ordinary Landscapes*. Edited by D.W. Meinig. New York: Oxford University Press, 11–32.

Massey, D. 1984. Geography matters. In *Geography Matters! A Reader*. Edited by D. Massey and J. Allen. New York: Cambridge University Press, 1–11.

Mitchell, D. 2000. *Cultural Geography: A Critical Introduction*. Malden MA: Blackwell.

Mitchell, D. 2001. The lure of the local: Landscape studies at the end of a troubled century. *Progress in Human Geography* 25(2): 269–81.

Mitchell, D. 2002. Cultural landscapes: The dialectical landscape – recent landscape research in human geography. *Progress in Human Geography* 26(3): 381–89.

Mitchell, D. 2003. Cultural landscapes: Just landscapes or landscapes of justice? *Progress in Human Geography* 27(6): 787–96.

Mitchell, D. 2008. New axioms for reading the landscape: Paying attention to political economy and social justice. In *Political Economies of Landscape Change*. Edited by J.L. Wescoat Jr. and D.M. Johnston. Dordrecht, The Netherlands: Springer, 29–50.

Mitchell, W.J.T. (ed.). 1994. *Landscape and Power*. Chicago: University of Chicago Press.

Murray, J. and K. Murray. 2006. *Burning New York*. Corte Madera, CA: Gingko Press.

Nascimento, A.D. and E.L. Nascimento. 1992. *Africans in Brazil: A Pan-African Perspective*. Trenton, NJ: Africa World Press.

Parry, W. 2011. *Against the Wall: The Art of Resistance in Palestine*. Chicago: Lawrence Hill Books.

Peteet, J. 1996. The writing on the walls: The graffiti of the Intifada. *Cultural Anthropology* 11(2): 139–59.

Pitanga, A. 1999. Where are the Blacks? In *Black Brazil: Culture, Identity, and Social Mobilization*. Edited by L. Crook and R. Johnson. Los Angeles: UCLA Latin America Center Publications, 31–42.

Robertson, I., and P. Richards (eds). 2003. *Studying Cultural Landscapes*. London: Arnold.

Rose, M. 2002. Landscape and Labyrinths. *Geoforum* 33(4): 455–67.

Sauer, C.O. 1963. The morphology of landscape. In *Land and Life: A Selection from the Writings of Carl Ortwin Sauer*. Edited by J. Leighly. Berkeley: University of California Press, 315–50.

Scheibel, D. 1994. Graffiti and "film school" culture: Displaying alienation. *Communication Monographs* 61(1): 1–18.

Schein, R.H. 1997. The place of landscape: A conceptual framework for interpreting an American scene. *Annals of the Association of American Geographers* 87(4): 660–80.

Schein, R.H. 1999. Teaching "race" and the cultural landscape. *Journal of Geography* 98(4): 188–90.

Schein, R.H. 2006. Race and landscape in the United States. In *Landscape and Race in the United States*. Edited by R.H. Schein. New York: Routledge, 1–22.

Schein, R.H. 2009. Belonging through land/scape. *Environment and Planning A* 41(4): 811–26.

Snyder, G.J. 2009. *Graffiti Lives: Beyond the Tag in New York's Urban Underground*. New York: NYU Press.

Soja, E. 1989. *Postmodern Geographies*. New York: Verso.

Webster, G.R. and J.I. Leib. 2001. Whose South is it anyway? Race and the Confederate battle flag in South Carolina. *Political Geography* 20: 271–99.

PART III

Spaces

Spaces of the Word

Paul C. Adams

"Some people," Miss R. said, "run to conceits or wisdom but I hold to the hard, brown, nutlike word."

The above passage from Donald Barthelme's short story "The Indian Uprising" (1969), seems oddly appropriate. But why? A word is small – the smallest free-standing unit of verbal meaning – and yet in the right soil (planted, as it were, in a sentence), it has the potential to branch and divide, forming a network of meanings, interrelated yet varied, branching out through time, space, and society. The nut metaphor suggests this much, but takes us further than that. A word is filled with potential to become, and whatever can be filled is by definition a container. A container with its husk, hull, or shell is emblematic of hardness, and the meaning of the word, in general, is a tough nut to crack.

Barthelme teases us by carrying the analogy too far. Nutlike, yes. Hard, maybe. But brown? Perversely, he overextends his (or rather Miss R's) metaphor, allowing it to go places it shouldn't. But here again he's on target. Reading or listening, we have to toss out some words that don't seem to say anything like nuts that fall down and lodge somewhere with all of their potential locked inside. We must toss the final adjective. So in a verbal tour de force, Barthelme both tells and shows us many things about words: small, even minimal, contained, yet capable of growing out beyond their shells to form a branching structure or process. And while words frequently fall by the wayside, who knows whether they may not eventually take root, effloresce, and make a difference?

In this chapter I will discuss the spaces of the word as realms of possibility. As indicated, these possibility-spaces include tree-spaces and container-spaces. In addition, words also constitute layer-spaces, particle-spaces, and area-spaces. Several branches of linguistics, including etymology, philology, semantics, sociolinguistics, cognitive linguistics, and computational linguistics provide the spatial metaphors I will employ here, indicating the general utility of space as a tool for understanding words as well as the benefit of engaging with these generally unfamiliar (to geographers) cognate disciplines.

While geographers have at times discussed particular words, such as "nature" and "culture," and the relations between these words and spatial processes, vanishingly few geographers have examined words as spaces in their own right. Likewise, while geographers have drawn on semiotics as well as on discourse analysis and critical theory, the roots of all of these fields in linguistics, and the peculiar insights of linguistics, have been noted only in passing. Lexicographer Tom McArthur identifies no less than eight distinct definitions of *word* (1998: 45–47), indicating complexities in linguistic approaches that have been lost in the translation of various theories and methodologies from linguistics to the various social sciences including human geography. The notion of words as spaces is fundamentally about thinking of words as systems of coherences (Foucault 1970 [1966]: xxi). Such coherence arises relationally and is constitutive of various types of relations between humans and both material and immaterial nonhumans. Words bring things together.

This chapter starts by briefly engaging with the concept of virtual space. The main part of the chapter introduces the following word spaces: tree-space, container-space, layer-space, particle-space, and area-space. We start by exploring spaces that are imposed on the word by dictionaries and other analytical devices – tree-spaces where words are products of branching etymological processes and capsule-spaces where words box-in certain meanings. We then move on to spatialities that can be discerned from word use, where words are understood as performances. In this section we shift from representations of space to representational spaces, to adopt Lefebvre's well-known (1991) terminology. I would maintain that thinking of words as spaces – any of the several spaces described here – offers far more latitude for debate than Derrida's notion of the word as disconnected from the world, empty of all relationships except to other words. Whereas for Derrida the lack of a divine word or logos reduces words to absence (such that words betray a profound emptiness), I would argue that what makes words so *useful,* so able to act and be acted on, is their ability to link, join, and bring together heterogeneous things by creating and occupying a range of distinct, structured, and structuring spaces.

Following encounters with various virtual spaces of the word, we will turn at last to a few words that geographers have scrutinized intensely – *wilderness, poverty,* and *culture.* These words are famously problematic. But whatever may be wrong with *wilderness, poverty,* or *culture* is, I will argue, wrong with all words. Taking this insight to heart, we might prefer to remain silent, but the fact that we do not remain silent serves to indicate the continuing need to occupy the spaces of the word.

Virtual Spaces of the Word

Geographers have associated the term *virtual space* with new media such as wireless devices, the Internet, and flight simulators. Such research should not obscure the ways in which virtuality was associated with "old" media such as the telegraph, sculpture, painting, photography, and the book (Adams 2009: 30–41; Shields 2002; Hillis 1996). However, it was speech, before all else, that opened up the first virtual spaces. Our early ancestors did not, as Lacan suggests (1977), sacrifice being on the altar of meaning when they began to speak. Rather, spoken language initiated a vibration or oscillation between the realm of being and the realm of meaning, which continues to this day. To be human is to engage with what Vygotsky called "inner speech" (1986 [1934]) not only when we speak, read, or write but even when we engage in seemingly nonverbal thought. Despite inhabiting words in this way, we are also always embodied and present in a material world. Thus "virtual space" is one pole of an ancient dialectic between our embodied presence in the physical world and our collective inhabitation and use of a virtual world. Virtuality is clearly more than simply a product of digital technology (Adams 2014).

William Gibson's (1984) reference to the "nonspace of the mind" is a foundation stone in the literature on cyberspace but it should be recalled that we used words for many thousands of years to enter what Michel Foucault called the "non-place of language" (1970 [1966]).[1] Famously, Foucault started *Les Mots et les Choses* by ruminating on a taxonomic

[1] The title of this landmark work has been rendered in English as *The Order of Things* but a more literal translation is *Words and Things,* indicating Foucault's intense interest in the relationship between word-making and world-making.

scheme in which animals were classified by categories including: "tame," "fabulous," "frenzied," "embalmed," "drawn with a very fine camelhair brush," and "having just broken the water pitcher."[2] Foucault argued that only in language could such a "heterotopic" classification scheme exist, yet he also pointed out that the language constructing such a scheme fails to point outside of itself. It is a heterotopia, and "heterotopias ... desiccate speech, stop words in their tracks, contest the very possibility of grammar at its source" (Foucault 1970 [1966]: xviii). Geographers eager to reattach Foucauldian theories to the built environment have forgotten this original meaning of the word *heterotopia* – a space opened up by language but incommensurate with and in fact cut off from physical spaces of matter and bodies.

Three things deserve specific attention in this regard. First, although geographers have discussed heterotopias and frequently claim to follow Foucault (e.g. Soja 1989; Barnes 2004; Saldanha 2008), they forget that the first heterotopia was a verbal construct that Foucault described as a space *functionally separate from the material world*. Second, pausing to reconsider this original heterotopia reminds us that virtual spaces made of words *may disrupt the logics of real-world spaces* evoking a sense that mutual understanding is a vain quest. Third, heterotopias exclusively in and of the word should interest geographers insofar as their properties can be understood in terms of spatial experience, and more subtly, in terms of human experience as always in some sense spatial.

The virtual spaces of the word are deeply ambivalent. Sometimes such spaces provide tools for organizing people, activities and objects in material, physical spaces. Sometimes they deepen the rupture between material and symbolic worlds. In any case, a thoroughgoing contemplation of word-spaces pushes us to go beyond diagnosing how discourses are infected by power, and beyond critiquing fraught terms such as *wilderness*, *poverty*, and *culture*. If textual deconstruction appears to be running out of steam (Thrift 2008), it is a sign that it is time to reengage with words by plugging them into the still new concept of virtual space. To do so, let us start by climbing a tree.

Tree-Spaces

In the nineteenth and early twentieth century, philologists saw themselves as explorers, drawing back the veils of ignorance – crusaders expanding the sphere of enlightenment. Redolent with this era's hubris, the abundantly credentialed Reverend Walter W. Skeat (LittD, LLD., DCL, PhD, FBA) proclaimed: "[T]he great gains that have resulted from the scientific study of comparative philology as applied to the Indo-germanic languages have been properly formulated and tabulated, to the explosion and exclusion of many hasty inferences that were both misleading and mischievous" (Skeat 1912: iii). His use of the term "Indo-germanic" implied that the European language family was rooted in northwestern Europe. This ethnocentric term eventually gave way to "Indo-European" (IE), with an implied center farther south and east.

Whether we think of a word, a language, or a language family as a tree, the notion of a tree-space implies interconnection, divergence, and rootedness. The cultural/linguistic hearth for the Indo-European languages presumably lay in the basins of the Volga and the Don Rivers; the Germanic subfamily grew out of what is today Denmark and southern Sweden; the Romance languages effloresced from Rome. The roots of *hound*, *house*, and

[2] These categories were ascribed by the fiction author Jorge Luis Borges to a Chinese encyclopedia.

cook can be traced to the Germanic hearth and the roots of "*canine*," *domesticity*, and *cuisine* can be traced to Rome, while all ultimately "go back" to Indo-European tongue and its hypothetical homeland. This "going back" is of course metaphorical and although linguists and philologists have no practical need to locate the geographical origins of words or tongues, their insistence on moving back to the root of a word is of interest to this audience because it intersects with historical geography. But the place of origin (here and now) remains only a stopping off point on a longer trip through virtual space. For example, departing from *radish*, we can travel down to the Latin *radix*, over to the Late Latin *radicīna*, and ascend again to *racine*, the French version of the word *root*. We could go back to the German *Wurzel*, which springs from a lower part of the linguistic tree and gives rise to the brewing term *wort* (the root material of beer). Meanwhile, *rhizome* (as entertained by followers of Deleuze) grows from the Greek word for "root"; it branches even lower on the Indo-European tree yet ends up as an equivalent theoretical term in multiple languages. Branches upon branches define a wordspace.

But even here we are not far from familiar geographies. Geographical separations, for example migration or a population's expansion across a geographical barrier such as a mountain range, desert, or water body, or the superimposition of a "hard" political border onto an existing linguistic region, can all give rise sooner or later to linguistic bifurcation. The subsequent branching may be slow or fast. The words for *two* in the Indo-European languages German, Greek, Russian, and Sanskrit – *zwei, dyo, dve,* and *dvi* – indicate relatively slow divergence in sound but the words for *know* – *kenne, gnostikos, znat*, and *jñāna* – show faster divergence within that family (see Figure 16.1).

Some linguistic roots have been unusually prolific when it comes to sprouting new shoots. According to Adler (1963: 55), the root *spec* from the Latin *spectare* (to look or see) has spawned a *spec*tacular number (246) of English words. While the reasons for slow versus rapid and sparse versus prolific branching are beyond the scope of this discussion, we can see that the tree model incorporates such variations quite well. This spatialization involves (a) a space-oriented perpendicular to time such that back becomes down, and (b) an imagined completion whereby one bridges gaps in sound with a kind of imaginary movement backwards then forwards or down then up. The particular rationality of the lexicon assumes the existence of a space where such branches are real things: "Pointing backwards and forwards at the same time, the dictionary had taken on the work of the search for the originals of words and, more importantly, the rational determination of meaning" (Benson 2001: 13).

This tree-space excites twenty-first-century linguists no less than nineteenth-century philologists. For example, computer programmers and linguists employ a derivative concept, Levenshtein distance, to quantify verbal difference. This technique consists in counting the minimum number of discrete alterations required to turn one sequence of phonemes into another. By this measure, the English *fish* is closer to the Swedish *fisk* (two changes) than to the French *poisson* (five changes). Averaging the linguistic distances between two languages across a standard list of word pairs produces a quantifiable measure of linguistic distance between any given pair of languages that have at some point branched apart (Wichmann et al. 2010). Languages that are close in terms of this Levenshtein distance arise from relatively recent branching. The new frontier of automated translation, interpretation, and voice recognition depends on building out various branching word-spaces in quantitative fashion with computer algorithms. However, all of this branching is separate from the question of word meaning, which produces its own explanatory and diagnostic spaces – boxlike and capsular.

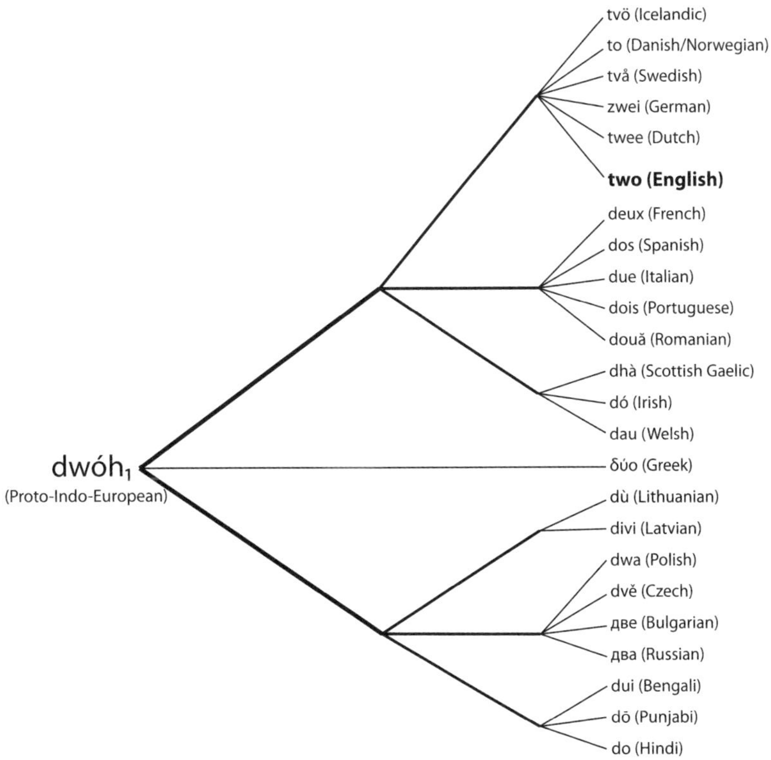

Figure 16.1 The word for *two* as a branching space in Indo-European languages
Source: Author's illustration

Container-Spaces

Phil Benson claims insightfully that a dictionary is not simply "a book about words, but also a book about the world viewed through the particular window of the word" (2001: 4). The lexicon frames, divides, and separates. Dictionary definitions pretend to keep the right stuff in and the wrong stuff out, spatializing the word as a neat and tidy container, although most definitions are once too narrow and too broad. A definition draws lines in a fuzzy virtual space of meaning, and to do so it simply ignores much that is fuzzy and indefinite about verbal meaning (Elbourne 2011). Far more than a simple repository or collection, the dictionary actually creates "lexicographical words" (McArthur 1998: 47). Perhaps the most interesting dictionary is the *Oxford English Dictionary* (*OED*), which ambitiously sought to capture every word in the English language at a time when this seemed like a vain aspiration. The first edition of the *OED* was compiled through the use of over a thousand wooden "pigeonholes," open-fronted boxes lining the dank walls of James Murray's backyard "Scriptorium" in north Oxford (Winchester 1998). From the 1880s until the end of his life, Murray used these boxes to sort and collate quotes that had been mailed in by volunteers. Target words were contained within the quotes, which were in turn contained by definitions in the emerging dictionary, all of which were organized in a single master container – the alphabetical order.

Combining *de-* (a Latin prefix meaning down to the bottom, completely, and thoroughly) with *finīre* (to end or finish), *definition* is an incisive act that cuts all the way down through the chaotic stuff of language and presumably brings an end to verbal confusion. This incision imposes a cellular spatiality onto language, transforming continuous gradations of difference into a finite number of boxlike meanings: A1, A2, B1, B2, B3, and so on. Transformation of the infinite (variation of meaning) into the definite(ion) with its chopped up, numbered, and lettered meanings, is the guiding principle in the lexicographic spatialization of language.

Peering closer into this matrix we can see exactly how this works. Consider the word *march*. It can mean the third month of the year, a disciplined and rhythmic way of walking, or a borderland. But for each of these meanings, there are various nuances or closely related meanings (subpigeonholes [cubicles within cubicles]). A march means any borderland, but also more specifically a contested borderland, so a small capsule of meaning is encapsulated within a bigger capsule.

Ironically, the *OED*'s compact edition of 1971 came in a sturdy cardboard box, internally subdivided into three compartments: two large spaces held the two volumes (A–O and P–Z) keeping them upright and dignified, while a third pigeonhole held a little drawer that in turn held a magnifying glass. These cardboard capsules concretized the dictionary's capsular logic. The entire system depended on *excommunicating* certain errant meanings along with all of the unspoken rules that attach symbiotically to the physical, embodied social contexts in which words are uttered. One looks in vain for instructions in the dictionary on how to make *march* mean one thing and not another thing!

Linguistics has been unpacked, unbound, and unboxed to a degree by the work of V.N. Vološinov. Rejecting the notion of a "usual" or standard meaning of a word, he instead stressed the "multiaccentuality" of words, arguing that "the meaning of a word is determined entirely by its context" (Vološinov 1973: 79). The presumption that words *have* usual or standard meanings is, on this account, a reactionary impulse that works to stabilize "the dialectical flux of the social generative process" that constitutes meaning itself (Vološinov 1973: 24). His approach – similar to but less radical than Derrida's – challenges the dictionary's abstract, containerized space, which has "homogeneity as its goal" (Lefebvre 1991: 287). His sensitivity to power embodied in language suggests another spatialization of the word, that of a performance, which spatializes the word as a position in multiple hierarchical layers.

Layer-Spaces

Ferdinand de Saussure is famous, in part, for his distinction between *langue* and *parole* (1983 [1972]), with the former being a static system of relations available to all speakers at all times, and the latter being *verbal performance* with its dynamism, fluidity, and particularity. This latter, performative aspect of language was brilliantly illustrated by William Labov, who empirically studied spoken language while avoiding what Chambers called the "axiom of categoricity" (Chambers 1995). Underlying such work is an assumption that a word performed in a particular site and situation means much more than the sum of its denotations or connotations. By pronouncing a word in a very particular blend of ways (depending on time, place, and social context), each speaker positions him- or herself relative to other speakers. A continuous spectrum of spoken performance is assessed by speakers in ongoing fashion according to an unspoken hierarchy of rightness, goodness, and power.

Verbal performances therefore respond to a "general agreement" (Labov 1972: 169), relating nuances of verbal performance to the social, physical, and symbolic spaces in which speech occurs. A layered space takes form through *parole* because varying verbal performances map onto higher and lower social groups, more or less formal situations, and more or less highly valued places. By speaking in a particular way in a particular place and a particular situation one takes up a position within multiple, hierarchically organized spaces.

In his classic 1972 study, "The social stratification of (r) in New York City department stores," Labov pretended to be an ordinary shopper and asked employees a directional question such as, "Excuse me, where are the women's shoes?" The questions he asked were varied with regard to the particular item of merchandise so that the answer would remain constant: "fourth floor." If he was on the fourth floor of a store, Labov would ask "Excuse me, what floor is this?" Unaware that they were participating in a speech study, his subjects replied "fourth floor" in accordance with their natural, unself-conscious speech patterns. To solicit a second, more emphatic pronunciation, he would reply "Excuse me?" His comparison of 264 such "interviews" indicated differences in the pronunciation that were layered systematically according to multiple hierarchies.

One such hierarchical layering was based on geographical place; the *r* sound was dropped least often in Saks Fifth Avenue, more often in Macy's, and most often in S. Klein. This finding matched the social profile of the stores: Saks catered to the wealthy, Macy's to a middle-class clientele, and S. Klein to the working class.

> *Saks is the most spacious, especially on the upper floors, with the least amount of goods displayed. Many of the floors are carpeted, and on some of them, a receptionist is stationed to greet the customers. Kleins, at the other extreme, is a maze of annexes, sloping concrete floors, low ceilings; it has the maximum amount of goods displayed at the least possible expense. (Labov 1972: 172)*

Employees of Saks were paid less than those of Macy's but they *borrowed* the high status of their surroundings in various ways, including with their formal verbal performances (Labov 1972: 177 n.5). The use of *r* (and conversely their avoidance of the casual/working-class/vernacular dropped-*r*) not only positioned people higher in a layered space of class but also helped confirm the layered model of social relations that constructed a particular store as "better," as a place for a higher class of customers. Conversely, Klein's and the customers in Klein's were positioned lowest in part through a devalued habit of dropping the *r* sound.

Labov also found that pronunciation responded fluidly to interaction itself. His question "Excuse me?" elicited an emphatic repetition that was more likely to employ the sounded *r*, suggesting that people often jump temporarily into a higher linguistic layer in an effort to improve their listener's comprehension. While speech performances varied by location, attitudes about "better" speech appeared consistent: the voiced *r* was treated as "better" speech "by at least some of the employees in all three stores" (Labov 1972: 175). The relation between locational and qualitative place elements is not mechanical; it involves fluid and changing performances within a shared construct of "higher" and "lower" that is mapped onto space, speech, status, and embodiment.

More generally, most subjects, if they are aware that their pronunciation is being studied, unself-consciously adjust their linguistic performance. If asked to read pairs of words that draw attention to pronunciation, for example "witch/which, foe/four, win/when ..." subjects will migrate upwards toward "standard" pronunciations. Less standard dialects can be elicited by asking subjects to read words from an unpaired list, while further shifts "down" toward the vernacular occur when subjects read a story out loud or recount a traumatic event (Chambers 1995: 19). Thus the layers already referenced here include many

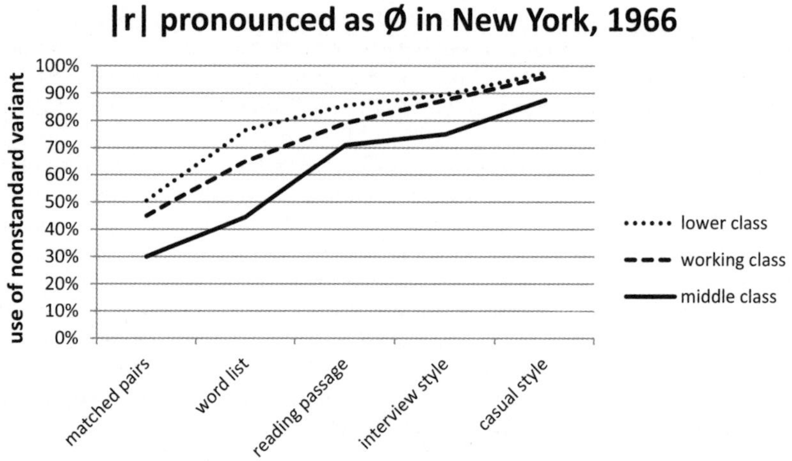

Figure 16.2 The nonstandard dropped *r* pronunciation in New York as a layer-space across three groups with two axes of stratification in five verbal interaction
Source: Author's illustration after Chambers 1995, p. 23, originally from Labov 1966

contingencies of verbal performance (see Figure 16.2). Tiny differences in pronunciation are therefore far from meaningless; speech varies systematically in ways that position speakers within multiple layers of geographical, social, and linguistic space.

Furthermore, *parole* organizes the world in layers, through distinctions that fall out of the neat boxes of dictionary meaning. Speakers located in particular places speak the "same" words in a range of different ways. Adding lexical meaning and its construction of space, we get something "more than representational" (Lorimer 2005). By speaking with a precisely calibrated but not necessarily conscious degree of standardness, speakers bring together multiple hierarchies and position themselves performatively within multiple layers of power, influence, meaning, formality, derivation, history, acceptability, and prestige.

Particle-Spaces

A somewhat different way to understand the act of speech is to consider words as particles. By this I mean that rather than retaining the word's location in verbal syntax and thinking of words as "joints connecting the limbs of a sentence" (Cicero, *Ad Herennium*, quoted in Yates 1966: 18), we can dissolve sentences into what might be called "statistical words" (McArthur 1998: 47). We are left with relative word frequencies, or at most with frequencies and measures of proximity such as the frequency of co-occurrence of two particular words in a sentence. Such measures provide barometers of social dynamics. When words become particles, the varying densities of certain words among various articulations and texts drive the climate of social life.

As James Pennebaker demonstrates (2011: 16), the "most common and forgettable words" in a language can be treated as indicators of "almost every dimension of social psychology." Densities of pronouns, articles, prepositions, conjunctions, and other seemingly insignificant "function words," averaged over large volumes of spoken or written matter indicate many things. For example, use of the word *I* increases among the suicidal, use of *we* to mean *I* indicates that one is throwing one's power around, and the use of *he*, *she*, and *you* in numbers outweighing *I* is a sign of dishonesty (Pennebaker 2011). Emotional responses to a perceived threat can also alter the comparative density of words. After the September 11, 2011 attacks, for example, American bloggers temporarily used more "we-words" and fewer "I-words," then returned to normal over the next 10 days (Figure 16.3).

Treating words as particles tells us a lot about attitudes and emotions, and also about forms of involvement in the world. The gendering of language, for example, is to a large degree a manifestation of the places of speech.

> *All people change their language depending on the situations that they are in. In formal settings, for example, people tend to use far fewer pronouns, more articles, and fewer social words – meaning most of us speak like prototypical men. When hanging around with our family in a relaxed setting, we all talk more like women. In short, the gender effects that exist in language reflect, to some degree, gender. But the context of speaking probably accounts for even more of our language choices. (Pennebaker 2011: 47–48)*

Thus, if we treat words as particles, counting them and comparing their relative densities across large amounts of verbal material, we obtain confirmation of the geographical contingency of the word and of subjectivity and identity as well.

In some cases, computational linguistics focuses on the degree to which each word in a text appears in proximity to every other word. Each word's set of unique proximities (distances from each other word in the span of a text) can be understood as a vector in an n-dimensional space. This space has practical utility, for example in the creation of machine-based algorithms used in speech recognition and translation (Sahlgren 2006; Schütze 1993). In this work, modeling the word as a particle simplifies the concept of verbal context, but it also reveals certain ties between words and their geographical contexts. By taking words out of their phrasal or syntagmatic contexts, we find that what makes small words meaningful is quite often the physical, geographical, or situational contexts in which communication occurs. Consider the statement: "Don't do it; wait until I get back." This phrase means almost nothing unless one knows what "it" is, who is sending the message, where "back" is, and so on. Such sentences are meaningful in context, precisely because we have learned how to extract meaning from the spatial and situational contexts where speech occurs and combine contextual meaning with verbal meaning. We are much more likely to hear this kind of utterance in place-based speech, like a conversation at the office or on a worksite, than in more placeless communications such as books and magazines. This approach shows the complexity of what it means to "place" the words we say, but we can go even further and treat words as areas.

Area-Spaces

We turn finally to the most subtle of the word-spaces discussed here. We are now interested in how people employ words to *carve out spaces of meaning*. This spatialization pertains to human activity in concrete situations. We start with the work of the linguist Benjamin Lee Whorf, who groped for spatial metaphors to capture the connections between certain words.

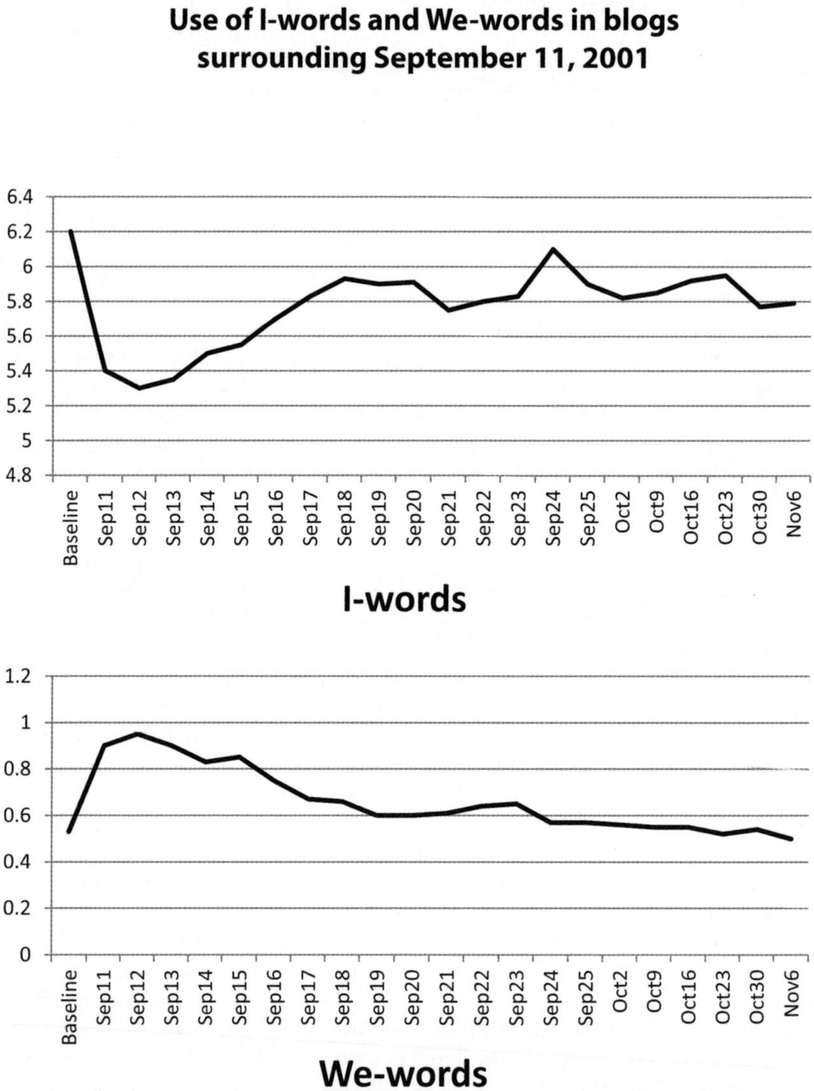

Figure 16.3 **The shift in relative densities of "I-words" (*I*, *me*, *my*, and *mine*) versus "we-words" (*we*, *us*, *our*) in blog entries following the terrorist attacks of September 11, 2001**

Source: Author's illustration redrawn from Pennebaker 2011, p. 118

> *I might say that my mental image of the [verbal] relation is not at all one of ideas hitched together by bonds of attachment which they possess like miniature hooks and eyes. It is more a concept of continuity, with the ideas as relative locations in a continuous medium. (Whorf 1956: 38)*

Whorf saw these "relative locations" of words not as subjective or personal, but rather as parts of a "common stock of conceptions" associated with use of the words in a particular language. One set of words he believed to be connected or adjacent in this way – *set, sink, drag, drop, hollow, depress,* and *lie* – were all connected to the conception *down.* Conversely, he believed the words *upright, heave, hoist, tall, air, uphold,* and *swell* were near (in some sense) to the conception *up* (Whorf 1956: 36).

Following Whorf in this direction takes us into a space where word-spaces are areas – potentially overlapping and intersecting yet also bordered by fuzzy boundaries. Areas of verbal meaning are imposed in culturally variable fashion on the continuous, embodied stuff of life. This understanding of words resides at a level called the subconceptual (Dade-Robertson 2011: 50–52) whereby "activation of one unit activates the others to which it is linked and the degree of activation depends on the strength of association" (Dellarosa 1988: 29; quoted in Dade-Robertson 2011: 51). Drawing on the writings of his professor Edward Sapir, Whorf argued that such verbal subdivision or partitioning of reality is not just applied retroactively to reality but actively constitutes reality in ways that vary from language to language. The linguistic relativity hypothesis embedded in this work asserts that the language one uses influences one's thought, behavior, and understanding of what exists. In place of the lexicographer's tidy boxes – we instead find a fuzzy-edged patchwork or pastiche. In place of an order *for* words we find an ordering of the world *by* words. While the popularity of this view has waxed and waned within the field of linguistics, from a hard-line "constitutivist" perspective that denies the possibility of thought without language to an opposing position that views thought as totally independent of language, today most linguists agree that our thought patterns are linguistically structured, if not by inner verbalization then at least by "a recursive system of hierarchical dependencies" internalized along with linguistic competence (Gomila 2012: 2, 107).

This is not to say that there is no external reality independent of words. Material, physical space can be seen as a challenge. Words can fail to map geographical, material spaces and places adequately. Whorf's insights originally emerged out of a period he spent working for a fire insurance company investigating fires: "[I]n due course it became evident that not only a physical situation *qua* physics, but the meaning of that situation to people, was sometimes a factor, through the behavior of people, in the start of the fire. And this factor of meaning was clearest when it was a LINGUISTIC MEANING, residing in the name or the linguistic description commonly applied to the situation" (1956: 135, emphasis original). In one case, people had been careless with matches around some "empty gasoline drums," assuming the drums to be "null and void, negative, inert" because they were commonly referred to as "empty." Unfortunately they were full of explosive vapors that eventually ignited. Other fire hazards arose similarly because verbal communication had attached labels to places and objects that in some way implied a *non-flammable* quality: a "pool of water," a "blower," and a pile of "scrap lead." Fires occurred because of what words failed to capture for the inhabitants of certain places: methane emanating from rotting material in the wastewater pool, sparks streaming from the blower, and flammable wax paper lurking between sheets of lead. These environmental details were not mapped onto places by the words people had been using to understand the places. Therefore the places were linguistically categorized in a way that left them ripe for disaster – which of course suggests that there exists a reality beyond language that we encounter either via language or despite language. The word may or may not occupy the area we need it to.

This linguistic model builds in certain key ways on the foundations laid by the Swiss linguist Ferdinand de Saussure. Saussure famously modeled the linguistic sign as a two-sided entity uniting signifier and signified, with one side being a mental representation of a sound pattern and the other side a concept of something in the world. Saussure showed that the subdivision of reality varies among languages carved up differently by their respective lexicons: "A language is a system in which all the elements fit together, and in which the value of any one element depends on the simultaneous coexistence of all the others" (Saussure 1983: 113). Developing his arguments, we could note that *child, infant, baby, girl, boy, daughter,* and *son* are not only related terms but overlapping and adjacent areas that mutually affect each other (see Figure 16.4 top). If one of the terms were missing from the English language, one (or more) of the others would have to expand to include the range of phenomena the missing term designated. French, for example, distinguishes between *boy* (*garçon*) and *son* (*fils*) but not between *girl* and *daughter* (*fille*), so the word *fille* covers a larger territory. The territory covered by the words *child, infant,* and *baby* in English is covered by only two terms in French, *bébé* and *enfant* (Figure 16.4 bottom). Conversely, French offers two distinct verbs, *savoir* and *connaître,* in place of the rather vague English verb *to know*. Such differences highlight the arbitrary verbal partitioning of reality, but the

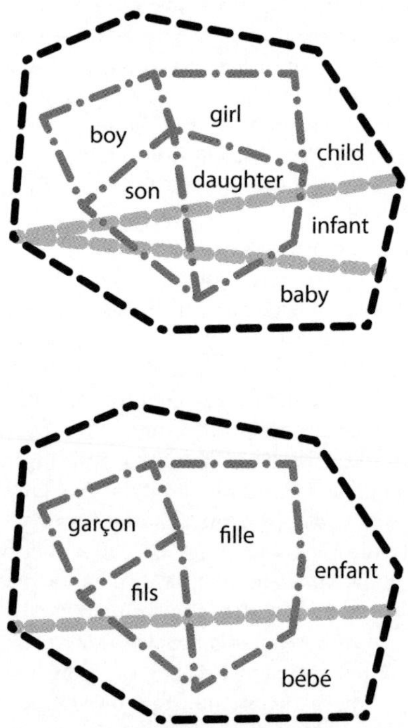

Figure 16.4 Conceptual diagram of words with related meanings as area-spaces in English and French. Divisions and overlaps are impressionistic.
Source: Author's illustration

fire hazards also show that partitioning to be more or less *useful* in mapping (a singularly unknowable) reality.

Thus, any given sign not only fuses signifier(s) to signified but also designates boundaries around certain types of phenomena and experiences, we assimilate this and that with the same name, and differentiate this from that with different names. Whorf shows this process as inherently *risky*.

Back to Geography

Geographers pay attention to words primarily as tools of the trade – resources for *earth writing*. Geographers have discussed toponyms (Herman 1999), place representations in texts and discourses (Livingstone and Harrison 1981), and words inscribed on landscapes and on maps (Iveson 2010; Ley and Cybriwsky 1974; Moreau and Alderman 2011). Driving these scattered engagements is a moral or ethical commitment to loosen up containerized concepts of the word and replace delimited word meanings with fuzzy, fluid boundaries that are sensitive to evaluative, progressive, and politically engaged thought. Drawing on Derrida, Dixon and Jones refer to a "grid epistemology" at the heart of categorization, whose "powers of segmentation fashion borders and supervise interrelations among objects and events in space and time" (1998: 251). The term *grid* evokes the lexical container-spaces discussed above and their "stable, stratified, and hierarchical ontology," while suggesting that this way of thinking structures the way we think as well as our movements and landscapes, ultimately encouraging surveillance and policing (Dixon and Jones 1998: 251). Intriguingly, just as social scientists including geographers have come to see borders everywhere, rather than just fixating on the lines adjoining political units (Balibar 1998; Paasi and Prokkola 2008), geographers are working to rupture the solid boundaries around certain words. In keeping with this project, geographers have given sporadic but intense scrutiny to particular geographically laden words and some insights pertaining to word-spaces can be gleaned from the geographical literature. I will present three examples – *wilderness, poverty,* and *culture* – and draw on the previous discussion to offer some suggestions regarding ways to move beyond the critique of lexicographical understandings of the word to a more nuanced exploration of word-spaces.

Tracing the historical evolution of the word and concept of "wilderness" from "the antithesis of all that was orderly and good" to its present status, which is tantamount to Eden itself, William Cronon contends that there is "nothing natural about the concept of wilderness" (Cronon 1995: 69). Wilderness appears to be essentially a word: "entirely a creation of the culture that holds it dear," and paradoxically "a product of the very history it seeks to deny" (Cronon 1995, 69). The word points outside of culture, but as a word it remains thoroughly human, completely cultural. Cronon asserts that *wilderness* is therefore "a serious threat to responsible environmentalism at the end of the twentieth century" (1995: 81). As in Whorf's analysis Cronon assumes that the words we use can pose a risk. Specifically, the "wilderness" label can induce blindness to anthropogenic impacts and the effects of culture on natural systems.

Similarly, in Lakshman Yapa's postmodern critique of poverty the word *poverty* is shown to exclude certain conditions and phenomena from consideration, thereby prescribing a predetermined set of responses, and ultimately functioning as the center of what Althusser (1969) calls a "problematic."

> *Poverty is a discursive/materialist formation. There is no real substantively bounded space called the poverty sector that can present itself as a tangible target for the economist's 'assault-on-poverty.' In fact, the concept of the poverty sector has diverted attention away from the complicity of development in the social construction of poverty. (Yapa 1996: 720)*

In undertaking the radical project of arguing that use of the word *poverty* leads to material deprivation, Yapa means to unravel harmful circuits of social power while showing the risk inherent in labeling. The term under scrutiny crystalizes a problematic that inflicts on certain persons the very conditions it seeks to explain.

Building on a similar set of concerns, Don Mitchell rejects *culture*, whether the term is instantiated as culture regions or used as a point of departure, like in the new cultural geography. While culture "is an incredibly slippery term" (Mitchell 1995: 104), in any guise the word denies social conflict by asserting the existence of *the culture* of a place, and quite often the *high culture* of that place (sometimes referred to as "Culture with a capital C"). Mitchell insists that any attempt to expose or critique "cultural struggle" ends up eliding the struggle and reifying "culture" as an ontological given, thereby supporting dominant ideologies (1995: 107). Thus, precisely like wilderness and poverty, culture is risky: "a very powerful name – powerful because it obscures just what it is meant to identify" (Mitchell 1995: 108).

In all three of these contributions, and in others like Cresswell's discussion of the *tramp* (2001) and Marston et al.'s rejection of *scale* (2005), one encounters the same general anxiety and concern with the risk of labeling: words are constructs but are treated as mere labels of real things in the world. As such they impose risks and harms on certain people, not least because they are made and used in contexts of *unequal* power; therefore their seeming naturalness serves to perpetuate existing power relations.

These were among the most notable contributions to a wave of geographical works extending from 1995 to 2005 in which certain heavily freighted words were deconstructed. While this engagement has been useful and instructive, it poses a problem in that there is nothing at all special about words such as *wilderness*, *culture*, and *poverty*. *All* words work the same way. Verbal targeting is at worst a kind of scapegoating, permitting blame to be pinned onto one individual word and artificially restricting a universe of risk to an individual word that is demonized, as if these critiques of meaning-making did not, themselves, depend on words.

What I want to suggest here is that the main target of this type of critique was (and still is) the *containerized word* – one of many spatializations of the word. There is a hope that by exposing the artificiality of one word's boundaries one can overcome the power-laden operations operating behind verbal communication in general. Of course, the object of critique is the word as container of meanings that subsequently shape actions in the world. But while we can certainly question the bounds around any given word, we should also, at the same time, be aware that what is the most risk-inducing is only one of the word-spaces discussed above: the basic operation of de-finition that reveals the word in a particular way.

More rarely, the critique may target the tree-spaces of etymological derivation, as if words such as *culture* or *development* were joined by a living connection to historically dubious, colonial, patriarchal, exclusionary, and exploitative trunk and roots. However, it is somewhat presumptuous to think that every use of a word in the present would fall to the ground like an apple unless supported by a particular tree of meaning. This way of thinking, it should be evident, depends again on a particular model of the word, not a really existing thing.

Simply acknowledging that the container-spaces and the tree-spaces are *tools* for understanding the word, and as such neither more nor less valid than layer-spaces, particle-spaces, and area-spaces, we would be able to expand and deepen our engagement with verbal mappings in general. The essence of my argument is that we must take particular care not to essentialize certain very particular word-spaces to the exclusion of other word-spaces. We should aim to say something about words in general rather than merely about a few scapegoat words as they appear in a few ontological lenses.

It is possible, then, to return finally to each of these troublesome terms and re-spatialize them. The saying or writing of *wilderness* could be seen as a way of positioning oneself opposite to the arbitrary exercise of power, endorsing a sociolinguistic layer that is troublesome to corporate-backed worldviews and neoliberal globalization, performing against and across strata of environmentally and socially exploitative social actors. Whether or not the word *wilderness* is a human construct, it may still be quite a useful word to draw attention to the limits of human power and the arrogance of technological fixes. In another vein, we could quantify the relative frequency of words associated with *poverty* in various texts, considering poverty's proximity not only to little words like *if* and *it* but also big words like *Constantinople* and *Timbuktu* (Seuss 1963). This quantitative approach, treating words as particles, may assist in identifying how it is that different segments of the media and differently positioned social actors leverage the concept of poverty in contrasting ways. With links to particular exotic(ized) places. Thus a computational linguistic analysis could achieve a good deal more than merely reiterating that the word is politically loaded. Finally, we could engage with *culture* by noting not only how the term is fraught with social conflict and rooted in exploitation and exclusion but also by exploring fuzziness and overlaps around its edges, and the ways it may be impinged upon by cognate terms like *cult, occult,* and *agriculture* and by neighboring terms such as *values, principles, beliefs,* and *the arts.* Even if we were to stick to the tree-spaces of that word, we could trace *culture*'s myriad branches – *kultur* (German, Swedish, Norwegian, and Danish), *cultura* (Spanish, Italian, Portuguese, and Romanian), *kultura* (Czech), and культура (Russian) – revealing it as something cosmopolitan and promiscuous, fond of fascism (sad to say) but also supportive of democracy, friendly to subordination as well as to emancipation.

In each case I have suggested that we move away from an excessive attachment to particular word-spaces and begin to address the multiple spaces of the word. I mean this advice to pertain to engagement with each and every word, and verbal reality in general. This may appear on the surface to overextend geography by treading too freely on the territory of linguistics. However, I would maintain that as geographers we have an opportunity and even an obligation to explore myriad spaces, both physical and virtual, even when the latter is as prosaic as the word. This will help us remain sensitive not only to nuances of meaning but also to nuances of performance, experience, agency, and power. Doing so, we would see new issues emerging around communications, in particular how communications constitute forms of movement, oscillation or cycling between virtual and physical spaces. Our circulation through the multiple spaces of words would become salient as part of the larger dynamism and flux that enlivens the spaces where life takes place.

References

Adams, P.C. 2009. *Geographies of Media and Communication*. Malden, MA, and Oxford: Wiley Blackwell.

Adams, P.C. 2014. Chapter 14: Communication in virtual worlds. In *The Oxford Handbook of Virtuality*. Edited by M. Grimshaw. Oxford and New York: Oxford University Press, 239–53.

Adler, M. 1963. How to read a dictionary. In *Words, Words, and Words about Dictionaries*. Edited by J.C. Gray. San Francisco: Chandler Publishing Company, 53–63.

Althusser, L. 1969. *For Marx*. Translated by Ben Brewster. London and New York: Verso.

Balibar, E. 1998. The border of Europe. In *Cosmopolitics*. Edited by P. Cheah and B. Robbins. Minneapolis: University of Minnesota Press, 216–29.

Barnes, T. 2004. Placing ideas: Genius loci, heterotopia and geography's quantitative revolution. *Progress in Human Geography* 28(5): 565–95.

Benson, P. 2001. *Ethnocentrism and the English Dictionary*. London and New York: Routledge.

Chambers, J.K. 1995. *Sociolinguistic Theory*. Malden, MA: Blackwell.

Cresswell, T. 2001. Making up the tramp: Toward a critical geosophy. In *Textures of Place: Exploring Humanist Geographies*. Edited by P.C. Adams, S. Hoelscher, and K.E. Till. Minneapolis: University of Minnesota Press, 167–85.

Cronon, W. 1995. The trouble with wilderness: Or, getting back to the wrong nature. In *Uncommon Ground: Rethinking the Human Place in Nature*. Edited by W. Cronon. New York: Norton, 7–28.

Dixon, D. and J.P. Jones III. 1998. My dinner with Derrida, or spatial analysis and postmodernism do lunch. *Environment and Planning A* 30: 247–60.

Elbourne, P. 2011. *Meaning: A Slim Guide to Semantics*. Oxford University Press.

Foucault, M. 1970 [1966]. *The Order of Things: An Archaeology of the Human Sciences*. Originally *Les mots et les choses*. New York: Vintage Books/Random House.

Gomila, A. 2012. *Verbal Minds: Language and the Architecture of Cognition*. Amsterdam: Elsevier.

Herman, R.D.K. 1999. The Aloha State: Place names and the anti-conquest of Hawai'i. *Annals of the Association of American Geographers* 89(1): 76–102.

Hillis, K. 1996. A geography of the eye: The technologies of virtual reality. In *Cultures of Internet: Virtual Spaces, Real Histories, Living Bodies*. Edited by R. Shields. Thousand Oaks, CA: SAGE, 70–98.

Iveson, K. 2010. The wars on graffiti and the new military urbanism. *City* 14(1–2): 115–34. DOI: 10.1080/13604810903545783.

Labov, W. 1966. The linguistic variable as a structural unit. *Washington Linguistics Review* 3: 4–22.

Labov, W. 1972. The social stratification of (r) in New York City department stores. In *Sociolinguistic Patterns*. Edited by W. Labov. Philadelphia: University of Pennsylvania Press, 168–78.

Lefebvre, H. 1991. *The Production of Space*. Translated by D. Nicholson-Smith. Cambridge, MA, and Oxford: Blackwell.

Ley, D. and R. Cybriwsky. 1974. Urban graffiti as territorial markers. *Annals of the Association of American Geographers* 64(4): 491–505.

Livingstone, D.N. and R.T. Harrison. 1981. Meaning through metaphor: Analogy as epistemology. *Annals of the Association of American Geographers* 71(1): 95–107.

Marston, S.A., J.P. Jones III, and K. Woodward. 2005. Human geography without scale. *Transactions of the Institute of British Geographers* NS30: 416–32.

McArthur, T. 1998. *Living Words: Language, Lexicography and the Knowledge Revolution*. Exeter: University of Exeter Press.

Mitchell, D. 1995. There's no such thing as culture: Towards a reconceptualization of the idea of culture. *Transactions of the Institute of British Geographers* NS20 (1): 102–16.
Moreau, T. and D.H. Alderman. 2011. Graffiti hurts and the eradication of alternative landscape expression. *Geographical Review* 101(1): 106–24.
OED. 1971. *The Compact Edition of the Oxford English Dictionary: Complete Text Reproduced Micrographically.* Oxford: Oxford University Press.
Paasi, A. and E.K. Prokkola. 2008. Territorial dynamics, cross-border work and everyday life in the Finnish-Swedish border area. *Space and Polity* 12(1): 13–29.
Pennebaker, J.W. 2011. *The Secret Life of Pronouns: What Our Words Say about Us.* New York: Bloomsbury Press.
Sahlgren, M. 2006. The Word-Space Model: Using Distributional Analysis to Represent Syntagmatic and Paradigmatic Relations between Words in High-Dimensional Vector Spaces. Dissertation submitted to the Department of Linguistics, Stockholm University, Sweden.
Saldanha, A. 2008. Heterotopia and structuralism. *Environment and Planning A* 40: 2080–96.
Saussure, F. de. 1983 [1972]. *Course in General Linguistics.* Edited by Charles Bally and Albert Sechehaye with Albert Riedlinger. Translated by Roy Harris. La Salle, IL: Open Court Classics.
Schütze, H. 1993. Word space. In *Advances in Neural Information Processing Systems 5.* Edited by S. J. Hanson, J.D. Cowan, and C.L. Giles. San Mateo, CA: Morgan Kauffman, 895–902.
Seuss, Dr. 1963. *Hop on Pop.* New York: Random House.
Shields, R. 2002. *The Virtual.* New York: Routledge.
Skeat, W.W. 1912. *The Science of Etymology.* Oxford: Clarendon Press.
Soja, E. 1989. *Postmodern Geographies: The Reassertion of Space in Critical Social Theory.* London: Verso.
Thrift, N.J. 2008. *Non-Representational Theory: Space, Politics, Affect.* London: Taylor & Francis.
Vološinov, V.N. 1973. *Marxism and the Philosophy of Language.* Translated by L. Matejka and I.R. Titunik. New York and London: Seminar Press.
Vygotsky, L.S. 1986 [1934]. *Thought and Language.* A. Kozulin (Ed.), Cambridge, MA: MIT Press.
Whorf, B.L. 1956. *Language, Thought, and Reality: Selected Writings of Benjamin Lee Whorf.* Edited by John B. Carroll. Cambridge, MA: MIT Press.
Wichmann, S., E.W. Holman, D. Bakker, and C.H. Brown. 2010. Evaluating linguistic distance measures. *Physica A* 389: 3632–39.
Winchester, S. 1998. *The Professor and the Madman: A Tale of Murder, Insanity, and the Making of the* Oxford English Dictionary. New York: HarperCollins Publishers.
Yapa, L. 1996. What causes poverty? A postmodern view. *Annals of the Association of American Geographers* 86(4): 707–28.
Yates, F.A. 1966. *The Art of Memory.* Chicago: University of Chicago Press.

17 ASHGATE **RESEARCH** COMPANION

Spaces of Mediated Sound

Michael Bull[1]

> *Inhabited space transcends geometrical space.*
>
> *Bachelard 1994*

> *Space becomes place as we get to know it better and endow it with value.*
>
> *Tuan 2001*

> *Pervasive digital devices have obvious spatial aspects: phones connect across distance, GPS locates people in space, computer games and streamed media synthesize spatial environments, personal stereos apparently confine the listener to a sensory container – all of these devices are distributed across space.*
>
> *Coyne 2010*

> *The music I listened to on my iPod consisted of upbeat tunes which make me cheery and positive for the day ahead such as Rihanna –"Diamonds," One Direction – "Live while we're young," Nicki Minaj –"Va Va Voom," Angel – "Wonderful" and Simple Plan – "Summer Paradise." These songs make me more focused. I felt I needed some music to inspire me for the day. The journey to work makes me very bored. This is why I feel the need to distract myself with multiple technologies … when I text people and use the Internet on my journey this stops me from being bored. I'm socializing and making use of my spare time. I often feel lonely when I travel so by using my iPhone and iPod this helps me remain happy and connected to people.*
>
> *Smartphone user*

Take a walk in any city today, sit in a café or take a train, and you will observe urban subjects texting while walking – their attention focused on the screen of their phone; others will be talking to absent others on their smartphones; still others will be reading from their iPad while simultaneously checking their e-mails or sit engrossed in the latest snippet from their Facebook account. These activities are often accompanied to the sound of music coming from the user's iPod or smartphone. These forms of technologically mediated behaviors described by Coyne (2010) question what it means for a person to inhabit public urban space. Indeed, it appears that public spaces are increasingly turned into utilitarian spaces of private mediated activity; we increasingly inhabit urban space through the use of range mobile technologies. This chapter focuses primarily, but not exclusively, upon the sonic dimension of urban experience. While mediated "habitation" remains multisensory, it is the sonic

[1] All empirical quotes derive from interviews conducted with the author between 2004 and 2012.

dimension of experience that remains the most mobile. Sound frees the eyes up enabling the subject to navigate space while the intense looking at the screen of a smartphone invariably inhibits movement.

The movement of people through cities has increasingly been a technologically mediated experience; from the sounds of the Muzak Corporation in the 1930s to the sounds of radios, the use of Walkmans, ghettoblasters, iPods, and smartphones. The mediated sonic experience of the city has a rich history. Sound, in this chapter, is conceived of as a specific way of "perceiving the world" (Geurts 2002) within which the consumption of technologically mediated sounds represents a significant "mode of being," a significant form of "corporeal immediacy" (Alter and Koepnick 2005).

This chapter focuses primarily on investigating a range of sonic experiences undertaken by Apple iPod, mobile phone, and smartphone users as they navigate their way through the city accompanied by their personal technologies. The sonic strategies analyzed below form an important part of the sensory reorganization of public space by users (Goggin 2011). The sonic uniquely permits users to reconfigure their relationship to urban space – to date, the majority of Western populations have the ability to create their own privatized sonic bubbles through both music reception and/or speech. Through the use of a range of technologies subjects are able to sonically embed, transcend, or negate the spaces they inhabit. These practices, historically, culturally, and technologically engendered enable citizens to redefine and reinscribe their understanding of private and public spaces both imaginatively and intimately (Bachelard 1994; Tuan 2001).

This chapter situates itself within a theoretical trajectory that understands space as becoming increasingly privatized in a variety of contexts. It does not claim that all urban space at all times is privatized – but merely demonstrates a range of privatizing tactics and strategies of embodied use. The paradoxical nature of this privatized urban experience is what is at issue in the following pages. Media technologies themselves embody a range of simultaneously private and structural affordances: meaning cannot be isolated from the structural conditions within which they arise. For example, the use of an iPod is both an inclusive act whereby the listener communes with the products of the culture industry and an act of auditory separation whereby users choose to live in their personalized soundworld. This personalized soundworld creates an alternative to the role of the media in sonically unifying the public spaces of the city. This results in a blurring of the experiential nature of public and private urban space. For example, as early as the 1930s the Lynds described the public role of radio-listening in the following terms, "When walking home in the hot summer evenings after window shopping on Madison Street," a Chicago man recalls, "one could follow the entire progress of *Amos 'n' Andy* from the open windows. By the 1940s, even in small towns like Honea Path, South Carolina, it was possible to practically hear the whole of *Grand Ole Opry* as it issued out of every house on the block" (Quoted in Loviglio 2005: xiv). Just as sounds can embed the subject into the space inhabited, so can they also repel. From recent examples of "sodcasting" whereby smartphone or iPod users point their phone outwards to demonstrate their musical taste to others on buses and trains – a twenty-first-century mini boom-box – to automobiles blaring their music from open windows in "their antisocial sociality redrawing the lines between public and private" (Gilroy 2004: 100), public urban space is a sonically contested space.

As public space is transformed into the private so, paradoxically, the private becomes public through the mediating role of communication technologies. How we experience one another and the world around us is necessarily mediated by the recognized and unrecognized cultural baggage with which we learn how "to be" in the world. The role of the media has increasingly conditioned this means, from the dulcet tones of Roosevelt's radio fireside chats in the 1930s and 40s to the growth of television in the 1960s. Subjects learned how to sit in the comfort of their homes with the mediated world flowing in, coded in waves of invisible radiation that beamed in domestic technologies such as the television. This mediated world – an audiovisual, one-dimensional representation – lures the subject with the very compression of its signal, to produce the appearance of "objectivity" in our encounter with the world. As David Morley states, television news flatters its "armchair imperialist viewers" into adopting a subjective position as "audio visual masters of the world," and the "guarantee" that television offers them is the "illusory feeling of presentness, this constructed impression of total immediacy … a televisual metaphysics of presence" (Morley 2000: 185). In parallel to this domestic "metaphysics of presence" has been its extension into traditionally defined "public spaces" of the city and elsewhere through the use of a range of mobile technologies from the automobile with its radio and hi-fi, to the boom box, Walkman, mobile phone, and now the smartphone. The one space mimics the other. While cities have traditionally been understood in terms of how space is shared (Simmel 1997; Sennett 1977; 1990), the use of mobile technologies has thrown into question the nature and meaning of the social spaces that we inhabit as well as questioning the nature of, and our need for, connectivity. This chapter traces these meanings through a range of mobile technologies that have redefined and reinscribed our understanding of the relationships between private and public spaces in the city.

Sonic Proximity, Distance, and the Transcendence of Space: Walkmans and iPods

While conducting interviews for a book on iPod culture (Bull 2007), I interviewed an upstate New Yorker who vividly described to me walking around New York listening to the New York Port Authority tapes of 9/11. These tapes are transcripts of telephone conversations between the authority and their staff on the ground as well as direct conversations between the inhabitants of the Twin Towers and the police authorities. The tapes, scratchy and partial in nature – inherently fragmented and unclear – possess, at least for me, an eerie sense of presence and immediacy. My interviewee described trying to make sense of what had happened in New York that day through listening to the tapes, and feeling a sense of connection to those events through his act of private listening. I didn't use this example in the book, feeling somewhat uncomfortable with it. However, it has remained firmly rooted in my mind as a metaphor for dislocated sonic connectivity in an urban culture – not to be taken in isolation but as part of a historical narrative of mediated connectivity in Western culture. Our subject is using his iPod, a pair of headphones, and the contents of his iPod to experientially embed himself into Ground Zero and its environs. His connection to Ground Zero is unique insofar as he is personalizing the experience of New York space. This imaginary reconnection is dependent upon the iPod itself. His experience, while unusual, highlights a central facet of contemporary urban experience as voiced by another New Yorker description of iPod use: "I enjoy having the soundtrack for New York streets. Having my own rhythm. I commute two hours a day. When I'm on the subway people listening to music on headphones often surround me. We each inhabit our own realities" (Karen).

The meanings attached to "we each inhabit our own realities" resonate philosophically, culturally, cognitively, and morally within Western culture, representing a complex set of relational issues associated with our understanding of space, place, and movement. The Apple iPod and, before that, the Sony Walkman are inherently technologies of sonic control; the placing of headphones around the ears permits a dramatic reorganization of the user's soundworld, in effect empowering the ears of the user. Technology thus transforms the power of the senses. Historically, the ears or hearing has always been considered a passive sense insofar as we are unable to close our ears at will; unlike the eyes, the ears are always open. The use of a Walkman or an Apple iPod changes this. For the first time users can traverse the noisy urban scene empowered precisely through filtering out the sounds of the city, to be replaced by their own private sound bubble provided by their own choice of music. Users frequently embark upon a range of strategies of sonic transcendence. Central to this is the construction of urban space as a "seamless space." Contemporary MP3 users both possess the ability and have the desire to unify urban space as they move from home, to the street, to the automobile, and to work, thereby transforming or denying the heterogeneity of the urban landscape passed through. The use of the mobile technologies like the iPod appears to bind the disparate threads of much urban movement together, both "filling" the spaces "in-between" communication or meetings and structuring the spaces thus occupied.

Sound, Technology, and Immersion

Users are able to traverse the noisy urban street, filtering out the sounds of the city and replacing them by their own private sound bubble. The auditory self of the iPod user thus increasingly inhabits acoustic space; sound becomes a habitual "way of perceiving the world" (Attali 1985: 4). Users both increasingly move to sound and are simultaneously moved by sound and in doing so they privatize sound itself (de Nora 2000). The origins of this privatizing auditory impulse are embedded in the cultural training and expectations of urban subjects through the use of a wide range of communication technologies from the telephone to the automobile (Douglas 2004; Flichy 1995; Sachs 1992). Sonic privatization is mediated and framed by Western cultural values as articulated in the work of Jonathan Sterne, who demonstrates that "audile technique was rooted in a practice of individuation: listeners could own their own acoustic spaces through owning the material component of a technique of producing that auditory space – the 'medium' that now stands for a whole set of practices. The space of the auditory field became a form of private property, a space for the individual to inhabit alone" (Sterne 2003: 160). The use of technologies like the iPod is merely the latest phase, or summation, of a historical trajectory of privatization. Technologies and values appear indissolubly linked.

This desire for immersive experience embedded in a range of everyday practices is intimately connected to the eradication or diminishment of the preexisting spatial soundworld. Frances Dyson has recently commented upon the intimate relationship between sound technologies and immersion: "Sound is the immersive medium par excellence. Three dimensional, interactive, and synaesthetic, perceived in the here and now of an embodied space, sound returns to the listener the very same qualities that media mediates: that feeling of being here now, of experiencing oneself as engulfed, enveloped, enmeshed, in short, immersed in an environment. Sound surrounds" (Dyson 2009: 4). The use of iPods and other MP3 players valorizes the "here and the now." Instrumental in creating this immersive state is the use of headphones, which transforms the user's relationship to the environment. Auditory privatization and headphone use are intimately connected. The headphone, in reempowering the ear against the contingency of sound in the world, bolsters the individualizing practices of sound reception precisely through this empowerment. In the fully mediated world of the iPod-user lies the dream of unmediated experience – of direct access to the world and one's emotions. It is a mediation that paradoxically conceives of experience in its immediacy – mediated experience, the sounds of the culture industry, the outside world sinking into silence. Sound both colonizes the listener and actively recreates and reconfigures the spaces of experience. Through the power of a privatized soundworld the world becomes intimate, known, and possessed.

The Privatizing Dispositions of Urban Culture

Retreat has become a dominant urban metaphor to describe strategies whereby citizens attempt to maintain a sense of "self" through the progressive creation of distancing mechanisms from the urban "other." Richard Sennett describes urban space as "a bland environment [which] assures people that nothing disturbing or demanding is happening 'out there.' You build neutrality in order to legitimize withdrawal" (Sennett 1990: 65). Urban retreat as a means to maintaining a subjective sense of balance or equilibrium can be traced back to the work of Georg Simmel, who described the urban subject as constructing a blasé attitude toward the physical nature of the city in order to achieve this aim. The blasé attitude negated difference through distancing itself from that which surrounds it: "things themselves are experienced as insubstantial. They appear to the blasé person in an evenly grey tone, no one object deserves preference over any other ... The self-preservation of certain personalities is bought at the price of devaluing the whole objective world" (Simmel 1997: 179). Simmel, in effect, became the first thinker to propose that a rich and full interiority was prefaced upon the negating of the urban environment that confronted the individual.

Thus, the dystopian image of urban life is prefaced upon a rejection of difference and indeed of physical presence. Urban life, from this perspective, becomes a dialectical process of freedom and insecurity whereby the urban citizen progressively retreats into their own cognitive or physical shell while simultaneously neutralizing the public spaces of the city. Urban retreat subsequently becomes the dominant metaphor in the dystopian image of urban life whereby the urban citizen attempts to maintain a sense of "self" through the progressive creation of distancing mechanisms from the "other." Technology both comes to the aid of, and furthers, this management of urban space and cognition. IPod use becomes a habitual "mode of being in the world" (Geurts 2002: 235) in which users choose to live in an increasingly privatized and "perpetual sound matrix" through which they "inhabit different sensory worlds" while sharing the same social space (Howes 2004: 14). Use, understood in this way, appears to represent a "device paradigm" whereby users withdraw from an engagement with the world around them in order to live in their circumscribed world of auditory pleasure. IPod users are representative of Bauman's urban citizens who "whatever company they may wish to enjoy (or are willing to tolerate) they carry with them, like snails carry their homes" (Bauman 2003: 98). Movement through the city is no longer "made up of chance encounters" (Lefebvre 2004: 30); indeed, iPod users never willingly interact with others while listening: "and I use my iPod in public as a 'privacy bubble' against other people. It allows me to stay in my own head. Sometimes I feel violated if I have to turn it off for an unplanned reason" (John). The breaking of the auditory bubble represents recognition of the fragility or contingency of auditory control.

The exclusion of, or transformation of the world beyond the user, coupled with the transformation of the user's "inner space" permits a restructuring of cognition, creating a free and orderly mobile space in which the user is able to successfully manage experience. Situations of cognitive conflict are avoided through a process of compartmentalization through which users focus upon the immediate task of control. The control of the self is managed through technological mediation in which the subject gives himself or herself over to the technology of the iPod. As such, users resemble Lasch's "minimal self" as they withdraw into a world small enough to exert total control over it. IPod use becomes representative "of the duality of modern culture: flight from others for the sake of self-mastery" (Sennett 1990: 44).

Intrinsic to this mastering of space and cognition is the strategy of "filtering" or "framing" experience, enabling users to remain focused in on themselves through the negating of the contingent nature of urban space. In this filtering stance, iPod use embodies a secessionist ethic. Secessionism refers to "a means of physically separating oneself from spatial configurations like higher urban density, public space, or from the city altogether" (Henderson 2006: 294). Secessionism is achieved through a process of filtering that heightens the user's cognitive control. This process of "auditory filtering" becomes for many users "second nature" as increasingly large areas of their lives are mediated through communication technologies such as the iPod.

Secessionist Values, iPod Use, and the Non-spaces of the City

For many theorists from Augé to Sennett, this denuded and privatized social is thought to reside in the streets we walk through, the buildings we pass by, the modern shopping centers we are inevitably drawn to, the anonymous spaces of airports, train stations, parking lots, and the endless motorways that many of us progressively live in as we shuttle backward and forward in our cars, on public transport. Augé in his analysis of urban space used the term "non-space" to describe an urban culture of semiologically denuded spaces – of shopping centers, airports, motorways, and the like. He thought of these spaces as if they had been dropped onto the urban landscape at random, as invariably architecturally bland: who can tell one shopping center from another, for example? Urban spaces from this perspective increasingly functioned as the endless transit zones of urban culture – emblems of the increasing mobile nature of urban culture.

Users of Walkmans, iPods, and the like transform any urban space into a non-space. The defining feature of the user's relationship to urban space is not necessarily how culturally situated they might be. For iPod users, urban "non-space" is not dependent upon the anthropological nature of the space itself, but increasingly upon the technologically empowered subjective response to that space, or indeed, the prior negation of that space through the cognitive predilections of the subject. Just as the placing of earphones over the ears empowers the ear, so the urban subject is free to re-create the city in their own image through the power of sound as the following iPod user so aptly describes: "When I plug in and turn on, my iPod does a 'ctrl+alt+delete' on my surroundings and allows me to 'be' somewhere else" (Wes).

IPod use permits users to control and manage their urban experience. In doing so time becomes subjectivized and speed brought into the rhythm of the user.

> *I view people more like choices when I'm wearing my iPod. Instead of being forced to interact with them, I get to decide. It's almost liberating to realize you don't have to be polite or smile or do anything. I get to move through time and space at my speed [and] my pace. (Andrea)*

IPod use potentially furthers the existing isolation of urban citizens that are articulated in, and embedded in, a range of technologies that enables urban citizens to carry out many traditionally public tasks with little or no interpersonal contact, which furthers the architecture of isolation articulated in the work of Sennett et al. Exchanges are increasingly taking place between subjects and machines in urban culture, making interpersonal exchange obsolete. Cognitively, consumers often expect, feel comfortable with, and desire no direct interpersonal communication while out in public: "Tracy expects to have wordless interactions with store attendants. When given a choice, Tracy will also use the 'You-Check' line recently available in her neighborhood's Fred Mayer, which allows her to scan her own purchases and credit card: 'I love it,' she says. In everyday life, she wants to 'get in and out'" (Jain 2002: 394). Thus, the normative foundation of the "non-places" of urban culture becomes etched into the social expectations of consumers as they partake of "public culture."

Urban infrastructures increasingly complement a range of technologies from the automobile to the iPod. The physical and cognitive zoning embedded in these technologies becomes second nature: "the basic idea of zoning is that every activity demands a separate zone of its own" (Kunstler 1998: 120).

> *I rarely even speak – I just hand them my credit card and say thank-you. (Mark)*

> *I tend not to notice people when I'm plugged in. I'm usually too preoccupied with myself to look at others. (Elizabeth)*

Progressive social withdrawal from the city both motivates much iPod use and furthers it:

> *I then started wearing it [the iPod] while shopping. I did it to control my environment and desensitize myself to everything around me. What I found interesting was that the more I wear my iPod, the less I want to interact with strangers. I've gotten to the point where I don't make eye contact. I feel almost encased in a bubble. (Zuni)*

The construction of privatized sonic landscapes permits users to control the terms and condition of whatever interaction might take place, producing a web of asymmetrical urban relations in which users strive for control.

The Vocalic Spaces of Privatization: Mobile Phone Use

If iPod users join up the spaces of the city in a continuous privatized web, then what of users who use either their mobile or smartphones to communicate with absent others? Mobile phones represent the world of the discontinuous – of punctured time – a world in which the contingency of the world becomes apparent with each unexpected call, received or not. Mobile phones construct mobile sound bubbles of discourse – simultaneously private and public as the user both speaks and listens. In the act of speaking, public space is transformed into private space thus puncturing and intervening in that space. Users often operationalize notions of a private/public divide in which the mobile phone represents an external intrusion into the private world and time of the user.

Caren is 26 years old and works in central London for a large media corporation. She commutes in daily to work on the underground from an outer London suburb. Caren lives alone and uses her commuting time to organize social activities for later in the day or week. Her use of the mobile phone while commuting is continual. The journey time of her commute is measured by the spaces in which uninterrupted mobile phone use is possible. Caren has become an expert on the geography of mobile phone availability on her routine journey to and from work:

> *I live in Woolston Green and I phone people from Finchley Road as you get a signal practically straight away there. And I'll phone and say, if I'm meeting someone, "I'm on my way," or "where are you?" Sometimes I phone because a friend of mine lives by me, but I'd have to go a different way home to see her, so I use the phone to check if she's in or not, or if she wants me to get a takeaway. (Caren)*

Caren micromanages her arrangements and subsequent traveling route, the time and space of commuting becomes oriented around arrangements and the meeting of friends, checking on availability, and acting accordingly – purchasing a takeaway meal to take to her friends, for instance. The city becomes a space of localized meetings. Caren, in distinction from those commuters who are going home to see their families and whose daily life revolves around the predictability of social arrangements, uses her "free-time" to generate social contact and to improvise her social arrangements with others. The mobile phone permits a possibility of near spontaneous social arrangements:

> *It [the mobile phone] gives you lots more opportunities. I probably would just go home all the time and never go out. I always think to myself when I'm on the tube, well maybe I do want to go out, and then I'll just phone to see who's in. It has opened up a whole new – I mean I never would have stood at a pay phone and phoned four people to find the one that was in! So now, I just sit on the train and then, because I can make plans there ... for those off the top, off the cuff, 'I just wonder if' things, a lot more of those happen now than ever would have. (Caren)*

Urban space becomes a space of social improvization, as a space orientated to future communication, orchestrated as a set of contingent possibilities with routes changed and activities transformed. Caren might arrange to meet at a friend's flat to watch a DVD. She will phone the friend from the rental shop to ascertain which DVD to rent. Similar arrangements are made concerning the ordering of food from a takeaway. Arrangement is also made while out and about in the city itself.

> *Well, I just say to a friend, "Just call me if you're in town," it's really nice to know you don't have to have a plan. If you both happen to be in town at the same time you can use the mobile to track one another down, which is great. It's like a homing beacon, "Where are you?" "I'm in M and S, where are you?" "I'm in Starbucks," "Okay, wait there, I'm coming." (Caren)*

Commuting time becomes a time and space for social arrangements; she rarely looks round at other people on the train, preferring to concentrate upon her mobile phone. When not arranging meetings, she spends time talking, which she describes as "just checking in" with friends.

For urban users such as Caren, using a mobile phone enhances her potential to lead a more spontaneous and active social life by being able to organize meetings while traveling, whereas previously she would have phoned from home after her commute, thus making arrangement more difficult and reducing her "free" time. Every public space becomes a potential place of talk with intimate others. When not arranging meetings, Caren uses the phone continually to "keep up" with close acquaintances and family:

> *I phone people on the bus or walking down the road, and so they're not really conducive to long phone calls. But because I've already spoken to them that day, I don't need a long phone call. I'll often phone people again when I get home, but the*

conversations don't carry much meat, just "Hello, how are you," or "I'm fine, alright, bye-bye." (Caren)

The use of mobile phones has permeated all areas of social life, rearranging the meaning of, and relations between work and home, of leisure and sociability itself (Castells 2007). Mobile phones have become an integral tool in the management of everyday life. In doing so the nature of public space itself has been transformed. Connor has argued that the very meaning of social space is "very largely a function of the perceived powers of the body to occupy and extend itself through its environment" (Connor 2000: 12). The sound of the voice colonizes the space it inhabits, and mobile phone talk is everywhere. Local customs of reserve become progressively eroded as individual mobile-phone users become more assertive in their public demonstration of talking to absent others. The mobilizing of public space for the engagement of technologically mediated and "private" intimacy "warms" up the space of the street for users as they commune with small numbers of intimate others. Urban space becomes decontextualized as the intimacy of a "cognitive" home is recreated in the public spaces of the street.

Mobile-phone use transforms representational space into a very specific form of vocalic space – a space of potential intimacy and warmth while all else that occupies that space is recessed, transcended. A denuded public space is transformed into a privatized intimate space in which "private" life gains greater visibility in a "public sphere emptied of its substance" (De Gournay 2002). One in seven urban citizens on average use mobile devices at any one time in urban space, thus transforming its meaning:

> *With a keitai, (a mobile), a girl can turn any space into her own room and personalise paradise ... The keitai is a jamming machine that instantly creates a territory – a personal keitai space – around oneself with an invisible, minimal barricade. (Fujimoto 2005: 97)*

Geographical space becomes recessed, as the speaker inhabits "another" space, as Bassett has noted: "phone space is often prioritized over local space" (Bassett 2004: 349). This very prioritization has relational consequences and speaks to the inherent prioritization of private space over shared social space. The use of mobile-phones represents an alternative way of filling up time as users habitually phone others in the public spaces of the city, "When you're walking to and from, I like to utilize my time so there's no dead time or down time. I'll do a quick 15 minute call to my mum, or to my brothers and friends" (Samantha). The street is turned into a utilitarian space of interpersonal discourse; time is accounted for in terms of its "usefulness" but also in terms of an ethic of "waste," stemming from users' increasing desire to multitask on a wide range of social activities (Gleik 1999): "I'm not very good at doing one thing at once. I always feel that if I can do two things then its better" (Samantha).

Streets walked through become secondary to the act of talking over the mobile phone. Lucy, a 32-year-old charity organizer from Brighton, describes the following scene:

> *It was a Monday night, it had been a lovely day and I thought, this is crazy, I've been in the flat all day doing bits and pieces. I'll go out for a walk along the seafront. Well, I spent almost the entire time walking along the sea front and back again, talking on my mobile phone. It was almost as if just walking wasn't enough for me. There was an element of wanting to tell people that it's ten o'clock at night and I'm walking along the seafront – aren't I a lucky girl. (Lucy)*

Lucy ended up not looking out to sea as she had originally intended, but rather talked to friends about looking out to sea and enjoying the experience. Experience appears to derive meaning through communicating it to others and in doing so destroys the very experience originally sought. Lucy does not notice who is in close proximity, "When I'm on the phone, it's my, my concentration is I'm talking to this person and what's going on around me is of secondary importance … I don't notice other people when I'm talking on the phone … I'm in my own little world." Neither is she inhibited about talking about private or intimate issues over the phone whilst in public space: "I work on the assumption that those people don't know me, I don't know them. So they can only hear half the conversation and it's not particularly going to be interesting to them anyway … I'm not aware of any reaction I might be causing." Public space becomes a blank and neutral canvas on which to write one's personal and intimate and mobile messages.

From iPods to Smartphones: Old Dispositions in New Technologies?

> *With the increasing popularization of location-aware technologies, the relationship between mobile technologies and places requires a new perspective because these technologies strongly influence how people interact with their surrounding space and how they understand location. (De Souza and Frith 2012)*

In 2012 the Apple Corporation sold four times as many iPhones as iPods. Does the introduction of smartphones with their ubiquitous multifunctionality make the present analysis of the mediation of public and private space historically passé as De Souza and Frith claim, or rather, does their use represent a continuation of past trends? The following pages demonstrate that the processes whereby users negate, transcend, and immerse themselves in public space are alive and well among users of smartphones. This is not to deny some significant transformative affordances embodied in the design of smartphones:

> *I enter the bus, pay and then sit somewhere towards the back on my own. I spend most of my journey on Facebook – pointlessly scrolling through – looking at my Facebook account – killing time. I might also send a text, call my mum or listen to music – then play games. (Jane)*

The affordances created through smartphone use do however complicate the auditory and audiovisual strategies encompassed by iPod use. Georgia, a 22-year-old, wakes up to her alarm on her smartphone; she often sleeps through the alarm, as she's grown accustomed to it. She wakes up and answers two text messages, gets up and goes for a shower, bringing her phone along with her. She has a shower, taking her iPhone with her, "Every day I shower to music as I find it relaxing and comforting. I always choose the same playlist as not only are the songs some of my favorites but also good 'morning songs' like 'Sunday Morning' by the Velvet Underground and Nico is very mellow and happy, and 'People Have the Power' by Patti Smith is very energetic and inspiring leaving me ready for the day ahead." She takes her phone downstairs still listening to music and makes breakfast while reading the paper. She checks the train times on her phone app and goes out where she meets her friend Frankie on the train to work: "despite being sat next to my friend who I spent most of the morning arranging to meet, now I am with her I am once again on my phone, preferring to play a game than make conversation. She is also playing a game, which means that neither of us make any effort to communicate." Georgia's response to the urban is similar to traditional mobile phone and iPod users. The technology merely allows her to engage in a wider range of mediating activities: "Whenever I'm walking on my own, even for a short amount of time – like walking from my home to the bus stop – I have to either call someone on the phone or listen to my music. I hate being alone." The privatizing themes of iPod use and the mediated absence/presence of phone use are embedded in Georgia's daily routines. The smartphone fulfills the multiple functions of the phone, the Internet, and the iPod.

Equally, Michelle describes her three-hour train journey from London to Norwich to visit her boyfriend, "I check my phone and make sure it is fully charged, it is necessary for me to have my phone fully charged so it will be able to handle the text messages, phone calls, the Internet and play music through my music playlist to last me the whole journey." While waiting for the train Michelle waits at the station. "I go on my phone to keep myself busy. When I'm bored and out in public I look to my phone in order to cope with the boredom. I text, call, go on Facebook, and whatever. Time goes quicker when I am doing something, and not just waiting around doing nothing." Before leaving she wants to pick up a birthday cake to take with her to Norwich, "I have to pick up a birthday cake in London. I have never been to the cake shop before. I use Google maps on my phone to direct me ... I am reliant on my phone to get me from one place to another. Instead of having to ask directions, my phone instantly tells me where the cake shop is and the quickest route to get to it." The privatizing strategies described by Michelle are similar to the secessionist tactics embodied in iPod use described earlier. Indeed, secessionism is enhanced by smartphone use. Users of smartphones continue to individualize city spaces through the use of a range of new apps available for users. While Michelle uses Google Maps to find places, others use applications like Yelp that enable users to find restaurants and spaces of consumption that others "like themselves" have already visited and commented upon. Whereas iPod users might compare themselves to other absent users who run to their iPods, for example, smartphone users can also look to see where other users "like themselves" might have visited – from wine bars to clubs to tourist attractions.

The street frequently holds as much interest for smartphone users as traditional iPod users. Indeed, smartphone users can move through a variety of applications including the use of music. Silva and Frith point out that a variety of GPS applications "create an individual experience of space for each user ... (contributing) to an increased commodification of locations (in which) public spaces might be more individualized" (158). These strategies of urban transcendence equally mirror those of iPod users:

> *I feel I can relax when I plug my earphones into my ear, and music drowns out the sounds of those around me. I am immune to the sounds of other people on the train, especially the young people in front of me, although they are sitting right next to each other; speak incredibly loudly so that the whole train can hear them. Listening to music changes the way I experience the journey. I love the fact that although I am in a public space, I am able to retreat into my own little world with the press of a button. I can just sit, relax and listen to my music which completely rids my mind of thoughts of the long and tiring journey I have to endure. (Kathryn)*

The use of mobile technologies from the Walkman through to the smartphone represents both a continuum and a shift within urban experience. The continuum represents new developments in the search for public privacy and a discounting of the "public" realm, while the transformation lies in urban citizens increasing ability and desire to make the "public" spaces of the city conform to their desires. As we increasingly inhabit "media saturated" spaces of intimacy, so we increasingly desire to make the public spaces passed through mimic our desires; thus, ironically, furthering the absence of meaning attributed to those spaces. This is the dialectic of an increasingly mediated and mobile culture. In the United Kingdom, a central platform of the incoming government of David Cameron was the idea that we all existed in the "big society," which we were all connected to and responsible for. Critics of the British Prime Minister's idea of the "big society" often said that it was too abstract. Maybe this is because our sense of the social has become abstract – increasingly taken away from the spaces that we more often than not live in – our sense of community is increasingly locked into the abstractness of the Web with its social networks – or in our mobile phones and iPods. In today's technologically mediated world is the desire for a physically shared social space merely nostalgic? If so, spare a thought for Alison who had been a regular Walkman user in the 1990s. She comments that, "In retrospect I wish I had not been stuck in my own head, so disconnected. People feel so alien to me now. They stand in line in front of me, dancing ever so slightly to their tune, often oblivious to what's happening around them and completely closed off from the niceties of the neighborly 'hello.'"

References

Alter, N. and L. Koepnick (eds). 2005. *Sound Matters: Essays on the Acoustics of German Culture.* London: Bergham Books.

Attali, J. 1985. *Noise: The Political Economy of Music.* Minneapolis: University of Minnesota Press.

Augé, M. 1995. *Non-Places: Introduction to Anthropology of Supermodernity.* London: Verso.

Bachelard, G. 1994. *The Poetics of Space: The Classical Look at How We Experience Intimate Places.* Boston: Beacon Press.

Bassett, C. 2004. How many movements? In *The Auditory Culture Reader.* Edited by M. Bull and L. Back. Oxford: Berg.

Benjamin, W. 1973. *Illuminations.* London: Penguin.

Bourdieu, P. 1986. *Distinction: A Social Critique of Taste.* London: Routledge.

Brandon, R. 2002. *Automobile. How the Car Changed Life.* Basingstoke: Macmillan Press.

Bull, M. 2000. *Sounding Out the City: Personal Stereos and the Management of Everyday Life.* Oxford: Berg.

Bull, M. 2007. *Sound Moves: IPod Culture and Urban Experience.* London: Routledge.

Bull, M. and L. Back (eds). 2004. *The Auditory Culture Reader.* Oxford: Berg.

Castells, M., M. Fernández-Ardèvol, J.L. Qiu, and A. Sey. 2007. *Mobile Communication and Society: A Global Perspective.* Cambridge, MA: MIT Press.

Connor, S. 2000. *Dumbstruck: A Cultural History of Ventriloquism.* Oxford: Oxford University Press.

Coyne, R. 2010. *The Tuning of Place: Sociable Spaces and Pervasive Digital Media.* Cambridge, MA: MIT Press.

De Certeau, M. 1988. *The Practice of Everyday Life.* Berkeley: University of California Press.

De Nora, T. 2000. *Music in Everyday Life.* Cambridge: Cambridge University Press.

Douglas, S. 2004. *Listening In: Radio and the American Imagination.* Minneapolis: University of Minnesota Press.

Dyson, F. 2009. *Sounding New Media: Immersion and Embodiment in the Arts and Culture.* Berkeley: University of California Press.

Flichy, P. 1995. *Dynamics of Modern Communication: The Shaping and Impact of New Communication Technologies.* London: SAGE.

Fujimoto, K. 2005. The third-stage paradigm: Territory machines from the girl's pager revolution to mobile aesthetics. In *Personal, Portable, Pedestrian: Mobile Phones in Japanese Life*. Eidted by M. Ito, D. Okabe, and M. Matsuda. Cambridge, MA: MIT Press.
Geurts, K. 2002. *Culture and the Senses: Bodily Ways of Knowing in an African Community*. Berkeley: University of California Press.
Gilroy, P. 2004. Driving while black. In *The Auditory Culture Reader*. Edited by M. Bull and L. Back. Oxford: Berg.
Gleik, J. 1999. *Faster: The Acceleration of Just about Everything*. London: Little Brown.
Goggin, G. 2011. *Global Mobile Media*. London: Routledge.
Henderson, J. 2006. Secessionist automobility: Racism, anti-urbanism, and the politics of automobility. *International Journal of Urban and Regional Research* 30(2): 293–307.
Howes, D. 2004. *Sensual Relations: Engaging the Senses in Culture and Social Theory*. Ann Arbor: University of Michigan Press.
Jain, S. 2002. Urban errands: The means of mobility. *Journal of Consumer Culture* 2(3): 419–38.
Kunstler, H. 1998. *Home from Nowhere: Remaking our Everyday World for the Twenty-first Century*. New York: Simon and Schuster.
Lefebvre, H. 2004. *Rhythmanalysis: Space, Time and Everyday Life*. London: Continuum Press.
Loviglio, J. (2005) *Radio's Intimate Public. Network Broadcasting and Mass Mediated Democracy*. Minneapolis: University of Minnesota Press.
Morley, D. 2000. *Home Territories: Media, Mobility and Identity*. London: Routledge.
Pieslak, J. 2009. *Sound Targets: American Soldiers and Music in the Iraq War*. Bloomington: Indiana University Press.
Sachs, W. 1992. *For Love of the Automobile: Looking Back into the History of Our Desires*. Berkeley: University of California Press.
Sennett, R. 1977. *The Fall of Public Man*. London: Faber and Faber.
Sennett, R. 1990. *The Conscience of the Eye*. London: Faber.
Silva, A. and J. Frith. 2012. *Mobile Interfaces and Public Spaces: Location Privacy, Control, and Urban Sociability*. London: Routledge.
Silverstone, R. 1994. *Television and Everyday Life*. London: Routledge.
Silverstone, R. 2006. *Media and Morality: On the Rise of the Mediaopolis*. Cambridge: Polity Press.
Simmel, G. 1997. *Simmel on Culture*. London: SAGE.
Sterne, J. 2003. *The Audible Past: Cultural Origins of Sound Reproduction*. Durham: Duke University Press.
Tuan, Y.-F. 2001. *Space and Place*. Minneapolis: University of Minnesota Press
Turkle, S. 2011. *Alone Together: Why We Expect More from Technology and Less from Each Other*. New York: Basic Books.

Spaces of Telemediated Sociability

Barney Warf

Today, more people are more connected technologically to one another than at any other time in human existence. For the bulk of the world's people, the Internet, mobile phones, text messaging, and various other forms of digital social media such as Facebook have become thoroughly woven into the routines and rhythms of daily life (Kellerman 2001; Thrift and French 2002; Dodge and Kitchin 2005). What does the enormous popularity of digital communications systems hold for how people relate to one another and view themselves?

This chapter situates digital communications within the wider notion of the networked society, and offers a brief empirical overview of the popularity of technologies that facilitate and expedite telemediated interpersonal interactions, including mobile phones, the Internet, and networking sites. Access to these technologies is socially and spatially uneven, of course, and the digital divide casts doubt on common assertions of universal access. Nonetheless, large (and rapidly growing) numbers of people have ready access to social media. Next, it focuses on the implications of telemediated connections for the construction of the self. Unlike the prevailing forms of socialization that have dominated historically, for many social media users the self is increasingly constructed through their online interactions. In contrast to the prevailing Western model of subjectivity of the autonomous individual, digital media allow for a new form of sociability that greatly enhances the importance of relational ties, leading, arguably, to a different form of the self than the historically accepted view of the self-contained, autonomous individual whose conception largely minimizes social interactions. The argument hinges on the notion of the networked self, beings so immersed in digital social media that their online identities, personas, and reputations are as central to their lives as their off-line counterparts. Networked selves tend to live at the center of webs of digital ties that bind space in complex and often unpredictable ways, so that conventional geographies of everyday life have limited relevance to understanding their outlook and behavior (Papacharissi 2010). Following Adams (2005), the networked self in many respects is "boundless" – that is, able to escape the physical and temporal limits of the human body. In remaking the self, it is argued that social media also change the nature of geographic relationships, facilitating the rise of a "flat ontology" in which scale and distance matter much less than they used to do so previously. The argument is supplemented with discussions of online communities, cyborg selves, the blogosphere, and digital panopticons.

Documenting the Rise of the Networked Society

Mobile phones, the Internet, and social media are all symptomatic of, and in turn, help to produce, what Castells (1996; 1997) famously labeled the network society. Castells distinguished earlier *information* societies, in which productivity was derived from access to energy and the manipulation of materials, from later *informational* societies that emerged in the late twentieth century, in which productivity is derived primarily from knowledge and information. In his reading, the time-space compression of postmodernism was manifested in the global "space of flows," including the three "layers" of transportation and communication infrastructure, the cities or nodes that occupy strategic locations within these, and the social spaces occupied by the global managerial class:

> *Our societies are constructed around flows: flows of capital, flows of information, flows of technology, flows of organizational interactions, flows of images, sounds and symbols. Flows are not just one element of social organization: they are the expression of the processes dominating our economic, political, and symbolic life. ... Thus, I propose the idea that there is a new spatial form characteristic of social practices that dominate and shape the network society: the space of flows. The space of flows is the material organization of time-sharing social practices that work through flows. By flows I understand purposeful, repetitive, programmable sequences of exchange and interaction between physically disjointed positions held by social actors. (1996: 412)*

He notes, for example, that while people live in places, postmodern power is manifested in the linkages among places and people, that is, their interconnectedness, as personified by business executives shuttling among global cities and using the Internet to weave complex geographies of knowledge invisible to almost all ordinary citizens. This process was largely driven by the needs of the transnational class of the powerful employed in information-intensive occupations; hence, he writes (1996: 415) that "Articulation of the elites, segmentation and disorganization of the masses seem to be the twin mechanisms of social domination in our societies." Flows thus consist of corporate and political elites crossing international space on transoceanic flights; the movements of capital through telecommunications networks; the diffusion of ideas through organizations stretched across ever-longer distances; the shipments of goods and energy via tankers, container ships, trucks, and railroads; and the growing mobility of workers themselves. In this light, the space of flows is a metaphor for the intense time-space compression of contemporary capitalism. Through the space of flows, the global economy is coordinated in real time across vast distances – that is, horizontally integrated chains rather than vertically integrated corporate hierarchies. In the process, it has given rise to a variety of new political formations, forms of identity, and spatial associations.

Telecommunications and social media simultaneously reflect and constitute the global space of flows. The rise in their significance is no accident. In the late twentieth century, post-Fordist capitalism, which relied heavily on the adoption of computers and the digitization of information, unleashed unprecedented possibilities for enhanced social and individual connectivity. Two key innovations that played a central role in this process were mobile telephony and the Internet.

Over the last 20 years, the mobile or cellular telephone has become the most widely used form of telecommunications in the world, surpassing even the Internet in numbers of users (Dekimper, Parker, and Sarvary 1998; Goggin 2006; Campbell and Park 2008; Comer and Wikle 2008; Ling and Donner 2009). Rapid decreases in the cost of mobile phones, and

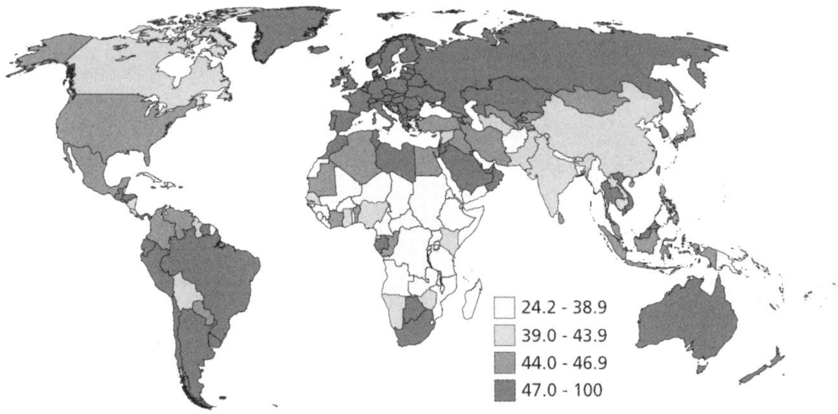

Figure 18.1 Mobile phone penetration rates, 2010
Source: Author, using data from International Telecommunications Union

the minimal infrastructure necessary for their operation (i.e. cell towers), have made them affordable for vast numbers of people, including in the developing world. In 2011, 59.6 percent of the world's inhabitants – 5.2 billion people – used mobile phones, more than 10 times as many as use landlines and far more than the 2.3 billion who used the Internet. The extent of mobile telephony worldwide is evident in Figure 18.1. Average penetration rates in 2010 exceeded that of landlines in every country, and in many there are more mobile phones than people. China has the world's largest population of mobile phone users (Dong and Li 2004; Ding, Haynes, and Li 2010). Even in sub-Saharan Africa, the world's least connected region, 10 to 50 percent of the population uses this technology (depending on the country). Moreover, mobile phone growth is explosive: between 2003 and 2010, the world's number of mobile phone users jumped by 187 percent, a rate even higher than that for the Internet. Given inequalities in incomes, literacy, gender barriers, and other dimensions of social life, this growth was unevenly distributed: while rates of increase were modest throughout the economically advanced world, in much of Africa and Central Asia they exceeded 1,000 percent in seven years.

The popularity of mobile communication technologies has enormous implications for the construction of identity, allowing users to interact digitally with one another to unprecedented degrees, even if these relations may lack much of the depth and emotional richness of face-to-face ties (Farman 2011). For example, the boundaries between private and public life have become increasingly porous as once-private conversations are held in public (Townsend 2000; Hampton, and Wellman 2001; Mäenpäa 2001; Fortunati 2002; Ling 2004; Pain et al. 2005; Ling and Campbell 2009). Mobile phones allow for improved coordination of activities, more efficient use of time while driving or walking, and greater security in case of emergencies. Often equipped with cameras, mobile phones allow for digital transmission of photographs as well, and, with smartphones, access to the Internet. It is not unlikely that mobile telephony enhances social cohesion (Ling 2010), although possibly at the cost of diminished rates of face-to-face contacts. For example, Sooryamoorthy et al. (2011) found in a study of Kerala, India, that mobile phone users were more likely to develop more nonlocal ties than were nonusers.

One of the prime applications of mobile phones is text messaging. In 2010, 74 percent of the world's mobile phone users, or 3.85 billion people, engaged in texting, sending a total of 6.1 trillion messages, or 192,000 per second (ITU 2010). Everywhere that cell phones are found, teenagers took the lead in adopting texting at rates far higher than their elders (Bolin and Westlund 2009; Lenhart et al. 2010). In the United States, where 93 percent of the population uses a cellular phone, the average user sends 534 messages per month, and one in three teens sends more than 3,000 per month (Lenhart et al. 2010). In poorer countries, texting is a popular substitute for voice traffic because it is considerably lower in cost. Mobile telephony's applications include instant messaging services such as Twitter, which has grown explosively. Starting in 2006, Twitter grew to include 140 million users worldwide in early 2012; the world sends more than 340 million tweets per day.

Perhaps the best exemplar of the network society is the Internet. In December 2011, roughly 2.3 billion people, or 32 percent of the planet's population, had Internet access. As numerous works have examined the social and spatial contours of cyberspace, they need not be recapitulated here (cf. Kellerman 2002). In the context of the networked society, the role of e-mail, which is by far the most common application of the Internet, should be emphasized. Instantaneous, free (or almost so), and asynchronous e-mail allows both one-to-one and one-to-many modes of communication. In 2012 more than 3.3 billion e-mail accounts existed, and the world sent 144.8 billion e-mail messages each day (Radicati 2012). E-mail is widely used in the business world (the typical corporate user exchanges 110 messages per day), and in addition to being an inescapable tool for professional and personal success, is also a prime source of information overload.

Internet usage is characterized by social and spatial digital divides at several spatial scales (Cooper and Compaine 2001; Crang, Crosbie, and Graham 2006; Goldfarb and Prince 2008; Korupp and Szydlik 2005; Stevens 2006). Globally, Internet access closely reflects the geographies of uneven development and the associated variations in wealth and power. Internet penetration rates vary greatly across the world (Figure 18.2): in economically developed countries, the vast majority of people have access, particularly in places such as Scandinavia, where Internet usage is essentially universal. In contrast, in the developing world Internet penetration rates are considerably lower, but rising rapidly. Digital divides also exist *within* countries, meaning that the poor, elderly, ethnic minorities, and rural areas exhibit lower rates of usage (Chakraborty and Bosman 2005; Mills and Whitacre 2003).

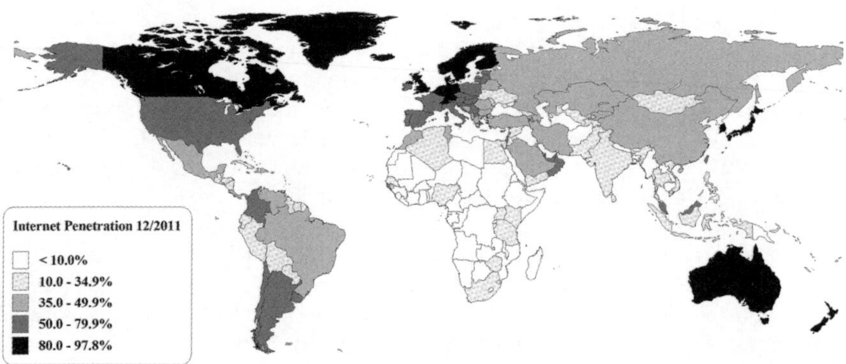

Figure 18.2 Internet penetration rates, December 2011
Source: Author, using data from www.Internetworldstats.com

However, the rapid rise in Internet users – approximately 15 percent annually – indicates that digital divides are rapidly changing. Finally, the growth of broadband services, including mobile ones, is erasing the boundaries between telephony and the Internet altogether (Arminen 2007; Kellerman 2010).

The networked society is also exemplified through digital social networks, which greatly expedite the creation of an online persona. Networking sites like Friendster, LinkedIn, MySpace, and Facebook began in the early 2000s (Table 18.1). Some are aimed at finding romantic partners (e.g. Match.com), while others such as YouTube allow sharing of digital content with everyone, including like-minded strangers, forming classic "communities without propinquity." Figure 18.3 reveals the growth in popularity of such networks: more than one-half of the US population used social media sites in 2011, and three-quarters of those under age 30 do so.

Table 18.1 Year of origin of selected social networking sites

1997	Six Degrees
1999	LiveJournal
2001	Cyworld
2002	Friendster
2003	LinkedIn, MySpace
2004	Flickr, Facebook
2005	YouTube
2006	Twitter

Source: Internetworldstats.com

Table 18.2 Facebook users and penetration rates, December 2011

	Users (*millions*)	Penetration rate
Europe	223	27.4
Asia	184	4.7
North America	175	50.3
Latin America and Caribbean	147	25.5
Africa	38	3.6
Middle East	17	8.4
Oceania	13	37.7

Source: Internetworldstats.com

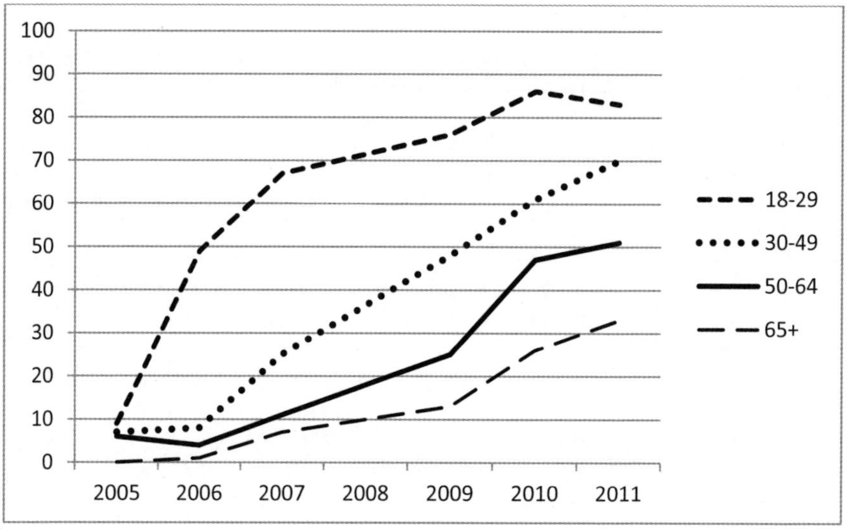

Figure 18.3 Percent of US population using digital social networks by age, 2005–2011
Source: Author, redrawn from Pew Research Center, www.pewinternet.org/Reports/2011/Social-Networking-Sites/Report.aspx?view=all

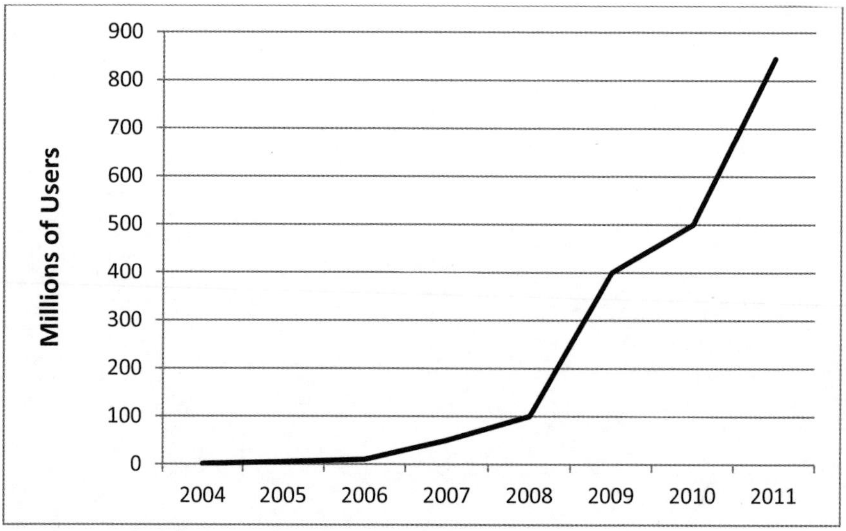

Figure 18.4 Facebook users worldwide, 2004–2011
Source: Author, using data from www.Internetworldstats.com

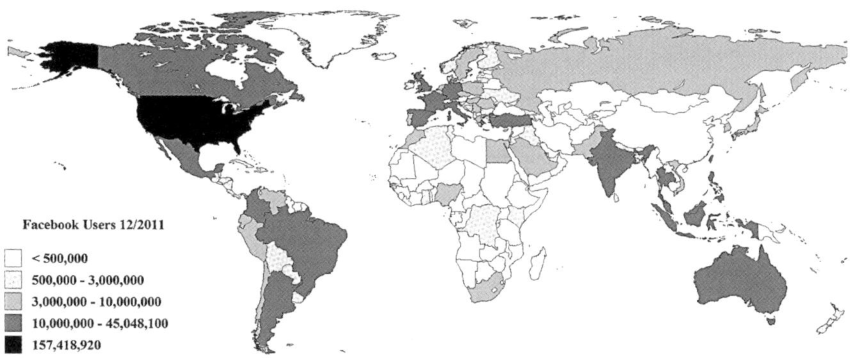

Figure 18.5 Map of Facebook users worldwide, December 2011
Source: Author, using data from www.Internetworldstats.com

Facebook is by far the most popular networking site in the world (Kirkpatrick 2010), with more than 845 million users in early 2012 (Figure 18.4), or 12 percent of the planet's population: if Facebook were a country, it would be the world's third largest. Its users are, naturally, unevenly distributed across the planet (Table 18.2; Figure 18.5). The United States, with 157 million users or half the population, forms the largest single national group of Facebook fans. The network is also popular throughout the Americas, Europe, South Asia, parts of Southeast Asia, and Australia and New Zealand. Within the United States, the highest Facebook penetration rates are found in relatively wealthy, educated states such as Massachusetts, New Jersey, Washington, and those with a large metropolitan area, such as Illinois and Georgia (Figure 18.6). Facebook has decisively trounced competing networking services such as Myspace, which in the eyes of many users has become relegated to ethnic minorities and low-income users (Miller 2007).

While it is the largest, Facebook is only one of several social networking sites worldwide (Figure 18.7). In Russia and neighboring states, the Kontakte network is popular. China has promoted its homegrown Qzone system, while in Brazil Zing reigns supreme. Dozens of other smaller sites also exist, such as Maktoob (in the Arab world), hi5.com (Mongolia), and Habbo (Finland).

Social Networks and the Networked Self

The rise of the network society has been manifested in new forms of individual identity and behavior that are decidedly relational in nature (Giddens 1991; Levy 1997). Correspondingly, relational perspectives on how people view themselves and one another have gained considerable purchase, specifically as these perceptions are telemediated through social media (Whatmore 1997; Valentine and Holloway 2002). In sharp contrast to views of disembodied, autonomous individuals who have dominated Western social theory since Descartes (most explicitly in that desolate creature *homo economicus*), or what Putnam (1981: 7) memorably called "brains in vats," relational theories of the self begin and emphasize its embodiment and social embeddedness. The construction and contestation of difference as a set of power relations in everyday is an integral part of this process (Pile 2008). In this light,

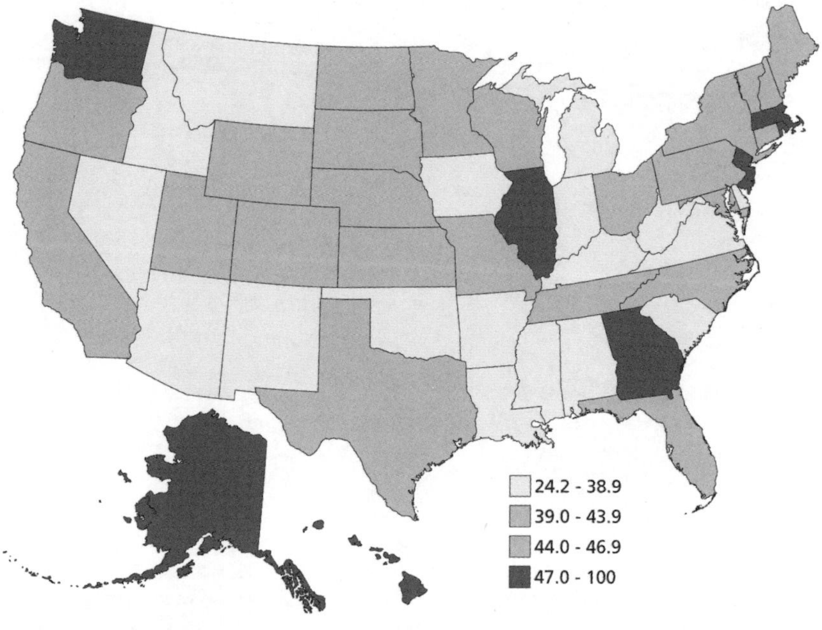

Figure 18.6 Map of US Facebook penetration rates, 2010
Source: Author, using data from www.Internetworldstats.com

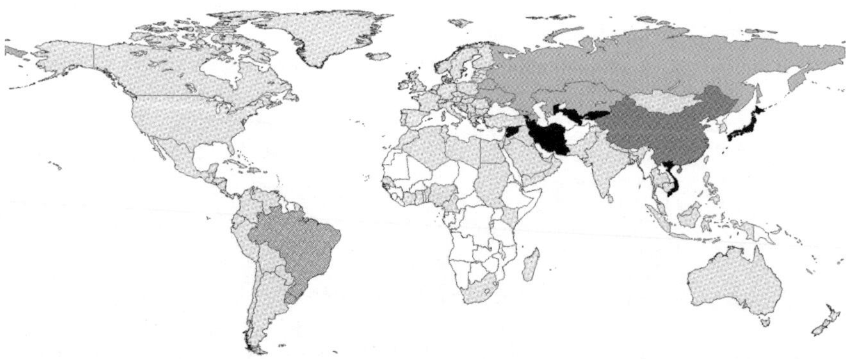

Figure 18.7 Dominant social networking service, 2011
Source: Author, redrawn from www.vincos.it/world-map-of-social-networks

identities are never fixed or given, but fluid, multiple, contingent, context-dependent, and always under construction.

An important theorization of this topic was offered by Granovetter (1985), who emphasized the embeddedness of the economy within wider circuits of culture. Granovetter famously differentiated between strong and weak social ties. Strong ties are characterized by high degrees of repeated interaction, trust, and emotional reciprocity, such as those typically found among family members and close friends. In contrast, weak ties tend to be more fleeting, utilitarian, and lack emotional depth. Generations of sociologists, such as Louis Wirth of the Chicago School, argued that urbanization tended to reduce the number of strong ties, enhancing alienation, and increase the number of weak ties, views that portray urban in a markedly negative light. In the context of post-Fordist information-intensive economies, weak ties vastly outnumber strong ones, and they are vital to the accumulation of social capital and career success.

Digital networks are ideal for cultivating webs of weak ties. However, the extent to which digital interactions can replicate or substitute for close interpersonal connections has been widely debated. The extensive literature on this topic reveals two contrasting positions (Nie 2001). For example, early analyses of the social impacts of the telephone asserted that it facilitated the formation of "communities without propinquity," groups of people with shared interests but lacking a common geographic location (Webber 1973). One body of literature holds that social media successfully replicate the emotional depth of face-to-face contacts (Hampton and Wellman 2001), that Internet users have *more* off-line social interactions than do nonusers (Castells 2001), and that digital interactions are displacing place-based communities as the primary vehicles of sociability. For example, the enormous popularity of massively multiplayer online role-playing games (MMORPGs) such as *World of Warcraft*, with 8 million players worldwide, reflects like-minded people defined by shared interests rather than spatial proximity (Li et al. 2010).

The contrasting interpretation maintains that precisely because digital interactions allow anonymity and disallow nonverbal cues (e.g. body language), they discourage the formation of intimate ties. From this perspective, the Internet and mobile phones complement, but do not substitute for, face-to-face interactions. Rather than create new interactions, the telephone enhanced preexisting social networks formed face-to-face (Fischer 1992). In the same vein, Wellman (2001a) argued that e-mail reinforced existing ties based on family or friendship, and that its use reflected a distance-decay effect as the physical location of the users increased. Haythornthwaite (2005) maintains that meaningful interactions via social media are invariably preceded or accompanied by earlier face-to-face ties. As a result, digitally mediated communities are typically ephemeral and lack significant levels of trust or emotional depth. Thus, telemediated interactions are ideal for sustaining weak ties, but less appropriate for the cultivation of strong ones. For example, Hampton et al. (2011) argues that the average Facebook user has 229 "friends," although an overabundance of such friends may actually undermine the capacity to sustain close, strong ties (Ellison et al. 2007; Tong et al. 2008). Telemediated ties have difficulty negotiating social difference: thus few Facebook users cultivate friends with people who are ethnically dissimilar to themselves (Vasalou et al. 2010).

Digital social media may actually make people less, not more, sociable. Turkle (2011) asserts that Internet and mobile phone use isolates users from one another and deprives them of intimate ties. In her view, telemediated ties lead people to feel alone even when they are together, and she blames texting in particular for an ostensible decline in conversational capacity: a new skill, for example, includes being able to maintain eye contact with one person while texting another. Internet interactions also shape users' self-perceptions: teenagers increasingly shape their identities by the expectations of their online audiences.

Because they confuse being connected with intimacy, heavy users of social media become unable to be alone, and thus often feel lonely. Not surprisingly, therefore, the growth of ersatz intimacy on Facebook has been accompanied by rising levels of loneliness in the United States (Marche 2012). Equally disturbing, the Internet may generate subtle but pervasive changes in brain structure, including shortened attention spans, echoing Postman's (1985) famous critique of the destructive effects of television (Jackson 2008; Carr 2010).

Forging close personal ties necessitates the exchange of tacit knowledge and the cultivation of trust. Ettlinger (2003) distinguishes between *emotive trust*, which includes an emotional component, and *capacity trust*, which centers on professional competence. While digitally mediated weak ties are helpful in the creation of capacity trust, they are considerably less useful in generating emotive trust, which relies on tacit information that is typically communicated face-to-face. Despite the increasing use of digital interactions, the creation of close interpersonal relations are never completely freed from the need for face-to-face contacts (Warf 1994; Stutzman 2006). In general, social media are a poor substitute for face-to-face ties, which are fundamental to the creation and transmission of what Storper and Venables (2004) call "buzz," the contextually specific dimensions of proximity and agglomeration. The reasons that face-to-face contact is so essential is that it permits body language (including handshakes, nonverbal gestures, and eye contact) and emotional cues, eliminates the possibility of anonymity that haunts digital encounters, and induces common feelings of belonging to a community that are prerequisite to the creation of trust, synergies, and mutual understandings that arise from dense networks of individuals in close contact with one another. As the considerable literature concerned with creativity, innovation, and competitiveness has demonstrated, networks that facilitate the exchange of unstandardized tacit knowledge are essential to the success of dynamic clusters, global cities, and post-Fordist centers of flexible production (Maskell and Malmberg 1999; Allen 2000). Florida's (2002) well-received notion of the "creative class" emphasizes the role of places in the creation of opportunities for both formal and informal interactions. In short, despite the often exaggerated rhetoric concerning the network society and digital technologies, face-to-face contacts are still an essential and fundamental part of contemporary economic and social life.

At the scale of the individual, digital media have changed "what a person can be" (Lanier 2010). The enormous enhancement of human extensibility offered by telemediated ties (Adams 2005) arguably has led to a far-reaching redefinition of the self: as social networks increasingly shift from a series of one-to-one ties to webs of one-to-many connections, weak ties have risen in importance the process of socialization. As a consequence, the geographies of everyday life have become greatly complicated, often involving complicated webs of interpersonal interactions filled by wormholes and tunnels, a notion that mirrors the rhyzomatic structure of the Internet and resembles the origami-like spatialities of post-structuralism (Murdoch 2006). Digital social media fold multiple spaces into the self, allowing "being at a distance." To the extent that weak digital ties reshape the self, they may blur the boundaries of the autonomous individual. Gergen (1991: 49) holds that this process generates the condition of "multiphrenia," "a world in which we no longer experience a secure sense of self, and in which doubt is increasingly placed on the very assumption of a bounded identity with palpable attributes." The post-structural subject, embedded in post-structural spaces and places, is located in multiple locations, and largely consists of an assemblage of interactions. Such a positionality allows people to present different sides of themselves to different audiences: a police officer may represent himself as a young girl in a chat room, or a corporate executive may live a secret double life online. In contrast to the modernist view of the subject, which holds it to be stable and coherent, the networked self consists of a pastiche of multiple selves, sometimes at odds with one another. As Jameson (1984: 63) put it, "the alienation of the subject is displaced by the fragmentation of the subject."

If digital media may be seen to blur the boundaries between the self and other, they also undermine the simple dichotomy between humans and machines, or to invoke the lingo of actor-network theory, between human and nonhuman actors (Latour 2007). Haraway's (1991) notion of cyborgs blurs the borders between bodies and machines, the natural and the artificial, as seamlessly integrated hybrids become increasingly widespread. Graham and Marvin (1996: 107) likewise noted that "Humans and machines (have) become fused in ways that make the old separations between technology and society, the real and the simulated, meaningless." In relying on digital networks, the post-structural subject becomes become part of a cybernetic system in which humans and nonhumans co-constitute one another.

As Diebert (1997: 182) notes, "the postmodern view of the self 'fits' the hypermedia environment – in ways that suggest it might resonate strongly as that environment deepens and expands." For example, the Internet has markedly changed traditional conceptions of what it means to be an author, allowing large numbers of people to become producers of information rather than simply its recipients, giving rise to what Ritzer and Jurgenson's (2010) call "prosumers" and what Bruns (2008) labels "produsage." Much of this change is due to the rise of Web 2.0, whose interactive capacities permit users to upload data and apply it in a manner tailored to their specific needs. Arguably, as Web 2.0 has produced large numbers of prosumers, it has generated a historically unprecedented democratization of knowledge. Criteria for truth change accordingly given the reliance on "crowd sourcing," which allows large, widely distributed groups to generate a common output (e.g. Wikipedia). However, this change has its costs as well, allowing information consumers to select only those sources that confirm their presuppositions and beliefs and never challenging them with alternative ideas.

An important difference between the networked self and its predigital counterpart is that digital media allow for a far greater degree of public visibility, decisively blurring the borders between public and private life. Increasingly, networked selves are performed in public. For many people, the digital, online self has become an extension of the nondigital, analog self; increasingly, it is difficult to separate these dimensions. Erving Goffman (1959) deployed a dramaturgical model to illustrate this idea, noting that everyone has a "front stage" as their public face. In this vein, Katz and Aakhus (2002) argue that mobile phone usage constitutes a public display of performance. Analogously, Facebook status updates publicize the details of private life on the Web. These digital selves are not passive reflections of the "real" person, they are an integral part of him or her, and reverberate to shape people's self-understandings. Digital social media form a version of a panopticon in which users monitor themselves to conform to the dictates and protocols of the Internet. Heavy users of Facebook, for example, micromanage their online presence. Little remains in this context of a purely private life when the public self is displayed so conspicuously in public (Debatin et al. 2009). In the age of Web 2.0, constructing and maintaining a digital self becomes an exercise in marketing, a means to affirm oneself in the eyes of friends, family, acquaintances, colleagues, and strangers (Livingstone and Brake 2010). There are, however, unsavory if unintended repercussions of this phenomenon: users who proudly post photos of themselves doing stupid or illegal activities, for example, may be chagrined to face future employers who use such material in their assessment of potential employees (Hill 2011; Waters 2011). For this reason, some users have begun to change their behavior off-line, as when college students on spring break curtail their typical wild partying for fear that pictures or videos of them may posted online and haunt them later (Alvarez 2012).

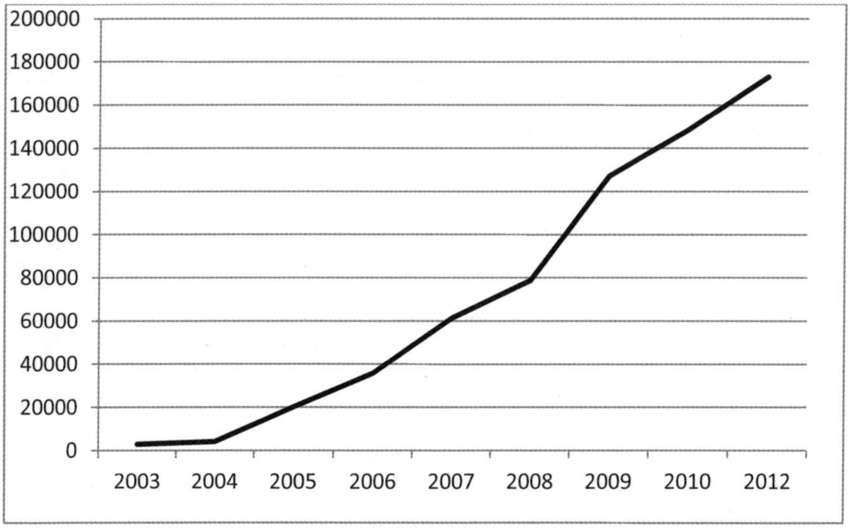

Figure 18.8 Growth in world's blogosphere, 2003–2011 (thousands of blogs)
Source: Author, redrawn from Technorati 2007 and SMI 2012

Another arena in which the digital, relational self unfolds is the blogosphere (Bruns 2008). The world saw roughly 173 million blogs in 2011 (Figure 18.8), and 30,000 more are added daily. Most bloggers are women, and half are under age 35 (SMI 2012). Like Facebook, blogs serve as vehicles for prosumers to post intimate material online, often with the options for readers to offer comments and feedback. Blogs and online forums may also allow anonymous comments, so that opinions expressed in them in many respects are more "real" than those conveyed face-to-face, in which the reputation of the speaker remains known and therefore vulnerable. An emerging literature on the geography of blogs has delved into the spatiality of this phenomenon (Gopal 2007). Frequently, blogs contain hyperlinks that connect them to other blogs, forming networks that vary widely in size and scope (Lin et al. 2007). As Fuller and Askins (2010) hold, blogs create "public geographies," or fleeting, transitory encounters with widely varying impacts. Some observers hold that blog networks can replicate the sorts of information that typically circulate through face-to-face contacts, allowing tacit knowledge to spread more rapidly and widely than ever before (Jones et al. 2010). Blogs thus are yet another vehicle by which digital capitalism blurs the boundaries between the private and the public, the local and the global, much as other digital communications have dissolved dualities such as economic/cultural, private/public, human/nonhuman, and local/global.

Finally, the very public visibility of the networked self raises serious concerns about digital privacy (Curry 1997; Kuzma 2011). Corporations that engage in data mining and targeted online advertising (e.g. Equifax Marketing) collect propitious volumes of information about individuals, including birth dates, incomes, favorite Web sites, and spending habits (Zook and Graham 2007). Political campaigns have begun to do the same. Large commercial or government datasets have been penetrated by hacker groups such as Anonymous or Germany's Chaos Computer Club, which steal tens of thousands of passwords at a time. The giant of search engines, Google, has been sued for using private information in services such as GoogleMaps (Gordon and de Souza e Silva 2011). Nor is abuse restricted to the private sector: Morozov (2011) gives disturbing examples of governments that use social media against their own citizens: Iran, for example, uses Facebook friends to arrest those who associate with known dissidents. Many social networking sites have become securitized (Pinkerton et al. 2011). The public digital data about private individuals reflects the panopticonic tendencies of contemporary capitalism to monitor and control their citizens' behavior, whether through recording of e-mail messages or closed circuit surveillance cameras, a process that Foucault would have no difficulty recognizing (Dobson and Fisher 2007).

Concluding Thoughts

Digital social media of one form or another, such as mobile phones, the Internet, Facebook, and blogs, are now used by the vast majority of the planet's population. Roughly two-thirds of the world uses mobile phones, one-third uses the Internet, and just over one-ninth subscribes to Facebook. Collectively, the human race now enjoys an historically unprecedented degree of connectivity. While Castells's (1996; 1997) view of the networked society emphasized interconnected elites – text messages, e-mail, Twitter, blogs, and Facebook allow substantial numbers of ordinary people to become linked with one another in ways never seen before. This state of affairs has emerged in an historical blink of an eye, and its implications have yet to be fully understood. One might argue that the telemediated self reflects the massive contemporary wave of time-space compression (Giddens 1991; Warf 2008). In a famous paper, Frederick Jameson (1984: 83) argued that postmodern hyperspace "has finally succeeded in transcending the capacities of the individual human body to locate itself, to organize its immediate surrounding perceptually, and cognitively to map its position in a mappable external world." Similarly, Massey (2005), in displacing the notion of place with that of networks and power-geometries, notes that the very meanings of "near" and "far" have themselves been profoundly transformed.

Undoubtedly, digital social networks have redefined the shape of human experience. Who is the digital individual when so much of one's identity circulates in computer networks beyond one's control? The relationality of digital spaces –that exist only by virtue of their interconnectedness – poses severe challenges to the long hegemony of the traditional Western model of the human subject: highly individualistic, lacking a body, and without social origins. Rather, the networked subject is explicitly relational: he or she exists only through ties to others, ties that are increasingly mediated digitally. Such a perspective problematizes the dichotomy between being "off-line" and "online," as many people exist in both simultaneously.

Digital ties can rarely offer the same degree of intimacy as face-to-face interactions, and thus are unlikely to lead to the creation of deep emotional experiences or the exchange of tacit knowledge. Social media, to use Granovetter's (1985) terminology, forge weak social ties rather than strong ones, meaning that networked individuals tend to have relations that are comparatively shallow, utilitarian, and transient. Although digital media allow for an unprecedented extension of the self over space, these interactions invariably reverberate to shape the self, requiring careful attention to one's online front stage. In the process, all users of digital media necessarily become cyborgs in which the boundaries between people and machines become so blurry that any difference is difficult to detect.

The rise of the networked, cyborgian subject is part and parcel of similar relational ontologies of place, a view that emphasizes the role of changing connections and interactions among locales (Massey 2005; Murdoch 2006; Jones 2009). Cheap, instantaneous, and ubiquitous digital media render obsolete the notion of place as a discreet, bounded entity; rather, people can be (albeit digitally) in several places simultaneously (Adams 2005). Thus Cosgrove (2008: 47) argues that "Places and landscapes are no longer thought of by geographers simply as bounded containers, but as constellations of connections that form, reform and disperse in space and over time." The geographies of relational space are fluid, mutable, and ever-changing (Abrams and Hall 2006). This line of thought has distinct parallels with the "flat ontology" of Delueze and Guattari, or geographies that are not bound by the insidious effects of scale (Marston et al. 2005). Similarly, globalization consists of relational spaces with a "fibrous, thread-like, wiry, stringy, ropy, capillary character that is never captured by the notions of levels, layers, territories, spheres, categories, structures, or systems" (Paasi 2004: 541).

Does place still matter in a relational, digitized, cyborgian world? Despite the hyperbole that digital media have conquered distance or rendered geography obsolete, physical location stubbornly remains important (Wellman 2001b; Papacharissi 2009; Gordon and de Souza e Silva 2011). Where a user's body is found, the ongoing significance of face-to-face ties, family, and local context, the digital divide in Internet access, and the spatiality of digital networks and the flows of information within them all attest to the enduring significance of place. A considerable geographical literature on embodiment has reflected on how bodies are sites of emotions and affect and are central to nuanced understandings of geopolitics (Nicley 2009), body-landscape relations (Macpherson 2010), aging (Antoninetti and Garrett 2012), and a host of other social phenomena. Why then, not also social media? By demonstrating the enduring power of location, even in an overwhelmingly digital age, this corpus of work points to the ongoing need to materialize the networked self, to ground it within prevailing social and cultural relations and spatial formations of which it is necessarily a part.

References

Abrams, J. and Hall, P. 2006. *Else/where: Mapping – New Cartographies of Networks and Territories.* Minneapolis: University of Minnesota Press.

Adams, P.C. 1995. A reconsideration of personal boundaries in space-time. *Annals of the Association of American Geographers* 85: 267–85.

Adams, P.C. 2005. *The Boundless Self: Communication in Physical and Virtual Spaces.* Syracuse: Syracuse University Press.

Allen, J. 2000. Power/economic knowledge: Symbolic and spatial formations. In *Knowledge, Space, Economy.* Edited by J. Bryson, P. Daniels, N. Henry, and J. Pollard. London: Routledge, 15–33.

Alvarez, L. 2012. Spring break gets tamer with world watching online. *New York Times*, March 16, 1.

Andrews, L. 2012. *I Know Who You Are and I Saw What You Did: Social Networks and the Death of Privacy*. New York: Free Press.

Antoninetti, M. and M. Garrett. 2012. Body capital and the geography of aging. *Area* 44(3): 364–70.

Arminen, I. 2007. Review essay: Mobile communication society. *Acta Sociologica* 50: 431–37.

Bolin, G. and O. Westlund. 2009. Mobile generations: The role of mobile technology in the shaping of Swedish media generations. *International Journal of Communication* 3: 108–24.

Bruns, A. 2008. *Blogs, Wikipedia, Second Life, and Beyond: From Production to Produsage.* New York: Peter Lang.

Butler, J. 1990. *Gender Trouble.* London and New York: Routledge.

Campbell, D. 2010. The new ecology of information: How the social media revolution challenges the university. *Environment and Planning D: Society and Space* 28: 193–201.
Campbell, S. and Y. Park. 2008. Social implications of mobile telephony: The rise of personal communication society. *Sociology Compass* 2(2): 371–87.
Carr, N. 2010. *The Shallows: What the Internet is Doing to Our Brains*. New York: W.W. Norton.
Castells, M. 1996. *The Information Age, Vol. I: The Rise of the Network Society*. Oxford: Blackwell.
Castells, M. 1997. *The Information Age, Vol. II: The Power of Identity*. Cambridge: Blackwell.
Castells, M. 2001. *The Internet Galaxy*. Oxford: Oxford University Press.
Chakraborty, J. and M. Bosman. 2005. Measuring the digital divide in the United States: Race, income, and personal computer ownership. *Professional Geographer* 57(3): 395–410.
Comer, J. and T. Wikle. 2008. Worldwide diffusion of the cellular phone, 1995–2005. *Professional Geographer* 60(2): 252–69.
Cooper, M., and B. Compaine (eds). 2001. *The Digital Divide*. Cambridge, MA: MIT Press.
Cosgrove, D. 2008. *Geography and Vision*. London and New York: I.B. Taurus.
Crang, M., T. Crosbie, and S. Graham. 2006. Variable geometries of connection: Urban digital divides and the uses of information technology. *Urban Studies* 43(13): 2551–70.
Curry, M. 1997. The digital individual and the private realm. *Annals of the Association of American Geographers* 87: 681–99.
Debatin, B., J. Lovejoy, A. Horn, and B. Hughes. 2009. Facebook and online privacy: Attitudes, behaviors, and unintended consequences. *Journal of Computer-Mediated Communication* 15(1): 83–108.
Deibert, R. 1997. *Parchment, Printing, and Hypermedia*. New York: Columbia University Press.
Dekimper, M., P. Parker, and M. Sarvary. 1998. Staged estimation of international diffusion models: an application to global cellular telephone adoption. *Technological Forecasting and Social Change* 57: 105–32.
Ding, L., K. Haynes, and H. Li. 2010. Modeling the spatial diffusion of mobile telephones in China. *Professional Geographer* 62(2): 248–63.
Dobson, J. and P. Fisher. 2007. The panopticon's changing geography. *Geographical Review* 97(3): 307–23.
Dodge, M. and R. Kitchin. 2005. Code and the transduction of space. *Annals of the Association of American Geographers* 95: 162–80.
Dong, Y. and M. Li. 2004. Mobile communications in China. *International Journal of Mobile Communications* 2(4): 395–404.
Donner, J. 2008. Research approaches to mobile use in the developing world: A review of the literature. *The Information Society* 24(3): 140–59.
Ellison, N., C. Steinfield, and C. Lampe. 2007. The benefits of Facebook "friends": Social capital and college students' use of online social network sites. *Journal of Computer-Mediated Communication* 12(4): 1143–68.
Ettlinger, N. 2003. Cultural economic geography and a relational and microspace approach to trusts, rationalities, networks and change in collaborative workplaces. *Journal of Economic Geography* 3: 145–71.
Farman, J. 2011. *Mobile Interface Theory: Embodied Space and Locative Media*. London: Routledge.
Fischer, C. 1992. *America Calling: A Social History of the Telephone to 1940*. Berkeley: University of California Press.
Florida, R. 2002. *The Rise of the Creative Class*. New York: Basic Books.
Fortunati, L. 2002. The mobile phone: Towards new categories and social relations. *Information, Communication, and Society* 5(4): 513–28.
Fuller, D. and K. Askins. 2010. Public geographies II: Being organic. *Progress in Human Geography* 34(5): 654–67.

Gergen, K. 1991. *The Saturated Self: Dilemmas of Identity in Contemporary Life*. New York: Basic Books.

Giddens, A. 1991. *Modernity and Self-identity: Self and Society in the Late Modern Age*. Stanford, CA: Stanford University Press.

Goffman, I. 1959. *The Presentation of Self in Everyday Life*. New York: Doubleday.

Goggin, C. 2006. *Cell Phone Culture: Mobile Technology in Everyday Life*. London: Routledge.

Goldfarb, A. and J. Prince. 2008. Internet adoption and usage patterns are different: Implications for the digital divide. *Information Economics and Policy* 20(1): 2–15.

Gopal, S. 2007. The evolving social geography of blogs. In *Societies and Cities in the Age of Instant Access*. Edited by H. Miller. Dordrecht: Springer, 275–93.

Gordon, E. and A. de Souza e Silva. 2011. *Net Locality: Why Location Matters in a Networked World*. New York: Wiley-Blackwell.

Graham, S. and S. Marvin. 1996. *Telecommunications and the City: Electronic Spaces, Urban Places*. London: Routledge.

Grannovetter, M. 1985. Economic action and social structure: The problem of embeddedness. *American Journal of Sociology* 91: 481–510.

Hampton, K. and Wellman, B. 2001. Long-distance community in the network society: Contact and support beyond netville. *American Behavioral Scientist* 45(3): 476–95.

Hampton, K., L. Goulet, L. Rainie, and K. Purcell. 2011. *Social Networking Sites and Our Lives: How People's Trust, Personal Relationships, and Civic and Political Involvement Are Connected to Their Use of Social Networking Sites and Other Technologies*. Washington, DC: Pew Research Center's Internet and American Life Project.

Haraway, D. 1991. *Simians, Cyborgs and Women: The Reinvention of Nature*. New York: Routledge.

Haythornthwaite, C. 2005. Social networks and Internet connectivity effects. *Information, Communication, & Society* 8(2): 125–47.

Hill, K. 2011. Will Facebook destroy your job search? *Forbes Magazine*, July 18. Available at: www.forbes.com/forbes/2011/0718/features-facebook-social-media-google-destroy-job-search.html (accessed April 20, 2012).

International Telecommunications Union. 2010. *The World in 2010*. www.itu.int/ITU-D/ict/material/FactsFigures2010.pdf.

Jackson, M. 2008. *Distracted: The Erosion of Attention and the Coming Dark Age*. Amherst, NY: Prometheus Books.

Jameson, F. 1984. Postmodernism, or the cultural logic of late capitalism. *New Left Review* 146: 53–92.

Jones, B., B. Spigel, and E. Malecki. 2010. Blog links as pipelines to buzz elsewhere: The case of New York theater blogs. *Environment and Planning B* 37: 99–111.

Jones, M. 2009. Phase space: Geography, relational thinking, and beyond. *Progress in Human Geography* 33(4): 487–506.

Katz, J. and M. Aakhus (eds). 2002. *Perpetual Contact: Mobile Communication, Private Talk, Public Performance*. Cambridge: Cambridge University Press.

Kellerman, A. 2002. *The Internet on Earth: A Geography of Information*. Hoboken, NJ: John Wiley.

Kellerman, A. 2010. Mobile broadband services and the availability of instant access to cyberspace. *Environment and Planning A* 42: 2990–3005.

Kirkpatrick, D. 2010. *The Facebook Effect: The Inside Story of the Company That Is Connecting the World*. New York: Simon and Schuster.

Korupp, S. and Szydlik, M. 2005. Causes and trends of the digital divide. *European Sociological Review* 21: 409–22.

Kuzma, 2011. Empirical Study of Privacy Issues among Social Networking Sites. *Journal of International Commercial Law and Technology* 6(2). www.jiclt.com/index.php/jiclt/article/viewFile/128/127.

Lanier, J. 2010. *You Are Not a Gadget: A Manifesto*. New York: Alfred A. Knopf.
Latour, B. 2007. *Reassembling the Social: An Introduction to Actor-Network Theory*. Oxford: Oxford University Press.
Lenhart, A., R. Ling, S. Campbell, and K. Purcell. 2010. *Teens and Mobile Phones*. Washington: Pew Internet & American Life Project. Available at: www.pewInternet.org/~/media/Files/Reports/2010/PIP-Teens-and-Mobile-2010-with-topline.pdf (accessed January 25, 2012).
Levy, P. 1997. *Collective Intelligence: Mankind's Emerging World in Cyberspace*. New York: Basic Books.
Li, F., S. Papagiannidis, and M. Bourlakis. 2010. Living in 'multiple spaces': Extending our socioeconomic environment through virtual worlds. *Environment and Planning D: Society and Space* 28(3): 425–46.
Lin, J., A. Halavais, and B. Zhang. 2007. The blog network in America: Blogs as indicators of relationships among US cities. *Connections* 27(2): 15–23. Available at: www.insna.org/PDF/Connections/v27/2006 1-2-3.pdf (accessed April 19, 2012).
Ling, R. 2004. *The Mobile Connection: The Cell Phone's Impact on Society*. San Francisco: Morgan Kaufmann.
Ling, R. 2010. *New Tech, New Ties: How Mobile Communication Is Reshaping Social Cohesion*. Cambridge, MA: MIT Press.
Ling, R. and J. Donner. 2009. *Mobile Phones and Mobile Communication*. Cambridge, UK: Polity Press.
Ling, R. and S. Campbell. 2009. The reconstruction of space and time through mobile communication practices. In *The Reconstruction of Space and Time: Mobile Communication Practices*. Edited by R. Ling and S. Campbell. New Brunswick, NJ: Transaction Publishers, 1–16.
Livingstone, S. and D. Brake. 2010. On the rapid rise of social networking sites: New findings and policy implications. *Children & Society* 24(1): 75–83.
Macpherson, H. 2010. Non-representational approaches to body–landscape relations. *Geography Compass* 4(1): 1–13.
Mäenpäa, P. 2001. Mobile communication as a way of urban life. In *Ordinary Consumption*. Edited by J. Gronow and A. Ward. London: Routledge, 107–24.
Marche, S. 2012. Is Facebook making us lonely? *The Atlantic,* May. Available at: www.theatlantic.com/magazine/archive/2012/05/is-facebook-making-us-lonely/8930/ (accessed April 22, 2012).
Marston S., J.P. Jones, and K. Woodward. 2005. Human geography without scale. *Transactions of the Institute of British Geographers* 30: 416–32.
Maskell, P. and A. Malmberg. 1999. The competitiveness of firms and regions: ubiquitification and the importance of localized learning. *European Urban and Regional Studies* 6(1): 9–25.
Massey, D. 2005. *For Space,* London: SAGE.
Miller, C. 2007. Class war: MySpace vs. Facebook. Forbes.com. www.forbes.com/2007/07/20/facebook-myspace-Internet-tech-cz_ccm_0723class.html.
Mills, B. and B. Whitacre. 2003. Understanding the non-metropolitan–metropolitan digital divide. *Growth and Change* 34(2): 219–43.
Morozov, E. 2011. *The Net Delusion: The Dark Side of Internet Freedom*. New York: PublicAffairs.
Murdoch, J. 2006. *Post-structuralist Geography: A Guide to Relational Space*. London: SAGE.
Nicley, E. 2009. Placing blame or blaming place? Embodiment, place and materiality in critical geopolitics. *Political Geography* 28(1): 19–22.
Nie, N. 2001. Sociability, interpersonal relations, and the Internet: Reconciling conflicting findings. *American Behavioral Scientist* 45(3): 420–35.
Paasi A. 2004. Place and region: Looking through the prism of scale. *Progress in Human Geography* 28: 536–46.

Pain, R., S. Grundy, S. Gill, E. Towner, G. Sparks, K. and Hughes. 2005. "So long as I take my mobile": Mobile phones, urban life and geographies of young people's safety. *International Journal of Urban and Regional Research* 29: 814–30.

Papacharissi, Z. 2009. The virtual geographies of social networks: A comparative analysis of Facebook, LinkedIn and ASmallWorld. *New Media & Society* 11(1–2): 199–220.

Papacharissi, Z. (ed.). 2010. *A Networked Self: Identity, Community, and Culture on Social Network Sites*. London and New York: Routledge.

Pile, S. 2008. Where is the subject? Geographical imaginations and spatializing subjectivity. *Subjectivity* 23: 206–18.

Pinkerton, A., S. Young, and K. Dodds. 2011. Weapons of mass communication: The securitization of social networking sites. *Political Geography* 30(3): 115–17.

Postman, N. 1985. *Amusing Ourselves to Death: Public Discourse in the Age of Show Business*. New York: Viking.

Putnam, H. 1981. *Reason, Truth, and History*. Cambridge: Cambridge University Press.

Radicati, S. 2012. Email statistics report, 2012–2016. www.radicati.com/wp/wp-content/uploads/2012/04/Email-Statistics-Report-2012-2016-Executive-Summary.pdf.

Ritzer, G. and N. Jurgenson. 2010. Production, consumption, prosumption: the nature of capitalism in the age of the digital 'prosumer.' *Journal of Consumer Culture* 10(1): 13–26.

Rodzvilla, J. (ed.). 2002. *We've Got Blog: How Weblogs Are Changing Our Culture*. New York: Basic Books.

Sheppard, E. 2002. The spaces and times of globalization: place, scale, networks, and positionality. *Economic Geography* 78: 307–30.

Social Media Influence. 2012. www.socialmediainfluence.com/2012/03/09/the-newest-threat-to-blogging-yep-pinterest (accessed April 20, 2012).

Sooryamoorthy, R., B. Miller, W. and Shrum. 2011. Untangling the technology cluster: Mobile telephony, Internet use and the location of social ties. *New Media and Society* 13: 391–410.

Stevens, D. 2006. Inequality.com: Money, Power and the Digital Divide. Oxford: Oneworld Publications.

Storper, M. and A. Venables. 2004. Buzz: Face-to-face contact and the urban economy. *Journal of Economic Geography* 4: 351–70.

Stutzman, F. 2006. An evaluation of identity-sharing behavior in social network communities. *Journal of the International Digital Media and Arts Association* 3(1): 10–18.

Thompson, L. and J. Cupples. 2008. Seen and not heard? Text messaging and digital sociality. *Social and Cultural Geography* 9(1): 95–108.

Thrift, N. and S. French. 2002. The automatic production of space. *Transactions of the Institute of British Geographers* 27: 309–35.

Tong, S., B. Van Der Heide, L. Langwell, and J. Walther. 2008. Too much of a good thing? The relationship between number of friends and interpersonal impressions on Facebook. *Journal of Computer-Mediated Communication* 13(3): 531–49.

Townsend, A. 2000. Life in the real-time city: Mobile telephones and urban metabolism. *Journal of Urban Technology* 7(2): 85–104.

Turkle, S. 1997. *Life on the Screen: Identity in the Age of the Internet*. New York: Touchstone.

Turkle, S. 2011. *Alone Together: Why We Expect More from Technology and Less from Each Other.* New York: Basic Books.

Valentine, G. and S. Holloway. 2002. Cyberkids? Exploring children's identities and social networks in online and off-line worlds. *Annals of the Association of American Geographers* 92(2): 302–19.

Vasalou, A., A. Joinson, and D. Courvoisier. 2010. Cultural differences, experience with social networks and the nature of "true commitment" in Facebook. *International Journal of Human-Computer Studies* 68(10): 719–28.

Warf, B. 1994. Structuration theory and electronic communications. In *Marginalized Places and Populations: A Structurationist Agenda.* Edited by D. Wilson and J. Huff. Westport, CT: Greenwood.

Warf, B. 2008. *Time-space Compression: Historical Geographies*. London and New York: Routledge.

Waters, J. 2011. Could you pass a Facebook background check? *Wall Street Journal,* July 25. Available at: www.articles.marketwatch.com/2011-07-25/finance/30745971_1_employers-pictures-and-comments-party-pictures (accessed April 19, 2012).

Webber, M. 1973. Urbanization and communications. In *Communications Technology and Social Policy.* Edited by G. Gerbner, L. Gross, and W. Melody. New York: Wiley, 293–304.

Wellman B. 2001a. Computer networks as social networks. *Science* 243: 2031–34.

Wellman, B. 2001b. Physical place and cyberplace: The rise of personalized networking. *International Journal of Urban and Regional Research* 25(2): 227–52.

Whatmore, S. 1997. Dissecting the autonomous self: Hybrid cartographics for a relational ethics. *Environment and Planning D: Society and Space* 15: 37–53.

Zook, M. and M. Graham. 2007. The creative reconstruction of the Internet: Google and the privatization of cyberspace and digiPlace. *Geoforum* 38: 1322–43.

Spaces of Volunteered Geographic Information

Ate Poorthuis and Matthew Zook

Open any recent geography article or book that discusses the Internet and you will find the opening sentences replete with the terms *new, change, proliferation* and *recent*. Apparently, something is brewing in digital space that makes geographers very excited. Clichés aside, it is clear that many of the most recent additions to the online world (e.g. Google Maps, Wikipedia, OpenStreetMap, Twitter) represent important changes to how we can think about spatial information and mapping practice as well as provide new ways for us to use and understand the space and places around us. Since this is a relatively recent phenomenon, there are a number of competing names for this process, including volunteered geographic information (VGI), neogeography, and the geoweb. While each term differs in what issues it emphasizes, they all seek to characterize the emerging and evolving ways in which space and place are practiced in the twenty-first century. While we are not entirely satisfied with any single term, we will use VGI in this chapter as it has the virtue of being an early, and thus widely used, term.

This chapter provides an overview of the onset and recent history of VGI and its effect on both spatial knowledge production and how we use and understand the space around us. Central to this review is a characterization of VGI as an integral part of already social spaces rather than as a separate layer "on top of" these spaces. Toward this end, it explores questions such as How does a Web site like Google Maps really change the way we live our everyday life? What does Wikipedia have to do with how we think about spatial knowledge? How are our understandings over places changing in concert with VGI? We review both applications of VGI in practice as well as how VGI is employed to study space and place. As noted already, VGI is not without its critiques and an overview would not be complete without trying to succinctly summarize the main issues and critiques of VGI.

The Genealogy of VGI

> You. Yes, you. You control the Information Age. Welcome to your world
> (*Time* 2006)

In the early days of the Internet, the Web was an amalgam of hyperlinked but fairly static pages. For most Internet users, the Web was largely a space of consumption, although some opportunities for creating personal content (e.g. hosting platforms such as Geocities) were available. This changed significantly in the early 2000s. A number of new technologies (e.g. Ajax, Flash, browser standardization) paved the way for the emergence of more interactive and user-driven practices of online content creation, commonly referred to as Web 2.0. Within this "new" version of the Web, users write their own blogs, comment on *New York Times* articles, hang out on social networks like Facebook, upload videos to YouTube, and share links to interesting sites via social bookmarking services. In short, the Web moved from a static space of largely top-down content production to a space where anyone with access can produce content via a dynamic web of ever-changing sites. Perhaps this change is best illustrated by *TIME* magazine's Person of the Year issue of 2006 where "You" was chosen as the most important person of the year.

However, this new Web brought more than just a shift in the sources of online content: it also made possible the incorporation of geospatial technologies within Internet applications. With sites and services such as Google Maps (released to the public in 2005) and low-cost GPS units (often integrated in mobile phones), it has become increasingly easy for users to make maps or produce spatially referenced data (e.g. geotagged photos and tweets). Turner coined this phenomenon "neogeography" and wrote one of the first do-it-yourself (DIY) manuals that outlined how Internet users could produce their own maps, create new mashups, and geotag their holiday pictures (Turner 2006). This kind of DIY process of data collection and spatial representation was something different. Before, making maps was squarely within the realm of the academic disciplines of cartography and geographic information systems (GIS). Now, producing maps and creating geographic information was no longer the exclusive domain of professionals but could be performed by anyone with access to a computer and an Internet connection. That was, at least, the narrative presented by conferences like O'Reilly's Where 2.0, which quickly became a standard for the emerging mapping technology community.

It is unsurprising that this new phenomenon quickly caught the attention of academia as well. Although others have written about the geospatial web before (Maguire and Longley 2005; Miller 2006; Zook and Graham 2007; Harvey 2007; Gorman 2007), it was Goodchild (2007) who coined the term *volunteered geographic information*, referring to the large numbers of ordinary citizens who provide all of this geographic information on a largely voluntary basis. Others referred to it as the Wikification of GIS (Sui 2008) or simply the geospatial web or geoweb (Elwood 2008). While none of these terms are perfect, we consistently use VGI throughout this chapter to retain clarity. However, we agree that the term *volunteered* geographic information is problematic as the voluntary basis of large amounts of geospatial information is questionable since, for example, not everybody might realize their smartphone is reporting locational data to the geoweb (Leszynski 2012).

Having explored the short genealogy of VGI, we turn to the significance of the phenomenon. Why did VGI turn out to be so important? The answer to this question is twofold, depending on two key (albeit not mutually exclusive) conceptualizations of VGI – data versus practice. First, if we think of VGI *as data*, an argument can be made that it is changing the way knowledge is produced in that a much larger group of (amateur) citizens have the opportunity to participate. While these opportunities remain shaded by long-standing societal divisions of class, gender, and race, the process of VGI as data production does change the traditional producer-consumer dichotomy. However, it also changes the sheer volume of data produced and how we make sense of it (i.e. the phenomenon of big data). The second conceptualization views VGI as not only information but as a platform that enables very specific phenomena or practices – for example, the role of Twitter in organizing the Occupy movement or the act of "checking in" to places via the social media services of Foursquare or Facebook. It is apparent that VGI is providing a means to reshape our everyday life as well. In geographic terms, VGI is changing the *space* we live in and how we perceive and produce the *places* that are meaningful to us. In the next section, we elaborate on the conceptualization of VGI as data and practice and explore the key ways in which they influence the organization of society and space.

VGI as Data: Changing Epistemologies

Although VGI has brought the concept of knowledge production by citizens under the attention of a wider audience, the concept itself is not new. While geographic knowledge has traditionally been produced by "experts" (e.g. the state or professional cartographers [Scott 1998; Harley 1989]), since the early 1990s critical geographers have engaged in a debate very much concerned with the interconnection between spatial technology and society (Pickles 1995; Sheppard 1993; Schuurman 2006; Sheppard 2005). One of several outcomes of this debate is public participatory GIS (PPGIS), which specifically emphasizes the importance of local knowledge and strives to use technology in a bottom-up, empowering and – naturally – participatory way (Sieber 2006). For example, Harris and Weiner (2002) outline the ways in which participatory GIS was used in South Africa to determine suitability of land for agriculture and the existence of forced removal during the apartheid: it turns out there are significant discrepancies between the "official" state data and data produced by white and black farmers.

There are many parallels between the emergence of VGI and the older discussion around knowledge production in GIS. Neogeography – a term often used interchangeably with VGI – implicitly places this new technology and its users against the old – *paleo* – GIScientists. Now anybody can use and produce geographic information. Likewise, when Goodchild coined the term *volunteered geographic information*, he emphasized,

> *[L]arge numbers of private citizens, often with little in the way of formal qualifications, [engage] in the creation of geographic information, a function that for centuries has been reserved to official agencies. They are largely untrained and their actions are almost always voluntary, and the results may or may not be accurate. But collectively, they represent a dramatic innovation that will certainly have profound impacts on geographic information systems (GIS) and more generally on the discipline of geography and its relationship to the general public. I term this volunteered geographic information (VGI). (Goodchild 2007)*

Although not explicitly stated by Goodchild, who focused more on user generated data for scientific studies such as citizen bird counts, the phenomenon of VGI means that most computer-literate citizens can now produce simple maps (mashups) ranging from general themes such as census data in one's neighborhood to personal maps of one's restaurant check-ins in previous years. If a street in a neighborhood is missing on Google Maps, a new street can be drawn in and uploaded to Google – by a private citizen, without expert knowledge or software. In short, VGI has allowed Internet users to move from simply being consumers of spatial information to also playing a role in the conscious and direct production of this data.

Moreover, and somewhat paradoxically, VGI also gave rise to the birth of what is often called "big data" based on the unconscious (and largely unseen) construction of vast amounts of spatial data on everyday life. All those check-ins, tweets, photos, and blog posts together produce billions and billions of data points each day and spatial or geographic information is a subset of this data. For example, the Library of Congress started archiving tweets in 2010 and their archive reached 170 billion tweets in early 2013, and it is still growing by half a billion data points each day (LoC 2013). However, while tweets (and other content) are made on a voluntary basis by private citizens, the ability to access this data – particularly in the aggregate to look for trends across society – remains elusive for legal and technical reasons. Even for the Library of Congress, the sheer size of the Twitter database created a tough nut to crack: although they are storing all that data, they have no way to effectively search, analyze, and use that data as of yet. As a result, big data research with VGI data has evolved into an industry dominated by technology experts (cf. IBM's Smarter Cities initiative) rather than geographers.

Within the social sciences, big data jump-started a turn to "computational" social science (Lazer et al. 2009; Torrens 2010). While research in the social sciences has often been hypothesis-driven, the onset of big data has increased the visibility of data-driven research. As the idea is often expressed, one only needs a large set of data, computational power, and some algorithms to uncover patterns already present within the data but hidden from plain sight. Take the case of a researcher interested in gentrification. A traditional urban geographer would operate under a certain hypothesis – say, cupcake shops and eyebrow-threading salons are first-wave predictors of gentrification in a neighborhood – collect data, and then empirically test that hypothesis and, if necessary, amend the existing theory. In the big data example, one could collect an amalgam of traditional (census) data and several VGI sources (e.g. Facebook, Twitter, Flickr). A data-driven approach would start from the data and look to uncover patterns within the data. One result might be that cupcakes, eyebrow-threading, and gentrification indeed go hand in hand but it might just as well uncover that plaid-patterned clothing is a much better predictor. Thus instead of testing existing theories, analysis of VGI data could generate new theories. This has led some to believe that, since the data is there, researchers only have to "dive in" (Miller 2010). Without taking sides in this debate, it is clear that analyzing the large VGI data sets presents significant analytical and technical challenges that belie the voluntary and amateur character of VGI: it requires tremendous resources and expertise to use and analyze big data.

So far we have looked at VGI as *data*. One can also conceptualize VGI as a process or social practice (Elwood et al. 2012). This perspective does not focus on the resulting product – data – but rather on the circumstances and processes of its production. From this perspective, a whole range of other important questions surface: Who is, and who is not, included in the making of VGI? What is represented through VGI and what can possibly be represented? And in what ways is the production of VGI interconnected with society at large? In the next sections, we explore the perspective of VGI as a process in more detail.

VGI as the Practice of Code/Space: Changing Space and Spatial Ontologies

VGI is part of a larger process of the interaction between information and communications technology (ICTs) and society that began with the first electronic computers of the 1940s and took network form when the first ARPANET computers were linked together in 1969. It would take until the early 1990s before the Internet would reach significant momentum in the Global North and yet another decade before the Internet would become ubiquitous and pervasive throughout most of the world. VGI is thus only the latest manifestation in a long line of significant technologies that have emerged and influence the sociospatial construction of our world. Unsurprisingly, since the late 1980s innumerable authors have analyzed and theorized on how the onset of the Internet and other information and communication technology is altering, amending, or perpetuating space. Whether it is called digital, virtual, or cyberspace[1] – the concept originates in fiction (cf. Gibson 1984) but has a long lineage in geography, from Castells (1996) and Harvey (1989) to the most recent work of Kitchin and Dodge (2011).

Interestingly, it was 1974 – the same year that Lefebvre wrote his well-known thesis on the production of space – when the term *Internet* surfaced. Without diving into a deep discussion of Lefebvre's thinking on space, it is important to touch briefly on two key points, as his conceptualization forms the basis for many contemporary thinkers on (cyber-)space of any kind. Lefebvre was one of the first authors to break away from the notion of space as some kind of abstract, empty container and assert that space is non-Euclidean. Instead of thinking of space as a container holding "things," Lefebvre argued that space is produced. Space as a product is never final. Space is produced, consumed, and reproduced in a never-ending and iterative process. As such, it is not the final product that is of interest but the process of the production of space. We should thus shift the focus of our attention away from "things in space" and toward "the actual production of space."

Adding to that (arguably already-confusing) redefinition of space is Lefebvre's somewhat tautological examination of the multiplicity of space: "We are confronted not by one social space but by many – indeed an unlimited multiplicity or uncountable set of social spaces which we refer to generically as 'social space'" (Lefebvre 1992: 86). Social space is thus an amalgam of countless social spaces. It becomes clear that space is a messy process – a mess that we try to tidy up by fitting space into neat analytical concepts. With this conception, Lefebvre likens social space to the flaky mille-feuille pastry. This delicious French treat has thousands of layers of crumbling pastry – so many that it becomes almost impossible to distinguish individual layers. Layers of pastry are interchanged with layers of cream or jam that are often oozing into the pastry itself, creating a pastry as intricate – dare we say messy? – as social space itself (see Figure 19.1). It is within this social space that VGI is practiced and produced. In fact, VGI is an integral part of the production of social space.

This conceptualization of VGI as part of an interconnected and messy layering of space stands in stark contrast to earlier visions of digital space. A large part of the early thinking on cyberspace and its consequences can be labeled as "naive" with hindsight. Many thinkers, especially in the popular media, assumed the Internet would make geographical differences smaller and smaller. Even relatively recently, the oft-cited Friedman (2007) defends this idea in his world-is-flat-thesis. A decade before Friedman, Cairncross (1997) made a similar claim: not only does history end (as Fukuyama claimed, 1992), the death of distance is near. After humankind gets rid of distance, telecommunications and the free market will dissolve the differences between rich and poor; between small and large. Unfortunately for those affected by these differences, distances, and geographies, geographers as varied as Harvey (2006) and Florida (2009) have shown otherwise in the last 15 years.

This death-of-distance discourse in popular media is closely related to what Graham (1998) calls the substitution perspective on cyberspace. It argues that territoriality and place are replaced by new technologies: cyberspace is thus replacing "human" space. This perspective is often used when people feel that progress is endangering how society used to function. Progress, in their eyes, leads to placelessness. Tuan shared this fear as well. In describing the sense of place of a "high-salaried executive," he writes, "He moves about so much that places for him tend to lose their special character" (Tuan 1977: 183). We see similar sentiments in Relph's discussion of place versus placelessness (Relph 1976) and Augé's nonplaces (1995). This is a fear that modernism leads to places that are wholly disconnected from the social fabric in which they are located: the strip mall, fast-food restaurant, or Disneyland.

[1] We do not prefer one over the other and will use digital, virtual, and cyberspace interchangeably throughout this chapter.

Figure 19.1 Space as a mille-feuille
Source: Photo by huppypie (www.flickr.com/people/huppypie/), Creative Commons license

In this case, online communities are alleged to form a complete substitute for the sense of belonging that place offers (Dodge and Kitchin 2001). Buliung (2011) alludes to this when he warns for a possible "extinction of experience" as a result of the virtual. But the phenomenon of VGI shows the problematic nature of that limited understanding of cyberspace. Place is very much alive – we only have to think of the digital cities of the 1990s, the place-based review sites of the early 2000s (e.g. Yelp, Google Maps), the hyperlocal social network sites (Foursquare, Facebook Places), and the augmented reality applications of the late 2000s (Billinghurst et al. 2014). Technology might change our sense of place but it nevers removes it completely. Instead, it mediates, alters, and augments our place-based experiences.

A much richer approach to cyberspace is what Graham terms "co-evolution": digital space and "real" material space produced in parallel and interactive processes. This dualism is present in Castells's (1996) thesis on the space of flows and the space of place – although he saw the space of flows overshadowing the space of places thus also echoing a bit of the substitution perspective. In both perspectives, digital place is another layer of space on top of preexisting, multiple layers of material space with less emphasis on the interactions between layers of virtual and material space than in our Lefebvrian view of VGI. In part this reflects the practice of cyberspace in the 1990s as a consumptive space rather than the more user-produced phenomenon of the Web 2.0 era. As a result, the coevolution conceptualization is more akin to a neatly layered cake such as *Spekkoek* where the layers are distinct and easily separate (see Figure 19.2) than to Lefebvre's intricately messy mille-feuille pastry.

This view on cyberspace was tied in part to the invisibility of cyberspace and the technology that enables it (although both Graham and Castells were well aware of this issue). Fiber-optic cables are buried underground and server's rooms are tucked away in nondescript buildings. It is hard to imagine that something one cannot see has links to what one can see. In 1996 Benedikt, an architect with an interest in cyberspace, asked, "One wonders why virtual worlds to this day look so similar to ours, then, rather than to the one envisaged by William Gibson in 1984 and 1986 and which he called 'cyberspace'" (Benedikt 2008 [1996]). That is a very valid question. If cyberspace is indeed disconnected from material space, why

Figure 19.2 Space as a layered cake (Indonesian/Dutch Spekkoek)
Source: Photo by Fabio Bruna, used under a Creative Commons Attribution-ShareAlike license: www.creativecommons.org/licenses/by-sa/3.0/

does it look so similar? The answer is, of course, simple. Cyberspace and material space are, in fact, interconnected. Graham (1998) terms this the recombination perspective. "The net cannot float free of conventional geography" (Hayes 1997 quoted in Zook et al. 2004). Virtual worlds are so similar to material worlds because it is impossible for us to completely disconnect from the material in which we are embedded. The social, cultural, and economic processes that we are part of shape the virtual space that we create. While separate layers, material space and digital space are overlapping in many ways and as such are best labeled hybrid spaces (see Figure 19.3).

The first scholars to explore the interactions between the material and the digital disagreed with the world-is-flat thesis of Friedman (2007) and were highly skeptical of the "technology as the great democratic leveler" thesis. In fact, they pointed out that, just like space itself, cyberspace is not free of power relations and hierarchies (Sheppard 2002). Cyberspace does not provide an opportunity to level the playing field, as is often thought, since access to cyberspace is not uniformly distributed. Cyberspace is unable to free itself of social, geographical, and historical constraints because new technologies are heavily embedded exactly within society, geography, and history. This is nothing new and is similar to the advent of other new communication technologies like telegraphy, radio, and telephony (Hugill 1999; Perkins and Neumayer 2009).

> *Like other telecommunications systems, the Internet is a social product, interwoven with relations of class, race, and gender, and inescapably subject to the uses and misuses of power. Telecommunications are not inherently emancipatory, freeing people from "the tyranny of distance," as they can be used to monitor everyday life, including credit cards, visas and passports, tax records, medical data, police reports, telephone calls, utility records, automobile registration, crime statistics, and sales receipts. (Warf 2001)*

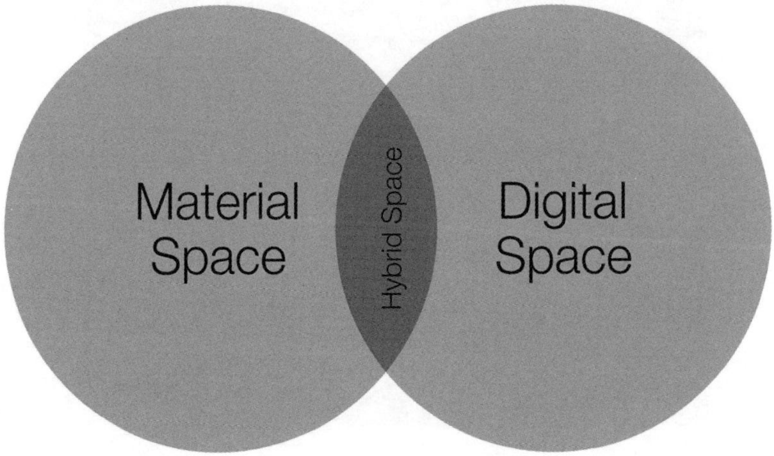

Figure 19.3 Overlapping material and digital space, yielding hybrid space
Source: Author illustration

Kluitenberg (2006) calls the overlapping parts "hybrid" space, where the "traditional" space is superimposed with a virtual space but the superimposition then fosters connections between the two. He gives the example of the flashmob – organized within the virtual through e-mails and text messages and then materializing and changing "real" public space when people – completely orchestrated through the virtual – synchronize their actions in the material. For those unaware of the virtual orchestration, the flashmob is difficult to explain, as its origin cannot be "seen" within the material.

Zook and Graham (2007) coin a different term for a similar concept. To capture the fact that material space impacts the digital and vice versa, they use the term "Digiplace." "DigiPlace is the understanding of a location based on and filtered through information about a place that is available in cyberspace" (468). They argue that Google Maps (particularly the way in which data about places is coded) creates variation within these Digiplaces. For example, searching for "gay and lesbian service organizations" yields more than 200 results in New York City but only two results are shown in San Francisco. While this result is unexpected (given the prominent nature of San Francisco's gay culture), it is an artifact of Google's labeling system; that is, removing the term "service" from the search produces many more results. Thus, representation of places is increasingly tied to the vagaries of online data and software associated with VGI.

Kitchin and Dodge (2011) go yet a step further. Relabeling the blending of material and digital space as code/space, they introduce the concept of transduction: the idea that space is continuously made and remade in a reiterative and transformative process. Similar to Lefebvre, they argue that space is not a fixed or static container but a process. Space continuously *becomes* through transduction. They add on to Lefebvre in saying that this process is often mediated through the digital – through *code*. Code/space emerges when software and space become mutually constituted in this process of transduction. Space, then, produces code and code in turn produces space. This takes the concept of "code is law" (Lessig 1999) one step further. In his thinking on the regulations in cyberspace, Lessig

Figure 19.4 Google Glass prototype
Source: www.en.wikipedia.org/wiki/File:Google_Glass_detail.jpg. Photo by Loic Le Meur. Used under a Creative Commons Attribution-ShareAlike license, www.creativecommons.org/licenses/by-sa/3.0/

was quick to see that it was certainly not the unregulated, free place people sometimes wish it would be. He draws a parallel with a "real" constitution[2] and argues that constitutions are never founded. Instead, they emerge, evolve, and get built in an incremental way. In the same way, it is code (both software and hardware) that regulates cyberspace. The novelty in Kitchin and Dodge's argument is that they not only acknowledge that code is "law" within the digital but also *outside* of the digital realm. Code can fundamentally change the material space we live in. For example, checking passengers into a flight is now completely dependent on software and the check-in space would fundamentally change if the software stops working (i.e. checking in and flying would become temporarily impossible).

From this theoretical discussion, it becomes undeniably clear that the material and the digital are indeed interwoven – be it via VGI data or VGI practice. While names for this interconnection abound – hybrid space, Digiplace, or code/space – what really matters is how volunteered geographic information impacts (the research of) our everyday lived spaces.

New Experiential Spaces of VGI

The data and practice of VGI are helping to create new experiential spaces in our day-to-day life. For example, Google's Project Glass prototypes show how daily reality might be *augmented* by a variety of digital information – ranging from bus schedules to Yelp reviews – via a pair of glasses! (See Figure 19.4.) Although the exact design of Google's futuristic project remains in development and beta testing, one does not have to look far to see how VGI interacts with daily life.

[2] A constitution here is more than just a legal text but refers to an architecture, as Lessig calls it, "that structures and constrains legal and social power" (Lessing, 1999: 5).

A striking example is the emergence of spontaneous parties or raves inspired by the Hollywood movie *Project X*. The plot of the movie centers around three high school friends who hope to become popular by throwing a party. Afraid nobody will show up, they even spread invitations on Craigslist. Of course, as word of the party spreads, things get completely out of hand. Although fictional, the concept has also occurred in real life. The basic premise is always the same: invitations are spread privately through social media but somehow go viral, too many people show up, and the event gets out of hand. A notable instance happened in the small Dutch town of Haren, where thousands of people came to a sweet-sixteen party when the girl who created the invitation forgot to set her Facebook event to "private." The results: 30 people were wounded and, after riots broke out, the town suffered millions of euros worth of damage (NOS 2012). Another example, from the city of Rotterdam, was a fake threat that was retweeted more than 500,000 times in a few hours, causing an entire shopping mall to empty out in panic (Kouwenhoven 2012). While not as flashy as Project Glass, the examples highlight how the digital is a tightly integrated part of the materiality of daily life.

Moreover, the number of interactions between the material and digital spheres is increasing. An average smartphone user might interact with hundreds of instances of VGI data and practice in a single day. Over breakfast on Monday, she might check the current traffic conditions on her commute as reported by thousands of other commuters automatically through their GPS navigating device. If an unexpected traffic jam arises en route, her device can even reroute her to a less busy road. On arrival at work, she updates her status on Facebook while attaching her work location. For lunch, she decides to try out a new restaurant and looks for well-reviewed restaurants nearby through Yelp. After work she uses a combination of Twitter, Facebook, and Foursquare to see where her friends are at that moment and arrange a meetup. She might even organize a date through one of the location-aware dating apps on her phone. Although not everybody is as connected as the woman in this example, it is easy to see that we do not need to be directly connected to some kind of VGI to be affected. For example, a rave review of a small restaurant, whose proprietor does not even know how to use a computer, could significantly impact the owner's life.

New Epistemologies of Applied VGI

Apart from using VGI in our personal lives, it can be used in a wide variety of other contexts ranging from purely academic research to city planning and crisis management. In urban planning, citizen participation has been a classic concern (cf. Arnstein 1969) and is often solicited through town hall meetings and surveys focus groups. Seeger (2008) describes how VGI – or what he calls "facilitated" VGI – can be used in the same context. Online interfaces can be used to solicit information on safe bike routes, placement of additional park benches, or georeferenced comments to design plans. Foth et al. (2009) even went as far as using the virtual reality world of *Second Life* as a complement to traditional community engagement strategies. On a larger scale, the "smart city" movement deploys VGI as one of the components in its promise to improve cities through the "smart" use of technology and data. Although it is easy to critique an overly technologically driven approach, the use of VGI in smart city projects –using citizens as sensors – might be of significant value for urban policy input.

In addition to government applications, VGI has been used in a number of other contexts, ranging from market research to monitoring of small-scale tourism (Brown and Weber 2012). In these more commercial settings, one could also argue that VGI constitutes free labor, often co-opted by commercial enterprise. Leszcynski (2012) theorizes specifically how the onset of VGI fits in the general process of the state "rolling back" from and market forces "rolling out" into the sphere of spatial information. Indeed, as private citizens can now create and update maps of their neighborhood (cf. OpenStreetMap and Google MapMaker), they are also specifically providing free labor for a task that would have traditionally be carried out by the state or paid company employees.

However, the applied use of VGI is most often heralded in crisis mapping or management. As the technologies behind VGI have made it much easier and faster to make and disseminate maps online, this is a powerful tool in times of crisis for local authorities, media, and NGOs alike. When destructive fires hit Southern California in 2007, several local media launched online maps that communicated the extent of the fire, evacuation notices, and other important news. The maps were updated every few minutes and informed millions of people with up-to-date information in a way that traditional media could not (Roche et al. 2011). Even though these maps made use of what we may term VGI-technology, they were still largely made in a top-down manner without the possibility of input from private citizens.

This changed with the introduction of platforms such as Ushahidi that provide more opportunities for Web 2.0 interaction. Ushahidi is an information-gathering platform that can be used by anybody to put specific information or testimonies "on the map" in times of crisis. It has been used during the earthquake in Haiti, violence in Palestine, and elections in Mexico. Anybody can add information to the map through the Web, e-mail, or text messages and the aggregated information can be used by individuals as well as local authorities that need to coordinate the crisis response. During the aftermath of the 2010 earthquake in Haiti, more than 3,000 testimonies were posted on Ushahidi, ranging from reports of people buried in the rubble to missing person reports (see Figure 19.5 below). One of the challenges for rescue workers on the ground was the lack of a good street map of Port-au-Prince. When you get a report of an incident on Rue Charlemagne, how does that information help you when you do not know how to get there? Additionally, existing maps were not accurate anymore, as the earthquake had destroyed parts of the local infrastructure. The OpenStreetMap community rose to that challenge and worked together to provide a complete basemap of the capital in a matter of days. Volunteers from around the world were tracing the latest satellite imagery to get up-to-date maps to the GPS units of the rescue workers on the ground (Roche at al. 2011; Zook et al. 2010).

In addition to the new experiential and epistemological dimensions of VGI, it is also important to understand how we might approach the spaces of VGI as a research object. In our theoretical discussion, we established that VGI has led to new spaces – a blend of the physical and the digital. But setting theory aside, what are these spaces like and how do we study them?

Graham et al. (2012) describe the case of the Bronze Soldier in Tallinn. The Soviet-erected statue is controversial since it represents the Soviet-occupation for most Estonians while the non-Estonian speaking part of the population (~25%) sees it as a memorial to the heroes of World War II. To add to the controversy, the statue was moved to a less central location in 2007. Within Google Maps and its embedded photos, the statue is represented very differently depending on the language used for the search. English-language content focuses primarily on the events surrounding the move of the statue in 2007, while Russian language content is often reminiscing about a distant past. On the other hand, Estonian content seems to just largely ignore the actual statue and focus on the surrounding features such as an adjacent flowerbed. In addition the statue's English Wikipedia page is home to a fierce debate on what the entry should say. Although the article itself is only 1,800 words, the discussion page weighs in at an impressive 70,000 words. It is here that we see how

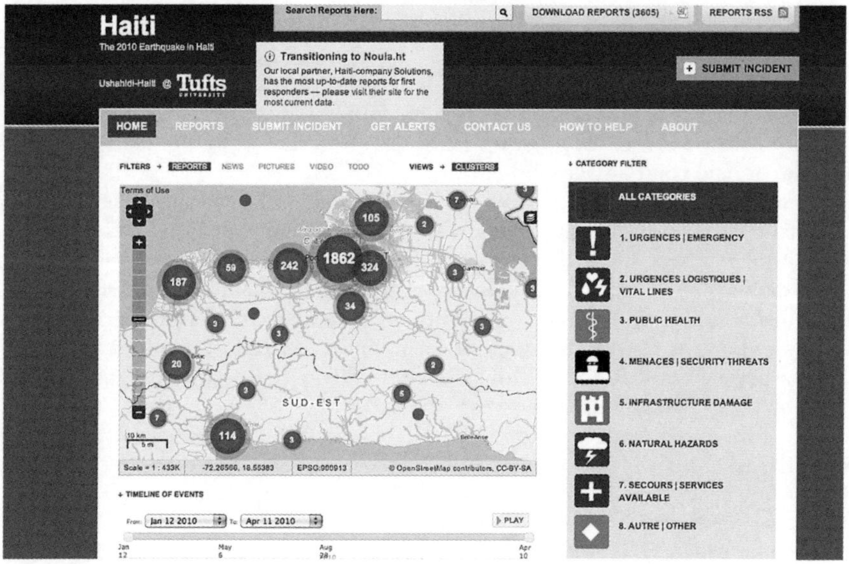

Figure 19.5 Screenshot of the Ushahidi Haiti project. Researching the code/space of VGI

Source: www.haiti.ushahidi.com

the digital and the material together form a hybrid space. Standing in front of the former location of the statue, a first-time visitor could be completely oblivious to the contestation surrounding the sculpture as the site is now a garden of wild flowers. Similarly, it is clear that the online representation is strongly rooted in – in fact, it could not exist without – the material world. It is only when we take the two together that we can fully understand the hybrid space of the Bronze Soldier in Tallinn.

The Bronze Soldier example shows how photos are a powerful medium in establishing the visual imagery that a certain place drums up. Instagram, the most popular photo-sharing platform to date, has a feature that allows users to explore other people's photos on a map. In similar vein, Flickr – Instagram's older brother – even has a map interface (www.flickr.com/map) that allows the user to search a specific city and peruse the most striking images from that place. It is clear that these photos are inherently spatial, especially since they can be tagged with their exact coordinates using the GPS in any smartphone. But what does a space look like through these platforms?

The city of Amsterdam was – and still is – known for its vibrant gay scene. Yet, in July 2009 only 11 pictures that referenced this aspect of the city were uploaded to Flickr. Apparently, Amsterdam is not a very *gay* place, at least when viewed through the lens of this hybrid VGI space at that time. Even though the gay scene might be very active, it doesn't show in the online representation of the city. But once a year this changes. Every summer the Amsterdam Gay Pride is organized, culminating in the canal parade in which hundreds of people party on boats parading through Amsterdam's canals. Many thousands of spectators stand along the canals waving, cheering, and, at least in 2009, uploading geocoded photos to Flickr. As a result, for this moment in time, the hybrid space of this Amsterdam canal and Flickr has produced an exceedingly *gay* place (see Figure 19.6). It is easy to spot the exact route of the canal parade, following the concentric canals in Amsterdam's inner city, and

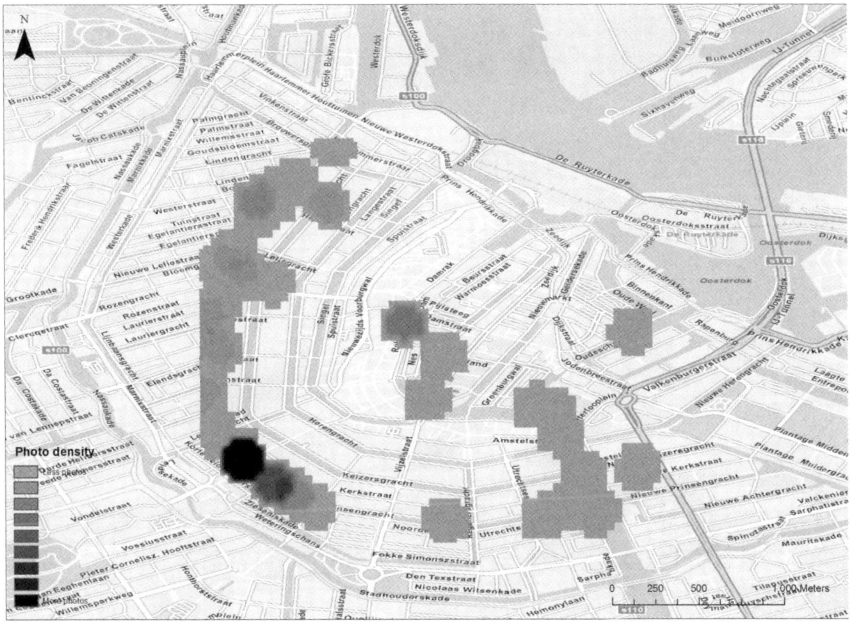

Figure 19.6 Flickr photo density referencing the term *gay* in Amsterdam, August 1, 2009
Source: Map by authors, based on geotagged Flickr photos

the two main party locations at the Leidseplein and the Reguliersdwarsstraat. The next day it is over. Flickr's cyberspace returns to only a couple of references per month. Gay place existed for one day, to only disappear completely the next day. The point here is not that VGI somehow causes this specific phenomenon. In fact, it mirrors closely similar cases where VGI did not play a role (Johnston 2002). Instead, VGI is one part of the process of producing a specific space. A process that might happen in similar or slightly different ways without VGI as one of the intricate layers in that flaky mille-feuille of space.

It is important to stress that the relation between the digital and the material is not one-way or linear. Instead, they are both part of a co-constitutive process in which people are consuming and producing these hybrid spaces via material and digital practices. For example, an Instagram user might use the Photo Map functionality to digitally explore new places before going out and taking a number of photos themselves. In the process, that user is consuming (by exploring a new place both digitally and physically) but also producing – by uploading new photos to Instagram and reproducing, or maybe slightly altering, the existing space in that location.

Concerns of Divides, Representations, and Privacy in VGI

The issue of access to ICTs – the digital divide – is important because it has such far-reaching consequences. Those without access or with constrained access might very well be (or become) the have-nots of today's society (Mitchell 1995).

> *Bluntly, for the very poor, simple access to networks may be next to impossible (Resnick and Rusk, 1996). Even within the most digitized of cities there remain large pockets of "off-line" poverty (Thrift, 1995), in which the poor and disenfranchised (typically the familiar litany of minorities) women, and the economically disadvantaged enjoy few of the benefits associated with the expansion of the Internet. Those who need the Internet the least, already living in information-rich environments with access through many non-Internet channels (such as newspapers and cable TV), may have the most access to it, while those who may benefit the most may have the least chance to log in. (Warf 2001)*

While the spaces of VGI represent an exciting area for research, it is important to recognize that this space is far from evenly distributed. In his analysis of accuracy in OpenStreetMap (OSM), Haklay (2010) points out that wealthy areas receive much better coverage than poorer neighborhoods. He quotes the founder of OSM in saying, "Nobody wants to do council estates. But apart from those socioeconomic barriers – for places people aren't that interested in visiting anyway – nowhere else gets missed." Other examples of the divided nature of VGI space are Microsoft's "avoid the ghetto" patent that would allow one's smartphone to avoid navigating through areas with high crime (Rogers 2012) and Kelley's (2011) discussion of how sentiments of fear in Foursquare "tips" might affect disadvantaged urban communities. A more innocuous example would be the recent uptake in using one's Klout – a metric that signifies a user's influence through social media – for coupons and discounts. No (or a relatively small) online presence means a lower Klout score and presumably no discount.

When we think back on the argument that sees technology (and by extent VGI) as the democratic "leveler," it is here that it becomes very clear that this is certainly not the case. Just as the digital is just one layer in that intricate amalgam we call space, the digital can never be the great force of democratization we would like it to be. If anything, it echoes (thereby slightly altering) the existing power configurations.

There are more indirect ways in which the digital divide is of significance for VGI. In traditional research – for example, the kind that informs policy – much effort is being put into gathering *representative* samples. Because of the digital divide, VGI is seldom representative but its sheer size makes it very tempting to create generalizations nonetheless. For example, IBM – as part of its Smarter Cities initiative – started marketing its Social Sentiment Index[3] software to cities in 2012. Based on data from a variety of online platforms, the software provides decision makers with a live pulse of public sentiment toward a range of subjects in different parts of cities. But how representative or "public" is this sentiment? Despite its million or billions of data points, it naturally excludes those who do not tweet, check-in, blog, or review online. Complicating the representativeness of VGI space is the quality of its data. For example, even on its home turf in the United Kingdom, OpenStreetMap data is still less accurate and less complete than the data collected by the UK Ordnance Survey. Note that the issue is much more nuanced than access to technology per se. For example, men contribute disproportionally more than women to a wide variety of VGI platforms (Stephens 2013).

Of course many VGI-related projects are specifically (if perhaps naively) designed to overcome the digital divide and lack of representation. OpenStreetMap volunteers have been active in training local mappers in a range of places (e.g. Kibera, Nairobi; West Bank, Palestine) to empower them in putting "themselves on the map." When data is completely missing, as was the case for urban planning practice, facilitated-VGI projects can be

3 www.ibm.com/analytics/us/en/conversations/social-sentiment.html

established as well and can be effective in collecting data that would otherwise be difficult to collect (Cinnamon and Schuurman 2012).

Lastly, the data and practice of VGI space raise important issues of privacy. Big data is often equated with a "big brother" government or entity encroaching on citizen's privacy through the use of a citizen's own data. But where does one draw the ethical boundary between public and private information for a platform like Twitter? A tweet can be sent to a few dozen friends and followers but then, completely unexpectedly, be picked up, taken out of context, and retweeted millions of times. Boyd and Crawford (2012) characterize it thusly: "Just because content is publicly accessible does not mean that it was meant to be consumed by just anyone" (p. 672). Elwood and Leszczynski (2011) even go a step further and argue that privacy should be reconceptualized as a result of big data. Moving beyond asking what privacy "is," they focus instead on the struggles over and renegotiations around privacy. Therefore, privacy has emerged as one of the key issues for consideration with the spaces of VGI.

Conclusion

On the surface, VGI is a set of tools – a digital technology – that enables anyone, including private citizens, to produce and consume spatial information with incredible ease. Popular platforms, such as Google Maps, Twitter, and Facebook, that many of us use on a daily basis are the poster children of this technology. But VGI is much more than "just" a technology. This chapter conceptualizes VGI as spaces of data and practice. It traces the genealogy of VGI and sketches the influence of VGI on the changing ways we understand and use space as well as its influence in the ways we can conduct research.

The ease with which we can now produce and consume spatial information via VGI has greatly contributed to the rise of "big data." This perspective on VGI – VGI as *data* – has the potential to significantly change the epistemologies of space. How do we know about space? Traditionally, this was the terrain of experts, often in the form of the state. Now, citizens can contribute to this knowledge all by themselves in a bottom-up fashion. In addition, the mere fact of having all that data at our disposal might also change how we do research. Some argue that the need for theory as a prerequisite of doing empirical research has diminished with the onset of VGI and big data. We no longer need a hypothesis to test theories through analysis of, for example, survey data. Instead, in data-driven research the data will not only provide answers, it might even provide the questions. We see this perspective – VGI as data – in practice in a wide array of fields, from IBM's Smarter Cities movement to crisis mapping and urban planning.

Second, if we think of VGI not only as data but as a process or practice, VGI is imbricated within the evolving fabric of everyday space. This is a more ontological perspective on VGI that has given rise to new, and often overlapping, concepts such as digiplace, code/space, and hybrid space. The essence of all these theories is that VGI – or the digital in general – is not just another layer on top of our existing material reality. Instead, it is meshed together with countless other "layers" of social space in a messy amalgam of flaky (albeit tasty) pastry or interactive and continuous unfolding spatial practice. This configuration of analytically separate but interconnected layers of space is by no means static. It is continuously being produced, consumed, and reproduced – never the same and always changing. We can see the effects of VGI on our everyday spaces even when we think of our own lives. We might use Google Maps to plot our travel route, which is dynamically updated based upon user-reported traffic jams; we might use Yelp to find well-reviewed new restaurants; or we might even find a date for Friday night using one of the location-aware dating apps. Less banal, we have also seen how the material and the digital are interconnected in the case of the contested statue of the Bronze Soldier in Tallinn or through digital photographs of Amsterdam's Gay Pride.

Undeniably, there are many important issues surrounding VGI, of which we have only touched on a few. The interrelated issues of the digital divide and (lack of) representation within VGI become even more pressing now that data like this is becoming popular as input for public policy and urban planning. Furthermore, the effects of the move to big data in relation to, for example, privacy are still difficult to recognize. Despite – or because of – the many issues and possibly harmful side effects, it has become uncontestable that volunteered geographic information has had a significant effect on both the configuration of spaces as well as how we learn about spaces.

References

Arnstein, S.R. 1969. A ladder of citizen participation. *Journal of the American Institute of Planners* 35(4): 216–24.

Augé, M. 1995. *Non-Places: Introduction to an Anthropology of Supermodernity*. New York: Verso.

Benedikt, M.L. 2008. Cityspace, cyberspace, and the spatiology of information. *Journal of Virtual Worlds Research* 1(1): 1–22.

Billinghurst, M., H. Bai, G. Lee, and R. Lindeman (2014). Developing handheld augmented reality interfaces. In *Oxford Handbook of Virtuality*. Edited by M. Grimshaw. Oxford and New York: Oxford University Press, 615–35.

boyd, d. and K. Crawford. 2012. CRITICAL QUESTIONS FOR BIG DATA. *Information, Communication and Society* 15(5): 662–79.

Brown, G. and Weber, D. 2012. Using public participation GIS (PPGIS) on the Geoweb to monitor tourism development preferences. *Journal of Sustainable Tourism* 21(2): 192–211.

Buliung, R.N, 2011. Wired people in wired places: Stories about machines and the geography of activity. *Annals of the Association of American Geographers* 101(6): 1365–81.

Cairncross, F. 1997. *The Death of Distance*. Boston: Harvard Business School Press.

Castells, M. 1996. *The Rise of the Network Society, Vol. I of The Information Age: Economy, Society and Culture*. Boston: Blackwell Publishing.

Cinnamon, J. and N. Schuurman. 2013. Confronting the data-divide in a time of spatial turns and volunteered geographic information. *GeoJournal*, 78(4): 657–74.

Craig, W.C.J., T.M. Harris, and M.D. Daniel Weiner. 2002. *Community Participation and Geographic Information Systems*. New York: Taylor and Francis.

Dodge, M. and R. Kitchin. 2001. *Atlas of Cyberspace*. London: Pearson Education.

Elwood, S. 2008. Volunteered geographic information: Future research directions motivated by critical, participatory, and feminist GIS. *GeoJournal* 72(3–4): 173–83.

Elwood, S. and Leszczynski, A. 2011. Privacy, reconsidered: New representations, data practices, and the geoweb. *Geoforum* 42(1): 6–15.

Elwood, S. Goodchild, M.F. and Sui, D.Z. 2012. Researching volunteered geographic information: Spatial data, geographic research, and new social practice. *Annals of the Association of American Geographers* 102(3): 571–90.

Florida, R. 2009. *Who's Your City?* Toronto: Vintage Canada.

Foth, M. et al. 2009. The Second Life of urban planning? Using NeoGeography tools for community engagement. *Journal of Location Based Services* 3(2): 97–117.

Friedman, T.L. 2007. *The World Is Flat*. New York: Picador.

Fukuyama, F. 1992. *The End of History and the Last Man*. New York: Free Press.
Gibson, W. 1984. *Neuromancer*. New York: Ace Books.
Goodchild, M.F. 2007. Citizens as sensors: The world of volunteered geography. *GeoJournal* 69(4): 211–21.
Gorman, S.P. 2007. Is academia missing the boat for the GeoWeb revolution? A response to Harvey's commentary. *Environment and Planning B: Planning and Design* 34(6): 949–50.
Graham, M., M. Zook, and A. Boulton. 2013. Augmented reality in the urban environment: Distorted mirrors and imagined reflections. *Transactions of the Institute of British Geographers*, 38(3): 464–79.
Graham, S. 1998. The end of geography or the explosion of place? Conceptualizing space, place and information technology. *Progress in Human Geography* 22(2): 165–85.
Haklay, M. 2010. How good is volunteered geographical information? A comparative study of OpenStreetMap and Ordnance Survey datasets. *Environment and Planning B: Planning and Design* 37(4): 682–703.
Harley, J.B. 1989. Deconstructing the map. *Cartographica: The International Journal for Geographic Information and Geovisualization* 26(2): 1–20.
Harvey, D. 1989. *The condition of postmodernity: An enquiry into the origins of cultural changes*. Boston: Blackwell Publishing.
Harvey, D. 2006. *Spaces of Global Capitalism*. New York: Verso.
Harvey, F. 2007. Just another private–public partnership? Possible constraints on scientific information in virtual map browsers. *Environment and Planning B: Planning and Design* 34(5): 761–64.
Hugill, P.J. 1999. *Global Communications Since 1844*. Baltimore: Johns Hopkins University Press.
Johnston, L. 2002. Borderline bodies. In *Subjectivities, Knowledges, and Feminist Geographies*. Edited by L. Bondi et al. Lanham, MD: Rowman and Littlefield Publisher, 75–89.
Kelley, M.J. 2013. The emergent urban imaginaries of geosocial media. *GeoJournal* 78(1): 181–203.
Kitchin, R. and M. Dodge. 2011. *Code/Space*. Cambridge, MA: MIT Press.
Kluitenberg, E. 2006. The network of waves: Living and acting in a hybrid space. *Open* 11: 6–17.
Kouwenhoven, A. 2012. Paniek na 580.000 tweets. *NRC Handelsblad*. May 12. Retrieved from www.nrc.nl.
Lazer, D. et al. 2009. Computational social science. *Science* 323(5915): 721–23.
Lefebvre, H. 1992. *The Production of Space*. Malden, MA: Blackwell Publishing.
Lessig, L. 1999. *Code and Other Laws of Cyberspace*. New York: Basic Books.
Leszczynski, A. 2012. Situating the geoweb in political economy. *Progress in Human Geography* 36(1): 72–89.
Library of Congress. 2013. *Update on the Twitter Archive at the Library of Congress*. Available from www.loc.gov/today/pr/2013/files/twitter_report_2013jan.pdf [accessed August 1, 2013].
Maguire, D.J. and P.A. Longley. 2005. The emergence of geoportals and their role in spatial data infrastructures. *Computers, Environment and Urban Systems* 29(1): 3–14.
Miller, C.C. 2006. A beast in the field: The Google Maps mashup as GIS/2. *Cartographica: The International Journal for Geographic Information and Geovisualization* 41(3): 187–99.
Miller, H.J. 2010. The data avalanche is here. Shouldn't we be digging? *Journal of Regional Science* 50(1): 181–201.
Mitchell, W.J. 1996. *City of Bits*. Cambridge, MA: MIT Press.
Netherlands Broadcasting Foundation. 2012. Schade Haren loopt in de miljoenen. Available at: www.nos.nl/artikel/421686-schade-haren-loopt-in-miljoenen.html [accessed October 1, 2013].
Perkins, R. and E. Neumayer. 2009. Transnational linkages and the spillover of environment-efficiency into developing countries. *Global Environmental Change* 19(3): 375–83.
Pickles, J. 1995. *Ground Truth*. New York: Guilford Press.

Relph, E.C. 1976. *Place and Placelessness.* London: Pion Ltd.
Roche, S., E. Propeck-Zimmermann, and B. Mericskay. 2013. GeoWeb and crisis management: Issues and perspectives of volunteered geographic information. *GeoJournal* 78(1): 21–40.
Rogers, K. 2012. Microsoft's "avoid ghetto" patent destined for failure? Available at: www.washingtonpost.com/blogs/the-buzz/post/microsofts-avoid-ghetto-patent-destined-for-failure/2012/01/10/gIQAX3PioP_blog.html [accessed October 1, 2013].
Schuurman, N. 2006. Formalization matters: Critical GIS and ontology research. *Annals of the Association of American Geographers* 96(4): 726–39.
Scott, J.C. 1998. *Seeing Like State.* New Haven: Yale University Press.
Seeger, C.J. 2008. The role of facilitated volunteered geographic information in the landscape planning and site design process. *GeoJournal* 72(3–4): 199–213.
Sheppard, E. 1993. Automated geography: what kind of geography for what kind of society? *The Professional Geographer*, 45(4), 457–60.
Sheppard, E. 2002. The spaces and times of globalization: Place, scale, networks, and positionality. *Economic Geography* 78(3): 307–30.
Sheppard, E. 2005. Knowledge production through critical GIS: Genealogy and prospects. *Cartographica: The International Journal for Geographic Information and Geovisualization* 40(4): 5–21.
Sieber, R. 2006. Public participation geographic information systems: A literature review and framework. *Annals of the Association of American Geographers* 96(3): 491–507.
Stephens, M. 2013. Gender and the GeoWeb: Divisions in the production of user-generated cartographic information. *GeoJournal* 78(6): 981–96.
Sui, D.Z. 2008. The wikification of GIS and its consequences: Or Angelina Jolie's new tattoo and the future of GIS. *Computers, Environment and Urban Systems* 32(1): 1–5.
Torrens, P.M. 2010. Geography and computational social science. *GeoJournal* 75(2): 133–48.
Tuan, Y.-F. 1977. *Space and Place.* Minneapolis: University of Minnesota Press.
Turner, A. 2006. *Introduction to Neogeography*, Sebastopol, CA: O'Reilly Media.
Warf, B. 2001. Segueways into cyberspace: Multiple geographies of the digital divide. *Environment and Planning B: Planning and Design* 28(1): 3–19.
Zook, M., M. Dodge, and Y. Aoyama. 2004. New digital geographies: Information, communication, and place. In *Geography and Technology.* Edited by S.D. Brunn, S.L. Cutter, and J.W. Harrington. Dordrecht: Kluwer.
Zook, M.A. and M. Graham. 2007a. Mapping DigiPlace: Geocoded Internet data and the representation of place. *Environment and Planning B: Planning and Design* 34(3): 466–82.
Zook, M.A. and M. Graham. 2007b. The creative reconstruction of the Internet: Google and the privatization of cyberspace and DigiPlace. *Geoforum* 38(6): 1322–43.
Zook, M. et al. 2010. Volunteered geographic information and crowdsourcing disaster relief: A case study of the Haitian earthquake. *World Medical and Health Policy* 2(2): 6–32.

Spaces of Affect

Paul Simpson

Recently, work in human geography has undergone an expansion of its epistemological boundaries. There has been an increasing interest in "how life takes shape and gains expression in shared experiences, everyday routines, fleeting encounters, embodied movements, precognitive triggers, practical skills, affective intensities, enduring urges, unexceptional interactions and sensuous dispositions … which escape from the established academic habit of striving to uncover meanings and values that apparently await our discovery, interpretation, judgment and ultimate representation" (Lorimer 2005: 84). Emerging from frustrations with the perceived overemphasis on textuality in post-structural analyses that so influenced human geography during the 1990s and beyond (Thrift and Dewsbury 2000), it has been argued that we need to pay more attention to the "dynamism immanent to bodily matter" and so to recognize the significance of *affect* to the experience and production of social spaces (Clough 2010: 207). As such, attempts have been made to "slow the quick jump to representational thinking and evaluative critique" so as to approach "the complex and uncertain objects that fascinate because they literally hit us or exert a pull on us" (Stewart 2007: 4).

This shift has not escaped the attention of media geographers. Media geography has for some time been interested in textual understandings of media and so how "Media intervenes and arbitrates the semiological chain of signifieds and signifiers, infusing signs with meaning, ideology and hegemony" (Lukinbeal et al. 2007: 1). However, there is more to media than textuality. We inhabit media as a kind of "aether," a "networked space" between bodies, technologies, and environments (Adams 2007). Media are both "representational and non-representational, lived and virtual, practised and performed, real and imagined." It is, therefore, important to attend to the role of "the affective and kinetic aspects of media" (Lukinbeal et al. 2007: 2). Media captivate us, manipulate us, excite us, scare us, make us happy, and make us sad.

In this chapter I am going to provide an overview of recent scholarship interested in the implications of media, space, and affect. I will start by providing an introduction to various understandings of affect and clarify a range of their key themes. The subsequent three sections will reflect on three key mediums of communication: film, video games, and sound, respectively. These sections will draw out a distinction between the relational affects of cinema, the interactive affects of video games, and the immersive affects of sound, and so how spaces of affect, and the spatial patterns and topologies associated with different kinds of mediated communication, differ with regard to the sensory modalities of the mediated communication taking place.

Geographies of Affect

Affect refers to the process of transition a body goes through when encountering another body. Such bodies can be human, animal, organic, or inorganic. A body can have a physical presence or can be something less concrete – an idea or an ambience. The emphasis here is on a "processual logic of transitions that take place during spatially and temporally distributed encounters" (Anderson 2006: 735). Thinking through affect implies that "the world is made up of billions of happy or unhappy encounters, encounters which describe a 'mindful connected physicalism' consisting of multitudinous paths which intersect" (Thrift 1999: 302). Elaborating this, Seigworth and Gregg (2010: 1) suggest that "Affect is an impingement or extrusion of a momentary or sometimes more sustained state of relation *as well as* the passage (and the duration of passage) of forces or intensities." Or put more simply, an affect "is a mixture of two bodies, one body which is said to act on another, and the other receives traces of the first" (Deleuze 1978).

And here's the rub. Affect *seems* to be a self-evident notion based around the interrelationships of bodies in space-time. However, affects are by no means easy to pin down and define (Thrift 2004). In fact, Massumi (2011: 153) states, "No general category understands the first thing about affect." Befitting its often fleeting and ephemeral manifestations, the concept has been present in a number of different academic traditions and has been understood in a number of senses. This in turn has led to a range of debates over its distinction from cognate phenomena like emotion and feeling. Therefore, in this section I aim to unpick some of the key themes/terms in work concerned with affect in geography to assist the reader in navigating the literature on this topic as well as provide a primer for the sections that follow.

Affect–Feeling–Emotion

Massumi's (2002) essay on "The Autonomy of Affect" has proved foundational to much of the work in geography on affect. This outlines how affect can be both tied to, and distinguished from, feelings and emotion. Here affects occur in relations between objects or entities and these interactions or affects are *felt* as intensities in the body (Anderson 2006). The affect is manifest in an alteration in a body's capacity to act. We can understand affect as "a kind of vague but intense atmosphere" and feeling as "that atmosphere felt in the body" (McCormack 2008b: 6). These can both be distinguished from emotions. While affect is "unqualified" and so "is not ownable or recognizable," emotion presents "a subjective content, the sociolinguistic fixing of the quality of an experience which is from that point onward described as personal" (Massumi 2002: 28). Emotions belong to the subject whereas affects exceed the subject. Affects are "transpersonal or prepersonal – not about one person's feelings becoming another's but about bodies literally affecting one another and generating intensities" (Stewart 2007: 128).

Here emotion and affect "pertain to different orders" (Massumi 2002: 27). Emotion relates to an "already established field of discursively constituted categories in relation to which the felt intensity of experience is articulated" (McCormack 2003: 495). This arguably restricts the movement of affective intensities by reducing them to the fixing and framings of meaning and significance. Emotion is the capture of affect, "the translation of the intensity of vitality affects' coming singularly together in the same event into recountable, codable, or formalizable content" (Massumi 2011: 153). As such, affects exceed the proper names that we give to apparently delimited emotions (Anderson 2009).[1]

Kinesthetics, Capacity, and Force

A further theme that comes up in many discussions of affect is "kinesthetics." Here a body has two simultaneous definitions. It is defined kinetically as being a composition of an infinite number of particles being at varying degrees of motion and rest, speed and slowness. Second, a body is defined dynamically by its capacity of affecting and being affected. Deleuze (1988) discusses this in terms of two fundamental affects: joy and sadness. Joy refers to a positive affection, an increased speed and motion, increasing our capacity to act. Sadness is a negative affection, a slowing down that reduces our capacity to act. Affects are then becomings: "sometimes they weaken us in so far as they diminish our power to act and decompose our relationships (sadness), sometimes they make us stronger in so far as they increase our power and make us enter into a vast or superior individual (joy)" (Deleuze and Parnet 2006: 45).

While this sounds quite simple, when translated to the situation of a body in the world, things become more complicated. Due to the shifting multiplicity of relations that we are always already entered into, we are affected/affecting in a multitude of ways. Equally, as suggested above, joy and sadness should not be equated with the representational logics by which we would normally interpret them: as meaning-filled emotions. Rather, they should be thought purely in terms of their relative status: as a pre-reflexive increase or decrease in a body's capacity to act.

Based on this, affect can be thought of both in terms of force and capacity. As a force, it might not always be all that forceful. It may modulate perpetually through bodily encounters. It might take place in the traumatic encounter of something that has a relatively lasting impact on what that body can, or can no longer, do. It may also be subtle and not noticed until some kind of threshold is past where such a shift in capabilities becomes evident. As a capacity, affect can be understood as "a gradient of bodily capacity … that rises and falls not only along various rhythms and modalities of encounter but also through the troughs and sieves of sensation and sensibility, an incrementalism that coincides with belonging to comportments of matter of virtually any and every sort" (Seigworth and Gregg 2010: 2). Affect here refers to the body's capacity to affect and be affected. The limits of what a body can do, and have done to it, are by no means fixed (Abrahamsson and Simpson 2011). Rather than "the" body, it is always "a body" that is singular in its specific manifestation in that moment of "its ongoing affectual composition" (Seigworth and Gregg 2010: 3). We cannot definitively know what a body can do (Deleuze and Guattari 2004).

Atmospheres

A final theme emerging in the most recent work on affect in geography has been an interest in "affective atmospheres." Here "the atmospheric suggests a relationship not only with the body and its immediate space but with a permeable body integrated within, and subject to, a global system: one that combines the air we breathe, the weather we feel, the pulses

[1] While there is not space to go into detail here, this relation between emotion and affect is not universally accepted and has been debated at some length (see Anderson and Harrison 2006; Bondi and Davidson 2011; Curti et al. 2011; Dawney 2011; McCormack 2006, Pile 2010; Thien 2005).

and waves of the electromagnetic spectrum that subtends and enables technologies, old and new, and circulates … in the excitable tissues of the heart" (Dyson 2009: 17). Such affective atmospheres draw attention to how affects can be "collective," can be transmitted between people, and so "'envelop and press upon life'" (Anderson 2009: 78). However, they also show how "There is no secure distinction between the 'individual' and the 'environment'" (Brennan 2004: 6). Atmospheres then "form part of the ubiquitous backdrop of everyday life" but a backdrop that is at the same time "forceful and affect[s] the ways in which we inhabit … spaces" (Bissell 2010: 272).

McCormack (2008a) suggests that affective atmospheres can be defined along two interrelated lines. We can view atmospheres in their meteorological sense as "a turbulent zone of gaseous matter surrounding the earth and through the lower reaches of which human and non-human life moves" (McCormack 2008a: 413). Secondly, there is their more specifically affective sense as "something distributed yet palpable, a quality of environmental immersion that registers in and through sensing bodies while also remaining diffuse, in the air, ethereal" (McCormack 2008a: 413). Therefore, atmospheres present a complicated and ill-defined spatiality. They are not simply spaces through which bodies move and "it is not easy to identify the 'where' of an atmosphere given '[t]hey seem to fill the space with a certain tone of feeling like a haze'" (Anderson 2009: 80, quoting Bohme). It is instructive to consider the roots of the term here: *atmos* indicates "a tendency for qualities of feeling to fill spaces like a gas" and *sphere* indicates "a particular form of spatial organization based on the circle" (Anderson 2009: 80). Atmospheres then "'radiate' from an individual to another" and so "envelope or surround" those individuals (Anderson 2009: 80).

These atmospheres come about through the relations of a multiplicity of (im)material bodies. This is not just a case of the physical interaction of material bodies. Rather, various forces emanate from the material entities present and the associations that may go with them. To consider atmospheres is not to be antirepresentational, but rather to require us to looks at how representations *also* play a role in the production of such atmospheres; how representations may be bound up in nonrational forms of communications that have an impact upon the body, but not necessarily in completely rational or reflexively considered ways. Mundane significations such as clothing, facial expressions, and even posture can play a part in how an atmosphere is registered in a body, though we might not be entirely aware of it as this registering takes place.

Such atmospheres hold a complicated relationship with the experiencing subject. They both "occur *before* and *alongside* the formation of subjectivity" (McCormack 2008a: 419). They require a subject to apprehend their presence but also, given that they emanate from a multiplicity of human and nonhuman entities, have an existence independent from the emergence of that subject. They are neither fully subjective nor fully objective; they can be experienced collectively but also intensely by an individual. They are not solely a product of the qualities of the bodies present for they exceed any causal relation. But they are not just constructed by a subject. They are, in fact, "always in the process of emerging and transforming … always being taken up and reworked in lived experience – becoming part of feelings and emotions that may themselves become elements within other atmospheres" (Anderson 2009: 80).

We do need to be careful though when thinking about the relationship between a body and the atmospheres it enters into. There is a danger of assuming an "outside-in" logic to the relationship between body and atmosphere (Dyson 2009). While illustrations of atmosphere are often presented in terms of a person walking into a room and "feeling" an atmosphere (Brennan 2004), it is also important to realize the significance of that body arriving (Ahmed 2010). Affective atmospheres will be experienced differently by each body depending on that singular body's susceptibility to being affected at that given time

(Bissell 2010) and will in turn bring something to that complex of relations and so potentially impact upon the composition and affectivity of that atmosphere. We need to be attentive to the "angle of arrival" of a body and the exchanges that take place between bodies and their atmospheric environments (Ahmed 2010).

Relational Affects

In thinking about the spatialities of affect produced in and through mediated communications it seems relevant to start with screens since "much of the world lives in the 'age of the screen', enmeshed in extensive and skillful assemblages dedicated to the production, circulation and consumption of moving imagery" (Lorimer 2010: 239–40). While moving images have been most commonly explored in terms of what they signify or represent, it is important also to recognize "the performative, haptic and affective dimensions to moving imagery" (Lorimer 2010: 240). Arguably, our "highly mediatized public sphere ... does not so much function to channel codes and signs, but to channel and amplify affects" (Carter and McCormack 2006: 241). It would appear this is particularly the case when it comes to thinking about cinema.

Cinematic Affects

Much of the work on film and geography has suggested that "the match of film and world ... is a matter of representation, and representation is in turn a matter of discourse, and discourse is, in part, the organization of images and the construction of narrative conventions" (Aitken and Zonn cited in Carter and McCormack 2006: 233; see Coulter 2010; Hillis 2010). However, recently work has drawn attention to how "Film engenders powerful affective currents and fields that are amplified and channelled in particular directions" (McHugh 2007: 36). As Carter and McCormack (2006: 240) have suggested, "the relationship between film and contemporary culture is not only a matter of interpretation. Nor can it be understood as a process operating according to the logics of discursively coded emotions. It is also a matter of the production and circulation of affects prior to yet also providing the grounds from which distinctive intensities of feeling emerge." It is appropriate then to think about how films actually work, what they *do*.

Colebrook (2002) suggests that cinema works by taking a number of images and connecting them into a sequence via the "inhuman eye" of the camera. In realist cinema certain techniques are used to present a clear and linear unfolding, a coherent and easily digested narrative, while ultimately drawing attention *away* from the work being done to organize images (Connolly 2002). However, there are cases where this sequencing of images is amplified. Significant here is the "liberation of the sequencing of images from any single observer, so the affect of cinema is the presentation of an 'any point whatsoever'" (Colebrook 2002: 31). While in our day-to-day life, we see the world from a specific embodied position and organize these perceptions into our own "world," "cinema can present images of perception liberated from this organizing structure" (Colebrook 2002: 31). Cinema's power here is not so much its ability to faithfully represent the world, but its ability to alter the perception of the everyday in novel ways by creating relations between images through techniques like irregular montage and irrational cuts, and so to create new worlds, transform "life," and produce a new sense of movement (Colebrook 2002, see Doel and Clarke 2007).

This altering of perception has been taken to an extreme in some recent Hollywood blockbusters. In the work of directors like Tony Scott and Michael Bay, "contemporary film editing is oriented not towards the production of meanings (or ideologies), but directly towards a moment-by-moment manipulation of the spectators' affective states" (Shaviro 2010: 17 [quoting Rodowick 2007]). Whereas traditional Hollywood cinema used editing to intensify storytelling while maintaining a fidelity to the space represented, "films like Michael Bay's 'Transformers' series no longer seem to be invested in meaningful expression, or narrative construction, at all" (Shaviro 2010: 118). Instead, rapid editing is used to affect the rhythm and pace of the movie's unfolding in such a way as to elicit user excitement. We end up with something like "a continual cinematic barrage, with no respite" (Shaviro 2010: 119); immediate affect over spatiotemporal (and so narrative) orientation.

Cinema here has quite direct and ultimately visceral effects on the viewing body and so disrupts any sense of stable identity in the viewer (Connolly 2002). As Colebrook (2002: 38) illustrates, "We can think of affect in terms of a form of pre-personal perception. I watch a scene in a film and my heart races, my eye flinches and I begin to perspire. Before I even think or conceptualize there is an element of response that is prior to any decision." It is important to note though that cinema, usually at least, does also include sound and so extends beyond such "watching" or solely the manipulation of images. Soundtracks can also have quite powerfully affective capacities.[2]

Pursuing an affective thinking of cinema, geographers Carter and McCormack (2006) explore the relationships between affect, film, and popular geopolitics through a discussion of the film "Black Hawk Down." With the power of film often articulated in terms of its representational capacities, Carter and McCormack go against work that sees "the affective dimensions of film … as a kind of aesthetic veneer to be stripped away while excavating an underlying discursive or ideological logic" (2006: 230). As such, they pay explicit attention to the affective dimensions of the film, and particularly "how the matter of affect is implicated in the emergence and popular enactment of geopolitical cultures" (Carter and McCormack 2006: 230). While film can (re)script and (re)envision forms of geopolitical intervention and perpetuate specific logics of perception, they argue attention also needs be paid to the performative logics at play here that "draw upon a repertoire of embodied and non-cognitive ways of knowing" (Carter and McCormack 2006: 233).

Carter and McCormack (2006: 238) show how an affective "sublime aesthetic of combat" is produced in the film. This emerges through the emphasis on the experience of combat over the film's geopolitical context in that "the film depicts a kind of decontextualized yet affectively charged experience of combat" (Carter and McCormack 2006: 239). Further, this also permeates the ways in which certain actors involved in the Somalia crisis are depicted – notably, their own explanations for their actions are not given. This gives the film a particularly ambiguous relationship to the broader geopolitical events of the time and, as such, allowed it to be reappropriated into the geopolitical context of post-9/11 American military activities. While aspects of specific signification and so identification are present (e.g. specific military uniforms, type of weaponry, military equipment, etc.) that both hold a contextualizing function and an affective potency in themselves, this reappropriation was possible because the film's "capacity to resonate [in a different context] was affective"

2 While I will discuss mediated sound later, one point to note is that such soundtracks are usually anchored to the spatial positioning of the screen and the action taking place therein. Cinematic soundscapes usually come to be associated with a specific spatial orientation relative to the action taking place on the screen/off-screen and so this can have implications for the immersive nature of the affects such sound creates – effectively, the relational positioning of the observer vis-à-vis the screen will still be maintained.

(Carter and McCormack 2006: 240), rather than being based on *actual* connections between those contexts.

Among these approaches to film, there is an evident relationality to the affects taking place. Images on screens come into relation with both other images and the spectator/observer to produce affects that are felt in the watching body. There is an "intensive geography" here in that "The sensual surface of the screen is something that we as viewers become one with, shape, and are shaped by ... . [A]s we move with the images, we are affected in such a way that our bodies and the spaces they are partially connected to change and produce" (Moreno 2007: 42). The spatiality of affect here lies in the in-between; "films ... communicate affective energies to us, some of which pass below intellectual attention while still influencing emotions, judgements, and actions" (Connolly 2002: 13). They do not belong to the content of the moving images, nor to the observer, but emerge in the interrelation of the two. Moving images therefore "touch us in a multisensory fashion" (Lorimer 2010: 243), they have something like a "'haptic visuality' or 'affective materiality'" (Lorimer 2010: 240).

"Post-cinematic" Affects

Taking these relations between screen-based media and the affective spaces they are based on and generative of further, Shaviro (2010) identifies a shift in the sorts of affective relations present toward what he calls a "post-cinematic" affect. This is post-cinematic in that "Film gave way to television as a 'cultural dominant' a long time ago, in the mid-twentieth century; and television in turn has given way in recent years to computer- and network-based, and digitally generated, 'new media'" (Shaviro 2010: 1). It is not so much that film has disappeared, but rather that it has been transformed in light of developments in digital technology.

Digitally produced media do not necessarily "imply, and does not take place within, the absolute perspectival space of ordinary perceptual experience" (Shaviro 2010: 6). Instead, they construct a relational space. Here, "there is no such thing as space or time outside the processes that define them ... Processes do not occur in space but define their own spatial frame" (Shaviro 2010: 15 [quoting Harvey]). Relational space therefore "varies from moment to moment, along with the forces that generate and invest it. It continually alters its curvature and its dimensions; it does not persist as a stable, enduring container for objects that would be situated solidly within in" (Shaviro 2010: 15–16).

This relationality is key to the distinction between cinematic and post-cinematic spaces of affect. Relational space is radically different from more traditional cinematic space. Cinematic spaces are indexical: "Their very materiality consists in the persisting chemical traces of objects that actually stood before the camera at a particular time, in a particular place" (Shaviro 2010: 16). This assumes some sort of space that existed prior to the film; it is a record of something that existed previously. Digital video does not require this preexisting space and so does not necessarily present this record of something existing previously. While digital cinema may involve the presence of an actor or scene in front of the camera in its production, "the video's *ontological consistency* does not depend, in the way that a film would, upon the fact of this prior physical presence" (Shaviro 2010: 16). This allows for even greater cinematic effects beyond those of analog cinema. Digital video can generate its own space, produce entire worlds, that can be modulated in a multitude of ways. The laws of space and time no longer have the same bearing on what a body can do and so bodies can be manipulated in previously unthought and unexplored ways.

Interactive Affects

Post-cinematic affects lead into another significant form of media that holds implications for thinking about the spatiality of affects, particularly in terms of relationality, digital manipulation, and the production of screen-worlds: computer games. Echoing the situation in work on cinema, Ash and Gallacher (2011) draw attention to the predominance of a representational focus in work on the geographies *in* video games. Work here has been largely focused on the ways in which computer games represent peoples, places, and concepts, and the political significance of this representation (see Shaw and Warf 2009). However, "The technical apparatuses of individual videogaming platforms require and produce very different forms of bodily practice" (Ash and Gallacher 2011: 353). There are multitude geographies *of* video games. Gamers actually explore game worlds and develop specific senses of space and place within them (Lammes 2008). Video games are practiced technologies that are experienced by gamers and as part of this video games are enrolled in the production of different affects for the gamer.

Ash (2009) discusses this in terms of the spatiality of the screen. While video games can represent specific places, it is also important to attend to "the spaces that images themselves produce" (Ash 2009: 2105). Video games produce an experience of a specific "world" for the gamer. However, "The sense of 'world' here is not of some stable and neutral thing which pre-exists users' interaction with it" (Ash and Gallacher 2011: 359). It is not that there is a preexisting abstract geometric space that the gamer explores in a distanced and purely rational way. Instead, these game worlds are experienced: "video games alter the relationship between the material and phenomenal by injecting activities of spatial movement and orientation onto a flat surface (the screen) and provide a new interface for a negotiation of this surface space (the control pad)" (Ash 2009: 2108). The sense of this game world is "of a processual world that actively emerges from the practices of users" (Ash and Gallacher 2011: 359), and so the interaction of the gaming body and the architecture of the game's designed world can be productive of different affects.

This affective interactivity of the worlds of video games becomes particularly evident when it comes to thinking about the activities of programmers and the processes of affective design they engage in (Ash 2010a). As with post-cinematic affects, there is a great deal of affective manipulation that can take place in the designing of video games. Using both overt and subtle techniques, "games designers are able to shape the spatial and temporal experiences of videogamers and their practices by manipulating the rules of videogames (albeit imperfectly)" (Ash and Gallacher 2011: 360). Game designers not only act as the architects of the spatiotemporal confines in which game play takes place but also can significantly alter the experiences and affects of the gamer, for example, by varying the responsiveness of controls, experimenting with the specific capacities and reactiveness of game avatars/characters, and so on. The ultimate aim of this is the proliferation of positive affects (ones that capture and maintain attention and so make the gamer want to play more) and the limiting of negative ones to those tied to a lack of gamer-skill (rather than poor game design, which might lead to frustration or, ultimately, the gamer becoming disenchanted with the game) (Ash 2010a).

That said, care needs to be taken so as to not ascribe too much efficacy to such designing of affects as "affective manipulation is necessarily a fragile achievement that is prone to failure and always reliant upon being continually reworked in the creative responses users develop in relation to the designed environments with which they interact" (Ash 2010a: 655). While the actions of gamers can be shaped by the rules of the game, in many games there is some degree of contingency to the outcomes of the relations of gamer and the game's architecture. We should consider the relationships between gamer and designed game environment as "a complex, problematic, and ongoing struggle between the openness and performative play of contingency and chance (which emerge through the techniques and intelligences that users develop as they become skilled at these games) and the mechanical systems and calculative rationalities through which these environments are designed" (Ash 2010a: 655). The intentions of the designers might not come to fruition as a result of the unintended responses of the gamer in certain circumstances.

Such interactions can shape the gamers' capacities to act and to be affected in that engagement with these game-worlds can ultimately "rewire the synaptic connections of the body in different ways, producing an altered phenomenality of how the world as such appears to humans" (Ash 2009: 2106). Ash (2010b) discusses this in terms of "teleplasty." Here a teleplastic technology refers to a technology that shapes the unconscious knowledges, capacities, and capabilities of bodies through the manipulation of spatiotemporal factors (Ash 2010b). Interesting here though is that "the teleplastic capacities of videogames do not simply derive from the images displayed on the screen (or the sound played through the speakers); they actively emerge from the relations between users and the game, which are mediated through the technological apparatuses of particular videogaming systems" (Ash and Gallacher 2011: 360). Such affects, and their resultant changes in the gaming body's capacities to act and be affected, then emerge through the *interactions* that take place in the playing of the game rather than from the gaze of a disengaged observer of a screen.

Through the interactive, world-producing nature of video games there is then an amplification of a relational, and here increasingly immersive and "captivating" (Ash 2013) spatiality to the affects emerging from a body's engagement with a screen-based media: "the screen is a connective plenum – it is a site which alters the relation between thought and movement and thus the status of the body's collective phenomenal field: its holistic being-in-the-world" (Ash 2009: 2106). This more existential understanding of the screen's spatiality is significant in that such a "Space implies the possibility of immersion, habitation, and phenomenal plenitude" (Dyson 2009: 1). In such an immersive environment, the gamer begins to become totally enveloped within and transformed by the "virtual environment" (Shaviro 2010: 124). Through the interaction of gamer and game space there is, in a sense, a shift from a "looking at" a two-dimensional image on a screen to an embodied "being in" the world of the game.

Going back to cinema for a moment, it is important not to overstate the distinction between computer game technologies and cinema. There is something of an immersion present in cinema and older screen-based media given that, as mentioned earlier, "We need only think of the almost palpable envelopment of film sound, and the way that lip sync unites three-dimensional sound with two dimensional image, producing an illusion of embodiment that owes its pervasiveness to the near impossibility of imagining voice and body as separate when the viewer feels his or her own voice embodied" (Dyson 2009: 14). However, new digital media go further in pushing toward an immersive affective spatiality, particularly through their interactive nature, and so in many ways aspire to what could be described as the phenomenality of sound – an emphasis on immersion in an environment experienced in a multisensory, embodied way. It is toward this spatiality of affect in terms of a fuller, embodied immersion that this chapter will now move by thinking about "sound affects."

Immersive Affects

Before thinking about this immersive nature of "sound affects" (affect associated with sound and music), it is important first to recognize the ways in which sound has been considered in geography. In general, much of the recent engagement with sound in geography has been in terms of the geographies of music (see Anderson, et al. 2005; Connell and Gibson 2003; Kong 1995; Leyshon, et al. 1995; Smith 1997). Like the work discussed earlier, in geography interested in cinema and video games, here music is treated largely as a text, as a medium that contains a message that depicts an idea of place/identity, rather than something that was actually experienced by a listener (see Cohen 1995; Keough 2011; Kong 1996; Leonard 2011; Morley and Somdahl-Sands 2011; Pesses 2011; Revill 2000). However, there has been a move toward attending to the more experiential, embodied aspects of listening to music and sound (see Anderson 2005; Anderson et al. 2005; Duffy and Waitt 2011; Morton 2005; Simpson 2009; Wood and Smith 2004; Wood et al. 2007). Geographers have become interested in what music *does* (Curti and Craine 2011); how the "qualities of sound" itself are experienced in the listening body and are significant to music's status as music and the worlds it produces (Duffy and Waitt 2011). Geographers have begun to realize how "Of all the arts, music is the most immediately moving, the most visceral and contagious in its effects" (Curti and Craine 2011: 139). Sounds, and music in particular, hold a significant capacity to affect our sense of self, and so perpetually enrolling us in ongoing processes of self (de)formation.

Immersed in Sound

Focusing on this experiential significance of sound/music, there is a significantly different spatiality to this, one more expressly predicated on immersion. While the screen-based media discussed above are primarily based around the transmission of light from the screen itself to the eye of the viewer, there is a different spatial logic to sound given the medium of its communication. While potentially originating from a speaker or other such technological source (see also Jackiewicz 2007), sound has a more voluminous nature and so takes the form of an atmospheric body. Echoing the discussion of affective atmospheres from earlier, rather than being orientated toward a spatially confined phenomenon or as having clearly defined parameters, sound is "Three-dimensional, interactive, and synesthetic, perceived in the here and now of an embodied space" (Dyson 2009: 4).

In listening, there is a "feeling of being here now, of experiencing oneself as engulfed, enveloped, absorbed, enmeshed, in short, immersed in an environment" (Dyson 2009: 4). There is a specific phenomenality of sound (how it is appears to us and so is experienced by us), given the way it surrounds us, "the fact that it is invisible, intangible, ephemeral, and vibrational" (Dyson 2009: 4). Sound enfolds with our bodies, "a folding of bodies where the outside becomes inside and the inside becomes outside" (Curti and Craine 2011: 139). It is not easy to maintain any kind of clear distinction between subject and object, body and world, self and sound; there is an intertwining as sound encounters and suffuses the body (Duffy and Waitt 2011). Sound presents itself as a "flow or process rather than a thing, a mode of being in a constant state of flux" (Dyson 2009: 4), much like the subject listening to it. Rather than being in relation *to* sound (as we might direct a look toward a screen), we are in fact always already *with* sound (Nancy 2007). It is not that the body-subject comes before sound and enters into relation with it, but rather that sound and self coexist and coevolve (Simpson 2009).

In essence, the body listening becomes an affective "resonance chamber":

> *a hollow column over which a skin is stretched, but also from which the opening of a mouth can resume and revive resonance. [...] A blow from outside, clamour from within, this sonorous, sonorized body undertakes a simultaneous listening to a 'self' and to a 'world' that are both in resonance. It becomes distressed (tightens) and it rejoices (dilates). It listens to itself becoming distressed and rejoicing. It enjoys and is distressed at this very listening where the distant resounds in the closest. (Nancy 2007: 42–43)*

We are penetrated by sound but also the source of it; affecting with sound and being affected by it. While the ears might be the primary organ of listening, we listen with our whole bodies – we can feel vibrational and resonant frequencies echoing throughout our corporeal being.[3] This affectivity of sound is not some kind of supplement, but is positioned as the very "condition of possibility" for the emergence of a body-subject.

Consequently, there is a different spatial orientation to the relationship between the listening body-subject and sound as opposed to a body looking at a screen: "Whereas seeing positions the subject symbolically as director of its look, always looking ahead toward the future, hearing subverts this role: the listener cannot control what is often overheard, what is muttered 'behind my back'. Immersed in sound, the subject loses its self, and, in many ways, loses its sense" (Dyson 2009: 4). Listening dislocates "the frontal and conceptual associations of vision with an all-round corporeality and spatiality" (Kahn cited in Duffy and Waitt 2011: 121). It is not as easy to direct our listening to a specific object of concern as it is to orient our eyes, nor to interrupt the sonorous arrival as "The ears don't have eyelids" (Nancy 2007: 14). Even if our ears are plugged, we begin to hear ourselves: the blood rushing through our veins, the high-pitch sounds of our nervous system's function, the ever-present movements of our corporeity (Finn 2011).

The spatiality of sound then is atmospheric: "there is sound, inasmuch as there is atmosphere; like a sense fog, it disappears when approached, falling beyond discourse as it settles within the skin" (Dyson 2009: 4). Sound spreads out in space, an ever-approaching sonorous present that is "immediately omni-dimensional and transversate through all spaces: the expansion of sound through obstacles, its property of penetration and ubiquity" (Nancy 2007: 13). With this expansive nature, "every surface becomes a topology that yields reflections and ... reveals a depth" (Dyson 2009: 5). Based on all of this, "the field of sound is not a chunk of divisible being, but is more like a state or quality, surrounding the listener, who is simultaneously hearing and being touched by the vibrating, engulfing, sonic atmosphere" (Dyson 2009: 135). That said, this very ubiquity also means that we tend to forget our immersion in our everyday soundscape (Atkinson 2011).

Violent Sounds

Despite this forgetting of our sonic atmospheres, it has been widely recognized that sound can have quite immediate and intensely affective effects. While sound can be affective in subtle ways (e.g. the creeping feeling of unease when a floorboard creeks in another room or when you hear movement in an empty house but can't ascertain the source [see Toop 2010]), one way in which this pervasive immersive nature of sound perhaps comes through most clearly is in the case of sounds that are pointedly disruptive, undesirable, or unwanted.

3 A great example of this comes in the music of Evelyn Glennie. She is a deaf percussionist who hears the music through her body. For further details, see www.youtube.com/watch?v=383kxC_NCKw.

Goodman (2010) discusses the ways in which sound can be deployed through various technologies to impact upon the way populations feel. More specifically, this interest is orientated toward the development of "a nonrepresentational ontology of vibrational force" that can attend to the production of environments where "sound contributes to an immersive atmosphere or ambience of fear and dread – where sound helps produce a *bad vibe*" (Goodman 2010: xv and xiv). This is key as "the sonic … body is always poised precariously in a processual disequilibrium with the acoustic environment, and … even minute perturbation of this environment can set in motion resonant events and generate and provoke unforeseen cultural mutations" (Goodman 2010: 12). Our embodied states are perpetually being modulated by variations in the rhythm, frequency, timbre, and so on of the sonic environments we find ourselves in. As such, human bodies are by no means at the center of this sonic atmosphere. Rather "a body [here] becomes merely another actual entity in a vibrational event, assuming not necessarily any more significance that the resonances between other entities within this nexus" (Goodman 2010). The body is simply a specific "transducer of vibration."

The use of "sonic booms" as "sound bombs" by the Israeli Air Force in the Gaza Strip provides a clear illustration of such sonic warfare. Generated by low-flying jets traveling faster than the speed of sound, this loud and deep-frequency sound effect had material effects on the body of the involuntary listeners, producing "ear pain, nosebleeds, anxiety attacks, sleeplessness, hypertension, and being left 'shaking inside'" (Goodman 2010: xiii). The aim of these attacks was to produce a specific affect: "the objective was to weaken the morale of a civilian population by creating a climate of fear through a threat that was preferably nonlethal yet possibly as unsettling as an actual attack" (Goodman 2010: xiv). Also, we can look to Goodman's discussion of the US "Ghost Army" stationed in Europe during World War II. Here sound and radio engineers were tasked with creating sound tracks of troops, tanks, and landing craft so as to provide a distraction and allow real troops to move unnoticed. This "sonic deception" acted to produce "an affective ecology of fear" that was confusing and distracting to the enemy (Goodman 2010: 42). In both these examples, sound was used to "modulate" mood; it was used a form of "acoustic violence" enacted through the "vibration and the trembling of temperaments" (Goodman 2010: xiv; also see Hill 2012).

This capacity of sound to affect can also be seen in slightly more mundane, everyday settings. We can think about the affects of unwanted sound in domestic environments. Here, "the breaching of sound across social and more porous physical thresholds" in domestic noise nuisance cases where music is played repeatedly and/or at loud volumes shows how there is little in the way of "sonic autonomy" when it comes to sound (Atkinson 2011: 20). We literally cannot escape it, being trapped by it in every corner of our homes. This also directs us again toward the importance of disposition. It is not so much that such noise possesses a negatively affecting quality in and of itself; the loud music is not necessarily "bad" music. It might in fact be a favorite song being played. However, such sound will affect us differently depending on how we are disposed toward it. In the context of a car, a run sound-tracked by our MP3 player, or when played on our own stereo, it might positively affect us. It might help us stay more alert, run harder, or relax. However, when we lose control over such sound and it spreads through "the aether of the urban soundscape" and through our windows, walls, and floors, we might find it "out of place, threatening to our well-being, suggestive of unpleasant experiences" (Atkinson 2011: 20). Sound's power to affect us modulates, shifts, ebbs, and flows as much as the sound itself; our "listening is always spatially and temporally contingent" (Duffy and Waitt 2011: 121).

However, such violence enacted by sound, both spectacular and mundane, is by no means a product of particular new technologies of amplification and mediation. Particularly since the increasing industrialization, and so noise, of Western society (Simmel 2002), there have been innumerable examples of highly pervasive and affective soundspaces being produced and negatively impacting on a variety of audiences (see Picker 2003). For example, Szendy (2008) draws attention to an interesting example here in terms of traveling musicians playing barrel organs in the public spaces of cities in the late eighteenth and nineteenth centuries. It was not only the violence of their mechanical reproductions toward the pieces arranged for them (e.g. the crude alteration of harmonies, the cutting of sections, etc.) that affected certain portions of the urban populace negatively. It was also that, given sound's properties of expansion and penetration discussed above, such sound often bled into the home and places of work of many urban inhabitants, disturbing their rest and leaving them with little respite from the ever-increasing sensory demands of modernizing urban life (Picker 2003). Here "the technological system constituted by instruments for the mechanical reproduction of music" represented "apparatuses that would end up in court accused of the worst crimes against music" (Nancy 2008: xii). Therefore, as Atkinson (2011: 14) notes, even a general background of "urban sound has a significant affective and behaviour-modifying influence and that such forces affect the broader ebb and flow of hearing bodies within the physical structure and spaces of the city."

Conclusion

In this chapter I have provided an overview of recent scholarship related to the implications of media, space, and affect. In doing so I have pursued two interrelated themes. Firstly, through a discussion of work on cinema, video games, and sound/music, I have drawn out how spaces of affect differ with regard to the sensory modalities of the mediated communication taking place. This was discussed in terms of screen-based and sound-based forms of mediated communication, though nuances have been shown in terms of the differences between broadly relational cinematic affects and more interactive video-game affects. Secondly, I have illustrated how there are different spatial patterns and topologies associated with different kinds of mediated communication, and so the affects they are generative of. This was discussed in terms of a progression from: (1) an affective relation between body and image(s) in various forms of cinema where the content of the screen-image, or the relations between screen-images, affects the viewer; (2) to a more interactive relationship between skilled body and video-game screens/technologies; (3) to an inescapable, immersive situation of body within a sonorous atmosphere when it comes to listening to mediated sound/music.

One thing that has been absent from this chapter has been a discussion of how to actually go about studying these various spaces and spatialities of affect in specific empirical settings. This question remains largely unanswered in recent geographic research (Latham 2003). While there have been various calls to reinvigorate research methods in human geography by variously drawing on approaches from performance studies (Thrift 2003); developing an open-minded experimentalism in how research is designed and conducted (Dewsbury 2010); experimenting a little with relatively familiar methods (Latham 2003); and by finding alternative ways to write research so as to be attentive to such affects (McCormack 2002), it is still not entirely clear how the substantial theoretical advancements made by work on affect can be explored and attended to "in the field." Key questions to be explored in future work are how we can attend to and articulate these complex, ephemeral, and ultimately diffused spatialities of affect? And how can we research the spatialities in/of affect and what methodologies should we employ?

That said, there have been some suggestive responses to this. Ash (2010b) has shown the potential of digital video in studying the minute variations of the body's responses to and interactions with various forms of media technology (see Lorimer 2010; Simpson 2011). In thinking about the experience of sonic environments, Duffy and Waitt (2011) have developed interesting forms of elicitation-based methods through the use of "sound diaries" to gain an insight into various mediated sonic experiences. These examples aside though, it is evident that more remains to be done in thinking through how we study the imbrications of affect, space, and various forms of mediated communication.

References

Abrahamsson, S. and Simpson, P. 2011. The limits of the body: Boundaries, capacities, thresholds. *Social and Cultural Geography* 12(4): 331–38.

Adams, P.C. 2007. The chilling tale of a haunted child (or how I learned to start worrying and love the media). *Aether: The Journal of Media Geography* 1: 4–7.

Ahmed, S. 2010. Happy objects. In *The Affect Theory Reader.* Edited by M. Gregg, and G.J. Seigworth. London: Duke University Press, 29–51.

Anderson, B. 2005. Practices of judgement and domestic geographies of affect. *Social and Cultural Geography* 6(5): 645–59.

Anderson, B. 2006. Becoming and being hopeful: Towards a theory of affect. *Environment and Planning D: Society and Space* 24(5): 733–52.

Anderson, B. 2009. Affective atmospheres. *Emotion, Space and Society* 2(1): 77–81.

Anderson, B. and Harrison, P. 2006. Questioning affect and emotion. *Area* 38(3): 33–35.

Anderson, B., F. Morton, and G. Revill. 2005. Practices of music and sound. *Social and Cultural Geography* 6(5): 639–44.

Ash, J. 2009. Emerging spatialities of the screen: Video games and the reconfiguration of spatial awareness. *Environment and Planning A* 41(9): 2105–24.

Ash, J. 2010a. Architectures of affect: Anticipating and manipulating the event in practices of videogame design and testing. *Environment and Planning D: Society and Space* 28(4): 653–71.

Ash, J. 2010b. Teleplastic technologies: Charting practices of orientation and navigation in videogaming. *Transactions of the Institute of British Geographers* 35(3): 414–30.

Ash, J. 2013. Technologies of captivation: Videogames and the attunement of affect. *Body and Society* 19(1): 27-51.

Ash, J. and L.A. Gallacher. 2011. Cultural geography and videogames. *Geography Compass* 5(6): 351–68.

Atkinson, R. 2011. Ears have walls: Thoughts on the listening body in urban space. *Aether: The Journal of Media Geography* 7: 12–26.

Bissell, D. 2010. Passenger mobilities: Affective atmospheres and the sociality of public transport. *Environment and Planning D: Society and Space* 28(2): 270–89.

Bondi, L. and Davidson, J. 2011. Lost in translation. *Transactions of the Institute of British Geographers* 36(4): 595–98.

Brennan, T. 2004. *The Transmission of Affect.* London: Cornell University Press.

Carter, S. and McCormack, D. 2006 Film, geopolitics and the affective logics of intervention. *Political Geography* 25(2): 228–45.

Clough, P. 2010. The affective turn: Political economy, biomedia, and bodies. In *The Affect Theory Reader.* Edited by M. Gregg, and G.J. Seigworth. London: Duke University Press, 206–26.

Cohen, S. 1995. Sounding out the city: music and the sensuous production of place. *Transactions of the Institute of British Geographers* 20(4): 434–46.
Colebrook, C. 2002. *Gilles Deleuze.* London: Routledge.
Connell, J. and C. Gibson. 2003. *Sound Tracks: Popular Music, Identity and Place.* London: Routledge.
Connolly, W.E. 2002. *Neuropolitics: Thinking, Culture, Speed.* London: University of Minnesota Press.
Coulter, K. 2010. Low fidelity: A national appeals in Rosenstrasse's funding, production, and use. *Aether: The Journal of Media Geography* 6: 14–37.
Curti, G.H. and Craine, J. 2011. Lark's tongue in aspect: Progressing the scapes. *Aether: The Journal of Media Geography* 7: 137–40.
Curti, G.H., S.C. Aitken, F.J. Bosco, and D.D. Goerisch. 2011. For not limiting emotional and affectual geographies: A collective critique of Steve Pile's "Emotions and affect in recent human geography." *Transactions of the Institute of British Geographers* 36(4): 590–94.
Dawney, L. 2011. The motor of being: A response to Steve Pile's "Emotions and affect in recent human geography." *Transactions of the Institute of British Geographers* 36(4): 599–602.
Deleuze, G. 1978. Seminar given on Spinoza, January 24, 1978. www.webdeleuze.com/php/texte/php?cle=14&groupe=Spinoza&langue=2.
Deleuze, G. 1988. *Spinoza: Practical Philosophy.* San Fransisco: City Lights Books.
Deleuze, G. and F. Guattari. 2004. *A Thousand Plateaus: Capitalism and Schizophrenia.* London: Continuum.
Deleuze, G. and C. Parnet. 2006. *Dialogues II.* London: Continuum.
Dewsbury, J.D. 2010. Performative, non-representational, and affect-based research: Seven injunctions. In *The SAGE Handbook of Qualitative Research in Human Geography.* Edited by D. DeLyser, S. Aitken, M. Craig, S. Herbert, and L. McDowell. London: SAGE, 321–34.
Doel, M.A. and D. B. Clarke. 2007. Afterimages. *Environment and Planning D: Society and Space* 25(5): 890–910.
Duffy, M. and G. Waitt. 2011. Sound diaries: A method for listening to place. *Aether: The Journal of Media Geography* 7: 119–36.
Dyson, F. 2009. *Sounding New Media: Immersion and Embodiment in the Arts and Culture.* London: University of California Press.
Finn, J. 2011. Introduction: On Music and Movement ... *Aether: The Journal of Media Geography* 7: 1–11.
Goodman, S. 2010. *Sonic Warfare: Sound, Affect and the Ecology of Fear.* London: MIT Press.
Hill, I. 2012. Not quite bleeding from the ears: Amplifying sonic torture. *Western Journal of Communication* 76(3): 217–35.
Hillis, K. 2010. Los Angeles as moving picture. *Aether: The Journal of Media Geography* 6: 1–9.
Jackiewicz, E. 2007. Harmony in my head. *Aether: The Journal of Media Geography* 1: 28–30.
Keough, S. B. 2011. Promoting and preserving cultural identity through Newfoundland Radio music broadcasts. *Aether: The Journal of Media Geography* 7: 75–96.
Kong, L. 1995. Popular music in geographical analysis. *Progress in Human Geography* 19(2): 183–98.
Kong, L. 1996. Popular music in Singapore: Exploring local cultures, global resources, and regional identity. *Environment and Planning D: Society and Space* 14(3): 273–92.
Lammes, S. 2008. Playing the world: Computer games, cartography and spatial stories. *Aether: The Journal of Media Geography* 3: 84–96.
Latham, A. 2003. Research, performance, and doing human geography: some reflections on the diary-interview method. *Environment and Planning A* 35(11): 1993–2017.
Leonard, K.P. 2011. Topsy-turvy Victoriana: locating life and death in Corpse Bride. *Aether: The Journal of Media Geography* 7: 27–41.

Leyshon, A., D. Matless, and G. Revill. 1995. The place of music. *Transactions of the Institute of British Geographers* 20(4): 423–33.

Lorimer, H. 2005. Cultural geography: The busyness of being "more-than-representational." *Progress in Human Geography* 29(1): 83–94.

Lorimer, J. 2010. Moving image methodologies for more-than-human geographies. *Cultural Geographies* 17(2): 237–58.

Lukinbeal, C., J. Craine, and J. Dittmer. 2007. *Aether*: A prospectus. *Aether: The Journal of Media Geography* 1: 1–3.

Massumi, B. 2002. *Parables of the Virtual: Movement, Affect, Sensation.* London: Duke University Press.

Massumi, B. 2011. *Semblance and Event: Activist Philosophy and the Occurent Arts.* London: MIT Press.

McCormack, D. 2002. A paper with an interest in rhythm. *Geoforum* 33(4): 469–85.

McCormack, D. 2003. An event of geographical ethics in spaces of affect. *Transactions of the Institute of British Geographers* 28(4): 488–507.

McCormack, D. 2006. For the love of pipes and cables: A response to Deborah Thien. *Area* 38(3): 330–32.

McCormack, D. 2008a. Engineering affective atmospheres on the moving geographies of the 1897 Andrée Expedition. *cultural geographies* 15(4): 413–30.

McCormack, D. 2008b. Geographies for moving bodies: Thinking, dancing, spaces. *Geography Compass* 2(6): 1822–36.

McHugh, K. 2007. Celestial fire. *Aether: The Journal of Media Geography* 1: 34–38.

Moreno, C.M. 2007. Affecting and affective social/media fields. *Aether: The Journal of Media Geography* 1: 39–44.

Morley, V. and Somdahl-Sands, K. 2011. Music with a message: U2's rock concerts as spectacular spaces of politics. *Aether: The Journal of Media Geography* 7: 58–74.

Morton, F. 2005. Performing ethnography: Irish traditional music sessions and new methodological spaces. *Social and Cultural Geography* 6(5): 661–76.

Nancy, J.-L. 2007. *Listening.* New York: Fordham University Press.

Nancy, J.-L. 2008. Forword: Ascoltando. In *Listen: A History of Our Ears.* By P. Szendy. Translated by C. Mandell. New York: Fordham University Press, ix–xiii.

Pesses, M.W. 2011. What's he building in there? The existential geography of Tom Waits. *Aether: The Journal of Media Geography* 7: 42–57.

Picker, J.M. 2003. *Victorian Soundscapes.* Oxford: Oxford University Press.

Pile, S. 2010. Emotions and affect in recent human geography. *Transactions of the Institute of British Geographers* 35(1): 5–20.

Revill, G. 2000. Music and the politics of sound: Nationalism, citizenship, and auditory space. *Environment and Planning D: Society and Space* 18(5): 597–613.

Seigworth, G.J. and M. Gregg. 2010. An inventory of shimmers. In *The Affect Theory Reader.* Edited by M. Gregg and G.J. Seigworth. Durham, NC: Duke University Press, 1–26.

Shaviro, S. 2010. *Post-Cinematic Affect.* Winchester: Zero Books.

Shaw, I.G.R. and Warf, B. 2009. Worlds of affect: Virtual geographies of video games. *Environment and Planning A* 41(6): 1332–43.

Simmel, G. 2002. The metropolis and mental life. In *The Blackwell City Reader.* Edited by G. Bridge and S. Watson. Oxford: Blackwell, 103–10.

Simpson, P. 2009. "Falling on deaf ears": A post-phenomenology of sonorous presence. *Environment and Planning A* 41(11): 2556–75.

Simpson, P. 2011. 'So, as you can see ...': Some reflections on the utility video methodologies in the study of embodied practices. *Area* 43(3): 343–52.

Smith, S.J. 1997. Beyond geography's visible worlds: A cultural politics of music. *Progress in Human Geography* 21(4): 502–29.
Stewart, K. 2007. *Ordinary Affects.* Durham, NC: Duke University Press.
Szendy, P. 2008. *Listen: A History of Our Ears.* New York: Fordham University Press.
Thien, D. 2005. After or beyond feeling? A consideration of affect and emotion in geography. *Area* 37(4): 450–56.
Thrift, N. 1999. Steps to an ecology of place. In *Human Geography Today.* Edited by D. Massey, J. Allen, and P. Sarre. Cambridge: Polity, 295–323.
Thrift, N. 2003. Performance and … *Environment and Planning A* 35(11): 2019–24.
Thrift, N. 2004. Intensities of feeling: Towards a spatial politics of affect. *Geografiska Annaler B* 86(1): 57–78.
Thrift, N. and J.D. Dewsbury. 2000. Dead geographies, and how to make them live. *Environment and Planning D: Society and Space* 18(4): 411–32.
Toop, D. 2010. *Sinister Resonance: The Mediumship of the Listener.* London: Continuum.
Wood, N., M. Duffy, and S.J. Smith. 2007. The art of doing (geographies of) music. *Environment and Planning D: Society and Space* 25(5): 867–89.
Wood, N. and S.J. Smith. 2004. Instrumental routes to emotional geographies. *Social and Cultural Geography* 5(4): 533–48.

21 ASHGATE RESEARCH COMPANION

Spaces of Mediated Performance

Katrinka Somdahl-Sands and Paul C. Adams

In late October 2012, a video went viral on the Internet. It showed a four-year-old girl wearing a pink "Hello Kitty" coat, her face streaked with tears, saying, "I'm tired of Bronco Bamma and Mitt Romney!" Off-screen, a woman asked, "That's why you're crying?" The girl nodded and choked back a sob. The woman responded, "Aw … it'll be over soon Abby, OK?" The girl nodded again with her eyes shut while the voice continued soothingly: "The election will be over soon, OK?" The girl sobbed "OK" (Tired of Bronco Bamma 2012).

Posted on October 30, the video received over 13 million hits by Election Day, one week later. In the absence of a digital camera and the Internet, Abby's actions and words would have remained merely a spontaneous emotional outburst. Mediated communication allowed the private expression to become a public communication, and helped translate personal emotion into something transpersonal, into affect. This transformation illustrates three closely related points we wish to address in this chapter: (1) the nature of performance is evolving in response to technological mediation, as (2) new media make possible novel kinds of connection and separation, thereby (3) intervening in public/private dialectics (e.g. enabling private expressions of emotion to become publicly circulated performances).

We start from the assumption that performances of any sort are defined largely by the sociotechnical contexts of mediation in which they "take place" literally and/or figuratively. This process now enfolds technologies as diverse as the personal computer, modem, telephone cable or coaxial cable, electromagnetic signal, html code, and MPEG and WMV code into our experience of performance. Rather than seeing media as containers or conduits through which performances are channeled from place to place, diffusing information, images, or representations *through* space, we make a case for a synthetic perspective in which media are structured by performances while performances are simultaneously structured by media, thereby creating hybrid spaces. The object under consideration when we study performance is therefore what Latour (2005) would call a *mediator* rather than an *intermediary*, a link that translates at the same time it connects. The social is thoroughly intertwined with technology through this process (Latour 2005; Braun and Whatmore 2010), so the space-time configurations we experience as we perform and witness performance are not natural, given, or fixed things, but rather are dynamic syntheses of the social phenomena constituting mediated gathering (Adams 1992).

To explore these ideas, we start by reflecting on the transformation that presence undergoes as performance is mediated, a shift that is key to the changing meaning of the public/private dialectic. We then turn to concepts of liveness versus reenactment, notions undergoing parallel reconfigurations. We move from there to consider fandom and "counterpublics" (Warner 2002). Lastly, we consider politics as mediated performance and mediated performance as political action.

Presence

Performance as we use the term here entails a dialectic between the space of the viewer and the space of the actor (Carlson 1989: 128). Traditionally, this dialectic calls for a particular place of performance as indicated by the long-standing need to have both parties *present* in order for a performance to *take place*. For thousands of years, people have come together to experience communal song and dance, Greek tragedy, vaudeville, ballet, wrestling. One had to get one's body to a *place* where other bodies were gathering if one was to witness or participate in any of these performances. To perform and to witness both required spatial proximity and some kind of bounded enclosure to separate a gathering from the rest of the world. Bodies were brought close in the performance environment, but not *too* close. There was always experimentation with closeness, separation, and enclosure; indeed, the evolution of performance in its various forms has involved playing with *the gap* between audience and performers, narrowing or widening it, bridging or breaching it, to produce very particular effects (Tuan 1982).

Bodily convergence and separation have acted together as "framing devices" (Kershaw 1992: 15). Such devices distinguish everyday performances in the Goffmanesque sense of "strategic interaction" (Goffman 1959; 1969) from the special class of actions that are *experienced as performances,* "done by an individual or group in the presence of and for another individual or group" (Schechner 1977: 30). A crucial gap always remains between Us and Them, alerting the "audience, spectators or participants to the reflexive structure of what is staged, drawing attention to its constructed nature, and more or less to the assumptions – social and/or political and/or cultural and/or philosophical, etc. – through which that construction is achieved" (Kershaw 1992: 15). This generally holds for conventional forms of performance, but in many ways mediated communication disrupts this state of affairs.

In noting this change, we must avoid the trap of imagining a pristine world before the age of media in which people enjoyed performance experiences that were wholly unmediated. In this scenario "the media" (meaning electronic and digital media) descended like aliens landing in an innocent world of person-to-person performance. Contrary to this scenario, we contend that mediation and "the media" are part of a long process of sociotechnical hybridization involving a range of technologies including language, architecture, and urban design as well as mechanical and electronic devices. The spaces of traditional performance, such as streets, squares, stages, theaters, and coliseums were media since they shaped waves and vibrations. Matter was the medium that not only held together an ephemeral group for the duration of each performance but also formed a container for sound and light. "Greek theater," for example, employed seats, sky, *skene* (backdrop), and surrounding landscape to mediate distinct genres of performance such as comedy, tragedy, and satire. By literally shaping the seen into a scene, architectural containers employed stone, plaster, wood, and other forms of matter to help the actors, actions, and props perform. Likewise, today's wires, waves, and coded signals do not simply *carry* performances; they hold, contain, bound, and shape sights and sounds in ways that constitute actions as performances.

For this reason, electronically and digitally mediated performances do not create an entirely new separation between the space of the performer and the space of the audience but instead rework elements of connection and separation that are preexisting and inherent in performance itself. This process invites questions. What aspects of proximity are achieved through technologically extended eyes and ears? What kinds of release from the literal geographies (e.g. the friction of distance) are afforded by technologically mediated performances? If performance spaces are now more often built with wires and digital codes than with wood, metal, stone, and plaster, then how is the social function of performance shifting in response to these new, more fibrous, and less massive materialities that support it? To answer these questions it helps to focus attention on the changing constitution of publics.

The Publics of Mediated Performance

In the event of mediated performance, the audience must be imagined (Warner 2002: 8; Litt 2012). This does not mean the audience is imaginary. Though hidden, silent, and publicly invisible at the moment of performance, the particular audience constituted by a mediated performance is present in the minds of performers who respond to it with particular patterns of action, sensation, and interpretation. This indicates a reworking of the gap between the space of performance and the space of the audience. The performer-audience relationship can be reinvented precisely because of this new kind of gap, which hides the audience from the performers and also from other audience members, while rendering performers visible to a virtually unlimited number of spectators. Performers and audience members must imaginatively piece together *who* it was that actually received *what* impression, *where* the performance constituted its ephemeral presence, and *how* it was perceived and received. Yet to communicate effectively in such a mediated context, one must "forget or ignore the fictional nature of the entity one addresses" (Warner 2002: 12).

It is never simply a matter of media appealing to "the public," since new media encourage gatherings associated with multiple, ephemeral, temporary, and contingent publics (Fraser 1990). These publics come "together" with assumptions "about what can be said or what goes without saying" and some publics "contravene the rules obtaining in the world at large, being structured by alternative dispositions or protocols" (Warner 2002: 56). New media also remain distinctly porous and permit the involvement of *counterpublics* whose "exchanges remain distinct from authority and can have a critical relation to power" (Warner 2002: 56). The Internet, social media, and Twitter simultaneously create and hide such counterpublics.

Thus by shaping waves and flows of energy, diffused over great distances and through all sorts of barriers, new media create affordances for new forms of expression. A key way they do this is through codes and other "soft" mechanisms that include and exclude the members of particular publics (Kitchin and Dodge 2011; Adams 2009). One example of inclusion/exclusion is the practice of "friending" on Facebook; another is the act of subscribing or "unsubscribing" relative to an e-mail listserv; yet another is by "following" someone on Twitter. New terms and new uses of old terms indicate a plethora of ways of including and excluding, which in turn correspond to new insides and outsides from the vantage point of these proliferating publics. In other words, performance spaces are linked in particular patterns and directions within the larger web of all possible connections, so as to form very particular social topologies (Adams 1998).

Taking these points into account, the onset of electronic and digital media over the past 150 years clearly has not created the amorphous masses or disempowered drones envisioned by the critics (Debord 1995; Kroker and Weinstein 1994; Brook and Boal 1995). Rather, it has created very particular configurations of attention and engagement, new separations as well as new forms of presence, and reconstitutions of both private and public realms. Abby's private emotional outburst became a public performance in a space defined by the protocols of YouTube and other social media, which is to say by their particular ways of linking social actors and actions. More generally, new publics and counterpublics form and reform as each mediated performance not only coaxes into being its own particular audience, shaped by the affordances of the medium, but each new audience constituted by this ongoing mediation of publics remains, as ever, subject to various "half-articulate struggles" (Warner 2002: 15) that wall it off in particular ways from the rest of the social world. It follows that countless new publics are reworking the public/private dialectic of social life – a situation that deserves much greater attention that it has been afforded thus far.

Transforming the Public/Private Dialectic

We have argued that mediated performances work in various ways to counterbalance the linear distance and separation between performers and audience members. This distance-reducing work often takes the form of fandom – an array of practices that make a "very real contribution to the social identity the products of [cultural] industries provide for us" (Harris 1998b: 42). Fandom is, of course, its own type of performance, engaged in spontaneously as a response to more obvious *performances*. Whereas textual analyses situate meanings in hermeneutic circles between texts and social contexts, studies of fandom are complementary in that they highlight the ways in which audiences engage performatively with specific texts, causing the hermeneutic circles to revolve. As recently as 1998, fandom was described as "profoundly untheorized" (Harris 1998a: 4), but the first decade of the twenty-first century has altered this situation, particularly with the blossoming of scholarly interest in reality television and social media. Of particular interest is how fans rework media texts and insert their own ideas and images into texts and intertextual spaces, creating "slash" and "mashup" products, recombinant creations facilitated by digitization. People "come to see themselves as 'owners' of texts … and believe that they contribute to the production of the text over time" (Harris 1998b: 48). This belief is justified because by blurring the distinctions between creators and producers and between audiences and consumers, the practices of fandom reduce the sensed separation between performers and audiences.

In computer-mediated-communication, in particular, we find performances that extend these boundary-dissolving dynamics. Consider a post by a MySpace user: "Are we still gonna go paintballing?" (boyd 2008: 124). Directed from a teenager to his friend, this fragment of private conversation is hard to pin down as either private or public: "In essence, Corey's friend is writing a purportedly private message to him in a public space for others to view. Corey will reply to the comment in kind, writing the answer on his friend's profile. By doing this, teens are taking social interactions between friends into the public sphere for others to witness" (boyd 2008: 124). The words in a posted message like this are not published in the conventional sense, nor are they sent through private channels like traditional postal correspondence. The sociotechnical context they occupy and at the same time help to recreate is a novel kind of performance stage where the structuring of public and private takes a hybridized form.

There are reasons for this hybridity and the avoidance of, say, cell phone texting, which would be unambiguously private,[1] as well as the avoidance of overtly public appeals such as "who wants to play paintball" that could be posted on a Facebook Wall or MySpace Testimonial page. The social milieu of a teenager is an environment that does not particularly value civility, and an open invitation would invite a clever and cutting comeback, whereas Cory's public/private question lies in wait, seemingly addressing a friend while coyly

1 Although experienced as "private" this is still subject to interception and may be subject to subpoena depending on state law.

engaging a public – he assumes a public performance space supplemented, enhanced, or embroidered with an enactment of private communications.

Performances in social media navigate the boundaries between public and private in new ways by embedding performances in code rather than in matter. Once again, it is helpful to note historical continuities as well as differences. Warner (2002: 77) elucidates a recurring aspect of communication: "Public speech must be taken in two ways: as addressed to us and as addressed to strangers. The benefit in this practice is that it gives a general social relevance to private thought and life." But something new is happening when a comment directed to a friend acts as *a public performance of a private tie*. This is the shift marked by the changing meaning of "friend" as in "friend me." One racks up a collection of performed friendships. "MySpace Friends are not just people that one knows, but public displays of connections" (boyd 2008: 129). Performance within social media does not just give a general social relevance to private thought and life; it self-consciously performs a particular private world within the scope of shared viewing that constitutes *a particular public* unlike earlier publics in certain ways.

For some observers, "cyberspace" implies absolute uniformity and homogeneity (Graham 2013) but we hold this to be an extreme view. We understand cyberspace as a heterogeneous aggregate of performance stages – the cyberplaces in which various types of performance occur. The rich dynamics of technologically mediated place are indicated by danah boyd who employs the term "networked publics," not only extending Fraser's (1990) arguments but also indicating that these publics form networks of connections across space and time bound by persistence, searchability, replicability, and invisibility (boyd 2008). Such network-based places can be refuges from authority, as online teenagers, for example, escape from parental surveillance into an interaction context that is (at least apparently) free of adult supervision and control. When parents attempt to intervene, teenagers employ aliases to enact a kind of barrier excluding the unwanted parental audiences. More generally, loss of privacy threatens "self-organized publics" (Warner 2002: 69) but social networking sites provide audience-feedback mechanisms that help users to "share clues about who is in the audience" (Litt 2012: 337) and subsequently re-bound various publics.

Nonetheless, the permeability of electronic boundary mechanisms means that there is a high risk of trespassing and leakage. A teacher supposes a Facebook posting will be read by the close friends she has "friended" but it can easily escape from that technological container and attract an audience of students, parents, and school administrators, with embarrassing and potentially costly consequences (Heussner and Fahmy 2010). A middle school student may send an online message to a few hundred Facebook-friends, only to have it intercepted, expanding the audience in a way that leads to expulsion from school (CBS 2012). These risks can be exacerbated by carelessness with regard to presentation of self, arising from the unwarranted presumption of privacy. Such slippage in identity-management often leads to efforts to reestablish new boundaries around one's performances. Consequently, more than two-thirds of users of social network sites report adjusting site settings so as to limit the access of certain others (Madden and Smith 2010). This reputation-managing activity indicates the pervasive theatricality of life – not simply in the old, Goffmanesque sense that people perform roles in order to be social, but in a new sense involving constant monitoring of the front-stage mechanisms constituting multiple publics. This ongoing identity management is a learned response; people in their twenties are 50 percent more likely than people over 30 to have deleted comments from their Facebook page or removed "tags" from online photographs (Madden and Smith 2010). Lovink describes this activity as "techno-sculpturing":

> *The cyber-prophets were wrong: there is no evidence that the world is becoming more virtual. Rather the virtual is becoming more real; it wants to penetrate and map out our real lives and social relationships. Self-management and techno-sculpturing become crucial: how do you shape the self in real-time flows? No longer encouraged to act out a role, we are forced to be 'ourselves' (in a form that is no less theatrical or artificial). We constantly login, create profiles, and post status updates to present our Self on the global marketplace of employment, friendship, and love. (Lovink 2011: 13)*

This focus on performing the self in mediated contexts is sometimes referred to as *self-work*, meaning a new form of labor entailing the "transformation of intimacy through its detailing and publicising" (Skeggs and Wood 2009: 231, 245). On this account, the new virtual spaces demand unpaid labor in image-management while imposing old divisions of class, gender, and race.

Such critiques miss some of the subtle dynamics involved in performing the self in new media environments. One wrinkle of this so-called self-work is the choosing of an avatar and/or screen-name. Game players often take the form of an avatar of the opposite sex (Consalvo and Harper 2009: 100) and many avatars have exaggerated sexual dimorphism – indicating masculinity with exaggerated muscles and femininity with exaggerated breasts and hips. While this cross-gender performance of the self in play may not moderate sexism and most likely accentuates it, it suggests the more general ludic impulses behind online constructions of self. A player of World of Warcraft indicates such a realignment of self from a woman's perspective: "I sort of like playing characters that I think look sexy … I sort of feel like it should bother me. But it doesn't" (quoted in Consalvo and Harper 2009: 107). Here the crafting of self is presented as a guilty pleasure that belies the grim utilitarianism implied by "self-work." Technological mediation introduces a creative gap between naturally and artificially embodied selves, bringing new forms of play (as well as work) into the performance of self. Mediated performances also rework time, especially via the construct of "liveness."

Liveness

Live performance used to be distinct from recorded performance with its ability to involve us directly – invoking a very special relationship between acting and the temporal construct of the now. The link to an actor was instant and therefore sensuous, actively receptive, intuitive, and noncognitive (Dewey 1934; Tuan 2004; Escobar 1994; Carlson 1996). New forms of performance may seem to abandon performance's "direct qualitative experience that is characteristically nondiscursive and hence nonrational" (Berleant 1970: 119) because they depend on the use of codes and software. But this critique presumes too much. The liveness of performance has not been abandoned or destroyed by new media, even if it has "been complicated in recent years … by the widening magnitudes of performance that seem to be leaving the theater behind" (Blau 2011: 247; see also Auslander 1999; Dixon 2011).

One element of continuity from old to new performance is the enduring popularity of television. The small (and now not so small) screen still has a vitally important role in redefining media in general and mediated presence in particular (Calhoun 2004: 4). A television program is perceived as embodying the here and now; television's construction of liveness is "basic to shaping the broad 'information background' to all public discourse" (Calhoun 2004: 4), and "the viewer of the television scene feels himself to be on the scene" (Lohr 1940: 3; see also Auslander 1999). Lenox Lohr, the former president of NBC, argued that "the most utilitarian feature of television lies in broadcasting events *exactly when and as they happen ... .* [t]elevision's essential properties as a medium are *immediacy* and *intimacy*" (Lohr 1940: 52, original emphasis), which lets people "see politics as practiced, sports as played, drama as enacted, news as it happens, history as it is made" (Dunlap 1947: 48).

The time-shifting that became available with the invention of the VCR, TiVo, Hulu, and the Internet did not fully undermine this experience of liveness. Televisual experience retains something of its essence as "a fleeting one-time, quasi live event" (Wurtzler 1992: 259). Earlier ruptures in shared experience revealed liveness as socially constituted and variable (Berger et al. 1972; Meinig 1979; Jay 1988). What is new since the 1960s is that as the viewing public has become more familiar with copies than with originals, and the originals have in many ways become secondary to and dependent on the copies, liveness itself has changed to include new forms of mediation. We must therefore reappraise when and how a temporally and geographically specific sense of liveness and presence is created through broadcast performances.

One does not simply watch the Internet but explores or surfs it – commenting, pinning, and posting – and one's engagement with other data devices takes place in the here and now, infusing the sense of being in place with the flow of multiple engagements with an evolving text. These actions suggest the prevalence of what feminist theorist Katie King would call "pastpresents, run together all in one word, in which pasts and presents very literally mutually construct each other" (2011: 12). Digital recording and transmission spread out the "now" of performance across space and time, a mediatization that has so shaped sensory norms that when confronted with a facsimile of a performance alongside an embodied performance, audiences often pay more attention to the screen bodies than the living, breathing bodies (Auslander 1999).

As performers use media of all sorts to transform spatiotemporal separation (Irish 2010), there is an obsession with immediacy in all of its permutations. Perhaps "real-time is the new crack" (Lovink 2011: 11) but it is more to the point to see

> *[T]he computer screen [as] a new type of theatre proscenium, in and through which to create new modes and interactive genres of theatrical (as well as social) performance. Hence the web can be considered as "the largest theatre in the world, offering everyone fifteen megabytes of fame." (Dixon 2011: 4)*

In his well-known essay, "The Work of Art in the Age of Mechanical Reproduction," Walter Benjamin (1936) traced the distinction between live and recorded performance, attributing *aura* to live performance as a consequence of the specialness of the moment of artistic creation and its singular position in space-time (Savage 2000). The notion of aura implies a link between the artwork as a unique and therefore valuable object and the unique time or times of its creation. Technological mediation fractures and multiplies this creative moment, in turn threatening to undermine notions of artistic value, at least those based on an auratic tie to a unique time-space origin (Auslander 1999: 50).

The line between the live and the recorded seems to be eroding. However, following Auslander (1999; see also Phelan 1993; Dixon 2011) we would suggest that new forms of liveness are available in technologically mediated reproductions. As distance, separation, place, space, and presence have evolved, so has liveness, becoming fluid, mutable, and prolific. It has been found, for example, that people smile more if they watch an amusing video with someone else than if they watch it alone, and surprisingly this effect remains even if the friend watching the video at the same time is in a different room or is only *believed to be* watching the video somewhere else at the same time (Fridlund 1991). Shared witnessing remains an emotionally potent experience despite mediation, and the mental response to liveness endures even if the bodies of audience members are separated in space and if the performance is prerecorded.

What mediation does is enable liveness to be distributed through time and space. Abby's tears were live for an entire week around the world. Online comments like Cory's paintball invitation are current as long as they remain near the top of a social media page. Liveness itself is not destroyed even if media unsettle the traditional associations between performance, space, and time. There is however a changed *sense of liveness*, detached from the semimetaphysical moment of artistic creation while remaining saturated with affective qualities:

> *Public discourse craves attention like a child. Texts clamor at us. Images solicit our gaze. Look here! Listen! Hey! In doing so, they by no means render us passive. Quite the contrary. The modern system of publics creates a demanding social phenomenology. (Warner 2002: 89)*

Historically, then, there was a radical potential in the synergy created through the physical performance place, the performers' embodied presence, and the willing engagement of the audience (Dolan 2001). These elements constituted liveness. We have argued that new places of mediated performance have their own radical potential to create forms of presence and liveness. Let us turn now to consider what this means for the politics of performance and for political performance.

Politics and Performance

We have seen how a child's confusion and frustration can become part of political discourse and affect through the dispersal of liveness and presence through a YouTube video. Unlike children, adults generally use media self-consciously and deliberately to bring political responses to various publics and their spaces and places. This politicization of performance draws on the long-standing political role of theater, which Václav Havel characterized as "a sensitive seismograph of an era, perhaps the most sensitive one there is; it's a sponge that quickly soaks up important ingredients in the atmosphere around it" (1990: 51). Similarly, he reflected on dance as politically potent as a manifestation of political resistance through

> *uncensored life, life that spits on all ideology and all that lofty world of babble; a life that intrinsically resisted all forms of violence, all interpretations, all directives. Suddenly, against the world of appearance and interpretation, here stood truth – the truth of young people who couldn't care less about any of that, who wanted only to live in their own way, to dance the way they wanted to dance, simply to be in harmony with their own nature. (Havel 1990: 49)*

Dramatizing and embodying emotion, participating in the flow of affect through theater and dance, one can be in tune with the mood of the time and simultaneously break new social ground – a dual role that has been crucial to the political power of in-place performance. These political potentials spill over into new media.

The political potency of dance depends simultaneously on the occupation of a very particular place, and on the mobilization of mediated discourses about the history and meaning of variously scaled places, including not only the stage (or street) where a dance occurs but also the surrounding city and society at large (Somdahl-Sands 2008). Bringing this idea into juxtaposition with the arguments of this paper, scale politics of performance are not a matter of either–or (either physical or virtual performance) but rather of both-and: dance now simultaneously *takes place* and engages with place-transcending, "virtual" discourses. Bringing together physical and virtual embodiment a thirdspace is "created through the dancer's actions which disrupt traditional methods of understanding the body in space, urban public spaces, and what audience members do" (Somdahl-Sands 2006: 612). This process involves not only the placement and movement of bodies in state territories and urban spaces but also a symbolic attack on norms, expectations, and values that circulate in the media.

Mediation extends and complicates the multiscalar political dynamics of performance. By working with and against mediated versions of reality, a performance at one scale resonates at another scale. As Craig Calhoun explains in connection with the dynamics emerging around the 1989 democracy movement in China, this political movement was on the one hand, "intensively focused on Tiananmen Square," while on the other hand it "existed in a 'metatopical public space' of multinational media and indirect relationships to a world of diverse and far-flung actors" (1989: 55). Whether engaged through nonviolent marches, protest occupations, hunger strikes, or other theatrical means, the political power of performance owes much to the strategic combination of place-based and mediated communications that together mobilize scale politics (Adams 1996).

If politics is about the struggle to define meaning, then we must not overlook the political struggles arising over the mediation of art and the ways in which mediated art engages in politics. To again take dance as an example, the hallmarks of this particular art form – its integration of space, time, and energy – may become a cause célèbre for campaigns against mediation. "Capture" in media can be seen to threaten dance's beauty, the poignancy of an existence so fleeting that it seems paradoxically to transcend time (Foster 2004: 39). In addition, between live and mediated dance there is a significant gap in regard to what can be seen, what gestures can be read, and how a dance is read as a whole. Watching a film or video of a dance, the audience can be "incredibly close to the performers, closer than we would ever be in a theatre, and [can] see every grain of dirt as it [clings] to the dancers' sweat" (Harass 2012), but this closeness is not merely an amplification. The screen body becomes something other than what it was, a creature of angle and focus, lighting, and editing style. Mediated performance therefore foregrounds a new political ideal of visibility based on repetition, multiplicity, manipulation, minimization of distance, and maximization of detail. From this translation emerges

> *an impossible oscillation between two poles of what was once seemed a clear opposition: whereas mediatized performance derives its authority from its reference to the live or the real, the live now derives its authority from its reference to the mediatized, which derives its authority from its reference to the live, etc. (Auslander 1999: 39)*

The filming of dance is consequently politicized through a heated debate about enhancement or loss, creativity or destruction (Barnes 1985; Noe 2012; Dodds 2001: 23). But mediation confers a unique political opportunity for dance to move more people, and do so in ways that are both pragmatic and ethical, as well as aesthetic and emotional (Reed 1998: 514–16).

This is not to confer on mediated political communication some sort of natural or automatic progressivism. As David Morley notes, media foreground the dominant constructions of the national community, creating a "national family" and a sense of "symbolic home" (2000: 105–27) that may quell political debate. However, "community" is always contested. Whether we consider television talk shows that give a public voice to women's issues, assisting in the construction of women as a public or cable and satellite television stations that bring some diversity to the "whiteness of the public sphere" or the Americanized dance performances of the Eurovision Song Contest, countercurrents roil the mediated construction of national community (Morley 2000: 116, 123; Edensor 2002).

It has been clear since the Nixon-Kennedy debates of 1960 that new media constitute new stages, drastically reworking the ways one can and must perform politics (Hellweg et al. 1992: 71–99), and the results are not always politically regressive. These reworkings are now apparent around the world even if media technologies are distributed unevenly and not everyone has access to every new medium (Lynch 2006). In poor countries, even a relatively privileged minority with access to communication technologies like mobile phones and the Internet can form the vanguard of a popular resistance movement insisting on government accountability and transparency (Fahmi 2009). It is increasingly clear that mediated performance of national identity works not only from the top-down, imposing standardized images and identities, but also from the bottom-up, disrupting such homogeneous national imaginaries.

Ai Weiwei

Thus we turn to the resistant scale politics of mediated artwork, as demonstrated brilliantly by the Chinese artist Ai Weiwei, who has become famous for exposing the ambivalences of modern Chinese aesthetics, culture, and politics. Weiwei gathered international acclaim for his architectural designs such as the "Bird's Nest" stadium used for the 2008 Olympics. Rather than retreat to comfortable popularity, and cash in on his cachet, he has instead employed both subtle and brutal means to highlight China's political opacity and to question nationalist iconography. By flipping off Tiananmen Square, swearing at the "motherland," posing nude in a cooking pot, ordering 100 million hand-painted sunflower seeds, welding together 1,200 bicycles, and dropping antique vases to the floor, he has made himself an icon of impropriety and irreverence, sometimes stretching and sometimes shattering nationalist imaginaries. There is something performative about all of his artwork. When not bodily performing the art, he sets in motion the gears of a collective performance as a means of reshaping matter, similar to the way Christo mobilizes a collectivity to bring his works into being.

Entirely consistent with this are his uses of new media. Adopting the role of public intellectual (Jacoby 2000), he has employed the Internet, Twitter, cell phones, and video to expose government brutality, corruption, and indifference. This mediated presence depends on the way he has branded himself across diverse media – using irreverence, absurdity, and profanity, along with an eye for beauty, to create and nurture a small Chinese counterpublic. Rather than merely call *for* democracy, he instead calls *out to* something – a nascent public that rejects the notion that China's cultural heritage is sacrosanct.

Perhaps the most famous of Ai Weiwei's political interventions was his effort to bring visibility and recognition to the thousands of children who died in the 2008 Sichuan earthquake. Ai Weiwei organized a team of supporters to canvas the region and collect information, ultimately compiling a list of 5,212 names of the children who had died largely because of faulty construction by government contractors and corruption of inspectors. On the first anniversary of the earthquake, he posted the list on his blog and released a video documentary about the quake. Authorities responded by shutting down his blog, so he turned to Twitter and established a large following, extending his campaign for government transparency through frequent tweets. For the two-year anniversary, he called on volunteers to record one name and upload the recording to an Internet team for compilation with the other children's names as a single sound file (Ai Weiwei: Never Sorry 2012). Digital editing telescoped the space and time between these separate speech acts, bringing them together in a collective online performance. These name lists – both visual and auditory – functioned as powerful memorials to the thousands of children who had lost their lives in the quake.

Weiwei's scale politics target the impulse to remain silent and invisible, to silence oneself for the sake of national unity. According to Evan Osnos, China correspondent for the *New Yorker*, "The question of what deserves to be public and what belongs to the public – that's what he's fighting about" (*Ai Weiwei: Never Sorry* 2012).

Technology can serve government authorities, for example permitting them to monitor the coming and going of dissidents through surveillance cameras (Curry 1997; Graham and Wood 2003; Crampton 2004), but it can also afford opportunities for various kinds of political performance. As Ai Weiwei attests, "Blogs and the Internet are great inventions for our time because they give regular people an opportunity to change public opinion" (Ai Weiwei: Never Sorry 2012). He was imprisoned for three months in 2011, but yet again translating experience into performance, he produced a goofy remake of the viral dance video "Gangnam Style" in which he twirls handcuffs in the air. His ability to remain a thorn in the side of Chinese authorities can hardly be explained except in light of his "lengthening digital shadow," which makes him "a nearly untouchable figure to authorities who might otherwise have stopped him" (Ambrozy 2011: xxiii, xxv).

This is not a placeless strategy by any means, nor is it a form of territorial contestation within given political borders. Instead, it is a hybrid of place-based and place-transcending strategies that is powerful precisely because it brings one type of power, at one scale, to bear on another type of power at a different scale (see Lipsky 1968). On his blog Weiwei wrote, "Nationalism is only a fig leaf for the feeble-minded, a tricky maneuver that prevents everyone from seeing the complete picture" (Weiwei 2011: 177). Through media he has appealed to, and developed, a public in China that is not "the Chinese public." The place-transcending power of the discursive and artistic appeal is used to provide both global and local leverage against the territorially bounded power of state authorities.

Conclusion

Mediated communication allows private expression to become public communication, translating personal emotion into affect that circulates transpersonally across multiple scales. This process was not initiated by the Internet or even by telecommunication and broadcast technologies; mediated performance is part of a long sociotechnical process whereby a range of technologies including architecture and urban design have become hybridized with human articulations and actions. Performance has for a long time undergone transformations in response to technological mediation. Today these transformations involve novel kinds of performance, creative and playful constructions of self, deliberate intervention in public/private dialectics, and new genres of political activism.

The crucial *who, what, where,* and *how* of performance are now shaped intimately by technological forms of separation, connection, inclusion, and exclusion. There is a reworking of the gap between the space of performance and the space of the audience. Into this gap a reinvented performer-audience relationship is growing like a weed. The performance of self is becoming more self-consciously performative and creative as people present themselves through various types of "posting" in public-private mediated spaces, techno-sculpturing their avatars and reworking the public-private divide at the heart of authorship by performing self through mashups of others' performances. In addition to posting, friending, following, subscribing, and unsubscribing are some of the ways we position ourselves relative to publics that are imagined, but not imaginary.

Presence and liveness used to anchor performance in the here and now. As performances have become hybridized with new technologies, presence no longer demands a single *here* and liveness no longer demands a single *now*. All of this might suggest a radically depoliticized space of public engagement – a politically ungrounded world of simulations, spectacle, surveillance, and voyeurism. In contrast, we offer the example of Ai Weiwei, whose performances in diverse communication media (including digital and more traditional media) creates multiple spaces of radical politics. We see risks and challenges, as well as opportunities within this scene, for both the politics and the poetics of performance.

Acknowledgments

Paul Adams wishes to thank the Department of Geography and the Environment at the University of Texas at Austin for a course reduction that enabled him to attend the UT Humanities Institute, and he wishes to thank the organizers and participants of the latter for a series of stimulating discussions that inspired his work on this project during fall semester of 2012.

References

Adams, P.C. 1992. Television as gathering place. *Annals of the Association of American Geographers* 82(1): 117–35.

Adams, P.C. 1996. Protest and the scale politics of telecommunications. *Political Geography* 15(5): 419–41.

Adams, P.C. 1998. Network topologies and virtual place. *Annals of the Association of American Geographers* 88(1): 88–106.

Adams, P.C. 2009. *Geographies of Media and Communication*. London: Wiley-Blackwell.

Ai Weiwei: Never Sorry. 2012. Directed by A. Klayman. United Expression Media/MUSE Film and Television.

Ambrozy, L. 2011. Introduction. In *Ai Weiwei's Blog: Writings, Interviews, and Digital Rants, 2006–2009*. Edited and translated by L. Ambrozy. Writing Art Series. Cambridge, MA: MIT Press.

Auslander, P. 1999. *Liveness: Performance in a Mediatized Culture*. London: Routledge.

Barnes, C. and A. Livet (eds). 1985. *Contemporary Dance*. New York: Abbeville Press.

Benjamin, W. 1936. The work of art in the age of mechanical reproduction. In *Video Culture: A Critical Investigation*. Edited by J. Hanhardt. Rochester, NY: Gibbs M. Smith, Inc/Peregrine Smith Books in association with Visual Studies Workshop Press, 27–52.

Berger, J., S. Blomberg, C. Fox, M. Dibb, and R. Hollis. 1972. *Ways of Seeing*. London: British Broadcasting Corporation; London and New York: Penguin Books/BBC.

Berleant, A. 1970. *The Aesthetic Field: A Phenomenology of Aesthetic Experience*. Springfield, IL: Charles C. Thomas, Publisher.

Blau, H. 2011. *Reality Principles: From the Absurd to the Virtual*. Ann Arbor: University of Michigan Press.

boyd, d. 2008. Why youth ♥ social network sites: The role of networked publics in teenage social life. In *Youth, Identity, and Digital Media*. Edited by D. Buckingham. The John D. and Catherine T. MacArthur Foundation Series on Digital Media and Learning. Cambridge, MA: MIT Press.

Braun, B. and S.J. Whatmore. 2010. *Political Matter: Technoscience, Democracy and Public Life*. Minneapolis: University of Minnesota Press.

Brook, J. and I.A. Boal (eds). 1995. *Resisting the Virtual Life: The Culture and Politics of Information*. San Francisco: City Lights.

Bruneau, T. 1979. The time dimension in intercultural communication. In *Communication Yearbook 3*. Edited by D. Nimmo. New Brunswick, NJ: Transaction Books, 423–33.

Calhoun, C. 1989. Tiananmen, television and the public sphere: Internationalization of culture and the Beijing Spring of 1989. *Public Culture* 2: 54–71.

Calhoun, C. 2004. Information technology and the international public sphere. In *Shaping the Network Society: The New Role of Civil Society in Cyberspace*. Edited by D. Schuler and P. Day. Cambridge, MA: MIT Press.

Carlson, M. 1989. *Places of Performance: The Semiotics of Theater Architecture*. Ithaca, NY: Cornell University Press.

Carlson, M. 1996. *Performance: A Critical Introduction*. London and New York: Routledge.

CBS. 2012. Three students expelled over Facebook posts about killing classmates [April 25, CBS online]. Available at: www.chicago.cbslocal.com/2012/04/25/3-students-expelled-over-facebook-conversation-about-killing-classmates [accessed December 31, 2012].

Consalvo, M. and Harper, T. 2009. The sexi(e)st of all: Avatars, gender, and online games. In *Virtual Social Networks: Mediated, Massive and Multiplayer Sites*. Edited by N. Panteli. New York: Palgrave/St. Martin's Press, 98–113.

Crampton, J.W. 2004. *The Political Mapping of Cyberspace*. Chicago: University of Chicago Press.

Curry, M.R. 1997. The digital individual and the private realm. *Annals of the Association of American Geographers* 87(4): 681–99.

Debord, G. 1995. *The Society of the Spectacle*. Translated by D. Nicholson-Smith. New York: Zone Books.

Dewey, J. 1934. *Art as Experience*. New York: Capricorn Books.

Dixon, S. 2011. Researching digital performance: Virtual practices. In *Research Methods in Theatre and Performance*. Edited by B. Kershaw and H. Nicholson. Edinburgh, UK: Edinburgh University Press, 41–62.

Dodds, S. 2001. *Dance on Screen: Genres and Media from Hollywood to Experimental Art*. 2nd ed. Hampshire, UK: Palgrave Macmillan.

Dolan, J. 2001. Performance, utopia, and the "utopian performative." *Theatre Journal* 53: 455–79.

Dunlap, O.E. Jr. 1947.*Understanding Television*. New York: Greenberg Press.

Edensor, T. 2002. *National Identity, Popular Culture and Everyday Life*. Oxford, UK: Berg.

Escobar, E. 1994. The heuristic power of art. In *The Subversive Imagination: Artists, Society, and Social Responsibility*. Edited by C. Becker. New York: Routledge, 35–54.

Fahmi, W.S. 2009. Bloggers' street movement and the right to the city: (Re)claiming Cairo's real and virtual "spaces of freedom." *Environment and Urbanization* 21(1): 89–107.

Foster, S.C. (ed.). 2004. *Crisis and the Arts: The History of Dada*. New York: G.K. Hall & Company.

Fraser, N. 1990. Rethinking the public sphere: A contribution to the critique of actually existing democracy, *Social Text* 25/26: 56–80.

Fridlund, A.J. 1991. Sociality of solitary smiling: Potentiation by an implicit audience. *Journal of Personality and Social Psychology* 60(2): 229–40.

Giddens, A. 1984. *The Constitution of Society*. Berkeley: University of California Press.

Goffman, E. 1959. *The Presentation of Self in Everyday Life*. Garden City, NY: Doubleday Anchor Books.

Goffman, E. 1969. *Strategic Interaction.* Philadelphia: University of Pennsylvania Press.

Graham, M. 2013. Geography/Internet: Ethereal alternate dimensions of cyberspace or grounded augmented realities? *Geographical Journal* 179(2): 177–82.

Graham, S. and D. Wood. 2003. Digitizing surveillance: Categorization, space, inequality. *Critical Social Policy* 23(2): 227–48.

Harris, C. 1998a. Introduction. In *Theorizing Fandom: Fans, Subculture, and Identity*. Edited by C. Harris and A. Alexander. Cresskill, NJ: Hampton Press, 3–8.

Harris, C. 1998b. A sociology of television fandom. In *Theorizing Fandom: Fans, Subculture, and Identity*. Edited by C. Harris and A. Alexander. Cresskill, NJ: Hampton Press, 41–54.

Harvey, D. 1990. Between space and time: Reflections on the geographical imagination. *Annals of the Association of American Geographers* 80(3): 418–34.

Havel, V. 1990. *Disturbing the Peace: A Conversation with Karel Hvížd'ala.* Translated by P. Wilson. New York: Vintage Books/Random House.

Hellweg, S.A., M. Pfau, and S.R. Brydon. 1992. *Televised Presidential Debates: Advocacy in Contemporary America.* New York: Praeger.

Heussner, K.M. and D. Fahmy. 2010. Teacher loses job after commenting about students, parents on Facebook. ABC News, August 19, 2010. Available at: www.abcnews.go.com/Technology/facebook-firing-teacher-loses-job-commenting-students-parents/story?id=11437248#.UKk30Id9KSo [accessed December 31, 2012].

Irish, S. 2010. *Suzanne Lacy: Spaces Between.* Minneapolis: University of Minnesota Press.

Jacoby, R. 2000. The last intellectuals: American culture in the age of academe. New York: Basic Books.

Jay, M. 1988. Scopic regimes of modernity. In *Vision and Visuality*. Edited by H. Foster. Seattle, WA: Bay Press, 3–38.

Kershaw, B. 1992. *The Politics of Performance: Radical Theater as Cultural Intervention.* London and New York: Routledge.

King, K. 2011. Networked reenactments: A thick description amid authorships, audiences and agencies in the nineties. Based on a paper presented March 7, 2008, to the Washington Area Group for Print Culture Studies. Washington, DC: Library of Congress.

Kitchin, R. and M. Dodge. 2011. *Code/Space: Software and Everyday Life.* Cambridge, MA: MIT Press.

Kroker, A. and M.A. Weinstein. 1994. *Data Trash: The Theory of the Virtual Class.* New York: St. Martin's Press.

Latour, B. 2005. *Reassembling the Social: An Introduction to Actor-Network-Theory.* Oxford and New York: Oxford University Press.

Lipsky, M. 1968. Protest as a political resource. *American Political Science Review* 62: 1144–58.

Litt, E. 2012. *Knock, Knock.* Who's there? The imagined audience. *Journal of Broadcasting and Electronic Media* 56(3): 330–45.

Lohr, L.R. 1940. *Television Broadcasting: Production, Economics, Technique.* New York: McGraw-Hill.

Lovink, G. 2011. *Networks Without a Cause: A Critique of Social Media.* Cambridge, UK: Polity Press.

Lynch, M. 2006. *Voices of the New Arab Public: Iraq, al Jazeera, and Middle East Politics Today.* New York: Columbia University Press.

Madden, M. and A. Smith. 2010. Reputation management and social media. Washington, DC: Pew Internet and American Life Project. Available at: www.pewinternet.org/~/media//Files/Reports/2010/PIP_Reputation_Management.pdf [accessed December 31, 2012].

Meinig, D.W. 1979. The beholding eye: Ten versions of the same scene. In *The Interpretation of Ordinary Landscapes: Geographical Essays*. Edited by D.W. Meinig and J.B. Jackson. New York: Oxford University Press, 33–48.

Morley, D. 2000. *Home Territories: Media, Mobility and Identity*. New York and London: Routledge.
Mumford, L. 1963. *Technics and Civilization*. New York: Harcourt, Brace & World, Inc.
Phelan, P. 1993. *Unmarked: The Politics of Performance*. New York and London: Routledge.
Reed, S.A. 1998. The politics and poetics of dance. *Annual Review of Anthropology* 27: 503–32.
Savage, M. 2000. Walter Benjamin's urban thought: A critical analysis. In *Thinking Space*. Edited by M. Crang and N. Thrift. London and New York: Routledge, 33–53.
Scarry, E. 1999. The difficulty of imagining other people. In *Human Rights in Political Transitions: Gettysburg to Bosnia*. Edited by C. Hesse and R. Post. Berkeley: University of California Press, 277–312.
Schechner, R. 1977. *Performance Theory*. New York and London: Routledge.
Skeggs, B. and H. Wood. 2009. The transformation of intimacy: Classed identities in the moral economy of reality television. In *Identity in the 21st Century: New Trends in Changing Times*. Edited by M. Wetherell. New York: Palgrave/St. Martin's Press, 231–49.
Somdahl-Sands, K. 2006. Cultural geographies in practice Triptych: Dancing in thirdspace. *Cultural Geographies* 13(4): 610–16.
Somdahl-Sands, K. 2008. Citizenship, civic memory and urban performance: Mission Wall dances. *Space and Polity* 12(3): 329–52.
Tired of Bronco Bamma and Mitt Romney. 2012. Posted by E. Evans. Uploaded on October 30. Available at: www.youtube.com/watch?v=OjrthOPLAKM [accessed November 4, 2012].
Tuan, Y.-F. 1982. *Segmented Worlds and Self: Group Life and Individual Consciousness*. Minneapolis: University of Minnesota Press.
Tuan, Y.-F. and T. Mercure. 2004. *Place, Art, and Self*. Chicago: Center for American Places.
Warner, M. 2002. *Public and Counterpublics*. New York: Zone Books.
Weiwei, A. 2011. *Ai Weiwei's Blog: Writings, Interviews, and Digital Rants, 2006–2009*. Edited and translated by L. Ambrozy. Writing Art Series. Cambridge, MA: MIT Press.
Wurtzler, S. 1992. She sang live, but the microphone was turned off. In *Sound Theory, Sound Practice*. Edited by R. Aldman. New York: Routledge, 87–103.

22 ASHGATE RESEARCH COMPANION

Spaces of Media Capital

Brett Christophers

While we often ignore or are not necessarily even aware of the fact, the vast bulk of the media we engage and consume in our daily lives – the television, film, radio, books, magazines, and so on – are produced and distributed commercially and thus according to commercial imperatives and prerogatives. Sometimes this commercialism is tempered, for instance where a media organization is state-owned and has public-service responsibilities to fulfill. More often, however, it is not, and profit maximization objectives are explicitly to the fore. As such, the "logic" of the media world and the commodities that circulate through it "must be situated," as Ronald Bettig (1996: 3) observes, "within the larger context of the logic of capital."

This chapter surveys recent research into the economic geographies of this nexus of "media capital," as I will refer to it. The chapter focuses for the most part on the activities of large, often transnational corporations, for the simple reason that media capital *is* highly concentrated. This is true, for most types of media, across the entire value chain, from development and production all the way through to final consumer-facing distribution. It has also tended to become *truer* rather than less true over time (large-scale consolidation rationalizing sometimes fragmented industries), and this despite various new technologies – the Internet perhaps foremost among them – appearing to hold the promise of more democratic ownership of capital (Wu 2012). Take, most starkly, the US media industry, as Ben Bagdikian has done in six successive editions of *The Media Monopoly* followed, in 2004, by *The New Media Monopoly*. When the first edition of the former was published in 1983, Bagdikian reported that 50 major corporations controlled the national media; but as he revised his text in each new edition, the number was gradually whittled down, first to 29 (by 1987), then 23 (1990), 14 (1992), 10 (1997), and finally six (2000 and 2004).

The first part of the chapter discusses the state-of-play of research into the spaces of media *production*, which is where the vast bulk of economic-geographical research on the media industries has long been – and remains – focused. That is to say, it explores recent empirical findings and theoretical refinements relating to the spatial structure of productive relations in the world of commercial media content creation. Despite that this is now a vast, long-standing, and well-rehearsed literature, it continues to spread and expand in all sorts of intriguing and revealing new directions.

The chapter argues, however, that for all the importance of the economic-geographical dynamics of media production, the heavy emphasis on this theme within the existing literature has been to the detriment of a fuller understanding of the geographies of media capital more broadly. Capitalized media organizations, after all, do much more than produce content; they package it, they market it, they license it, they distribute it. As such, in the second and third sections of the chapter, I explore two other areas of research into the spaces of media capital, which remain much less developed than research into production

geographies but which offer considerable promise for original research contributions in the future. The first concerns the wider spatial organization and strategies of the companies that control the global media, such companies typically existing and operating well beyond the sites merely of original production. Second, and related to this, there is the crucial matter of distribution relations. What do we know about the spatial flows of contemporary media, and about the spatial market structures put in place by media organizations to enable, manage, and profit from such flows? This is the subject of the final section.

Clustered Capital

It is on industrial location – *where* media production activities take place – that most geographical research into media economies has focused. This research has repeatedly and forcefully demonstrated that commercial media production activities have a tendency to agglomerate or "cluster" in particular cities, with Los Angeles (i.e. Hollywood) being the archetypal example. Such agglomerative tendencies, of course, are not unique to the media industries; but various authors (e.g. Currid and Connolly 2008) have suggested that the tendency is *more* pronounced in the media sector than elsewhere. The central theoretical thrust of the large literature on media clustering has been that the phenomenon evinces a profound spatial logic, effectively consisting of the enhanced competitive and creative performance deriving from proximity.

Recent research in this area builds accretively on a number of formative interventions in the 1980s and 1990s by, most notably, Michael Storper and Susan Christopherson (Christopherson and Storper 1986; Storper and Christopherson 1987) and Allen Scott (2000). Notwithstanding the materiality of these studies, however, we cannot fully appreciate the intellectual lineage of contemporary cluster research unless we look considerably further back in time, and especially to the groundbreaking work of the English economist Alfred Marshall. While the industrial agglomerations studied today differ in important ways from those analyzed by Marshall a century earlier, contemporary research suggests that economies of localization – in the media industries as well as others – continue to arise, for the most part, from what Paul Krugman (1991: 70) calls "the standard Marshallian trinity of labour market pooling, supply of intermediate goods, and knowledge spillovers."

Most recent studies of the clustering of media production activities are concerned with the three industries that have long constituted the staple of such research: film, television, and recorded music. Yet the same phenomenon has been diagnosed in relation to a range of other media subsectors, among them magazine publishing (Heebels and Boschma 2011) and video game development and publishing (Dyer-Witheford and Sharman 2005). In the early years of the Internet, plenty of commentators predicted that *this* medium would be different, and that pressures toward dispersion would win out. But Leamer and Storper's (2001) contrary suspicion – that agglomerative tendencies, not least those associated with the understanding and trust underpinned by face-to-face contact, would again hold sway – has proven largely accurate (e.g. Cooke 2002; Arai et al. 2004).

All of which is not to suggest, of course, that media production activities *always* cluster together, according to some relentless and undeviating spatial logic. They do not, and there are, in the literature, plenty of examples of the emergence of alternative spatial configurations of productive media capital. Norcliffe and Rendace (2003), for instance, have charted the historical shift in the North American comic book production industry from a geographically concentrated, Fordist-like mode of organization to a model with a much more deconcentrated spatiality and a very different social economy. Yet, as ever, the exceptions

serve to prove the rule: on the whole media production, *especially* where heavily capitalized and consolidated, does occur in clusters. Indeed, a veritable cottage industry of "media cluster" studies has materialized in recent years as if to reinforce the point (e.g. Cooke and Lazzeretti 2008; Karlsson and Picard 2011).

It would be a mistake, however, to think that the literature on such clusters is homogeneous and repetitive. While one could be forgiven for rolling one's eyes at evidence of yet *another* cluster formation, nuances in fact abound. Clusters, for example, by no means exhibit the same internal characteristics or equivalent levels of economic performance, even within the same media subsector (Cook and Pandit 2007; Britton et al. 2009). They are, moreover, differentially incorporated into wider circuits of productive and financial capital, a fact whose importance has been increasingly recognized in recent years (Coe 2000a; Krätke 2002; Coe and Johns 2004).

It is also the case that different scholars emphasize different dynamics in seeking to account both for the emergence and endurance of media clusters, and for their varying fortunes. Theoretical consensus, in other words, remains elusive. Scott, in his book *On Hollywood* (2005: 24), pegs Los Angeles's rise to prominence in the US film sector to "the vigorous system of productive organization that evolved out of the disparate collection of branch plants that had drifted into [Southern California] in the six or seven years before 1915." More generically, Harald Bathelt (2005) sees processes of knowledge creation, sustained by external linkages, as decisive in explaining the growth and reproduction of media clusters. Richard Florida and colleagues (2010), discussing music clusters more specifically, argue for the significance of "scale and scope economies." And Michael Curtin (forthcoming), in turn, points to three sets of factors – another explanatory trinity, then, but reworked from Marshall's original version – as enabling particular cities to emerge as leading media clusters during the global era.

Finally, and perhaps most importantly of all, clusters are not stable, and nor therefore is our knowledge of them; they evolve, and so must research into this evolution. Old clusters stagnate. New clusters emerge. Sometimes they emerge in ways that are effectively complementary to existing agglomerations, as has occurred with the growth of "satellite" centers of production – either within the same country, or overseas – in the music (Brandellero and Pfeffer 2011) and film and television (Lukinbeal 2004; Elmer and Gasher 2005) sectors. (In the latter context, the most famous and exhaustively researched such satellite location is Vancouver in Canada [Coe 2000b; 2001; Scott and Pope 2007; Barnes and Coe 2011].) At other times, new clusters materialize more-or-less independently of existing centers of production rather than as adjuncts to them, and come to represent competition rather than auxiliary outposts. Among other things, research into such competitive clusters questions – explicitly or implicitly – the long-term sustainability of Hollywood's long-standing dominance of global media production (Scott 2000; Curtin forthcoming). Might the growing role of non-US media clusters such as Mumbai, Paris, Milan, and Tokyo be viewed as a portent of changing macropatterns of industrial location? It seems likely this question will remain at the core of research into the spaces of media capital for the foreseeable future.

Transnational Capital

From an economic perspective, one of the most conspicuous and important attributes of the core commodities of the media industries is their typically trivial costs of reproduction. Once one copy of a television program or a piece of recorded music has been produced, for instance, it generally costs very little – and in the digital age, often nothing – to produce another.

The vast bulk of such costs are incurred up front. This economic attribute has quite a wide range of implications for the structure and dynamics of media economies (Hoskins et al. 2004). One such implication, however, is especially pertinent to our discussion of media capital's spatiality. This is that the media industries are, almost by their very nature, geographically expansionist: if it costs an immaterial amount to produce extra copies of a commodity, then it would be commercially irrational *not* to endeavor to sell that commodity to as many people – and geographic markets – as possible. To be sure, other, nonproduction-related costs will ordinarily be incurred in seeking to penetrate new markets. Nevertheless, and certainly relative to other industries, low marginal production costs inscribe an expansionary impulse at the very heart of the commercial media.

It is no surprise, therefore, that the media should figure centrally in the vast literature on economic and cultural globalization and on the intermingling of these two phenomena (Appadurai 1996; Rantanen 2004; Lule 2011). But how exactly has – and does – media capital, in the shape of the large corporate organizations that largely constitute it, embraced and effected globalization? The rest of this chapter explores the answers that recent research has provided to this critical question. In the present section, the focus is mainly on the spaces of corporate capital: where, and in what ways, media organizations have *themselves* globalized. In the final section, the focus shifts to the generalized spatial structures and frameworks – often grounded explicitly in geo-legality as well as geo-economics – put in place *by* media organizations and state institutions to facilitate and coordinate the resulting global flows of media commodities.

Perhaps the most obvious and recognizable respect in which the spaces of media capital are increasingly *globalized* spaces is in the shape of foreign direct investment (FDI). This refers to the process whereby media organizations from one country establish or acquire permanent operations in another country. Television, as we shall see, represents a prime and now long-standing example of media-sector FDI, and is unarguably the most heavily researched. But it is not unique. Recent research has highlighted the prevalence of FDI strategies across almost the full gamut of the media industries. Tian et al. (2008: 234), as one example, have discussed the importance of FDI in book publishing, noting that "most of the activity" in the sector, in most geographic markets, is "accounted for by a handful of large-scale, foreign-owned multinationals exploiting the benefits of global economies of scale and distribution." Johns (2006) reports a comparable phenomenon in the world of video game publishing, showing that the bigger publishers – both integrated with console manufacturers (Sony et al.) and not (e.g. Electronic Arts, Sega) – typically boast proprietary operations in all three of the main geographic markets for such games (the United States, Europe, and Japan).

The television sector has of course been a primary locus of media-capital FDI, in particular during the past two decades. Once satellite and cable television began to expand the broadcast capacity of household television around the world beyond the narrow confines of traditional terrestrial delivery, established American networks rapidly internationalized to fill the emerging bandwidth. Think of MTV or Discovery Channel. By the time of its twenty-fifth anniversary in 2006, MTV was reported to be the owner of channels in 28 languages and 168 countries (Ulaby 2006). Discovery Communications has been equally relentless in its globalizing ambition. Since the launch of its first channel (Discovery Channel) in the United States in 1985, it had, by 2008, expanded to the point that its bouquet of television channels was available – in part or in whole – in 170 countries (Mjos 2009: 3).

American television's extremely visible FDI-based expansion into international television markets only served to add, in the 1980s and early 1990s, to the robust existing critique of so-called American cultural imperialism (Schiller 1976). While some scholars of global media capital and culture still find this latter label somewhat useful (Mirrlees 2012), the term

globalization has, in the past decade-and-a-half, usually been preferred. Partly this preference has to do with increasing unease with the connotations of the term *imperial*. But it also has to do with the fact that "media globalization" in its contemporary guise is clearly not solely a US-driven phenomenon. All sorts of media products have enjoyed global or near-global commercial success in recent years, and while many are indeed US-originated, many are not.

Jeremy Tunstall's critique in *The Media Were American* (2007) – he had published an influential book entitled *The Media Are American* three decades earlier – is particularly interesting in this respect. For Tunstall, one key signifier of the supposed decline in American dominance of global commercial media is that even the most successful US-owned international television channels such as the MTVs and Discoverys have only very small niche audiences around the world.

This is, of course, true; and Tunstall *may* be right that US media organizations are now materially less powerful on the global media stage than they were in the 1970s and 1980s. Yet the key point to be made for our present purposes is that Tunstall's envisioning of the transnational spaces of corporate media capital seems altogether too narrow. Yes, FDI is one vital way in which media organizations globalize. But it is not the only one. Remaining for now in the realm of television, one is left wondering after reading Tunstall, what about all the US-produced programming aired on the major domestically-owned channels in non-US markets? Just because US *channels* have small audience shares in foreign markets does not mean that US media *products* – and thus US media capital – have a minimal presence there. *Mad Men* does not lose its Americanness, nor (more pointedly) its American producers their ability to extract rents from its distribution, simply because it is broadcast overseas on non-American channels.

More generically, we need therefore to recognize that the transnationalization of media capital occurs through export as well as FDI. Think here of film rather than television. It is seldom the case that the leading movie theater chains in, say, European territories, are US-owned and operated. But does that imply a limited influence for US media capital in the European film market? Clearly not: in the mid-1990s, some three-quarters of all movie tickets bought in Western Europe were for Hollywood output (Miller et al. 2005: 17). Simply because control over the extraction of economic value at the point-of-sale is more distant, and thus arguably not quite as direct, does not make this any less a space permeated with US media capital.

Even when adding export activities to FDI, however, we still have a far too simplistic overall picture of the spaces of transnational corporate capital in the media environment. We have essentially assumed so far, for example, that a media property – a film, video game, or piece of recorded music – is produced in one place (likely a clustered production milieu) before then being distributed and consumed. Yet increasingly, for individual media products, the spaces of production *itself* are multiple in terms of both geographic location and corporate identity: specifically, in both film and television, the last two decades have seen a significant increase in the phenomenon of co-production, whereby companies based in different territories work together on discrete projects and are each (or, in the case of three or more participants, all) credited as producers.

There are innumerable examples of high-profile television and film co-productions from recent years. 2009's *Inglourious Basterds* was, to take just one example, a co-production between Germany's Studio Babelsberg and the production vehicles of Bob and Harvey Weinstein (The Weinstein Company) and of Quentin Tarantino and Lawrence Bender (A Band Apart). In the film world, production companies typically come together, as they did in this case, specifically to work on individual projects, forming bespoke corporate entities to manage the economics of those projects and those projects alone. This happens in television, too, but in the latter case one also sometimes finds co-productions occurring within the context of much wider, longer-term partnerships. An important example of this would be the far-reaching joint venture between the UK's British Broadcasting Corporation (BBC) and America's Discovery Communications, which was established in 1998 and extended in 2002 (to 2012) and again in 2010 (to 2014). While the venture covers many areas of business (including channel ownership and distribution), co-production is at its core, with marquee coproduced output including, to date, *The Blue Planet*, its follow-up *Planet Earth*, and the various installments of the *Walking With* … franchise.

Studies of cross-border film and television co-productions (e.g. Tinic 2002; Christophers 2006; Morawetz et al. 2007; Cole 2008) have demonstrated that they have a number of different rationales. Finance is certainly a critical one: with ever-heightening demands on production values in the international marketplace, the number of production companies with the financial resources to fund high-quality projects on a stand-alone basis gets ever smaller. Other companies need to find partners. They do so, moreover, to pool resources beyond merely financial ones: technical and creative resources, of course, are all differentially distributed as well, and partnering with companies with complementary resources and skills is often seen as preferable to attempting to develop or acquire them. Then there are more specific rationales: securing multiple national tax benefits, for instance, and avoiding or exploiting "cultural" regulations such as local-content quotas.

What then should we make of co-productions in respect of the spaces of media capital? They clearly represent further evidence of the latter's transnationalization. But, given that this transnationalization is occurring in the realm of production as opposed to distribution, does it offer counter-evidence to the clustering phenomenon? Some writers have intimated that it does (Cole 2008). And yet with co-productions often involving participants themselves located *in* clusters (albeit in different countries), perhaps their rise should be seen not as a trend away from clusters so much as evidence of growing cross-border collaboration *between* clusters – in ways that suggest, nonetheless, that geographic proximity is not the be-all and end-all of competitive advantage in the media industries.

Meanwhile, if our original, simplistic picture of transnational media capital presumed uni-locational production dynamics, it also presumed that transnationalization involved some sort of substantive boundary-crossing. If companies themselves were not moving overseas through FDI, then at the very least their output was. Today, however, the international geography of media capital is much more complex than this latter assumption allows. Often, in turns out, what links together different national media spaces is not the companies or products circulating within them but merely product *ideas*, or *formats*.

Again, television is the clearest example of this phenomenon. *Big Brother*; *Weakest Link*; *Idol*; *Who Wants to Be a Millionaire?* – all these, and countless others besides, are examples of shows where the entity transferred from one country to another is a concept or structure for a program rather than a program per se. The buyer pays the seller a license fee for the exclusive right to exploit the program format within its particular territory, and then proceeds to produce a *new* program – albeit within the generic editorial parameters that the format effectively represents. The formats business has become a substantial and highly lucrative one in the past two decades. The major European format hothouses such as Endemol and FremantleMedia – and the format development business *is* a Eurocentric one – often participate overseas in the local production of their own formats. But often, they do not. In such instances, television format circulation and its geographical economy of rent accretion constitutes perhaps the most "virtual" of all forms of transnationalization of media capital.

Territorialized Capital

Having thus far considered spaces of media capital from the perspective primarily of the companies that make up the media industries, our focus in this final section of the chapter will be on the spatiality of media *markets*. As we will see, one of the most striking and enduring features of the world of commercial media has long been its rigid territorialization. Not only are the rights to distribute media products typically delimited and exploited on a territory-by-territory basis, but the very product itself often differs substantively between territories – and not only in the case of the television format business discussed above. New technologies, assuredly, have posed considerable challenges to existing architectures of media market geo-segmentation; but despite such challenges, fundamental, legally enforceable territorial boundaries remain widely in place.

Before examining what those boundaries look like and the types of threats they face, however, it is worth pausing to ask *why* the global media market crystallized, early on, as a series of interlocking but commercially separable national economic spaces. The simplified answer is that this configuration of things has always suited those organizations with the power to shape international distributional frameworks – which is to say, the major producers of media content with potential global appeal. Whether it be books, films, television programs, or video games, there has always been a clear commercial logic to market segmentation by territory. It allows, inter alia, for the differentiation of content (ranging from relatively substantial differences to those as minor as that between the *Philosopher's Stone* [UK] and the *Sorcerer's Stone* [US] in the first *Harry Potter* book); for differentiation by price (based on ability to pay); and for differentiation by timing of release. In short, it has conventionally been thought that more cumulative revenue can be extracted from a media property if it is released sequentially into differentiated geographic markets than singularly into an undifferentiated global market. That these differentiated geographic markets would typically be *national* was more-or-less inevitable given the predominantly national locus of boundaries in key areas such as language, currency, legal and regulatory apparatus, distribution platforms, and the like.

The case of recorded music is an emblematic one. In the "traditional" world of vinyl, cassette tapes, and compact discs, music copyright – the right to reproduce music and distribute it for financial gain – has invariably been licensed on a strictly national basis: in other words, territory by territory. This has been the preferred approach of the leading record companies (the "majors"). And it has also been encouraged and reinforced by the powerful collective rights management societies that represent smaller rights-holders and negotiate copyright licenses on their behalf with commercial users. Indeed, territorialization is engrained in the very fabric of such organizations: "[M]ost ... collective rights management societies currently derive their existence from rights granted or entrusted to them on a national (territorial) basis" (Hugenholtz et al. 2006: 22).

Consider, similarly, book publishing. As Esposito (2011: 15) explains, the distribution of physical books has never been a straightforward matter. "Books must be warehoused and shipped; demand must be carefully estimated in advance (the hardest trick in the book business); shipments of titles must be coordinated with publicity efforts; a network of sellers and resellers (the supply chain) must be assembled and made to work in coordination." In part because of these logistical challenges, Esposito continues, "most publishing throughout the twentieth century was national. A book was published first in, say, London for the UK book market and then trading partners were found to take on the distribution of the title in the U.S., Australia, etc."

Ultimately, however, in the worlds of books and music and of other commercial media, territorialization, as suggested above, is about *control*. It is about the giant corporations of media capital *creating* spatial markets in such a way as to maximize *their* control over product release and thus their revenue outcomes. Johns (2006: 171) makes this particularly clear in her excellent analysis of global production networks in video-game publishing. Splitting the world into (in this case) the macro-regions of North America, Europe, and the Asia Pacific enables the console manufacturers "to gain a greater degree of control than would be possible in a truly global system." How so? "Publishers are required to submit code to the console manufacturer's base in the region in which they are located. For example, a UK-based publisher wishing to publish a game on PlayStation2 has to submit code to Sony Computer Entertainment Europe (SCEE). If accepted, SCEE will publish the game and manufacture games suitable for PAL territories. If the publisher wishes to sell the game in the USA, they are required to begin the whole submission process again with Sony Computer Entertainment America (SCEA)." This is not a problem for the handful of large independent publishers with publishing houses on both sides of the Atlantic, or of course for the vertically integrated, multinational console manufacturers themselves. But most European publishers do not have registered offices in North America; the cost would be prohibitive.

A final media subsector deserving of attention in relation to questions of market territorialization is that of television and film. Here, as in the case of recorded music, rights have always been disassembled and allocated on a country-by-country basis. Take television. The BBC might acquire the rights to an American television drama series for the UK market; TF1 might do so for the French market; Sverige Television for the Swedish market; and so forth. One of the most striking and widely discussed implications of this approach has long been enormous disparities in the prices paid for the same program by broadcasters in different territories: population size, average income levels, and degree of buyer competition in each territory all contributing to such disparities. In the mid-1990s, for example, the price per commercial hour (50 minutes) of imported American programming was reported to range from \$20,000–\$100,000 in the UK to as little as \$200–\$250 in Zimbabwe (Hoskins et al. 1997: 69).

In the world of commercial media production and exploitation in general, however, one of *the* key effects of the development of the Internet over the past decade-and-a-half has been to throw down a fundamental challenge to such widespread historical practices of market – and thus media capital – territorialization. This challenge has been keenly felt in all of the subsectors discussed above, with the partial exception of video-game publishing. For, the recorded music, book, and television and film sectors have all witnessed revolutionary developments in the digital reproduction and online delivery and consumption of content. And, in the process, many of the most formidable technological and logistical – if not commercial and legal – obstacles to direct global media delivery have simply disappeared. If a small producer in Argentina wanted to sell an e-book or MP3 music recording or MPEG4 video to a customer in South Korea, it would not be technically difficult for them to do so; the "friction of distance" has, in large part, dissipated.

As we shall shortly see, technical developments alone are not necessarily sufficient to dismantle territorialized market structures that have been in place – and have handsomely served the owners of media capital – for many decades. Plenty of commentators have argued that such a dismantling *will* (and for some, should) be the effect of the Internet. But to anticipate as much is not only to underestimate media capital's investment, in every sense of the word, in market geo-segmentation. It is also to overlook important lessons from recent history: the Internet is not the first technology to threaten dissolution of strict media market territorialization, and past challenges have, for the most part, been successfully resisted.

Perhaps the most notable and instructive example of such a challenge has been that posed to national television markets by the growth in satellite television technologies from the early 1990s. Traditional technologies of consumer broadcast television delivery – terrestrial and cable – suited the territorialization of rights perfectly since they were and are typically nationally circumscribed infrastructures. (Even if the BBC had *wanted* to broadcast an acquired program direct to overseas viewers, it could not technically have done so.) But the advent of direct-to-home satellite broadcasting irrevocably undermined this neat territorial circumscription: all satellites have spatial "footprints" within which their signals can be received, and none of these are coterminous with the boundaries of nation-states. Most encompass numerous national territories. As such there is, with satellite-based television broadcast, always the possibility of consumers in one country picking up broadcasts intended and legislated only for – because based on the ownership of *rights* only for – a foreign market.

Christophers (2009: 149–56) discusses several examples of how these "spillover" effects of satellite broadcasting can play out and can threaten the conventional architecture of territorialized rights. Such examples typically relate, of course, to television rights with high economic value across multiple national markets; and few rights are more valuable, in the contemporary international broadcast economy, than those associated with English Premier League football. It is thus not surprising that all manner of disputes have arisen over the years involving actual or perceived infringements of legal national monopolies on the exploitation of such rights. Interestingly, these disputes have related to alleged infringements in both geographical "directions" – both outwards *from* the UK, and inwards *into* the UK. In the former case, for instance, there has been concern that households and commercial establishments in continental Europe can pick up and decrypt signals broadcast by UK broadcasters who own (only) the UK rights; in the latter case, the concern is with the signals of foreign broadcasters, with rights to broadcast only in their respective foreign markets, being received and watched *in* the UK.

The whys and wherefores of these often seemingly paradoxical economic-geographical transgressions need not detain us here. What is important in the present context, rather, is their cumulative impact – which, to date, has been extremely limited. In other words, despite satellite broadcasting posing a very obvious *technical* challenge to the continued territorialization of television rights exploitation; and despite numerous instances of this challenge being *practically realized* in actual viewing behaviors – the major rights holders in the international television marketplace continue to sell their rights explicitly for national use. They remain confident that, individual infringements notwithstanding, this is still the most profitable and secure way to proceed. And, equally important, they remain *allowed* to do so by the terms of national and international copyright laws.

Which begs, of course, an obvious question: will the Internet, if not satellite broadcasting, be the death of territorialization (and not only in television but also in the markets for e-books, digital music, and other media)? The technical possibilities for direct transnational delivery are certainly unprecedented. Where satellite enables broadcasters to reach audiences in more than one territory, the Internet allows retailers of digitized content of all forms to reach, simultaneously, a literally *global* audience. Granted, there are technical means of limiting circumvention of territorial consumption restrictions on the Internet (e.g. "geo-blocking"; see, e.g. Boyle and Whannel 2010: 356), just as there are with satellite reception (encryption and viewing cards). Yet with the Internet, the commercial possibilities appear so revolutionary, and the challenges to the geo-economic status quo so profound, that it is hard to imagine the territorialization of media rights remaining quite as hegemonic and unaffected as it has to date.

At present, research into this particular issue remains somewhat thin on the ground. Christophers (2009: 156–60) discusses the online television/video market. But perhaps more revealing of the tensions at stake and of the generally glacial pace of change currently visible in the market is the case of recorded music. There has, as Santos (2009) reports, been pressure for change, including from regulatory authorities. She highlights in this regard the European Commission's 2005 *Recommendation on Collective Cross-Border Management of Copyright and Related Rights for Legitimate Online Music Services*. Santos argues, however, that the commission's appetite for legislation in this area has since waned. There have, moreover, been high-profile examples of online music retailers (most notably Apple's iTunes) being *required* to operate on a country-by-country basis within the EU, even where their preference was seemingly for an EU-wide deal. Due in large part to the problems associated with uncoupling artists' public performance rights from their territorial moorings, commercially substantive, genuinely pan-European licenses remain a rarity in the online music world. Overall, steps toward deterritorialization are thus "somewhat hesitant, still uncoordinated" (ibid.: n.p.).

In short, the situation remains in flux. Much more research is needed, to understand both recent developments and the shifting strategies of media capital. It is nonetheless clear that most observers do continue to expect a gradual weakening of the traditional territorialization model. As Esposito (2011: 16) writes in the book publishing context: "The digerati will win this one; it is only a matter of time … Publishers with clout will demand global ebook rights; over time the practice will become increasingly widespread and then universal." Furthermore: "It is probable that print rights will get caught up in these negotiations." What is also clear, however, is that there will be continued struggles over such developments – technically, commercially and, not least, legally. "The law," predicts Santos (2009: n.p.) in relation to the aforementioned music example, "will probably get there after the market does."

Concluding Comments

The one constant in the world of commercial media is, of course, change: change in the nature of the content created by producers and demanded by consumers; change in the patterns of production, distribution, and consumption of that content; and change, perhaps most conspicuously of all in recent years, in the technologies deployed for such production, distribution, and consumption. The digital revolution has already had, and will inevitably continue to have, deep-seated implications for the commercial possibilities associated with the delivery of mediated information and entertainment.

And with new technologies come, very often, new players in the commercial media environment. Sometimes these new market actors are new companies entirely: Google, for instance, is now one of the largest media companies in the world, with market-leading positions in areas ranging from Internet search and advertising to video-sharing (through subsidiary YouTube); but 15 years ago, it did not even exist as an incorporated company. In other cases, the "new" actors are existing companies that exploit new technological developments to enter market spaces in which they did not previously participate: think of Apple, formerly "just" a consumer electronics and software manufacturer, and its entry into the digital media market with iTunes. New technologies frequently foment, in short, a blurring of lines between conventional industrial sectors. The development and ongoing iteration of products such as Google TV and Apple TV is, in this respect, symptomatic.

Meanwhile, if new technologies tend to presage new corporate positionings and institutional borders, they often *also*, in the process, give rise to new spatial configurations of media capital. I have sought to flesh out something of the basic nature of these configurations in this chapter; it is the shifting empirical substance of such configurations that ongoing research into the spaces of media capital must attempt to grapple with, articulate, and analytically illuminate. As the Googles and the Apples of the world come increasingly not only to partner with, but *compete* with, the NBCs and BBCs and the Bertelsmanns and Sony Musics, what are the implications for the spaces of capitalized media production? for the spaces of media capital – the companies that constitute such capital – per se? and for the spatiality of the markets put in place *by* media capital, and through which such capital constantly circulates? Such questions can form the bedrock of a rich future research agenda at the interface of economic geography and media geography.

Acknowledgments

Many thanks to Barney Warf and Paul Adams for reading and commenting on the chapter. Remaining errors of fact or interpretation are mine.

References

Appadurai, A. 1996. *Modernity at Large: Cultural Dimensions of Globalization.* Minneapolis: University of Minnesota Press.

Arai, Y., H. Nakamura, H. Sato, T. Nakazawa, T. Musha, and K. Sugizaki. 2004. Multimedia and Internet business clusters in central Tokyo. *Urban Geography* 25: 483–500.

Barnes, T. and N Coe. 2011. Vancouver as media cluster: The cases of video games and film/TV. In *Media Clusters: Spatial Agglomeration and Content Capabilities.* Edited by C. Karlsson and R. Picard. Cheltenham: Edward Elgar, 251–77.

Bathelt, H. 2005. Cluster relations in the media industry: Exploring the "distanced neighbour" paradox in Leipzig. *Regional Studies* 39: 105–27.

Bettig, R. 1996. Copyrighting Culture: The Political Economy of Intellectual Property. Boulder, CO: Westview.

Boyle, R. and G. Whannel. 2010. Three interviews. *Convergence* 16: 355–68.

Brandellero, A. and K. Pfeffer. 2011. Multiple and shifting geographies of world music production. *Area* 43: 495–505.

Britton, J., D. Tremblay, and R. Smith. 2009. Contrasts in clustering: The example of Canadian new media. *European Planning Studies* 17: 211–34.

Christophers, B. 2006. Circuits of capital, genealogy, and geographies of television. *Antipode* 38: 930–52.

Christophers, B. 2009. Envisioning Media Power: On Capital and Geographies of Television. Lanham, MD: Lexington Books.

Christopherson, S. and M. Storper. 1986. The city as studio; the world as backlot: the impact of vertical disintegration on the location of the motion picture industry. *Environment and Planning D* 4: 305–20.

Coe, N. 2000a. On location: American capital and the local labour market in the Vancouver film industry. *International Journal of Urban and Regional Research* 24: 79–94.

Coe, N. 2000b. The view from out West: Embeddedness, inter-personal relations and the development of an indigenous film industry in Vancouver. *Geoforum* 31: 391–407.
Coe, N. 2001. A hybrid agglomeration? The development of a satellite-Marshallian industrial district in Vancouver's film industry. *Urban Studies* 38: 1753–75.
Coe, N. and K. Johns. 2004. Beyond production clusters: Towards a critical political economy of networks in the film and television industries. In *Cultural Industries and the Production of Culture*. Edited by D. Power and A. Scott. London: Routledge, 188–204.
Cole, A. 2008. Distant neighbours: The new geography of animated film production in Europe. *Regional Studies* 41: 1–14.
Cook, G. and N. Pandit. 2007. Service industry clustering: A comparison of broadcasting in three city-regions. *Service Industries Journal* 27: 453–69.
Cooke, P. 2002. New media and new economy cluster dynamics. In *Handbook of New Media*. Edited by L. Lievrouw and S. Livingstone. London: SAGE, 287–303.
Cooke, P. and L. Lazzeretti (eds). 2008. *Creative Cities, Cultural Clusters and Local Economic Development*. Cheltenham: Edward Elgar.
Currid, E. and J. Connolly. 2008. Patterns of knowledge: Cultural production and the geography of advanced services. *Annals of the Association of American Geographers* 98: 414–34.
Curtin, M. forthcoming. Media Capital: The Cultural Geography of Globalization. Oxford: Blackwell.
Dyer-Witheford, N. and Z. Sharman. 2005. The political economy of Canada's video and computer game industry. *Canadian Journal of Communication* 30: 187–210.
Elmer, G. and M. Gasher (eds). 2005. Contracting Out Hollywood: Runaway Productions and Foreign Location Shooting. Lanham, MD: Rowman & Littlefield.
Esposito, J. 2011. One world publishing, brought to you by the Internet. *Publishing Research Quarterly* 27: 13–18.
Florida, R., C. Mellander, and K. Stolarick. 2010. Music scenes to music clusters: The economic geography of music in the US, 1970 – 2000. *Environment and Planning A* 42: 785–804.
Heebels, B. and Boschma, R. 2011. Performing in Dutch book publishing 1880–2008: The importance of entrepreneurial experience and the Amsterdam cluster. *Journal of Economic Geography* 11: 1007–29.
Hoskins, C., S. McFadyen, and A. Finn. 1997. *Global Television and Film: An Introduction to the Economics of the Business*. Oxford: Clarendon Press.
Hoskins, C., S. McFadyen, and A. Finn. 2004. *Media Economics: Applying Economics to New and Traditional Media*. London: SAGE.
Hugenholtz, B., M. van Eechoud, S. van Gompel, L. Guibault, N. Helberger, M. Rossinim, L. Steijger, N. Dufft, and P. Bohn. 2006. The recasting of copyright and related rights for the knowledge economy. European Commission DG Internal Market Study. Available at: www.ec.europa.eu/internal_market/copyright/docs/studies/etd2005imd195recast_report_2006.pdf.
Johns, J. 2006. Video games production networks: Value capture, power relations and embeddedness. *Journal of Economic Geography* 6: 151–80.
Karlsson, C. and R. Picard (eds). 2011. *Media Clusters: Spatial Agglomeration and Content Capabilities*. Cheltenham: Edward Elgar.
Krugman, P. 1991. *Geography and Trade*. Cambridge, MA: MIT Press.
Krätke, S. 2002. Network analysis of production clusters: The Potsdam/Babelsberg film industry as an example. *European Planning Studies* 10: 27–54.
Leamer, E. and M. Storper. 2001. The economic geography of the Internet age. *Journal of International Business Studies* 32: 641–65.
Lukinbeal, C. 2004. The rise of regional film production centers in North America, 1984–1997. *GeoJournal* 59: 307–21.

Lule, J. 2011. *Globalization and Media: Global Village of Babel*. Lanham, MD: AltaMira Press.
Miller, T., N. Govil, J. McMurria, R. Maxwell, and T. Wang. 2005. *Global Hollywood 2*. London: British Film Institute.
Mirrlees, T. 2012. *Global Entertainment Media: Between Cultural Imperialism and Cultural Globalization*. New York: Routledge.
Mjos, O. 2009. *Media Globalization and the Discovery Channel Networks*. New York: Routledge.
Morawetz, N., J. Hardy, C. Haslam, and K. Randle. 2007. Finance, policy, and industrial dynamics: The rise of co-productions in the film industry. *Industry and Innovation* 14: 421–43.
Norcliffe, G. and O. Rendace. 2003. New geographies of comic book production in North America: The new artisan, distancing, and the periodic social economy. *Economic Geography* 79: 241–63.
Rantanen, T. 2004. *The Media and Globalization*. London: SAGE.
Santos, A. 2009. Experimenting with territoriality: Pan-European music licensing and the persistence of old paradigms. *Duke Law & Technology Review* 7.
Schiller, H. 1976. *Communications and Cultural Domination*. New York: M.E. Sharpe.
Scott, A. 2000. *The Cultural Economy of Cities: Essays on the Geography of Image-Producing Industries*. London: SAGE.
Scott, A. 2005. *On Hollywood: The Place, The Industry*. Princeton: Princeton University Press.
Scott, A. and N. Pope 2007. Hollywood, Vancouver, and the world: Employment relocation and the emergence of satellite production centers in the motion-picture industry. *Environment and Planning A* 39: 1364–81.
Storper, M. and S. Christopherson. 1987. Flexible specialization and regional industrial agglomerations: The case of the US motion-picture industry. *Annals of the Association of American Geographers* 77: 260–82.
Tian, X., B. Martin, and H. Deng. 2008. The impact of digitization on business models for publishing: Some indicators from a research project. *Journal of Systems and Information Technology* 10: 232–50.
Tinic, S. 2002. Going global: International coproductions and the disappearing domestic audience in Canada. In *Planet TV: A Global Television Reader*. Edited by L. Parks and S. Kumar. New York: New York University Press, 169–85.
Tunstall, J. 2007. *The Media Were American: US Mass Media in Decline*. New York: Oxford University Press.
Ulaby, N. 2006. MTV at 25: From upstart to parent network. NPR. Available at: www.npr.org/templates/story/story.php?storyId=5595384.
Wu, T. 2012. *The Master Switch: The Rise and Fall of Information Empires*. London: Atlantic Books.

Index